LEGALIZING MISANDRY

Legalizing Misandry

From Public Shame to Systemic Discrimination against Men

PAUL NATHANSON and
KATHERINE K. YOUNG

McGill-Queen's University Press
Montreal & Kingston · London · Ithaca

© McGill-Queen's University Press 2006
ISBN-13: 978-0-7735-2862-8   ISBN-10: 0-7735-2862-8

Legal deposit first quarter 2006
Bibliothèque nationale du Québec

Printed in Canada on acid-free paper

This book has been published with the help of a grant from the Canadian
Federation for the Humanities and Social Sciences, through the Aid to
Scholarly Publications Programme, using funds provided by the Social Sci-
ences and Humanities Research Council of Canada.

McGill-Queen's University Press acknowledges the support of the Canada
Council for the Arts for our publishing program. We also acknowledge the
financial support of the Government of Canada through the Book Publishing Industry Development Program (BPIDP) for our publishing activities.

Library and Archives Canada Cataloguing in Publication

Nathanson, Paul, 1947–
    Legalizing misandry : from public shame to systematic discrimination
against men / Paul Nathanson and Katherine K. Young.

Includes index.
ISBN-13: 978-0-7735-2862-8   ISBN-10: 0-7735-2862-8

1. Misandry – Canada.   2. Misandry – United States.   3. Sex discrimination against men – Canada.   4. Sex discrimination against men –
United States.   I. Young, Katherine K., 1944–   II. Title.

HQ1090.N367 2006   305.32′0971   C2005-902483-6

Typeset in 10/12 Sabon with Frutiger display by True to Type

Contents

Acknowledgments

We would like to thank the many people who helped make this book possible. Some responded to our requests for legal and statistical information: Augustina J. Kposowa, Grant Brown, and Brian Jenkins. Christopher Gray read several chapters and offered his comments. Jane Aiken has granted us permission to publish some of her material. Nicolas Lambe and Tara McPhail helped us with our legal citations. Our editor, Ron Curtis, read the manuscript very carefully; he not only corrected typos but also provided many worthwhile editorial suggestions. Finally we are grateful to the Social Sciences and Humanities Research Council for its financial support.

Introduction

One sure sign of danger at any time and in any place is a segment of the population that society considers unworthy of attention. No wonder more boys than girls face the future with apathy and drop out of school.[1] Worse, far more young men than young women are committing suicide. Ditto for old men and old women.[2] Males are not faring well at all in a society that is now focused explicitly on the needs and problems of females and is often hostile to the very possibility that males might have any distinct needs and problems of their own. Rapid social change and depression have been listed as causes of these problems, but the question is why these factors affect men, especially young men, much more than they do women.

These are complex problems, to be sure, and have more than one explanation (as we will show in *Transcending Misandry*, the third volume of this trilogy; the first volume, *Spreading Misandry*, was published in 2001). Underlying many explanations, though, is a distinctly gynocentric worldview. Being woman-centred, by definition, gynocentrism ignores the needs and problems of men. (The irony is that it was originally adopted to correct the biases of an androcentric, or man-centred, worldview.) And because gynocentrism now has both official status (in law) and quasi-official status (in institutional policies), its bias has become deeply embedded in public policy. That status has created and even institutionalized a new double standard, one that favours women instead of men and that, in turn, has created many additional problems: psychological, political, and – above all – moral ones. It is hard to know precisely how these problems affect boys and men personally, but it is worth noting that no large-scale study has ever been done to find out. It would be folly to ignore the warning signs mentioned above, in our opinion, but that is precisely what has been happening.

At least one bar association has seen fit to threaten male dissenters, concluding a report on women with a stern warning. Men, it says, will try to stop affirmative action, deny their bias, refuse to understand the nature of systemic barriers to women, or even institute a backlash with stereotypes embedded in misogynistic messages, anecdotes, myths, and homilies or "accusations ... [that women are] 'whining' or being 'provocative' when legitimate complaints are raised."[3] From our point of view, this report – one that relies on its own stereotypes – has gone beyond gynocentrism and embraced misandry.

Gynocentrism is the self-centred counterpart of androcentrism, and misandry is the sexist counterpart of misogyny. From the very beginning of this volume, we must be as clear as we were in the earlier volume about one thing. We define hatred as a collectively shared and culturally propagated worldview, not a personal emotion such as dislike or anger. Ultimately, this worldview is always expressed as "our" contempt for "them." Misandry, as such, has never been either legal or illegal. In a technical sense, therefore, it cannot be legalized in the same way that, say, marijuana can be legalized. Nonetheless, overt expressions of hatred toward specific groups are indeed illegal. Our point here is that hatred toward men is just as unacceptable morally as hatred toward any other group and should therefore be just as unacceptable legally.

Some people are aware of misandry but fervently believe that hatred toward men should be regarded as a legitimate exception to the general rule against hatred toward other groups. Most people find it hard even to notice misandry. The very idea seems counterintuitive. Men, according to conventional wisdom, have all the power. Therefore, presumably, they are immune to all serious harm. Besides, no one has ever called explicitly for discrimination against men or against any other segment of the population. After all, modern democracies and their legal systems are based explicitly on the rhetoric of equality. Yet many people have called explicitly for discrimination in favour of women – that is, legal measures to solve problems faced only by women. As a result, women have gained special protections: for example, the right to job security and benefits during pregnancy. These reforms, which were originally welcomed in the name of fairness, were soon extended to include measures such as affirmative action. Designed to "level the playing field," these measures were supposed ultimately to create equality by institutionalizing temporary inequality (although it was by no means self-evident that they could ever be terminated, no matter how much conditions might change, without a major political upheaval).

The goal was to raise the prospects of women, advocates explained, not to lower those of men. The result, nonetheless, was that gynocentrism and even misandry entered through the back door. Feminists explained the need for these legal measures by blaming the problems of women directly and exclusively on men, who were the scapegoats. Women were a victim class, said feminist lobby groups, and men the oppressor class. If men suffered from the new discrimination, they added, then so be it; men were collectively guilty and deserved collective punishment. No wonder many people, including some men, accepted the notion that it was morally acceptable to impose legal obligations, penalties, and restrictive conditions on men but not on women. No wonder, also, that they found it morally acceptable to use hate legislation as a way of protecting women and minorities from negative stereotypes but not to as a way of protecting men from equally negative stereotypes.

By now, our legal systems are based firmly on double standards. No matter how liberal, no matter how complacent, men who end up in court over conflicts with women soon discover these double standards not only in connection with custody and child support but also in connection with accusations of domestic violence and even in the reversal of such basic legal principles as the presumption that they are innocent unless proven guilty. Discrimination against men is by now so pervasively institutionalized that it is best described as systemic and characteristic of the legal system as a whole. Here, then, is the connection between the attitudes generated by misandry in popular culture and their institutionalization in policy and law.

Before proceeding, it is worth pausing to review what we said in *Spreading Misandry*. That book was primarily about the various ways in which men are seen by society and the negative stereotypes of men that became pervasive during the 1990s. Our goal was to demonstrate that misandry had become deeply embedded in popular culture. Though by no means the only interesting pattern that could be found in popular culture, it was very common and had not yet been explored systematically by other scholars.

Popular culture takes many forms. We discussed it in connection with the entertainment industry and some of its offshoots: movies, television shows, comic strips, greeting cards, and so on. Even though the productions we examined revealed a profoundly misandric worldview, they usually did so indirectly, implicitly, and unintentionally (except, of course, for talk shows and newsmagazines). As feminists had been doing for thirty years (not without initial resistance from skeptical commentators), we pointed out their sexist subtexts, according to which men may be stereotyped as either evil or inadequate; a few exceptions are allowed for "honorary women" (that is, either minority men or men who have "converted" to feminism).

Most of *Spreading Misandry* was devoted to description. But toward the end of it (and leading directly to this book), we discussed what underlies misandry. This phenomenon did not originate spontaneously at the grassroots level but was initiated and is still promoted by a segment of the academic elite that is affiliated with one branch of feminism. We called that branch "ideological feminism," for two reasons.

First, we wanted to distinguish it from the egalitarian feminism of the 1960s, which is probably still the most popular form of feminism, at least on the conscious level and in theory. Equality is a noble ideal. After publishing our first book, in fact, we found that many egalitarian feminists – especially those with sons – were willing to take seriously our observations on the negative portrayal of men in popular culture and even on the origin of that negativity in other forms of feminism. Although they supported the reforms that had improved women's lives over the past century, they recognized that reforms carried too far were creating injustices for men and boys (which would not bode well for society as a whole in the long run). Two wrongs, they agreed, did not make a right.

Second, we wanted to link ideological feminism with other political ideologies on both the political left and the political right. Throughout *Spreading Misandry*, we referred specifically to ideological feminists or feminist ideologues. And of course it was understood that some women are indifferent to feminism and others hostile to it.

Ideological feminism is the direct heir of both the Enlightenment and Romanticism. From the former it takes the theory of class conflict, merely substituting "gender" for "class" and "patriarchy" for "bourgeoisie." From the latter it takes the notion of nation or even race, focusing ultimately on the innate biological differences between women and men. The worldview of ideological feminism, like that of both Marxism and National Socialism – our analogies are between ways of thinking, not between specific ideas – is profoundly dualistic. In effect, "we" (women) are good, "they" (men) are evil. Or, to use the prevalent lingo, "we" are victims, "they" are oppressors. This particular feminist worldview reveals several additional and closely related features that are characteristic of ideologies on both sides of the political spectrum: essentialism (in this case, calling attention to the unique qualities of women), hierarchy (alleging directly or indirectly that women are superior to men), collectivism (asserting that the rights of individual men are less important than the communal goals of women), utopianism (establishing an ideal social order within history), selective cynicism (directing systematic suspicion only toward men), revolutionism (adopting a political program that goes beyond reform), consequentialism (asserting the belief that ends can justify means), and quasi-religiosity (creating what amounts to a secular religion).

We defined ideological feminism very precisely. Trouble is, discussing feminism is often tantamount to discussing personal and collective identity. And identity is seldom established and never defended on the basis of argument or negotiation. No matter what we say, some feminists are going to accuse us of attacking all feminists or even all women. Yet doing that would be counterproductive, because it would imply that some of our offending claims are indeed true of all feminists or all women and must therefore be defended.

Our larger point was that gynocentrism and its misandric fallout – the cumulative results of ideological feminism – have transformed elite culture. They have become pervasive enough in academic, legal, and political circles to pass for conventional wisdom. They have become ways of thinking that seem self-evident and thus require no explanation, let alone justification.

In view of all this, it is worth remembering our primary conclusion: that contempt for men – the idea that men can be classified only as evil or inadequate, or as honorary women – has been a recurring theme in popular culture for over a decade. We did not conclude that contempt for women has been absent from popular culture, by the way, although we did point out that misogyny, unlike misandry, has been carefully monitored, declared politically incorrect, and publicly excoriated.

When *Spreading Misandry* was published in 2001, the topic was hot enough for journalists to cover – we were interviewed for many newspapers, radio shows, and television shows – but not hot enough to be taken seriously by most of them. In some cases, it was the equivalent of a publicity stunt; the goal was to hook readers or viewers with sensationalism – prejudice against men, of all people! – not to explore a social problem with profound moral implications. Print journalists often admitted that men had been portrayed unfairly in popular culture during the 1990s but pointed out that the situation had changed. The culture wars, they declared, were over. Misandry (though not necessarily misogyny) was gone, they opined, along with titillating jokes about Bill Clinton. Men and women were now getting along just fine, thank you very much. How did they know that? By asking a few of their co-workers at the water cooler. Their attitude might be explained as naive optimism, unconscious denial, political strategy, ideological ridicule, or whatever. The point is that many – not all, by any means, but many – of those who direct public opinion found it either desirable or necessary to trivialize our warning about the increasing polarization of men and women (along with other groups making use of identity politics) in our society. We respond to our critics in appendix 1 of this book.

In this second volume, *Legalizing Misandry*, we focus on the interface between popular culture and elite culture at the end of the twentieth century and the beginning of the twenty-first. This is the realm not of movie moguls and media mavens but of lawyers, legislators, and journalists, a realm that not merely reflects a worldview created by others but creates, institutionalizes, and even enforces that worldview.

To create a symbolic, or structural, framework for all this, we use two closely related metaphors: litigation and revolution. The early stages of most great revolutions of the last few hundred years – those of the English, the French, and the Russians, for instance – were marked by litigation (trials of monarchs blamed for the misery) that led to revolution.

First, consider the metaphor of litigation. In part 1 we show that men as a "class" have been put on trial in the court of public opinion by journalists exploiting the emotions generated by sensational events, and that they have been found guilty by a hung jury of academics or professionals manipulating evidence to fit their postmodern or ideological theories but undermining scholarship in the process. These first four chapters describe an important cultural phenomenon that pervaded society in the late twentieth century and therefore provide a historical context for the discussions of legal theory that follow.

Parts 2 and 3 are specifically about men in the courts of law, the ways in which public perceptions of men (and women) have been translated into the legal codes and public policies of both the United States and Canada. Why two countries? Because public perceptions of men and women in both countries are almost identical. Unlike legal and political structures, they do not stop at the border. But our comparative study does two things. First, it shows that Canadian ideologues have been able to extend the influence of feminism much more deeply than American feminists into education, law, bureaucracy, and society at large, with the result that it is undermining the very structure of liberal democracy. Second, it shows that some American feminists are trying to achieve precisely the same things and often in very similar ways. This should be a wake-up call to American legislators and justices, who might still have enough legal or political clout to do something.

Beginning with part 2, then, we move from the metaphor to the daily reality of litigation. Leading the way are ideological feminists. But because they have carefully disguised their role by using euphemisms and other fronts, their influence has often gone unnoticed. Chapters 5 and 6, which are about men and rights, show that the prevalent legal rhetoric favours rights of women and undermines rights of men. Whether intentionally or not, feminists who support that point of view have placed the whole notion of human rights on trial. Part 3 (chapters 7, 8, and 9) is about the prevalent legal rhetoric on sex – that is, the male sex. Intentionally, ideological feminists have placed the whole notion of sex, or at least sex between women and men, on trial.

Part 4 is about men and society from a more theoretical perspective. In chapter 10, we show that the scholarship on which society depends has been severely undermined by feminist ideology. As a direct result, equality has been severely undermined, not merely because of public "debates" over sensational or grotesque public scandals and not merely because of legislation promoted by interest groups but also – ultimately – because of an ideological worldview that has been actively promoted for several decades in schools, colleges, and universities. The result is a gynocentric worldview (ostensibly a mere correction of the older, androcentric one) accompanied by misandry (ostensibly an unfortunate side effect).

That brings us, in chapter 11, to the metaphor of revolution. This has been a "quiet revolution" and thus both less costly and more effective than most of the noisy ones that end up in bloody streets and coups d'états. The doctrines of ideological feminism have been introduced so quickly, so cleverly, and so subtly that most citizens – including most lawyers and legislators – have not even recognized what has been happening. And most of those who have are quickly silenced by a reign of terror uniquely suited to the needs of a quiet revolution: that of political (and sexual) correctness.

Bear in mind that what follows is about the moral and philosophical implications of law, not law per se. Even though this or that ruling can be legitimated by legal precedent or legal analogy, for instance, it cannot necessarily be legitimated morally or philosophically. Lawyers, judges, and even legislators more and more often ground their opinions, interpretations, or reinterpretations, either directly or indirectly, on questionable ideological principles. And feminist ideologues (some of whom happen to be lawyers, judges, or legislators) have done precisely the same thing by arguing that the fundamental premises of legal theory must be reexamined in view of their own theories or even epistemologies. In fact, it is precisely the attempt to legalize and bureaucratize – and thus institutionalize – feminist epistemologies that constitutes the essence of what we call a quiet revolution.

PART ONE

Men on Trial:
The Court of Public Opinion

We begin this book with several high-profile legal or quasi-legal cases that, one way or another, put men collectively on "trial" in the court of public opinion. We focus on journalism – with its reliance on the expertise of academics and other experts – instead of the entertainment industry and examine more closely not only the interaction between popular and elite culture but also content as distinct from form (cinematic conventions, say, or the manipulation of symbols). Moreover, we focus on direct, explicit, and intentional manifestations of misandry instead of indirect, implicit, or unintentional ones.

The case studies here reveal public perceptions not only of the real problems faced by many women but also perceptions of the alleged evils or inadequacies that characterize all men. We discuss the McMartin witch hunt (child abuse, or satanic-ritual abuse) in chapter 1, the Bobbitt affair (wife abuse) in chapter 2, the Hill-Thomas debate (sexual harassment of women) in chapter 3, and the Montreal Massacre (murder of women) in chapter 4. The men in these cases were conceptualized by journalists and other commentators as oppressors, the women as victims, and the men were presumed guilty until or unless they could defend themselves.

Each of these events immediately took on a life of its own, apparently arising spontaneously from popular outrage but in fact arising partly or even mainly from perceptions that had been promoted for years by ideological feminists and had gradually been absorbed by many other people, including men. Some were the usual suspects, including journalists, say, and talk show hosts. Others, however, were professionals: social workers, psychologists, psychiatrists, other clinicians or therapists, and so forth. They were featured in the mass media as "expert witnesses" – that is, interpreters of events that were sometimes not merely sensational but often grotesque and bizarre.

For some of the ideological feminists involved, evil was the result of male biology. (We will explore that topic elsewhere.) For others, however, it was "merely" the result of masculine socialization, which had convinced men of their own superiority and turned women into objects that may be sexually exploited or even killed. And even though ideological feminists did not manage to convince everyone that all men were implicated in the crimes of a few, they did establish the generally accepted rhetorical framework of public debate.

By the end of the century the verdict seemed clear: guilty as charged. As a result, these social problems, which had always evoked fear in women, became political trump cards among ideological feminists. No matter what the individual men involved actually did, they were generally believed to represent men as a class. Consequently, the accused were presumed guilty before court proceedings had ended, or had even begun, and their guilt was maintained even when the courts decided otherwise.

1

Children v. Demons:
The McMartin and Other Witch Hunts

If you are unable to remember any specific instances like the ones mentioned above but still have a feeling that something abusive has happened to you, it probably did.[1]

Sensational cases like that of "Sybil"... [were] welcomed by feminists who saw it as the ultimate consequence of women's victimization and loss of self.[2]

Believe it or not, public furore over satanic ritual abuse during the 1990s was at least partly a public referendum on the status of men, even though some women, too, were caught in the web of fear mongers. According to Mary deYoung, this was really a "new type of sex crime ... discovered during the 1980s: the abuse of very young children in rituals performed by robed and hooded satanists who also happened to be their day care providers. Satanic-ritual abuse appeared to be epidemic ... and the McMartin Preschool was its first *locus delicti*. The cultural response to the McMartin case had all of the characteristics of what sociologists call a moral panic: it was widespread, volatile, hostile, and overreactive."[3]

But the sudden emergence of satanic-ritual abuse – that is, of attacks on people for allegedly engaging in it – was only one manifestation of a problem. Others, very closely related in both time and description, were associated with multiple-personality disorder, recovered-memory syndrome, boy molesters, and predator priests. They all manifested themselves as what could be described metaphorically as either witch hunts (when focusing, as we do here, on the targets) or moral panics (when focusing on those who target them). No matter how grotesque in form and dire in effect for the accused and their families or communities, these were surface phenomena, symptoms of an underlying disease: a pervasive and pathological anxiety over sexuality in general and male sexuality in particular.

In this chapter (which is linked with chapter 7), we discuss how these witch hunts unfolded, how they spread so quickly, and why some of them

eventually subsided. Before concluding, we discuss the two underlying anxieties – the moral panics – that generated these witch hunts: collective stress
coupled with perceptions of guilt over sexual urges and an ideological
worldview that identifies men with evil.

The most dramatic witch hunt, the one that became paradigmatic, began
with accusations of satanic-ritual abuse against the McMartin Preschool, a
family-owned business in Bakersfield, California. Most of the parents were
respectably middle class and upwardly mobile. Judy Johnson was a recently
separated mother living in the district. When she found out that there was
no opening for her son at McMartin, she dropped him off in the school-
yard anyway. One day the boy came home with a reddened anus. Johnson,
immediately jumping to the conclusion that he had been molested by someone at the school, accused Raymond Buckey, the only male teacher at
McMartin. When a medical examination of the boy proved inconclusive,
Johnson hired a detective. She informed him that her son had told her of
perverse sexual activities at the school, activities that involved not only him
but other children as well. At this point, the boy was given another medical. The doctor, though inexperienced in these matters, gave a cautious
diagnosis: the boy, he said, *might* have been molested.

   Johnson's detective sent letters to approximately two hundred families.
Parents were asked to question their children about activities that might
have occurred under the pretence of having their temperatures taken – oral
sex, fondling, sodomy, and so on. In addition, the letter named Buckey as
the primary suspect. After repeated questioning, many of the children confirmed what their parents suspected. Now, the legal system was called in.
A similar case had already occurred, by chance, in Bakersfield. Parents
were advised immediately to take their children for professional evaluation
by social workers. Buckey and other members of the McMartin family
were eventually indicted by a grand jury.

   Once the story was publicized by journalists, a feeding frenzy ensued.
With every retelling of the story, its details became more lurid and more
horrific. Further questioning of the children revealed that they had been
molested in a specifically satanic context. The children now told

tales about the ritualistic ingestion of feces, urine, blood, semen, and human flesh; the
disinterment and mutilation of corpses; the sacrifices of infants; and orgies with their
day care providers, costumed as devils and witches, in the classroom, in tunnels under
the center, and in car washes, airplanes, mansions, cemeteries, hotels, ranches, gourmet
food stores, local gyms, churches, hot air balloons. And they named not only the seven
McMartin day care providers as their satanic abusers, but their soccer coaches,
babysitters, next-door neighbors, and even their own parents, as well as local busi-

nesspeople, the mayor's wife, who was said to drive around town with the corpses of sacrificed infants in the back of her stationwagon, news reporters covering the story, television and film stars, and members of the Anaheim Angels baseball team.[4]

Johnson mobilized for war with the help of other parents, journalists, psychiatrists, lawyers, government officials, community activists, and so on. All of them took this bizarre nonsense very seriously.

It was also taken very seriously by Congress. In 1984 the social worker who had diagnosed satanic-ritual abuse testified that the McMartin Preschool "was an 'organized operation of child predators' that 'serves as a ruse for a larger, unthinkable network of crimes against children' that has 'greater financial, legal, and community resources than any of the agencies trying to uncover it.'"[5] By the time Johnson died of alcoholism, two years later, approximately fifty other McMartinesque events had taken place. And after another five years, approximately fifty more.

While all this was going on, a closely related witch hunt was emerging that involved an apparent epidemic of multiple-personality disorder. The personalities of patients are supposedly fragmented, two or more of them being said to co-exist within the same body; patients believe that they are "possessed" by one or more of these personalities. This phenomenon has a long history in the imagination of Western civilization. In Mark 5:5–15, for example, Jesus heals someone who has been possessed by many demons. More recently, the idea has taken secular and fictional form in the story of Dr Jekyll and Mr Hyde. The most recent parallel of all, which has been presented in several movies, takes psychiatric form. Among the earliest was *The Three Faces of Eve* (1957), starring Joanne Woodward as a woman who has taken on two additional personalities as a way of escaping from painful memories of sexual trauma in her childhood. But as Carol Milstone points out, it was *Sybil* (1976), starring Joanne Woodward (once again, though not the protagonist) as a woman with no fewer than sixteen personalities, or "alters," that generated widespread interest among psychiatrists and other professionals.[6] One thing, though, had changed radically during the previous twenty years. Then, the problem was considered extremely rare. Now, it was considered extremely common. The same thing happened in Canada. By 1990 the province of Manitoba had set up the Satanic Cult Committee, whose mandate was not only to heighten public awareness of these "epidemics" but also to train therapists, counsellors, and other health care professionals. In 1994, Milstone writes, there were no fewer than three thousand of them.

According to Elizabeth Gleick, witch hunts for satanic-ritual abuse and multiple-personality disorder were closely related to a third and simultaneous witch hunt. Targeted were those ostensibly responsible for "recovered memories" of incest."7 Many thousands of parents, almost always fathers, were accused of molesting their own children. So horrific were the experiences of these children, apparently, that they had repressed all memories of them. But many could "recover" these memories as adults, experts said, with the aid of psychologists or psychiatrists. Among the most infamous cases was that of George Franklin, whose daughter, Eileen Lipsker, suddenly "recovered" her memory of a childhood trauma and accused him of having raped and killed her friend more than twenty years earlier. Although Franklin was convicted in 1990, the court decided in 1995 to overturn the conviction because no corroborating evidence had ever been presented.

After the Sybil case was investigated by the American Psychiatric Association, Milstone observes, "repressed" and "recovered" memories became part of common parlance and the focus of an "industry" – in the derived sense of networks of professionals in cooperation with bureaucrats. They began to spin off textbooks, scholarly articles, college courses, academic conferences, public workshops, training videos, talk shows, and highly profitable lecture tours. The "experts" told the public – mainly in the United States and Canada – that curing the disorder could involve up to eight or even ten years of expensive therapy, including long-term hospitalization in specialized wards. They did not always tell the public, however, that therapy involved hypnosis and injections of the drug Amytal (often called truth serum and known for increasing suggestibility). Nor did they tell the public that diagnostic features could include not only startling symptoms such as "lost time," hallucinations, panic attacks, schizophrenia, and manic depression but also a host of symptoms so common that they could apply to almost anyone: "glancing around the therapist's office, frequent blinking, change of posture or voice, rolling the eyes upward, sudden laughter or anger, covering the mouth, hair falling forward, scratching an itch, touching one's face or chair, changing hairstyles, or wearing a particular colour of clothing or jewellery ... drinking alcohol." In children, diagnostic features could be equally common: having "imaginary playmates, being lonely, truant, sexually precocious or delinquent."8

Because information was so readily available to the public, not all patients even waited for specialists to diagnose this problem. In any case, some reported not merely two or three "alters" but dozens or hundreds. And they reported not only incest and molestation but also satanic rituals, out-of-body experiences, near-death experiences, and alien abductions (the latter, for some reason, were seldom taken seriously by the public as real events). Not all patients got well, either; some became more depressed or even suicidal.

The stakes were very, very high. And it was all taken very, very seriously. "Hokey as the MPD [multiple-personality disorder] field is starting to sound, one must be reminded that North America's post-Sybil MPD wildfire is fueled not by fringe elements but by the most powerful institutions in the medical establishment – the American Medical Association, the National Institute of Mental Health, the World Health Organization, the Canadian Psychiatric Association, the Canadian Medical Association, the International Society for the Study of Multiple Personality Disorder and Dissociation, and university medical schools such as Harvard."9

Another witch hunt, not as pervasive but continuing and still worthy of headlines, erupted over an alleged epidemic of boy molesters. In *Harmful to Minors: The Perils of Protecting Children from Sex*, Judith Levine discusses the case of a boy named Tony, his younger sister Jessica, and their mother Diane.10 In 1993 Tony, then twelve years old, was doing well at school, although he sometimes got into trouble (hardly an unusual problem). He had a "fierce" relationship with Jessica, fiercely affectionate and fiercely antagonistic (hardly unusual among siblings). One night, he and Jessica played at touching each other. And before you could say "molestation," Tony was accused by social workers of having made inappropriate advances toward her. Their case was based on statements from Jessica at school, statements that she later recanted (although officials explained her recantation away as a result of "accommodation syndrome") and that, in any case, could not be supported by any evidence. Jessica accused her mother Diane, too, of behaviour that was construed as inappropriate. In a flash, the children were removed from Diane's home and given to foster parents. The case dragged on for years. In the end, due to the efforts of at least one appalled social worker, Diane regained custody of her children. The family had been fractured for three years, though, and the children had "learned" a few things. Tony had learned that the adult world would betray and punish him for no reason, and Jessica had learned how to take advantage of her sexual power: how to intimidate others by threatening to accuse them of inappropriate behaviour and how not to feel "bad guilt" for being an informant (even, presumably, if the information was based on fantasy or malice). Which was worse, one might well ask – as we will on more than one occasion in this book – the disease or the cure?

Other cases, Levine points out, did not have such "happy" endings. Preadolescent children, usually boys, were institutionalized routinely for displaying what adult professionals considered an untoward interest in sex, even though no one had ever made an adequately scientific study of "normal" sexual behaviour in children. Once incarcerated in "therapeutic" settings, these children were classified officially as child molesters – the alleged molesters were almost always boys – and expected to confess as quickly as possible. Those who failed to do so were said to be in denial and subjected to behaviour modification techniques of a kind that would result in law suits among adults, denied personal privacy of any kind, and forced into humiliating acts of "atonement" such as apologizing on their knees. Given their pathologized identity, many of these children actually came to believe that they would end up as adult molesters. And a few, no doubt, would.

Thousands of people who are still very upset over the episode of "predator priests," or "priest pedophiles," would be outraged that we classify it as a witch hunt. The major difference between this phenomenon and those that are now commonly known in retrospect as witch hunts is that most of the accused in this case might really have been witches – that is, guilty. We say "might," because the number of priests who actually molested children, at least 80% of whom were boys,[11] will never be known despite the official tally, since most of these cases have been settled out of court (although many civil suits are still pending) and most of the accused have never been tried and either convicted or acquitted.[12] This problem is no mere technicality, even though we usually assume that an admission of guilt is conclusive. Ignoring it, in fact, would be tantamount to ignoring due process. And that is a major feature of every witch hunt. Even so, it would be foolish – and certainly foolhardy – to claim that most of these priests were actually innocent of the charges against them; most of them, in all likelihood, really were guilty.

But that was true also of the McCarthy witch hunt of the late 1940s and early 1950s. Whether the McCarthy hearings were necessary or not, one thing is clear: some of those accused by the House Committee on Un-American Activities really were guilty of the charge against them; they were either Communists themselves or knew of Communists but did not reveal their names. What defines a witch hunt is not the innocence or guilt of those charged but the emotional intensity, the loss of control, that accompanies charges and corrupts the process of deciding on innocence or guilt. According to that definition the church scandal is just the most recent in a long line of witch hunts that overtook society in the late twentieth century and that continue into the twenty-first.

It is hard to ignore the fact that the moral panics over satanic-ritual abuse, multiple-personality disorder, recovered-memory syndrome, and boy molesters were multiplying rapidly just when stories of alien abduction were also multiplying and just before panics over predator priests. Was this entirely a coincidence? If the other phenomena are taken seriously, no matter how bizarre, why not alien abductions as well? In a recent book, Elaine Showalter has noted some distinct parallels, as has Stephen Rae, in an essay for the *New York Times Magazine*.[13] "Abductees" are subjected to sexual abuse (experiments involving their sexual organs, say, or being forced to mate with the aliens), and like their counterparts, they repress their memories for two reasons. First, they find their experiences too horrifying. Second, they know that no one will believe them. They consequently experience intense but inexplicable emotional pain and are now offered forms of therapy similar to the therapy given to their counterparts (notably, hypnotic regression). Rae discusses the work of Harvard's John Mack:

To help abductees shed their isolation, Mack set up the Program for Extraordinary Experience Research. He helped them recover memories in hypnotic screamathons. When combined with breathwork, Mack says, hypnosis undoes the repression of memory imposed by the aliens. As the traumas are brought to consciousness, relived with "feelings of terror, rage and grief as intense as any I have encountered as a psychiatrist," their power was dissipated ... [Mack] acknowledges that it is possible to implant false memories under hypnosis, but only memories of inconsequential events – an issue at the center of fierce debates over recovered memories of Satanic cults and childhood sexual abuse.[14]

It could be argued that those who consider themselves abductees are, in reality, merely denying more mundane forms of sexual abuse. Yet people in both groups have made precisely the same claim: that what they experienced was true, not a delusion, no matter how impossible or unacceptable it might sound. And people in both groups have demanded to be taken seriously on the same grounds: their demonstrated intelligence, social respectability, civic responsibility, mental health, and so forth. In that case, the argument could be reversed: the victims of satanic cults and incest were denying more *bizarre* traumas.

In fact, both advocates for and detractors of people who claim to have recovered memories of sexual molestation might be wrong. Hallucinations are common experiences that occur to ordinary people under ordinary circumstances but also in connection with sleep paralysis, a disorder experienced by at least 8% of the population during that twilight state between waking and sleeping. It involves three elements: a sense of paralysis, the presence of strange and sinister beings, and sexual stimulation. This condition, says Carl Sagan, results when less oxygen than usual flows to the brain. At one time the sinister beings were called succubi and incubi or fairies. Nowadays they are called "aliens." Whatever they are called, these beings are said to have sexual relations with their human victims. Sagan might have added that a far more acceptable name, these days, would be that of the victim's father, brother, uncle, or even mother. "Is it possible," asks Sagan, "that people in all times and places occasionally experience vivid, realistic hallucinations, often with sexual content with the details filled in by the prevailing cultural idioms sucked out of the Zeitgeist?"[15] Obviously, it is possible in some cases.

In its coverage of this topic, CBS's *48 Hours* noted in 1994 that some twenty-five million Americans claimed to have been abducted by extraterrestrials! At a meeting of alleged victims, the camera noted a bulletin board with this quotation from William James: "A new idea is first condemned as ridiculous and then dismissed as trivial, until finally, it becomes what everybody knows."[16] The point is this: maybe the alleged abductees really are a bunch of crackpots, but those who had recently been called crackpots themselves – those whose claims about incest had been dismissed for decades by experts under the influence of Freud[17] – were hardly in a position to call others crackpots for making almost identical claims. On the contrary, they were in an ideal position to demand extensive research on behalf of those who claimed to have been sexually molested by extraterrestrials. Fortunately, they did not.

The "alien abductions" did not lead to a witch hunt. After all, no one could take an alien from outer space to court. And very few people ever took the alleged victims seriously. Moreover, they have included both women and men in roughly equal numbers. This episode fills out the social, cultural, and historical background against which to examine the witch hunts and raises an interesting question: Why are millions of people willing to take some bizarre phenomena seriously but not others? Because some phenomena have more political clout than others do.

Why did the witch hunts spread so quickly? Several explanations have been offered. Referring to Elaine Showalter's "hystories," Carol Tavris notes that they are "constructed by vested interests protecting their professions and incomes, ignorant psychologists, greedy opportunists who see a way to make a fast buck on the insecurities of the vulnerable, ideologues of the right and left, and clergy and politicians drunk on elixir of moral righteousness."[18] In the case of satanic-ritual abuse, panic was spread by both professional and grassroots groups. Among the former, the most obvious were journalists, who, not surprisingly, adopted hyperbolic imagery and a somewhat hysterical tone. The television industry had a vested interest in dramatic exposés and provocative interviews, all of which were "politically correct." (Although the term truly belongs within ironic quotation marks, we must use it so often that adding them every time would be irritating; for a discussion, see appendix 4.)

Then, as now, being a victim was actually a badge of pride. Those who embarked on their twelve-step programs were well aware of this. The ceaseless parade of victims – especially the victims of childhood sexual traumas – was a fascinating sequel to the spectacle of an earlier time. Unlike the bearded ladies and alligator men once exhibited at freak shows to evoke curiosity and pity, these survivors were exhibited on the talk show circuit to evoke pity and solidarity. The former had been victims of nature, after all, but the latter were victims of evil. The old side shows had been not only bizarre but also edifying, so that a viewer could think, There, but for the grace of God, go I. The new ones were still bizarre, but they were also edifying in a different way. A viewer could now think, There, *by* the grace of God, go I. "Sympathetic professionals" also appeared on television.

During the bitter years of McMartin, they not only received a great deal of local, national, and international news attention, but also appeared on television talk shows and primetime newsmagazines. They took to the lecture circuit, gave testimony in government-sponsored hearings, addressed conferences of child abuse professionals, consulted with other professionals as other satanic day care cases began cropping up across the country, and testified as experts in the criminal trials of day care providers. And in each interview, each presentation, each consultation, the story of McMartin was told and re-told in communities that were being primed for the moral panic by the telling.[19]

As Richard Gardner points out in *Sex Abuse Hysteria: The Salem Witch Trials Revisited*, accusations were encouraged by the therapy industry, which had a vested interest in fanning the flames of hysteria and a constant supply of new cases.[20] Levine makes it clear that the flood of accusations against boy molesters, like those against other targets, was led by professional experts with financial interests, apart from any others. At first, in the early 1990s, there were no treatment facilities for "children who molest." Just over a decade later, there were 50 residential and 390 nonresidential ones in the United States. The head of one told Levine that establishing a program was a "business decision."[21] The programs were not based on any empirical data. A few cases were reported, and the experts declared a state of emergency, having diagnosed an "epidemic" of juvenile molestation. There was a great deal of anxiety over the "negative pairing" of sex and aggression (even though both are universal features of human existence in both adults and children and not necessarily "negative"). Once the mass media took up this new cause, the number of demands for solutions increased. That encouraged other experts to set up new treatment programs and to seek massive funding. An industry was born.

Popular therapeutic self-help books came into their own at this very moment. Potential accusers did not have to consult psychotherapists to conclude that they had been victims of horrific treatment at the hands of their fathers or even grandfathers. They had only to pick up a self-help manual. One of these was particularly popular. *The Courage to Heal*, by Ellen Bass and Laura Davis, functioned as a modern equivalent of the *Malleus maleficarum*, the primary textbook used by witch hunters of the late Middle Ages.[22] The new version was available to millions, though, not only to an educated ecclesiastical elite. According to Bass and Davis, any woman who even suspects that she was sexually molested, even if she cannot actually remember the event, probably was molested. (Bass and Davis referred only to women; the fact that men, too, reported being sexually abused by their parents, even by their mothers, was clearly of no interest to them.) The book provides a simple checklist of symptoms and explicitly encourages readers, with leading questions, to diagnose recovered memory syndrome. The book was soon accompanied, says Showalter, by countless "hystories" spread over the Internet, talk shows, and the self-help networks of the "recovery community," stories that quickly developed "their own conventions, stereotypes, and structures."[23]

Grassroots groups participated, too, in the spread of witch hunts, both willingly and ably. By 1984, parents had formed an organization called Believe the Children. Their activism had grown "in sophistication from wearing buttons and carrying hand-painted signs to establishing a clearing house on satanic ritual abuse, replete with a speakers' bureau, a support network for parents, police, and prosecutors involved in other satanic day care cases, and a referral list of sympathetic professionals."[24]

Because the spread of mass hysteria at the end of the twentieth century, as in earlier centuries but much more quickly and effectively, was no accident, we should take it very seriously as a symptom of social pathology. "The stories we tell," writes Gleick, "say a lot about our fantasies, our fears, and our preoccupations."[25] Even if only for that reason, Showalter refrains from urging the abolition of psychiatry.[26]

Some patients have remained sincerely and profoundly convinced that the events in question occurred, even though no evidence was ever found to substantiate widespread incest or satanic cults – let alone victims murdered for ritual purposes. But the hysteria generated by some of these witch hunts has subsided. At any rate, multiple personality disorder, along with satanic-ritual abuse and recovered-memory syndrome, are now cultural and historical memories that intelligent people would like very much not to recover. (The priest pedophiles have been stopped, although the emotional impact of their discovery has not yet receded, and the boy molesters are still "discovered" now and then.) We are left to pick up the pieces.

The witch hunts ended for at least three reasons. First, they had gotten out of hand. As in the Salem witch hunt of 1692, too many people were threatened by the possibility of false accusations. And too many professionals, both legal and therapeutic, realized that they had better save their personal and collective reputations by returning to the status quo ante. Second, it was too hard to convict people without evidence. Worse, both the alleged victims and the alleged malefactors began to sue for damages. Milstone is by no means the only one to suggest that respectable professionals were either unprofessionally gullible and negligent or criminally responsible for destroying countless lives. Some former patients, now convinced that they had been duped, have initiated lawsuits against therapists and institutions. Others have made formal complaints to medical organizations. The False Memory Syndrome Foundation has been established in Philadelphia by accused parents, who encourage other parents in their situation to challenge courts that produce no hard evidence of molestation.

And what about McMartin? By 1986, 80% of the surveyed residents of Los Angeles County believed that the McMartins were guilty of crimes almost inconceivably horrific. Nevertheless, charges were dropped against five of the seven who were originally charged, due to lack of evidence. Raymond Buckey and his mother Peggy McMartin were sent to trial. This ordeal lasted twenty-eight months, then the longest criminal trial on record. It consumed 64,000 pages of transcripts and cost $13 million. After nine months of deliberation, McMartin was acquitted of all charges and Buckey of most. A hung jury on eight charges, however, meant that he had to be tried a second time. Finally, all charges were dropped against him. And what of Judy Johnson herself? "The mother of the little boy who never shared his dark secrets with anyone, and who never could even pick out Raymond Buckey's picture form a photo lineup, was institutionalized for a while with the diagnosis of paranoid schizophrenia after she told detectives that her ex-husband had also sodomized her son, and that an intruder had broken into her house and sodomized the family dog."[27]

The third reason for the end of the witch hunts was that professionals and clinicians began to rethink the theories that had led to, or at least had been used to explain, them. With growing criticism of the therapeutic movement's contribution to the witch hunts, the Sybil case itself was investigated. One of two psychiatrists who had written it up, Herbert Speigel, said in an interview that "Sybil" had been highly suggestible and that all her "alters" had been created under hypnosis by his colleague on the case, Cornelia Wilbur. Speigel had come to have serious doubts, in any case, about the patient's abuse by her mother. Being cautious, he attributed her false memories to some unconscious interaction between her and her therapist. He wanted to challenge the dubious notion of recovered memories, in short, but he did not want to risk accusing anyone of immoral and illegal behaviour.

It was only in the late 1990s that psychiatrists themselves began to challenge the whole theory of recovered memories. Some recognized that the therapies offered were providing disturbed patients with an attractive but also a powerful and false explanation for their suffering and that many of their professional colleagues were exploiting these patients. As a therapeutic device, "remembering" childhood traumas was very effective. It did what all therapies must do, by providing a powerful explanation for suffering: my pain has a cause that can be identified and thus eliminated. It replaced chaos with order: bad things do not just happen; bad people make them happen. It replaced neurotic guilt with what was considered healthy rage: the bad person is someone else, not me. Unfairly blaming others, even parents and usually fathers, offered an irresistible alternative to anxiety, confusion, and even mere regret about the vicissitudes of everyday life. On talk shows, observers in studio audiences often said that the fathers must have done something to cause so much unhappiness. And this was often true, because people are never perfect. But did they cause it in this particular way? Were there no other causes for unhappiness? Do adults have no responsibility for making choices leading to their own unhappiness? Finally, must we rely on the old adage that "where there's smoke there's fire"? There might be, sure, but there might not be.

Any patient who sought this kind of therapy might indeed have suffered childhood distress or even trauma of some kind, possibly, though not necessarily, of a sexual nature. But were the therapists beyond scientific, let alone moral or legal, accountability? As Richard Gardner points out, the crusade mounted on behalf of the new therapy provoked a witch hunt not merely in the metaphorical sense of the postwar McCarthy hunt but in a quite literal sense.[28] The parents of the patients were accused of having worshipped the Devil, in other words, of being witches according to the definition of that word held in old Salem. Then, as now, the "experts" relied on testimony that sounded plausible in the immediate cultural context but had little or nothing to do with hard evidence. There was only one major difference between this witch hunt and those of the sixteenth and seventeenth centuries: the people accused and destroyed by unverifiable allegations were usually men, not women. We will return to that topic.

Professionals and clinicians re-examined some case studies of parents, moreover, including fathers who had been unjustly attacked in court and even imprisoned. Evidence of the rethinking could soon be found not only in books and articles[29] but also on television.[30] One segment of *Prime-Time Live*, for example, indicated that the psychiatrists were now divided between those who specialized in satanic-ritual abuse therapy and those who challenged the professional competence, the moral integrity, and even the mental health of their colleagues. The former believed that members of Satanist cults, who, they claimed, indulged in the torture and ritual murder of their own children, numbered somewhere between the tens and hundreds of thousands. Due to the trauma of watching these sinister events, or even being forced to participate in them, survivors repressed the memories. Later, as disturbed adults, they turned to therapists who helped them remember. But it took more than some rethinking by professionals to end the hysteria. Eventually, patients changed their minds and accused their therapists of implanting false memories through suggestion, hypnosis, and other manipulative techniques. Police departments admitted that they could not come up with any corroborating evidence.

Child abuse, even if it has nothing to do with Satanism and is not an epidemic, remains a serious problem. But must we take at face value virtually any story of childhood molestation? Elizabeth Loftus – often called as an expert witness in court because of her research on memory – says no.[31] Her research on twenty thousand subjects showed that memories of any kind are distorted in about one quarter of the subjects merely through the power of suggestion or if they are supplied with incorrect information. Moreover, says Loftus, violent events actually decrease the accuracy of memory. Memories are weakest when associated either with low levels of arousal (such as boredom or sleepiness) or high levels of arousal (stress or trauma). In short, memory is fragile and disintegrates gradually. It is prone to suggestion, moreover, not autonomous. Loftus and colleagues have also shown that even imagining a false event increases subjective confidence that the event happened and that subjects can confuse dreaming and waking events when presented with a list of them. She writes that "63 percent can 'recover' nonexistent memories of being exposed [as infants] to colored mobiles while in their hospital cribs – a literal impossibility since the nervous system is not developed enough to lay down explicit memories in the first few years of life."[32]

Other scholars eventually began to sift the wheat from the chaff. In *Suggestions of Abuse: True and False Memories of Childhood Sexual Trauma*, Michael Yapko claimed that many of the charges were probably the result of hypnosis.[33] In *Victims of Memory*, Mark Pendergrast told the story of his own experience with an accusation of incest.[34] Like Yapko, Pendergrast refrained from consigning all accusations to the category of false memories, but he did describe memory as "plastic" and subject to unwitting manipulation for various purposes. His experience with his two daughters is a case in point. They were in their early twenties when they began "feminist therapy." Shortly thereafter, they accused him of having molested them as children. Their therapist advised them to change their names, move to other cities, and cut off all contact with him. But when Pendergrast went into therapy himself, in an effort to retrieve his own memories of what had happened, he could only remember one occasion on which he had wept in front of his daughters. This, they claimed, was evidence of "emotional incest."

In *Remembering Satan*, Lawrence Wright discusses the bizarre case of a man who developed his own false memories of molesting his daughters and the consequent guilt, under the impact of accusations.[35] According to one reviewer, John Goddard, Wright fails to make a necessary distinction between sexual trauma and other traumas. Wright points out that children who witnessed the most horrific scenes in Nazi death camps remember them vividly in adult life. Why, he asks, should only sexual scenes be repressed? But according to Goddard, "Wright is mixing apples and oranges. Witnessing a parent's murder might be shocking, but the event has nothing in common with being sexually violated by the very person on whom the child depends for love, nourishment and physical survival."[36] *Might* be shocking? *Nothing* in common? Please! Adult notions of sexuality make the advances of parents seem shocking, not anything inherent in caressing.[37] Children themselves often play or experiment with their sexual organs until they are warned not to do so by adults. (Children's experimentation is a complex problem, though, and responsible parents provide their adolescent children with cultural guidelines for sexual behaviour.) The motifs of reversal and betrayal are by no means confined to sexual encounters between parents and children. In the Nazi death camps, children learned that adults were ready to kill them instead of protect them. A world that had once made sense, moreover, now made no sense at all. And yet they remembered everything! To claim that anyone would find it easier to live with memories of Auschwitz than to live with memories of sexual encounters is not merely a psychological absurdity. It is a moral outrage.

But were there any underlying factors involved in the witch hunts and moral panics? Were millions of people actually predisposed to believe that such bizarre scenarios were actually occurring? If witch hunts result from underlying social tensions and anxiety projected outward onto convenient targets, which anxiety was projected onto the particular targets discussed in this chapter?[38] There were indeed at least two underlying factors. In this section, we will consider one of them: pervasive and enduring stress at the collective level.[39]

The series of witch hunts that began with McMartin lasted a decade. Taken together, they could be described as a "collective stress reaction in response to a belief in a story about immediately threatening circumstances."[40] This is how DeYoung, in particular, explains the perplexing hysteria over satanic-ritual abuse.[41] During the 1980s, she explains, more and more women were moving into the work force and had to depend on daycare for their children. Yet they became deeply ambivalent over what was happening. On the one hand, they and their children had "covenantal relationships," which were based on bonding and emotional expressiveness. On the other hand, they and their employers had "contractual relationships," which were based on negotiation and exchange. Many women felt guilty, either consciously or subconsciously, for not taking care of their own children, and they worried about the quality and safety of their arrangements. They felt trapped, in short, between necessity and risk. It was a no-win situation. The tension that all this generated made those who worked at daycare centres convenient targets, scapegoats. Almost overnight, the situation became highly combustible; only a single lighted match was necessary to provoke an explosion. And that was provided in 1983 by McMartin.

Eventually parents found ways of exerting more control over daycare centres. They could drop in at any time, observe or participate in activities, chaperone outings, sit on boards, and so on. Many states enacted legislation to screen potential daycare workers, moreover, checking for psychiatric problems and character flaws. Once the original and underlying psychological problem had been resolved, there was no longer any need for the remedy.

But the demise of that witch hunt, says Levine, did not mean the end by any means of a more generalized anxiety. The sexual revolution had made sexual activity freer from restraint and more visible than ever before. A flood of pornography was now accessible to both adults and children on the Internet, cable television channels, and even (in slightly toned down form) on network television. One possibility haunted parents: if other people got the idea that anything goes, and they surely would in such a permissive and hedonistic age, then they would see no reason to refrain from pedophilia. Not many parents drew the further conclusion, at least not consciously, that they and their children might actually want to indulge in forbidden sexual activities. That possibility would have threatened the longstanding cultural taboo on incest, the relatively recent notion of childhood innocence, and the fragile accommodation that society had reached in connection with deeply rooted ambivalence toward sexual activity of any kind at all.

According to historian John Demos, the late medieval and early modern witch hunts occurred after crises.[42] During the crises themselves, people were so busy coping that they had no time to think about causes or rail against scapegoats. The witch hunts began only after things had calmed down. Only then did they kill those whom they perceived as instigators or their surrogates. Bear in mind that witches were closely associated not only with deviant religious activities but also with deviant sexual ones. As we have said, modern witch hunts differ from earlier ones in only one significant way: the targets are much more likely to be male than female.

All the witch hunts discussed here were linked, we have already suggested, by a sexual subtext that was represented within the family circle by the parents' molestation of their own children[43] and outside the family circle by molestation of other children.[44] Not so obviously, the witch hunts were linked by an ideological subtext as well, the ideological manipulation of stress to advance feminist political goals. The source of evil was symbolically represented by men (the victimizers) and the source of goodness by women and children (their victims). Yet at no time during the controversy did the specific topic of gender come up for public discussion; no one noticed that most of the people attacked (and many of the victims) were either men or boys.

Although it was easy to deny that millions of people were fiendishly sacrificing babies in their suburban basements, it was not so easy to identify
the connection between ideological feminism and a witch hunt that
targeted primarily men. So far, that connection has remained hidden, and
ideological feminism has remained fashionable in academic and political
circles.

The ideologues who intentionally or unintentionally, directly or indirectly, encouraged the accusations against men purported to explain the
world in terms of victims and oppressors and therefore made victimhood
politically useful. When victims go public even today, they do not merely
elicit support from other victims or potential victims but also reinforce the
ideological claim to collective victimization, along with its supposed corollary of collective righteousness and its actual consequence of collective
power. In this case, the fact that some of the accusers were men was ideologically irrelevant as long as most of the accused, too, were men.

Who would have had a vested interest in connecting repressed memories with sexual misconduct, especially incest? Although some mothers
were accused of heinous sexual misconduct, or at least of having done
nothing to prevent it, fathers were the primary suspects. Anyone who
wanted to heap suspicion on fathers, or on men in general, would have
found the phenomenon politically useful. And some feminists – not all, but
some – fell into precisely that category. Their demonization of men had
already surged by the 1990s, as we will show throughout this book, and
the witch hunts provided an ideal opportunity to score political points.
Not only were there reasons to suspect all or most men of wanting to rape
women,[45] it seemed, but there were reasons to suspect in addition that all
or most fathers wanted to rape their own children. Carol Tavris has noted
that "[s]ensational cases like that of 'Sybil' ... [were] welcomed by feminists who saw it as the ultimate consequence of women's victimization and
loss of self."[46]

The ideological worldview of activists was highly dualistic, a characteristic feature of ideology. At the individual level, troubled people – and those
who "recovered" memories of sexual traumas were always troubled people, which is why they sought out psychologists or psychiatrists – found the
source of their troubles in what had supposedly been done to them by others, rather than in their own attitudes or behaviour. At the collective level,
too, they found the source of suffering not within their own group but in
another one – that is, in men (although, in cases involving daycare, where
very few men worked, many women were accused). The source of evil was
externalized, in other words, and the world was polarized between "us"
and "them." Another characteristic feature of ideology is essentialism. In
this case, women or girls were stereotyped as innocent victims by nature
and men or boys as sinister molesters by nature. Yet another characteristic

of ideology is the belief that ends can justify means. In this case, advocates for the victims of satanic ritual abuse and incest were convinced that any measure – even distorting the justice system to make prosecutions easier – could be justified.

That a movement devoted to "survivors" of incest and a generalized suspicion that all men, just beneath the surface, are rapists and molesters originated almost immediately after the advent of ideological feminism was almost certainly not a coincidence. Nor, given the number of cases based on false memories, was it due to the fortuitous discovery of a hidden problem. Incest has always existed, no doubt, but it was widely believed in the 1990s to be prevalent.

DeYoung points out that male teachers were accused far out of proportion to the number working in daycare.[47] In 1983, only 5% of daycare workers were male. But in a survey of thirty-five major cases, 49% of those charged were male. As a result, men fled the field to find greater security in fields conventionally assigned to them. Daycare was even more feminized, in short, and men even more demonized. If feminists can argue that it was no accident that women were the primary targets of witch hunters several centuries ago, we can surely argue that it is no accident and hardly surprising that men are the primary targets of modern witch hunters. Consider the rhetoric generated at precisely this moment in history by ideological feminists, according to whom all of history is a conspiracy of men against women. The hysteria generated by this modern witch hunt has contributed in no small measure to the creation of misandry. American society, thanks at least partly to the Puritan tradition, has never been comfortable with sex. But now, thanks at least partly to the beliefs of ideological feminists, the level of discomfort has reached an unprecedented high – unprecedented even in Victorian times.

This is not to say that even the most ideological feminists deliberately set out to create a panic. But they did contribute significantly to an atmosphere in which it was easy to single out men or boys as scapegoats, as the chief suspects for any social problem – especially those in which girls or women were likely to be identified as the primary victims. In addition, many feminists promoted pop psychology, which had become a characteristic feature of talk shows that were addressed primarily to women. Hence the extensive use of psychotherapeutic language. Without both the feminist movement itself and the recovery movement that was closely associated with it, in short, we would probably not have been engulfed in the hysteria over satanic rituals and recovered memories.

It is not entirely surprising, therefore, that Showalter received death threats from those with emotional or political investments in the notion of "recovered memory syndrome."[48] Loftus received similar treatment. "She has been called a whore by a prosecutor in a courthouse hallway, assaulted by a passenger on an airplane shouting, 'You're that woman!' and has occasionally required surveillance by plainclothes security guards at lectures."[49]

Men were the main targets of the witch hunters discussed here, though not the only ones. In the following chapters, we discuss episodes in which major segments of the population targeted only men as the collective source of evil. The polarization of society along sexual lines was so obvious and so pervasive, in fact, that many journalists and other cultural observers could not help but comment on it.

2

Wives v. Abusers:
The Bobbitt Affair

The retail clerks who send [Lorena Bobbitt] letters of support, the homemakers who cackle wildly every time they sharpen the butcher knife, are neither "tired of hearing about victims" nor eager to honour them. They're tired of *being* victims. And they're eager to see women fight back by whatever means necessary.[1]

Sitcoms routinely portray women hitting men, almost never portray men hitting women. When he fails to leave, it is not called "Battered Man Syndrome"; it is called comedy.[2]

On 23 June 1993, Lorena Bobbitt sliced off the penis of her husband John. Journalists immediately went into a feeding frenzy. What case could symbolize more graphically, they must have thought, the war between the sexes? In the trial that followed, Lorena was found not guilty of maliciously wounding John. The reason? She had been driven, during a moment of "temporary insanity," by an "irresistible urge." After four years of physical and sexual abuse from John, it was argued officially, she had suddenly gone berserk. Unofficially, though – and this is very important – it was said that she had acted in self-defense, even though John had been fast asleep at the time and had already been found not guilty of raping his wife, at least on that occasion.

The trials of Eric and Lyle Menendez took place at almost exactly the same time, and their attorneys used almost exactly the same defense. The brothers had been driven during an irrational interlude to kill their parents. After years of physical and sexual torment by their parents, the boys had suddenly gone berserk. They believed, however, that they were acting in self-defense, even though their parents were watching television and eating ice cream at the time. In the Menendez trials, neither jury was able to reach a verdict. But the pleas of self-defense in the two spectacular Menendez trials generated a storm of controversy.

In this chapter, which is linked with chapter 9, we discuss comments on the trials from various sources within popular culture and comments on domestic violence from a panel of experts in social work. These comments reveal misandry as a fundamental premise of ideological feminism.

On 4 February 1994, Ted Koppel's *Nightline*, presented a special "town meeting" on the implications of the three trials, one for Lorena Bobbitt and one for each Menendez brother.[3] "Is Abuse an Excuse?" was the title of the meeting, and in the opinion of some guests, but not others, abuse clearly was an excuse. This conflict reflected widespread disagreement between men and women. The men on Eric's jury wanted a verdict of guilty, for instance, and the women did not. Several of the latter made it clear, moreover, that the dispute among jurors was unusually bitter. What accounts for all this?

From the very beginning of the show, it was clear that no one really cared about the people actually involved in these lurid trials. What everyone did care about were the social, legal, and political (but not, unfortunately, the moral) implications. The discussion on the show – and everywhere else – might have been clarified considerably if everyone had acknowledged this. Several supporters of Lorena tried to trivialize the controversy over temporary insanity. Why, they asked, is everyone so concerned about a few unrepresentative cases? After all, the temporary insanity defense is risky and used only by those who can afford to pay for the most expensive lawyers, investigators, psychologists, or other expert witnesses. And even then, they are usually unsuccessful.

Alan Dershowitz, a controversial professor of law at Harvard, noted the obvious by observing that those most anxious to legitimate prior abuse as a factor mitigating guilt were politically motivated: "These aren't psychologists," he said in connection with some of the expert witnesses called in by defense lawyers; "these are advocates, and this is advocacy psychobabble. What we're hearing is people who are politicians, who have a political agenda. It's not that we're learning more about the mind, we're learning more about the politics of certain movements."[4] Dershowitz carefully refrained from identifying the particular movement. He received a smiling but rhetorical reply from Lenore Walker, the psychologist from Rutgers who gained fame in some quarters and infamy in others for introducing the legal notion of Battered-Woman Syndrome (which we discuss in appendix 3)[5]. "And what is that political movement," she asked rhetorically, "to end violence?"[6]

At issue during this debate was not compassion for Lyle and Eric Menendez, two men who took the law into their own hands, but compassion for Lorena Bobbitt and other women who do the same thing. It was clear to everyone that the underlying topic was ideological feminism. Not all panelists even bothered to substitute "abused people" for "abused women." Although many feminists had seen the Menendez brothers and their trials as nothing more than sideshows, they felt an urgent need to legitimate the Menendez defense strategy, which they would have liked to see used more often on behalf of women.

Their political motivations notwithstanding, psychologists must be taken seriously in cases of this kind. One expert noted that suffering leads women such as Lorena to lose control. But the same argument could be applied to almost everyone. It could certainly be applied to most of the men now locked away in prisons for crimes such as murder and rape, crimes generated at least partly by extremely stressful home environments involving hopeless poverty, alcohol or other drugs, gang violence, and the absence of fathers. Some were driven by irresistible urges that could not be cured even after years of therapy. Nevertheless, these men are seldom declared to have been temporarily insane. Men who injure women are always evil, it would seem, no matter what their state of mental health. Women who injure men are always out of control, on the other hand, no matter what their state of moral awareness.

Lisa Kemler, Lorena Bobbitt's lawyer, tried to place the discussion of abused women in a different, presumably less controversial, context: "I don't think that anybody sitting around here would have any trouble with a death-camp inmate who reacted, finally, and struck out at his guard and killed him."[7] Although it is true that a few inmates in the Nazi death camps did kill their guards, these acts were the result of remarkable control, not loss of control. No one would dream of arguing for the temporary insanity of inmates at Auschwitz or Treblinka who used violence to escape. Lorena's defenders, on the other hand, were inconsistent. The official argument, which held sway in court, was that she had lost control and therefore deserved pity. The unofficial argument, however, which held sway among her supporters in the court of public opinion, was that because Lorena had taken control by defending herself, she deserved admiration and even emulation by women in similar circumstances. But logic would not have allowed the argument to go both ways. Either Lorena was out of control, or she was not.

Some feminists on *Nightline* who understood the logic and acknowledged it openly were not satisfied with the temporary insanity defense. For them, it was merely an expedient measure made necessary by the current state of legal practice. They would have gone further. Although she later contradicted herself, Walker probably spoke for millions: "I'm not sure I would have used an insanity defense in this case. I think you could have made just as good an argument that this was self-defense." "Most battered women," she observed, "are not mentally impaired."

Why, then, had the notion of temporary insanity become so widely accepted in the present? "For years," according to Jeff Greenfield's voice-over on the show, "American culture has been heavily influenced by the language of therapy, of recovery, the language that defines millions of us as victims of one sort or another. And it's language that has come to dominate ... the American talk show."[8] No wonder people had come to believe that much or even most of their unhappiness can be blamed on others. As a result of the incessant talk about sickness, evil had been abolished and sin medicalized. "Maybe what we're really worried about," said Greenfield, "is that a culture that seems more comfortable with explanations than with judgments is a culture that's losing its sense of what is right and what is wrong."[9]

Greenfield might have been right, in one sense, but precisely the opposite could be said in another sense. The rhetoric of victimization inevitably takes on moralistic overtones. How could it be otherwise? For every victim, after all, there must be a victimizer – or, more to the point, a class of victimizers. Even though victims had come to be seen in ever more complex terms, victimizers had come to be seen in ever more facile ones. Victims had come to deserve nothing other than compassion, in popular opinion, and victimizers nothing other than denunciation and punishment. Victims had come to seem thoroughly or even innately good and victimizers thoroughly or innately evil (even though neither makes any sense, because moral agents must by definition be free to choose between good and evil). Victims had come to have no moral responsibility for their own behaviour, but victimizers had come to have total moral responsibility for theirs. The result was a bizarre combination of moral relativism in relation to "us" (that is, victims of childhood trauma, physical or psychological addictions, low self-esteem, or whatever) and moral purism in relation to "them" (the victimizers). Charles Sykes, who wrote *Nation of Victims*, put it very bluntly: "In a sense," he said, "we've sanctioned revenge for people who can claim to be victims."[10] Even though a few social commentators do speak out now and then, no evidence suggests that much has changed in this respect since the 1990s.

It would be folly, as Greenfield pointed out, to underestimate the symbolic significance of law. Some panelists were therefore careful to adopt moderate positions. Instead of agreeing with the verdict of not guilty, which would have legitimated revenge and vigilantism, they advocated a verdict of guilty but with extenuating circumstances to mitigate punishment. This was the position, for example, of two legal experts: Lynn Tepper, a judge of the Florida Circuit Court and member of the governor's Battered Women's Clemency Review Board, and Patricia King, a law professor at Georgetown University. "I personally am appalled at the message we're sending in these cases," said King, "I'm a hardliner. You commit a crime, you kill somebody, you mutilate them, you go to prison. Maybe you get mitigation in the sentencing."[11] Yet she said also that "we are putting [all] the weight on the criminal justice system ... The jury is stuck with the fact that we have not dealt, up until that point, with any of these issues, at any other place in our system, effectively."[12]

And this is surely true. The legal system itself cannot possibly solve every problem; many other social and cultural systems must be brought into action. The answer is not to look the other way when citizens take the law into their own hands, therefore, but to provide them with shelter and assistance before they resort to violence.[13]

The immediate problem created by the Bobbitt verdict was not vigilantism, however – millions of women were not ready to copy Lorena by castrating men physically[14] – but they were ready to exploit her by castrating men psychologically. Whatever their political leaders considered expedient to say on national television, the fact is that millions of ordinary women revelled vicariously in the lurid symbolism of revenge. For them, Lorena's behaviour was unfortunate, perhaps, but expedient nevertheless as a message to men. What message did they want to send? Presumably, it was simply this: abuse us at your own risk. But what message were men likely to hear? The most benign was surely that we had already moved one step beyond the debate over legalizing castration as a way of dealing with sex offenders toward legitimating it legally and even morally as a symbol of rage. A more sinister one was that we had already moved one step beyond acknowledgment of the anger inspired by injustice toward promotion of the revenge inspired by hatred. As a result, the level of moral, legal, and political discourse was lowered beyond recognition.

Although men were certainly anxious about the implications of Lorena's case, they were reluctant to call into question their security and identity as men – let alone their sympathy for women – by saying so. The prevailing atmosphere thus inhibited men still further in their search for the distinctive "voice" they would have needed in order to participate in any genuine dialogue with women. As so many observers noted, all that most men could do was to make "nervous jokes" about John Bobbitt, someone who was supposed to represent them as a class – that is, as potential victims in the eyes of men and as potential rapists in the eyes of women.

Lorena Bobbitt was the only participant in her sordid case that anyone – either women or men – even tried or appeared to take seriously. Some feminists were diplomatic enough to dissociate themselves from her. For example, on one segment of NBC's newsmagazine *Now*, Susan Estrich, herself a victim of rape and an author on the subject, said that: "Mrs Bobbitt is no hero of mine. And I don't think she should be the hero of any woman in this country who believes in the law. Mrs Bobbitt is a woman out of

control. I have a lot more respect for women than to make her our symbol."[15] Many other feminists, though, allowed Lorena to merge with the
very icon that ideologues had been promoting for twenty or thirty years:
the innocent female victim of men who fights back against one of them.
And if the way that she fought back was emotionally and morally repugnant to men, or even to many women, then so be it – or so much the better. To us, this was the really disturbing thing.

According to Jamie Lee Evans, a rape crisis counsellor in San Francisco,
we "don't need a judge or jury to tell us whether or not Lorena's telling
the truth. Lorena came forward herself, said this man was battering her,
this man was raping her. That's all we need to know to know that
Lorena's telling the truth."[16] Never mind that, as mentioned, a jury had
already found John Bobbitt not guilty of raping his wife, at least on that
occasion, a fact that seems to have escaped every one of the jurors.[17]
Never mind that the whole point of a trial in our legal system is to replace
subjectivity with some measure of objectivity in the search for truth.
Never mind that those who bypass the legal system are nothing more than
vigilantes. Evans observed also that "John Wayne Bobbitt is a big deal,
because it's a man's penis being mutilated. If it was a woman's vagina
being mutilated, no one would care."[18] Really? Had she been living on
Mars for the previous ten or fifteen years? Had she never heard of the
furore over the ritualized genital mutilation of African girls? If a man had
mutilated his wife's vagina – or, more to the point, cut off his sleeping
wife's breast and thrown it out the window – he would have been burned
in effigy throughout the country and hunted down by vigilantes. Besides,
how would public indifference in either case make retaliation morally
acceptable?

Answering that question was irrelevant to Barbara Ehrenreich and, if
her analysis was correct, to most other women as well. Her essay "Feminism Confronts Bobbittry" appeared in *Time*, which no one can accuse of
being a marginal magazine, an organ of political radicals; on the contrary,
it has always been the mainstream newsmagazine par excellence. The article was extremely revealing. Ehrenreich made it clear that Evans was by
no means an extremist and was not, therefore, fair game for trivialization
as a member of some lunatic fringe. Lorena's trial indicated the existence
of a "huge divergence ... between feminist intellectualdom, on the one
hand, and an average female cafeteria orator, on the other." According to
her, "feminist pundits are tripping over one another to show that none of
them is, goddess forbid, a 'man hater.'" Obviously, Ehrenreich saw nothing wrong with being a man hater. "And while the pundits are making
obvious but prissy-sounding statements like 'The fact that one has been a
victim doesn't give one carte blanche to victimize others,' the woman in
the street is making V signs by raising two fingers and bringing them

together with a snipping motion."[19] Well, what if it did sound "prissy" to remind people of fundamental moral principles? Fear of ridicule has certainly never stopped ideological feminists from making "obvious but prissy" statements in the interest of women. (Consider the familiar dictum that no man ever has a right to force himself on a woman, even a woman who suddenly changes her mind about having sex.) If the statements Ehrenreich attributed to pundits were so obvious, moreover, how could she have explained the fact that so many women, by her own account, were oblivious to them?

According to Ehrenreich, feminist intellectuals were a bunch of elitists. Internal conflicts had rendered them out of touch with ordinary women. Among these conflicts was "the great standoff over the subject of victimhood."[20] On one side were the specialists in domestic violence, such as Walker, who saw Lorena Bobbitt as a martyr. On the other side were those, such as Naomi Wolf, who believed that women should stop whining and get on with the business of seizing power.[21] But this conflict was based on a false dichotomy; it was a red herring. The two positions were not mutually exclusive but, on the contrary, mutually reinforcing. The easiest way to attain power in our society, after all, is still to attain the sacred status of victimhood. Women do not have to stress either victimhood or power. They can stress both. They can have their political cake, in other words, and eat it too.

Millions of women understood that the rhetorical conflict meant nothing. As Ehrenreich pointed out, they saw no need to wait around while the ideological theorists and political strategists figured out a politically correct way of acknowledging this. She admitted that "organized feminism" had fostered a new "beyond bitch" attitude. Ignoring the stereotypes of men that had become prevalent after more than two decades of ideological ranting, she explained the new attitude as a result of nothing more than impatience created by raised expectations. Of great importance, in any case, was the fact that so many ordinary women identified themselves with Lorena not only as a victim but also, mainly, as one who took revenge by taking the law into her own hands, who fought back "by whatever means necessary."[22] If this last phrase sounds familiar, it is because ideologues on both the political left and the political right are far from being the only ones to use it. So do terrorists.

The terms of this controversy were usually limited on both sides to practical ones: how to advise jurors, what effect sensationalism has on the administration of justice, whether a verdict was likely to polarize the nation, and so forth. If Lorena had been found guilty, for example, how could women have been expected to protect themselves? If Lorena had been truly not guilty, on the other hand, how could we have expected to endure as a society based on the rule of law? Underlying these problems, though, was a question of profound importance. Can ends justify means? The belief that they can has always been attractive and has been applied, overtly in the cases of national socialism and communism, although it was seldom openly proclaimed before modern times. If ends can justify means, however, then virtually nothing can be inherently wrong and virtually anything can be justified for one reason or another.

In itself, the unofficial verdict in the Bobbitt trial was not morally problematic, because even the most traditional moral systems recognize self-defense in the context of immediate physical danger as the one end that really can justify what would otherwise be an unacceptable means. In other words, it is the lesser of two evils. However, many cases that come to court, including Lorena's, do not involve immediate physical danger. As long as potential assailants are doing something else – as long as they are sleeping, for instance – no physical response is necessary. Because the ideologues refused to admit this, they had to argue that a good end (the elimination of potential danger) had justified an evil means (a pre-emptive strike). But what they really meant was that the collective end (helping women as a class) justified the collective means (punishing or threatening men as a class).

Ehrenreich herself, it should be clearly noted, really did believe that ends could justify means. She challenged her colleagues in the feminist establishment not for accepting this idea, after all, but merely for doing so surreptitiously. Why, she wondered, were they ashamed of accepting it? In fact, she argued, most women knew better. Those who rejected the label "feminist" did so not because it carried the connotation of hating men, she opined, but because "it has come to sound just too damn dainty." Ehrenreich's concluding paragraph made her moral and legal position clear. "Personally," she wrote, "I'm for both feminism and nonviolence. I admire the male body and prefer to find the penis attached to it ... But I'm not willing to wait another decade or two for gender peace to prevail. And if a fellow insists on using his penis as a weapon, I say that, one way or another, he ought to be swiftly disarmed."[23]

This mentality, which supposedly makes sense not only in emotional terms but on practical grounds as well, is, ironically, most likely to prove very impractical – unless, of course, practicality is defined in terms that exclude gender peace or even gender interaction. If a relationship can be maintained only on the basis of fear felt by either the woman or the man, it is hardly worth maintaining at all.

The debate over Lorena Bobbitt did not occur in a vacuum. How to understand the reasons for domestic violence and what to do about offenders had been hotly debated by social workers and academics in the preceding

decade. Ideological feminists, many of whom were themselves professionals in the field, were actively involved in these debates. They promoted
their cause with statistics on the extent of domestic abuse by men – some
of which, as we observe in both chapter 10 and appendix 3, were highly
dubious – challenged the interpretations and clinical practices of others in
the field, and mobilized public opinion by playing on the fears of women.
(For a detailed examination of the ideological "discourse" on domestic violence, see the case study in appendix 13.)

On one level, this chapter (along with that appendix, which is closely
related) has been about hostility expressed physically in the home. On
another level, it has been about hostility expressed verbally in both popular and elite culture. What happens when people who might have engaged
in dialogue turn instead to something resembling warfare? It is especially
in the context of domestic violence that ideological feminists have encouraged the rhetoric of victimization. By far the most successful and important of their projects, one that combines therapeutic and moralistic features, has been the political movement focused on victims of domestic
violence. Feminists have brought it to public attention as an urgent social
problem, and with good reason, but they have done so by supporting three
extremely dubious assumptions: that almost all human beings except
white heterosexual men can claim to be victims of abuse for one reason or
another, that victimhood can be equated with innocence, and that victimization in the past can eliminate moral responsibility for losing control in
the present.

Where there are victims, presumably – but not always logically – there
are victimizers. Ideological feminists have denied, trivialized, or excused
the abuse of men by women. If they had not, they realize, some central
pillars of their worldview would have collapsed: that all social problems
can or even must be explained in terms of power, that men have all the
power, and that men are encouraged to use it against women. As we have
argued, profound essentialism and dualism – "we" are by nature good;
"they" are by nature evil – are characteristic of every ideology, including
feminist ideology. No wonder the debate over domestic abuse has been so
fierce!

The debate goes on and on and on. Arguments for one side are refuted
with counterarguments and those, in turn, with other counterarguments.
One side of the debate has produced websites with extensive bibliographies
and links on "husband battering"[24] and the other on "gender asymmetry."[25] Given how much both men and feminists have at stake here, it
seems clear that this debate will continue for a long time. But the game of
"comparative suffering" (a topic that we will discuss in *Transcending
Misandry*) is of very dubious moral value. It assumes that human suffering

can be quantified and then exploited for political purposes. We suffer more, each side says, than you do. We deserve compassion, therefore, and you do not. As if one premise follows logically and morally from the other.

Of importance here, in any case, are not the precise numbers. By now, everyone agrees that some men are battered by women. No matter what the numbers are on either side, the problem would still be serious and would still undermine some key planks in the political platform of ideological feminism.

3

Workers v. Harassers:
The Hill-Thomas Debate

What the hearing lacked and what I and others found missing was balance in terms of credibility – mine certainly equalled Thomas' – in the matter and balance in terms of process – the weight of the Senate and the Executive should not have been used against an individual citizen called upon to participate in a public process.[1]

This is a circus! A national disgrace! ... a high-tech lynching for uppity blacks who in any way deign to think for themselves.[2]

The problem of sexual harassment, like other problems studied by feminists, is a serious one. We will discuss various legal remedies for it in chapter 8 and some closely related topics in chapters 7, 9, and 10. For the time being, consider an event that crystallized public opinion on the topic. Between 11 and 13 October 1991, millions of people huddled around their television sets to watch the confirmation hearing of Clarence Thomas, a black man who had been nominated several weeks earlier as a justice of the Supreme Court. A seismic event, it was reported on the news all day and every day and discussed on every talk show. It was said to have changed America. It certainly polarized America: men versus women, blacks versus whites, conservatives versus liberals. Almost anything that could be said about any public event was said about this one.

In this chapter, we discuss the hearing itself and its immediate aftermath, the problems that surfaced in connection with it, some responses from women, and some of the effects.

Thomas had never been a popular candidate for a job on the Supreme Court. During the evaluation hearing, he evaded some controversial positions – he actually claimed never to have discussed abortion with his friends and fellow lawyers – and glossed over earlier statements about legal principles such as natural law. Still, his confirmation was all but assured by

11 October. Then, suddenly, he was struck by a bolt of political lightning: an accusation of sexual harassment made by Anita Hill, a law professor at the University of Oklahoma who had once worked for Thomas at the Equal Employment Opportunities Commission.

According to Hill, Thomas had repeatedly asked her for dates. After being rejected on each occasion, he subjected her to offensive discussions of pornography. Hill had hoped that her accusations would remain anonymous and confidential. When someone leaked her story to the press, though, she defended her position in the full glare of public debate. The climax, as it were, came when Hill accused Thomas of boasting about the size of his penis. This confirmed a common stereotype of black men. With that in mind, Thomas accused her, or at least her supporters, of racism (even though Hill herself was black). His confirmation hearing, he observed, had turned into " a high-tech lynching of an uppity black man" who dared to take unpopular positions. According to Jean Bethke Elshtain,

those who were hoarse in their defense of Hill, and more generally in their pious and politically correct assertions about gender and power and knowledge, might have taken the trouble to observe that they themselves were complicit in the construction of the black male as a paradigmatic sexual suspect. The tendency to portray black men as sexually rapacious, with a propensity to rape, has long been an unsavory theme in many (white) feminist tracts. In Susan Brownmiller's *Against Our Will*, for example, the "feminist classic" that helped to spur the obsession with rape, and the conflation of rape with sex in the minds of radical feminists, it is asserted that the allegations of white women against black men in the Jim Crow South were to be credited, because white women and black women formed a single oppressed category against men. In Brownmiller's words, "The sexual oppression of black women, and all women is commonly shared," under slavery and into the present.[3]

Overnight, this confrontation became the hottest story since, well, since anyone could remember. Most viewers agreed that an already acrimonious and politicized hearing had turned into an even less edifying spectacle. Had the charges of sexism and racism not been so serious, it might indeed have been what many were already calling it: a circus, a sideshow, or, as one commentator put it, a sequel to *Sex, Lies, and Videotapes* that could have been called *Sex, Lies, and Stereotypes*.[4] At least some viewers must have wondered what people in Europe and elsewhere were thinking as they watched senators listening intently to fantastically lurid stories about pubic hair, penises, and pornography. Millions of viewers dropped everything else, even baseball games, to avoid missing a single sordid detail. When it was all over, on 14 October at 2:00 A.M., the committee adjourned after having only achieved a stalemate. The decision itself came on 16 October: Thomas was confirmed by the smallest margin since 1881.

But there was nothing amusing or trivial about this bizarre and even grotesque "ordeal by word." The hearing itself bore more than a passing resemblance to the McMartin witch hunt of the 1990s, the McCarthy witch hunt of the 1950s, and even to the Salem witch hunt of the 1690s. Not surprisingly, many people came away more cynical than ever about the processes and institutions that supposedly sustained justice. Moreover, there was nothing edifying or encouraging about the public response, which would have been far less disturbing had it been motivated merely by the kind of self-righteousness generally associated with prurience. Instead, it was motivated largely by the kind of self-righteousness generally associated with political ideologies of both the political left and the political right. As a result, what might have been an opportunity for a public debate between men and women (though probably not a genuine dialogue) turned into a public harangue directed against men by women. What happened, in fact, provides an ideal case study of precisely what we hope this book will help us avoid in the future.

Elected officials have always tried to be politically correct (a topic that we discuss in appendix 4), especially when they appear every day on television. Yet some are convinced that politically correct positions are also morally correct. No wonder sanctimonious posturing was common in the Hill-Thomas case and intellectual probing rare. The situation was similar in living rooms, newsrooms, offices, cafeterias, and bars across the land (in Canada no less than the United States). Not surprisingly, it was the subject of monologues on late-night talk shows and at least one episode of a situation comedy.

Given the overtly feminist worldview of *Designing Women*, it was almost inevitable that one episode would include some explicit comments on the Thomas hearing.[5] No attempt was made to ensure that both sides were given a fair hearing. On this episode, Mary Jo and Julia have a fight with Allison over the Hill-Thomas affair. Mary Jo and Julia support Anita Hill, and Allison supports Clarence Thomas. Mary Jo and Julia are the moral and political heavyweights on this show. Allison is the pretty but ditsy "belle" who need not be taken seriously. She is the proverbial "straw man" whose statements are all stereotypical, uttered only to be refuted by polemical declamations from the others. The studio audience responds to everything Allison says with hoots or boos, of course, but to everything Mary Jo and Julia say with applause. In a way, the atmosphere of this episode is like that of a revival meeting, replete with testimonials and denunciations. Even Anthony, the token (black) man, is exploited for political purposes to assert that Thomas does not represent black people.

The ostensible story for this episode, Allison's birthday party, all but disappears under the weight of these diatribes; the characters are merely mouthpieces for ideological rhetoric. The show concludes with a montage of snapshots from the Thomas hearing. At the very end is a still photo of Anita Hill. Her head downcast, her eyes closed, she looks like a perfect martyr for the faith.

During the hearing itself, the senators obviously had to hear all the evidence in public if they were to avoid the accusation of not taking women seriously, but going public meant that they could be accused of pandering to popular opinion and political pressure. How, one might well ask, could they have allowed a public trial – and this was a kind of trial – without the slightest shred of evidence to support the testimony of character witnesses on either side? In the end, the illusion of justice was preserved but, as partisans on both sides have angrily observed, though for different reasons, not necessarily justice itself. The allegations had been discussed openly, but both the process and the result were widely condemned. Some commentators argued that merely being exposed to such a hideous invasion of his personal life made Thomas a victim of injustice. Others argued that the same was true of Hill, and in addition, of course, they were outraged by the final decision.

Either Hill or Thomas must have been lying, it was said over and over again, because the two stories contradicted each other. If either of them was lying, nobody will ever know which one (although it is safe to say that everybody has an opinion on the matter). Because no substantive evidence was introduced on either side, the whole trial was based entirely on her word against his. The good senators eventually had to come down on one side or the other, based at least in theory solely on who had given the better performance. Some proclaimed Hill's performance more "credible" or "powerful" than that of Thomas. Others proclaimed the reverse. No wonder so many people over so many years have commented on the unreality or theatricality of public life in America.

The senators, along with many viewers and commentators, made assumptions that can be summed up in a syllogism: either Thomas or Hill was lying; people lie to cover up improper behaviour; ergo, either Thomas or Hill had behaved improperly. As a result, the senators speculated about possible motivations that Hill might have had for lying. No other way of solving the case occurred to them. But what if the initial assumption was based on a superficial examination of the possibilities? Suppose that Thomas really had said what Hill reported, that he really was lying and Hill really telling the truth. Would knowing that have truly settled the matter to everyone's satisfaction? Probably not. Consider the following two scenarios.

Thomas and Hill might indeed have discussed pornography and dis-agreed, as lawyers and academics often do, about its legal, sociological, political, and psychological significance. In view of the controversy sur-rounding this subject, Thomas could legitimately have urged Hill to exam-ine it more carefully. If so, his refusal to acknowledge any discussion of pornography at all would indeed have been a lie. But how else could he have defended himself in the self-righteous atmosphere of this hearing and the increasingly puritanical atmosphere of this society?

On the other hand, Thomas might indeed have found discussions of pornography erotically entertaining. Does everyone really agree that dis-cussing pornography is inherently either immoral or unhealthy (which we discuss in chapter 7)? If not, should a discussion of the kind reported by Hill be considered sexual harassment? For those who could answer yes to the question, the only matter worth considering was the truth of Hill's alle-gations. For those who could answer no to the same question, on the other hand, the situation was far more complicated. What mattered for them was not what Thomas had said to Hill but how she *interpreted* what he had said. Since her interpretation now corresponds to the law of the land, the legitimacy of laws governing sexual harassment is at issue here.

To be effective and legitimate, laws must be based on consensus. If they are not – prohibition of liquor under the Volstead Act comes to mind – they are ignored, flouted, or resisted in one way or another by large segments of the population. This, in turn, generates cynicism and brings both the courts and the legislature into disrepute. Judging from the public response to this hearing, it is clear that no consensus underlay current laws defining sexual harassment. Ideological feminists had already succeeded in attaining a very broad legal definition of it, but they had failed to convince many men and even some women that this definition was appropriate. And these feminists were willing to hold Thomas responsible for events of ten years earlier, even though both cultural and legal standards had been very different then. This presents us with the problem of anachronism. Support for Thomas was possible even for some who believed that he was lying, consequently, and hostility toward Hill was possible even for some who believed that she was telling the truth.

Had either scenario been considered, much of the resulting anger might have been avoided. There would have been no need to protect Thomas by trying to prove that Hill was motivated to lie about him, either by political malice or by neurotic fantasies. She might have been telling the truth about events, in fact, but interpreting them from a point of view that was, to judge from the public response, highly debatable. Moreover, there would have been no need to protect Hill by trying to prove that she had remained silent for fear of losing her job. Instead, it would have been necessary to find out when she had adopted her current point of view. Ten years earlier, she might have considered her situation uncomfortable but not serious enough to require legal attention. Finally, there would have been no need to accuse her, as distinct from some supporters, of political opportunism or cynicism. Like many other women during those ten years, she might have become deeply convinced of a moral responsibility to speak out. Even though this scenario would not have provided any explanation for the larger ideological struggle in which both Hill and Thomas were pawns, it would have provided a perfectly reasonable explanation for both Hill's initial delay in coming forward with the accusation and her strong desire to come forward with it later.

Although both Hill and Thomas were subjected to inquiries about their private lives and attacks on their personal integrity, many observers felt sympathy for only one of the two "stars" in this production. Hill's supporters claimed that she was the chief victim – indeed, the only victim. And she was a victim in some ways. For instance, she was accused of fabricating the entire case out of romantic delusions. This was both demeaning to her and frightening to all women whose jobs were threatened. Moreover, Hill had to risk her personal and professional reputation by going public without any supporting evidence. We believe that her status as a victim was greatly exaggerated. And some women, including Elshtain, agree. She observes that the melodrama

was presented as the primal and prototypical engagement between a powerful male and a "passive" female. "Passive," that is, by Hill's own account. Although Thomas insisted on seeing Hill as a resourceful, energetic and competent woman, she staked out the ground of her own helplessness, which extended even to her conversations and acquaintances. "I was very passive in the conversation," she reported, referring to a casual discussion with several people about her reaction to the news that Thomas had been nominated to the Court. When Senator Arlen Specter asked, "Excuse me?" she repeated the sorry but, as it turned out, politically shrewd refrain: "I was very passive in the conversation." Hill's representation of herself in such reactive terms struck me at the time as pretty unbelievable. I could not help noticing that she was seen by others (not only by Thomas) as a woman quite capable of making her own way through the world and pressing her own case. A female co-worker testified that "when I worked with Anita Hill and I knew her ... she was not a victim. She was a very tough woman. She stood her ground. She didn't take a lot of anything from anyone, and she made sure you knew it." Clearly Hill was, and is, not only capable, but also ambitious.[6]

Elsewhere, Elshtain notes one implication of this focus on female passivity. "Dusting off hoary stereotypes of male lust and female sexlessness, presenting a world in which sex is what men 'do' to women, is one of the more disturbing features of contemporary feminist argumentation; and now, in the wake of the Hill-Thomas affair, it is working its way into our government and our politics."[7]

At some level of consciousness, Hill must have realized that beyond her immediate difficulties, she had an ultimate advantage over Thomas. If he was found guilty, she would become a heroine. And if he was found innocent, she would become a martyr. No matter what happened, in other words, Hill would be glorified by a large and vocal segment of the population for having given maximum visibility to the cause of women. Thomas, on the other hand, would be tainted for having been unable to prove that he had not indulged in some hideously wicked behaviour.

In view of this situation, some comments by Hill's supporters were tendentious. It is true that witnesses talked about her private life, but what they said paled by comparison with what she said about the private life of Thomas. After all, it was his allegedly monstrous penis and the most intimate details of his allegedly vile and disgusting personal life that the whole nation was talking about.

Again, it is true that one senator accused Hill of perjury, which later brought indignant cries of "shame" from Senator Edward Kennedy. But if we reject the old stereotypical notion that women lie in cases of this kind, why accept the new stereotypical notion that women don't lie? Obviously, both women and men are capable of lying, especially when they believe that doing so can be justified politically. And this truly was an ideal opportunity to promote political goals, because Thomas was known to oppose not only new legislation against sexual harassment but also abortion and affirmative action. In the absence of any concrete evidence, how could the senators ignore this possibility?

In several disturbing ways, this event followed the script of a rape trial. First, given the lack of concrete evidence, lawyers have often questioned the female plaintiff's personal integrity and credibility, as they did with Hill. Second, given the same lack of evidence, these trials focus heavily on performance in court. Some people might have supported Hill not because of her evidence but because of the way in which she conducted herself. Third, notwithstanding ideological claims to the contrary, public opinion nowadays is usually with the alleged victims of men. This alone would have worked against Thomas, but still, because of his positions on abortion or affirmative action, many people already disliked him. Finally, some people support the alleged victim merely because of group solidarity. In this case, Hill's supporters knew that many women really are victims of sexual harassment and many of them probably believed that "women don't lie." Even though it was Hill who attacked Thomas, therefore, many viewers were convinced that he had originally attacked her. As the "true victim," she was attacking him only in retaliation.

Whatever Hill's intentions – let us assume here that they were sincere and even altruistic – the fact remains that both she and the cause she has come to represent benefited from this experience in the following years. Even as she arrived back home at the University of Oklahoma, students and colleagues were ready to welcome her as a martyr for the cause of women. And millions of people all over the country – not a majority, but a very sizable minority – joined them in spirit. For years now, she has been sought eagerly for speaking engagements not only by talk-show hosts but by serious journalists, academics, and feminists. From the beginning, it was clear that any publisher would jump at the chance to work with her. And she did publish a book in 1997.[8] In some very important ways, then, Hill's prospects have been greatly enhanced by this trial.[9]

Now, though, think about all this from the perspective of Clarence Thomas. Although Thomas had some advantages over Hill, since he was a man (albeit a black man) of considerable authority, he was also a man openly attacked by many for his political beliefs. Moreover, since the accused is presumed innocent unless proven guilty, the burden of proof was on Hill, not Thomas. It was perfectly appropriate, therefore, that the senators gave him the benefit of their doubt. In the court of public opinion, on the other hand, Thomas was being accused by someone who, as Hill's supporters pointed out, spoke for millions of innocent victims. By virtue of this fact alone, it was he who had to dispel initial suspicion, not Hill. In the end, Hill could not prove beyond a reasonable doubt that he was guilty. But neither could Thomas prove that he was innocent. The senators were less willing than the nation to give him the benefit of the doubt. Just over half of the former found Thomas innocent, but two-thirds of the latter did. Clearly, most people chose to ignore their lingering doubts. But, as Thomas himself sadly observed, those doubts would always remain and continue to cast a shadow over his moral integrity (and over the integrity of the Senate and the Supreme Court as well).

As one savvy journalist put it, "What we had here was a victim-off, a contest to see who was the most convincing victim. And I think that Clarence Thomas won that in that he was the more immediate victim of the lynch mob that was coming after him and he was also a more passionate victim than ... Anita Hill. But I think that the search for victim status which is probably the highest status a public figure can aspire to in America right now was really what was going on."[10]

One more question. Assuming for a moment that Thomas had really said some offensive things to Hill, would that justify the penalty that might have been imposed on him? Although Hill herself did not intend to humiliate him before the entire nation, once word had leaked out, her supporters demanded that he be tried publicly, knowing that one false move in his own defense would destroy him. Can we really compare what Hill might have endured temporarily because of Thomas to what he would have had to endure permanently because of her? No matter how unpleasant her experience might have been ten years earlier, Hill had prospered over the years. Had she won this case, though, his career would have been utterly ruined.

From the start, it was obvious to everyone that more important matters than the conduct of either Hill or Thomas were at stake. Unfortunately, only two were actually discussed in any depth: the brutal process of confirming nominees to the Supreme Court, including the fact that feminists were mobilizing to prevent the addition of a conservative Republican to the Supreme Court, and the fact that many women want protection from sexual harassment. Other matters, including many that underlie these, were usually ignored.

The hearing presented several problems. One was defining "sexual harassment." According to one survey of popular opinion in the aftermath of this case, 41% of Americans believed that sexual harassment occurs when a woman's boss or superior flirts with her; 64%, when he is accustomed to putting his arm around her; 74%, when he tells sexual jokes to her; 77%, when he pressures her for a date; 80%, when his speech includes either direct or indirect sexual references; 87%, when he asks her to have sex with him; and 91%, when he insists on discussing pornographic acts with her.[11]

Of great interest here is the fact that listening to the boss discuss pornography is considered an even more definitive feature of sexual harassment than actually being asked to have sexual relations!

Thomas was not accused of raping Hill or even of touching her. And he could not truly be accused of intimidating or blackmailing Hill, because her job was never at risk; on the contrary, he continued to promote her throughout her career.[12] He was accused, actually, of nothing more than repeatedly asking Hill for a date and saying vulgar things to her. His alleged use of language was called "outrageous," "unspeakable," "grotesque," "vile," "perverted," "appalling," "heinous," "psychopathic," and even "insane." Although some commentators argue that offensive talk can indeed be a crime for which the culprit ought to be punished, their argument can be challenged. The world is not always a nice place. Consequently, adults must be expected to face at least some degree of adversity or conflict with courage and dignity. The Constitution guarantees all Americans the right to pursue happiness but not happiness itself.[13]

Moreover, a double standard was clearly at work in the Thomas case, since it was and still is considered politically correct for women to make what used to be called lewd remarks. This is demonstrated every night of the week on television in reruns of *The Golden Girls*. Three of the characters – Blanche, Dorothy, and Sophia – say hardly anything without making crude sexual innuendoes. Blanche speaks incessantly of her lovers and their physical endowments, along with her own. One aim of the early feminist movement was precisely to abolish the double standard by which men, but not women, were free to indulge in sexual play and sexual talk. But a new double standard has replaced the old. We are now asked to believe that women are liberated when they talk about male bodies, no matter how crudely, but that men are sexist when they do the same thing about female bodies.

Why should anyone assume that men, unlike women, will tolerate a double standard? If women may use the term "sexual harassment" in connection with something beyond intimidation or blackmail – indecent exposure, assault, rape – then surely men may do so as well. (Whether women or men should use the law to do so is another matter, though, because not everything that is immoral must be illegal as well.) For women, sexual harassment has come to mean the creation of an atmosphere in which men either directly or indirectly express their sexual interest in women. To be harassed in this sense might mean having to reject repeated advances, feeling discomfort due to crude discussions of sex, being exposed to posters of nude women, or merely finding copies of *Playboy* around the office. For men, however, sexual harassment might mean the creation of an atmosphere in which ideological stereotypes of men are commonplace or in which men are made to fear questioning prevalent ideological assumptions, including those on which company policies are based. Underlying the feminist movement is the assumption that conditions need to be improved precisely because they were created by men. To varying degrees, therefore, every branch of feminism is also a movement dedicated to the critique of this or that group of men or of men as such. Which raises an interesting question: If men should not be allowed to keep copies of *Playboy* in their offices, why should women be allowed to keep copies of *Ms*. in their offices? In fact, it would be hard to find an issue of any mass-market magazine addressed to women that fails to include at least one article that would be offensive to men by implying that they are not merely different from women but inferior. And many of these magazines go further, focusing attention on the ways in which men victimize women. Why should men not feel intimidated by women who reflect this worldview even in casual conversations and who believe that men have no reason for resenting repeated attacks on "the male model" of working, thinking, feeling, speaking, and so forth?[14]

Those men and women who want to be part of the solution rather than the problem will have to acknowledge that gender-related stress in the workplace – or, to use the current expression, "sexual harassment" – is a problem for both sexes. It might take different forms in each case, but its effect is the same: feeling threatened, manipulated, trivialized, or disrespected *as* men or *as* women. From what was said during and after the Thomas hearing, though, it is obvious that the old double standard has not merely been turned on its head but also institutionalized by law. How can any moral or legal definition of sexual harassment work unless it is acceptable, or at least tolerable, to both women and men?

Another problem was the current glorification of political correctness, which was a serious impediment to freedom of speech. It would have been political suicide for any journalist or commentator even to question a feminist position; for a senator it would have been like questioning biblical authority in a fundamentalist community. Although the senators themselves were male, they made every attempt (though sometimes unsuccessfully) not to speak *as men* on national television. In one way, that was helpful; they had to address the needs of women as well as men. In another way, though, it was not: they effectively "silenced the voice" of men per se in an extremely important public debate that concerned men no less than women.

Yet another problem with the hearings was created by feminist interpretations of harassment. These draw, says Elshtain, on critiques of objectivity in scholarship (which we will discuss in chapter 10). "I and my reality," said Hill at the hearing, "did not comport with what they accepted as their reality."[15] Commenting on this statement, Elshtain remarks that "these words pithily and a little chillingly capture a controlling idea of our blinkered cultural and academic life ... To go beyond the reality of perspectives to the claim that there are only perspectives, that facts themselves are arbitrary inventions and that there is only 'my reality' and 'your reality' is to embrace nonsense. And to go still further and argue that the conditions of knowledge change with a change of gender, that men and women inhabit disparate epistemological universes, is to embrace not only nonsense, but dangerous nonsense."[16] (More about all that in chapters 8 and 9.) "If the controversy about Hill and Thomas has been so susceptible to ideological distortions," Elshtain continues, "and if the dogma that knowledge is power has lent itself so smoothly to the discussion of sexual harassment, it is because knowledge is elusive in this particular instance, not because knowledge is generally impossible. There are such things as the facts."[17] It is very hard to establish the facts; witnesses are seldom available. There might be only circumstantial evidence, which is often based on "perceptions." "That is why Hill can continue to say, in some of her post-hearing public talks, that 'women

should be supported *regardless of proof.*' She is hiding a political statement behind an epistemological hardship."[18] In short, harassment cases
are almost always ambiguous. Even the official terminology – defining
words such as "unwelcome" and "pervasive" – are understood in various ways. The result, says John Cloud, "is a thicket of rulings. Since
1991 juries have returned well over five hundred verdicts on sexual
harassment decisions that often contradict one another and send mixed
signals about how we should behave any time we meet a co-worker we'd
like to see after five."[19]

America's legal system rests on a fundamental premise: that the accused
is innocent unless proven guilty beyond a reasonable doubt. This premise
does inhibit prosecution to some extent, but it also prevents persecution.
Supporters of Hill pointed out correctly that the difficulty in finding evidence to substantiate claims in cases of this kind means that many victims
prefer to remain silent. But what is the appropriate solution to this problem? Must we overturn the moral and legal basis of our society by declaring that accusations with nothing more substantial than hearsay to support
them should be believed merely because they are made by women? Or that
the accused should be presumed guilty instead of innocent? Some ideological feminists would answer both questions in the affirmative. Already convinced from the beginning that Hill had a legitimate case, therefore, they
were outraged that not everyone came to the same conclusion. Justice, they
said, had been denied. We have always known that guilty people are sometimes exonerated and innocent people sometimes convicted. Our legal
system is not perfect. But Anita Hill did have her day in "court." As it
happened, she lost. Citizens are guaranteed the right to be heard, not some
right to be believed.

Several years after the Hill-Thomas hearing, its legal and political fallout
had still not settled. Women did not stand idly by. Dissatisfied with the fact
that not everyone believed Hill (although an increasing number did), Jane
Mayer and Jill Abramson reopened the "national dialogue" with another
look at the case in *Strange Justice.*[20] Of primary interest to them are the
"other women" who were not allowed to testify in 1991. The authors conclude that Thomas was the liar, not Hill. As mentioned, this, in itself, could
not prove that he had been a sexual harasser. Much of the evidence discussed, however, has nothing to do with events that either did or did not
take place.

The authors focus attention on Thomas's character. For them, the mere
fact that Thomas enjoys porn is enough to qualify him as someone with an
evil character. They interview the owner of a video store, who says that
Thomas was a regular in the x-rated section. They report that he
could find nothing worth salvaging from his first marriage except his

collection of *Playboy* magazines and that his own mother had once called him a bully. The implication is obvious: any man who likes to look at beautiful women must be the kind of man who would harass them.

By 1996, Hill herself had written a book, *Speaking Truth to Power*, which includes an "Open Letter to the 1991 Senate Judiciary Committee." "What the hearing lacked and what I and others found missing," writes Hill in her letter, "was balance in terms of credibility – mine certainly equalled Thomas' – in the matter and balance in terms of process – the weight of the Senate and the Executive should not have been used against an individual citizen called upon to participate in a public process." Well, should the weight of institutions such as the Senate and the Executive have been used instead against Thomas? He, too, was a citizen. "Neither the issue of harassment nor the nomination," writes Hill, "was served by a presumption of my untruthfulness." Indeed, this presumption should not have been made. But Hill implies that it should have been made against Thomas. Elsewhere, Hill writes that "anything less than a balanced approach condemns women to second-class status and the Court to members who abuse power and authority granted to them in a public trust."[21]

The problem of balance underlies Hill's whole discussion, but judging from what she writes elsewhere, it is clear to us that she understands balance from the perspective of ideological feminism. Would a more balanced approach of this kind not merely turn the problem on its head by condemning men to second-class status? Hill writes that "since sexual harassment was central to the nominee's qualifications, the members of the committee should have educated themselves on the issue before them. Evidence that you failed to do so lies in your use of social myths to explain my testimony, your refusal to utilize information provided by experts on sexual harassment, and your deviation from your own procedural rules in hearing the testimony as presented." But how should the senators have educated themselves? Obviously to Hill, by exposing themselves to feminist indoctrination. Hill argues that the experts in question should have been formally trained in the psychology and sociology of sexual harassment. Because the ones who get that training are almost always feminists, she clearly refers to them. Hill does not actually say that, of course. What she does say is that the investigation "should be handled by a non-partisan body or individual in the role of neutral fact finder, experienced in investigating sexual harassment."[22]

Hill writes that the committee should have considered only "competent information." When there is no clear-cut evidence that favours the female plaintiff's case, she implies, the assessment should be based on women's general integrity, a recommendation that is based, in turn, on the "finding" of one survey that only 3% of the harassment claims filed are baseless and that 97% of the cases go unreported. "Women rarely use harassment claims to escape responsibility for the problems in their lives," Hill continues. "However, when, without fully investigating it, you presumed that my claim was a frivolous or spite claim, you advocated action based on the exception rather than the rule."[23] But statistics are notoriously unreliable in political controversies and thus cannot provide a very firm foundation for justice. That "97%" is not even a statistic of actual cases, moreover, but an estimate of experiences that were never reported. Given current debates over the inflation of statistics by feminist and other ideologues (appendix 2), should at least think twice before using even statistics as evidence.

"One of the greatest disservices that the Judiciary Committee did," writes Hill, "was to unnecessarily blur the lines between the nominee's public and private behavior." But following the feminist dictum that "the personal is political," she considers it justifiable to assess the personal lives of candidates, especially if they are seeking jobs that involve law – jobs at the Supreme Court, say, or the Department of Justice. It is one thing when homicide or sexual assault is involved. In those cases, even private matters are appropriately discussed in public. But Hill refers specifically to sexual harassment. Must we assume that her private dealings with Thomas should be discussed in public? Elsewhere, she makes the same point: "Thus, the information about his behavior was relevant regardless of whether it fit within the definitions of behavior which was outlawed."[24]

Hill's strategy, a common one among ideologues, is to expand definitions and thus encourage the broadest possible legal interpretation (a strategy that we discuss in chapters 8 and 9). By making anything and everything in the private domain subject to public scrutiny, of course, you can increase the likelihood of finding some source for a smear campaign. It is true that the private and public domains do intersect in some legal contexts, and the former can be relevant when assessing candidates for public leadership. But this does not mean that the personal should necessarily be political. If Hill's case had been one of quid pro quo, if she had been able to prove that Thomas had offered professional advantages or job security in return for sexual favours, okay, case closed. But that was hardly the case. What she advocates, therefore, is a radical change in the judicial system. Any change of that kind should surely be a topic of public debate, not merely of a declaration.

Here is another of Hill's claims: "Often, absent a court ruling, a person offering evidence of illegal activity cannot establish with certainty that the information that they are seeking to present represents a violation of the law. Placing the burden of obtaining a court ruling or otherwise establishing a violation with absolute certainty does not serve the public interest in making a thorough determination about the nominee."[25] This approach relies on a reversal of the ad hominem argument. It is based on the assumption of her integrity in particular and that of women in general, not on actual evidence of illegal or even immoral behaviour.

Had there been an adequate sexual-harassment procedure in place, Hill believes, her claim could have been processed within seven to ten days.[26] Nevertheless, it took Hill herself ten years to make that claim in the first place. And had there been an adequate sexual-harassment procedure in place, Hill believes, there need not have been a public hearing. This would have prevented embarrassment for both her, she says, and the government (although she obviously does not care about that of Thomas). But the danger of procedures without hearings – and that is precisely what some feminists want – is the absence of cross-examination, which becomes especially important if sexual-harassment officers have been trained to think in a particular way and thus to control the process for ideological purposes.

Ironically, the feminists who were so vociferous in their condemnation of Clarence Thomas behaved very differently when two other political leaders – Senator Robert Packwood and President Bill Clinton – were charged (one formally and the other informally) with sexual harassment. At least some commentators have explained this double standard in connection with political opportunism: Packwood and Clinton, unlike Thomas, used their legislative power in ways approved of by feminists.

Gloria Steinem played the social constructionist card – that is, the political card – by proclaiming that Packwood's actions should be explored and judged "in context." And what context might that be? The answer is simple: the context in which Packwood [could] be counted on to deliver the votes that various women's groups (NARAL) [National Abortion and Reproductive Rights Action League] and the Women's Legal Defense Fund, among others) wanted delivered on abortion, affirmative action and other matters. Politics and politics alone accounted for the reluctance of these national tribunes of the weaker sex to respond to a blatant, egregious and (finally) an admitted string of offenses. Eventually their hands were forced by local outrage and national publicity. No such patience, however, with Clarence Thomas.[27]

Feminist opinion on Clinton's escapades was very divided. "What is immoral is not President Clinton's having normal sexual impulses," argues one. "What is immoral is hating someone as much as Clinton's detractors do, just for the purpose of destroying him."[28] Wendy Kaminer presented a less emotional argument for letting Clinton off the hook: "Instead of quaintly accusing Clinton of defiling women, feminists should reconsider their commitment to policing minor instances of sexual misconduct at the expense of sexual privacy, free speech and a view of adult women as independent beings capable of discouraging, initiating or consenting to sex."[29] For some reason, these arguments were never applied to Clarence Thomas. One female observer put the opposite point of view very bluntly: "Not one of the women involved in the Clinton soap opera took legal action at the time they claim they were sexually harassed. Now they appear to be on the bandwagon to enrich themselves one way or another. They make me feel ashamed to be a woman."[30]

Sometimes art imitates life. Men, too, had their say – at least in the movies. Since the Hill-Thomas affair, at least two movies were about sexual harassment: *Disclosure* and *Oleanna*. Both have been discussed as if they were sociological textbooks. In fact, of course, they are not. The former could be classified as entertainment and the latter as art. Neither claims to be a definitive statement, covering every possible situation that could be identified with sexual harassment. Each presents one situation in particular and asks viewers to find room for it in their perception of the problem. How well each one succeeds depends not on how closely it adheres to statistics but on how closely it adheres to human nature – or, to put it another way, on how much viewers actually care about the characters (a criterion that applies no less to popular entertainment than to high art).

Disclosure, which is based on a novel by Michael Crichton,[31] was reviled by critics, who were chiefly interested in it as a political statement. They were annoyed by the fact that it oversimplifies a complex social problem by making its victimized male protagonist too innocent and its female villain too guilty. Never mind that the latter allows someone to stick his penis in her mouth before running off, which could be interpreted – as it certainly would be in connection with a female victim – as an insidious suggestion that the protagonist "enjoys" being sexually harassed and thus deserves it.

In real life, the critics argued, innocence and guilt in connection with sexual harassment are not so easily identified. Considering the political and ideological rhetoric surrounding this problem, however, it is hard to avoid the conclusion that these critics were being both disingenuous and opportunistic. How often is the charge of oversimplification used to defend men accused of sexual harassment or to attack the women who accuse them? Very seldom. In fact, this approach would itself be attacked relentlessly as "blaming the victim." What the critics truly disliked about this movie was the mere fact that it shows a man being the victim of a woman's sexual harassment. Anyone who lives in the real world knows that women are neither more nor less capable than men of using power, wherever they find it, to manipulate or intimidate. The possibility of women using it in the office more and more often as they attain positions of power would surprise no one were it not for the constant stream of rhetoric from ideologues who claim that only men are selfish and "hierarchical." Thank God for Amanda on *Melrose Place* and Samantha on *Sex and the City*!

Not all feminists agreed with the attack on *Disclosure*. Not all agreed, in other words, that either the author or the director felt threatened by an unpleasant "fact" of their sex: that men routinely flirt with, and thus harass, women at work. In one editorial, Eve McBride offered some good reasons for thinking twice about this problem.[32] Whether intentionally or otherwise, she suggested, women are just as likely to flirt as men. Only 5% of the cases that end up in court involve men suing women for harassment. On the other hand, only 5% of the corporate supervisors are women. Men complained only about harassment, which they defined in connection with an imbalance of power, not about flirting. Can we assume that all the women complained about harassment? Maybe they complained merely about flirting but interpreted flirting with their equals as harassment. Unlike harassment, flirting really is about sex rather than power.

In view of all this, consider what has been said about *Oleanna*, which is both a play and a movie. Critics acknowledge that this work opens up the discussion of sexual harassment. Here, too, a man is falsely accused by a woman of sexual harassment. In this case, though, the woman (a confused student) is emotionally appealing and the man (a self-centred academic) is emotionally unappealing. Ideally, viewers would feel at least some sympathy for both. In fact, they seldom do. This egregious situation is due more to the social and political context, however, than to anything lacking in author David Mamet's artistry. Many men are too defensive to admit that a woman might have good reasons for deciding to take control of her life. Many women, on the other hand, are too defensive to admit that doing so dishonestly and maliciously is morally unacceptable. Unfortunately, critics often discourage the defensiveness of men but encourage that of women. Even *Oleanna*, which is nothing if not a sincere attempt to see both sides of a complex problem, has been dismissed as "male-driven."[33] The implication here is that complexity itself constitutes the problem. On the subject of sexual harassment or any other gender problem, in other words, the only worthwhile works are those that present only one side – the side of women. Male-driven productions are bad, but female-driven ones are just fine. So much for the "national dialogue" supposedly initiated by the Hill-Thomas affair.

Sometimes, on the other hand, life imitates art. Sexual harassment does work both ways. Even at the risk of being ridiculed or trivialized, more and more men are willing to sue for damages. One man sued the University of California for $2.5 million after a lecture in which the female students were taught how to masturbate in order to avoid the "hardship" of sexual relations with men. Craig Rogers said that he had felt "raped and trapped" when a "psychology professor told intimate anecdotes about her sex life and allegedly made flippant remarks about male genitalia."[34] Another high-profile case involved eight male employees of the Jenny Craig diet company. The men claimed to have been denied promotions and subjected to a hostile work environment involving demeaning remarks about them because of their sex.[35]

The effects on men of the entire debate about sexual harassment were negative, to say the least. On trial for sexism in the Hill-Thomas case, according to virtually every journalist and commentator, was not merely one man but all men. But defending men even then was like defending black people in the South of fifty years earlier. It was just not done by respectable folks. The fourteen senators hearing this case were all men, but as everyone knew, their interpretation had to be politically correct. If Thomas had been found guilty, therefore, few senators would have dared to challenge the current ideological interpretation of sexual harassment. Indeed, Thomas himself said that anyone guilty of the allegedly heinous behaviour attributed to him should be severely punished. If the fallout from his ordeal had been confined to vague attitudes that surfaced on sitcoms, there might be no need for this book. As we intend to show, however, it settled like radioactive dust over the entire legal system.

Moreover, not only men were on trial. Even boys, young boys, were. How else can we explain some of the absurd accusations that were taken very seriously by both lawyers and journalists at the same time? In 1996, for instance, Jonathan Prevette (in North Carolina) and De'Andre Dearinge (in New York) found themselves at the heart of a national debate over sexual harassment in elementary schools. Prevette, who was six years old, had kissed his female classmate. Dearinge, who was seven, had not only had the audacity to kiss a female classmate but also to pull a button off her skirt (in homage to a story-book bear whose coveralls were missing a button). Prevette was suspended from school for one day, Dearing for five. Their schools relented, in the wake of massive public scorn, but the debate continued on every talk show. Schools have found it necessary to crack down on sexual harassment, and sexual harassment has been defined ever more broadly. Where do we draw the line? And on what basis?[36]

Sexual harassment is by no means a one-way street even in elementary schools. Not only are some boys victims, but some girls are victimizers. Girls indulge in harassment just as often as boys, even though their ways of harassing boys are seldom understood or acknowledged. Girls shame boys by calling them sissies, fairies, wussies, and so on. Any boy who performs inadequately in sports – and most boys do – is well aware of that. So are effeminate boys, shy boys, frail boys, sensitive boys, intellectual boys, or even just boys who are near-sighted enough to require glasses. And gender stereotypes are by no means the only ones to be exploited by children. But as one commentator observes, schools have "singled out certain kinds of bad behaviour for harsher treatment than others. If every 7-year-old who struck another during school hours was suspended, classrooms would be half empty. Yet even though hitting is surely more serious than a kiss on the cheek, sexual-harassment policies tell children that boys who kiss girls are committing a graver offense than girls who strike one another."[37] According to an official notice distributed to high schools in Ontario, sexual harassment includes calling another student some demeaning name such as "chick" or "babe." It advises the "victims" to call either an emergency response number or a rape-crisis centre!

During the Thomas hearing, women across the country were interviewed. Over and over again, they said incredulously: "After twenty-five years of feminism, men still don't get it." Clearly, there is something these women, too, still "don't get": the obvious fact that hostility between men and women, or any other groups, can be resolved only through negotiation, not by presenting one side with an ultimatum. But if only the position of women is granted legitimacy, how can men participate in negotiation? After twenty-five years of feminism and increasingly ideological rhetoric, men and women are further apart than ever.

It is true that women have won many legal and political battles. And it is true that they are better off in many ways than ever before. Even so, the conflict with men goes on. And that, in itself, is one of the chief problems still facing women. It would be naive to imagine that this kind of conflict can ever be completely eliminated, but have we done all we can do? And if not, what has gone wrong? Why was the golden opportunity of the Hill-Thomas affair, not taken to explore the possibility of a new approach? Even if women win every battle and punish every offending man, after all, their victories will not be worth much if they generate sullen resentment from men. The goal of social harmony will continue to elude us unless, by some miracle, the opportunity is taken for a true dialogue between men and women. Even during the hearing, some commentators called for dialogue on sexual harassment. Judging from what they said, though, it became clear that what they really wanted was a monologue by women addressed to men, not dialogue between two groups with two legitimate points of view. No one, for example, suggested that women, along with men, might have to rethink their definition of sexual harassment (let alone their assumptions about freedom of speech, pornography, and sexuality itself).

So far, there is no obvious reason for optimism. Sexual harassment was less noticeable in earlier generations, partly because there were fewer women in the workplace. What changed, beginning in the 1960s, was not merely the fact that more women were working outside the home but also the fact that many of those women wanted – and still want – two things in particular: exciting careers and exciting sex. This mentality has been most consistently and evocatively represented by the magazine founded by Helen Gurley Brown, *Cosmopolitan*, but it has been expressed also in other magazines and on every talk show. Even the most hidebound men must be aware by now that many women do see the workplace as a venue for seduction or flirtation. Those who want men to agree that the workplace is not an appropriate context for sexually charged talk (let alone flirtation or seduction) will have to convince women to do more than lobby for new regulations or new laws. They will have to convince women to stop giving men double messages – that is, to reject, publicly and consistently, the "Cosmo girl" mentality. That mentality has recently been widely disseminated by *Sex and the City*, a television show about the sexual and emotional lives of four working women in New York.[38] Because this show is massively popular among women – even as we write these words, no doubt, feminists doing graduate work in "gender studies" and "cultural studies" are preparing dissertations on it as a "transgressive" or "subversive" show that has provided an effective "site" for the "empowerment" of women – and because they see nothing wrong with women being on the make in any setting, it is clear that advocates of stricter rules of decorum in the workplace have a tough job waiting for them.

The Hill-Thomas affair made apparent what had long been hidden: not so much the lamentable fact of intimidation or blackmail in the workplace but the fact of sexual polarization almost everywhere. Merely by making an unsubstantiated accusation, one woman had the power not only to delay the confirmation of a judge to the Supreme Court and not only to precipitate a nationwide campaign for her point of view but also to stop the entire nation in its emotional tracks. And yet supporters of Hill shouted the message that women have no "voice" in America. A healthy society might have been able to avoid polarization. Although many were ready and able to challenge old assumptions about women and their needs, no one was ready to challenge current assumptions about men and their needs.

At the very least, the Hill-Thomas affair has focused attention on how complex sexual harassment cases can be. It is no easy matter to sort out the facts when evidence consists of "he said, she said" and when the hearing process is procedurally flawed. But the Hill-Thomas affair should focus attention also on the ways in which some feminists exploit high-profile media events for ideological ends. In this case, that means allowing women alone to define harassment and doing so in a way that classifies heterosexuality in general and male sexuality in particular as inherently dangerous for women or even evil. From our perspective, only one scenario is unambiguously in the category of sexual harassment – arrangements made on the basis of quid pro quo – and should remain illegal.

Ultimately, it was not merely what Thomas was alleged to have said that outraged many feminists but what he thought or felt. Many people now believe that straight men harass women simply by expressing admiration for female beauty (a controversy that we discuss in chapter 7). For a straight man to do so, they say, is not merely inappropriate in some contexts – inconvenient, clumsy, or even vulgar – but also oppressive and thus evil. We disagree. And if there is nothing inherently wrong with thinking about heterosexual attraction, how could there be anything inherently wrong with talking about it? At issue are only two matters: the extent to which sexual behaviour can be controlled and the extent to which it should be controlled. So far we have heard a great deal about what can happen with too little control and very little about what could happen with too much control. Contrary to what commentators have said repeatedly, the ultimate result of the Hill-Thomas affair might not be more men who are reluctant to hire women for fear of being sued on the slightest pretext – employers can be sued for sexual discrimination if they refuse to hire qualified female applicants – but more men who are reluctant even to fraternize with women (let alone "commit" to women). At some point down the road, more than a few men might decide that pursuing relationships with women is no longer worth the risk of being sued for speaking incorrectly.[39] As one observer noted, "The use of the terms 'unwanted' or 'unwelcome' sexual attention creates a catch-22 for males, who rarely know whether a pitch will be 'welcomed' until it has been made."[40] Even so, only those who are psychologically naive or ideologically pure could ever imagine that men and women can work together without being attracted to each other from time to time. Therefore, we will have to find a way of negotiating the acceptable limits of sexual behaviour.

Men will abandon forms of behaviour that fail to attract women, but they will not become trained seals. Both men and women will have to rethink their positions, because no lasting and genuine reconciliation has ever been dictated by an ultimatum from one side. We do need to recognize that the workplace is not a proper context either for vulgarity or for flirting that involves physical contact. But we need to recognize also that the new etiquette must be based on something other than prissiness at best or ideology at worst. And we need to establish mechanisms, such as mediators or ombudsmen, to resolve most conflicts before employees resort either to sexual harassment policies or to legal measures. Apart from avant-garde lesbians, feminists generally refrain from arguing explicitly that heterosexuality (or male sexuality) is inherently evil. Nonetheless, they attack things associated with it. This will never do.

4

Martyrs v. Murderers:
The Montreal Massacre

[It is] not an individual act. It is not just one man hating women. It is the social and political reality we live in. [1]

This incident is very unusual. If people are going to use this as a political issue, they are missing the point ... I don't feel this is a continuum of persecution."[2]

Feminists have separated violence against women from other forms of violence. For ideologues, in fact, it has become both the ultimate and the original sin. We discuss the specifically legal aspects of violence against women in chapter 9, but for the time being, we focus on one particular event of this kind and its fallout in public opinion.

Americans are familiar by now with the phenomenon of high school shootings, and some observers have wondered why the shooters are always maladjusted boys.[3] The victims, however, are both boys and girls. But in a case of mass murder at a university in Canada, not only was the victimizer male but all his victims were female. Consequently, the event became a touchstone not only of public debate but also of ideological rhetoric. We refer to the murder of fourteen women by Marc Lépine at the University of Montreal's École Polytechnique. This event sent shock waves through every segment of Canadian society and was discussed even on American talk shows.

In this chapter, we discuss the massacre itself and its immediate aftermath, the public response to it, the institutionalization of its ideological interpretation in quasi-religious forms, its institutionalization in political form, and the extent to which the feminists involved in promoting that interpretation have contributed to sexual polarization.

Journalists told this story over and over again for weeks. It was described as follows in a local newspaper:

At first they viewed it as a prank, some kind of collegiate farce in keeping with the festive spirit that marked the second-last day of classes at the University of Montreal's École Polytechnique. The man was young, about the same age as most of the roughly 60 engineering students gathered in Room 303 on the second floor of the yellow-brick building sprawled across the north slope of the mountain in the heart of the city. He entered the classroom slowly a few minutes past 5 on a bitterly cold afternoon. There was a shy smile on his face as he interrupted a dissertation on the mechanics of heat transfer. In clear, unaccented French, he asked the women to move to one side of the room and ordered the men to leave. The request was greeted with titters of laughter. "Nobody moved," recalled Prof. Yvan Bouchard. "We thought it was a joke." An instant later, Bouchard and his students discovered that what they were confronting was no joke.

Shots: The young man who would later be identified as a 25-year-old semirecluse named Marc Lépine, lifted a light, semiautomatic rifle and fired two quick shots into the ceiling. "You're all a bunch of feminists, and I hate feminists," Lépine shouted at the suddenly terrified occupants of Room 303. He told the men to leave – they did so without protest and, as one of the young women attempted to reason with him, the gun-toting man opened fire in earnest. Six of the women were shot dead. Over the course of the next twenty minutes, the young man methodically stalked the cafeteria, the classrooms and the corridors of the school, leaving a trail of death and injury in his wake. In four separate locations scattered around three floors of the six-storey structure, he gunned down a total of 27 people, leaving 14 of them dead. Finally, he turned his weapon against himself, blowing off the top of his skull. Most of the injured and all of the dead except for the gunman himself were women. This week, the city and the nation will mourn again ... as a funeral service is held for 11 of the victims at Montreal's Notre Dame Roman Catholic church.

It was the worst single-day massacre in Canadian history. And the very senselessness of the act prompted an outpouring of grief, indignation and outright rage. The City of Montreal and the Province of Quebec declared three days of mourning. Vigils were mounted in cities and towns from coast to coast. Churches held memorial services. Prime Minister Brian Mulroney and his wife, Mila, travelled to the school to offer their condolences on behalf of the rest of Canada. "It is indeed a national tragedy," he said. Earlier, with the flag atop Parliament fluttering at half-staff, the Prime Minister had asked a hushed House of Commons: "Why such violence in a society that considers itself civilized and compassionate?"[4]

We have no way of knowing precisely what was in Lépine's mind when he resorted to mass murder, let alone what was in his mind during the years leading up to that event. His friends and relatives, moreover, have for obvious reasons been reluctant to talk about him. Anyone who discusses Lépine at all, therefore, must rely to some extent on hypothesis. And every hypothesis must rely to some extent on invading the privacy of his family. On the other hand, we have several reasons for proceeding to walk where devils fear to tread. For one thing, journalists and psychiatrists began almost immediately to speculate on who or what could have produced this person. We are interested here in public perceptions, moreover, rather than biographical data. And the public perceptions generated a fierce and politically motivated debate over whether Lépine was an ordinary man or a highly aberrant one. It would be irresponsible to avoid speculating, therefore, even if we must resort to words such as "could have" or "might have." We are willing to suggest that Lépine was severely disturbed by perceptions of himself in relation not only to women but also, and perhaps more significantly, to men.

Strangely enough, Lépine's relationships with women were not particularly problematic. Although he is not known to have had sexual relations with any women, he did enjoy casual friendships with several. He liked Gina Cousineau, Jean Bélanger's girlfriend. When he and Bélanger got together, she often came along. "We were always together," she recalled, "the three of us."[5] At a high school reunion, Lépine expected to meet Bélanger. The latter never showed up, but Cousineau did. Lépine spent the evening with her and her new fiancé. Lépine's friendship with Dominique Leclair, on the other hand, could have been based on the fact that she felt sorry for him. Unlike many of the others who worked at St Jude de Laval Hospital, she took a protective interest in him. His third female friend was Sylvie Drouin. Hoping to become an engineer, Lépine began a prerequisite evening course. Drouin was his lab partner, and he became particularly fond of her. But she describes the relationship as difficult at first. He was very severe with her, constantly giving orders, calling her "Fraülein." After two weeks she told him to back off or get another partner. After that, they got along well. He helped her with her work; he walked her home. Occasionally, she visited him.

Lépine's relationships with the women in his own family were more problematic. He was probably not very close to his sister Nadia, who used to taunt him by calling him Gamil, his legal but unwanted name. His mother, Monique, probably presented him with a deeper problem. After her divorce, she resumed her career as a nurse, which meant that she had to place her children in the care of relatives, and saw them only on weekends, when she expected them to do housework. Even as a child, Lépine was asked to take care of the house. "He never really had a summer job or anything like that," according to Bélanger. "Instead, his mother paid him to stay at home and do the chores."[6] He might have blamed her for moving the family from Pierrefonds to Cartierville, thereby ending his friendship with Bélanger. In his suicide note, Lépine described this move as the beginning of the end.

Even though Lépine showed hostility toward women only at the very end, he might well have always envied them. His mother was the breadwinner; he was the househusband. His mother was the director of nursing at St Jude's;

he washed the floors there. Sylvie was accepted by the University of Quebec in Trois Rivières; he was rejected. There is some evidence to suggest that Lépine found this situation shameful and compensated through fantasy. For example, he invented a story for Cousineau about being fired from St Jude's and a woman taking his place there. Moreover, he invented a story for Drouin about being accepted for engineering at the University of Montreal.

Lépine's anxiety over his own inferiority to women, over the replacement of men by women, might well have resulted in his hostility toward women who took on nontraditional roles. Reacting to the story of a policewoman who had saved a man trapped inside a burning house, he observed that women should not be on the police force; he thought that they were not "big enough or strong enough." This troubled him so much that he made the effort to find out the names of all six women on the Montreal force. The last straw for him might have been the fact that Drouin, whom he had tutored, would be able to study engineering but that he would be unable to do so. If Lépine had been romantically interested in her, moreover, he might have interpreted their last meeting as a rejection. After the massacre, she observed that "I had come away ... with a very strange feeling like I would never see him again, that I didn't want to see him again, and I didn't. I told him I might call in the summer but I never did."[7]

Bear in mind that Lépine blamed feminists in particular, not women in general, for ruining his life. He might have harboured some resentment toward the women in his own life, either because he thought that they had rejected him or because they were successful and took jobs away from men. Before the massacre, nevertheless, there is no evidence of deep hostility toward them. There is evidence, on the other hand, of severe hostility toward some of the men in his life.

Bélanger was the only friend that he retained from childhood. As children, they had bought old gas masks and an old helmet at an army surplus store. According to Bélanger, "It wasn't that he had a fascination with war ... it was just things we found interesting, like, hey, they actually wore this stuff."[8] He and Bélanger used to shoot pigeons with their pellet guns. "It wasn't for the killing, though," observed Bélanger. "He wasn't like that, 'yeah, I want to kill.' It was just fun. We were kids."[9] As they got older, the two designed and built electronic gadgets and sound-effects systems from abandoned radios. They were close friends. Nevertheless, Bélanger's friendship ended when the Lépine family moved to another part of town. Lépine made no other lasting friendships with men. During the last summer of his life, Eric Cossette was his roommate. When Cossette moved out, Lépine's cousin Michel Thiery took his place. There is no indication that either relationship was a particularly close one. In all these cases, circumstances intervened and prevented the continuation of relationships. Lépine might have interpreted these circumstances as rejection.

Several things stand out about Lépine's father, Liass Gharbi. An immigrant from Algeria, he eventually became a successful businessman. According to Stanley Selinger, he "was a very bright guy. He spoke a number of languages and was a fantastic salesman. A slick dresser. He could sell the Brooklyn Bridge to anyone."[10] At first, the family lived well. They had big cars, glitzy parties, and a thirty-room mansion rented at a country resort. But Gharbi lost everything when his company collapsed. Even before that, he had showed signs of severe psychological problems.

Gharbi had been abused as a child. As often happens in these cases, he abused his own child Marc by beating him. Moreover, Gharbi had a habit of rubbing his crotch against women at parties and even against complete strangers. These sexual proclivities made relationships with women problematic, especially with his wife. He ignored her in public and cut her off in conversation. Sometimes, he beat her. Gharbi confessed to having had children outside of marriage. When Lépine was seven and his sister five, their parents divorced. Gharbi cut off all contact with the family. Lépine hated his abusive father to the point of refusing to take his name.

Monique realized that her son needed a surrogate father. When he was fourteen, therefore, she enlisted the help of Ralph, a Big Brother. For about three years, Lépine, Bélanger, and Ralph had good times together, but Ralph disappeared late in the fall of 1981, when the boys were seventeen. When Bélanger asked Lépine what had happened to Ralph, Lépine shrugged and said that he had gone back to Europe. But when Bélanger persisted, Lépine told him that Ralph was gay, had assaulted a child, and was in jail. Although no official charge against Ralph has been traced, it could be that Lépine himself had been sexually approached or seduced. If there was any truth to his allegation against Ralph, though, yet another man had betrayed his trust.

To understand the role of men in Lépine's life, we must also consider his interest in that classic collectivity of men: the army. In the years immediately following the separation of his parents, Lépine had enjoyed a good relationship with his uncle, a former paratrooper who had trained with an elite group of special forces in the United States. He taught Lépine how to use a gun. Shortly after the incident with Ralph, Lépine returned to his old interest in military life. Hoping to sign up with the armed forces, he went to the local recruiting office. No one knows exactly what happened. According to official military records, Lépine had been interviewed, assessed, and found to be unsuitable. He himself acknowledged in his suicide note that he had been rejected for antisocial behaviour. At least someone, therefore, had noticed that Lépine was something *other* than a healthy, well-adjusted, ordinary young man. Shortly before the massacre, his room was filled not with sadistic pornography in which women are portrayed as victims but with videos, books, and pictures about war in which men are the victims.

This seems to be an anomaly. He killed women, after all, not men. It could be explained, at least partly, as projection of the extreme negativity he felt for men (including himself) onto women – more specifically, onto women who seemed to be prospering at his expense and especially onto those who were accepted into engineering. "Why should women be engineers," asked Lépine of one victim, "and not men?"[11] He must have realized that feminism had successfully promoted the presence of women in nontraditional jobs such as engineering or police work. This realization could explain why he singled out for attack female students who were studying engineering.

Clearly, Lépine had difficulty assimilating the notion of manhood. It is reasonable to suggest, therefore, that he had a very inadequate sense of masculine identity and, moreover, an inadequate sense of personal identity. Even though some people have described him as ordinary, it is clear on closer examination that he was maladjusted even in childhood. Except when in the company of his friend, Bélanger, he was extremely withdrawn. He always wore a baseball cap pulled down over his forehead as if to make his face invisible. Years later, he was still wearing a baseball cap to work and to school. Judging from the comments by fellow workers about his inappropriate behaviour, we conclude that Lépine's self-esteem was not very high. According to Dominique Leclair, "I was kind to him because he was so hyperactive and nervous. Everyone else tried to avoid him because he was a bit strange because of his shyness ... He was always rushing things. He would never be calm." He raced the food carts the same way he did everything else. Always in a hurry. Soup got spilled. Dishes got broken. Finally, he was put on the food serving duty in the cafeteria. But the steamy kitchen atmosphere made his acne worse. Dominique recalls: "The employees would say they didn't want him to serve them their lunch because of his acne ... Lépine was becoming loud, always making cracks and telling jokes. No one laughed."[12]

Even so, Lépine did well in high school. At junior college, he took courses in the pure sciences. He did not do well in the first term, failing several courses, but he did very well in the second. During the final term, nonetheless, he suddenly quit and applied to the University of Montreal for engineering. After being rejected, he went to work as a menial in St Jude's Hospital. This same pattern – quitting after succeeding – was repeated seven years later. Having almost completed his studies in computer programming, he abruptly quit. Was his self-esteem so low that he was willing to quit within sight of success in order to confirm his own sense of himself as a failure? Why would anyone want to confirm something so negative? Because it provides at least one consolation, albeit a neurotic one: life is painful but nonetheless consistent and comprehensible.

Not one but two events took place at the University of Montreal on 6 December 1989: a massacre and a suicide. And the two are clearly connected. The former was consciously associated with Lépine's experience of women. Both the former and the latter might have been subconsciously associated with his experience of men. Lépine was a boy who had long suspected that he could not become a man. Even so, he was attracted to machismo. And it is precisely those men who feel unsure of their manhood, those who have "something to prove," who often resort to machismo. To Lépine, the only way to prove himself might have been to kill the enemy. In doing so, however, he defied society. Killing himself was his last act of self-loathing, his last act of defiance, or both.

At least some people will be reminded here of what happened, albeit on the collective level, in Germany just before the Nazis rose to power. Because of their catastrophic defeat in the Great War, many Germans had come to see themselves not only as losers but also as victims. Needing a scapegoat to maintain their identity, especially since German soldiers had not been defeated in the field, they came to see the Jews (traditionally defined by their otherness) as those who had "stabbed Germany in the back." The solution, they believed, was to reverse this situation. Consequently, they came to believe that the Jews were, in fact, an inferior race and that they themselves were the master race. In that case, exterminating those who were trying to subvert the natural order seemed to make sense. Although some of the Nazis were opportunists, others were true believers. They truly believed that the Jews were a sinister and threatening force that had to be destroyed in the interest of German survival. Using this as a model, we can better understand Lépine's pathological behaviour. He could well have seen himself as both a loser and a victim. If so, he would have tried to reverse the situation by attacking those he perceived as winners and victimizers: namely, feminists.

At least one feature of the public response to this event is beyond debate: the tragedies of fifteen human beings were deliberately exploited by some feminists, both male and female, for political purposes. Those who led the way exploited not only the grief of bereaved families but also the confusion of society as a whole.

Lépine's attitude toward women was of little or no importance, according to some people, even though all his victims were women. The mass murder, they argued, could be explained best in terms of one individual's psychosis – his inner demons, in other words, as distinct from his thoughts about social organization or political conflict or any other aspect of the outside world. "This incident is very unusual," said Helen Morrison, a psychiatrist whose specialties for almost two decades had been serial and mass murders. "If people are going to use this as a political issue, they are missing the point ... I don't feel this is a continuum of persecution."[13]

Some feminists, on the other hand, focused exclusively on the fact that all

Lépine's victims were women. This, they believed, was of crucial importance. His behaviour could be explained only in terms of the widespread misogyny that Lépine supposedly shared with many or even all other men. "It is not accidental in this misogynous society," said Maria Eriksen, a professor of women's studies at the University of Calgary, "that men kill women."[14] Similarly, Erin Graham of Vancouver Rape Relief said, it "is not an individual act. It is not just one man hating women. It is the social and political reality we live in."[15] Jennifer Bankier, writing in a bulletin of the Canadian Association of University Teachers, put it this way: "Commentators who attempt to reduce Lépine's rampage to the act of an insane and isolated individual don't understand the nature of madness. Insanity begins with a human being who holds values and assumptions about the world. Madness often operates by distorting this person's sense of proportion so that they act on their pre-existing views in extreme ways that a sane person would not."[16]

Actually, though, madness operates far more often by distorting perceptions, not merely the sense of proportion. The result might have little or nothing to do with any pre-existing views, moreover, unless perception is distorted suddenly at some point after infancy. In that case, though, it would do much more than merely give permission, as it were, to act on long-repressed urges. Even sane people, after all, have malevolent fantasies from time to time. What prevents them from acting on these fantasies is not merely external constraints but the complexity and ambivalence of their inner worlds. People hate and love at the same time. It is by no means self-evident, in short, that Lépine did only what sane men – ordinary men – would have done had they lost their sense of proportion.[17] Indeed, many sane people do lose their sense of proportion, adopting all sorts of crazy ideas, but still never resort to murder and suicide. No matter how hard it often is to distinguish between the sane and the insane, between the neurotic and the psychotic, there is a qualitative and crucial difference. Deliberately blurring this distinction for political purposes is not only contemptible but dangerous.

Bankier goes on, though, to blur other distinctions as well. "Although Lépine's murderous actions attract universal condemnation, his underlying objection to women (and, by analogy, members of other equity-seeking groups) who move out of their traditional spheres to occupy or transform 'white men's jobs' is shared and acted upon by many sane individuals through more moderate but nevertheless destructive behaviour. Such conduct is discriminatory but not irrational."[18] Bankier's main point is that any discriminatory act is tantamount, morally, to murder. Once again, though, she ignores a crucial distinction. Murder is not like any other act. Murder involves death, not merely malice. Murder is ultimate, therefore, not merely extreme. We have all committed murder "in our hearts" at one time or another. Does that mean we all belong on death row or in some institution for the criminally insane? Bankier's argument clearly makes sense on ideological grounds and therefore works very effectively to mobilize resentment, but it makes no sense on moral or psychological grounds.

Please note, however, that women were not the only ones to jump on this ideological bandwagon. According to one Larry Finkelman, a psychologist at the University of New Brunswick, Lépine was just an ordinary man who lost control. "We need to recognize that there is a spectrum of violent behaviour towards women and that most of us occupy, or have occupied, a place on that spectrum. We need to look at ourselves honestly and acknowledge the discomfort that part of ourselves may be more like Marc Lépine than we care to admit."[19] According to Edward Renner (along with two female co-authors), "it is common, ordinary men who are dangerous to women and children ... Being an ordinary man cannot continue to be the basis for a discount, because it is ordinary men who are a clear and present danger to women and children. That danger exists in the context of everyday social relationships, but rarely results in visible external physical harm."[20] Men become "male feminists" for various reasons. Some, no doubt, are truly altruistic. Others find it professionally useful to ally themselves with the academic avant-garde. Still others find it psychologically useful to separate themselves from the negativity associated with maleness.

In politically correct circles, gay men are almost always considered exceptions, honorary women, even though gay people are by no means immune to violence.[21] Facts notwithstanding, they are excused as an "equity-seeking group."[22] As one observer put it, "[t]he whole absurdity of making Lépine representative of anyone other than himself is revealed if we review the groups which could be inculpated by these tactics. Lépine could be held to represent 1. males; 2. white males; 3. North American males; 4. Canadian males; 5. québécois males; 6. Montreal males; 7. École Polytechnique males. The only grounds for choosing "white males" over the other possibilities is that this happens to be the group one wishes to inculpate."[23]

Those who identified all or most men with Marc Lépine pointed to the statistics of violence against women. They told people that one woman in four would be sexually assaulted at some time in her life, half of them before the age of seventeen, and that one million Canadian women would be abused by their partners every year.[24] However imprecise these figures might be and however tendentious the research methods behind them might have been (topics that we discuss in appendix 3), they should not be ignored. In a study of homicides of women in eighteen industrialized nations between 1950 and 1980, moreover, Rosemary Gartner, a professor of sociology at the University of Toronto, found that women who move into nontraditional roles run a higher risk of being killed.[25] Gartner explained this finding in terms of a violent backlash. The fact that Lépine killed women in engineering would support her position. Just after the massacre, indeed, there were several phone calls from men who either approved of what Lépine had done or threatened similar acts. At Mount St Vincent University in Halifax, for instance, security was increased for a vigil after anonymous callers threatened violence against its largely female student body. At its office in Ottawa, the National Action Committee on the Status of Women received a call from a man who said, "Marc is not alone." When Montreal psychologists established a hotline to counsel people shaken by the tragedy, they were shocked to receive calls from a handful of men with comments such as this: "I am very happy Lépine did it. You psychologists are just like those women, and I am coming to your office to kill you all."[26] Clearly, there is a major problem. At issue here, once again, is only how to interpret the problem and thus solve it.

We believe that neither extreme position – that this tragedy was the result of one crazed individual or that it was the result of pervasive misogyny – is adequate. To understand Lépine, we must consider him as both an individual and a member of society. He fitted the classic definition of a psychotic: someone who is utterly out of touch with reality. No wonder his letter included references to his return, after death, for revenge. He used bizarre fantasies to cope with paranoid delusions. What actually went on in Lépine's mind can never be known. And as one individual, in any case, he is of no historical or cultural importance. Of great importance, though, is the particular form that his psychosis took.

In this sense, we agree with those who focus attention on the fact that his targets were women. In another sense, however, we disagree with them. Granted that the victims were all women and that this says something important about our society. But precisely what does it say? In the opinion of some, this case of mass murder says that we live in a society characterized by the hostility of men toward women. In our opinion, the mass murder and public response to it say that we live in a society characterized by profound polarization between men and women (but also between other groups). It could be argued that the targets of hostility selected by individuals are likely to be those identified by the collectivity in any particular time and place. Scapegoats thus reflect major social or cultural "fault lines," which are given various names. In Quebec, there were, and are, two major ones: the gulf between speakers of French and English and the gulf between men and women (the old gulf between Catholics and Protestants having become insignificant due to secularization). It is not surprising that a severely disturbed person, whatever the biographical origin of his pathology, would express his fear and anger in terms of one targeted group or the other.

Some feminists used the event as an excuse to propagate their own position: that men, as a class, are sinister beings involved in a historic conspiracy against women. Lépine, they argued, merely did what most men would like to do, what most men believe that they have some moral right to do.

The only difference between him and most other men, they claimed, was that the latter are too inhibited by fear of the consequences. According to this interpretation, Lépine was not deranged in any way but just an ordinary man, a man like all other men. Those who proclaim that all men are mass murderers at heart, of course, could be accused of sexism just as easily as those who claim that all women are whores or witches at heart.

The notion that all men are murderers under the skin is not a new idea, but it raises an interesting question. If the underlying humanity of men is perverted by evil, if our society teaches men to hate women, how can we explain the fact that most men do not, in fact, resort to murdering women? Can it be seriously maintained that these men are restrained merely by fear of being thrown in jail? If so, the only sensible solution would be to get rid of men altogether by locking them up in concentration camps or killing them in death camps. If not, then what does prevent these men from acting on their sinister impulses?

It would be very hard indeed to prove that most men hate women and take delight in fantasies of women writhing under torture. Some women explain this anomaly in terms of gynocentrism. If there are good men, from that point of view, they are good only due to influence by women or feminism. But it would make much more sense simply to acknowledge that men, like women themselves, are not all alike. Moreover, it would make sense to acknowledge that our culture itself is not uniformly malevolent toward women (or, for that matter, benevolent toward men).

According to a woman interviewed on *Canada* AM, this mass murder was of interest to feminists for proving that men see women as appropriate victims or targets. A cartoon made the same point in graphic terms. In one box, identified by the biological symbol for maleness, is a collection of violent and pornographic videos along with a machine gun. The latter is pointed at another box, identified by the biological symbol for femaleness, which contains nothing but a dart board.[27] Ignored by both the interview and the cartoon is the fact that men have been trained for centuries to believe precisely the opposite: that other men, but not women, are the appropriate targets of aggression. Even schoolboys are usually well aware that hitting other boys in the playground might earn them prestige, but not hitting girls. Whenever atrocities occur, moreover, journalists routinely describe them as events in which women and children (as distinct from civilians) or men, women, and children (as distinct from people) are killed. What makes these events tragic, apparently, is that women or women and children are killed rather than merely men.

Women have been, at least until very recently, protected by a powerful taboo. Like all other taboos, this one was sometimes broken. Until now, though, it remained a taboo. But when taboos break down, they do not always fade away gently and gradually. Sometimes, the process releases a powerful urge to do precisely what had once been forbidden. Even so, the fact that women are the objects of violence does not necessarily indicate that men have singled them out as desirable targets. It might simply mean that women have lost their special protected status. That makes them more like men, not more unlike men. No longer protected by a taboo, they are subject to the same violence to which men have always been subject. Says Helen Morrison, "I see violence as an equal-opportunity behavior."[28]

The idea that women have come of age – that women no longer want or need to be protected, like children, or placed on the proverbial pedestal – has been actively promoted by feminists. This might not be the only reason for their loss of protected status, but it is surely one of them. Popular culture, too, has promoted the idea of "empowered" heroines. They fight like men and kill like men. Think only of movies such as *Charlie's Angels* and television shows such as *Dark Angel* and *Alias*. The message to men has registered: women want to be treated just like men. The problem, of course, is the way that men are taught to treat other men.

The kind of violence that assumes most political importance is invariably violence against women. Indeed, it is usually listed as a distinctive or even unique social problem. But what about violence against men, who are still, after all, the majority of those killed as a result of violent crime? Apparently, murder is only heinous when women are singled out as the victims. "The initial accounts were horrifying ... But the national revulsion increased dramatically when it became clear that the 25-year-old killer, Marc Lépine, had deliberately singled out women as his victims and spared the men."[29] No one recalled the TWA flight that had been hijacked only a few years earlier in Lebanon. In that case, it was the men who were singled out as victims; the women were allowed to leave with the children (who were not necessarily their own children). Even at the time, no one asked about this sexual differentiation.

One answer to this question, which no one ever asks, is that masculine identity, both historically and cross-culturally, has been predicated partly on men's function as protectors of women and children. Men have been socialized, in fact, to sacrifice their lives if necessary to maintain this ideal. This is why many observers wanted to know why none of the male students in Lépine's class risked their lives to save the female students (although some observers did realize that, despite the cultural rhetoric, these young men were utterly unprepared for heroism).[30] The most obvious, direct, and dramatic example of the twentieth century was recalled in the movie *Titanic*, which is historically accurate enough to show the authorities placing women and children into the lifeboats but barring men. Unfortunately, it blunts the impact of this custom, somewhat jarring to the self-consciously egalitarian mentality of later generations, by showing the female character Rose rushing below deck – and thus risking her life – to save Jack. He drowns in the end, but the politically correct point has been made that women can be just as heroic as men – even though the event itself went down in history as a moment of specifically masculine heroism par excellence.[31]

Why would the murder of women be more significant than the murder of men? One feminist answer would probably be that the former is the paradigm of all violence. But is it? A gynocentric ideology, as we say, encourages women to believe that all of history revolves around themselves. Consequently, they often find it difficult to accept the possibility that men might be motivated by needs, desires, or problems that have little or nothing to do with women. Lépine said that he was specifically motivated by hostility toward feminists, however, so feminists were correct in arguing that this particular event should not be dismissed as just another act of random violence. But was their own analysis of it any less superficial or biased than the others?

Underlying the exclusive preoccupation with female victims might be the belief that male victims deserve no attention, because men are the victimizers, the chief culprits as well as the chief victims of murder. This attitude is highly problematic for two reasons. First, it is based on the old notion of collective guilt. This or that male victim might be innocent as an individual, some would argue, but this makes no difference in view of the "fact" that men are guilty as a class. Feminists have argued persuasively that there is something inherently wrong with the whole idea of blaming victims (at least when the victims are women). But these arguments are based on logic. In our society at this time, feeling is more important. Those who ignore male victims want revenge, in short, not justice.

Over and over again, Marc Lépine's example has been used to prove that boys are socialized in destructive ways. And we agree. But Lépine's example raises a very interesting question. Precisely why are boys socialized in destructive ways? Even though parents might not be aware of any link, the attitudes and even games that they themselves have inherited and passed on to their sons are related to the skills that their sons might need someday. These skills might be useful to society on the battlefield and in the boardroom, to be sure, but not necessarily to individual men in daily life.[32] Just as girls are encouraged to develop the relational skills necessary for promoting social harmony (the ability to communicate feelings, for example, and the ability to intuit those of others), many boys have been encouraged to develop the combative skills considered necessary to protect society and provide for their families. The hippies, who withdrew into themselves and thus failed to change the basic structure of society (or vice versa), were thus doomed to become aberrations. Their notion of masculinity, a relatively peaceable ideal, was overtaken by earlier ones, although it should continue to provide us with an expanded sense of the possibilities inherent in manhood.

An event as dramatic and shocking as the Montreal Massacre might have provoked real discussion. A few people did write books and articles, many of them heavily ideological, about this event and its aftermath.[33] Others relied on political ranting and ideological slogans. Many commentators relied on the obvious, instead, solemnly declaring that the socialization of boys eventually has destructive effects on women. Few, if any, observed that it eventually has destructive effects on men as well. According to Herbert Pascoe, a forensic psychiatrist at Alberta Hospital, many men share Lépine's resentment against successful women. "The fact is," he observed, "that many men feel inadequate and inferior in their relations to the opposite sex. And this can show up in some very unpleasant activities."[34] But precisely why do men feel so threatened by women? According to Gartner, the movement of women into higher-paid occupations once reserved for men might "be perceived, consciously or unconsciously, as a threat to the traditional male dominance in society."[35] As far as it goes, this explanation makes sense. Lépine did say that he felt threatened by women in nontraditional occupations. But, once again, why?

Gartner's explanation was ideological. Men have all the power, according to her, and are unwilling to share it with women. Case closed. What immediately and obviously threatens many men, however, is not so much loss of dominance as loss of security. When affirmative action means that men are excluded on biological grounds from jobs that would otherwise have been open to them, for example, feeling threatened is a realistic response to injustice. But for most men, we suspect, the threat is also a loss of *identity* — that is, the loss of any remaining sense that they can make a distinctive, necessary, and valued contribution as men to society. Not all men are intellectually inclined, and thus not all think about these things in connection with social and cultural problems. Not all men are graduates of what could be called the Oprah Winfrey School of Psychology, moreover, and thus not all are aware of their own emotional vulnerability. Nevertheless, there really is no obvious solution to the pressing problem of masculine identity in a society that allows men to choose only between a negative identity – all men are Marc Lépine – and no identity at all.

To grow up, children must become increasingly independent from their parents. We all need at least some autonomy. Yet too much autonomy represents pathology, not maturity. To be a mature human being cannot mean complete self-sufficiency; we live in communities, not in isolation. We depend on each other, not only ourselves. We must be prepared not only to serve the needs of others, therefore, but also to receive the services of others. To put it another way, we not only need others but also need to be needed. When men are told that women are autonomous, that women do not need men, anger (though not hatred) is a perfectly reasonable response. And the overwhelming message to men from feminists really has been that women do not need them.[36] Because no healthy identity can be formed unless it is based on the possibility of making a distinctive, necessary, and valued contribution to society – we will repeat that point several times, no matter how irritating it becomes, because it lies at the heart of our thesis – men have good reasons for finding this situation extremely threatening. They are neither "unmanly," therefore, nor paranoid. Usually men are either unwilling or unable to admit that they feel threatened by women (or anyone else, for that matter). But Lépine did just that.

In Lépine's world there was still one sphere of activity that had not yet completed the process of sexual desegregation: combat. Like many other boys, therefore, he turned to the only role model that had not yet been claimed by women and that was, therefore, still distinctively masculine. The fact that he was fascinated by movies about men who are reduced to dangerous beasts or machines of destruction – these often have titles such as *Predator*, *Terminator*, and *Lethal Weapon* – should be taken as a dire warning of what can happen when boys are denied the possibility of form-ing identity in healthier ways.

Lépine's act of mass murder was only the first act of a drama that was to be enacted on radio and television, in the newspapers, and in the collective imagination. And it should certainly be remembered in the way that simi-larly shocking events are publicly remembered. The only question is how to do that in a responsible way. In this section, we examine two particular manifestations of this phenomenon: quasi-religious liturgies and shrines.

Even two years after the event, it had already been institutionalized through public ritual: gathering at monuments, ringing church bells on 6 December at precisely the moment when Lépine opened fire, presenting anniversary editorials in newspapers and on television, and attending reli-gious or secular memorial liturgies. These liturgies are very revealing. We went to one in 1991 at McGill University. It focused on a contrast between the current nightmare of a world designed by men and the dream of one designed by women.

The room was filled with women; approximately 10% of those who attended were men. On the "altar" were fourteen candles, which were lit, one by one, before each speaker sat down. This corresponded, hardly by coincidence, to the use of six candles at events commemorating the Nazi Holocaust. In both cases, the result amounts to a ritual of the community's civil religion.[37]

From beginning to end, music played an important part in creating the atmosphere of a religious event. The liturgy was preceded by a musical pre-lude, followed by a musical postlude, and divided by a musical interlude. The latter, Beethoven's String Quartet, op. 18, no. 1, Adagio, began on a funereal note but ended with a light movement that, in this context,

suggested the triumph of women, of ideological feminism, or both. Music
is a highly emotional element in every liturgy, and it was used on this occasion for precisely that reason.

Central to this event was a seemingly less traditional feature: ribbons.
Like the poppies handed out at memorial services on 11 November,
Remembrance Day in Canada, these white ribbons identified those with the
approved attitudes or beliefs and united them in solidarity. Both poppies
and ribbons are reminiscent of the ashes distributed in churches on Ash
Wednesday. And both are reminiscent, ultimately, of the bread and wine
distributed at every eucharist. As with all sacraments, the ribbon is held
(albeit implicitly) to be an "outward and visible sign of an inward and spiritual grace." Putting on ribbons, not surprisingly, reminded us of exchang-
ing the peace just after confession and just before receiving communion.

The liturgy proper began with a musical prelude by Bach (Partita in A
Minor, op. BMV 1013), which was played on the recorder by a man. This
was followed by a "liturgy of the word." It consisted of verbal presentations, almost all of them by women. One speaker, a man, represented
McGill's Internal Students' Society. His presentation, of the kind commonly
found in evangelical services, took the form of a testimonial against male
violence. He told his story to let others know that redemption was still possible for all who accept the true faith. Converts to the cause, those who saw
the light, were presumably saved at this point. Then, during a "liturgy of
the table," the ribbons were distributed and exchanged. Just before leaving,
participants sang a hymn, "Bread and Roses," which had been adapted
from a 1912 poem by James Oppenheim. The liturgy concluded with
believers being sent out into the world on their mission to save others from
the Original Sin, as it were, of patriarchy.

Men were visibly and literally marginalized on either side of the altar and
pulpit. On one side of the altar stood a man filming the event for television.
One piece of equipment, whispered someone nearby, looked "phallic."

One speaker, who represented the Jewish Women's Circle of McGill's
Hillel House, presupposed both dualism and essentialism: violent men versus nonviolent women. From the pulpit she observed "how dangerous" it
is for women to live in our society (even though statistics show that it is
even more dangerous for men). Women and men, she averred, do not share
the same outlook and the same power (presumably because men are all
powerful and brutal, while women are all powerless and loving). "We as
women really are victims," she went on, "and we as men really are the perpetrators of violence." Next, she observed that women are "angry and that
we need to be angry." Calling attention to the white ribbons worn by supporters, she asked those present to "pledge our lives to end that violence."
In conclusion, she noted that people must first mourn (although two years
had passed) and then work for change.

The next speaker, equally dualistic and essentialistic, represented the McGill Women's Union. Continuing the polarizing rhetoric, she argued that men and women have different notions of honour. Male honour has to do with killing, whereas female honour has to do with fidelity. Moreover, men are concerned with facts and women with feelings. And men lie, women do not. "Even about the facts," she observed, "they have continually lied." Women must "take seriously the truthfulness between women and among women." For several minutes, she continued to rant ideologically, discussing the differences between "them" and "us."

Another speaker, who represented McGill's Department of Philosophy, noted that it is consistent with feminism to use events of this kind for political purposes. In fact, she referred indirectly to an analogy between the mass murder by Lépine of women and the mass murder of Jews by Hitler. Remembering these events, memorializing them, is a strategy for survival. It counteracts the tendency to forget, which would make everyday life more tolerable. Because (ideological) feminists base their worldview (exclusively) on the experience of women, she argued, they are surely correct in appropriating Lépine's victims for political purposes. She was saying the obvious, but it had the effect of empowering those who might still feel queasy about exploiting personal tragedies for political purposes. At least some of us wondered, however, if all this was consistent with moral principles. Besides, the same way of thinking could be – and has been – used by men to acknowledge their own collective experience of vulnerability and pain during the two world wars. That, however, was deliberately ignored. The speaker concluded with the (unrelated) thought that love is stronger than death and hope better than despair. This was followed by applause.

Yet another speaker, who represented McGill's Sexual Assault Centre, made use of "linguistic inflation" (a political strategy that we will discuss in chapters 8 and 9), as if there was any need to inflate the impact of this particular event. First, she said that Lépine's act constituted "violence on the largest scale" (thus ignoring the violence at Passchendaele, say, or Iwo Jima). Then, moving in a different direction, she discussed other problems faced by women: everything from the loneliness of being at home to the alienation of "family conspiracies" of father and son versus mother. For her, these problems were suitable parallels with Lépine's mass murder. Finally, she noted that women suffer from self-hatred. They cannot protect themselves, she argued, because they think that they deserve to suffer. But since events like this one, as she well knew, have precisely the same effect on men, we must assume that she was hoping for deeper polarization between the sexes, not deeper understanding between them.

Pilgrimages, too, are part of the civil religion under discussion here. Every year on 6 December, people gather at Montreal's memorial park on Queen Mary Road and Decelles – only a block from the University of

Montreal. Seven stone markers, each engraved with a victim's name, are arranged on each side of a path. Benches are provided for visitors. That is all. This memorial park is very understated, though not ineffective, especially when compared to the one in Vancouver. That city's Thornton Park has been turned into a much more dramatic pilgrimage site. Fifteen stone monuments, shaped like coffins, form a circle. The fifteenth is not a coffin for Lépine, of course, but a focus for the others. An inscription on it begins as follows: "Murdered, December 6, 1989, University of Montreal." On the other side is a list of the fourteen names. These are repeated, one by one, on the other stone coffins. The inscription continues by noting that this monument is dedicated to "all women who have been murdered by men. For women of all countries, all classes, all ages, all colours."

Forming a second circle are several hundred small tiles, each donated to pay for this park. Some are from government departments. The "Ministry of the Attorney General"[38] has this to say: "That this tragic event served to raise awareness and educate us all about violence against women." Some tiles sound more like promos or commercials than anything else: "Human Resources Development Canada is pleased to have supported the Women's Movement Project through the Canadian Jobs Strategy Operations." The Public Service Alliance of Canada adopts a more humble tone: "Local 20088." Some tiles convey simple messages: "Ministry of Women's Equality: stopping violence against women."[39] Others are more longwinded: "In loving memory of the women killed on Vancouver's downtown East Side, we dream a different world, when the war on women is over." We find it striking that one tile says, "Creating a lesbian."

In Ottawa, the flag on Parliament Hill now flies at half mast every 6 December. On that day, citizens are exhorted to remember not only the fourteen women killed by Lépine but also other women who have been "murdered by men." This gesture is supposed to parallel one on 11 November. On that day, citizens are exhorted to remember Canadian soldiers killed not only in World War I, after which the custom began, but also in World War II and any other wars.

On 6 December 2001, the flag was lowered not only on Parliament Hill, however, but also on every federal building across the country. Because that never happens on 11 November, it was obvious immediately that an ideological battle had been waged and won behind closed doors by feminists. Their female victims, apparently, were more important than male victims. An enormous debate erupted, forcing the minister responsible, Sheila Copps, into crisis-control mode. She simply denied having had any connection with this travesty.[40]

A few weeks earlier, on 11 November, a similar problem had gone virtually unnoticed. According to one newspaper editorial, "the poppies are reminders of man's weakness as well as of men [sic] and women's strengths and sacrifices in difficult times."[41] A few decades ago, the word "man's" might have referred to the human race. But not now. The word "weakness" refers explicitly to male human beings as distinct from female ones, to men as distinct from women. "Strengths and sacrifices," on the other hand, refers explicitly to both men and women. Men had caused the war, in other words, but men and women together (and supposedly in equal numbers) had done what they could to end it. But this editorial was hardly the first to indulge in historical revisionism. For years, journalists have referred to the men and women who fought in wartime for their country by choice, even though Canadian women have never done so and have never been expected or even allowed to do so and even though American women have only recently begun to enter combat zones.[42]

We turn now from quasi-religious memorials for the victims to overtly political assaults on the alleged victimizers. From the very beginning, public response to the slayings was profoundly divisive among both men and women. In fact, Montreal was engulfed in a hurricane of hatred. Like a sudden squall of racism or anti-Semitism, the forces set in motion were very soon beyond the control of anyone. Provoked by sorrow, fear, and anger, fed by ideological malice and opportunism, and sustained by ignorance and confusion, it provided a brief glimpse of an abyss swirling in darkness just beneath that surface of the civility that is necessary to maintain social order of any kind.

There was never any doubt that this event would have political repercussions. Overtly political statements were made at the mass funeral itself and are still made at every annual memorial service. What follows is a discussion of one: the parliamentary debate over a royal commission on gun control in the specific context of violence against women, which was published in 1991 as a government report called *The War against Women*.[43]

Implicit in the title itself was the very dubious assumption that violence against *men* is not a serious problem, as if men were somehow guilty by virtue of being male and thus members of an oppressor class unworthy of the public concern expressed in the form of a government study.[44] The title would have been unthinkable without one underlying belief: that violence against women, or the threat of it, is the true foundation on which our society rests. And that belief, in turn, was based on another assumption: that the behaviour of men can be explained solely in terms of their attitude toward women. From the gynocentric perspective of those who instigated this report, in short, all of history revolves around women – that is, around themselves.[45] Consequently, all of history can be seen as a conspiracy of men against women, a conspiracy to keep women helpless by threatening them with violence. Almost by definition, women were classified as innocent victims and men as evil oppressors. Because the rhetorical gauntlet had been thrown down, as it were, everyone had to take this title seriously. Unfortunately, not many actually questioned its legitimacy in the first place.

Obviously, there was no literal war going on between men and women. The report's title was intended only as a metaphor, to be sure, but was that metaphor helpful? The authors clearly hoped that readers would take the title seriously not only on the individual level of Marc Lépine and his female victims but also on the collective level of all men and their female victims.

Metaphors are analogies, not equations, and on the collective level this metaphor works more effectively in reverse. It could be argued that ideological feminists acting in the name of women have declared war on men. The former are heavily armed, as it were, with very sophisticated political and academic weapons. They have organized themselves politically in opposition to "the patriarchy." More specifically, they have established a wide variety of organizations to coordinate their efforts and achieve their goals. They have leaders to represent them. They raise money through both private agencies and government bureaucracies. They are proud to acknowledge their affiliations and goals. And one of these, for a particular group of women, is to establish the idea that men are responsible for virtually all of human suffering. The parallels with ideological wars of the twentieth century, albeit metaphorical ones, are not exactly hard to imagine.

The use of military language is dangerous, however, because it encourages people to take extreme positions. Once war is declared, people have no choice but to defend themselves. And once this rhetoric is endorsed by the state, what had been a psychological and moral conflict becomes a legal and political one. But raising the stakes is a risky business. The women who proposed this government study wanted to send several messages. To women they wanted to say, The best way to defend ourselves as a class is to attack men as a class. To the nation, they wanted to say, Women are justified in attacking men, because we do so in self-defense. To men, however, they wanted to say, We consider you enemy aliens, and if the best defense is an attack, then so be it. In that context, why should men not take legal steps to protect themselves? Do we really want to move into a situation like that? If not, we will have to abandon the rhetoric of war.

It is clear to us that even though both random physical attacks on women by men and organized political attacks on men by women are common, there is no war between the sexes. And even though millions of men and women continue to marry, on the other hand, there is no peace between the sexes. On the contrary, there is escalating conflict, whether it is expressed in terms of physical violence or political exhortation. Both men and women are locked into the paradoxical and illusory rhetoric of self-defense. Canadians merely gave it official status in *The War against*

Women. Ironically, though, some women have actually declared war against men.[46]

It was in this atmosphere, only one month before the government study was proposed, that Andrea Dworkin had urged members at a conference of the Canadian Mental Health Association "to stop men who beat women ... get them jailed or get them killed."[47] In other words, she had supported vigilantes. Soon afterward, the same measure – arming women – was advocated by the National Firearms Association, Canada's gun lobby.[48] This approach would have reintroduced capital punishment through the back door, as it were, long after it had been abolished by the government. Moreover, it would have legitimated vigilantism long after it had been abolished in virtually every industrialized nation.[49] Although some participants at Dworkin's conference later admitted that killing offenders might not prove acceptable to most people, the fact is that a court acquitted a woman for doing precisely that only five days after the study had been proposed in Parliament.[50] Because the woman in question had been terrorized by her husband on a regular basis, no one dreamed of charging her with first-degree murder. Because he had already put the gun aside, though, shooting him was not quite an act of self-defense. Nor was it, as she claimed, "accidental." No matter how difficult or painful, she did have some choices to make at that point. Shooting him was only one of these. The point here is that by acquitting her, the jurors legitimated a prevalent desire for (at least vicarious) revenge.[51]

Unfortunately, justice and law are not synonymous; the two might or might not coincide. Even in this secular age, after all, the ethical heritage of Judaism and Christianity remains reasonably intact and accessible. Neither Christians nor Jews (since the early rabbinic period, which began approximately 2,500 years ago) believe in equating "an eye for an eye" with justice. On the contrary, justice is possible only in a context of reconciliation. No justice worthy of the name, in other words, can be said to exist unless it leads to peace, unless both parties in a dispute are satisfied that many of their needs have been fulfilled. It would be a serious mistake to underestimate the enduring power of this idea whether in its original religious context or translated into a secular one.

Because the purpose of a government study is to promote law reform and because the effect is to provide symbolic recognition for the official values of society, its implications must be taken very seriously. *The War against Women* undermined at least two legal principles that are fundamental to any democratic society. One is that no group should be singled out for attack by the state. In this case, the citizens of an entire class identified by a biological characteristic – maleness – became the object of governmental suspicion and therefore of public prejudice. Another principle is that the accused are presumed innocent unless proven guilty. In this case, an entire group was clearly presumed guilty unless it could be proven innocent. And no attempt was made to do that.

In view of all this, what alternatives might have been considered by Parliament? There were at least two: a government study of the causes of violence in general (including, but not restricted to, violence against women), and a government study of the increasing polarization of men and women (including, but not restricted to, hostility of men toward women). Neither was suggested. And neither would have been taken seriously even if it had been proposed, in all likelihood, except as an alleged example of misogyny masquerading as liberalism.[52]

The first alternative would have allowed the study of specific biological and cultural factors leading to violence against women but without making the following assumptions even before research began: that the world revolves around women (which is to say, the attitude of men toward women); that history is nothing other than a pervasive conspiracy or war of men against women; and that men might as well have been programmed by nature to be violent. There is a profound difference between deliberately promoting a preconceived position (no matter how noble it might sound) and sincerely trying to describe reality in all its complexity (no matter how imperfectly) before proposing a solution. The former is usually called "propaganda."[53] The latter is scholarship.

But many would have objected to this alternative. They would have raised two main questions. First, would it not have diverted attention and tax dollars away from women? Sure, to some extent. But since we have reason to believe that the problem does indeed extend beyond the scope of any inquiry on violence against women alone, no amount of attention or money spent on more specific problems would have sufficed.

Second, would a more general inquiry not have trivialized women by turning their distinctive problems into examples of a larger one? Actually, no. Like every other social problem, violence against women has its own distinctive features, and if they were the only victims of violence, it would make sense to focus attention on them alone. But since women are not the only victims or even the primary ones, it follows logically that additional variables must be involved. Ideologues would deny this, of course. They believe that violence against women is caused by some unique or primal hatred; therefore, it is the model for all other forms of violence. But neither of these beliefs can be established on a foundation of hard evidence. Consequently, the government study of violence against women was seriously compromised from the very start by ignoring or setting out to eliminate all factors apart from the attitudes of men toward women and all explanations apart from those based on a conspiracy theory of history or the notion that (male) biology is destiny. But if the answer is known even before research begins, why bother to have a government study in the first place?

Relating the problem of violence against women to that of violence in general merely acknowledges the obvious. Both women and men are human beings. Their experiences can be understood, therefore, in terms of principles applied to everyone by historians, psychologists, anthropologists, and so forth. To argue otherwise would mean claiming that the experience of women is not merely unique but "uniquely unique." And that claim, an ontological or even metaphysical one, could be supported only by theology. To assert that women are victims in a "uniquely unique" way, for example, would mean that they are the victims of some "uniquely unique" force of evil. That would make all men demonic beings or satanic agents of some kind, an implication, as we showed in *Spreading Misandry*, that can be found even in popular movies. It is precisely by insisting that violence against women is *like* other forms of violence, having many causes and many variables, that we can avoid the kind of witch hunts familiar from the pages of history.

The second alternative would have been a government study of the increasing polarization of men and women. Consider the advantages of this approach. It would have acknowledged reality, no matter how inconvenient some people might have considered it: a conflict with active participants of both sexes. Moreover, it would have acknowledged additional problems: violence against women, violence against men (whether by other men or by women), and reasons for violence by men such as genetic abnormalities, developmental problems, divorce, alcoholism, and drug addiction. In other words, it would have encouraged the consideration of factors and points of view that were ignored in the published report. At the very least, this approach would have raised the fundamental question of why so many men, conditioned by the same society, do *not* resort to violence against women or even against other men. By examining culture as well as nature, it would have avoided the implication that one segment of society, biologically defined, was being morally attacked from the outset and would have included the specific problem of sexism in both forms, misogyny and misandry. The scope would thus have been neither too broad nor too narrow. It would have helped us to understand why more men than women kill, for instance, but without succumbing to stereotypes and the propagation of hatred.

Given the realities of political life, though, how would a government study of that kind have functioned? For one thing, both men and women would have required equal representation. Merely insisting on an equal number of male and female experts would not have done the trick, however, because political leanings do not necessarily correspond to physiological types. Some men, for example, consider themselves feminists. To make this kind of study work would have meant either of two solutions: eliminating (male or female) commissioners known to have already adopted political positions or balancing them with (male or female) commissioners known to care about the condition of men as well as that of women – and also, of course, to have studied the condition of men no less thoroughly than that of women. This would have generated acrimonious debate, to be sure, but debate is part of both scholarship and government. The experts would have been in a better position to produce sound scholarship, in short, than believers in the same ideology. A government study of this kind might have gone beyond debate. If chosen wisely, commissioners could have fostered a different form of communication. It would have been an experiment, sure, but so are all attempts at social engineering.

The problems noted in this government report were very serious ones, requiring both study and action. To argue against this or that explanation for a problem afflicting women is not to deny its existence, its gravity, or the need for a solution. A government report on either violence in general or the polarization of men and women might have been very useful (to the extent that any government report is more than just an exercise in political expediency). This one, on violence against women alone, was of value only to those who wanted a particular political position endorsed by the state. Any government study, though, would have proven self-defeating unless a significant number of the commissioners, not merely a few token men, were both willing and able to challenge all partisan claims. And potential commissioners of that kind would have been – and still would be – extremely hard to find.

The potential response of men, of male citizens and taxpayers, was considered irrelevant. Men are in a no-win situation. They can either be politically correct but ineffective or politically incorrect and equally ineffective. From the very beginning, when the study that resulted in *The War against Women* was first proposed in Parliament, the situation was engineered in such a way that few would have dared to present an opposing point of view. And those who did could have expected to pay a heavy political price: public ridicule.

But there is nothing shameful in feeling threatened, certainly not when the threat is real. And men are increasingly willing to acknowledge this. Ironically, ideological feminism has caused more and more men to think of themselves, as women now do, in terms of their identity as a group. Fewer and fewer men, therefore, will be manipulated into silence by anyone who accuses them of being "unmanly" or "insecure" for defending their identity as male human beings.

Despite its divisive rhetoric, the immediate effect of *The War against Women* was less than dramatic. Included among its recommendations to Parliament, after all, were some sensible but hardly revolutionary suggestions. One, for instance, was that more emphasis should be placed on putting dangerous criminals behind bars and keeping them there. Another was that the sale of guns should be more strictly controlled. Many of these suggestions were legislated. But has the result been peace negotiations between men and women? Hardly. The level of violence against women did go down, to be sure, but so did the level of violence in general. The level of rhetoric, on the other hand, went up. Way up. And even as the rhetorical stakes were raised, moreover, so were the ideological ones. A significant cultural and emotional boundary was crossed. Those who might have hesitated before using extreme language no longer have any reason to do so – not after the government of a liberal and reputedly staid, even polite, society used it in official documents.

No event could possibly have illustrated more dramatically than the Montreal Massacre, along with its aftermath, the extent to which men and women had become polarized. Because Lépine targeted not merely women but feminists, moreover, it raises an important question: To what extent have ideological feminists contributed to the general climate of hostility between men and women? Because the advocates of any revolution are bound to generate fear and anger, it is logical to conclude that the rise of increasingly hostile forms of ideological feminism has had at least some historical impact on men. Some men feel profoundly threatened by it, and sometimes – when they are threatened by loss of identity or loss of custody, say, and not loss of illegitimate privileges – with good reason. It is at least conceivable that this partly explains the fact that male suicides have increased dramatically over the past twenty years. Is it entirely coincidental that "the rate of suicides among Canadian women remained nearly constant over the same period"?[54]

Ideological feminists believe that women are fundamentally autonomous and have no need for men, except as sperm donors; men, they add, are fundamentally dependent on women and therefore make demands on them (the result being oppression). Apart from anything else, this means that women are not only innocent bystanders in the conflict between the sexes (wanting only to leave men alone) but also passive (wanting only to be left alone by men). Ideological feminists deny, however, that women are passive. In fact, they say, history revolves around women. But that raises questions about even the alleged innocence of women. As active historical agents, after all, they cannot leave men alone; at least sometimes, they make demands that conflict with those of men.

Ideological feminists have produced several theories to explain social problems, but these are hardly the only theories. One member of Parliament described the debate over *The War against Women* as a "very painful experience."[55] In a democratic society, though, it would surely be even more painful for reports to go through Parliament without any opposition or debate. Our way of life, represented by the legislature, recognizes no way of thinking that is beyond challenge. It is far from self-evident, at any rate, that those who opposed the report did so out of indifference. No one could deny that something had to be done about violence against women. What should have been denied were ideological theories that purported to explain or solve the problem. It should not have been acceptable to assume that any man who questioned ideological positions or proposals was too "insecure," too stupid, or too evil to be taken seriously as a responsible citizen. At that point, theory became doctrine.

Women really do need to defend their lives. But men, whether they realize it or not, need to defend their lives as well. Moreover, they need to defend some sense of identity, no matter how that might be defined, without which their lives would be meaningless. We do not believe that women have no reason to protest when their safety is endangered – they surely do – but we do claim two closely related things in addition. First, women sometimes choose very inappropriate ways of doing so. Second, men have good reasons for protesting. In short, both men and women, as groups, have something vital to defend.

Despite a pervasive fear that thousands of other Marc Lépines were ready to murder women, or feminists, nothing like that actually happened. Yet everyone realized that something very significant had taken place – even in the United States, where the Montreal Massacre was discussed on news and talk shows – and that nothing would ever be quite the same again.

For Canadian men, at any rate, the time had come to think seriously about maleness and masculinity. A few men agreed with the feminist theory that all men were rapists and killers under the skin, but many more men reacted to that theory with revulsion. At least some of the latter, in fact, began to realize the urgent need for articulate and sophisticated forms of self-defense – that is, new gender theories and new political or legal strategies. For Canadian women, the time had come to translate radical theories into action. Most feminists believed that they had reached a turning point in their struggle to change society. And they were correct. During the next few years, they redoubled their efforts to rewrite every law governing relations between the sexes and thus bring about a new society. The rest of this book is about what they achieved. American feminists did not write a great deal about what had happened in Montreal, but it might not be entirely coincidental that their legal efforts to change society reached a new height at precisely that historical moment.

PART TWO

Rights on Trial: Money Matters

In part 1, we discussed widely accepted perceptions of men in popular culture, continuing what we began in *Spreading Misandry* but focusing on the interface between popular culture and elite culture. We argued that those perceptions are, in fact, shaped primarily by the ideological branch of feminism. In part 2, we examine the ways in which these perceptions have affected the fundamental structures of society – that is, national constitutions, legal systems, and bureaucracies. Our basic point is that ideological feminism is no longer merely a point of view adopted by a few pretentious journalists or ranting academics. It has been institutionalized. It has become the law. And this has taken place largely due to the pressures exerted by feminist interest groups.

In stable democracies, those who want radical change do not require violent revolution. There are much easier and more effective ways for them to achieve their goals or at least to enhance their power. Constitutional modification – a formal amendment, say, a new rule, or a judicial interpretation – can be a very effective mechanism. This was certainly true for American blacks, who have used litigation to improve their position. According to Christopher Manfredi, the most successful interest groups have reliable sources of money and expert legal advice. They work toward long-term goals, accumulating valuable experience at each stage of the game. Political bargaining, sponsoring test cases, intervening in cases, infiltrating the courts as researchers and judges, and litigating for a new framework by which to settle disputes, redistribute goods, or introduce new court-ordered policies are furthered by lobbying, making political contributions, or influencing the mass media. Gradually, in short, outsiders can become powerful insiders.

Everyone knows that interest groups, or lobby groups, play a major role in democracies, but not everyone knows how effective those of women have been. In some cases, that is all to the good; women really have required reforms. In other cases, it is not. The reforms have either intentionally or unintentionally punished men (which is a moral problem) and thus contributed heavily to social fragmentation or even polarization (which is a political problem). In the name of reform and equality, we have institutionalized revolution and inequality. Gynocentrism has replaced androcentrism. Misandry has replaced misogyny. New problems have replaced old ones. Or old ones have remained and merely taken on new forms. For instance, many new laws – or new interpretations of old ones – discriminate against men instead of against women. They do not do so directly or explicitly, of course, because that would mean formal renunciation of anything remotely recognizable as equality. And that would require, apart from anything else, tearing up constitutions and barricading the streets. Instead, they do so indirectly or implicitly.

Our aim here is to examine the constraints, if any, that are placed on feminist lobby groups in the United States and Canada. The two countries have somewhat different legal systems (even though both are rooted, apart from civil law in Quebec, in the British legal tradition). Why discuss both here? Because both countries have been heavily influenced in the recent past by a common worldview promoted by the United Nations. Based either explicitly or implicitly on postcolonialism, the international version of postmodernism, it is highly receptive to what we have identified as ideological feminism, along with various national, racial, and ethnic ideologies. But one country is less constrained by political structures than the other is. Canadians have found it easier than Americans to implement the legal changes that are promoted by the United Nations. Canada, in short, is what the United States would be like with a twentieth-century constitution instead of an eighteenth-century one.

In both countries, using different mechanisms, advocates of feminist ideology have secured the collective economic interests of women and either ignored or attacked the collective economic interests of men: the individual women and men involved, their particular circumstances, have been considered of little or no importance. Because the resulting systemic discrimination against men has been achieved in subtle ways – incrementally, for instance, rather than suddenly – many people, including men, have either failed or refused to recognize that a major shift has taken place. As a result, misandry has been legalized – that is, misandry has taken the form of systemic discrimination against men.

In chapter 5, we discuss the transformation of rights (originally defined in terms of freedom from state interference) into entitlements (defined as state obligations). And in chapter 6, we do so in connection with child support.

5

Women's Rights v. Human Rights: The Case of Entitlements

If you interpret the term "equality" as it has typically been interpreted ... you will maintain the inequality of the sexes. Women, in particular, will remain the perpetual economic, social, and political underclass that women now are.[1]

If Stanley Fish really means what he says [about affirmative action], he should immediately resign his ill-gotten, unmerited position as professor of English and law at Duke University so that it can be filled by someone from a group that has been "bought, sold, killed, beaten, raped, excluded, exploited, shamed, and scorned for a very long time."[2]

Men and women are biologically different in a few – not many, but a few – basic ways. This was considered self-evident throughout human history until circa 1965. Women can bear children, for instance, and men cannot. Men are more muscular and slightly bigger, on average, than women. And men have more testosterone than women do. Feminists have debated the relevance of these differences incessantly. Some trivialize them, arguing that the sexes are interchangeable for all practical purposes and should therefore qualify for equality under the law. Other feminists (or sometimes, when it suits their needs, even the same ones) exaggerate these differences, arguing that women are innately vulnerable to men and should therefore qualify for either special protection or even special advantage under the law in order to level the playing field. Still other feminists, ideological ones, often add that women are innately superior to men – more caring, more just, more peaceful, more knowing, or whatever – and therefore qualify as the vanguard of a radically new order.

Men and women are (still) culturally different, too, for various reasons. In the past, androcentric biases relegated elite women to the domestic sphere and the masses of women to unpaid labour in the fields or poorly paid labour in the factories (although the masses of men were hardly better off in those very same fields and factories). This gender system left most women unprepared to participate fully in society. They were disadvantaged in connection with jobs, divorce, remarriage, widowhood, single motherhood, and so on. Ideological feminists go beyond this observation and insist that these cultural differences are not merely the accidental results of biology or the exigencies of history but the intended results of an oppressive patriarchal society. Men deliberately exploit biological differences or invent cultural differences, they claim, in order to subordinate women. In other words, these differences reveal a misogynistic conspiracy.

Whatever the reason – and there is plenty of room for debate on that score – the fact is that women have had some serious disadvantages in the public realm and have therefore needed reforms. (Men have had some serious disadvantages of their own, which we will discuss in *Transcending Misandry*.) Most feminists use the rhetoric of equality, which is our political lingua franca, to discuss these reforms. And who would ever oppose equality? Trouble is, there are two or three competing paradigms of equality. Each has been used as a framework in which to solve the problem of intentional or unintentional discrimination against women by increasing their rights.

After an introduction on the problem of how to define words such as "discrimination," "rights," and "equality," we review the legislation on equal rights, the moral status of affirmative action programs and pay equity programs, and how these programs affect men and human rights. Our goal is to move beyond both gynocentrism and androcentrism.

The word "discrimination" is problematic because it can be used in both descriptive and pejorative senses. Like most people today, we use it in a pejorative sense; for practical purposes, we refer to discrimination against this or that. But the word need not be used in that way, because the ability to discriminate, to make distinctions, is a necessary part of human existence. The law discriminates with good reason, for example, between criminal and acceptable forms of behaviour.

As for the word "rights," the story is more complicated. It was originally used in connection with freedom from tyranny by the state. The goal was personal liberty. This perspective gained momentum throughout the eighteenth-century Enlightenment and was first institutionalized in the new American republic. According to the Declaration of Independence, every American has a right to "life, liberty, and the pursuit of happiness." The implications were eventually spelled out more precisely in the Bill of Rights. From the beginning, it was clear that not all Americans actually enjoyed liberty. Slaves, for instance, did not have the rights of other Americans. This brings up the closely related word "equality."

After the Civil War, legal inequality was much harder to justify (except, for almost a hundred years, in the South). One group after another demanded practical access to equality of opportunity, which is what most theorists now call "formal equality" or "procedural equality." How to achieve that? Until very recently, the answer was clear: by applying the same rules, in the same ways, to all citizens. American feminists followed the same pattern, at first, as American blacks had followed. They demanded legal and social adjustments so that women could pursue their goals, especially in the public sphere, just as effectively as men could. They wanted a gender neutral society, in the language of today, or a gender blind one – the hallmark of a liberal democracy.

But things have changed. Michael Ignatieff and others have argued that we are witnessing an international rights revolution, a significantly new way of thinking about rights and equality that has evolved over the past few decades.[3] The rhetoric among feminists has changed profoundly as they try to liberate women from all traditional roles and to redesign society accordingly. This has meant acquiring and then mobilizing a new set of rules to advance their own understanding of women's rights and gender equality. These changes have become embedded in the institutional structures of the governments of Europe and Canada and in international treaties and conventions.

According to the new rhetoric, rights are primarily about entitlements and protections granted by the state. The new goal, which most theorists call "substantive equality," amounts to equality of result. (Both "formal equality" and "substantive equality" are manipulative terms. By implication, only "substantive equality" is "substantial" and thus legitimate or acceptable. Also by implication, "formal equality" is reduced to something that can be dismissed as merely "pro forma" or "procedural" and thus illegitimate and unacceptable.) The ultimate model for equality of result, in any case, is Marx's classless society, in which personal merit has little or nothing to do with the distribution of wealth, although that model has come down to us in Western countries as the slightly less utopian welfare state.

How to achieve equality of result? Precisely by *not* applying the same rules in the same ways to all citizens as individuals – that is, by applying them differentially to correct for disadvantages due to race, sex, language, or whatever. Many feminists now demand "gender balance," or "gender equity." Closely related is the narrower demand for "pay equity," a scheme to redress the fact that women as a group earn less than men as a group. That problem has involved either systemic wage discrimination or occupational segregation because of historical notions about women's work and men's work.

The new way of thinking is most fully exemplified in documents produced by the United Nations that we discuss in appendix 6. As a result, new policies are expanding the political power of women. Ideological

feminists lobby both that organization and their own governments to institute equality of result. Because they have trouble getting this done through
the front door of legislative change, they introduce it through the back
door of bureaucratic change. First, they attain incremental changes in documents of the United Nations. Once they are signed by their own governments, the road ahead is clear. Bureaucrats modify policies accordingly
with "guidance" from women's organizations that are affiliated with the
United Nations. Only those directly involved know what is going on.

Many of the most influential American feminists are eager to adopt the
new rhetoric, but the Constitution places some constraints on them. Some
politicians contend that even the Equal Rights Amendment would only
reinforce equality of opportunity, although that conservative interpretation
could be their way of selling the amendment. Because the new rights
rhetoric has become deeply embedded in public opinion, thanks partly to
the talk shows, legislators have managed to change at least some laws
accordingly. But they do meet strong resistance from those who point to a
long constitutional tradition. The most influential Canadian feminists are
just as eager to adopt the new rhetoric, and the Canadian system places few
constraints on them. We could sum up the difference as follows. The
American position is characteristic of both liberalism and conservatism,
ironically, with its focus on the individual. The Canadian position is characteristic of ideology, on the other hand, with its focus on the collectivity.
By the latter, note well, we refer not to society as a whole but to fragments
of it defined by race, sex, and so on.

Between these two positions is a third, one that has already been widely
institutionalized in both countries but has never been acknowledged by
those who demand equality of result. This position adapts equality of
opportunity to accommodate pregnant women and new mothers in the
workforce, allowing a few exceptions to general rules but without endorsing equality of result. Those who insist on the latter have incorporated
these accommodations into their own program, which makes equality of
opportunity seem less inclusive. In any case, they remain dissatisfied. They
still demand equal representation. The law, they claim, must require that
women fill at least half of all managerial jobs in the public world: corporate, legislative, judicial, and so on.

Equality of opportunity was institutionalized first in the United States.
Both before and just after the Revolution, however, only elite white men
were eligible to vote; most men, along with all women, were not. But things
began to change in the mid-nineteenth century. In 1848, the first Woman's
Rights Convention was held in Seneca Falls, New York. Twenty years later,
the Fourteenth Amendment was passed. It guaranteed equal protection to
men and women under the law. According to section 1, "No state shall ...

deprive any person of life, liberty, or property, without due process of law; nor deny to any person within its jurisdiction the equal protection of the laws."[4]

The Fifteenth Amendment, ratified in 1870, declared that "the rights of citizens to vote shall not be denied or abridged ... on account of race, color, or previous condition of servitude."[5] This amendment gave the vote to some black men – those who were literate, say, or owned property – but to neither white nor black women. Some feminists were vocally hostile, in fact, to the possibility that black men might get the vote before white women.[6] After decades of political agitation, women finally won the right to vote in 1920. According to the Nineteenth Amendment, the "right of citizens of the United States to vote shall not be denied or abridged by the United States or by any state on account of sex."[7] This remains the only specific constitutional guarantee of equal rights for American men and women.

It all adds up to equality of opportunity, and the Constitution is thus consistent with classical liberal theory. According to Anne Peters, "the American Constitution does not explicitly provide for equality of men and women before the law. Differential treatment based on gender must conform to the general equal protection principles under the Fourteenth and Fifteenth Amendments. These clauses do not explicitly spell out a specific standard of protection."[8] Still, they have been interpreted by the Supreme Court to solve the problems faced by women. "The Supreme Court stressed that the Constitution proscribes 'archaic and overbroad generalizations,' or 'overbroad generalizations based on sex which are entirely unrelated to any differences between men and women or which demean the ability or social status of the affected class.'"[9] Accordingly, the functional position of the United States is equality of opportunity in a *modified form*. Included in that category are modifications to ensure that women do not lose their jobs and benefits due to pregnancy, for instance, or for being mothers of infants.[10]

As we say, though, many feminists want more than that. They want equality of result and government-sponsored measures to achieve it. The best-known measure is affirmative action. Because of their constitutional documents, says Peters, some Americans oppose affirmative action in theory but often allow it even so. This anomaly can be traced back to the Kennedy administration's attempt to deal with the racial crisis by establishing affirmative action for blacks, which led women to demand affirmative action for themselves. But many feminists are unwilling to admit that equality of opportunity has been attained by modifying it in a way that "realistically reflects the fact that the sexes are not similarly situated in certain circumstances."[11] Instead, they appropriate these modifications as examples of "substantive equality." This makes it easier for them to continue struggling toward their ultimate goal: officially recognized equality of result. They want explicit references in the Constitution to special "protections" for women, presumably for the additional security but also because of the additional status that they would confer.

American feminists have spent more than 150 years campaigning for the Equal Rights Amendment. A precursor was first introduced as the Lucretia Mott Amendment in 1848 and revised in 1943 as the Alice Paul Amendment. Inspired by the civil rights movement, feminists mobilized again in the 1960s. In 1972, it was approved by Congress as a proposed Twenty-seventh Amendment, which had to be ratified by three-quarters of the states within seven years.[12] Section 1 reads as follows: "Equality of rights under the law shall not be denied or abridged by the United States or by any state on account of sex." Section 2 adds that Congress "shall have the power to enforce, by appropriate legislation, the provisions of this article." And section 3 concludes that "[t]his amendment shall take effect two years after the date of ratification."[13]

The amendment was not ratified by enough states, but supporters agitated for – and won – an extension. By the new deadline, 1982, they still lacked three states. Since then, the Equal Rights Amendment (minus any deadline on the ratification process) has been reintroduced as a bill in each session of Congress. And advocates point out that one amendment originally proposed by James Madison in 1789 (and sometimes called the Madison Amendment), took 203 years to ratify. In that case, they would not need to campaign once more for the original thirty-five states; they would need only three more states. This position was deemed worthy of consideration by the Congressional Research Service in 1996. Ratification bills intended to test this "three-state strategy" have been introduced into the fifteen states that have not yet ratified it.[14]

Even though some feminists claim that the Equal Rights Amendment would promote a narrow, or conservative, interpretation of gender discrimination in order to facilitate its ratification – justices could use the test of strict constitutional scrutiny in deciding whether equality has been denied or abridged on account of sex – it has not been ratified by the required number of states, partly because of considerable tension between equality of opportunity and equality of result. Nevertheless, American women have secured the passage of many laws on affirmative action and pay equity. Although polls have shown considerable American support for affirmative action, those who advocate equality of opportunity (even in a modified form) have criticized it for undermining individual freedom, being unfair to white men, coming in through the back door of administrative guidelines and court decrees rather than through direct political processes, undermining competition by benefiting minimally qualified candidates, making it hard to deal with competing group interests in a nation of immigrants, and conferring greater benefits on white women than blacks of either sex, for whom affirmative action was originally designed.[15] This antipathy toward entrenched affirmative action could explain why the United States has never ratified a document that was signed back in 1980: the United Nations Convention on the Elimination of All Forms of Discrimination against Women (which we discuss in appendix 6).

Affirmative action did get in, gradually, through the back door. The term was first used in 1935 by the National Labor Relations Act, or Wagner Act, which was part of the New Deal. According to that legislation, the National Labor Relations Board was required to insist that employers stop unfair employment practices. This could mean taking "affirmative action," reinstating employees either with or without back pay. In 1961, President Kennedy's Executive Order 10,925, which set up a committee on equal employment opportunity, redefined affirmative action as an active way of counteracting discrimination. Even this, however, was expressed in partially negative terms: "The [government] contractor will take affirmative action to ensure that applicants are employed ... without regard to their race, creed, color, or national origin."[16] In 1965, President Johnson amended that order with Executive Order 11,246, which made the following statement mandatory for all government contracts: "[T]he contractor will take affirmative action to ensure that all applicants are employed, and that employees are treated during employment, without regard to their race, color, religion, sex or national origin."[17] In 1971, under President Nixon, a revision of Implementing Order 4 to Executive Order 11,246 defined affirmative action as the commitment by contractors to specific procedures and goals that would give preference to particular sexes and races (also described as "women and minorities") in order to achieve equal employment opportunity in federal jobs according to a schedule. Affirmative action-plans required by this legislation targeted women and four ethnic groups.[18] Meanwhile, in 1963 the Equal Pay Act was passed to prohibit sex discrimination for similar work in similar conditions.[19] All these laws and their subsequent amendments provided a federal mandate for affirmative action. Legislation referred to "targets" and "goals," however, rather than to quotas, although quotas were sometimes required by courts.

Affirmative action was buttressed in 1978 by guidelines on sex discrimination. Government contracts were now awarded on the basis of affirmative action policies. To qualify for contracts, institutions had to file reports if they found an inadequate number of women or minorities, redress any "imbalance" by active recruitment, include these new recruits in management training programs, and so on.[20] In short, affirmative action came in largely through "administrative agencies and courts, not the legislature."[21] It has been embraced by the private sector, moreover, which has established independent affirmative action programs.

Minority businesses gained government support with the Public Works Employment Act of 1977 and Public Law No. 95-507 of 1978. This legislation authorized set-aside programs, so that some procurement contracts would go to these businesses. But after these programs were challenged under the Clinton administration, the Supreme Court eliminated them both in the military and elsewhere.[22]

Title VII, an amendment of 1997 to the Civil Rights Act of 1964, included a statutory prohibition of employment discrimination on the basis of race, colour, religion, sex, or national origin.[23] But this prohibition, too, had to meet several criteria. Advocates had to demonstrate some legitimate need to correct an "imbalance" in the workplace (although evidence of earlier discrimination was irrelevant), provide empirical evidence to support their claim, avoid "unnecessary burdens" on or unnecessary infringements on the rights of those who were "dispreferred" (a euphemism for "discriminated against"), demonstrate that this mechanism would be more effective than other ways of correcting the problem, and make it "flexible" enough to be discontinued if the labour market was negatively affected. It would be negatively affected if the need to reach hiring "targets" because of affirmative action conflicted with the need to fire people because of economic conditions, for instance, or if people hired on the basis of race or sex were less qualified than other candidates.

Affirmative action has been introduced in education, too, especially in connection with policies governing admission to universities. These policies have been challenged. One of the major cases, in 1978, was *Regents of the University of California v. Bakke.*[24] The Supreme Court struck down explicit quotas for minority applicants (16% in this case), although it did allow universities to include "birth" traits such as skin colour as "plus factors" (along with other traits such as special talents, having parents who had attended the university, and region of residence) to create a "good mix" of students. These policies were once more under attack by the late 1990s, this time in two cases at the University of Michigan.[25] In June 2003 the Supreme Court supported Michigan's affirmative action policy for law students but overturned the one for undergraduate students. According to the justices, the former considers race or ethnicity (African Americans, Native Americans, and Hispanics) as nothing more than a "plus" factor, one variable among others, and therefore passes the constitutional test of strict scrutiny. The latter, by contrast, automatically awarded twenty points out of one hundred for race or ethnicity, thus making it a decisive factor for minimally qualified applicants.

American judges analyze the merits of affirmative action claims according to constitutional and statutory provisions. Policies must comply with the Equal Protection Clause of the Fourteenth Amendment and be assessed by the appropriateness of goals and means – taking into consideration race or sex. When the government mandates affirmative action, it uses a strict test, or standard, of legitimacy. The government must have a compelling interest, in other words, and the means must be narrowly tailored, although justices have often debated which standard should be used, because the choice of test greatly influences the outcome.[26]

All this legislation resulted in a new bureaucracy. According to a list of all departments in the government, several are devoted explicitly and exclusively to women.[27] The Department of Justice's Violence against Women Office does research involving statistics, suggests ways of ending violence against women, staffs hotlines, provides links to coalitions and advocacy groups, lobbies for better laws or policies, and gives grants to state governments.[28] The Department of Labor's Women's Bureau is intended to "promote profitable employment opportunities for women, to empower them by enhancing their skills and improving their working conditions, and to provide employers with more alternatives to meet their labor needs by advocating for equitable employment standards, policies, and programs" and "to empower women to enhance their potential for securing more satisfying employment as they seek to balance their work-life needs."[29] Two more agencies are devoted explicitly to the wives of federal officials: the Office of the First Lady and the Office of Mrs Cheney (or the wife of any other vice-president).

Canada, too, began by recognizing equality of opportunity, and, as in the United States, it was achieved in stages. But Canada, unlike the United States, has officially replaced that ideal with equality of result. Its institutionalization is due largely to one ideologically oriented feminist organization: the Legal Education and Action Fund, or LEAF.[30] Here is the story.

The Canadian feminist movement began in the nineteenth century with demands for suffrage (achieved in 1928 for the women of every province except Quebec, where it was achieved in 1940) and recognition as "persons" under Canadian constitutional law (achieved in 1928).[31] But the big push for feminists began during the 1970s, when Parliament officially adopted a national policy of "multiculturalism." This policy was originally intended, in the form of federal bilingualism – the Official Languages Act was passed in 1969 – primarily as a way of dealing with sharp conflict between Canada's two founding communities: the English and the French. But the underlying notion of "pluralism" was soon extended to women.

In 1970, the Royal Commission on the Status of Women made 167 recommendations. To lobby for their implementation, about thirty feminist groups created the National Action Committee on the Status of Women. It now represents approximately seven hundred groups.[32] This organization became closely linked with government through the Canadian Advisory Council on the Status of Women, which was established by the federal government as a privileged channel by which feminist groups could make their demands directly to the government. As Christopher Manfredi has put it, this is a political advocacy group within the government itself.[33]

Two major legal cases in the 1970s did not bode well for women. In *Lavell v. Canada*, the Supreme Court upheld Canada's Indian Act, which said that Indian women, but not men, would lose their Indian status (with its entitlements) if they married non-Indians.[34] In this case, equality before the law was defined by the Court as "equality of treatment in the enforcement and application of the laws."[35] In other words, they applied equality to enforcement but refused to challenge the law's inherent inequality. In *Bliss v. Canada*, the Supreme Court denied benefits under the Unemployment Insurance Act to women who stopped working during pregnancy.[36] There was no discrimination, said the justices, because the problem was caused by nature. Both decisions were understood as restrictive interpretations of equality.

But Canada ratified the United Nations Convention on the Elimination of All Forms of Discrimination against Women in 1980. And it was partly with this convention in mind that a joint parliamentary committee held hearings between 1980 and 1981 to encourage feedback from major interest groups on Canada's proposed Charter of Rights and Freedoms. Several of these groups – among them the National Action Committee on the Status of Women, which was by then a coalition of 230 groups, the Canadian Advisory Council on the Status of Women, the National Association on Women and the Law, and several aboriginal women's groups – presented briefs. They wanted most of all to change the draft of section 15, the one on equality, and they were successful on most but not all counts. They lobbied with other groups, according to Manfredi,[37] for a charter with very general language and hence interpretive flexibility.[38] Due to the efforts of these groups, the term "non-discrimination rights" (which connotes negative ones) was changed to "equality rights" (which connotes positive ones). Moreover, these groups convinced the government to include "sex" in the affirmative action clause of section 15(2). They did not, however, convince it to include "marital status," "sexual orientation, " or "political belief" in that clause; eliminate the "reasonable limits" clause;[39] or insist on an equal number of women and men on all courts. Even so, women had won a major constitutional victory.

Of interest here are two sections of the Charter, which became law in 1982. Sections 15 and 28 must be seen as operating together. According to the first part of section 15, "[e]very individual is equal before and under the law and has the right to the equal protection and equal benefit of the law without discrimination and, in particular, without discrimination based on race, national or ethnic origin, colour, religion, sex, age or mental or physical disability." According to the second part, that "does not preclude any law, program or activity that has as its object the amelioration of conditions of disadvantaged individuals or groups including those that are disadvantaged because of race, national or ethnic origin, colour, religion, sex, age or mental or physical disability." Now consider section 28: "Notwithstanding anything in this Charter, the rights and freedoms referred to in it are guaranteed equally to male and female persons."[40]

In Charter cases, the courts must decide whether your claim of discrimination is "'reasonable,' given the important factors in the social environment affecting your case."[41] The key words, for us, are "reasonable" and "social environment." To interpret the Charter, authorities use the Oakes test, which defines "reasonable" in connection with section 1 of the Charter, which "guarantees the rights and freedoms set out in it subject only to such reasonable limits prescribed by law as can be demonstrably justified in a free and democratic society."[42] The limits are

- that the government had an important social goal or good in mind when it made the problematic policy or law (a "pressing and substantial object");
- that the violation of your rights actually advances this goal (the "rational connection" between the action which limits your right to equality and the furthering of this important goal);
- that your rights were not affected more than is reasonable or necessary (the "minimal impairment" of your right to equality);
- that there is a balance between the good done by the law and the bad effect on your rights (the balance between "salutary" (positive) and "deleterious" (negative) effects of the law).[43]

The Canadian government actually helps some of those who want to challenge its own laws. Under the Court Challenges Program, it provides funding for cases intended to challenge laws that might be considered discriminatory according to the Charter.[44] "The Court Challenges Program is committed to realizing the equality rights of Canada's historically disadvantaged groups and the language rights of Canada's official language minorities."[45] The term "historically disadvantaged groups" is extremely important in this context as a de facto amendment to the Charter. It has been used to qualify some groups for special protection – women but also "visible minorities" (whom we discuss in appendix 7) – and disqualify others regardless of individual need or even of collective need in the present.

In 1989, *Law Society of British Columbia v. Andrews* became one of the most important cases on equality.[46] Ostensibly about whether noncitizens may practise law in Canada, it was really about the definition of equality. Justice William McIntyre "defined discrimination as a distinction, whether intentional or not but based on grounds relating to personal characteristics of the individual or group, which has the effect of imposing burdens, obligations, or disadvantages on such an individual or group not imposed upon others, or which withholds or limits access to opportunities, benefits, and advantages available to other members of society."[47] He said also that some group characteristics might be added to those listed in section 15 of the Charter. If so, anyone having those characteristics would be classified as part of a "distinct and insular minority" that deserves protection such as affirmative action. This position was reaffirmed several months later, according to Manfredi, when Justice Bertha Wilson defined minorities as groups subject to "stereotyping, historical disadvantage or vulnerability to political and social prejudice."[48]

That definition led in 1989 to the unanimous decision of *Brooks v. Canada Safeway*, which overturned *Bliss*. The Court argued that the "capacity to become pregnant is unique to the female gender."[49] It is discriminatory, therefore, not to provide pregnant women with benefits. *Bliss* had argued that the law was not responsible for biological differences. *Brooks* admitted the need to eliminate systemic discrimination caused by biological differences, which is precisely what Americans had done by interpreting amendments on equal protection in ways that allowed them to modify equality of opportunity so that they can accommodate the special needs of women.

In its 1985 "reference document" on the United Nations Convention on the Elimination of All Forms of Discrimination against Women, which Canada had signed, the government agreed that "discrimination" means "differentiations based not directly on sex, but rather on traits correlated with it, such as height or pregnancy or being a part-time worker (or, to put the issue in another way, whether discrimination in *both effect and intent* is prohibited)."[50] This definition includes systemic discrimination: "indirect, impersonal and unintended discrimination that is a result of inappropriate standards which have been built into employment systems over the years."[51]

Because discrimination against women is pervasive and affects every aspect of women's lives, feminists claimed, society must use every means at its disposal to correct the problem. And because the effects of discrimination can be expressed quantitatively – with statistics on employment, benefits, crime, and so forth – it is easy to document the negative effects of discrimination and eliminate them. To do that is to institutionalize equality of result. Canadians have been more successful than Americans in introducing the term "substantive equality" into government documents and thus institutionalizing it. According to the Court Challenges Program, for instance, funding is given for "cases that advance substantive equality as opposed to formal equality. A formal equality approach considers that equality is achieved when individuals or groups are treated the same, even if the impact of a certain policy is not equal. A substantive equality approach, however, requires that a law be examined to determine whether it has a differential impact on individuals or groups."[52] Never mind, once again, that equality of opportunity can be modified to accommodate particular circumstances.

Canadian officials have been less ambivalent than American officials about affirmative action. With the demand in Canada for equality of result came the demand for affirmative action. Among the first steps to be taken was the Federal Contractor's Program, which was initiated in 1986. This program applies to local organizations that employ one hundred or more people and receive $200,000 or more annually in federal goods or services. These organizations must hire preferentially from four groups that have historically been the victims of discrimination: women, visible minorities, aboriginal people, and people with disabilities. And they are required to meet "targets" on schedule.

Justice Canada (also known as the Department of Justice) has been a major player in the debate over equality. In the 1980s it began to argue for the need to correct systemic discrimination, eliminate discrimination based on sexual orientation, and establish affirmative action and pay equity.[53] Its Human Rights Section produced a paper on systemic discrimination and began to pay for briefs by various "equality seeking" groups. These groups claimed that courts are authorized under section 15 of the Charter to order the implementation of affirmative action programs.[54] (These programs are constitutionally based in Canada, unlike the United States, because of the Charter.) In 1991, Justice Canada organized a National Symposium on Women, Law and the Administration of Justice, which led to the publication of a three-volume work.[55] Leading feminist academics and organizations were invited to participate. The results included many recommendations on how to change laws, the legal process, and work in the legal profession. They amounted to a blueprint for social revolution. Among the changes demanded were the following: establishing "zero tolerance" for discriminatory behaviour; ending systemic discrimination and reviewing all government laws and policies with that in mind; including "sexual discrimination" among the grounds for discrimination; and declaring that "heterosexual privileges must be amended (tax law, family law, and so on) including ... the definition of 'spouse' and 'family' to include common law and same-sex partners and family units."[56] In response came the "Action Plan of the Department of Justice on Gender Equality," which required more bureaucratic appointments for women, more "feminist" judges and justices on the Supreme Court, enforceable pay-equity legislation, and so on (although it did not demand that women should hold 50% of all jobs or refer explicitly to "substantive equality"), as recommended by the United Nations.

In 1993, the Canadian Bar Association produced a report called *Touchstones for Change*, which explicitly rejected formal equality, even in modified form, and explicitly endorsed substantive equality.[57] The former "fails to address the reality of existing inequality and results therefore in the perpetuation of these inequalities."[58] The latter's aim, by contrast, is "the redress of existing inequality and the institution of real equality in the social, political and economic conditions of different groups in society."[59] In fact, this report confidently predicts a radical transformation of the legal profession in precisely these terms.

In 1995 pay equity was given legal status under Canada's Employment Equity Act. "The purpose of this Act is to achieve equality in the workplace so that no person shall be denied employment opportunities or benefits for reasons unrelated to ability and, in the fulfilment of that goal, to correct the conditions of disadvantage in employment experienced by women, aboriginal peoples, persons with disabilities and members of visible minorities by giving effect to the principle that employment equity means more than treating persons in the same way but also requires special measures and the accommodation of differences."[60]

Before the third World Conference on Women, held by the United Nations at Beijing in 1995 (which we discuss in appendix 6), Status of Women Canada formed two committees: the Canadian Beijing Facilitating Committee and the Canadian Preparatory Committee. Together, they prepared a national report. After Beijing, the Canadian government – more specifically, Status of Women Canada – produced *Setting the Stage for the Next Century: The Federal Plan for Gender Equality.*[61] This document revealed plans to implement Beijing's Platform for Action within five years.[62]

In 2001, Status of Women Canada made available a document called "Canadian Experience in Gender Mainstreaming."[63] Judicial decisions and policy debates under sections 15 and 28 of the Charter, it says, have led to the recognition that identical treatment of women and men does not produce equal outcomes. Therefore, it continues, we need to demand them. Arguments for equality of result "have been made in relation to employment opportunities and pay, spousal support, sexual assault, sexual harassment, sexual orientation, pregnancy, pensions and violence against women." (Status of Women Canada is a government office, remember, but it acts also as a lobby group for women. Note the link between "equal outcomes" and "substantive equality.") In addition, a new argument follows: "Gender-based analysis can prevent costly legal challenges under the Charter and at the same time promote sound and effective public policies."[64] In other words, forget litigation. Bureaucracy itself can take care of everything. Just leave it to us!

The following statement of commitment leaves no doubt that gender-based analysis is really woman-based, or gynocentric, analysis: "The federal government is committed through the Federal Plan [*Setting the Stage for the Next Century*, which we have already mentioned] ... to ensuring that all future legislation and policies include, where appropriate, an analysis of the potential for different impacts on women and men. Individual departments will be responsible for determining which legislation or policies have the potential to affect women differentially and are, therefore, appropriate for a consistent application of a gender lens."[65] The word "men" appears, to be sure, but – as the very next line indicates – only as a token gesture.

Interpretations of the Charter have institutionalized equality of result as a goal. This clearly distinguishes Canadian law from American. (Passage of the Equal Rights Amendment, the struggle for which is far from dead, would open up very similar possibilities in the United States. This is why feminists still want it). But all legislation that results from feminist agitation for equality of result, whether in the United States or Canada, is based on the assumption that women constitute a victim class. (Some feminists believe that women constitute the original and even the ultimate victim class.) Ergo, women both need and deserve special protection. And by "special" we refer to protection that infringes on the rights of other citizens. Like every other segment of society, women are indeed victims in some ways. But not because they have no power today as a "class." On the contrary, few segments of society have more political clout than women. In fact, women have become one of Canada's unofficial victim classes. And men, by implication, have become Canada's official oppressor class. Male citizens may be denied equality under the law, in other words, by virtue of the nefarious activities of their ancestors – which is to say, by virtue of the biological characteristics that they share with male ancestors.[66]

It is true that feminists have not had it all their own way. Wary of increased government expense, the courts have sometimes used section 15 of the Charter to eliminate specific benefits, to level downward rather than upward.[67] Feminists have not yet made dramatic gains in the purely political realm, although, during the Meech Lake talks on constitutional reform, they almost succeeded in creating a Senate with equal numbers of men and women. Nonetheless, the courts have generally complied with feminist demands. From framing the Charter to litigating successfully, with important gains even in unsuccessful cases, feminists have taken the offensive.[68] They have made tremendous gains in both the legal and economic realms.

"In effect," says Manfredi, "a key institution of the state – the Supreme Court of Canada – has given positional support to the collective aims of a significant social movement. The advantage of using this technique compared to other tactics – such as lobbying, advertising, and electoral support – is that the policies associated with these legal victories have acquired a preferred status by virtue of their association with important constitutional

principles. Once achieved, policy victories based on constitutional litigation ... endure remarkably well."[69]

Not surprisingly, Canada appointed several strong feminists to the
Supreme Court. Bertha Wilson, the first woman appointed, explicitly called
for radicalism: "I would like to ask you where would we be without the
strident voice of the extremists who have the pristine courage to call ugly
things by their proper names ... Just look at history – it is the vigour and
energy of the extremist who paints issues in bold colours that has been the
engine of historical change, whose voice has been a clarion call to action
and who will brook no delay."[70]

No wonder American feminists see Canada as a success story. Consider
timing. The Charter was written and debated when the feminist lobby was
already well established and ready to take up legal and political challenges.
Canada was already a welfare state, more like European countries in this
respect than the United States. And that suited many Canadians, who had
long sought an identity to distinguish themselves from Americans. (In fact,
it could be argued, Canadian identity consists primarily of whatever makes
them unlike Americans.) By 1986, Catharine MacKinnon (who is discussed
in chapters 7, 8, and 9) could comment that under

the Charter, Canadians have a unique opportunity to advance sex equality. You
have a chance to make it real in Canada. I contrast this with the existing situation
in the United States, where there is not even one equal rights amendment. Canada
has two, section 15, the more abstractly framed provision, and section 28, the more
substantively framed provision. Each has many separate sub-clauses conferring
guarantees in various metaphorical relations to the law: beneath it, before it, and
so on ... If you interpret the term "equality" as it has typically been interpreted –
including by American courts and mainstream commentators in the Anglo-
American jurisprudential tradition – you will maintain the inequality of the sexes.
Women, in particular, will remain the perpetual economic, social, and political
underclass that women now are. Our inferiority, our powerlessness, our relative
negligibility, will be maintained as it has been, both by acts of positive government
and by acts which are so socially systematic that they have seldom needed positive
law to guarantee them, for example, spousal rape and the pornography industry.[71]

MacKinnon urged Canadian feminists to reject equality of opportunity
because, judging from the American experience, it gave white men the few
advantages that women already had. Custody law had been dramatically
changed for the worse, in her opinion, because fathers had now been given
equal opportunities in court (a claim that we discuss in chapter 6). Moreover, husbands could now be awarded alimony. In fact, men now had
access to women's schools and jobs. She lamented the prevalent belief that
the best way to improve things for women was to do so for men as well –

even though she admitted that this approach has given women "nominal access" to traditional domains of men, including blue-collar jobs and military jobs, along with more than nominal access to athletic activities. Mac-Kinnon believed that this approach – men and women are fundamentally alike – could never work, because it fails to account for the fact that men and women are fundamentally different. Moreover, it does not take into account

the most systematic social disadvantages, the sex-differential abuses of women. In these abuses are included not only segregation into less valued jobs, but also the range of issues of violence against women which have been systematically tolerated by virtually every government in the world, despite cultural differences or formal equality guarantees. These include the massive amount of rape and attempted rape about which virtually nothing is done; the sexual assault of children apparently endemic to the patriarchal family; the battery of women which is systematic in our homes; prostitution, women's fundamental economic option; and pornography, which makes inequality sexy to the tune of $8 billion a year in the United States alone ... The fundamental issue of equality is not whether one is the same or different. It is not the gender difference, it is the difference gender makes ... To be on the bottom of a hierarchy is certainly different from being on the top of one, but it is not simply difference that most distinguishes them. It is, in fact, the lesser access to resources, privileges, credibility, legitimacy, authority, pay, bodily integrity, security, and protection that is effective for you: less of all of what is valued in society ... It is an issue of systematic male supremacy and how it shall be ended. Confronting this problem leads to a much more substantive approach to the notion of equality. It leads to the principle that to be equal is to be non-subordinate: not to be subordinated.[72]

Given her long involvement with the Canadian women's Legal Education and Action Fund (LEAF),[73] it should come as no surprise that MacKinnon's interest in Canadian law is revealed in several books and articles.[74]

Another American, Carol Gilligan, has entered the annals of Canadian legal history. The proceedings of a conference organized by the Canadian Bar Association in 1992 included a paper by Kim Campbell, who was minister of justice and attorney general (but would later, briefly, become Canada's first female prime minister). Campbell drew directly on the work of Gilligan, especially *In a Different Voice*.[75] In that book, says Campbell, the feminist icon "got us thinking in a new way about the differences between men and women. The response of two eleven-year-olds to a moral dilemma suggests that boys have an 'ideal of perfection' and that girls have an 'ideal of care' ... Although we have to be careful about importing analysis from the United States and making blanket assumptions, I believe that in Canada, today, men and women do live different realities which give each sex a unique perspective. Women can and do bring something different to the practice of law, to judging, to the political process."[76]

Campbell elaborated by quoting Annette Baier, who had said that if Gilligan "is right about the special moral aptitudes of women, it will most likely be the women who ... are the ones with more natural empathy, with the better diplomatic skills, the ones more likely to shoulder responsibility and take moral initiative, and the ones who find its [sic] easiest to empathize and care about how the other party feels."[77] She believes that women are morally superior to men, in other words, not merely different from men. After observing that men were becoming more open to "women's ideas, voices and realities," Campbell concluded by noting that many men were taking responsibility for their violence by wearing white ribbons on 6 December, when, as we saw in chapter 4, Canadians remember the fourteen women shot by Marc Lépine.

According to an influential report by four psychologists – Faye Crosby, Aarti Iyer, Susan Clayton, and Roberta Downing – affirmative action can be justified on several grounds.[78] For one thing, they argue, numerous surveys show that it is popular; students approve of it – or, if not of affirmative action itself, then at least of its goal (which, however, is not exactly the same thing). This is not a moral argument, of course, because anything can be popular but still not be morally justifiable. The authors argue primarily not on moral grounds but on grounds of pragmatism or expediency. Affirmative action works, they say; other mechanisms, such as high school or even undergraduate grades and aptitude tests, do not.

Specifically, we contend that all measures of merit include an element of subjectivity and that they are, therefore, influenced by both historical and current prejudice. We also see that psychological factors such as stereotype threat influence how members of target groups perform, causing some tests to underestimate their actual merit. On the basis of numerous social psychological studies, we claim that members of the target groups cannot be relied on to come forward themselves and that other, fair-minded people are usually unable to detect unfairness in the absence of aggregate data. The implication is that affirmative action, with its reliance on the analysis of systematic aggregate data, is needed if fairness is to be achieved by rewarding and utilizing merit, regardless of gender or ethnicity.[79]

This pragmatism is actually a slightly veiled form of postmodernism, the philosophy that is routinely exploited by feminist and other ideologues. The key word here is "subjectivity." Because no test is perfectly objective, ideologues say, we should embrace subjectivism – this is a characteristic and even fundamental requirement of postmodernism – by deliberately, albeit somewhat indirectly, selecting students according to sex and race or ethnicity. Crosby and her colleagues use verbal magic to state their point. They declare that fairness involves "rewarding and utilizing merit, regardless of gender or ethnicity." This goal is attainable, they add, only after affirmative action has done its work by eliminating prejudice. But because postmodernism denies that the requirement for eliminating prejudice – objectivity – can ever exist, it follows that affirmative action can never complete its work. No matter what they say in public, therefore, ideologues consider affirmative action a permanent necessity and not merely a temporary expedient.

Elsewhere, Crosby and her colleagues move in precisely the opposite direction. They find it expedient to argue for "the importance of using objective methods for identifying discrimination rather than relying on the good intentions of individuals for rectifying such problems. The studies also show the specific importance of implementing practices that require organizations to collect and examine systematic, aggregate data for comparative purposes. Systematic comparisons based on aggregated data are at the core of affirmative action."[80] People can be objective when selecting and analyzing data for affirmative action, apparently, but not when grading or testing.

However, the very idea of aggregate data (in this case, the total percentage of men compared to that of women) highlights a serious problem that is often mentioned in connection with admitting students and also with hiring members of the faculty. The truth is that female undergraduate students, and even female graduate students in some fields, outnumber their male counterparts at many universities. So why not establish affirmative action for male students in specific fields? Because, say advocates of affirmative action, men still dominate the university as a whole – that is, when you consider the "aggregate" of all those who make up a university, including members of the faculty who began teaching long before women began entering their fields. Aggregate data can be used to show that male students are advantaged, although the reverse can be used in the context of hiring. Is using the former really a measure of objectivity? Remember that affirmative action has been used to correct for fewer women than men in some fields but not for fewer men than women in fields such as social work, education, or nursing.

Crosby and her colleagues are inconsistent. They say that most law schools give more weight to LSAT scores (60%) than to undergraduate grades (40%). This is a problem for women, they add, because the LSAT scores of female students are lower than those of their male counterparts, even though their undergraduate grades are higher. But they argue elsewhere that both grades and tests are inherently subjective. On what basis can they say, therefore, that female undergrads are actually better students than male undergrads and are thus more deserving of entry to law school? Besides, would Crosby and her colleagues have even noticed a problem in the reverse situation – that is, if male students were getting higher grades but lower LSAT scores? Not likely.

Everyone knows that affirmative action "works" in the sense of promoting the interests of target groups. How could it be otherwise, when the state uses law deliberately to favour them? It does not necessarily work, however, in the sense of fostering good education. Success comes with a cost. Crosby and her colleagues actually admit that in a study of eighty thousand students at twenty-eight prestigious universities, "the special admits graduated from college, attended and graduated from professional and graduate schools, and held professional jobs at the same rate as did the other students. The special admits did, however, differ from the other students in two salient ways. First, they had lower grade-point averages than did the comparison groups both during their undergraduate education and during their professional or graduate training. Second, decades after graduation, those who were special admits were more likely than their White counterparts to be active civic leaders."[81] But who knows what "civic" means? It could mean political activism for more affirmative action.

The stated goal of affirmative action is always a "diverse" student population. Why? Because that produces a wider variety, advocates say, of opinions and perspectives. And that, in turn, makes students more adept at "problem solving" or coping with the real world after leaving university. What sounds good in theory, though, does not always work so well in practice. This defense of affirmative action in the name of diversity is problematic for several reasons (apart from the fact that it relies on the notion that ends can justify means).

In the first place, we do not know that sexual or ethnic diversity actually adds up to *intellectual* diversity. And that, presumably, is more to the point in a university than the genetic pool of its students. Sexual or ethnic diversity might lead to tolerance. On the other hand, it might lead to stronger support for sexual or ethnic ideologies. If so, the end result would be greater polarization and therefore greater intolerance than ever before. Indeed, ideological intolerance is already rampant in the university and has been during the entire period of affirmative action. In this conformist and censorious atmosphere, not many university teachers actually encourage independent thought that is based on critical analysis of fashionable political ideologies. On the contrary, many encourage students to stamp out whatever can be classified as politically incorrect (see appendices 4 and 7). Some students might report teachers who create a "hostile environment," for instance, even if only by questioning a feminist doctrine. Other students might launch or participate in hate-mail campaigns against teachers who write books or articles that challenge gay ideology. This might well prepare students for an increasingly *polarized* society beyond the university, true, but only by exacerbating the problem.

In both the United States and Canada, universities and other institutions are eligible for government-funded research grants only if they adopt affirmative action programs. This approach is based on two assumptions. First, men and women are equally intelligent. In other words, men are inherently no more capable than women and should not outnumber women on the faculty. Okay, we can live with that. Second, the unequal numbers of men and women can be explained only by discrimination. This assumption is debatable, to say the least. Hostility toward women might explain the rejection of female applicants in a few cases today, but that is by no means the only possible explanation, because equal numbers of men and women might not apply in the first place.[82] Not all graduates actually want to teach in universities, after all. This is particularly true of those with professional training in fields such as medicine, dentistry, nursing, social work, law, architecture, education, occupational health, physical and occupational therapy, psychology, library science, engineering, management, and ordained ministry. Although some of these fields are indeed still dominated by men, others have long been dominated by women. And some of the newer ones are now identified by both women and men as ideological rather than academic. Besides, many women decide to interrupt their academic careers and, for a few years after graduation, stay home with their children. Even if the relative paucity of women on the faculty of any given department really could be traced directly to sexual discrimination, however, the most obvious solution would surely be to discourage sexual discrimination and not to promote it by substituting one kind of discrimination for another. According to Grant Brown,

Preferential employment practices meet none of the normal conditions for compensatory justice: that the very person who perpetrated a civil wrong must compensate the very person who was harmed, and that the compensation must be commensurate with the harm suffered. Treating individuals merely as members of groups, and transferring employment benefits and harms between them willy-nilly on that basis, cannot be deemed "compensatory justice" or "rectification" for past wrongs, without doing violence to the concepts of compensation and rectification. Indeed, it is the very essence of bigotry to wish to bring harms upon a person simply because he belongs to the same group as someone who (let's suppose) has harmed a member of a group to which you belong.[83]

It could be argued that opposing affirmative action is tantamount to supporting those who, no matter what they say in public, are motivated by bigotry. But Jews who oppose affirmative action know better, because they have experienced its dark side. Stephen Stern points out that Jews have "never proposed or favoured legislation forcing employers to preferentially hire them in order to make amends for over two thousand years of past suffering. Indeed, they have fought tirelessly for the removal of all quotas and all references to one's skin colour or ethnic heritage in matters pertaining to hiring, firing, or promotion. They have, to their eternal credit, simply demanded that merit be the only criterion."[84]

Actually, "never" is not the best word. Jews did not seek affirmative action in earlier times, it is true, because no state offered to the Jewish community or any other minority community the possibility of improving its condition. More recently, some Jews have ignored their own history by supporting affirmative action for minority groups or women. But Stern's point is worth taking seriously. Jews, represented disproportionately among liberals in most public debates, tend to be more skeptical about affirmative action than many other communities. In living memory, after all, it was used against them. Our own university, McGill, maintained a quota to limit the number of Jews until the early 1960s.[85]

But suppose that the unbalanced sex ratio really was a result of discrimination and required correction. The underlying assumption is that the end (encouraging departments to hire more women) could justify the means (discouraging them from hiring men). As we have mentioned, this principle is an essential premise of all ideologies, whether on the political left or the political right. In every case, adherents believe that their own particular end is worthy enough to justify what would otherwise have to be considered immoral conduct. Not surprisingly, many of the worst catastrophes in history have been done in the name of some greater good.[86]

In a famous article for the *Atlantic Monthly*, Stanley Fish threw down the academic gauntlet to those miscreants who persisted in opposing affirmative action.[87] He implied that oppressed communities have some moral right to oppress other communities, although he did not phrase it so blatantly. For him, official discrimination against white Americans is justifiable because of official discrimination against black Americans in the past. Never mind that no one alive today either experienced centuries of slavery or inflicted it. Moreover, as John Field pointed out in his letter to the editor, Fish ignored the historical fact that most communities engaged in the persecution of other communities have always tried to justify themselves by pointing back to their own persecution. That creates two moral problems.

First, the target population might or might not have been involved in the original persecution. From Fish's point of view, Jewish (Israeli) injustice toward Palestinians could be justified on the grounds not of Palestinian injustice toward Jews (Israelis) but on those of Nazi injustice toward Jews. Second, the original persecution might or might not have been real at all. Hitler and at least some other Nazi leaders sincerely believed that Jews had been persecuting Germans through economic exploitation, capitalist (or communist) manipulation, or whatever. Albeit unwittingly, Fish justified the Nazi persecution of Jews.

It all amounted, said Field, to a rejection of the golden rule and all our efforts, no matter how inadequate, to create a more egalitarian society. "The idea was to be color-blind. It is a great ... ethical principle ... and it should not be so lightly cast aside. We may be terribly flawed, but we are at least trying to figure out how not to be in spite of advice like Fish's."[88] The idea of colour-blind justice is not without problems, however, which we will discuss in a moment.

But from Fish's point of view, and that of many others who support affirmative action, what appears to be discrimination is not really discrimination at all, because discrimination is motivated by malevolence but affirmative action is motivated by benevolence. For this reason, Fish dislikes the term "reverse discrimination," which "fails to distinguish between inequities whose production is intentional and inequities that follow in the wake of a policy not designed to generate them."[89] Actually, the term "reverse discrimination" really is inappropriate but not for that reason. Discrimination is discrimination, no matter what the motivation, and it should not be disguised by suggesting that it is somehow a second-order phenomenon, a reversal of the real thing.

No wonder, as Steven Yates points out, public discourse has been contaminated by Orwellian euphemisms: "equal opportunity" now refers to preferential treatment, for instance, and "racism" to a statistical imbalance.[90] It is true that motivation must be considered in any moral debate. Because people are moral agents only to the degree that they can actually make moral choices, the motives for those choices must always be considered in assigning guilt or innocence. But motivation is notoriously hard to establish, partly because people are not necessarily open about it, partly because they are not necessarily aware of it, and partly because it is not necessarily unambiguous in the first place. Fish tried to finesse his way out of this attack, in any case, by responding that "oppression is not the agenda here; affirmative action is not a revenge strategy even if it is experienced as such by those who are caught up in the backwater of its effects."[91] In other words, a legitimate interest of some unfortunate citizens – in this case, their ability to earn a living – is expendable.

Motivation notwithstanding, the result is not only "justice" for some but also injustice for others. There is no moral basis for this trade-off unless you argue that affirmative action is a necessary evil. To make that point, you must use the analogy of a just war in which killing the enemy is a necessary evil. But no one could seriously argue that affirmative action is a spontaneous reaction to the threat of being attacked or killed by ruthless enemies, a reaction unmediated by the subtle moral considerations required in everyday life. On the contrary, advocates of affirmative action claim that it is founded precisely on subtle moral considerations. No matter. There is for many an ideological basis to affirmative action. Men (or at least white men), they believe, make up an oppressor class and therefore deserve to be punished.

But this presents another extremely disturbing moral problem: eliminating the individual as a significant factor in moral debate. People are no longer individual moral agents. They are nothing more than representatives of some collectivity – a class, say, or a race. This focus on the collectivity would be perfectly consistent with totalitarianism, but it is an utter contradiction of the moral framework of liberal democracy in the modern Western world. For affirmative action to be effective, the individual rights of men must be sacrificed in favour of the collective rights of women. This particular problem can hardly be dismissed as a remote or irrelevant abstraction by Canadians, in particular, since it lies at the very heart of the enduring conflict between Quebec (which favours collective rights in order to support the notion of its own sovereignty as a "nation") and the rest of Canada (which presumably favours individual rights, including those of anglophone Quebecers, but which actually favours collective rights when doing so seems politically correct).

Besides, the notion of collective rights is only one side of this coin. Flip it over, and you find the notion of collective guilt, which has had a long and depressing history of its own. One of the more notorious examples has been the belief among some Christians that their Jewish contemporaries, no less than those of the first century, were ontologically defiled by guilt as the "deicide people." More recently, this idea has been used to legitimate a variety of profoundly dualistic worldviews in which the source of evil is projected onto some easily identifiable group of "others," whether defined by their class, race, language, or sex. If the problem is solely due to "them," of course, then "they" are rightly punished en masse as scapegoats for all of "our" suffering. Even innocent individuals are thus considered guilty for being members of a class or race. Lee Dembart asked the obvious question: If Fish insists that white male aademics are living off ill-gotten gains, why does Fish himself not resign?[92] Fish responded by claiming that Dembart took the idea too far, that race or sex should be merely "one ingredient" in hiring decisions, "not as a special favor but as a recognition of the positive contribution such groups might make to an ongoing enterprise that has not one but many goals."[93] Sure it does. And none of these goals, presumably, gives political goals priority over academic ones.

Affirmative action for women is intended to end discrimination against women. To that end, it institutionalizes, at least for the time being, discrimination against men. One underlying assumption is that discrimination itself should not be identified as the problem. For the sake of social justice, some would argue, governments routinely discriminate in favour of some groups and against others. Using this analogy, it would seem that opposing a policy of discrimination at a university would be tantamount to opposing any government intervention and, by implication, any attempt to attain social justice.

Consider one of the most obvious examples of government discrimination: taxation as the redistribution of income, which is also the foundation for every service provided by the state. In one way, to be sure, the analogy holds. Taxation can be used against one class (the rich) in favour of another class (the poor). But the analogy is too seriously flawed to be morally useful. Citizens are taxed on the basis of their incomes as individuals, after all, not their membership in a biological category. Theoretically, every individual who is required to pay really can afford to pay, and every individual who is supported really does need to be supported. The goal of taxation is to distribute wealth more fairly among classes, but it operates at the level of individual responsibility and need. This is not the case with affirmative action. If a man and a woman were to apply for the same job under those conditions, it could not be argued that the woman needs it more than the man. The man would be rejected in favour of the woman simply because of the biological fact that he is a man, not because of anything to do with him as an individual. The discrimination involved in taxation is calibrated according to individual circumstances, in short, but the discrimination advocated for universities and other institutions involves targeting people according to innate characteristics.

Even those who find affirmative action disturbing on moral grounds often argue that it is the lesser of two evils: either continuing the current "policy" of covert discrimination against women, in this case, or adopting a new policy of overt discrimination against men. But this principle is legitimate only when the two evils are very different. Waging war against Hitler involved incalculable suffering for the soldiers and civilians on both sides, but the alternative was to cooperate with a form of evil that would have destroyed everything worth living for in the first place. It would be very hard, on the other hand, to differentiate on moral grounds between the evil of discriminating against men and that of discriminating against women. Both are evil for precisely the same reason and in precisely the same way. If it is wrong to discriminate against women, then it is wrong to discriminate against men. In fact, it is inherently wrong to discriminate against any group of human beings.[94]

Some argue that the *ultimate* goal of affirmative action is to hire people on the basis of personal ability, not sex. Because the proper sex ratio had not yet been achieved, its immediate goal – to be achieved by "interim policies" – is to correct the imbalance. Equality, in other words, is to be achieved through inequality. Morally, though not pragmatically, that is a contradiction in terms. We say that it is impossible to honour the principle of equality in one situation by mocking it in another.

Returning now to the case of affirmative action in the university, it might be argued that the primary academic objective is to recruit and hire "excellent women scholars." That objective is clearly a political priority, however, not an academic one. Using the term "excellent women" cleverly disguises the fact that this proposal has nothing to do with academic priorities (promoting excellence) and everything to do with political ones (promoting women). Why elide these two principles? To answer this question, we must examine an underlying belief about the university, the academic institution par excellence: that it is a microcosm of the larger society. Because this belief is now so commonly held that it passes for conventional wisdom in some circles, many people imagine that they no longer need to support or even state it. It has become an assumption.

But the university is not and never can be a microcosm of the larger society.[95] It represents one particular segment of society with one particular task: the search for truth. (In the age of deconstruction, it must be reasserted that truth, no matter how elusive under the finite conditions of human existence, no matter how ambiguous and incomplete it remains in our perception, must remain the goal.) From this it follows that the distribution of various social groups in the larger society need not be mirrored perfectly in the university (just as they need not be on, say, a basketball team). From the same premise, moreover, it follows that the university need not be and indeed should not be directly involved in social engineering – if it were, it might easily be reduced to nothing more than a government agency or an ideological factory, acting on the basis of whatever is considered politically expedient. Tax dollars are used to support universities, true, which is why politicians argue that the student body should represent the taxpayers demographically. But tax dollars are used to pay for highways, too, even though not all taxpayers own cars. Ditto for primary and secondary schools, even though not all taxpayers have children. Inherent in the democratic system, no matter how cynical it can be, is a residue of altruism. Some things, including universities, are so valuable to society as a whole – unless they are undermined by ideology masquerading as scholarship – that everyone should participate in paying for them.

At this point, we must acknowledge a belief of our own. We believe (although we cannot prove) that truth leads to justice. We believe that there is no such thing as justice, in fact, unless it is based on truth. Consequently, seeking truth is an indirect way of seeking justice. Those who seek justice make use of scholarship as graduates or as participants in the larger world. The university itself, however, must not be turned into a tool by or for those who think that they know best how to reorganize society.

Even those who accept the primacy of political considerations over academic ones – in this case, the principle of proportional representation in the university as a microcosm of society – are surely both logically and morally obliged to apply them consistently and thoroughly. After all, the composition of society can be classified according to many criteria, not only according to sex or race. Using the same arguments, it would be reasonable for every group that considers itself distinct on grounds of ethnicity, religion, political affiliation, geographical region, class, language, disability, or whatever to demand the same preferential treatment as women in order to ensure their proportional representation on university faculties. If the mere fact of belonging to these groups were the ultimate criterion, the one that trumps purely academic criteria, they should be satisfied with nothing less. But would that help the university fulfill its distinctive mandate or justify its specific raison d'être? To answer that question, think of the bureaucratic and political nightmares that would ensue if every job were to become the potential prize sought by dozens of competing groups. Once the principle of proportional representation is accepted, then it must be applied consistently. Otherwise, every identifiable group, no matter what the criterion on which its identity is based, would have cause for charges of immoral or illegal discrimination.

Now, what if femaleness is not entirely unrelated to scholarship? Scholarship thrives in the context of intellectual debate, and intellectual debate can occur only in the context of differing points of view. It is true that the life experiences of women can generate distinctive points of view. Some might argue, therefore, that giving them preference makes sense even in scholarly terms. But advocates of this position often ignore several problems (which we discuss more fully in chapter 10). For example, this idea would not apply to women alone. If the distinctive perspectives of women are sought by means of quotas or targets, why not those of every other group that can claim some distinctive point of view?

Besides, the mere fact of having a distinctive point of view means little or nothing in itself. When hiring teachers and researchers for a university, it is the ability of applicants to subject their own points of view to critical analysis, to use them in scholarly ways, that should be of primary concern. Otherwise, a distinctive point of view would be synonymous with an ideological one. And in some fields – mathematics, say, or electrical engineering – different life experiences should make no difference whatsoever to the outcome of research. Not unless we agree with Hitler, who demanded that "Jewish physics" be replaced by "Aryan physics."

Some say that female students and teachers are at an inherent disadvantage because they find fewer mentors or role models on the faculties of universities than their male counterparts. Even if only for that reason, they say, universities should make the hiring of women a priority. But this idea makes no sense – except, of course, to ideologues who believe that "feminist scholarship" (based on the notion of a "female epistemology," which we discuss in chapter 10) is inherently different from (read: superior to) "masculinist scholarship." There is no reason why scholars must have some biological qualification to serve as mentors. Mentors are scholars, not icons of sex, race, ethnicity, religion, or anything else. At issue is not whether scholars can serve as role models for life itself but only whether they can serve as models for scholarship. It is good for women to see other women succeed in attaining high academic offices, but this alone is not a prerequisite for women to become scholars themselves. Otherwise, how could we explain the existence of female scholars in the past and present? There was a time, not so long ago, when very few Jews were highly placed or even present in the university. (In those days, quotas were used to keep Jews out, not to get them in.) Very few Jewish students allowed that to prevent them from becoming scholars. For specifically Jewish role models, they turned to the Jewish community. For academic ones, they turned to the academic community. It should be noted, moreover, that some men have been successfully "mentored" by women. Our point here is not that the presence of female scholars should make no difference at all to female students but that it should not be a factor in evaluating the actual scholarly potential of female candidates for jobs.

Should the criteria for assessment be the same for male and female applicants? Some people say no. In doing so, they raise the old spectre of a double standard. But, they add, have universities not always used double standards for one reason or another? Why not be honest about it? Because, in our opinion, that line of "reasoning" makes no moral sense. Openly acknowledging a vice does not turn it into a virtue; the latter does not follow from the former. Those who deliberately and overtly institutionalize unfairness are in no way morally superior to those who do the same thing unwittingly or covertly. Otherwise, we would have to admit that legalized apartheid in South Africa was somehow more acceptable than the informal racial segregation in other places. But wait. The new double standard, say advocates of affirmative action, discriminates in favour of the vulnerable instead of the powerful. Should that not make it morally acceptable? No, because the vulnerability of one group is merely foisted onto another. That amounts to nothing more than playing musical chairs.

Ignoring the need even to argue the case for a double standard, some claim that because of family responsibilities, women often take longer to complete their degrees than men. That looks bad on a résumé. But why should length of time be a criterion for hiring someone – female or male – in the first place? Surely it is the degree itself that indicates scholarly ability, not the length of time it takes to complete. (We should be able to assume that those who linger too long without a good reason will not be awarded degrees in the first place.)[96] Of course, those who do take longer to complete their degrees are older than other candidates. But why should anyone – female or male – be rejected on the basis of age? Insisting on scholarship as the sole criterion would solve the problem without creating a new one, without adding a biological criterion that has nothing to do with effective performance on the job.

According to another claim, hiring committees should recognize explicitly that the career paths of female applicants are often different from but as valuable – "equally valuable" – as those of male applicants. But what does "equally valuable" actually mean? Is it a reference to working part-time versus full-time? To taking several years off versus continuing without interruption? To teaching alone versus teaching, publishing, and sitting on committees? How can it be said that all these choices are equally valuable? Equally valuable to whom? To the women in question? To society? To the students? To the university? To the academic world? Making these choices should be possible, yes, but not pretending that one choice is as good as another from any perspective at all. Life always involves choices. No one can have it all, not even men. When men choose to devote their lives to scholarship alone, they choose also, by default rather than by intent, to have minimal contact with their families.

The term "equally valuable career paths," moreover, refers primarily to the establishment of "alternative" criteria for promoting women with no time for research and publishing, partly because women often feel obliged to sit on many committees just to ensure female representation.[97] Although universities do reward academics who make truly outstanding contributions to administration – they are run primarily by academics who choose this career profile – they still maintain the fundamental importance of research and publications, especially for tenure. But if women refuse to be bound by the expectation of research and publishing, why not men? Given a real choice, men might indeed want to spend more time with their families (or their hobbies, or anything else). Unless we want to continue sending the message that fatherhood is irrelevant, we will have to encourage men, and not only women, to consider "equally valuable career paths" and entice men, not only women, with the provision of daycare facilities. On the other hand, many men and women might simply feel better suited to teaching or administration than to research or publishing.

In addition to moral problems affirmative action creates some purely practical ones. Like so many medical cures, after all, this one can bring with it some very unpleasant side efects. Some of these might prove even worse than the original disease – and not only for men but for women as well. Why, for instance, should men not express resentment over discrimination against them? You would have to be very naive, for instance, to imagine that men do not resent affirmative action for women. At a relatively abstract level, it is easy to agree that access to jobs should be no more difficult for women than for men, even if that means the gradual displacement of men as a dominant group in the academic world – as long as the process of displacement reflects scholarly integrity. It is not so easy to agree that they themselves, or their sons and the male students whom they have been preparing, should be sacrificed in the interest of social engineering. That would amount to their displacement as individuals – and by a process that makes a mockery of both scholarly and moral integrity. No one willingly becomes a pawn to be moved around in the interest of others. Even martyrs always *choose* to sacrifice themselves for others, after all, which is why they are considered holy and not crazy. Similarly, no man, unless he has a name such as Trump or Rockefeller, is going tell a woman: Here, take my job, I don't need it. To ignore that simple fact of life is folly for women who are hoping for a genuine improvement in relations between the sexes. They cannot reasonably expect to institutionalize discrimination against men *and* receive respect from those men.

If practical considerations were the only ones that mattered for institutions, there would be no controversy over affirmative action. It is precisely because the easiest and most practical solutions are often questionable on specifically moral grounds that we need to discuss them in the public square. Otherwise, why not embrace some form of totalitarianism? There was some truth in the old saying about Mussolini, that he at least made the trains run on time. If efficiency were the main criterion in matters of this kind, then we would have to declare democracy itself hopelessly inefficient and replace it with some other system.

Fish and other advocates of affirmative action have surely been correct in complaining that many opponents react to it blindly and, in some cases, even maliciously. That "discourages any serious consideration of the injuries affirmative action seeks to redress."[98] The idea of affirmative action arose for a reason; discrimination was a major problem. Moreover, as many advocates of affirmative action have pointed out, the bias that causes discrimination is often subtle and even unintentional. Standardized tests, for example, have been found to favour those with specific cultural backgrounds. The only question is how to remedy that situation.

Why not fight fire with fire, replacing one form of bias or discrimination with another? Those who ask that question might not be cynical themselves, but they rely on arguments that are inherently cynical. Others say that we should fight fire with water, as it were, using insight to replace bias and prevent discrimination. They might be naive, to the extent that they believe in a system based on equality, or at least the quest for equality, but they rely on arguments that are inherently moral.

For some people, justice means that resources must be shared in amounts proportional to the size of each segment of the population. That premise underlies equality of result, once again, and of proportional representation. For others, even a right to freedom from discrimination should be limited if another group's constitutional right to the same thing is ignored when collective goals conflict with individual ones. Governments may use corrective measures such as affirmative action, they argue, but only if some attempt is made to balance competing interests, only if these corrective measures are limited in scope and duration.

But we suggest that affirmative action creates a moral problem even when limitations really are in place. Why? Because the same problem can be solved in other ways, assuming that safeguards are in place to ensure selection on the basis of merit. Proper education from an early stage to make everyone competitive on the basis of merit would surely be preferable on a moral level to the introduction of a double standard and, on a practical level, to the devaluation of beneficiaries as second raters. The same would be true of remedial education and training programs.[99]

Once group identity is linked with special treatment, how can the latter be ended without attacking the former, even after the original problem has been solved? Once claims are defined in nebulous and unverifiable ways, how can any outsider tell when the original problem no longer exists? And once groups are allowed to operate without checks and balances, how can the principle of "justice for all" be maintained? Advocates of affirmative action seldom even acknowledge these problems. (We discuss them in appendix 7.)

Closely related to affirmative action is pay equity. This, too, involves many moral problems. No discussion of pay equity should avoid its verbal context. Some feminists like to replace the word "equality" with the word "equity." They associate "equality" with an abstract or even mathematical way of thinking, that way of thinking with historical notions of "blind" justice, and those notions, in turn, with maleness. These same people associate "equity," on the other hand, with a more personal and allegedly more humane way of thinking (never mind its common use in the world of finance, which is not notably humane), that way of thinking with fairness or caring, and that caring, in turn – thanks partly to Gilligan – with femaleness. Besides, this rhetoric renders slightly less harsh or obvious the inherent contradiction that underlies affirmative action: creating inequality in the name of equality. But the two are by no means synonymous. The notion of equality supports "equal pay for equal work," but the notion of equity supports "equal pay for work of equal value."

Various criteria are used to establish work of equal value. Every scheme classifies jobs into various tasks – categories and subcategories – and assigns each a numerical value. These are added up to indicate appropriate salaries.

Pay equity requires the use of gender neutral job evaluation methods. Gender neutral job evaluation is intended to assess the relative value of all jobs within a workplace based on a common set of factors. In general, the most common evaluation factors used include skill, effort, responsibility and working conditions. The reported aggregate gender wage gap is a statistical indicator of women's wages relative to men's wages. It is usually calculated by dividing the average annual earnings of women by the average annual earnings of men. The gender wage gap varies depending on labour market experience, unionization, occupation, industry, educational attainment, and age, among other factors. The pay equity wage gap is that portion of the wage gap that is not explained by factors such as labour market experience, hours of work, educational attainment and unionization. It is commonly understood that the pay equity wage gap results from systemic wage discrimination.[100]

Critics have pointed out that "disaggregation" – separating every task and assigning it a numerical value – makes it easy to skew the scale in favour of women. Without actually labelling jobs as women's jobs, for instance, equity agencies can list the skills required – skills that are often still associated primarily with women – and give them higher status. This means that employers would have to pay higher salaries for them. Collectively, these upgraded "gender-neutral" jobs would improve the economic status of women as a group (or, to use the jargon in a slightly different way, as an "aggregate"). Moreover, the advocates, or watchdogs, are always members of women's groups.

In any case, the whole system of collective bargaining between employer and employee is breaking down under the weight of pay-equity schemes. Unions use market-survey data to bargain for men's wages and then run to human rights tribunals on behalf of the women who are thus left behind. The unions want their female members to cash in, of course, and have supported pay equity in a big way. Listen to this comment from the AFL-CIO:

Equal pay has been the law since 1963. But today, nearly 40 years later, women are still paid less than men – even when we have similar education, skills and experience. In 2000, women were paid 73 cents for every dollar men received. That's $27 less to spend on groceries, housing, child care and other expenses for every $100 worth of work we do. Nationwide, working families lose $200 billion of income annually to the wage gap. It's not like we get charged less for rent or food or utilities. In fact, we pay more for things like haircuts and dry cleaning. Over a lifetime of work, the 27 cents-on-the-dollar we're losing adds up. The average 25-year old working woman will lose more than $523,000 to unequal pay during her working life. And because we're paid less now, we have less to save for our futures and we'll earn smaller pensions than men. Half of all older women receiving a private pension in 1998 got less than $3,486 per year, compared with $7,020 per year for older men. These figures are even worse for women of color ... *Equal pay helps men, too.* Men in jobs usually or predominately held by women – sales, service and clerical positions, for example – are also victims of pay bias. The 4 million men who work in predominately female occupations lose an average of $6,259 each year ... The 25.6 million women in these jobs lose an average of $3,446 a year.[101]

But this figure of 73% is an "aggregated" one. It does not mean that any particular woman earns that much less than any particular man. Nor does it account for any global discrepancy. The implication is that discrepancies are due to sexist discrimination against women, but discrepancies can be due to other factors. Given the educational patterns of earlier generations, for instance, older women are still less often part of the workforce than older men. Not all women, moreover, either have or want full-time jobs. When their salaries are factored in with all others, the resulting figure indicates only that women as a group earn less than men as a group. The fact is that women themselves have made choices: to have children or not to have children, to work or not to work, to work part-time or to work full-time. Unions come out ahead either way, but the system does not. Because of the enormous sums of money at stake, a whole industry has grown up around pay equity: researchers, job evaluators, consultants, and so forth.

In a society that is truly interested in fairness, equity agencies would have to demonstrate fairness to citizens of both sexes. Otherwise, the situation could become dire. Some men would eventually fight back. Others would withdraw into cynical isolation. Still others, to judge from the statistics on suicide among boys and young men, would give up hope in life itself. Neither scenario would enhance democracy, which depends on the transparency of justice for all citizens. Any agency with the authority to oversee pay equity or to inform the public about it, in short, must represent the public as a whole.

Someone should examine the various "options" proposed by equity programs with precisely this goal in mind. Doing so would mean analyzing documents submitted to them with the aim of identifying explicit or implicit biases against either women or men. This approach would evaluate definitions of "gender," underlying ideological presuppositions or sources of authority, double standards, openness to manipulation, and so on. Nothing of the kind is likely to happen.

Pay equity is supposed to increase the value of women's traditional paid work. At the same time, it decreases the value of men's traditional paid work. We are thinking of work traditionally assigned to men and based on characteristics of the male body. Manual labour, historically done by men, is sometimes considered less valuable than clerical labour or of no value at all, due to mechanization (although it is also necessary and sometimes dangerous, factors that should make it valuable). Even before the Industrial Revolution, physical labour had a relatively low social status; upper-class men and even middle-class men shunned it. (We will discuss the history of the male body in *Transcending Misandry*). Until very recently, though, it could still provide at least lower-class men with a healthy sense of identity. It was still based on some contribution to society that was distinctive, necessary, and publicly valued. And that, as we have already said several times, is the sine qua non of any healthy identity. Cross-cultural and historical evidence indicates that no society has been able to ignore this need. Our society, far from trying to solve the problem of ignoring it, has actually found ways to exacerbate it. At the very least, we need programs to help men retool for the information age. Should the government take steps to upgrade workers in male ghettoes just as it now does to upgrade workers in female ghettoes? Should it see the obligation to train more men, especially unemployed men, for white-collar work?

And what about risk? Note that risk – this is an important variable, because the work-related accident is a major cause of death for men – is seldom if ever a criterion in pay-equity programs. "Work place accidents are ... a major killer of men. 98% of all the employees in the ten most dangerous professions are men and 94% of all those who die in the workplace are men."[102]

If we are going to level the playing field, truly, we will have to end the current domination of pay equity discussions by women's advocacy groups both within and beyond the government. In one research paper, Morley Gunderson and Paul Lanoie begin by supporting (or seeming to support) pay equity programs but conclude by rejecting them.[103] They point out, for example, that many aspects of these programs seem innocuous enough but hide severe problems. They present three "typical" case studies: a manufacturing company staffed mainly by blue-collar men, a public hospital staffed mainly by women, and a newly established telecommunication company staffed by both men and women.[104] At this point, the authors present an important definition. "Target efficiency refers to the extent to which a program assists as many persons in the target group by as much as possible without having the benefits spillover [*sic*] into the non-target groups. In the case of pay equity, the target group would be *persons* in female-dominated jobs whose pay is 'undervalued,' although the real target is likely to be *women* in such female-dominated jobs."[105]

Gunderson and Lanoie admit that the procedures are complex, so complex that they can easily be manipulated in favour of women – the target group – especially in the private and nonunionized sectors (although the very same procedure could be managed or manipulated in the public and unionized sectors to the detriment of men.) They discuss the benefits of pay equity for a few men in female-dominated jobs but point out that these benefits undermine the ultimate goal of closing the wage gap between men and women, because men can take advantage of "leakage" from the female target group. In other words, any improvement in the pay of a few men detracts from the improvement of all women in relation to men. Clearly, advocates of pay equity do not want to help men in female-dominated work. Although advocates of pay equity sometimes use this possibility in propaganda directed at men, they view it as a negative factor in the larger picture.

The authors note that some employers hire experts even before receiving complaints of discrimination, because the complicated procedures required by law would probably be misunderstood without them. And misunderstanding them would waste time and cost money. This is work for the experts! And thousands are ready to become experts in this growth industry.

Some economists, they point out, argue that wage fixing in the case of pay equity amounts to price fixing. It ignores market forces that would naturally correct some problems, including the problem of employees who stay in undervalued jobs, say, or employers who "downsize." Advocates of pay equity reject that argument by claiming that the market created discrimination in the first place. Other economists support employers who complain about the high cost of pay-equity programs, noting that money is merely transferred from employers to employees. Consumers or taxpayers (or possibly other workers) absorb the cost, they say, adding that there are hidden costs to pay equity at every stage of a complex and technical procedure. Design, implementation, and administration involve committees, job evaluators, consultants, and lawyers.

Gunderson and Lanoie describe the bureaucratic duplication involved in pay-equity programs, which would involve separate plans for each organization, for each bargaining unit within each organization, and for nonunionized employees. And the resulting complexity, apart from anything else, has given rise to legal wrangling. Organizations require tribunals to adjudicate the almost inevitable conflicts. When one side challenges a decision, the result can be costly for litigants and defendants. "These real resource costs are 'eaten up' in the process; they represent shrinkage in the pie that can otherwise be distributed to the parties. As aptly stated by Fudge and McDermott ... '[T]hat is the final beauty of pay equity: it consumes so many resources there is little left for anything else.'"[106] The only people who make money are the professionals, in other words, not those who were actually supposed to earn more money.

Given all this complexity and the need for experts, say Gunderson and Lanoie, the system can hardly be transparent. Worse, the experts are by no means impartial. Because pay-equity programs are designed to improve women's wages, these experts have vested interests in furthering the cause of women by promoting their own obscurantism, complex methods, and bloated bureaucracies. The end result is that these programs develop lives of their own. Therefore, Gunderson and Lanoie recommend reversion to the "complaints-based approach" and add that "there is no evidence that the original needs for the [complaints-based] program have dissipated over time in that the discriminatory pay gap that could be reduced by pay equity has now been closed."[107]

Feminist calls for equality, or even equity, sound at first like nothing other than calls for justice. Lurking just below the surface, though, is often the call for gynocentrism. Whatever its underlying motivation, gynocentrism has already been institutionalized, either directly or indirectly, in laws or interpretations of them, constitutional amendments or interpretations of them, and bureaucracies at every level of government. The rhetoric has functioned like that of motherhood. Who (except for some feminists) would ever oppose that in public? Equality is not only the legitimate expression of egalitarian feminism, therefore, but also the ideal front for ideological feminism. Not only are students exposed to gynocentric indoctrination, but so are legislators, judges, bureaucrats, corporate managers, and employees.

Here is one example. The National Judicial Institute, established by the Canadian Judicial Council in 1988 "to provide continuing education courses for federally appointed superior court judges," has since 1992 provided "gender sensitivity" seminars.[108] The institute's program on gender equality consists of "a 30-minute video, printed materials and an afternoon panel discussion." Both the video (which is used in connection with admission to the bar) and the printed materials (which are taken from a book edited by feminist professors Sheilah Martin and Kathleen Mahoney)[109] preclude any real discussion of gender, because they present only feminist interpretations of the Charter and therefore only feminist takes on problems such as domestic violence, custody and support, sexual assault, and systemic discrimination.

Systemic gynocentric bias has led to more than a demand for quotas, usually known as "targets." It has led also to a demand for social and cultural (though not political) revolution. Ideological feminists measure progress according to a "female standard" and in view of "female knowledge." Ideological feminists denounce equality of opportunity, insisting on equality of result. Ignoring the fact that the former has been greatly modified over the past thirty years to suit women, they claim that modifying it has prevented a critique of what they believe is the "phallocentricity" of knowledge. Women have nothing to learn or gain, in other words, from the experience of men.

There is no reason not to suppose that women, as they earn seniority, will rise to the top. But consider the current debate over pay equity in Canada, which erupted anew in 1998 when the Human Rights Tribunal ruled that the federal government had underpaid two hundred thousand federal employees in female-dominated jobs. It was not only the high cost of corrective measures that caused an outcry, by the way, but also the fact that federal employees were already overpaid. In 1997 the Canadian Labour Congress found that the employment of women in the public sector had risen by 47% between 1976 and 1996, whereas that of men had actually fallen by 14%. In fact, female employees had become the majority, and their average earnings were almost double those in the private sector. Canadian women earned a better hourly wage two years after graduation, moreover, than did men.[110] And more women were hired more quickly than they would have been without affirmative action.

No policy is going to eliminate the wage gap between men and women, because women (or men) who stay home with their children will lose financially. Even when governments provide special measures – family bonuses, tax breaks, and so forth – they do not make up for lost income and therefore lower pensions.[111] Not unless we resort to some form of totalitarianism and eliminate the freedom to make choices. Nevertheless, we can mitigate the problem in two ways: by providing people with a variety of incentives and thus of choices, and by providing them with parental leave.

At the heart of this controversy is the fact that women, historically, have been more closely involved than men with rearing young children. Until recently, most were not part of the paid labour force. One result was economic vulnerability in the event of widowhood and divorce. Special protections have been introduced to prevent their vulnerability, and many women have been able to choose between working at home and working in the larger world. But many women who stay home to rear children will eventually want to rejoin the labour force, especially in view of extended life spans. To make that possible without penalizing those who choose to stay at home with children, we would have to do at least two things very effectively: offer a wide variety of educational and retraining programs and eliminate *age* discrimination. For some reason, that form of discrimination is seldom mentioned by anyone advocating either affirmative-action programs or pay-equity programs. And yet it is rampant.[112]

We do take seriously the fact that women as a group – though not necessarily as individuals and seldom, nowadays, as young individuals – earn less than men. And we do take seriously the fact that some jobs should be reclassified, if not because of malicious discrimination (which is probably very rare) then because they have changed with the advent of new technologies (which is probably very common). But there is surely no need to evaluate society in exclusively economic and political terms. Ultimately, every society must be evaluated in moral terms as well. Advocates of pay equity, like the advocates of affirmative action already discussed, invite moral evaluation, in fact, because their schemes are all premised on "fairness." Even if they could bring about a fairer distribution of wealth, their schemes would still be morally flawed. They are based firmly, inherently, and irrevocably on the dubious principle that ends can justify means, which involves sacrificing the interests of some people to serve the interests of other people. And for those who do not care about moral principles, there is this to think about: the cynicism that flows directly from any practice based on systemic discrimination and political or economic manipulation. For evidence of that, look at the moral collapse of societies in eastern Europe after decades of communism.

So where does all this leave men in the age of social engineering? In theory, Canadian men should be included in sections 15 and 28 of the Charter under "sex." In fact, that claim has been resisted by interpreting the Charter in connection only with "historically disadvantaged" groups. Men, it is assumed wrongly, have not been historically disadvantaged. But men in our time really have become disadvantaged as the official victims of institutionalized double standards. Men have become the sacrificial victims of society, to put it bluntly, because the economic interests of women have taken precedence over the economic and sometimes other interests of men.

Here is one example. In *Weatherall v. Canada*,[10] the Supreme Court ruled that the frisk-searching of male prisoners by female guards was acceptable but maintained that the frisk-searching of female prisoners by male guards remained unacceptable.[113] One reason for the double standard was to ensure the job security of female guards. This trumped the right to privacy of male prisoners. But the reason actually cited in one authoritative source involved "historical, biological and sociological differences between men and women."[114] It is most unlikely that any judge would condone inequality for women on the grounds of their biological characteristics, which would be explained away as the social constructions of a patriarchal society (except, of course, when biological characteristics could be cited as grounds for inequality in a positive sense and thus for entitlement). As for historical (or sociological) differences, which are of immediate interest to us here, the ruling clearly suggests that male prisoners, unlike female ones, deserve no privacy. Why not? Partly because this case involved the conflicting interests of guilty prisoners and innocent guards, to be sure, but mainly because our society has historically ignored the notion that men value privacy as an essential feature of human dignity but has nonetheless insisted on the notion that women do. Men have not been conditioned to feel inhibited by modesty, but women have been. Exposing men to the prying eyes of women does not constitute a violation of their human dignity, supposedly, but exposing women to the prying eyes of men does.

At issue here is whether privacy should be considered an essential feature of human dignity, not whether Canadian notions of masculinity or femininity have fostered it. Either way, the judgment in this case is very disturbing. It reveals an underlying double standard: recognizing the histori-cal conditioning of women but not that of men. If privacy is an essential feature of human dignity, the judge might have considered the possibility that Canadian culture has historically disadvantaged men by denying it to them but not to women. If privacy is not an essential feature of human dig-nity, on the other hand, why allow it for female prisoners?

Most men are not in prison. Most have jobs. And almost all need jobs. Older male employees, those who are preparing to retire, are unlikely to be affected by affirmative action or pay equity (unless men, but not women, are actually fired on principle in the event of downsizing). Slightly younger men might be disappointed if their promotions go to women. But young men, those planning or beginning their careers, are paying the full price for affirmative-action programs or pay-equity programs. Even those who get jobs realize that their chances of getting better ones, or even ones at the same level, have been diminished. And these mechanisms are not only for women but also for minorities, which means that young men will always be at the bottom of the hiring pool. Even minority young men will have to wait until minority women are hired. They realize, at some level of con-sciousness, not only that their prospects are dimmer than those of young women but also that society does not care about the prospects of young men.

When the system is expanded to include other groups, this problem is magnified, despite the rhetoric about diversity. Writing about what might be "the greatest policy achievement in recent history," Katherine Boo observes that "over the past decade significant numbers of formerly welfare-dependent black women have successfully entered the work force. But what about black men?"[115] The fact is that black men are in bad shape. Welfare reform has opened a "chasm between the status and prospects of black women and those of the men they might marry. A grim home economics: In the 1990s the employment of young black females dramatically increased, despite the fact that many of those working women were single mothers. Meanwhile, the employment of their less-encumbered male counterparts stagnated, even in a period of unprecedented economic expansion."[116]

A higher proportion of black women than white women are employed. And not only at menial jobs. They earn, on average, 96% of what white women earn. That is a major achievement. A much lower proportion of black men than white men, however, are employed: 30% lower. And that figure excludes men in jail. "Set aside the profound emotional implications of this gender gap [and think about] the loneliness of newly working women struggling to raise children by themselves; the resentment of men watching female contemporaries succeed, with considerable government assistance, in jobs at which they themselves have failed or from which they've been displaced by women."[117]

The underlying cause, according to Boo, is feminism (in our terminology, gynocentrism). Men in general and black men in particular, she argues, have been ignored. The "grave predicament of the contemporary black male, and its fundamental connection with the fate of black children, has managed to slip quietly through two distinct cracks: the one between competing special-interest blocks of the poverty industry, and the one between the hardened ideological categories of right and left."[118]

Paul Offner has commented on the funding patterns of what he calls the welfare-industrial complex and the resulting neglect of black men: "The emotional testimony at congressional hearings on welfare reform is inevitably going to be about day care, or welfare time limits, or definitions of activities that qualify as work ... because women and children are the social-services constituency – the individuals with whom the government and the nonprofits interact. Men are barely on the screen, except as dead-beat dads."[119] Consider also the depressing effects of political expediency on both sides of the political spectrum.

If there is less rigorous discussion about how, now, to create opportunity for black males, it may be because the political utility to such a debate is uncertain. Drawing acute distinctions between the deserving and the undeserving poor, the political right resists heavy investment in a child-abandoning, work-resistant, lawbreaking population. Buttressing the right's position is the fact that previous federally funded efforts to put young black males to work have produced few appreciable results. The left, meanwhile, is reluctant to advocate for men in the face of the considerable needs of women.[120]

What does Boo suggest? How can we create hope for struggling black men and, by implication, for struggling men in general? "What if unemployed fathers who owed child support were mandated to participate in work-related activities or community service? What if they then received stipends while learning skills or searching for jobs with the assistance of community-based programs that have established a track record in helping women?"[121]

Social engineering is a very blunt instrument. It affects not only those immediately involved in this or that scheme but also society as a whole. Affirmative-action programs and pay-equity programs are only two symptoms – we will discuss several others in the following chapters – of a much more pervasive phenomenon: the apparently paradoxical trend toward both extreme collectivism and extreme individualism at the same time. We say "apparently," because the paradox is more apparent than real.

First, consider the trend toward extreme collectivism, which is revealed not only in the rise of political ideologies based on group identity, including feminism, but also in the rise of state control that has emerged as a direct result of their utopian programs. These utopian programs must be imposed on society. Or, to put it another way, the state must control people more and more rigorously – economically, legally, and politically – in order to attain not merely equality of opportunity but equality of result. Second, consider the trend toward extreme individualism. At one time, men and women pooled their resources as family units within larger units, or classes, defined by economic status, religion, ethnicity, and many other things. In our time, women (and, by default, men as well) are seen as autonomous individuals within rival classes. When income statistics are compared, they are often understood (falsely) in connection with the earning capacity of individual women versus individual men. Few think about the interdependence of men and women in family units as a significant factor. This is hardly surprising, since the goal of many feminists – the ones we classify as ideological – is not merely sexual equality or even "equity" but autonomy and even separation from men (about which we will say much more in chapter 8). So far, this autonomy has been realized most fully by individual women (although some feminists would like to attain collective autonomy as well). The result is a rapidly fragmenting society of more or less autonomous individuals controlled directly by the state in ways not mediated, as they once were, by family or community.

This debate over entitlements shows that human rights are threatened on an international level. Human rights once referred to the rights of men, women, children, and religious communities. They are now being redrafted in the name of "gender balance" to focus exclusively on women's rights (which we discuss in appendix 6). Because this is a controversial departure, officials use the term "human rights" anyway as a front. Occasionally, they give a nod to the old worldview by throwing in references to "men and women" or "girls and boys." But they do so mainly to counter any charge of overt discrimination.

We are by no means the only ones to think about these problems. Jean Bethke Elshtain, for instance, suggests that there are three models for understanding rights in connection with men and women. One is "sex polarity," which assumes that men and women are categorically different and might as well belong to different species. This sex polarity has both ontological and hierarchical implications. In the past, women were devalued. Now, men are devalued. This rhetoric, which is always about power, often resorts to analogies such as slavery and war. As we have pointed out elsewhere, this is the rhetoric of conspiracy.

The difference between earlier generations of male disparagers of women and current disparagers of men by women is that the language of rights was not available as a central category in the rhetorical struggle. Rights, then, traffics as a variant on power-talk, as the emblematic relationship between male and female as separate categories is that of oppressor and oppressed. Sex polarists cannot, by definition, think their way out of, or through, this static formulation. Or, perhaps better put, they can get out of the oppressor/oppressed and master/slave pairing only through the obliteration of one category: thus men must be "feminized," and the more virtuous and saintly sex must triumph for the scenario to play itself out to a desired end.[122]

Elshtain's second model, "sex unity," ignores the difference between male and female bodies as "a source of identity ... the object of epistemological wonder and understanding."[123] From this point of view, men and women are interchangeable, especially since the advent of reproductive technologies such as surrogacy or ex utero gestation, which get around the most obvious difference.

Elshtain's third model is "sex complementarity." This "begins from a stance of ontological equality and equal dignity that is nonetheless compatible with different roles and offices ... [It] affords a sense of partnership, of what it means to be in community and in communion. Framed with this understanding in mind, rights become signs of human dignity, marks of 'the same' and 'the distinct' simultaneously. This latter position is philosophically richer but it complicates matters politically and requires a more nuanced understanding of the way rights structure our identities both with and against multiple bodies – family, church, neighborhood, and state."[124]

Human rights developed within the Western tradition of formal rights, which were based in turn, observes Elshtain, on both the classical idea of universal law and the Christian one of natural law. Rights were immunities, inhering in people as such, from interference by the state. With the development of market economies, however, rights as immunities became rights as entitlements.

Entitlements place me in a different position towards both the state and my neighbor. Rather than serving an interpositional role – the state is not permitted to do certain things because so to do would violate human dignity – rights now affords us a way to couch a particular claim – I am entitled to certain things, because I belong to one of a proliferating number of possible human categories (male, female, young, old, handicapped, minority, etc.) ... Tethered to an adamantly individualistic understanding of the human person, rights as entitlements denies any weight to principles of belonging, obligation, and community or communal identity. In this adversarial version of rights, the tethering of self to community is severed – at least in theory – and the transitive nature of rights is lost. Rights as immunities, as inherent markers of human ontological dignity is the understanding of rights in general to which Christians are most indebted and toward which they can make the strongest contribution.[125]

When rights as immunities turned into rights as entitlements and when group identities – determined by sex, for instance, or race – were presupposed, rights became adversarial. "Not only that. A world defined by rights as adversarial possessions, increasingly lodged in a presupposition of pre-given group identities' (by gender or race, for example), promotes or requires a flattening out of human identity. We are all bundles of needs and claims ... What separates us one from the other is not our human distinctiveness but the fact that some are oppressors, others oppressed; some hegemonic, others object."[126] Elshtain concludes that the sex-polarity position has aligned with the adversarial approach to human rights and to human rights themselves "as a way to get and to hold power."[127] For those who disagree, too bad. They, presumably, are the products of false consciousness.

Elshtain's position on human rights is very close to our own. Like her, we believe that ideological feminism not only polarizes the world into "us" versus "them," women versus men, but also places these ontologically different groups into a hierarchy. Men were above women in the past, but the reverse is true today. It should be needless to say – but clearly is not – that two wrongs do not make a right. We would prefer to get beyond the androcentric view that "human" means "man" but also the gynocentric one that "human" means "woman." We would prefer to see human beings, in short, with stereoscopic vision. In the context of human rights, this would mean seeing the bodies (and histories) of men and women as both different and similar. The latter would surely make sense in view of the fact that men and women are members of the same species.

The word "equality" is almost universally accepted in the United States and Canada as the highest political goal of society, but how many people – how many voters – are actually aware that it can be defined in two radically different and opposing ways? Among those who do, how many realize that advocates of one definition want not merely to modify the other definition but to replace it? Or that each definition represents not merely a political position but a worldview?

Equality of opportunity, even in its current modified form, emerged from the worldview that created both countries (though not, of course, the recent Canadian Charter of Rights and Freedoms). It encourages society to reduce the gulf between rich and poor and currently tries, with varying degrees of success, to prevent anyone from falling below a minimal level of economic security, but does not replace personal responsibility with state regulation. Equality of result has emerged much more recently from a worldview that promotes very different notions of (among other things) the state, the community, the citizen (or individual), and the law. It insists that society must distribute wealth evenly according to a mathematically calculated paradigm. And to achieve that goal, it does replace personal responsibility with state regulation.

The older worldview accommodates both liberalism (which encourages the active pursuit of amelioration) and conservatism (which places that within a larger moral context). It therefore requires negotiation and compromise in connection with reform. The newer worldview accommodates neither liberalism nor conservatism. It therefore tolerates negotiation, or compromise, only in connection with immediate political expediency. Fundamentally utopian, it strives for revolution – if not political revolution in the narrow sense, then cultural revolution in the broad sense – rather than reform. To succeed, its advocates must wipe the slate clean and start over again. MacKinnon certainly understands this and, taking her feminist theory of the state to its logical conclusion, says so unequivocally. And lots of people, including legislators, like what they see of it.

The "contested" definition of "equality," then, is by no means a trivial matter, of importance only to hairsplitting academics or nitpicking lawyers. At stake is a worldview and its vision of society.

6

Maternal Rights v. Paternal Rights: The Case of Children

In family law disputes, women are often fighting for the safety of themselves and their children, while some men are fighting to maintain power and control. Making custody and access decisions less formal will not cause violence to disappear; it will simply remove the few existing protections for women and children.[1]

Today, simply being a divorced father instantly subjects you to being treated with contempt by your state government. State agencies universally regard mothers as their customer to serve and protect, and fathers as forced supplier, not gender-neutral parents of the same children.[2]

Consider the following case, that of a well-to-do household. "Michael" goes to court in the hope of having the judge reduce his family-support payments. On the surface, his case seems preposterous. After all, he earns $158,000. The judge rejects his plea, perhaps not surprisingly, and orders him to continue paying his former wife $7,153 every month. But that amount represents 96% of his take-home pay; after deductions, he takes home $7,455 every month. And after making his family-support payments, he has only $302 on which to live. The fact is that even single men on welfare in his city actually receive more money: $520. His son and former wife, on the other hand, are hardly living at the poverty line. Was Michael evil enough to have deserved this situation? Neither infidelity nor physical violence caused his divorce. Nor, for that matter, did "psychological violence." It was caused, according to his wife, by the fact that he spent too much time at work. When the local newspaper ran a story on deadbeat dads, nevertheless, his sixteen-year-old son had this to say: "Dad, did you read that article in *The Star*? Well that's what I think of you."[3]

Controversies over the rights of children often involve controversies over the rights of women and men, and the former usually take precedence over the latter – even if children are deprived as a result. Discussion has been heavily dominated by a galaxy of interconnecting "interests": feminist

advocacy groups lobbying for the economic betterment of divorced mothers, specialized government bureaucracies that rely almost exclusively on
feminist analysis, collection agencies with vested interests in getting more
money from noncustodial parents (that is, by and large, from fathers), and
assorted academic experts, clinicians, lawyers, and journalists. Collectively,
they have been called the child-support industry. Because some participants
are government or social-service bureaucrats not engaged in commerce as
such, this phenomenon is industrial in a derived but interesting sense.
Many thousands of these people now earn their livings, after all, by cater-
ing to needs created within their own bureaucracies. (More about industrialization of that kind in chapter 7.) Despite the differences between American and Canadian law, the situation in one country is basically the same
as that in the other.

   After an introduction on the history of custody arrangements, we will
review the legislation governing divorce, custody, and child support, some
prevalent misconceptions about fathers, some of the resulting legal problems, the current debate over law reform, and the link that this debate
reveals between gynocentrism and misandry.

Most people in our society now expect that the custody of children in cases
of divorce or separation will be awarded to mothers. It was not always so.
Roman law automatically awarded custody to fathers, a practice that continued in Western countries long after the fall of Rome. Only in the nineteenth century were questions raised about it. After a landmark case in
Britain, judges awarded custody of children under the age of seven to their
mothers and children over seven to their fathers. This practice produced
the "tender years doctrine." But even that doctrine, which recognized the
importance of both mothers and fathers, was doomed by the Industrial
Revolution. For one thing, more and more fathers worked in factories. By
default, women became the primary caregivers at home. Moreover, fewer
and fewer fathers taught trades to their sons. The importance of fathers for
children, in short, was no longer so obvious.

   By the 1920s, both society and the courts presumed (barring unusual circumstances) that custody of children should be given to their mothers.
Even though legislators introduced gender-neutral laws in the 1960s,
judges still presumed that maternal custody was in "the best interest of the
child."[4] And few fathers, on the advice of their lawyers, were prepared to
argue with them in court. Even fathers who did argue seldom won custody.[5] At the moment, things are beginning to change. Not, of course, to
the presumption of paternal custody. The trend is toward joint, or shared,
custody. But even that has been attacked by many feminists.

   Child support is closely related to divorce and custody. Everyone agrees
that parents, both custodial (usually mothers) and noncustodial (usually

fathers), should provide economic support for their children. But child-support arrangements, which might otherwise be settled according to the child's best interest, are now usually settled according to the wife's best interest, with child support often elided through legalistic legerdemain into wife support. Even when they suspect that something is wrong, few men know precisely what it is. Nonetheless, many have had to think carefully about the concrete problems caused by separation from their children after divorce. Fathers have begun to mobilize for law reform, in fact. Because at least some women can see the need for even divorced fathers to remain actively involved with their children – something that current laws often discourage – this wing of the men's movement is likely to find grudging acceptance from them.

The controversy over divorce, custody, and child support is complex – partly because of the byzantine legal principles that now govern family life but mainly because of the ideological rhetoric that governs discussions of it.[6] Two arguments in particular function as trump cards; merely alluding to them, which is done over and over again in every possible context, drives every other consideration out the window. One argument is that men demanding rights as fathers are dishonest and actually have no interest in their children. What they really want, allegedly, is to control their former wives. The other argument is that many of these men are actually violent or perverted. Giving them a legal right to joint custody, therefore, would mean exposing women and children to danger. These arguments and similar ones (which we document in appendix 9) are flawed on close examination, but constant repetition has by now made them seem like conventional wisdom. Repeat a lie often enough, someone once said, and it becomes the truth.

In the United States, child support has been regulated at the federal level by resorting to the Constitution's Commerce Clause. Section 8 describes the power of Congress to collect taxes, provide for common defense, and promote general welfare; article 1 gives Congress the authority to "regulate Commerce with foreign Nations, and among the several States, and with the Indian Tribes." What can commerce possibly have to do with child support? The convoluted reasoning is that people who owe support might try to avoid payment by moving across state lines. This can be prevented by federal authorities, advocates argue, because "interstate commerce" is regulated by the federal government. But child support is surely not commerce. Never mind. Even though the intention of the Commerce Clause was originally to facilitate free trade across state lines, according to Wendy McElroy, it was gradually given broader interpretations.[7] Feminists saw in those interpretations ideal opportunities to further their own interests, using the Commerce Clause to argue for federal, or "interstate," regulation of child support. Federal jurisdiction not only solved the immediate problem of men crossing state lines to avoid child support but also gave the problem a higher profile and provided efforts to solve it with better funding. How did we get to this point?

The story began in 1975. Feminist groups were delighted when President Ford established the Office of Child Support Enforcement (OCSE). He warned them, even so, that this office would amount to a federal intrusion into the powers of both states and families. No matter. There were more important things to worry about. Stephen Baskerville shows how interest groups, including some feminist ones, "demonized divorced fathers into 'deadbeat dads' and then criminalized them."[8] Men who refused to pay up were the topic of a journalistic feeding frenzy. The problem, it was said, had become a national scandal (even though the Government Accounting Office noted that "95% of fathers having no employment problems for the past five years pay regularly; 81% in full and on time").[9] Taking its marching orders from public opinion as mediated by journalists and talk show hosts, as usual, legislatures across the country raced to come up with corrective measures.

The federal program increased in size ten times between 1978 and 1998.[10] Bill O'Reilly, the host of one talk show, declared a national "epidemic of child abandonment in America, mainly by fathers."[11] Senator Evan Bayh attacked "irresponsible" fathers in several speeches. Liberal Democrat Al Gore promised voters harsher measures against "deadbeat dads" if he was elected and promised to imprison more of them. Even earlier, President Clinton had urged his administration to plan a "crack down" on irresponsible fathers. To track them down, officials were given two new resources: the Directory of New Hires (which lists all new employees in the country) and the Federal Case Registry (a massive surveillance system that monitors between sixteen and nineteen million citizens). And Republicans, never soft on maintaining the traditional family or afraid to call for law and order, soon followed suit. President George W. Bush announced a $320-million program to "promote responsible fatherhood," and Congress considered a bill to "reconnect fathers with their families." Sounds okay. But the underlying plan was that of the Democrats, according to Baskerville. Both parties wanted to extract more money from fathers.

Here, though, is the background story. Society experienced a "divorce revolution" and the rise of a "divorce culture."[12] Divorces are usually initiated by women, as it happens, at least partly because feminism has convinced them of the need for greater autonomy – which is to say, liberation from men and marriage. Trouble is, divorce involves a financial strain on women (and men). Experts produced exaggerated statistics on the sorry economic plight of women following divorce, which led to anxiety for women but also to guilt for society as a whole. And that, in turn, led to successful political action by and for women as victims of men. In practical terms, the result was to reinforce the claim that wives should get enough money from their former husbands to maintain their standard of living before divorce. Those who could not get it directly as alimony found ways of getting it indirectly as a by-product of child support. Third, many women claimed sole custody. Some believed that children belonged, in effect, to their mothers. Others were genuinely worried about violence or molestation by the fathers.

Congress passed welfare legislation in 1984 that required states to adopt not only guidelines for the payment of child support but also formulae to increase amounts. Baskerville notes that these guidelines and formulae had been promoted by the OCSE, which argued that making noncustodial parents (usually fathers) pay more would get custodial parents (usually single mothers) off welfare.[13] In other words, an important but hidden goal was to solve a larger problem than the poverty of children: the "feminization of poverty." The trouble was that many of these fathers were themselves on welfare; few were economically stable enough to pay higher amounts or even the current amounts. As a result, the government could not collect enough to take many mothers off welfare. No one cared that men on welfare or with low incomes were impoverished due to new demands. The Bradley Amendment (or Omnibus Budget Reconciliation Act) of 1986 altered the Social Security Act to prevent "retroactive modification of child support awards or arrearage for any reason, ever."[14] That was just the beginning.

In 1988, the net was expanded to catch more middle-class fathers, even though there was no evidence of need, and the amount of money expected from them was increased. The new guidelines targeted not only those on welfare, in other words, but also those not on welfare. Being employed, they could presumably pay at higher rates than those who were unemployed. As a result, federal collection agencies could show evidence that they were collecting more money for women and tightening the screws on "deadbeat dads."[15] The Family Support Act required state agencies to administer all cases (not only welfare cases), garnish the wages of all noncustodial parents automatically (including those with spouses who did not require the money), introduce paternity-testing programs, and deny passports to noncustodial parents who owed more than five thousand dollars. In addition, it required written explanations for not following state guidelines from judges who adapted them to particular circumstances and therefore seldom went against the guidelines.[16]

The Child Support Recovery Act of 1996 made "the willful failure to pay a past due support obligation [of more than $5,000] with respect to a child residing in another state a federal offense ... A first violation ... is punishable by two years imprisonment and/or a fine. The F.B.I. has primary investigatory jurisdiction. Additionally, Special Agents of the Office of the Inspector General of the United States Department of Health and Human Services have been given authority to investigate violations ..."[17] The aim was to prevent noncustodial parents from changing jobs, concealing assets, using false names and social security numbers, moving to other states in order to avoid paying (or moving after being served notice of contempt of court for not paying), and so on. Some situations, according to this act, require immediate intervention by the federal government: when custodial parents or their children need expensive medical care, have problems due to handicaps, or are threatened with eviction. Other situations involve federal charges: bankruptcy fraud (concealing assets), bank fraud, tax evasion (false statements), or other crimes.[18] Offenders may be fined, in addition to being charged for the amount in arrears, or imprisoned.

The Welfare Reform Act of 1996 allowed the federal government to improve its methods of surveillance with potential seizures in mind. By 1998, for instance, all companies would have to report new employees and their wages to a new central data base. By 1999, all financial institutions would have to comply with government requests for information on accounts; non custodial parents in arrears would lose their driver's or other licences. Child support orders would have to include health coverage (in addition to basic child support). And states would have to identify 90% of unmarried fathers or lose their federal reimbursements and incentive payments.

Also in 1998 the Child Support Recovery Act was amended by the Deadbeat Parents Punishment Act. This measure increased both the status of violations and the penalties. Here was a formal act of Congress that used the very informal word "deadbeat" in its title. That alone should have made citizens suspicious. Although the gender-neutral word "parents" followed it, everyone knew that "dads" were targeted. Mothers were almost always given custody of children, after all, and fathers given instructions to pay for their support.

The Hyde-Woolsey Act,[19] introduced in 1999 but never passed, involved the Internal Revenue Service. This act would have required "all employers to withhold child support payments and send them to the I.R.S. The I.R.S. would then distribute the withheld amount to custodial parents owed child support. The bill would also [have treated] child support obligations as taxes for purposes of penalties and interest related to failure to have them withheld by employers."[20] Amounts were already being withheld by employers, of course, but bringing in the Internal Revenue Service would have introduced an even more aggressive collection agency with more extreme penalties for infractions. This bill, however, died in committee.

More recently, in 2000, the Department of Health and Human Services ruled that noncustodial parents owing more than $2,500 in child support would no longer be eligible for food stamps.

In Canada, child support is defined by the federal Divorce Act of 1985 and the Federal Child Support Guidelines of 1997.[21] Underlying these guidelines is the Formula for the Tables of Amounts Contained in the Guidelines. Child support is *collected*, on the other hand, by provincial agencies. In Ontario, for instance, the Family Responsibility Office is in change of collections under the Family Responsibility and Support Arrears Enforcement Act of 1996. This office receives all support orders and enforces them. It operates by garnishing wages, bank accounts (up to 50%), and funds from federal sources such as income tax refunds or employment insurance benefits. If necessary, it reports noncustodial parents to the credit bureau, seizes their bank accounts or other assets (including registered retirement saving plans), suspends their passports, suspends their driver's licenses, and takes them to court.[22] Canadian legislation serves the same purpose, in short, as American legislation.

Many observers have pointed out that our culture fosters a whole lot of misconceptions – no pun intended – about fathers. In the first part of *Divorced Dads*, Sanford Braver challenges those who have collectively had a profound and pervasive influence on the American legal system governing divorced fathers.[23] A psychologist who led the largest federally funded research project on divorced fathers,[24] he isolated six primary "myths" about divorced fathers: that they are usually the ones who either initiate divorce or trigger it by abandoning their families,[25] that they usually have most of the legal advantages in negotiating divorce and custody arrangements,[26] that they experience a climb in their standard of living and their ex-wives a decline,[27] that they are in better emotional health than their ex-wives,[28] that they seldom bother to continue supporting their children,[29] and that they seldom bother even to stay in contact with them.[30]

Do husbands abandon their marriages more often than wives? Some people argue that men have more to gain economically from divorce than women and that they are therefore more likely than women to initiate proceedings. Other people argue that men are more irresponsible than women and thus more likely to cause the problems that lead to divorce. Still others argue that there are too many women looking for husbands;[31] men are in a better bargaining position than women and therefore in a better position to find new partners or at least to initiate divorce proceedings when things go wrong.

But the fact is that approximately two-thirds of divorces in the United States are initiated by women,[32] and the rate is even higher in Canada.[33] From the ideological perspective of some feminists, the reason is very simple. Marriage, they believe, is an inherently patriarchal institution and thus inherently oppressive for women even without violence. No wonder they want out. But studies have shown that other explanations are more likely. "If women can anticipate a clear gender bias in the courts regarding custody," writes Candis McLean, "they can expect to be the primary residential parent for the children. If they can anticipate enforcement of financial child support by the courts, they can expect a high probability of support monies without the need to account for their expenditures. Clearly they can also anticipate maintaining the marital residence, receiving half of all marital property and gaining total freedom to establish new social relationships."[34] If they stand to gain so much from divorce, in other words, why put more effort into making the marriage work? This is an interesting, but cynical, explanation. According to Baskerville's more charitable one, divorcing women no longer feel loved or appreciated.[35] But there are other explanations.

In order to find out why men and women initiate divorce proceedings, economists Margaret Brinig and Douglas Allen conducted a massive study of divorce, analyzing all forty-six thousand divorce suits filed during 1995 in four states: Connecticut, Virginia, Montana, and Oregon.[36] Although one reason for women is to get away from violent or adulterous husbands, "in the state with the best records of grievances, Virginia, only 6 percent of divorces were granted on grounds of violence, and husbands were cited for adultery only slightly more often than wives." Another reason is "the belief that your partner is no longer good enough for you. The classic example is the guy who takes a trophy wife after dumping the high-school sweetheart who sacrificed her own potential to put him through medical school, but a woman can be similarly tempted to leave a husband who is less successful than she is."[37] What then?

The solution to the mystery, the factor that determined most cases, turned out to be the question of child custody. Women are much more willing to split up because – unlike men – they typically do not fear losing custody of the children. Instead a divorce often enables them to *gain* control over the children.

"The question of custody absolutely swamps all the other variables," Dr. Brinig said. "Children are the most important asset in a marriage, and the partner who expects to get sole custody is by far the most likely to file for divorce."

The correlation with custody is so strong, Dr. Brinig said, that she has changed her view about the best way to preserve marriages and protect children. She previously advocated an end to quick no-fault divorces, but she now believes that the key is to rewrite custody laws.[38]

Robert Seidenberg discusses yet another explanation, one that should be taken seriously by researchers at least as a possibility.

Abandoning one's children is not a "normal" thing to do. It is natural for a father to love his children. For most fathers only extreme circumstances could force the breaking of this bond. Consider too, how difficult it must be to pick up and leave, not only one's children, but one's home town, family, friends, and job, and how difficult it is to enter an underground cash economy – all to avoid supporting *one's own children*! Someone would literally have to be crazy to do this, unless there were extraordinary pressures to uproot.

For fathers who have gone many rounds with the courts, lost their children, had their property seized, had their wages garnisheed [*sic*], and spent time in jail, flight becomes a rational alternative. Deadbeat Dads are men who have "voted with their feet." They would more appropriately be called "Refugee Dads" or "Fathers in Exile."[39]

The second misconception is that divorced fathers are better equipped than mothers to negotiate separation,[40] divorce, and custody. Although both men and women complain about their problems, many people are prepared to believe that women – members of an official or unofficial victim class – are at a relative disadvantage. Feminists have argued, and not only in this context, that laws were made by and presumably for men.[41] Or that the judges are usually men. Or that men are richer than women and can afford better lawyers. Or that men are more aggressive and thus better equipped for legal battles. Braver points out that not one of these arguments is legitimate, certainly not now. And he is not the only one. "In terms of commanding federal dollars, electing politicians, enacting legislation, controlling academic discourse, and influencing media to promote their cause," writes Seidenberg, "the feminist movement is one of the most powerful political forces in the United States today. Unfortunately, the public, including the middle-class professional men most affected by custody litigation, still tends to perceive feminists as the near-powerless victims they portray themselves to be. Judges, however, are astute political creatures; they understand the extent of feminist political power and act accordingly."[42]

The third misconception is that divorce brings men a higher standard of living and women a lower one. It would be hard to exaggerate the importance of this claim. Yet several investigators have shown that this assumption is false. Here is what happened. Lenore Weitzman published *The Divorce Revolution* in 1985, reporting that while the average mother lost 73% of her income after divorce, the average father gained 42%.[43] This "fact," supposedly discovered by the Harvard researcher, has been cited as grounds for divorce and custody legislation ever since. As Geoffrey

Christopher Rapp and others have pointed out, however, Weitzman got the math wrong. Other researchers were unable to duplicate her findings, and she was unwilling to provide them with access to her files. No matter. Since 1985 her startling but false figures have been quoted repeatedly by politicians, academics, social workers, lawyers, judges, and journalists.[44] Rapp, who works for CNN, pointed out that Weitzman's claim "has become one of the philosophical bases for deciding child custody and property division in divorce cases. It has also altered public perceptions of men, women and divorce. It was cited hundreds of times ... and was regarded so clearly as holy writ that President Clinton cited it too in his budget proposal ... as part of his attack on deadbeat dads."[45] Eventually, of course, the full story came out. It was a hoax, just like the one about violence against women peaking on Super Bowl Sunday, the one about 150,000 women dying every year from anorexia, and so on (which we discuss in appendix 3). But the damage had been done, and not everyone really cared about why or how.

The fourth misconception is that divorced fathers are more satisfied than mothers, emotionally, with the results of divorce and loss of custody. As for divorce itself, Braver writes that ex-husbands find it harder to let go of their wives than for ex-wives to let go of their ex-husbands.[46] (On the other hand, he adds, ex-husbands find it easier than their ex-wives to let go of their anger.)[47] Ex-husbands often find it harder to adjust to divorce than their ex-wives. "The one who leaves the marriage holds all the power. Consequently, the one being left – most often the man – feels utterly powerless because he can do nothing to prevent the breakup of the marriage.[48] This is a matter not so much of losing power but of losing self-esteem. Women, by contrast – even if we judge only from what they so often tell Oprah Winfrey on television – often feel "empowered" by divorce.

Loss of custody presents a much more severe emotional problem. Custodial parents, almost always mothers, gain valued roles. As they become breadwinners and heads of their households, their self-esteem grows. But noncustodial parents, almost always fathers, lose these valued roles. As a result, their self-esteem withers.[49] Besides, divorced mothers usually have more extensive support networks than divorced fathers. At the very least, they usually have their children to provide them with emotional support.

Gender expectations make the problem even worse for divorced fathers. Men are expected to suffer in silence no matter what happens to them. "Whereas a mother who has lost custody of her children elicits ... immediate sympathy for the hurt the loss must cause her, fathers are somehow expected not to suffer equally when the same happens to them."[50] Indeed, they are usually suspected of having caused their divorces in the first place.

But what about "visitation rights"? Braver agrees with David Blanken-horn, a pioneer on this topic, who says that divorce and fatherhood, by def-inition, are irreconcilable. The challenge for many is almost insurmount-able. A father with permission to receive his children as visitors must

devise, essentially unassisted, an entirely new household for those occasions when his children come to visit. He must start over, reinvent everything, construct an alternative family life with his children – complete with new rules, new routines, new expectations, and new father-child relationships. Most crucially, he must accomplish this feat in a home in which his children do not live ... [and in which] virtually all parental control resides with the custodial parent. Compared to the mother, the father is largely without power or even knowledge ... Visiting father-hood almost always becomes disempowered fatherhood, a simulacrum of paternal capacity.[51]

The result, as everyone knows, is that fathers in this position focus on merely entertaining their children and supplying them with presents. In other words, they try to become big friends rather than real fathers. And children can tell the difference. They know that love and respect cannot be bought.

A system that can take away most of a seriously involved father's income has driven many to destitution and some to suicide.[52] According to sociologist Augustine Kposowa, longitudinal studies show that divorced men are nine times as likely as divorced women to commit sui-cide.[53] Given the draconian measures taken by countless bureaucrats and sixty thousand plainclothes agents – garnishing the wages of delinquent fathers, using computers to trace their whereabouts, revoking their licenses (even if their jobs depend on driving), confiscating their assets, and throwing them in jail but not necessarily allowing them any contact with their children – how many of us would not, placed in that position, become desperate?[54]

The fifth misconception is that divorced fathers seldom bother to sup-port their children. According to the study by Brinig and Allen, couples are statistically less likely to divorce in states that presume joint custody. And when they do, fathers are less likely to lag behind in their child support payments. In fact, the compliance rate is 87% to 90%.[55] "'Custody is now a way – in some marriages the only way – for women to achieve a real show of force over men,' Dr. Brinig said. 'If you remove that distortion, it's apt to change the way men and women relate to each other and to their kids. Fathers are likely to spend more time with kids if they can expect to still see them if the marriage doesn't work out. Women will be more likely to see men as parenting partners, and less likely to use divorce as a power play.'"[56]

For all the feminist rhetoric against deadbeat dads, Ronald Henry notes, "when mothers are ordered to pay child support, their compliance rate is lower than that of fathers."[57] Braver, too, discusses this problem.

Virtually all the researchers who arrived at the conclusion that fathers are overwhelmingly not paying child support used only one source of data in arriving at their findings: the custodial mothers ... The same bias, of course, would likely apply to any answers given by the non-custodial parent ... For the Census officials and other researchers to come to their conclusions by asking only mothers and not allowing fathers to be heard, is equivalent to a judge making a decision in a case after denying one party to a disagreement the opportunity to take the stand. No judge would think of doing this, and our system of justice specifically precludes it, because we intuitively realize that people tend to tell their story in a way that makes themselves look good and their adversary look bad ... mothers furnish the information about whether they are receiving child support, and divorced mothers can hardly be considered unbiased sources ... Not a single one of the previous researchers or census officials indicated that questioning only mothers may have been a problem. Nowhere in any published reference to the figures was the appropriate qualifying phrase "according to the custodial parent" included.[58]

The sixth misconception is that divorced fathers spend little or no time with their children. They are known as "runaway dads." Has there been an epidemic of fathers abandoning their children? Braver found that very few fathers did so. Those who did, moreover, almost always did so because of unemployment. Actually, he argues, mothers are implicated in the problem.

According to the evidence we examined, vastly fewer fathers than conventional wisdom recognizes appear to have stopped seeing their children and become the runaway dads the bad divorce-dad image portrays. And what about the ones who *have* disconnected from their children? The answer ... suggests that non-visitation, which is undeniably harmful to most children (as well as the father), is caused substantially by mothers' recalcitrance. Clearly, in the view of fathers, more contact is prevented by the choices of the custodial parent, not by their own choice. And most disturbing, many fathers whose visitation rights have been trampled on have little legal recourse to become what society loudly proclaims it wants of them: to be a father to their child.[59]

Some fathers do become "runaway dads," true, but that is no reason for the system to encourage this phenomenon.

At least six problems are inherent in our legal systems: systemic bias against fathers, gross inefficiency, Kafkaesque bureaucracies, scams that serve the interests of everyone but fathers and children, the criminalization of fathers, and vested interests.

Systemic bias against fathers prevails in the methods used to calculate child support payments. Some of these methods were created for welfare families but extended to middle-class families, for instance, which distorts calculations for the latter.[60] Here is a partial list of the flawed assumptions on which they are based:

- authorities use various mathematical models to calculate support payments, but each is of dubious value for one reason or another;[61]
- they ignore the income of custodial parents, which leaves all costs to non-custodial parents;[62]
- they assume that children should have the same standard of living as they had before, even though this is usually a very unrealistic goal for non-custodial parents, who must support two or more households instead of one;[63]
- they assume that the amount collected from non-custodial parents should rise as their income rises, even though income has nothing to do with the actual cost of maintaining children;[64]
- they assume that non-custodial parents will have little or no contact with their children,[65] even though they might live together almost half of the time, and they therefore ignore the fact that noncustodial parents must pay not only for all expenses while the children are living with them but also for all expenses while the children are living with their custodial parents;[66]
- they assume that only custodial parents deserve tax breaks such as credits and deductions;[67] and
- they assume that the amount should be fixed and therefore unrelated to specific or changing circumstances such as the ages of children (costs varying considerably according to age), the existence of previous or later children, and even the fact that some "children" have become adults.[68]

We would add here that these schemes are flawed for political reasons, too. According to Roger Gay, the amounts awarded are often increased arbitrarily because of pressure from feminist lobby groups.[69] Fathers pay heavily in lawyer and court costs to fight these arbitrarily increased amounts.

One result of systemic bias against divorced fathers is to support the assumption that they become "deadbeat dads" due to lack of interest in their children, since the law penalizes those who actually do try to take an active interest in their children. Why be surprised or even shocked, therefore, when many fathers act accordingly? This is a self-fulfilling prophecy. Another result is to support the glorification of single mothers. If single mothers can do everything necessary for their children, helped only by child support payments or welfare payments, then why expect fathers to take an active interest in family life at all? (Did we say "glorification"? Yes, we did. More about that in due course.) Yet other results include destitution and occasionally even suicide.[70] Consider the case of a Canadian man. He had been married to his employer, a physician who had paid him a handsome salary and wrote off the expenses for tax purposes. When they divorced, he had to take an eight-dollar-an-hour job. Nonetheless, he was required to pay child support based on the much higher salary earned previously. He lost more money by trying to get the payment adjusted to his new circumstances. (Noncustodial parents are forced to spend a lot of money, by the way, if they decide to challenge court rulings.) Once, when he was two days late, his ex-wife tried to have him jailed. Forced to live in his car, he committed suicide in 1999 by inhaling the exhaust fumes.[71]

The second problem inherent in our legal systems is inefficiency. Nicholas Riccardi and Greg Krikorion present some telling examples of injustice in the United States due to sheer inefficiency – inefficiency that, we strongly suspect, would never be tolerated if women suffered from it. Officials of Los Angeles County have admitted, for instance, to going after the wrong men for child support payments approximately 350 times a month.[72] Many men are never even informed of their child custody hearings and are then charged huge amounts in arrears, although required payments are sometimes impossibly high in any case. They must pay up, moreover, even if access to their children is legally denied or illegally prevented. And when their wages decline, their required payments do not. According to K.C. Wilson, the evidence of compliance with American child support legislation is less than edifying after two decades of reform. "Billions of dollars a year, hundreds of thousands of fathers in jail, seized assets, suspended licences, terminated business, and government taking on the management of all child support has not [increased] compliance."[73] And what does all that mean for women? "Single mothers are no better off. Indeed, [the system] may be counter-productive."[74] Wilson suggests several reasons. The system is impersonal. Many of these men are in jail, too, which hardly helps them pay up. The amounts required, in short, push too many men beyond their ability to pay.[75]

The third problem involves Kafkaesque bureaucracies. Some cases are truly ludicrous. One American father had to support an adult. Why? Because child support ends only when children leave school, under federal law, which can occur many years after they come of age. A minor was forced to support a child of the adult woman who had been convicted of statutorily raping him. An octogenarian invalid was forced to support a child of the housekeeper who had assaulted him. A man shackled with an electronic ankle bracelet was forced to support his twenty-one-year-old "child" at college even though his twelve-year-old child lacked medical care.[76] In Canada, too, fathers have been forced to support adult children. These cases are anomalous, it is true, but enough of them occur to indicate the need for correction in the name of, if nothing else, common sense.

The fourth problem involves scams. Fostered directly or indirectly by systemic bias against fathers, scams often indicate collusion between public and private interests. Robert Williams, a paid consultant with the United States Department of Health and Human Services, created a scheme to increase the amount of child support significantly: two and a half times as much as the earlier system. When Congress produced a deadline for states to adopt his scheme if they wanted to continue receiving federal funds, many did so. Meanwhile, Williams was developing his own child support consulting business and collection agency: Policy Studies Inc. By 1996, he had more contracts than anyone else in the private sector. Moreover, the number of his employees had grown from three to five hundred, and his company received between 10% and 32% of all the money collected.[77] When child support payments were high, there were many delinquents. When collection was left to the private sector, therefore, he made a lot of money. As for the states, they made between 6% and 10% on each dollar collected. In addition, they received two-thirds of the operating costs of the scheme and 90% of the computer costs. The federal government spent over $2 billion in 1996, according to Baskerville, which meant that California was able to collect $144 million and New York $49.1 million.[78]

Officials and scholars often rely on questionable or even false statistics, as Lenore Weitzman and the bureaucrats who were influenced by her did, to legitimate the bias. In Canada, however, the government itself actually resorted to covering up its bias. Remember the formula that was appended to the Guidelines? This was appended only in theory. It was very hard for anyone to find either the formula or information about it. Even members of Parliament had not seen it when they passed the guidelines into law! After almost two years, an eight-page report on the formula was published.[79] And its circulation list was very restricted.[80] The Family Law Committee of the Canadian Bar Association was excluded, for instance, as were justices of the Supreme Court. Member of Parliament Roger Gallaway had to invoke the Freedom of Information Act to get his copy. "Documents recently released by the Department of Justice under a Freedom of Information request," writes Alar Soever, "indicate that a conscious decision was made by the Department of Justice to limit circulation of this report."[81] We find it astonishing that someone had to use the Freedom of Information Act to find basic information on the economic condition of so many citizens. But that is how ideological interest groups operate: behind the scenes rather than in full view, very often, or through bureaucracies rather than legislatures.

According to evidence presented by Soever, at any rate, the Child Support Team of Justice Canada, which created the formula, feared that releasing it would raise awkward questions. And with good reason. They must have known that it would inevitably result in serious disadvantages for noncustodial parents, including those who make their payments. Knowing that publication would be delayed, the Child Support Team noted in a summary for the minister of justice that its focus had been on implementation rather than theory and that, in any case, the document was too technical for anyone who was not a mathematician or an economist! Why, then, tax the intelligence of ordinary citizens?[82] Glenn Cheriton points out, moreover, that officials removed two male economists from the child support team and left only female lawyers.[83] This arrogance would have caused an uproar if word had leaked out in time.

The most common kind of scam involves paternity fraud: when a woman cheats on her partner and gives birth to another man's baby but her partner nevertheless has to pay child support.[84] The problem faced by Carnell Smith, for instance, is not only ludicrous but also disturbing. Here is his story. American law presumes that children born within wedlock are those of the husband. So why does Smith, who is not the biological father of his former girlfriend's child, still have to pay child support? He took his case through the lower courts. Unsuccessful, he took it to the Supreme Court. On 12 June 2002, the Supreme Court refused to hear it.[85] But many paternity tests, 28% of them in 1999, reveal that the presumed fathers are not in fact the biological ones.[86] Smith's case rested on the grounds of "fraud deception," because the "victim is persecuted for the actions of the guilty party" (that is, the biological father).[87] This is unheard of in any other circumstances. We will return to one important implication of this case. Meanwhile, here is another case.

Damon Adams had a DNA test which showed that he was not the father of a ten-year-old girl born during his former marriage. But the Michigan court rejected this evidence and ordered him to continue paying $23,000 a year in child support. Adams, like many other men across the country, lobbied the state legislature to prohibit paternity fraud. Approximately a dozen states have done so.[88] But others, including Michigan, cite what they consider more important interests. "Most states design their family laws," writes Martin Kanisdorf, "to protect what they call 'the interests of the child.' That means siding with the child's financial and emotional needs and against supposed fathers who want to avoid paying for tricycles and braces. Taxpayers also have a big stake in child support collections, which have grown to $18 billion annually and cover 20 million children. If men who are paying child support no longer have to and authorities can't find the real fathers, welfare agencies will get the bill for family assistance."[89] In other words, the laudable goal of protecting children gives the state license to disregard the rights of adult citizens and even to reward those who violate the law. Kanisdorf's overtly cynical mentality is evident from his assumption that the only fathers affected are rich men who cannot be bothered to pay for the necessities of children, even, in some cases, the children of wives who are having affairs with other men. If biological fathers cannot be found (which might not be a problem in the first place if everyone was given a DNA test at birth just as everyone is now fingerprinted at birth), then it is surely more fitting for a community to bear the cost out of compassion than for innocent citizens to be punished out of sheer political expediency. That turns them into scapegoats for public fear and outrage over social breakdown.

Moreover, Kanisdorf ignores one important need of children: the need to know who their biological fathers are and thus who they themselves are. Has that become irrelevant to legislators? As one father, paying $1,400 a month for a child whom he has never met and who was the result of his wife's adultery, put it, "I can get out of jail for murder based on DNA evidence, but I can't [use DNA evidence to] get out of child support payments."[90] Meanwhile, financially strapped, he and his new wife and their three children live with his in-laws, and he has lost his driver's license for missing support payments.

There are women who deliberately become pregnant by refusing to take the pill, not telling their partners, and then refusing to have abortions. Nonetheless, some of them claim child support. This situation prompted Peter Wallis to sue his former girlfriend. "Some say that it is his responsibility to ensure that such an 'accident' does not happen," says Mary Ann Sieghart. "He could have worn a condom. That is true, but a relationship in which people are living together, as these two were, presupposes a certain level of trust."[91] Moreover, says Sieghart, this case brings up an analogy that should disturb women. They are allowed either to abort or not to abort, after all, and with or without the knowledge of fathers. But what about an analogous right to choose for men? Wallis did not choose to have a child (which makes him analogous to a woman who fails to use contraception), but he could not insist on an abortion (even though a pregnant woman would be allowed to end her pregnancy) and therefore ended up by being ordered to pay child support for years to come. Women who make mistakes are allowed an escape clause, in short, but men who make mistakes are told to shut up and pay up.

In view of all these scams concocted by both private individuals and public institutions, Baskerville comments on how hard it would be for Americans not to believe "that a lucrative racket now is cynically using our children as weapons and tools to enrich lawyers and provide employment for judges and bureaucrats. Rather than pursuing ever greater numbers of fathers with ever more draconian punishments, the Justice Department should be investigating the kind of crimes it was created to pursue – such as kidnapping, extortion and racketeering – in the nation's family courts."[92] The statistics on fathers who abandon their families are insignificant, he adds, when compared with those that indicate "the scale on which families are being taken over by a destructive and dangerous machine consisting of judges, lawyers, psychotherapists, social workers, bureaucrats and women's groups."[93]

Paternity fraud is a problem in Canada, too.[94] A man in Ontario was forced to pay the full amount for a son, even though the boy had been kept away from him since birth and even though the boy's adoptive father, too, was paying the full amount. Listen to the morally dubious reasoning proclaimed by the Court of Appeal in that case: "While it is true that neither [the child] nor Mr. Zaver has had the opportunity of a personal relationship with the other, Mr. Zaver has had a holiday from support for many years. There is no indication that it will be an undue financial burden for him to pay support in accordance with the Ontario guidelines."[95] This is why fathers are now lobbying to make DNA testing mandatory at or before birth and also to abolish the obligation of paying child support in cases of fraud.

The "experts" have said very little about the biological connection between fathers and their children. That silence has been challenged by fathers who demand DNA tests to establish paternity and thus eliminate the possibility of being forced to pay for children who could and should be supported by their biological fathers. Some women resist that change. For one thing, it might reveal that they have had liaisons with men other than their current husbands or partners. If the latter turn out not to be the biological fathers, moreover, these women might be left with all the expenses. At any rate, the current system is one of several factors that combine to blur the biological facts and trivialize the biological importance of fatherhood. (More about single mothers and reproductive autonomy for women in due course.)[96]

This desire to blur biological facts helps explain another ruling of the Ontario Court of Appeal, letting mothers have sole authority for providing their children with surnames. It said that "a mother can acknowledge a father for custody or child support reasons but does not have to acknowledge him on a birth registry for naming purposes."[97] Here is the reason cited by Justice Kathryn Feldman: "[T]here will be circumstances where a mother will have the ongoing responsibility for the child, and should not be forced to have the child linked by name with the biological father."[98] How to explain the discrepancy between acknowledging him when it comes to paying for child support but refusing to do so when it comes to naming his child? This explanation was offered: "Because acknowledgement involves a volitional act of admitting knowledge of a fact, it is possible for a person to acknowledge something to be true in one context, but to decline to do so in another context."[99] This double talk amounts to sheer moral expediency. According to earlier rules, if "the mother acknowledges the father in the birth registry and both parents certify the child's birth but do not agree on a surname, the child shall be given a surname consisting of both parents' surnames hyphenated in alphabetical order."[100] The same controversy arose in British Columbia. That province's Court of Appeal had made a similar ruling the year before. But when it was appealed to Canada's Supreme Court, the judge ruled that fathers should, in fact, have their names on birth certificates.[101]

The fifth problem inherent in our legal systems is that divorced fathers are criminalized in both the United States and Canada, directly in the former and indirectly in the latter. In the United States, all noncustodial parents – and they include those who *do* comply with child support regulations – are now being monitored by the criminal-justice system and thus being treated as criminals or potential criminals. "Under the guise of pursuing deadbeat dads," writes Baskerville, "we now are seeing mass incarcerations without trial, without charge and without counsel, while the media and civil libertarians look the other way. We also have government officials freely entering the homes and raiding the bank accounts of citizens who are accused of nothing and simply helping themselves to whatever they find – including their children, their life savings and their private papers and effects, all with hardly a word of protest noted."[102] Not only are problem cases filtered through criminal enforcement agencies, moreover, but so are all cases of child support. Otherwise, states would not be eligible for federal funds. "This both further criminalizes the fathers and enables the government to inflate the amount of collections it makes," says Baskerville, "which helps divert attention from the fact that the program operates at a consistent loss."[103]

This creates a situation that would endanger any free society. "Never before," said the *Washington Post*, "have federal officials had the legal authority and technological ability ... to keep tabs on Americans accused of nothing."[104] Fathers are under surveillance merely because they *pay* child support. The situation is ominous, according to Steve Dasbach, in view of the precedents in totalitarian societies. "[G]overnment bureaucrats will soon have the power to deny you a job, and the ability to monitor your income, assets, and debts ... This law turns the presumption of innocence on its head and forces every American to prove their innocence to politicians, bureaucrats, and computers."[105] And surveillance is by no means the only problem. As Baskerville points out, guilt and innocence are fatally blurred "since officials are monitoring citizens who owe [money for child support], those whose obligations are paid up, and those who are not under any order at all. The presumption of guilt against those who are obeying the law was revealed by one official who boasted to the [*Washington*] *Post* that 'we don't give them an opportunity to become deadbeats.'" When a noncustodial father is charged with civil contempt, he "must prove his innocence without a formal charge, without counsel, and without facing a jury of his peers."[106] The burden of proof is often on defendants. And fathers are put in jail without trial. "Those who face trumped-up accusations of child abuse also must prove their innocence before they can hope to see their children. Yet now it is well established that most child abuse takes place in the homes of single mothers. A recent study from the Department of Health and Human Services, or HHS, found that "almost two-thirds [of child abusers] were females." Given that male perpetrators are not necessarily fathers but much more likely to be boyfriends and stepfathers, fathers emerge as the least likely child abusers."[107]

Canadian laws governing child support are civil, not criminal. Even so, courts have the authority to put offenders in jail. In some ways, civil law creates even more problems for the accused than criminal law. In criminal cases, after all, defendants are entitled to lawyers and legal aid. Not so in civil cases. The courts need not provide either in default hearings, for instance, if defendants lack proof of insufficient income.

The sixth problem involves vested interests, which people at all levels of the legal system want to protect. Think of the political factors involved. American judges are appointed at the higher levels and elected in some states at lower levels. Either way, the process is a political one. Elected judges are politically influenced by public opinion, after all, and appointed judges are selected according to the recommendations of committees made up of lawyers belonging to the political party in power and appointed by the elected governor or legislators. Court judges are "elected or appointed by commissions dominated by lawyers who have an interest in maximizing litigation. Family court judges wield extensive powers of patronage, thanks to their power to appoint attorneys and expert witnesses."[108] Worse, they are in league with enforcement agencies. No wonder family court judges are often honoured by enforcement groups. Seidenberg puts it this way:

There are intrinsic and extrinsic political influences that come to bear on the judge's decision-making habits. By intrinsic politics I mean the judge's immediate constituents – those people and organizations the judge comes in contact with on a regular basis – the people who might have some say about his reappointment. Essentially this means the lawyers who appear before him, the local bar association, and the representatives of two large bureaucracies – the Child Support Enforcement Agency and Child Protective Services. Frequently, Child Support Enforcement and Child Protective Services are housed in the same building as the court ... The extrinsic politics involves the larger political picture: such as the electoral influences on the state legislators (some of whom may also be lawyers who appear before the judge) and the popular mood.[109]

Moreover, notes Baskerville, we should consider another form of vested interest in the United States. The National Child Support Enforcement Association, according to its own website, consists of "state and local agencies, judges, court masters, hearing officers, district attorneys, government and private attorneys, social workers, caseworkers, advocates, and other child support professions," as well as "corporations that partner with government to enforce child support."[110] He sees the American family court system itself as a major problem, calling it a "secretive" institution that operates behind closed doors, seldom records proceedings, and keeps no statistics on decisions."[111]

In other words, it is made up entirely of people who have a financial interest in having children separated from their fathers. Setting child support levels is a political process conducted largely by groups that benefit from divorce. Parents are largely excluded. In about half the states, the guidelines used to set child-support levels are devised not by the legislature but by courts and enforcement agencies, and in all states the courts and enforcement agencies play a dominant role in setting the guidelines. Under the separation of powers we do not normally permit police and courts to make the laws they enforce and interpret, since this would create an obvious conflict of interest.[112]

Feminists, too, have vested interests in these courts. Women are the ones who most often seek divorce, after all, and want to win custody. Not surprisingly, they often end up on the commissions reviewing guidelines by representing "custodial parent advocacy groups." Men are the ones who most often have to pay child support. Until very recently, however, they had no advocacy groups to represent them.

In the Canadian system, too, vested interests can be found at every level. F.L. Morton and Rainer Knopff have written about the "Court Party,"[113] for instance, referring to a coalition of groups from academics to legal departments in government, law reform commissions, human rights commissions, administrative tribunals, and the courts themselves. (We discuss these topics in chapter 10.)

With all this in mind, consider this discussion of vested interests with the words of Seidenberg:

The most *overt* discrimination in the United States is not against women, or blacks, or hispanics, but against men in a specific situation – divorce-custody proceedings.

Other groups may suffer broader and deeper discrimination. The discrimination against blacks, to take an obvious example, affects more people in numerous areas of life. But the largest part of this discrimination is subtle or hidden because no one today would want to be labelled a racist. The discrimination against men in divorce-custody proceedings, on the other hand, is blatant and shameless. Protective orders, which evict men from their homes at a moment's notice, are issued without evidence; restraining orders are issued without testimony; at times custody is awarded without testimony; and false child abuse allegations against fathers are rampant.[114]

It is hard to avoid the conclusion that the whole system, whether in the United States or Canada, is corrupt. And that is a dangerous situation in any society, because it fosters rampant cynicism. At a public meeting in Toronto, family-law lawyer Gene Colman noted that "gender bias is indeed a reality in Canada's courts."[115] Because most Canadian laws are written in gender-neutral terms, "the problem lies not with the wording of the laws, but with the judicial interpretation of the statutes as applied to the facts of individual cases."[116] Apart from anything else, he added, this encourages disrespect for the judicial system. Colman referred to family-law lawyer Carey Linde, who had observed that these interpretations result from "judicially assumed presumptions" that "have never been put to the test of evidence, but spring from and are maintained out of gender biases still ingrained in the system."[117] He referred also to criminal-law lawyer Edward Greenspan, who had observed that "feminist influence has amounted to intimidation, posing a potential danger to the independence of the judiciary" and that "feminists have entrenched their ideology in the Supreme Court of Canada and have put all contrary views beyond the pale."[118] These are very serious charges, especially because they come from lawyers: insiders with professional experience of the system. Because justice must not only be done but also be seen to be done, Canadians would do well to take these charges seriously.

What about reform? We have reached a turning point. Until recently, we heard heated rhetoric from only one side: mothers and their advocates. Now, though, we hear it from the other side as well: fathers and their advocates. Reform, therefore, is at least possible.

The American child-support industry now affects enough men to have generated dozens of books that are critical of the system, and most of these books are read by both Americans and Canadians. We have already mentioned Braver's *Divorced Dads* and Seidenberg's *Father's Emergency Guide*, but there are many others.[119] Divorced fathers have organized support groups, too, some of which can be found within local communities and on the Internet. They function in two basic ways. First, they offer therapy; hapless fathers write in to tell their stories. Second, they offer ideas. Some are directed toward individual fathers in need, others toward society as a whole. Among the latter are proposals for law reform that are often accompanied by advice for those willing to take action as lobbyists.

One website provides visitors with an eighty-five page manual on how fathers can beat the system.[120] The rhetoric is overtly confrontational. "Powerful tips and information," according to the first page, that "those in the system don't want you to know about [t]hat will help you get the most out of the family court system and help make the system more accountable to you, your family and to all families who may be taken advantage of by the system after you."[121] It is very similar in both purpose and tone to the kind of manual that has been addressed to women for many years – and can still be found at many feminist websites (which we illustrate in appendix 9).

Among the many practical tips given at this site are the following: have witnesses present whenever possible when dealing with the courts and with the social workers or psychologists assigned to your case; tape or videotape interactions with them whenever possible; do background checks on everyone assigned to your case – judges, lawyers, and clinicians – to learn about flawed methods, examples of unaccountability, dissatisfied clients, political or ideological affiliations; hire your own experts so that opposing reports can be challenged; insist on seeing written reports by all those involved so that you can check their interpretations and statistics; file complaints against anyone involved who exhibits (or tries to hide) any sign of bias; and go public if these complaints are ignored.

The mobilization of fathers has already led to some minor legal reforms in the United States. The Deadbeat Parents Punishment Act of 1998, for instance, streamlined the process for deciding which cases require federal investigation and prosecution. These cases must be referred from a United States attorney's office, now, not from individual lawyers or advocacy groups. This change offers some protection to fathers in these more serious cases (although it hardly compensates for increasing the status of violations and penalties in the first place, which, as we have already mentioned, the act also does). Some states have introduced joint-parenting legislation. Others have now adjusted or even forgiven arrears.[122] Still others have fixed an even worse problem, which gives men in Carnell Smith's position some basis for hope. Ohio and Georgia, at least, have passed legislation that exonerates men after DNA tests prove that they are not the biological fathers of children in question.

Moreover, the authority of Congress to interpret the Commerce Clause broadly – that is, to use the official lingo, overbroadly – is being challenged.

Under the Child Support Recovery Act, as we have observed, failing to comply with an interstate court order for child support has been a criminal offense. According to the Supreme Court, however, this act goes beyond the authority of Congress under the Commerce Clause.[123]

In Canada, the Ontario Court of Appeal agreed in 2003 that the Federal Child Support Guidelines should be used with caution. The story is worth telling here. Joseph Contino had applied to reduce the amount of child support for his son, because he now had physical custody of the boy for 50% of the time. The judge agreed and changed the amount from $550 to $100 a month, citing the shared-custody rules in section 9 of the guidelines. The mother appealed this decision, and it was overturned by another judge who actually increased the amount to $688, citing the best interest of the child. Once again, Contino challenged the status quo. He brought his case to the Ontario Court of Appeal, which ruled that it should indeed be assessed according to the rules for shared custody. This time, the judges calculated that Contino owed only $399 a month.[124] The guidelines were still useful in providing some level of predictability (for the child) and objectivity (for the judge), they ruled, but they should not be used mechanically – which is to say, without considering the particular circumstances of specific people.[125]

Finally, remember the Ontario case in which a judge ruled that a father's surname need not appear on a birth certificate? That ruling might turn out to have been a legal landmark, because the Supreme Court overturned it on the ground that sexual discrimination against men by the lower courts had violated section 15(1) of the Charter, which stipulates sexual equality.

Advocates of equal rights for divorced fathers and mothers want more reforms. For one thing, they want a presumption of joint custody. American fathers, as we say, have already won that reform in two states, and Canadian fathers are lobbying for it at the federal level. McLean points to evidence from the United States. According to one study,

states which obtained high levels of joint physical custody awards in 1989 and 1990 showed significantly greater declines in divorce rates in the following five years, compared with other states. Divorce rates declined nearly four times faster in states with high joint physical custody (known in Canada as shared custody), compared with states where shared custody is rare. As a result, the states with high levels of shared custody now have significantly lower divorce rates on average than other states. States that favoured sole custody, on the other hand, also had more divorces involving children.[126]

In addition, fathers want better models for calculating child support payments. In the United States, R. Mark Rogers and Donald Bieniewicz argue that "each parent has an equal duty to bear the financial costs of rearing children. It only follows that both parents have an equal right to share the cost offsets of tax benefits attributable to the same children."[127] To achieve this, they developed the Cost Shares model, which is based on actual expenditures in single-parent households in various categories, the average gross income of both parents, and a fair distribution of tax benefits.[128]

In Canada, fathers propose legal recognition of at least three underlying principles to improve the guidelines. They argue that "child support is for the care and maintenance of children; [that] ... both parents have an equal duty to support their children; [and that] ... all relevant circumstantial information may effect the amount of the award."[129] The information might include ability to pay, for instance, or ability to take care of yourself after paying. In addition, they want several other modifications. Any legitimate child support scheme should be not only logically and legally coherent but also based on a clear definition with "criteria to determine whether the presumptive award is just and appropriate ... It is also apparent that the law must ... make a relational statement about the obligations of the parents and provide the courts with the proper authority to consider all relevant factors before making a final judgment."[130] The court should calculate a separate payment for each child, which would prevent noncustodial parents from being forced to support adults. (As it is now, once again, some fathers must pay until the youngest child reaches maturity.)[131] And calculations should be based on the real cost of rearing children, which should be shared by both parents according to the income of each. These measures would require a new formula. It all boils down to acknowledging the actual time spent by the children in each household and the actual cost of each stay.[132]

One possible bulwark against the unfair existing formula that underlies the guidelines, says Soever, is the Divorce Act. The purpose of child support payments, according to the Supreme Court's interpretation, is "maintenance of the children, rather than household equalization or spousal support."[133] This interpretation could be used to reverse the formula, which states that its purpose is to equalize "the financial circumstances of the two households," to make the households "equally well off" through the transfer of payments. The formula transforms child support into "household support," says Soever, which contradicts the Divorce Act.[134] Because the term "household support" is more nebulous than either "child support" or "spousal support," instead of being used for children at all, it might be used for almost anything receiving parents want. That arrangement does little for children, but it clearly does a great deal for custodial parents. "Child support" or "spousal support" turns into "household support" or "domestic support" and "equality" into "equity."

Another possible bulwark against injustice to divorced fathers might be Canada's Charter of Rights and Freedoms. For Soever, this legislation should be used to support the claim that economic hardship for men created by the formula constitutes discrimination under section 15 (which presumably guarantees sexual equality).

A parliamentary committee listened to Canadian fathers and studied the merits of joint parenting. In a report called "For the Sake of the Children," it proposed an interpretation of the Divorce Act that would presume (barring unusual circumstances) that arrangement. This should have solved at least some problems, right? Not so fast. Ideological feminists refused to stand idly by. In fact, their rhetoric heated up. They used a primary feminist strategy that we have already mentioned and will mention again: creating social and economic change through linguistic legerdemain – ideally, by establishing new terms and, alternatively, by creating new definitions or new interpretations of existing ones. Using the Internet, they mobilized their constituencies to isolate any potential legal changes that might benefit fathers. In both the United States and Canada, then, officials have used language to suggest change in the direction of joint parenting but nonetheless have actually prevented real change. (For a detailed discussion, see appendix 9.)

Because only adults are involved in public debate and because our book is about men in relation to women, much of this chapter has revolved around the conflicting rights of fathers and mothers. In this section, we will pay particular attention to the link between gynocentrism (laws that attend to the needs of women alone) and misandry (rhetoric that turns fathers into "deadbeats" or worse, even if most of them obey the laws). Directly or indirectly, however, the needs of children are always involved as well. And in spite of all the rhetoric on both sides about divorce being better for children than the alternative, in spite of all the jive talk about "quality time," the fact is that – from the perspective of children – a divorce can be disastrous (unless, of course, the marriage has involved violence or extreme psychological damage).

In the United States, 75 percent of juvenile delinquents, 71 percent of pregnant teenagers, and 90 percent of teenage runaways, are children from fatherless homes. Such statistics are endless. Whether the subject is gang involvement, drug abuse, alcoholism, scholastic failure, or teen suicide, the incidence among children from fatherless homes far exceeds the incidence among children from homes where the father is present. Our culture's hostility toward men has reached a dimension where it no longer affects only individual families, but is tearing apart the social fabric.[135]

Beyond the needs of adults and even of children are those of society as a whole. Without major reforms to the legal systems discussed in this chapter, society will become even more fragmented and polarized than it already is. We are already moving toward a society in which women have colonized reproduction, along with childrearing, and men will have less and less incentive to participate fully in family life and more and more penalties if any problems arise. Think of all this as a series of symbolic messages.[136] Some are sent to boys and men, others to girls and women. Some are about society, others about identity.

One message to girls and women is that they should strive for complete autonomy. That means liberation, freedom, or even separation from men. And that reveals a profoundly gynocentric worldview. But it reveals a profoundly misandric one, too, because it implies that all men should be kept under permanent suspicion of being violent, selfish, and controlling. This much is clear not only from the laws under discussion but also from the ideological rhetoric about those laws.

At one time – in this respect, the world of only forty years ago now seems as remote as that of four hundred years ago – single mothers (and their "illegitimate" children) were stigmatized. They were the objects of either scorn or pity. In our time, they are not merely exempt from any stigma but seen as role models. To get this far, we had to go through several transitions.

The first was from single mothers as immoral women to single mothers as victims. And from the ranks of victims, as we have been told for decades by talk show hosts and political activists, come heroes. There is nothing heroic in being a victim at the individual level, to be sure, but there is a reward that translates directly into political power on a collective level: uncritical public sympathy. Designated victim classes, not only women in general but single mothers in particular, are lauded merely for enduring and triumphing over obstacles. Underlying this glorification at the emotional level is manipulation at the political level. Here is one example, the response of a journalist to a Swedish study on the many problems faced by children of single parents. "If we accept," writes Janet Bagnall, "that parents are doing the work of bringing up children on behalf of all society – and I think we should – then single parents clearly need more help."[137] And by "single parents," she means single women: "It is not fair to expect a single person to keep it together for herself and her children."[138] She does not consider that reducing the number of single mothers in the first place would be an even better solution than spending more tax dollars on them and thus encouraging the phenomenon. That would involve a radical rethinking of conventional wisdom on divorce, let alone of feminist ideology. Not surprisingly, single mothers organize politically, with massive support from feminist organizations, for economic support from governments.

The next transition was from seeing single mothers as victims to seeing them as heroines or role models, which coincided with the transition from single motherhood as a phenomenon primarily of the lower class to single motherhood as a phenonemon of the middle and upper classes as well. Many of these women were not undereducated and underemployed victims of irresponsible men. They were sophisticated and upwardly mobile executives, entrepreneurs, professionals, and academics in their thirties. Rather than wait for the right man to come along and, if they waited too long, face the prospect of having to "marry down" or not at all, they preferred to have children right away. Rather than put their careers on hold while caring for young children, in other words, they chose to have their cake and eat it too by combining motherhood and career. Caring for children took time away from work, true, but looking for husbands took up even more time. Besides, these women had the financial resources to pay not only for daycare but also for part-time or full-time nannies. In short, these women decided to have it all. Whether this was a blessing for their children or not, of course, that was another matter. Researchers are still troubled by the problem of fatherless children – this is now emerging as a major topic of academic and political debate – but there are still feminists who advise women not to worry as long as they can provide their children with "quality time" and, perhaps, supply them with "father figures."

One result of this second transition has been the evolution of what is best described as a "single-mothers industry." Like every other industry, this one relies on a growing number of customers and a growing cadre of professionals and experts to service them. It was featured by Susanne Hiller in Canada's *National Post*.[139] The rate of increase for single mothers since 1991, according to Jane Mattes, was four times as high as the rate for married mothers.[140] At least four factors explain the new mentality. First, social acceptance. Single mothers can now expect massive support from their families and friends. Second, the development and industrialization of reproductive technologies. Women who lack husbands or "relationships" with men need no longer wait around as their biological clocks run down. At ReproMed, according to Cathy Ruberto, about 30% of the clients from 2000 to 2001 were "single women in a hurry to become mothers."[141] Third, the "rights revolution." This boils down to the belief that what you want is what society owes you: a right. And fourth, the glorification of heroic single mothers in popular culture (due partly to the glorification of female autonomy by feminists). This factor closes the circle, because it forms the basis for public support.

Women at all levels of society are affected. Consider the iconic status of single mothers such as Calista Flockhart and Angelina Jolie. But not all the women who choose to become single mothers are television or movie stars. Many are just highly educated and upwardly mobile career women. Some of them would like to marry some day, and others would not. What they all really want, with or without husbands, are babies. And organizations such as Single Mothers by Choice, headed by Mattes, are happy to help them out. Not that they need much help in this age of day care and sperm banks or in vitro clinics. Even single women who do not choose mother-hood, the ones who have "accidents," are often portrayed as victims (gar-nering sympathy) who become heroes (garnering admiration) for rearing children alone. No wonder that one single mother interviewed by Hiller said that she had "never received a negative comment."[142] Do these women consider the possibility that their children need fathers? Some do, but they are content with "father figures." Another woman told Hiller that her son "has a grandfather and a stepgrandfather. He has male influences and is a real boy."[143]

The Library of Congress lists no fewer than sixty books on single moth-ering and single parenting.[144] And, as usual, television shows reflect social trends. Consider Miranda on *Sex and the City*, Rachel on *Friends*, Ellenor on *The Practice*, Viveca on *Family Law*. Odd exceptions? Hardly. Refer-ring to the new single mothers, in general, Jane Bock observes that they "have altered the way we look at this issue because they've been successful as single mothers. They are legitimizing single parenthood as an appropri-ate life choice."[145] Legitimate? Appropriate? In which ways? By whose standards? The number of American single mothers between thirty-five and thirty-nine, which reached a new high in 2000 – 64,523, according to the National Center for Health Statistics – is still low in absolute terms but very high in relative terms: six times as high, in fact, as the figure for 1965. This, even as single motherhood among teenagers is declining![146]

Complete reproductive autonomy for women has for years been a major plank in the political platform of ideological feminism. It has been exem-plified best by the Feminist International Network of Resistance to Repro-ductive and Genetic Engineering (FINRRAGE), an organization that is pre-occupied mainly with new reproductive technologies such as in vitro fertilization, although it is equally opposed to "older" technologies such as surrogacy.[147] Members meet regularly, publish a journal, hold conferences, and lobby governments for bans on the use of reproductive technologies. In 1989, Canadian members got the government to set up the Royal Com-mission on New Reproductive Technologies, which produced a report urg-ing the government to take a "cautious" approach – albeit not quite as cau-tious as the original instigators had wanted.

Among the more prominent members of FINRRAGE was Gena Corea. In *The Mother Machine*, she claims that the new reproductive technologies amount to new ways for men to control women.[148] In other words, the participation of men in matters that affect reproduction is just another way of maintaining patriarchal control over women's bodies. Given this point of view, it is hardly surprising that Corea refers to the "subversive sperm" and accuses some countries of "gynocide." By the latter, she refers to sex-selection techniques that would result in the mass killing of female fetuses. But Corea refrains from accusing countries that conscript young men for combat of "androcide."

At the heart of Corea's work is the symbolism of reproduction, what she sees as the continuing problem of society turning women into "breeding machines." Never mind that the same society could be accused of turning men into economic or war machines. Corea would agree, if pressed, but what she fears most is that the "patriarchal urge to self-generate" will lead to artificial wombs or cloning and thus make even these "breeding machines" obsolete and turn reproduction over entirely to men. Never mind that the same technology could be used for parthenogenesis, or asex-ual reproduction, which would make the male contribution obsolete and even lead, by another route, to "androcide." For Corea and her ideological colleagues, new reproductive technologies require a political response, not only for the sake of a few infertile women who have been culturally pres-sured into thinking of themselves as inadequate on that account but for all women. At stake, ultimately, is their identity as women. That is partly why ideological feminists argue for female autonomy. Taken to its logical con-clusion, that means placing reproduction itself in the exclusive control of women. From this it follows that new or old technologies promising female autonomy – contraception, abortion, and artificial insemination by donor – are highly desirable; only those that might lead to male autonomy or at least require negotiation between men and women – sex selection, surro-gacy, and in vitro – should be banned.

Another message to girls and women is that they may feel free to extract as much money from men as they can. As we said in chapter 5, "equity" is a key code word for feminists. Ideological lobby groups have found both direct and indirect ways of embedding it in the fabric of law. What would either the American or the Canadian Supreme Court say about a case challenging the legality of child support systems? Feminists would almost certainly argue that the principle of equity should take precedence over any other consideration. In short, financial equity for women would trump financial support exclusively for children (not to mention equity for men). They would never say so, of course. They would have to do some serious window dressing. But politicians of all stripes are good at window dressing.

One message given to boys and men is discouraging, to say the least: fatherhood can be a nightmare – legal, financial, and emotional – due to the laws governing divorce, custody, and access. These laws are not going to prevent all men from investing in family life, certainly not those who consider marriage a religious covenant, but they have already made many other men think twice before becoming involved in what could easily become a no-win situation. Why invest so heavily in family life, after all, if your children can be taken away from you or even turned against you so easily? At the very moment when men have begun to think about being fathers in ways that their own fathers never considered, being more physically and emotionally available than ever before, they hear that fathers are disposable – except as a financial resource, of course, and ultimately not even as a financial resource, given their replacement by the state and the glorification of single mothers.

Closely related to that message is another: that the bond between mother and child is both emotionally and erotically so powerful, in any case, that not even the bond between mother and father can compete. One overtly political implication is the ultimate autonomy of mothers in family life. One covertly political implication, though, is the ultimate irrelevance of fathers in family life. This message is so prevalent that it surfaces in discussions not only of popular culture in general but also of pornography and even romance novels in particular (which is why we discuss this point of view, based on the psychoanalytical theories of feminists such as Mary O'Brien and Nancy Chodorow, in appendix 5.)

The same laws send an additional and even more disturbing message to boys and men. This one is specifically about women: avoid strong relationships with those who could easily use the law to exploit you or manipulate you into poverty. Men who try cohabitation either as a prelude to marriage or as an arrangement preferred to marriage, for instance, find more and more often that their legal and financial obligations – thanks partly to "palimony" but mainly to the laws we have been discussing here – are almost the same as those of marriage. And the success rates of both arrangements are not exactly encouraging. If things continue moving in the same direction, more and more men will come to believe that the risks of long-term relationships with women outweigh the potential benefits. This is already a problem in Canada, and it could become much worse.

The legal changes brought about directly or indirectly by ideological feminism are just as misandric (though couched in the rhetoric of self-defense) as the artifacts of popular culture that we examined in *Spreading Misandry*.

To conclude, here is a suggestion that no one else has (yet) made: mandatory courses outlining the legal consequences of separation or divorce, especially when children are involved, for every couple preparing to marry (and, on prudential grounds, for every couple planning to cohabit). It is safe to say that very few potential husbands or fathers have even the faintest idea of what these legal consequences would be. They might think twice before entering any marital or quasi-marital relationships at all, true, but even that might be better than waking up too late to the painful reality of being taken to the cleaners by their ex-wives and – worst of all – losing their children. The only alternative to cynicism would be to reform the system so that fathers would have a significant legal investment in family life and would thus be more likely than some now are to make an emotional investment in it as well.

PART THREE

Sex on Trial:
From Liberation to Separation

So far, we have concentrated on economic battles between women and men as they have been waged in courts of law due to legislative changes. We turn now to political battles, also waged in courts of law due to legislative changes, over the meaning of sexual acts. At issue is not whether violence against women (or men) should be taken seriously. Clearly, it should. At issue are the ways in which that has been done.

Everyone agrees that violence is a bad thing and that legal measures are necessary to curb it. But violence *against women* has become an ideological trump card. Every political demand of feminists is backed up, ultimately, by the assertion that failure to comply is tantamount to endorsing violence against women. Everyone agrees that harassment is a bad thing, moreover, and that legal measures are sometimes necessary to curb it. But what happens when many other forms of behaviour, though lamentable, are elided with the ones that cause serious physical or economic harm? Two things.

First, the serious nature of these problems is trivialized. Second, and more important, the polarization between men and women is widened. Although more and more women look with suspicion on the legal measures proposed – and often attained – by ideological feminists, the fact remains that few are either willing or able to reverse the process.

For one thing, many women have been convinced that they ought to fear even the most trivial attentions from men. Also, many women are convinced that every measure taken to protect women from men is at least a symbolic step in the right direction. A few women, however, believe that these measures are necessary for a quite different reason: to discourage contact of any kind between the sexes. These are the ideological feminists, those who believe that heterosexual relations – including those wanted or even initiated by women – are inherently corrupted by a "power imbalance" that renders women utterly incapable of giving their consent. In that case, every heterosexual act involves the rape of a woman. Very few women would agree with that conclusion, but very few are prepared to argue against the inherent logic of an ideology that begins with the isolation of patriarchy – that is, men – as the ultimate source of all problems for women throughout history.

The result is what could be called the victimization industry, a congeries of professional networks, political associations, and lobby groups advocating ever more inclusive definitions of victimization, ever more laws to punish violence, ever more dubious ways of overriding the principle of due process, and ever more serious penalties for those found guilty.

We turn now to several disturbing problems. All of them involve either violence or the threat of violence. And all of them are explained by ideological feminists as evidence of an inherently violent worldview that must be destroyed, root and branch. Even though we discuss these problems in separate chapters, bear in mind that many feminists do *not* see them as separate topics.

In chapter 7, we discuss the legal implications of pornography. In chapter 8, we discuss what has been called the sexual harassment industry, along with its legal implications. Women have indeed come a long way over the past forty years. What began as liberation during the sexual revolution – the adoption of a single standard for women and men – has turned into a legal system that directly or indirectly, explicitly or implicitly, fosters the separation of women from men. In chapter 9, we discuss the most serious problem of all, the touchstone and ultimate trump card of ideological feminists: their legal interpretation of sexual assault, which has come to include everything from touching a woman to raping her. All three have important political implications, of course, as well as other cultural ones.

7

Power v. Pleasure:
The Case of Pornography/Prostitution

Rapists and pimps, representing the interests of normal men, some of whom rape, some of whom buy, seem to have the law of gravity on their side ... No matter what lie they tell, it passes for truth, because the hatred of women underlying the lie is an accepted hatred, a shared and unchallenged set of prejudiced assumptions.[1]

In our sample, men tended to show more activity than women in brain regions associated with *visual* processing ... [which could] shed light on why men so avidly support the worldwide trade in visual pornography.[2]

For many nonideological women and even for many "sensitive" men, the very act of enjoying the sight of pretty women – even fully clothed women – is now equated with sexism. Ken Tucker speaks for them in his review of *The Apprentice*, a reality show in which contestants vie for a job with tycoon Donald Trump. Tucker refers to "Kristi Frank, the camera crew's go-to girl for shots summarizing the action because (and yes, I'm indulging in the sexism *Apprentice* thrives on) she's great looking – but contributes little to most competitions."[3] The fact that a (presumably male) camera crew pays more attention to a woman's looks than to her knowledge might well be sexist. (The functional equivalent would be women who pay more attention to a man's wealth and power than to anything else about him, Trump himself being an excellent example of men in this category.) But Tucker is troubled merely by noticing the fact that Kristi is "great looking." And he assumes correctly that the readers of a mainstream magazine will agree with him. What troubles Tucker has been given a name by feminists: the "objectification of women." It lies at the heart of current controversies over pornography and prostitution (but also at the heart of controversies over sexual harassment and violence against women, which we discuss in the next two chapters).

After a brief introduction on the relation between pornography and prostitution, we will review the legislation governing both and continue with discussions of the various feminist positions on them: the belief that both are based on the subordination and objectification of women, which makes these industries inherently misogynistic; the belief that both should be tolerated in order to avoid abrogating freedom in one form or another; and the belief that both should be valued as venues for the liberation of women from outdated notions of female sexuality. Before concluding, we will provide a larger context for this debate, present some reasons for tolerating pornography and prostitution, and discuss the double standard that has characterized most discussions of this topic.

Feminists have produced a voluminous literature on both pornography and prostitution. Actually, they comprise one topic rather than two. Although they are enacted in different ways and controlled by different laws, ideological feminists claim that the underlying phenomenon is identical. Every basic reason that they cite for opposing one, in fact, they cite for opposing the other as well. And this book is organized with their point of view in mind. According to even moderately ideological feminists, both pornography and prostitution "objectify" women and therefore, they say, lead directly or indirectly to violence against women. According to more radical ones, such as Andrea Dworkin and Catharine MacKinnon, pornography

is a systematic practice of exploitation and subordination based on sex that differentially harms women. The harm of pornography includes dehumanization, sexual exploitation, forced sex, forced prostitution, physical injury, and social and sexual terrorism and inferiority presented as entertainment. The bigotry and contempt pornography promotes, with the acts of aggression it fosters, diminish opportunities for equality of rights in employment, education, property, public accommodations, and public services; create public and private harassment, persecution, and denigration; expose individuals who appear in pornography against their will to ... hatred ... and embarrassment and target such women in particular for abuse and physical aggression ... promote injury and degradation such as rape, battery, child sexual abuse, and prostitution and inhibit just enforcement of laws against these acts; contribute significantly to restricting women in particular from full exercise of citizenship and participation in public life, including in neighborhoods; damage relations between the sexes; and undermine women's equal exercise of rights to speech and action guaranteed to all citizens.[4]

Even when a discussion is explicitly about pornography alone, therefore, readers should bear in mind that it is implicitly about prostitution as well. In all respects except for the specific laws that regulate each, the two topics are most effectively discussed together rather than separately. (They are very closely related also to sexual harassment and even to violence against women, which we discuss in chapters 8 and 9).

Pornography and prostitution can be discussed as industries in two senses, neither of which is what usually comes to mind at the mention of the word "industry." They are industries in the commercial sense, albeit disreputable and sometimes illegal ones, because they are defined by the transactions of small businesses. In fact, pornography and prostitution are two venues of the same industry. In the former, customers buy visual or verbal images of sexual objects. In the latter, they hire sexual objects themselves. Both venues are associated with other ones, in turn, and these are part of an underground economy. They involve criminal and often violent activities, in other words, such as drug dealing, pimping, and even what amounts to slavery. Yet not all prostitutes are uneducated minors who have run away from abusive fathers or uneducated women who have run away from abusive husbands. In fact, not all are even female. The ones known as call girls work in a very different social, cultural, and economic environment. In some societies, the prostitutes known as courtesans enjoy no small degree of status. Consider the geisha of Japan. Our point here is that criminal activities are often entailed by pornography and prostitution as these are currently organized but not inherent in them.

Pornography and prostitution have also generated new industries of a different kind. As we said in the previous chapter, the word "industry" can be applied usefully to jobs that involve the fallout from social and legal problems. Like the children of divorce, the "victims" of pornography and prostitution have become the focus of intense interest by a vast array of specialized agencies, municipal offices, academic departments, federal offices, and so on. These industries are defined not by commercial transactions but by the public policies created by networks of closely related private and public bureaucracies.

Porn is a little more complicated, in some ways, than prostitution. Some feminists acknowledge a distinction between porn that directly or indirectly threatens the safety of women and porn that merely titillates men (but also, according to feminists as different as Helen Gurley Brown and Camille Paglia, women as well). This porn is sometimes called erotica. Other feminists acknowledge no such distinction, although some of them find it politically expedient to do so for legal purposes. They believe that even the most innocuous pictures of naked women should be seen as one end of a misogynistic continuum that ends in rape. Following that pattern of thought, they believe that even the most innocuous act of heterosexual intercourse should be seen as one end of precisely the same misogynistic continuum. For these ideological feminists, in other words, the very act of intercourse between a man and a woman is tantamount to sexism in general and rape in particular. They are in the minority, but their influence can hardly be exaggerated.

As for prostitution, it includes a wide range of phenomena. One of them could be classified as industrial; people pay prostitutes for their services. But this is often accompanied by contextually related – though not inherently related – phenomena that include pimps, violence, the trade in drugs, and abuse of one kind or another.

In the United States, pornography is defined along a constitutional continuum. At one end are images of real children who are engaged in sexually explicit activities. These images are not protected by the Constitution. The involvement of children is carefully monitored by federal laws. The authority for this comes from sections of the federal Criminal Code on porn, sexual abuse, sexual exploitation of children, selling or buying of children, sexual exploitation of minors, activities relating to material constituting or containing child porn, coercion for prostitution, and so forth.[5]

At the other end are images of real adults who are engaged in sexually explicit activities. These images are protected. Between these two extremes are ambiguous images: "explicit material created without the benefit of a live child model but which appears to depict an actual minor, or produced by having an adult pose as a minor and later presented or sold as if it depicted ... an actual minor, arguably falls somewhere in between."[6] The Child Pornography Prevention Act of 1996 (CPPA) was supposed to modernize existing legislation by bringing it into the computer age. Sometimes, computer manipulation of images makes it possible for children (like adults) to be involved even when they know nothing at all about what is going on. Included among illegal images of children, for instance, are those that have been manipulated, enhanced, or wholly generated by computer technology. In 2002, after several years of legal wrangling over constitutionality, the Supreme Court ruled in *Ashcroft, Attorney General, et al. v. Free Speech Coalition et al.*[7] that the Child Pornography Prevention Act

prohibits speech that records no crime and creates no victims by its production. Virtual child pornography is not "intrinsically related" to the sexual abuse of children. While the Government asserts that the images can lead to actual instances of child abuse, the causal link is contingent and indirect. The harm does not necessarily follow from the speech, but depends upon some unquantified potential for subsequent criminal acts ... The contention that the CPPA is necessary because pedophiles may use virtual child pornography to seduce children runs afoul of the principle that speech within the rights of adults to hear may not be silenced completely in an attempt to shield children from it ... That the evil in question depends upon the actor's unlawful conduct, defined as criminal quite apart from any link to the speech in question, establishes that the speech ban is not narrowly drawn. The argument that virtual child pornography whets pedophiles' appetites and encourages them to engage in illegal conduct is unavailing because the mere tendency of speech to encourage unlawful acts is not a sufficient reason for banning it ... The overbreadth doctrine prohibits the Government from banning unprotected speech if a substantial amount of protected speech is prohibited or chilled in the process ... that the CPPA should be read not as a prohibition on speech but as a measure shifting the burden to the accused to prove the speech is lawful raises serious constitutional difficulties.[8]

Prostitution is governed by the Victims of Trafficking and Violence Prevention Act of 2000. It prohibits activities connected with prostitution across state lines. This approach is based on the Constitution's Commerce Clause. Division A is the Trafficking Victims Protection Act: "trafficking" refers to the use of fraud or coercion to rape, abuse, torture, starve, imprison, or psychologically abuse girls or women.[9] Citing what had been found by Congress, division A held that trafficking in the national and international sex trade is a modern form of slavery and the fastest-growing source of profit for organized crime.[10] When it comes to local prostitution, whether on the street or in brothels, state law governs, rather than federal law. Prostitution is illegal everywhere except in some parts of Nevada.[11]

In Canada, the legal situation is somewhat different. Part V, section 163 of the Criminal Code covers several activities, including making, printing, publishing, distributing, circulating, selling, or keeping "in his possession" – the legislators did not bother to use gender-neutral language – "any obscene written matter, picture, model ... which publicly exhibits a disgusting object or an indecent show." This material has as its "dominant characteristic ... the undue exploitation of sex, or of sex and any one or more of the following subjects: crime, horror, cruelty and violence." The only exception is for material that serves the "public good," presumably something artistic or educational.[12] Section 163(1) prohibits not only using minors – that is, anyone under eighteen, even though the legal age of consent is fourteen – in the production of porn but also providing them with access to it. In 2002 it became illegal to post child porn on the Internet.[13] In the same year, Bill C-20 was proposed to clamp down even more heavily on child porn. Although this bill died, a similar one was proposed in 2004. Measures included eliminating the defense of artistic merit,[14] even though a case in 2001 maintained the loophole.[15]

Canadian prostitution is mainly under federal jurisdiction, although municipalities have been allowed to "regulate or license indoor activity."[16] Federal laws against various aspects of prostitution date back to Canada's first criminal code. These laws were updated by the Soliciting Law of 1972. In 1983, the Special Committee on Pornography and Prostitution (also known as the Fraser Committee) recommended that prostitution be legalized but also that its venues and circumstances be restricted. In 1985 the Communicating Law – this name is unfortunate, to say the least, since many Christian churches use precisely the same word for participation in holy communion – prohibited "communicating in a public place for the purpose of buying or selling sexual services."[17] Legislators allowed a limit on freedom of expression according to the "reasonable" test, which must balance "the salutary and deleterious effects of the law."[18] The Communicating Law was challenged in several court cases. They argued that it violated both freedom of expression and freedom of association as guaranteed by sections 2b and 2d of the Charter of Rights and Freedoms.[19] Nonetheless, the Supreme Court upheld this law.

Prostitution is regulated also by sections 210 to 213 of the Criminal Code.[20] Section 210 makes it a criminal offense, punishable by imprisonment for not more than two years, to own and manage a bawdy house, work in one, be found in one (without a lawful excuse), or rent space to one. Section 211, directed at pimps, is about transporting people to bawdy houses and getting them involved with prostitution. Both 210 and 211 involve summary charges (once known as misdemeanors).[21]

Section 212 is about manipulating and controlling prostitutes, which is to say, about pimps. It prohibits procuring and soliciting. Offenders may be imprisoned for up to ten years. And if they procure prostitutes under the age of eighteen, up to fourteen years. Even if they procure someone under eighteen for "consideration," they are guilty of an indictable offence and liable to imprisonment for up to five years.

But section 213, about communicating in public for prostitution, is really the main one. According to subsection 1 of section 213, "every person who in a public place or in any place open to public view (a) stops or attempts to stop any motor vehicle, (b) impedes the free flow of pedestrian or vehicular traffic of ingress or egress from premises adjacent to that place, or (c) stops or attempts to stop any person or in any manner communicates or attempts to communicate with any person for the purpose of engaging in prostitution or of obtaining the sexual services of a prostitute is guilty of an offence punishable on summary conviction." According to subsection 2, "public place" includes motor vehicles that can be seen by the public. In short, this law tries to prevent communicating in public, because it creates a "nuisance" for the community that many people want most to eliminate. Out of sight, out of mind.

In 1998, Justice Canada produced its "Report and Recommendations in Respect of Legislation, Policy and Practices Concerning Prostitution-Related Activities," which revisited the legislation to see if anything should be changed or added.[22] The report revealed many differences of opinion. Some arose during consultations with advocacy groups for women and prostitutes. Others arose from conflicts within the working group. After discussing the pros and cons of each proposal, the latter made several recommendations but also admitted that "there was a great deal of confusion about the current legal status of prostitution in Canada."[23] Those testifying did not always know precisely what was legal, for instance, or illegal. "Although prostitution in Canada is not illegal, most prostitution-related activities are. This creates confusion among the public and does not tell prostitutes or customers where and under what circumstances they can meet."[24]

Street prostitutes, defined in section 213, were the main focus of these discussions. They had always been the main target of police, for two reasons.[25] First, they were associated with an unwholesome atmosphere in neighbourhoods. Second, they were associated with violence at the hands of both pimps and customers. These two problems are closely related, because eliminating street prostitutes from communities means merely moving them to less visible places such as dark streets and parks, industrial districts, or remote country roads. And doing so makes it easier for criminals to hide their drugs and their assaults and murders.[26] The working group acknowledged this but pointed out that not much could be done legally at the local level, because Canadian laws governing prostitution are federal. Some members of the working group worried that the current legislation penalized the poor (prostitutes) and favoured the rich (residents and landowners or business owners). More expensive prostitutes, who plied their trade discretely, were not bothered by the police; others, who did so on the streets, were routinely arrested by the police.[27]

Feminists influenced the report, even though they could not always agree on precisely what would be best for women. One solution was to create harsher penalties for prostitutes.[28] Some feminists disagreed because that would make life even harder for them. A second solution was to create separate offences for prostitutes and customers.[29] A third was for the police to leave prostitutes alone and arrest only their customers.[30] Some feminists considered it a good way of bringing more customers to court than ever before. Appearing in court involves mandatory fingerprinting and photographing, after all, which make it easier to track repeat offenders from one place to another and from one offence to another. This measure, some believed, would actually deter customers, because most would be ashamed to appear in court in these circumstances.[31] Because this solution would eliminate specific offenses for prostitutes, however, some feminists worried that the police would charge them instead merely for loitering. Other feminists worried that this, in turn, would merely give prostitutes longer criminal records than they already had, because fingerprinted prostitutes, too, would be easier to track.[32]

Therefore, although some members wanted harsher sentences or sentences only against customers, the working group did not recommend these measures. They believed that section 213 referred merely to a "nuisance offence," that the rate of recidivism was low, and that legislation was unlikely to solve the problem of street prostitution in any case. Instead, the working group recommended that federal, provincial, and territorial governments provide better resources for prostitutes, including "safe accommodation, crisis intervention and counseling for those who desire assistance in leaving the sex trade ... [and] treatment and counseling particularly with respect to sexually-transmitted diseases and alcohol and drug abuse."[33]

Some members wanted to help prostitutes leave the business by providing them with job training and job placement. They pointed to a program for prostitutes in Toronto called Streetlight, which includes a day-long class about choices and an eight-week "life skills program." Funds generated by a "john school" pay for the latter. Similar programs exist in Ottawa and Edmonton.[34] The working group "urged [communities] to recognize the importance of specialized exit programs."[35] Some members of the working group argued that fear of violent reprisals makes it hard for prostitutes to present evidence against customers and pimps. Therefore, officials should come up with strategies to "help equalize this power differential."[36] They could use screens in courtrooms, closed-circuit TV or videotapes, out-of-court testimony, or phone tapping. The working group recommended these measures.

As for customers, the working group was even more divided. There was a hot debate over measures to punish them – revoking or suspending their driving licenses, impounding their cars, and shaming them. Some American communities broadcast the names of customers. Other communities send letters to the homes of clients, a measure that has been known to cause divorces. The working group failed to reach a consensus but recommended continued study of these measures.

In John Lowman's estimation, the mixed messages of Canadian law on prostitution have made the "john" into a folk devil.[37] The "john schools" set up by some Canadian communities are designed to "reeducate" customers at their own expense, either on a pre-charge basis (which eliminates the necessity of appearing in court) or a post-charge basis (when attendance at these schools functions as the sentence or part of it). The day's curriculum typically includes lectures by experts on how street prostitution damages neighbourhoods, by ex-prostitutes on how much suffering the "trade" caused them (which, we are told, helps these ex-prostitutes "heal"),[38] and by medics on sexually transmitted diseases. The working group recommended that communities be allowed to decide for themselves about the usefulness of john schools but also "urged [them] to recognize the importance of specialized exit programs for female, male and transgender prostitutes who wish to leave the sex trade as an integral component of the community's attack on street prostitution."[39] Yet other strategies involved prostitutes and members of communities meeting together to resolve differences, through mediation if necessary.

The most extreme position on pornography and prostitution is surely that of Catharine MacKinnon and her pal Andrea Dworkin, so a brief introduction to their work is in order here. The former is a very prominent lawyer, academic, and activist, [40] the latter a very well-known writer and activist.[41] Dworkin is often dismissed by liberal feminists, expediently, as a member of the lunatic fringe. In other words, they either say or imply, she need not be taken seriously. Yet we do take her seriously. After all, MacKinnon does.[42] And MacKinnon has had a major impact on legislation not only in the United States, her own country, but also in Canada.

As a lawyer, MacKinnon is probably more directly influential than Dworkin. Her legal strategies are evident in *Toward a Feminist Theory of the State,* where she discusses "feminist jurisprudence" in the context of a radically transformed society. Elsewhere, she discusses the need to focus attention on civil cases rather than criminal ones.[43] Because criminal cases require a very stringent standard of evidence, jurors must be convinced "beyond a reasonable doubt," which makes it hard to convict men. In civil suits, on the other hand, jurors are convinced merely by a "preponderance of evidence." That makes it easier than it would otherwise be to sue men and win.

MacKinnon uses her background in political science to analyze the politics that keeps women subservient. She opposes both the political right (with its morality talk) and the political left (with its freedom talk). Both, she believes, keep violence against women invisible and irrelevant.[44] She is openly hostile toward those, including women, who disagree with her and routinely accuses them of insensitivity to women's pain (since they reject the politics of victimization) and selling out to men (by playing the political game of "divide and conquer").[45] She is much more hostile to men, of course. Even the best of them, she taunts, are cowed by the mass media. Others are, well, men. MacKinnon's entire worldview is based on power – that is, the power that men have over women (and, by implication, the power that women should have over men).

As MacKinnon sees it, the problems faced by women are all due, directly or indirectly, to a titanic conspiracy of men against women. The conspirators come from both sides of the political spectrum, are driven by sex and money, and bring together a wide range of pursuits such as journalism, entertainment, publishing, crime, teaching, research, and law. Their power is seldom obvious. When challenged, she says, they resort to the First Amendment as an opportunistic way of protecting their interests. Politicians, lawyers, and academicians, she claims, have all cowered before this political bloc.[46]

Even though MacKinnon relied heavily on Marxism, at first, feminism led her to the belief that a new and independent analysis was necessary for women.[47] Dworkin agrees. When it comes to women, she says, the political left sold out and thus directly or indirectly joined the right. Only women now remain on the left: "Far to the left, off the mainstream continuum – at least as currently articulated in popular discourse – are women whose politics are animated by a commitment to listening to those who have been hurt and finding remedies that are fair."[48] All men belong, moreover, to the culture of "dead white males." Listen to her:

In addition to romanticizing forced sex and celebrating sexual exploitation, the Left has joined the Right in defending the culture of dead white men: protecting it from criticism or change; keeping it inviolate, immune from contamination by creative persons not dead or white or male. The culture of dead white men, built on the bodies of silenced women and colonialized people of color, has become a weapon to keep living women of all races silent. Like a private club that keeps out all but an elite few, art and books especially are used to tell the emerging women – emerging not only from silence but often enough from hell – that they are not good enough or important enough or worthy enough to be listened to. The proof of their insignificance is in their suffering: having been raped or beaten or prostituted. Was Aristotle? Was Descartes? Why listen to women who are more pleasing laid out flat, legs spread, than standing up, talking back, talking real? Why should the men of liberation interrupt the liberatory act itself to listen to the person whose hole he was sticking it in? And if I were to say that hole is not empty space waiting to be filled by anyone or anything, what would my authority be? How do I know? But he knows – every "he" knows.[49]

As we say, many feminists argue that Dworkin is nothing more than a vocal member of the radical fringe. Why take Dworkin or any other extremist seriously? And why pay the price, in any case, for doing so? Men who take ideological feminism seriously and speak out against it are routinely attacked as misogynists (even though the same accusation is flung at men who fail to take it seriously). But remember that MacKinnon is Dworkin's chief collaborator. And no one can accuse her of living on the fringes of legal or political circles. Au contraire. Professionally, MacKinnon is a member of the academic and legal elite.[50] In other words, her ideas almost inevitably influence the feminist mainstream. These two, but especially MacKinnon, have had an enormous impact on legislation to protect women from men.

Martha Nussbaum understands Dworkin's approach as retributive, being based on revenge. She takes a close look at Dworkin's novel *Mercy*, which tells the story of a woman named Andrea (surely no coincidence, especially when many of the details of this woman's life match those of her own biography of abuse by men).

This novel does not read like a novel because its form expresses the retributive idea that its message preaches. That is, it refuses to perceive any of the male offenders – or any other male – as a particular individual, and it refuses to invite the reader into the story of their lives. Like Andrea, it can't tell him from him from him. The reader hears only the solitary voice of the narrator; others exist for her only as sources of her pain. Like the women in the male pornography that Dworkin decries, her males have no history, no psychology, no concrete reasons for action. They are just knives that cut, arms that beat, penises that maim by the very act of penetration. Dworkin's refusal of the traditional novelist's attention to the stories of particular lives seems closely connected with her heroine's refusal to be merciful to any of those lives, with her doctrine that justice is cruel and hard.[51]

By now it should be clear that we are dealing not only with culturally promoted gynocentrism but also with legally promoted misandry, which is the point we are trying to make throughout this book. Dworkin's men are generic objects, not human characters. It is easy, therefore, to treat them – and punish them – as a class. Whether any man is guilty or not of any specific crime, he must pay along with others of his class. "The inclination to mercy is present in the text only as a fool's inclination toward collaboration and slavery. When the narrator, entering her new profession as a karate-killer of homeless men, enunciates the 'politic principle which went as follows: It is very important for women to kill men,' a voice within the text suggests the explanations that might lead to mercy. As the return of the narrator quickly makes clear, this is meant to be a parody voice, a fool's voice, the voice of a collaborator with the enemy."[52]

MacKinnon's basic argument against porn is that women are doubly "violated" by it: first by its production and then by its consumption. Even if it does not lead to the physical violation of women, she opines, the mere sight of porn, the very existence of it, constitutes a violation of women. From this point of view, one finding of researchers seems particularly interesting. The keywords describing oral sex in clinical terms get a lukewarm response from users of the net, but those describing it in more imaginative terms (such as "choking") get an enthusiastic response. "Such findings," writes one journalist, "may cheer antipornography activists; as Dworkin puts it, 'the whole purpose of pornography is to hurt women.'"[53] But is it? This would certainly be news to the gay men who enjoy porn – unless, of course, you argue that they secretly hate men and want to hurt them. Because almost every feminist assumes that the appeal of porn is not merely vulgar but sinister, this claim is worth discussing here in more detail.

Dworkin believes that pornography and prostitution are based on a "commerce in women," a free market where women are bought and sold. A woman, she argues, "is meat in [a man's] marketplace; he is the butcher who wields the knife to get the right cut; and he communicates through the cutting, then the display of the body parts. She is worth more in pieces than she ever was whole."[54] Elsewhere, she refers to the "colonialization of women's bodies for male pleasure."[55] This process, she says, is based on male sexual force (which supposedly brings men pleasure) and male sexual exploitation (which brings a few of them fortunes). And all this depends on "dominance and submission as a dynamic and the 'objectification' of women as a fundamental element of pleasure."[56] Commerce itself is okay, says Dworkin, unless it involves the exploitation of labour. (She must be using that word in its popular sense of excessive exploitation, because its technical sense can refer merely to anyone who works for others.) But commerce in human beings is not. That amounts to buying and selling people, to slavery.[57]

Many feminists are troubled by the existence of pornography and prostitution because they believe that these not only "objectify" women (a word that we discuss below) but also place women in a subordinate position and therefore both condone and encourage violence against them. MacKinnon and Dworkin pointed out that efforts to curb or reform it have been notoriously unsuccessful. With that in mind, they promoted a series of amendments to the ordinances of several cities. The idea was to ban porn for violating women's civil rights, preventing them from participating freely and fully in public life due to either violence or fear of violence. Their best-known campaigns focused directly on porn, but their opposition to prostitution was based on the same reasoning. In Indianapolis, the city council found that

Pornography is a systematic practice of exploitation and subordination based on sex, which differentially harms women. The bigotry and contempt it promotes, with the acts of aggression it fosters, harms women's opportunities for equality of rights in employment, education, access to and use of public accommodations, and acquisition of real property; promotes rape, battery, child abuse, kidnapping and prostitution ... and contributes significantly to restricting women in particular from full exercise of citizenship and participation in public life.[58]

In its amended ordinance, write James Jacobs and Kimberly Potter, the city "prohibited the production, distribution, exhibition, or sale of pornography and the display of pornography in any place of employment, school, public place, or private home ... created a civil cause of action for persons coerced, intimidated, or tricked into appearing in a pornographic work; and ... provided victims of sexual violence a cause of action against sellers of the pornography."[59] In *Hudnut v. American Booksellers Association*, a case of 1986, this ordinance was challenged by the Seventh Circuit Court of Appeals (a challenge that was later upheld by the Supreme Court).[60] At issue were the First Amendment (which protects freedom of speech) and the definition of porn (which was too broad or vague).

MacKinnon and Dworkin proposed an even stronger ordinance for Minneapolis, but it was challenged and struck down for similar reasons. Porn, according to the Minneapolis proposal, is

a concrete description of the materials the pornography industry makes and sells: graphic sexually explicit materials that subordinate women and others. It is not a description of any ideas ... By contrast with the Indianapolis version of the ordinance, this definition is not restricted to violent material. This is because the violence of pornography is not limited to materials that show violence. Women are coerced into materials that show no violence. Rapists use materials showing what appears to be consenting sex to stimulate their rapes and to select their targets. Children are abused to make pornography that shows no violence. Pornography showing no violence is violently forced on women and children.[61]

The Minneapolis ordinance would have prevented coerced performances to be used for porn, although their definition of "coerced" was debatable. Among the facts not allowed by the defense, according to the Minneapolis ordinance, would have been that

the person is a woman or ... [that] the person is or has been a prostitute ... [that] the person has attained the age of majority ... [that] the person is connected by blood or marriage to anyone involved in or related to the making of the pornography ... [that] the person has previously had, or been thought to have had, sexual relations with anyone, including anyone involved in or related to the making of the pornography ... [that] the person has previously posed for sexually explicit pictures with or for anyone, including anyone involved in or related to the pornography at issue ... [that] anyone else, including a spouse or other relative, has given or purported to give permission on the person's behalf ... [that] the person actually consented to a use of a performance that is later changed into pornography ... [that] the person knew that the purpose of the acts or events in question was to make pornography ... [that] the person showed no resistance or appeared to cooperate actively in the photographic sessions or in the events that produce the pornography ... [that] the person signed a contract, or made statements affirming a willingness to cooperate in the production of pornography ... [that] no physical force, threats, or weapons were used in the making of the pornography ... or [that] the person was paid or otherwise compensated.[62]

Most of these stipulations make sense, but the last five are highly problematic indeed. MacKinnon and Dworkin defended them by arguing that most of the women who appear in porn are poor and powerless. Therefore, they are incapable of giving informed consent to the publishers. And therefore, their participation is "coerced." This is the same argument used elsewhere against any sexual relations between men and women, according to which women are "powerless" almost by definition. Therefore, they are incapable of giving men informed consent. And therefore, all sexual relations between them and men are "coerced" – which is to say, they are rapes. Apart from any other problems – and we can think of several very important moral ones – one is of particular importance in a specifically legal context: the assumption that grown women must not be treated as adults and held responsible for their own behaviour.

MacKinnon and Dworkin argued that no one would use the First Amendment to challenge this ordinance, because that document does not protect people from coercion. Moreover, the ordinance would have banned only the "graphic, sexually explicit subordination of women, whether in pictures or words ..."[63] Clever wording would have excluded not only highbrow literature but also middlebrow movies and even some lowbrow erotica. (This was a concession to political expediency; both MacKinnon and Dworkin believe that all sexually suggestive representations of women are, in fact, degrading forms of "objectification" and really ought to be banned.) In short, the ordinance was designed to avoid challenges. Nevertheless, this ordinance and many similar ones were defeated. According to MacKinnon, these defeats were due to a conspiracy of liberals and pornographers, a "cabal" that included some misguided women who chose either foolishly or deceptively to support an abstraction – freedom of expression – over the civil right of women to freedom from real fear.[64]

McKinnon's role in this matter began during the 1980s.[65] She won some cases and lost others. Her most important victory came in 1988. As a consultant to the Legal Defense and Action Fund (operated by the National Organization for Women) in *Louis Robinson v. Jacksonville Shipyards*,[66] she argued that porn constitutes a "hostile environment" for women; displaying it in the workplace, therefore, qualified as sexual harassment under Title VII of the Civil Rights Act of 1964. MacKinnon's efforts to make porn illegal in the United States were ineffective in all cases except for that one, which linked porn with a "hostile working environment" and therefore with sexual harassment. What did her in most often was the First Amendment, a cornerstone of the legal system and even of national identity.

For various reasons, MacKinnon has been more successful at banning porn in Canada than in the United States. She has worked closely with the Legal Education and Action Fund (LEAF) for many years. In *R. v. Keegstra*,[67] she provided an important affidavit and a factum for LEAF's intervention before the Supreme Court.[68] Here is MacKinnon's own summary of the case: "LEAF had successfully argued before the Canadian Supreme Court that racist and anti-Semitic hate propaganda violates equality and multiculturalism rights under the new Charter, so criminalizing such expression is constitutional."[69] In other words, the government may limit freedom of expression in order to promote the equality of traditionally disadvantaged groups.[70] Even though this particular case was not specifically about porn, it provided a basis for an extremely important one that was: *R. v. Butler*.[71] Donald Butler defended his right to own and distribute porn against criminal prosecution under Canada's obscenity law. To do so, he cited Canada's Charter of Rights and Freedoms. In other words, he challenged "the constitutionality of section 163 of the Criminal Code, which prohibits the sale of 'obscene' materials ... any publication a dominant characteristic of which is the undue exploitation of sex, or of sex and any one or more of the following subjects, namely, crime, horror, cruelty and violence."[72] Dworkin sent LEAF a letter in which she argued against using criminal law because it requires a higher standard of proof than civil law and thus results in fewer convictions. MacKinnon agreed, but she decided nonetheless to work with LEAF. The Court ruled that the government may limit freedom of expression in order

to prevent harm to society rather than to impose any particular standard of public or sexual morality. According to the Court, obscenity is harmful because it communicates a degrading and dehumanizing message that is "analogous to that of hate propaganda." Consistent with LEAF's position, the Court declared that the particular harm avoided by regulating pornography is "the degradation which many women feel as 'victims' of the message of obscenity, and of the negative impact exposure to such material has on perceptions and attitudes towards women."[73]

Please note, however, that this ruling involved a double standard. Material that degrades women (even if produced by and for gay women) is now illegal in Canada, but material that degrades men (even if produced by and for gay men) might remain legal.

Every case is about the specific behaviours of specific people and their effects on other people, of course. *Butler* was specifically about several films that allegedly depict women in ways that are harmful to all women. Every case sets a legal precedent, moreover, being directly or indirectly about similar behaviours by similar people. That is why judges not only cite legal precedents but also discuss legal and social consequences. Not surprisingly, the court focused very heavily on pornography as a phenomenon that can harm women (and therefore society as a whole). Unfortunately, the court barely paid lip service to pornography as a phenomenon that can harm men.

Now and then, to be sure, the court describes material that "could be said to dehumanize men or women."[74] But these statements are extraneous to the main arguments and do not form any consistent pattern. They give the impression, therefore, of being inserted to make the discussion politically correct. After all, the Charter does guarantee sexual equality. It is hard, therefore, to take these statements seriously. Moreover, some statements actually cast doubt on the very possibility that pornography can have harmful effects on men. Consider the following: "Harm in this context means that it predisposes persons to act in an anti-social manner as, for example, the physical or mental mistreatment of women by men, or, what is perhaps debatable, the reverse."[75] Nowhere does anyone acknowledge that popular culture – mainstream popular culture – routinely portrays men in negative ways and that some women act accordingly, whether in connection with mental mistreatment of men or (as we show in chapter 9) physical mistreatment. Nowhere, moreover, does anyone acknowledge that gay porn routinely presents men as "willing victims" of other men. To acknowledge that, of course, would be to provoke a political conflict with gay people.

Even though the Charter does require equal treatment under the law for women and men, therefore, that requirement remains an empty abstraction when the needs of men are at stake. Public rhetoric about equality notwithstanding, the legal system remains mired in notions that generate inequality. This is an example of what we call "systemic discrimination" against men. It seems most unlikely that any Canadian official would try to clamp down on pornography produced by and for *gay* men on the grounds that it degrades *men*. Anyone inclined to do so, at any rate, could hardly use *Butler* as a precedent.

In addition, the Supreme Court agreed with LEAF that it was unnecessary to prove the existence of a causal link between porn and violence. It was necessary only to show the existence of a "reasoned apprehension of harm."[76] Moreover, it was easier to solve the problem by banning obscene materials than by restricting them. This was indeed a major victory for MacKinnon in her – and LEAF's – campaign to outlaw porn. She and Dworkin concluded that

in the United States, our Anti-Pornography Civil Rights Ordinance – together with related legislative initiatives against the harms of racist hate speech – has helped to trigger an escalating constitutional conflict between "speech" rights guaranteed by the First Amendment and "equality" rights in the principles underlying the Fourteenth Amendment. In our neighbor nation to the north, Canada's Supreme Court has determined that racist hate expression is unconstitutional (*Keegstra*) and that society's interest in sex equality outweighs pornographers' speech rights (*Butler*). Taken together, these two rulings are a breakthrough in equality jurisprudence, representing major victories for women and all people targeted for race hate. We wish that U.S. constitutional consciousness were so far along.[77]

Calling *Butler* "a stunning victory for women,"[78] MacKinnon praised Canada for being "the first place in the world that says what is obscene is what harms women, not what offends our values."[79] Several years later, though, she was back-peddling real fast. In a press release of 1994, she and Dworkin responded to criticisms that *Butler* was being used by Canada Customs to stop feminist, gay, and lesbian materials – including some books by Dworkin herself! – from entering the country.

They began their defense by arguing that "Canada has not adopted our civil rights law against pornography. It has not adopted our statutory definition of pornography; it has not adopted our civil (as opposed to criminal) approach to pornography; nor has Canada adopted any of the five civil causes of action we proposed (coercion, assault, force, trafficking, defamation)."[80] After describing the history of their involvement in the case, they argued that there had been a long-standing practice by Canada Customs to stop gay and lesbian materials. Therefore, the current situation had had nothing to do with *Butler*. Besides, they argued, *Butler* had actually improved the situation for gays, because restrictions could no longer be based on the ground that some works are immoral but only on the ground that they would harm women (which gay porn, at least the kind addressed to gay men as distinct from gay women, would not do). Even so, they had to acknowledge one anomaly. Lesbian porn would be caught in the net, after all, if it were suspected of harming women.[81] Obviously, neither MacKinnon nor Dworkin believed that men, with their godlike power, could be harmed by anything. Or cared one way or the other in any case.

Clearly, the war on porn has been waged on different battlefronts in the two countries. Americans have resisted the idea of making it illegal (although they have done so in connection with the involvement of children) mainly because of the importance they attach to freedom of expression. Canadians, on the other hand, have resisted the idea that freedom of expression is more important than the equality of "historically disadvantaged groups." And those groups, they say, include women. The Canadian definition of (illegal) porn ostensibly excludes erotica, but it includes not only the link between sex and crime, horror, cruelty, or violence but also the "degradation" of women for the pleasure of men.[82] Yet the latter is a very vague notion. As MacKinnon and Dworkin themselves have argued, after all, it can be identified with any sexual contact at all between men and women.

Before concluding our discussion of this extreme position, it is worth pointing out that not everyone who agrees with it can be identified with radical feminists. Who could be more mainstream that Gloria Steinem? It was she who led a crusade against a controversial movie, *The People vs Larry Flynt*, with an essay in the *New York Times*.[83] Her main point was that this movie about the publisher of *Hustler* magazine had cleaned up the image of an evil man. Instead of protesting, critics had glorified the movie along with the man himself as a tribute to his crusade for freedom of speech. There is something deeply disturbing, to be sure, about both Flynt

and his magazine. Month after month, it reproduces images that are neu-
rotically grotesque, not erotically beautiful or innocently playful. Should
they be banned? If not as obscenity, which is notoriously hard to define,
then as hate literature?

These questions were surely worth asking. But Steinem's own bias added
nothing to the debate. "My question is: Would men be portrayed as inviting, deserving and even enjoying their own pain and degradation, as
women are in Mr. Flynt's life work?"[84] Actually, they are. For decades, in
fact, men have been portrayed in precisely that way. Not usually in connection with sex, it is true, although there have been some notable cases of
that. One example would be Somerset Maugham's *Of Human Bondage*,
either in print or on film. Philip, the protagonist, is nothing if not masochis-
tic in his love for a cruel waitress. Far more common, though, is the
masochism expected of men in connection with war and other kinds of violence. If you are going to argue against violent porn for dehumanizing
women, you should at least be prepared to argue against other material for
dehumanizing men.

Not all feminists have joined the crusade against porn. Some liberal feminists, for instance, want to safeguard freedom of expression. In *Defending
Pornography*, Nadine Strossen argues that censorship does more harm than
good to women. To oppose porn, she says, is to undermine the argument
for women's equality and autonomy. If men are allowed to enjoy porn,
after all, then why not women? This is a technical argument for legal equality. Maybe Strossen believes that most women, unlike men, would choose
not to act on this form of equality. But how many feminist or other critics
of her book have challenged the idea that porn is a necessary evil, which
implies that sex itself is no more than a necessary evil? In his article on this
topic for *Time*, at any rate, Philip Elmer-Dewitt mentions not one. Because
he makes it clear that porn is "a guy thing," statistically, the implication is
that there is something necessarily evil about men themselves. Strossen's
attitude to porn, and therefore to sex, is by no means unusual, although it
is unusual for a feminist.[85]

The notion that sex is a necessary evil at best has had a long history,
unfortunately, in the West. During the Hellenistic period, gnosticism – a
profoundly dualistic worldview that was characterized by extreme polarization between matter or "flesh" (which had negative connotations) and
spirit or mind (which had positive ones) – entered both Greco-Roman and
Jewish writings. It entered early Christianity, therefore, from not one but
both of its primary sources.[86] The result, which can be seen in writings as
early as those of St Paul, was an aversion to the material world in general
and to sex in particular. Given their belief that the world was about to end,
the earliest Christians reacted appropriately. It became clear to them very

quickly, however, that the Second Coming and establishment of God's Kingdom would be postponed. In that case, they would have to plan for the future of a Christian social order. And they did find ways of affirming sex within marriage for practical purposes, partly by drawing on the mainly pre-Hellenistic Old Testament tradition, which had a relatively "high" view of sex and marriage.

Catholics are ambivalent about sex to this day, because they acknowledge the authority of two quite different (though not contradictory) traditions. According to Augustinian theology, sex transmits Original Sin, along with life, from one generation to another. According to natural law, sex within marriage has the legitimate function of procreation. The result is a reasonable compromise. Procreative marriage is a legitimate ideal for most people, but asceticism is an even higher ideal for the few.

Most Protestant communities have rejected monastic asceticism, along with many other features of the Catholic worldview, but have nonetheless fostered more subtle forms of the ascetic ideal. This is true especially of Calvinists, who created the founding cultures of both the United States and English Canada. Some Protestants have looked with greater suspicion on sensual or even aesthetic pleasure of any kind, in fact, than Catholics have. But all Christians are tied to founding documents – including, at least, the New Testament itself – that are ambivalent about material existence in general and about sexual behaviour in particular.

No matter what its historical origin, the fact remains that profound anxiety about sex is very common in our culture. And this is true of feminists no less than of other people. Some feminists argue that (heterosexual) sex is an unnecessary evil. Others argue that it is a necessary evil. Still others that it is liberating.

Some feminists question the primacy of "objectification" in connection with pornography and prostitution. In *Sex and Social Justice*, Nussbaum argues that MacKinnon and Dworkin have "totalized" it.[87] (We would add that they have endorsed a totalitarian mentality.) As evidence, she points to MacKinnon's statement that "[a]ll women live in sexual objectification the way fish live in water."[88] Nussbaum identifies at least seven ways of understanding objectification: instrumentality, denial of autonomy, inertness, fungibility (that is, interchangeability with other objects of the same type), violability, ownership, and denial of subjectivity. Some are morally problematic, she suggests, but others are problematic only in this or that context. Still others are necessary or even desirable. Nonetheless, Nussbaum applauds MacKinnon and Dworkin for two things.

First, she applauds them for describing the socialization of women into subservience and the resulting deformation of their desire – that is, the alleged "eroticization of male power" and female passivity.[89] According to

MacKinnon and Dworkin, women are culturally conditioned to be sexually aroused by male power and men by female powerlessness. As for the former, this has probably always been true about men as providers, if only because a mate with access to material resources – economic power – has always been in the interest of any woman and her children or potential children. Moreover, the wives and children of men with high prestige – social power – often enjoy additional advantages. But MacKinnon, Dworkin, and Nussbaum are referring to something else entirely, something far more sinister: sexual aggression – physical power – as the ultimate source of erotic appeal. Women, they say, have been conditioned to find male brutality *sexually* attractive. This comes dangerously close to the notion that women are masochists and want to be raped (which would, in any case, be a contradiction in terms). When rapists say so, the implication is that women are biologically programmed to enjoy rape and culturally programmed to deny it. In that case, there can be no such thing as rape. In other words, "no" really must mean "yes." When some feminists say the same thing, however, the implication is that women have been culturally programmed to enjoy what amounts to rape. And all acts of heterosexual intercourse really are rapes, from this point of view, because women, dupes of "the patriarchy" one and all, have been rendered incapable of truly giving their consent. Yes, women want to be raped, they argue, but only because men have made them that way! This point clearly lies at the very heart of what MacKinnon and Dworkin, along with Nussbaum, are saying.

Moreover, Nussbaum applauds MacKinnon and Dworkin for extending the "Kantian" tradition of demanding that people – in this case, women – be treated as ends and not merely as means to other ends. But she adds that objectification actually can occur within relationships characterized by equality and mutuality. Nussbaum argues, *pace* MacKinnon and Dworkin, that it is indeed morally permissible or even desirable to treat the other (temporarily) as passive or inert, see the other's genital organs as wonderful objects, or surrender autonomy to the other. Porn might even be useful in the effort to overcome puritanism, she says, and delegitimate the repression (by men, presumably) of female eroticism. (Judging from the productions of both popular and elite culture, we suggest that it would be hard to imagine a society less puritanical or less sexually repressed than our own is at the moment – with the notable exception of feminists who insist on "sexual correctness.")[90] Nussbaum is less certain than MacKinnon and Dworkin, in this context, that "bad objectification" is rooted in "deformed desire," in the "eroticization of male power." It might be rooted, she admits here, merely in a culture of commodification.

In any case, Nussbaum opposes even civil ordinances against porn. These, she says, would probably be administered inadequately. Worse, they would jeopardize "expressive interests" (such as elite literature, say, or photography) and even prevent us from learning about sexism. Besides, it might be very hard to establish a causal relation between porn and any particular harm (although that would present no problem in Canada, where lawyers need only show a "reasoned apprehension of harm.") Although Nussbaum does not believe that porn should be illegal, she does believe that it is immoral. And she wants impressionable young men, at least straight ones, to know why. She has no use for those who excuse porn by saying that "boys will be boys" or even canonize pornographers in the name of free speech.

Because Nussbaum sees herself as a liberal, she protects freedom of speech from legal controls and subjects it instead to moral controls. The idea is still to eliminate porn, of course, but not by abridging freedom of speech. We believe that her moral argument against porn is somewhat facile. Only in an ideal world would we treat all people in all circumstances as ends in themselves rather than as means to other ends.

But this is not an ideal world. To act on this moral premise, to treat everyone as a "thou" instead of an "it,"[91] would make daily life impossible. The fact is that we must make distinctions between the few people we love intimately and the many other people we live and work with. We must "use" or "objectify" the latter, even though we should do so respectfully. In some situations, especially within families or communities, that might involve reciprocity based on mutual obligation or common cause. In others, it might involve simple (but generous or at least adequate) payment for services rendered. No one should seriously believe in any moral obligation to set every commercial transaction, say, within the context of a "meaningful relationship" or one based on "mutuality and equality." In short, treating people as the means to some other end is not *necessarily* immoral.[92]

Two arguments, easily confused, refer to means and ends. One of them, which we do not make here, is about the end *justifying* the means – that is, about a noble end justifying an evil means. For two reasons, we are not suggesting that porn be justified as the evil means (tolerating the objectification of people) that is necessary to attain a noble end (maintaining freedom of speech). First, we do not believe that any evil means (except killing in self-defence) can be justified by any noble end. That is why we oppose all ideologies, which rest on precisely that belief. Second, we do not believe that either sex or (nonviolent) porn is inherently evil in the first place.

The other argument, which we do make, is about people *as* either means or ends. We argue here that all people are ultimately ends in themselves, but we have just acknowledged that some legitimate or even necessary interactions with other people in daily life would be impossible on that basis. We see no harm in treating other people as the means to other ends in some circumstances as long as doing so does not involve harm. And there is nothing harmful, at least not on secular grounds, about sex between consenting adults.

Another problem with antiporn rhetoric is that "objectification" and "domination" are very nebulous words and have therefore easily been turned into ideological jargon. Given the interest of ideological feminists in litigating their way to power, that should come as no surprise. How many people actually think about what "objectification" means or ask whether it is always evil, or, for that matter, if women alone are objectified? How many people actually think about the various ways in which people can "dominate" each other, moreover, or realize that women can be no less adept at it than men?

Wendy McElroy, too, argues against the censorship of porn (and, by implication, the banning of prostitution). But she has a different reason. Instead of classifying erotica as a necessary evil, she classifies that kind of porn as a good thing for women no less than for men. Having interviewed women who work in the industry, in connection with her book *XXX: A Woman's Right to Pornography*, she notes that, far from being victims, these women are liberators.[93] In fact, they are members of the "sexual elite." They make their own choices, for one thing, including the choice of discarding outmoded sexual mores. They enjoy what they do, moreover, because they could not put on convincing performances otherwise. But McElroy goes further. She rejects the notion that their (male) employers are wicked exploiters. Even they, she says, have moral standards. Violence, being fantasy, is always simulated. And not all violent fantasies are permitted. McElroy conludes that the main problems for these women (assuming that only women are involved) are relatively low pay from their employers and even less respect from the public.

McElroy's main point is simply that erotic porn is good for *women*. It gives them a safe place to be sexually playful in an otherwise dangerous world. It stimulates their imagination, encouraging women to explore their own sexuality beyond conventional boundaries. But some readers will draw the conclusion that these boundaries were established by men and thus constitute the real exploitation: tying sex to marriage and reproduction, for example, and demeaning women who actually enjoy sex. So women can turn feminist theory on its head but still come out attacking men! Men are evil both for encouraging women to participate in pornographic behaviour and for failing to do so. Either way, it would seem, men are wrong.

In both the United States and Canada, there has been plenty of conflict over freedom of expression. Should we limit free speech to prevent discrimination? Or should we limit discrimination by preventing free speech? This brings us to the topic of hate literature. According to Jacobs and Potter, the modern nation has had a long history of trying to suppress dangerous forms of free expression. Why allow anyone to promote prejudice based on race, nationality, or ethnicity? Jacobs and Potter conclude that "unlike most other countries in the world, in the United States these laws have not withstood judicial scrutiny or political judgment. Tolerance for vile expression is the price we pay for the right to free speech."[94] The Indianapolis ordinance promoted by Mackinnon and Dworkin inspired Harvard Law School professor Laurence Tribe to point out that "the First Amendment similarly protects advocacy ... of the opinion that women are meant to be dominated by men, or blacks to be dominated by whites, or Jews by Christians, and that those so subordinated not only deserve but subconsciously enjoy their humiliating treatment ... It is an inadequate response to argue, as do some scholars, that ordinances like that enacted by Indianapolis take aim at harms, not at expression. All viewpoint-based regulations are targeted at some supposed harm."[95]

The Canadian Civil Liberties Association has gone to court over freedom of expression and succeeded in 63% of its cases. It has failed, however, in challenging the censorship of pornograpy and hate speech.[96] Former executive director Alan Borovoy argues that liberalism is now deeply threatened by Charter litigants on the political left (even though his own organization had had close ties with the Canadian trade unions).[97] And, according to F.L. Morton and Rainer Knopff, *Butler* involved an activist and innovative approach to the interpretation of existing laws – in this case, those that censor obscenity – to square with feminism: "No longer would the law be interpreted as a bulwark of public morality against sexual depravity; it would now be seen primarily as a way of protecting women and children against male oppression. Consensual erotica would thus be distinguished from the objectification of women for the pleasure of men."[98]

At the heart of this debate is how we understand sexuality. We need to place it in a larger context. This will involve a brief discussion of male biology and cultural evolution.

Magnetic resonance imaging (MRI) records blood flow in the brain. Bright yellow and deep orange on the computer screen reveal which parts are being stimulated, and that, in turn, reveals the chemicals involved and their functions. Men and women who claimed to be deeply and happily in love were studied, using MRI, as they looked at pictures of each other and pictures of other people. The finding showed differences between most men and women. "In our sample, men tended to show more activity than women in brain regions associated with *visual* processing whereas women showed *more* activity in regions associated with motivation and attention," writes Helen Fisher, and "this male brain response may shed light on why

men so avidly support the worldwide trade in visual pornography."[99]
Fisher speculates that the connection between visualization and penile
arousal is due to the evolutionary importance of recognizing a suitable
reproductive partner. Women find reproductive partners not so much by
looking at men but by remembering which ones are most likely to provide
for them and their infants (which ones are not only strong but also smart,
fearless, generous, and so forth).

Suzanne Frayser, an anthropologist, points out that the instinctive
aspects of sexuality in human beings are always set within a context of cultural meaning,[100] that is, nature and culture are correlatives; culture guides
nature – our physical urges – to meet the reproductive needs on which we
rely for survival as families, as religious or ethnic communities, and even as
a species. We rely much less on instinct than other animals and much more
on adaptability. Culture must be flexible enough for adjustments to new
situations or environments but also conservative enough for protections to
ensure the intergeneration cycle – to ensure that most men and women are
brought together, produce children, and care for them until they reach
maturity and renew the cycle. Marriage – this institution is characteristic of
all societies, at all times, and in all places – is the cultural mechanism that
does these things.[101]

Even though marriage as a norm is universal, not all its features are;
some are nearly universal and others variable. In some societies, marriage
is mandatory, although exceptions are sometimes tolerated. In others,
exceptions are either officially or unofficially allowed. These might include
monastics, prostitutes, single people, and gay people. Given this general
mandate to ensure collective continuity, societies have handled sexuality in
various ways. Some overtly or covertly allow premarital sex. Others overtly
or covertly allow extramarital sex after marriage for men. Still others do so
for men but also for groups of women such as courtesans. That arrangement has been common throughout history but is now attacked by feminists as "male chauvinism," "patriarchy," "phallocentrism," or whatever.
Nonetheless, its underlying rationale should not be understood so reduc-
tively. Faithful wives make it possible for husbands to know who their own
children are and thus encourage fathers to invest resources in their children
accordingly. And at least before the welfare state, this was important to
women, who would otherwise have been on their own. They intuited that
this was a trade-off: of their own desire for sexual variety for protection
and resources.

Officially monogamous systems such as our own have placed prohibitions on sex outside marriage, the goal being to foster exclusive bonds
between men and women. These prohibitions have led in some cases, unofficially, to extramarital sex – usually, at least in the past, on the part of men.
And that, in turn, has led to feminist attacks on the double standard. But

most people in our society have inherited an even worse problem in the early Christian belief that sex itself is a sign of "carnality" and thus of sin. This attitude toward the material world, including that of the human body, has had profound effects by now even on secular people. When Nussbaum claims that any sexual activity is inherently contaminating unless it can be cleansed by or subordinated to some "higher" purpose, she consciously or unconsciously continues a long Western (but by no means a universal) tradition.[102]

Sorry for that digression. Back now to the point. In the past, people linked sex outside marriage mainly with prostitutes or with courtesans, their elite counterparts. In a symbolic sense, though, they linked sex outside marriage also with pornography. The latter is much more prevalent now, after the advent of technologies that make mass production and distribution possible, than it ever was. It not only competes with prostitution but also displaces it to some extent. After all, porn eliminates some of the problems that prostitution presents: unwanted pregnancy, say, and sexually transmitted diseases. Because prostitution involves people (no matter how objectified) rather than merely pictures, on the other hand, it still has one obvious advantage over pornography: a greater illusion of intimacy. From a comparative perspective, at any rate, it is clear that prostitution and pornography have been banned mainly in monogamous traditions. And even in these traditions, they have often gained unofficial acceptance. The only question is why. We do not believe that feminists have provided an adequate answer. We do believe that they, like the Christians that some of them despise, are products of cultural and religious history.

Every society must promote the intergenerational cycle through some form of marriage. With continuity thus ensured, it can afford to tolerate exceptions to the norm. In our time, the main exception, at least in secular circles, is consensual sex between adults who are neither married nor "in committed relationships." These people, especially those who intend to marry, do not threaten the norm of marriage. Nor do they threaten the stability of any particular marriage. As long as contraception prevents unwanted pregnancies, we see no harm to anyone (except to the extent that they deny themselves, even temporarily, the psychological or spiritual richness associated with marriage).

By extension, we see nothing inherently wrong with porn. It need not threaten the institution of marriage. First, consider the least problematic context: porn as fantasy for unmarried adults, whether straight or gay, couples or individuals. Through fantasies, people explore sensations. And eroticism is about sensations, in this context, not emotions or ideas. Both men and women enjoy physical sensations. Sexual pleasure is derived not only from seeing and touching, by the way, but also from hearing, smelling, tasting, and so on. It is surely unnecessary to assume that male or female lovers who enjoy licking and even nibbling each other are engaging in murderous fantasies. The pleasure here is in the act itself, not what it might lead to in some other context.

Porn as fantasy is closely linked with the desire for play. Whatever else porn might be, after all, it is surely play. Like many other species, human beings like and perhaps even need to play. Sometimes play involves physical activity, sometimes mental activity, and often both. The word "play" refers to activity that has no obvious or immediate usefulness. It has a function, true, but an indirect one. Play helps people, adults no less than children, move beyond the here and now that would otherwise monopolize their attention and prevent them from thinking about new or different possibilities. In this sense, the content of play is less relevant than the activity. Play is an end in itself but also the means to some other end. Play creates new ways of perceiving and experiencing the world. Or, putting it in slightly different terms, it fosters our ability to adapt and thus to reduce the threat of change.[103]

There are some good reasons for tolerating pornography and prostitution, which is not to say that there are good reasons for celebrating either.

Human existence would surely be easier if people had no need for sex apart from procreation. Maybe it would be easier if only we could control that need more effectively than we have. But would we be happier? To answer that question, think about the quality of life in societies that make the most intense efforts to control or deny human nature: totalitarian ones. Even if these societies could make people happier, which they do not, they would still be likely to fail in the long run. Tightly controlled societies endure only as long as conditions remain stable, as they do in relatively isolated societies (although even these, according to the current generation of anthropologists, are never either completely isolated or completely static) but not in modern ones.[104] Because they discourage innovation, the basic requirement for which is freedom of thought and the basic training for which is freedom to play, societies that depend very heavily on orthodoxy and conformity discourage the kind of adaptability required to face change effectively. The most obvious example of inflexibility in recent times, of course, is that of Eastern Europe under communism.[105] But another example, the one that is most prevalent here and now, is surely the mentality inherent in ideological feminism.

Like communism, ideological feminism is utopian. Ignoring the ambiguity and ambivalence that have always characterized human existence, it directly or indirectly proclaims that society would be happy if only it was more thoroughly controlled by the state. In other words, it focuses attention heavily on power, believing that women have less power than men (which is true in some ways though not others) but also believing that power itself should be the primary factor in creating a new and presumably better society. For women to prosper, in other words, they must control men by wielding more power over them (even though Marilyn French and some other ideological feminists assert that "power over" is a distinctively "male" preoccupation). We have argued here and elsewhere in this book that every society must use culture to create order by controlling nature but also that no society worth living in can be based entirely or even primarily on doing so.

At the very least, we should acknowledge the need for a single moral standard and a single legal one. If porn is bad because it dehumanizes women, it is surely just as bad because it dehumanizes men (either those men who are depicted in porn or those who use it). And if it is bad for men to create or buy porn, then it is surely bad for women to do the same thing. But how many women actually use porn? Very few, if you confine your inquiry to the most obvious equivalents. (At least some readers of *Playgirl*, in fact, are probably gay men.) Very many, on the other hand, if you consider various functional equivalents.

In *Spreading Misandry*, we discussed the dehumanization of men in popular culture, especially in movies and on television shows. Think now about romance novels, which are written by and for women. In these books – sold at every supermarket, this formulaic genre is probably more lucrative than any other – men are reduced to the wealthy fantasy objects of female protagonists (a topic that we discuss in appendix 5).[106] Consider also "women's magazines" and "teen 'zines." In these publications, women or girls learn how to "catch" and "hold" men or boys. They do not present readers with coarse or vulgar pictures, to be sure, but they do encourage readers to objectify and even manipulate the opposite sex. And what about soap operas? These shows manage to objectify both sexes, actually, because both are presented as sexually and financially predatory.

By far the most disturbing venue for objectifying and even dehumanizing men, though, would be the books and articles written by feminist ideologues. These publications encourage readers – either overtly or covertly, directly or indirectly – to feel contempt for men as inferior beings or even to hate men as the source of all suffering and evil throughout history. The usual justification is based on the assumption that men have such godlike power that nothing can damage them. This, we believe, is a false and dangerous assumption. It implies that women are justified in using any means short of violence (although Valerie Solanas advocated even violence)[107] to promote a social, economic, and legal revolution. Classic (but by no means rare) examples would include the following feminists: Robin Morgan, author of *Demon Lover*;[108] Marilyn French, author of *Beyond Power* (a massive compendium purporting to show not only that men are both evil and inferior to women but that so is maleness itself in just about every species)[109] and *The War against Women*;[110] Andrea Dworkin, author of *Intercourse*; and Catharine MacKinnon, author of *Toward a Feminist Theory of the State*. The list could go on and on. These authors implicitly deny the full humanity of male people.

The fact that some of these authors – not all but some – stop short of basing their claims on maleness itself does not make the sinister creatures that they describe recognizable as real human beings. They are not the complex, ambivalent, and confused people who actually co-exist in daily life with equally complex, ambivalent, and confused women (much less those who actually live with women in imperfect but mutually sustaining relationships). From what these authors say, it would seem that (straight) men have only "one thing" on their minds: not merely having sex with women but having sex with *unwilling* women – or, failing that, using some other, closely related way of subjugating women. Even though feminists of this school seldom claim that evil is genetically produced by the distinctive chromosome carried by men, they do claim that evil is culturally produced by the genetically defined class of men. The difference between these two claims, the latter ensuring that men are found morally guilty for deliberately choosing evil, is nothing if not subtle. At best, these feminists either say or imply, men are the creations of dark cultural forces that are so ancient, so titanic, so pervasive, so malevolent, and so implacable that they might just as well be genetically encoded. If men were to stop being evil, they would have to stop being men at some profound level. Only those who see the light and convert to feminism of one kind or another, as it were, are redeemable. And even then ... If this message does not qualify as hate literature, the obvious parallel being anti-Semitic literature, it is hard to imagine anything that would. So far, though, no one has suggested that we use hate legislation to ban this stuff.

Every society should acknowledge, and most do, that not everyone is going to marry and that trying to impose life-long asceticism on people who do not is unfair. In any case, if pornography and prostitution are made illegal, many people will meet their needs illegally and often in ways that are dangerous for society. Since some people will disobey the law no matter what, that argument does not in itself provide a good enough reason to legalize their behaviour, but it does provide a good enough reason to weigh the pros and cons very carefully.

Now, what about pornography or prostitution *within* marriage? Most people would reject them, because our marital tradition is monogamous (although it is becoming serially monogamous). The trouble with both pornography and prostitution, they might say if they get beyond the vulgarity or their own prudishness, is that they introduce a third party, or at least an image of one, to the marriage. The analogy is to adultery. There is some truth to that in theory. But there is ambiguity, too, in reality. Most societies and religious communities, especially monogamous ones, make massive efforts to encourage fidelity within marriage. And to some extent, pornography – along with masturbation – detracts from the centrality of a spouse. Fear of pornography and prostitution can easily become excessive, true, as it has in Western religious traditions. But the underlying problem should not be dismissed as trivial.[111]

On the other hand, these same things could actually be useful – more useful, at any rate, than in clandestine forms. Think of what can happen when one spouse is sexually withdrawn. One solution would be to dissolve the marriage, but doing so would have a negative effect on any children (apart from anyone else). Another solution would be for the sexier spouse to make use of a legal safety valve: an erotic picture, say, or a prostitute. Religious people will baulk at that suggestion, and for good *theological* reasons, but this book is not addressed exclusively (or even primarily) to religious people. It is about law, and that must apply to all people.

It is safe to say that both pornography and prostitution within marriage are morally and psychologically ambiguous. The threat to marriage and society, at any rate, is far from certain. No one would argue that looking at erotic pictures and masturbating, consorting with prostitutes, or even casual coupling with friends would be an effective way of satisfying the deepest human needs that are represented by marriage. These needs include not merely amusement, not only companionship (or even holiness, for religious people), but also enduring relationships that promote the continuity of families in particular and society in general. But human nature is complex, and we do not live in an ideal world. Not everyone can find a way to link sex with love. Even while promoting the ideal of marriage, many societies have recognized the need for compromise by implicitly tolerating other sexual outlets. In short, society should presume that erotica is legally acceptable, even if religious communities find it morally unacceptable, and that adult citizens should use their freedom to see or read whatever they want to see or read. We would not be justified in banning pornography and prostitution, therefore, although we would be justified in regulating them very carefully.

We have argued that there are some good reasons for tolerating both pornography and prostitution. But not in all contexts. We refer specifically to contexts involving violence and minors. Some have seen them at one time or another, pictures of people choking partners during oral sex or of torturing them for erotic pleasure. Others have even experienced acts of this kind with prostitutes. Maybe these are not just innocent fantasies; maybe they reveal at least the secret desire to inflict pain. Maybe, though not necessarily. They might in fact be merely fantasies, daydreams that explore the forbidden.[112] As a form of play, porn can be linked with both anarchy or violence and artistic or intellectual creativity. The link is inconvenient, to be sure, but not necessarily evil. The case against "rough sex" or sado-masochism can be made effectively, but it is more complicated than meets the eye.

Here is an analogous situation: the imaginative exploration of murder in mainstream movies. Everyone recognizes that these movies are fictional. Moreover, they are placed within a moral framework. Until the day before yesterday, as it were, moviegoers were always expected to believe that murder is indeed evil and that those who do evil will be brought to justice. But critics of violent porn might say that because it is more or less hidden from view, it lacks that moral framework. Its defenders might reply that it allows people to explore fantasies that have nothing to do with the real world, ones that they would never act out in real life. And they might add that the moral framework is sometimes very ambiguous in mainstream movies, particularly in some recent ones, but also even in earlier ones. You have only to think of one famous scene in *Gone with the Wind* (which we discuss in appendix 5). Rhett carries Scarlett, against her will, up to the bedroom and has "his way" with her. Next morning, however, a delighted Scarlett wants more of the same from Rhett. Well, was she raped or not? And if so, are viewers – female viewers – justified in enjoying the fantasy? Should this movie be banned or the scene excised by censors?

A similar question arises with respect to violence on television. It is true that a few viewers go out and copy the violence they see on television, and there is some evidence that children and adolescents who watch a lot of violent shows are more likely than others to become violent in the future.[113] But most viewers, by far, do nothing of the kind. Clearly, then, some *additional* factor or factors must be involved in cases of antisocial behaviour. If additional factors were not involved, one might ask feminists who want to ban porn why they do not want to ban television as well? And if not all forms of television, why not at least some forms? Possibly because feminists present porn as a threat to women alone (despite gay porn), which makes it easy for them to conceptualize porn as a "women's issue." They can hardly say the same of violence on television, which presents at least as many male victims of violence as female ones. But if violence against women is intolerable, why not violence against men as well? Is the latter acceptable merely because in many cases both the culprits and the victims are men, as if the victims somehow deserve their fate by virtue of their common maleness?

The problem of ambiguity aside, would women actually be safer if men were denied outlets such as porn or prostitution? Who knows? In the papers collected for *In Harm's Way*, McKinnon and Dworkin, along with many others, present evidence of porn leading directly to violence against women, although they say little or nothing about gay porn leading to violence against men or even about lesbian porn leading to violence against women.

Can pornography and prostitution lead to violence? Of course they can. Must they do so? Are they inherently evil? Not unless human nature itself – and, in this context, most people would think of male human nature – is evil. Here is the implicit deductive argument that underlies this entire discussion: All men like porn; porn is evil; all those who like something that is evil are themselves evil; ergo, all men are evil. There are those who believe precisely this. When people discuss porn in the public square (and even within religious communities, which often agree with radical feminism on that particular topic), they should at least acknowledge one of the several things at stake: the condemnation of an entire group of people on biological grounds.[114]

But something must still be done about pornography and prostitution (although minors are already protected). Like so many other unregulated or deregulated industries, they can cause serious harm. Apart from any ways in which they endanger women in particular, after all, they are currently operating in ways that endanger society as a whole. Partly because of their marginal status as underground operations, for instance, both are heavily associated with drugs and violence. The solution most commonly proposed by ideological feminists in the United States and Canada is to ban them, or at least try to do so. At stake in that solution, especially in connection with porn, is freedom of expression, which raises several questions. Is society more in danger from the absence of freedom or the misuse of freedom? Is society more in danger from conformity or nonconformity? We suggest that no solution will work unless it accepts ambiguity and therefore compromise. From this point of view, it would make sense for the law to presume that people are free to conduct their lives as they see fit but also to limit that freedom – and freedom is always limited to activities that do not endanger others – when either violence or minors are involved.

What, then, would we actually suggest in the way of law reform? As for pornography, we see no reason to oppose the production of erotic imagery. On the other hand, we support the current prohibition of material that either depicts or involves minors in its production. In addition, we would encourage legislation against violent porn but not against vague ideas of the "subordination of women." And as for prostitution, we see no reason to oppose payment for sexual services. To put it bluntly, we would stop the prosecution, even persecution, not only of adult prostitutes but also of their adult customers.

Although some erotic pornography is classified as art and although high-end prostitutes live and work in very comfortable conditions, pornography and prostitution are heavily associated with the lurid and the sordid. Why tolerate these industries? Because, whether some people want to admit it or not, both pornography and prostitution serve a very widespread need. And not only for men. As Frederick Mathews points out in connection with a study by the National Juvenile Prostitution Survey, half the juvenile prostitutes reported that they had been approached by female customers or female pimps, or "procuresses." Of these prostitutes, 62% were male and 43.4% females.[115] Women do enjoy watching the Chippendales "dance," watching steamy soap operas, and reading romance novels. And all those things are forms of porn, albeit ones that most people consider respectable.

Many who turn to either pornographic images or prostitutes are unable to find sexual gratification in more satisfying ways – that is, in the context of marriage or some other durable relationship, rather than in the context of a business transaction. These people lack the money, good looks, personality skills, or whatever, to attract spouses. And far from being an inherent threat to marriage, as we say, pornographic images and prostitutes might actually prevent at least a few marriages from disintegrating due to affairs; people pay for them, after all, without loving them. Those involved in these industries – male or female, gay or straight – would become providers of a service like any other. Not love, which cannot be hired, but sex. This is particularly important in the case of prostitutes. In a regulated industry – and prostitution is regulated in some European countries – they could participate in the economy: paying taxes but also collecting sickness or unemployment insurance, old-age pensions, and so on. Government inspection or supervision, moreover, could provide them with healthier working conditions and eliminate pimps.

Lowman's approach might be helpful. "We should repeal all the prostitution laws," he says, "and start over."[116] He continues by suggesting that four principles should guide legislators: considering the procurement of minors for prostitution "as an abuse of power, not a prostitution contract" (by which he must mean an abuse of prostitution); using ordinary criminal laws to protect prostitutes from violent customers and pimps; using ordinary civil laws to control street life in the interest of bystanders and residents; and helping prostitutes establish businesses for themselves in "appropriate locations." To these, we would add the following: replacing the double standard for prostitutes and their customers with a single one. If we refrain from treating prostitutes as criminals, then we should refrain from treating their customers as criminals – unless, of course, the latter indulge in violence or other criminal activities.

If we ban violent pornography for leading to violence against women in real life, for instance, then we should ban violent popular culture as well – that would include movies, songs, and even some segments of news shows – for leading to violence against everyone. If we ban it for expressing hatred against women, then we should ban feminist books and other productions that express hatred against men. If we ban merely erotic porn for objectifying women, then we should ban romance novels, along with ideological diatribes for "objectifying" men.

If we ban porn intended for straight people, moreover, then we should ban porn intended for gay people. Little is said in public about gay porn, because gay men and women are considered oppressed groups, or "equity seeking groups," and therefore immune to criticism. The fact is, however, that many gay people like porn and some resort to prostitutes. Feminist lesbians try hard, nevertheless, to dissociate themselves from gay men on this topic. Their porn is said to be superior, somehow, to gay male porn. One lesbian, for example, argues that she and her friends prefer "art porn" to the vulgar and raunchy stuff gay men prefer. "Its more sophisticated strategies of hiding, showing and implying sexuality are far more interesting than two-hour videos of badly shot humping. Perhaps, just perhaps, we dykes are more sexually complex beasts than our gay brothers, needing more than dicks in holes to get us off. And, as we've suspected all along, women turn to other, more fulfilling, sources to arouse and satisfy their fantasy selves unlike those straight boys who still haven't figured out that 'Here clitty, clitty' won't get girls the least bit wet *or* wild."[117] Well, la-di-da.

MacKinnon and Dworkin are clearly at one end of the feminist continuum, even of the ideological feminist continuum. They are radicals, or, as we would say, ideologues. But they are neither loony nor stupid. On the contrary, they are rational and brilliant. And their arguments are sophisticated. Given the initial ideological premises, these arguments proceed clearly, logically, and consistently to articulate a coherent worldview. This worldview is in profound and irreconcilable conflict with other worldviews, however, including the one that we support. And the evidence indicates that their worldview is rapidly becoming the dominant one in our society, the one that sets the tone for legislation. Anyone who thinks that our society is moving away from polarization between men and women, therefore, should think again.

At the heart of our dispute with MacKinnon and Dworkin is not merely what they say about men but what they do not say about hatred. They would never admit to hating men. After all, "hating" is not a word that most people apply to themselves. But that is partly because of how they define the word "hatred." If it refers to emotional antipathy, then it would be easy to deny any accusation of hatred. Even MacKinnon and Dworkin like some men. On that basis, they could say honestly that they do not hate all men. But as we have pointed out elsewhere, hatred should not be used as a synonym for emotional antipathy, or anger, toward this or that individual. It should be used instead to describe a distinctive phenomenon: the deliberate cultural propagation of contempt for a whole segment of the population – a race, a class, a sex, or whatever – *per se*. In this respect, it would be hard to read anything by MacKinnon or Dworkin that could not be classified as hate literature. They present male people – all of them, even the few likable individuals who try to mitigate the inherent malevolence of their own maleness – as thoroughly contaminated by malice toward women, by evil that they have chosen collectively. Feminists under their influence would find it very hard not to have contempt for men as a class and foster legislation that puts men in their place as those who would harass, batter, rape, and kill women if only they were allowed to do so. At the very least, converts would find it hard not to discourage any fraternization whatever between women and their inferiors. If this reminds you of racism, it is no accident. Even though they eschew the crude notion of biological determinism, they foster the slightly more sophisticated notion of cultural determinism (applied, however, to a group that is biologically defined). Hence the need to destroy the current culture, root and branch, and replace it with another.

8

Separatists v. Integrationists: The Case of Sexual Harassment

Men who sexually harass say [that] women sexually harass them. They mean they are aroused by women who turn them down. This elaborate projective system ... is surely a delusional structure deserving of serious psychological study. Instead, it is women who resist it who are studied ... The assumption that in matters sexual women really want what men want from women, makes male force against women in sex invisible. It makes rape sex.[1]

What we may have thought of, with self-hatred and guilt, as a dirty childhood game is reinterpreted as child sexual abuse. The flattering wolf-whistle becomes sexual harassment. The pile of dirty dishes in the sink no longer occasions self-rebuke and a sense of personal failure, but rather anger at an unreconstructed husband. It is not simply that the interpretation of the experience changes: the very experience and the emotions associated with it are different too.[2]

Early in 2004 a controversy erupted over a claim by Naomi Wolf, famous until then for two feminist tomes: *The Beauty Myth*[3] and *Fire with Fire*.[4] In a major article for *New York Magazine*, she accused literary scholar Harold Bloom of having placed his hand on her thigh twenty years earlier.[5] She had been a senior at Yale, he her much older prof, and the two had been enjoying dinner and wine in her apartment at her invitation – presumably, on a purely scholarly basis. "The next thing I knew, his heavy, boneless hand was hot on my thigh."[6] Bloom left after the alleged act, and Wolf threw up. (How would she have reacted, one cannot help wondering, if her assailant had been a handsome young man with a slender, sinewy hand?) But her ordeal did not end. In fact, the trauma has continued to torment her ever since. According to Wolf, "the transgression ... devastated my sense of being valuable to Yale as a student."[7] First, she claims, her grades went down due to rage and depression. Then she failed to get a Rhodes scholarship on the basis of Bloom's recommendation (although she later clarified early reports by saying that his letter had been written before the incident in question took place).

But now, after months of getting nowhere with officials at Yale and no doubt empowered by her own journey into feminism, Wolf went public, although she had already alluded to this event in college talks. Why then? To save other women, at Yale and elsewhere, from the same horror, not so much from an inappropriate romantic overture, because Yale and other universities have long since brought in new codes of professional etiquette, but from an indifferent academic bureaucracy. At the very least, she must believe, both Bloom and Yale should be suitably punished in the court of public opinion for her suffering. Why not sue either Bloom or Yale? Because the university's policy on sexual harassment is clear. It gives alleged victims two years, not two decades, to report events of this kind. And besides, Bloom had indeed taken no for an answer; even Wolf does not allege that he had continued his advance toward her.

Some people have argued that Wolf was justified in protesting not only the way that she was abused by a professor twenty years earlier but also the way that she had been abused much more recently by academic bureaucrats. Others have argued that Wolf ignored the gains of women. Wolf, writes Anne Applebaum, has "reduced herself to a victim, nothing more. The implication here is women are psychologically weak: One hand on the thigh, and they never get over it. The implication is also women are naive, and powerless as well: Even Yale undergraduates are not savvy enough to avoid late-night encounters with male professors whose romantic intentions don't interest them."[8] Still others have argued that Wolf applied the standard of our time to the ways of an earlier time; she sought not justice but notoriety and succumbed to the victim mentality that permeates our politically and sexually correct society by almost equating a man's hand on a woman's thigh with rape.[9] And if you think that this controversy emerged out of nowhere, read on.

After a brief introduction on the historical context, we review the legislation governing sexual harassment and continue by discussing the ideological assumptions that have influenced recent legislation, several strategies that are used to institutionalize the position of ideological feminists, the ways in which formal legislation has influenced the less formal policies of institutions such as the university, "heterophobia" (which, though never acknowledged by feminist ideologues and seldom even noticed by other feminists, is both an assumption and a strategy), and the effects of this debate.

By the 1960s, women, including highly educated women, had become a major part of the labour force. The men who worked in their offices and factories, unfortunately, did not always welcome them for purely professional reasons. Some men bartered jobs or promotions for sexual favours, an arrangement that is usually known as quid pro quo. Other men did not welcome women at all. Seeing the workplace as a symbol of masculine identity, they tried to discourage women and thus get rid of them. Still other men made them uncomfortable, often unwittingly, by displaying pictures of nude women here and there or making risqué jokes now and then. All of these things, which came to be called "sexual harassment," led women to mobilize for legal and quasi-legal measures to protect themselves. These measures have been nothing if not controversial, and we will discuss them in the following pages.

But first we must acknowledge our particular indebtedness to Daphne Patai. She has commented extensively on sexual harassment. Because her analysis of ideological assumptions and strategies amounts to a brilliant exposé of feminism's dark side, we have drawn heavily on her work. She argues that misandry is indeed pervasive in contemporary feminism, and not merely on the fringes.[10] She argues also that it is revealed most strikingly among those feminists who have deliberately generated what she calls the "sexual harassment industry." At any rate, Patai is important here for three reasons. First, she identifies the strategies that ideological feminists use to move from the fringe to the mainstream. Second, she highlights the link that they make between sexual harassment in the workplace and sexual harassment in other forms: pornography, prostitution, rape, domestic violence, and so on – all of which, for ideologues, are variants of the same phenomenon. Third, she intuits that ideologues see the source of all these problems not merely in male sexuality but in heterosexuality. This last insight was the missing link in our own theory of misandry.

American legislation on sexual harassment has proliferated. Title VII of the Civil Rights Act of 1964 does not refer explicitly to sexual harassment, but it does refer to discrimination by "race, color, religion, sex, or national origin." The same title established the Equal Employment Opportunity Commission, its job being to implement and enforce the act. In 1972, title IX of the Education Amendments extended the scope of the Civil Rights Act to include institutions that receive federal funding.[11] In addition, it established formal grievance procedures. In 1976 the federal case of *Williams v. Saxbe*[12] and in 1980 that of *Alexander v. Yale University*[13] extended the idea of discrimination based on sex to quid pro quo sexual harassment.

American feminists found it very hard to find legal grounds for charging men with "subtle crimes" such as "offensive behaviour." Apart from anything else, charges of this kind led to countercharges of obstructing free speech. But the Equal Employment Opportunity Commission provided a loophole. Its 1980 guidelines extended the concept of sexual harassment to include "unreasonably interfering with a person's work performance or creating an intimidating, hostile, or offensive work environment." The guidelines were used in *Moire v. Temple University School of Medicine*[14] and a few years later in *Meritor Savings Bank v. Vinson*[15] (a case we discuss below).

According to the Civil Rights Act of 1964 illegal discrimination had to be intentional. The Civil Rights Act of 1991, however, removed that requirement. The emphasis was now on "disparate impact," or effect, not intention. In 1992 the Campus Sexual Assault Victims' Bill of Rights[16] – this is binding on all universities that receive federal funds – required authorities to revise their policies in ways that protected those making charges of sexual harassment. By 1993 it was no longer necessary for plaintiffs to show even that they had been harmed by the allegedly offensive behaviour. According to guidelines established by the Equal Employment Opportunity Commission, sexual harassment included conduct that merely created "an intimidating, hostile or offensive working environment."

Canada took similar measures. The *Canada Labour Code*, according to a reader-friendly pamphlet, "establishes an employee's right to employment free of sexual harassment and requires employers to take positive action to prevent sexual harassment in the work place."[17] And sexual harassment includes "any conduct, comment, gesture, or contact of a sexual nature that is likely to cause offence or humiliation to any employee or that might, on reasonable grounds, be perceived by that employee as placing a condition of a sexual nature on employment or on any opportunity for training or promotion."[18] Sexual harassment includes, among other things, the "displaying of sexually explicit, racist or other offensive or derogatory pictures."[19] Employers must have a policy in place and make "every reasonable effort" to make sure their employees do not experience harassment. Employees who do, though, have a right to complain without revealing their identities "unless disclosure is necessary for the purposes of investigating ... or taking disciplinary measures."[20] When alleged harassers are found guilty, employers must take disciplinary action. Unsatisfied victims have a "right to take a complaint under the Canadian Human Rights Act."[21]

One assumption of those who advocate legislative change in both Canada and the United States is that only women encounter sexual harassment. Catharine MacKinnon claims precisely that.[22] According to her statistics, moreover, as many as seven out of ten American women experience sexual harassment at least once in their lives. But these statistics are highly questionable (as we show in appendix 3).

Another assumption, articulated most effectively by MacKinnon (usually with Andrea Dworkin) is that sexual harassment constitutes merely the tip of a patriarchal iceberg. She believes that men find women sexually attractive precisely *because* women lack power and are oppressed. To satisfy their sexual inclinations, therefore, they must continue to subordinate or oppress women. It works the other way, too. She believes that women find men sexually attractive – which is to say, that women have been culturally conditioned to find men sexually attractive – precisely *because* men have power and are oppressive. The upshot of her argument is this: to eliminate one factor (the power of men over women) requires us to eliminate the other (heterosexual attraction) as well. The more difficult we make it for men to act out their sexual impulses, no matter how trivial or even welcome these might seem to patriarchally programmed women, the better off women will be. Clearly, MacKinnon wants to marginalize or even demonize ordinary men – all men, not only deviant men. For her, in fact, the only deviant men would be those who *agree* with her theory.

This last point is worth discussing in more detail. For MacKinnon, the mystifying power of men is not merely pervasive in this particular society at this particular time but inherent in the way things always have been and always will be whenever men and women interact – even here and now, when women wield power in everyday life. Hence her dictum that sexual harassment "is done by men to women regardless of relative position on the formal hierarchy."[23] Obviously, the ultimate solution would be to prevent women from coming into any contact at all with men.

Both MacKinnon and Dworkin recognize the possibility of consensual arrangements between women but not between women and men. Because they believe that all women in our society are subordinate to all men, even if they actually earn more money than men or outrank them, it follows for them that no woman in any circumstance is actually capable of freely giving consent to sexual relations with any man, much less of actually wanting sexual relations with any man. Every heterosexual act, therefore, is defined in terms of violence. That is merely one point on a continuum, one that begins at the seemingly innocent end with friendly heterosexual relations, continues with sexual harassment, and ends with rape.

Before the Messianic Age, though, women will have to live with men. What ideological feminists want, Patai points out, is to "alter the terms of the negotiation so that women hold all the cards."[24] When the words "unwanted" or "unwelcome" become "routinized, it will be difficult to challenge such a privileging of one sex's 'wants' over the other's, for merely to raise a question about it invites the retort that one is promoting oppressive behavior toward women (or is selling out to the patriarchy)."[25] Never discussed, says Patai, is women's own allure created by gesture, dress, and so forth. This, too, is a kind of power. "The message is clear: Women are never at fault. They need not examine their own ways. They need only to learn when and how to file complaints, although, interestingly, even this recourse is never construed as a 'power' in their possession. Only men have power, and it is men, not women, who need to change."[26]

Those two fundamental assumptions – that only women encounter sexual

harassment and that sexual harassment (like rape) is based on the eroticization of male power over women – have led ideological feminists to adopt several strategies in their quest for a feminist utopia. We have already referred,
both in this chapter and in the previous one, to two extremely effective
strategies of ideological feminism: expanding the definition of one crime to
include forms of behaviour that were once not classified as crimes, or reinforcing old claims with new ones, and eventually generating something that
approaches hysteria. This strategy requires them to keep upping the ante.
Just as pornography and prostitution can be forms of rape, so can sexual
harassment. We call this strategy "linguistic inflation," because words or
ideas can be debased and thus made trivial (unintentionally or not) just as
currencies can be debased and thus made worthless. Here is Patai on the topic.

As I have repeatedly stressed, the SHI [Sexual Harassment Industry] does not
attempt to differentiate between instances of indisputable abuse and mere expressions of sexual interest. Each is taken to be as egregious as the other. The key concept by which male-female interactions are being redefined is "power differential,"
the presence of which contaminates any sexually tinged word, gesture, or look and
turns it, potentially, into "sexual harassment." This persistent inability or refusal to
draw distinctions cannot be taken as accidental. Male sexual interest is not simply
being construed, or interpreted, as "power." It has actually been redefined as such.
The slow and continuous expansion of efforts to regulate personal relations, now
extending even to consensual relationships between adults, is a particularly clear
example of the stigmatizing of male sexuality in and of itself. True, women and
homosexuals are occasionally caught in the trap, but this seems an unintended consequence; they are not the main targets – as the sexual harassment literature has
made clear from its very inception. Sexual harassment is first and foremost an act
committed by powerful males against powerless females. The infantilization of
adult women implicit in this view does not seem to trouble many of those who pro-
fess feminism.[27]

The original problem, quid pro quo harassment in this case, is now understood as the mere tip of a colossal patriarchal iceberg – that is, a vast and
eternal conspiracy of men to objectify, subjugate, subordinate, and otherwise oppress women. According to MacKinnon, "economic power is to
sexual harassment as physical force is to rape."[28]
    The new definition of sexual harassment became dinner-table conversa-
tion in connection with Anita Hill's allegation against Clarence Thomas,
but it was established as law in *Vinson*. MacKinnon represented Mechelle
Vinson in this case, which provoked a landmark decision, according to an
article in US *News and World Report*, because it redefined sexual harassment by expanding it to include the experience of a hostile work environment.[29] But this article neglects to mention what really changed after this

case. According to *Newsweek*, it involved far more than a hostile work-place: it involved rape. Vinson "claimed that her supervisor fondled her in front of other employees, followed her into the lady's room, exposed himself and, on several occasions, *raped* her."[30]

Now consider a chart that appeared in the same article. A survey in 1987 (before the Hill-Thomas affair) found that 35% of the sample included "sexual remarks" as a defining feature of sexual harassment; 28% included "suggestive looks," 26% included "deliberate touching," 15% included "pressure for dates," 12% included "letters and calls," 9% included "pressure for sexual favours," and 8% included "actual or attempted rape or assault."[31] Two conclusions can be drawn from these figures. First, the definition of sexual harassment now includes rape itself. Second, the definition of rape now includes sexual harassment. Since 1986, it is worth repeating, rape and "sexual remarks" have been merely two ends of a single continuum, two manifestations of a single phenomenon. If someone who rapes can be charged with sexual harassment, therefore, why should someone who merely makes "sexual remarks" not be charged with rape? Clearly, a major change took place between 1980, when the Equal Employment Opportunity Commission based its guidelines on civil rights legislation, and 1986, when the Supreme Court based its definition in *Vinson* – a case that could have been argued on the grounds of rape or indecent exposure – on feminist ideology.

Patai, too, comments on the recent tendency of "experts" to conflate mere words or gestures that make women uncomfortable with serious offenses.[32] Linguistic inflation works in two ways because the process, once set in motion, is self-perpetuating. The goal is to protect women from men by making interaction between the sexes increasingly hard. But the increasingly ugly consequences for men who do interact with women require increasingly grandiose justifications. This problem is solved, observes Patai, by expanding and magnifying – we would say almost "sacralizing" – the notion of sexual harassment as a counterpart of rape. Ideological feminists transform accusers first into victims and then into "survivors," as if they had been brutally assaulted, tortured, or persecuted.[33] Until the late 1980s, in fact, the word survivor was used most often in connection with two horrors: the Nazi death camps and cancer. Only then did feminists expand on "survivor" by applying it to molestation, domestic violence, and sexual harassment. "By means of semantic contamination," says Patai, "a seamless continuum exists between passing comments, criticism in the classroom (which 'silences' women students), and criminal sexual assault."[34]

As Patai points out in connection with MacKinnon's belief that verbal hostility is tantamount to rape (a controversy that we discuss in chapter 9), MacKinnon "could not seriously maintain that 'I hate you, dumb cunt' is the same thing as killing a woman in a misogynistic rage."[35] If words are made to seem like deeds, they become as damaging as deeds. But Patai notices that MacKinnon is nothing if not clever. She justifies linguistic inflation on the basis of speech-act theory, which tries to show that words *are* deeds. When hearing a word becomes an experience of violation, then sexual harassment becomes a self-fulfilling prophecy. Ideological feminists want something more than mere equality with men, whether in the university or in the workplace. The whole point of inflating the harms of sexual harassment is to inflate the severity and pervasiveness of evil that can be attributed to men and therefore to justify the separation of women from men – that is, to undermine the movement toward the integration of men and women. (Some ideological feminists imply the desirability of sexual separatism on psychological or psychoanalytical grounds, as we point out in appendix 5, without actually demanding it on political grounds.)

Here is an example of linguistic inflation, albeit a hypothetical one, from Katie Roiphe. A new female student considers it sexual harassment when a guy flirts with her at a college party – even though he refrains from actually touching her. As college life goes on, she experiences more incidents of this kind. Now a feminist, she believes in the "zookeeper" approach: training the "beast" to behave in acceptable ways. Here is a real account:

Susan Teres ... said, at the 1992 Take Back the Night march, that 88 percent of Princeton's female students had experienced some form of sexual harassment on campus. Catharine MacKinnon, a professor of law and the chief architect of American legal harassment policies, writes that "Only 7.8 percent of women in the United States are not sexually assaulted or harassed in their lifetimes." No wonder. Once you cast the net so wide as to include everyone's everyday experience, identifying sexual harassment becomes a way of interpreting the sexual texture of daily life, instead of isolating individual events. Sensitivity to sexual harassment becomes a way of seeing the world, rather than a way of targeting specific contemptible behaviors. In an essay attempting to profile the quintessential harasser, two feminists warn in conclusion (and in all seriousness) that "the harasser is similar, perhaps disturbingly so, to the "average man."

As one peruses guidelines on sexual harassment, it's clear where the average man comes in. Like most common definitions, Princeton's definition of sexual harassment includes "leering and ogling, whistling, sexual innuendo, and other suggestive or offensive or derogatory comments, humor and jokes about sex." MacKinnon's statistic includes obscene phone calls. These definitions of sexual harassment sterilize the environment. They propose classrooms that are cleaner than Sesame Street and Mr. Rogers's Neighborhood. Like the rhetoric about date rape, this extreme inclusiveness forces women into old roles. What message are we sending if we say We can't work if you tell dirty jokes, it upsets us, it offends us? With this severe conception of sexual harassment, sex itself gets pushed into a dark, seamy, male domain ...

If someone bothers us, we should be able to put him in his place without crying into our pillow or screaming for help or counseling. If someone stares at us, or talks dirty, or charges neutral conversation with sexual innuendo, we should not be pushed to the verge of a nervous breakdown. In an American College Health Association pamphlet, "Unwanted sexual comments, jokes or gestures" are characterized as "a form of sexual assault." Feminists drafting sexual harassment guidelines seem to have forgotten childhood's words of wisdom: sticks and stones may break my bones, but names will never harm me."[36]

It could be argued that Roiphe has gone to the other extreme, claiming that all problems can be solved by wielding a sharp tongue. But many of them, surely, can be.

Linguistic inflation would never have been an effective strategy had it not been for another ideological strategy. Every law is supposed to be reasonable. But reasonable according to which standard? Or, to be more precise, in connection with the dominance of postmodernism, *whose* standard? Surely not that of a reasonable person, ideological feminists argued, because male and female persons have totally different ways of thinking about or experiencing the world. Men do so from a position of power, supposedly, and women from one of subordination. Their gynocentric approach "encouraged feminists to pursue new theories that would better reflect the women's view of office flirtations."[37] They began to argue that harassment charges should be judged from the viewpoint of a reasonable woman, not a reasonable person. And they emphasized "woman," not "reasonable."[38] What they meant by a "reasonable woman" was by no means self-evident.

In *Louis Robinson v. Jacksonville Shipyards,*[39] a federal judge in Florida declared in 1991 that pictures of nude women displayed on the wall of a dry dock were legitimate evidence of what a reasonable woman could consider sexual harassment.[40] This case institutionalized an aspect of MacKinnon's position on porn. And in San Francisco, a federal appeals panel ruled that a female agent of the Internal Revenue Service could sue a fellow agent "for pestering her with sexual innuendoes in conversation and love letters."[41] The court declared that "a reasonable woman" could consider this conduct "sufficiently severe and pervasive to ... create an abusive working environment."[42] These two cases and an increasing number of other court cases opened up the possibility that almost any aspect of men's conduct – the guidelines of the Equal Employment Opportunities Commission consume no fewer than thirty-one pages – could be grounds for "reasonable women" to accuse them of sexual harassment. "Thus, a woman's subjective judgment of men's actions, regardless of their intent, became the standard by which complaints could be judged."[43] Merely feeling uncomfortable is now cause for litigation. The "reasonable woman" is not someone whose goal is to rely on reason and cultivate objectivity, after all, but someone whose goal is to rely on emotion and cultivate subjectivity.

Feminists argued not merely that the collectivity of women alone should define sexual harassment but also that the individual woman alone should be able to establish when it has taken place. And the courts have accepted this. The law's point of view, legal experts say, is that of the victim. "As one attorney for employers put it, 'If one woman's interpretation sets the legal standard, then it is virtually up to every woman in the workplace to define if she's been sexually harassed.' This puts sexual harassment in the same category as violations of college speech and behaviour codes, which often turn on the feelings of the aggrieved rather than on any objective and definable offense. But if feelings are trumps, how do we know when sexism and harassment end and hypersensitivity or even ideology begins?"[44] According to the guidelines of the Equal Employment Opportunity Commission, claimants must show that the "purpose or effect" of some behaviour interferes with their ability to work and thus creates an "intimidating, hostile, or offensive work environment."[45] As in a famous theological dispute of the Middle Ages,[46] one tiny word has sparked a conflagration: the word "or," as in "purpose or effect." Women no longer need to prove that men actually intended to be offensive. They need only allege that a "reasonable woman" could have interpreted his behaviour in that way. "This set the stage," writes Patai, "for the elevation of women's word to the level of law – which was precisely the goal of feminist activists."[47]

To be universally acceptable and therefore effective, law must be based on objective criteria. Something is either legal or illegal. It either did or did not take place. But this standard no longer applies to laws that affect women. Instead, radical subjectivity applies.[48] Ultimately at issue here and elsewhere in this book is the privileged position of subjectivity in feminist (and postmodernist) thought. Privileging subjectivity has had important consequences not only for jurisprudence but also for scholarship. (We discuss the link between epistemological subjectivism and ideological feminism in chapter 10). At issue here is the ultimate authority that feminists – and not only ideological ones – attribute to experience (the celebrated subjectivity that they associate with women) instead of to reason (the supposedly arid or even destructive objectivity that they associate with men, even though they undermine the position of female scholars by doing so). Apart from anything else, they hope to obviate the need for rational argument and rely instead on emotional ranting. Appealing to what women "know" (and what men either do not or cannot know) has been popular among feminists for decades. Ideological feminists believe that women have an innate advantage when it comes to feeling. (Misogynists agree, ironically, but consider their reliance on feeling an innate disadvantage.) The glorification of feeling, often accompanied by the denigration of thinking or logic, is characteristic of the pervasive therapeutic emotionalism that is best illustrated by the daytime talk shows on television and the rampant popularity of pop psychology. Witness the public response to Princess Diana's death.[49]

In another sense, though, the "reasonable woman" is someone whose goal is to rely on neither the objectivity of reason nor the subjectivity of emotion but on a hybrid that could be called "subjective reason." We refer by that oxymoron to objectivity in the service of subjectivity, or reason in the service of ideology (which is by definition about "us" versus "them" and therefore subjective). In other words, the "reasonable woman" is really an *ideological* woman, one who has been trained to think in "ideologically reasonable" ways.

At first, the trouble was that not many women had been suitably trained to recognize signs of their own oppression. They needed expert advice, training manuals, support groups, counselling sessions, and so on. Which they got. The results have been serious. Feelings of discomfort were transmuted into feelings of a hostile environment. And due process disappeared for the accused. No matter. Except, of course, to men. Given everything that Patai has said about the background of this "reasonable woman" standard, it would be tempting to call it the "reasonable ideologue" standard. There would be no point in doing so, however, because reason is not a significant feature of ideology. The appeal of all ideologies, whether on the political left or the political right, is primarily emotional. In order to exploit collective identity for political purposes, after all, every ideology must first establish and support it.

Ideological feminists make a direct link between experience and interpretation. Celia Kitzinger, for instance, observes in the second epigraph to this chapter that what we now call "sexual harassment" is a "social construction" (just as sexuality is).[50] "It is not simply that the interpretation of the experience changes: the very experience and the emotions associated with it are different too."[51] Kitzinger could have added that women are being taught precisely how to reinterpret things. Patai puts it this way: "Unlike battery and sexual assault, where the hurt resides in the action itself, the injury in much of what is today labeled sexual harassment arises in the *interpretation* women are being taught to adopt as a guide to understanding others' words and gestures."[52] Everyone wants to legislate safety for women, but ideological feminists want to legislate comfort for women.

Another strategy could be called "victimology." To Patai's point, we add the following. The preoccupation with victimology has a complex history. It involves not only ideological feminism but also pop psychologism and neo-Romanticism, both of which glorify emotion at the expense of reason and both of which are strongly supported by various branches of feminism. Victims are people. They are citizens. But so are the accused and even the condemned. Our legal systems do bend over backward, as it were, to ensure that the accused are given every opportunity to defend themselves. They are mere individuals, after all, confronted by the massive power of the state.

Victims of sexual harassment share one set of characteristics: vulnerability and (often) femaleness. Victimizers share another set: power and (often) maleness. Forget the real world; rhetoric is what really counts here. Completely ignored is women's own harassment of male professors and students, because "in such a perspective, an individual woman's 'professional power' is always trumped by a male's (including a male student's) 'social power.'"[53] This attitude is not an abstraction, of interest only to ideological theoreticians and their opponents. It is a fact of everyday life in the classroom and the workplace.

Having already discussed the strategies of law reformers in our review of the legislation on sexual harassment, we turn now to the less formal counterparts of this legislation: quasi-legal measures that include the codes or policies established by institutions such as universities and corporations. Better to err on the side of caution – that is, on the side of those who would throw all caution to the winds in their zeal to convict sexual harassers (especially government officials responsible for either withholding grant money or taking punitive legal action that would lead to financial damages) – than on the side of justice. The major impact of recent legislation is not to be seen in the few cases that make it into court, surely, but in the fact that all private companies and public institutions now protect themselves with quasi-legal sexual-harassment codes.

Aside from instituting definitions that are too broad and too ambiguous, these codes often ignore due process, which contributes to the chilling, and even polarizing, effect on relations between men and women. Of greatest importance here, however, is that one sex has gained the upper hand. Women alone have been allowed to decide what is or is not permissible. And men – most of those accused so far have been men – have been saddled with the burden of proof. In short, they are guilty unless proven innocent. This perception, fostered by both law and policy, fosters the more general perception that men are evil. This is no longer a matter of gynocentrism, which might, at least in theory, be justified as a corrective to androcentrism. It is a matter of institutionalized, legalized misandry.

Many universities have come up with codes of "sexual correctness" to match their codes of political correctness. In some cases, the authorities adopt them formally. In other cases, the students adopt them informally. At Antioch College in Yellow Springs, Ohio,[54] students require verbal permis-

sion not only for every stage in the process of seduction – including kissing, touching, and even looking – but also on every occasion of seduction.
This new norm is called "communicative sex." Patai refers to the message
that this sends to men, who are assumed to be the seducers, but not only
to men. "Looks, gestures, sighs, hints, the back-and-forth of sexual play –
all would be delegitimized if explicit verbal consent were to become the
sine qua non of 'legal sex.'"[55] Given the constant threat of litigation, moreover, sensible men would have to insist on written permission. Just try to
make a romantic movie out of that.

In a contribution to "Hers," in the *New York Times Magazine*, Francine
Prose provides a case study of what sexual harassment can mean in an
American university.[56] Prose introduces herself as a feminist. "I write about
'women's issues.' I teach in writing programs and am painfully aware of the
pressures facing young (and older) female writers. I find myself more often
than not taking the woman's side. I believed Anita Hill."[57] But in the case
of her friend, Stephen Dobyns, she takes the other side.

Dobyns, a writer and teacher of creative writing, was brought before an
academic tribunal. At a party, he had splashed a drink in the face of a student who had overheard him talking about her breasts – that is, she had
overheard him asking a colleague to stop looking at them – and she had
filed a formal complaint. Two other students came forward to say that
Dobyns had destroyed their ability to function both in class and as writers.
Although Prose acknowledges that her friend acted inappropriately, she
does wonder if his guilt pertained to any sensible definition of sexual
harassment. As she points out, no one accused Dobyns of trying to
exchange good grades for sexual favours. He did not sleep with students or
even proposition them. Nor did he engage in the kind of hectoring that
used to define the word "harassment." He was accused of using "salty language" – not even in the classroom, but at a party.

The point made by Prose is not that throwing drinks at people should be
considered acceptable behaviour but that some female students have
returned to a view of womanhood (and manhood) that bears an eerie like-
ness to that of much earlier generations.

Victorian damsels in distress, they used 19th-century language: they had been
"shattered" by his rude, "brutish" behavior. After testifying, they seemed radiant,
exalted, a state of being that, like so much else, recalled "The Crucible," which used
the Salem witch trials as a metaphor for the Army-McCarthy hearings.

Are these the modern women feminists had in mind? Victorian girls, Puritan girls,
crusading against dirty thoughts and loose speech? I thought of all the salty words
I have used in class – words that could apparently cost me my job – and of my own
experience with sexual harassment: the colleague who told me that his department
only hired me because I was a woman; if they could have found a black woman,

they would have hired her. Such words were more damaging than anything he could have said about my breasts. But no one could have accused him of harassment: he didn't make a pass at me or refer to a sexual act.[58]

In the end, Dobyns was found guilty of verbal sexual harassment. The tribunal recommended that he be suspended, without pay, for two years, expelled from the campus (except the library), required to put in two hundred hours of community service, and ordered to pay one of his accusers $600 for wages she had lost in connection with "mental suffering."

Here is another case, this one from Canada. Early in 1994, the government of Ontario issued its "Framework Regarding Prevention of Harassment and Discrimination in Ontario Universities."[59] This document opens with a proclamation: "The government of Ontario has adopted a policy," it reads, "of zero tolerance of harassment and discrimination in Ontario's universities."[60] The government quickly went into reverse after the text was leaked to a newspaper in Ottawa only two weeks before the deadline for action, leaving academics outraged by what they considered a real threat to freedom of speech.[61] Critics worried about the whole idea of "zero tolerance." Listen to William Leggett, the principal of Queen's University in 1994.

In a most unfortunate omission, the [policy] made no mention of the importance of approaching discrimination and harassment prevention in ways that uphold the traditions of academic freedom and free speech which are central to our educational mission, our research functions and the proper carrying out of our social responsibilities. Promoted in an inappropriate manner, the demand for a harassment-free environment may inhibit the free exchange of ideas and the debate that are essential to the intellectual vitality of a university. A distinction needs to be made between, on the one hand, affirming the right to voice in an academic setting unpopular ideas that may be perceived as wounding or hurtful and, on the other, the gratuitous abuse of that right for purposes that are not academic but merely offensive.[62]

Tom Darby of Carleton University argued that the document was an attempt to impose political correctness on the university. He and others believed that it represented "an ill-considered stab at social engineering that attempts to impose a climate of complete civility on university life at the cost of free intellectual inquiry."[63] Bill Graham, president of the University of Toronto Faculty Association, noted that civility does not, in fact, lie at the heart of university life. "What you have to do while protecting human rights," he wrote, "is recognize that universities are the very places where you should be offending people sometimes. Part of the purpose of university is to examine, question, and criticize the basic beliefs of our society and the various groups in it. You have to challenge people."[64]

Some academics might have noticed an additional problem but refrained from mentioning it (partly because it had already been embedded in law). The policy's definition of "sexual harassment" is exceedingly broad. Examples cited include not only "gestures, remarks, jokes, slurs, taunting, innuendo, threats" and so on, but also "physical, verbal, or sexual assault."[65] According to Canadian law, "sexual assault" is the term for what was once called "rape." What troubles us is not the inclusion of rape as an offense (although that would surely be prosecuted by the state as a criminal offense and not merely by the university as an infraction against its harassment policy) but the implication that rape is merely one end of a continuum that includes what most people would consider trivial and unrelated phenomena. We must assume that the government of Ontario has established ideological feminism as its official philosophy.

Allegedly "stunned" by the hostile response to its policy, Ontario officials tried to mollify critics by claiming that it was intended merely as a guideline to support policies already in place at universities, not as a new policy to be backed by coercion. But if policies were already in place, why the alleged need for further guidelines? Other officials, both bureaucrats and academics, tried to trivialize the controversy by arguing that everyone had been overreacting. "People can come forward with complaints," said Dale Fogle, a sexual-harassment officer at Wilfrid Laurier University, "but that doesn't mean complaints will rule the day. It has to be weighed and find its way through procedural channels. It's just not going to result in some big chill on freedom of speech."[66] But how many people would risk the harrowing experience of going through these procedural channels? It is so much easier and safer to remain silent on controversial topics. According to the policy's defenders, common sense will prevail. Yes, but whose common sense? (In this case, the characteristic question of postmodernists is addressed to postmodernists themselves.) Besides, we should have laws that cannot be so easily misused.

Graham pointed out that this government policy would allow officials to censor remarks in class about the rights of gay people, because those remarks would infringe on the rights of religious fundamentalists. The same policy would prohibit a course on feminism or one taught from a feminist perspective, moreover, because it would inevitably produce a negative atmosphere for male students. But if this highly politicized document was written by "ideologues and fundamentalists," as critics claimed, then it was clearly written with no intention whatsoever of allowing the inherent logic of "zero tolerance" for harassment and discrimination to prevail (a problem that we discuss in appendix 4). On the contrary, only politically correct groups would be given protection.

Ideological feminists involved in policy reform euphemistically call one strategy for dealing with harassment "reeducation." Those found guilty of sexual harassment – and sometimes even those found innocent – are required to participate. Patai discusses what this really means in the context of a university. It often involves more than threats, lectures, readings, and discussion groups. In fact, it often involves what could be called a "conversion experience," followed by "repentance" and "atonement." The latter is expressed as an act of public contrition or at least a letter of apology – reviewed first by the "trainer," of course, and then submitted to an official of the department, as well as one from the Equal Employment Opportunity Commission.

Due process at institutions such as universities would include the following: a presumption of innocence until or unless the accused is proven guilty; precisely stated accusations; separation of investigators from judges to avoid conflicts of interest; access of the accused to legal counsel from the start; and hearings in which the accused can face their accusers and call witnesses in their own defense. The current lack of due process is endorsed by many feminists, according to Roiphe, who believe that

academic freedom and due process are simply more platitudes generated by the old boy network. They dismiss any concern about fairness with their image of the ranks of male professionals united against the slim victim. Sexual harassment has assumed such grand proportions in the minds of these feminists that they are not concerned with the machinations of the disciplinary system, however Kafkaesque. To many feminists ... who are interested in cleansing the university of harassers, a few casualties of justice along the way seem like a small price to pay.[67]

In any case, "reeducation" should remind everyone of brainwashing, which is more intense, to be sure, but which has the same goal.

Finally, consider another strategy. Of great interest here, explains Patai, is the urge not merely to punish men for stepping out of line but to shame them publicly for doing so, which might remind some readers of the stocks used in seventeenth-century New England and elsewhere or of the self-criticism rituals once required in many Marxist or neo-Marxist communities. Roiphe has documented the horrors of antiharassment wish lists, which often include plans to publish or publicize the names of alleged harassers – the "walls of shame," for example, that are advocated by many on college campuses. Those who advocate institutional policies of this kind seldom pay any attention to the need for due process, not surprisingly, which would be assumed in a court of law.

Even if no conclusive result is reached by the investigators, observes Patai, those accused of sexual harassment remain under suspicion. Sexual harassment experts appear before tribunals with a "harasser profile," which provides a script by which to interpret all testimony.[68] Even when the accused are actually found not guilty, they are still often punished by being required to attend "workshops." The idea is for a company or university department to demonstrate zeal in attacking sexual harassment. "One can think of few other areas," adds Patai, "in which even the failure to find any evidence of wrongdoing is always accompanied by protestations of total commitment to ferreting it out nonetheless."[69] Actually, we can think of several. We have already discussed this very thing in connection with child abuse, say, and child support. But Patai is correct in a way, because ideological feminists see all of these as aspects of one problem and therefore adopt the same strategies to deal with all of them.

Worst of all, says Patai, some people will be accused unjustly. Their names will never be cleared, because secrecy surrounds the whole process.[70] Yes, yes, some say, a few people will be treated unjustly according to these new rules. A few people will be accused falsely. But so what? Most harassers are punished, they say, and that discourages other potential harassers. The end, presumably, justifies the means. Shaming accused harassers is, not surprisingly, just like shaming the customers of prostitutes.

Because the expanded definition of sexual harassment reflects the worldview of those consciously or unconsciously opposed to heterosexuality, lesbians have clearly won a major victory. This conclusion takes us to what Patai calls "heterophobia" and also back to what MacKinnon calls the "eroticization of male power." Both are examples of what we call misandry. Among the many forms taken by misandry in popular culture have been the notions of ridiculing, bypassing, dehumanizing, and even demonizing men. Translated from the reel world to the real world, and the other way around, these tactics encourage sexual segregation – in Canadian parlance, sexual separatism – instead of sexual integration.

Some comentators refuse to believe that most people are heterosexual by nature (though reinforced by culture). In other words, they believe that heterosexuality is nothing more – nothing less, to be more precise – than an invention, a "social construction" perpetuated, or perpetrated, by men, precisely in order to oppress women. If so, then the cultural conditioning of so-called heterosexual women can be overcome with suitable ideological training. Failing that, women must escape from the tyranny of heterosexuality by separating themselves as much as possible from men.[71] How else can we explain the lengths to which feminists have gone in trying to eliminate what many other people, including many women, regard as trivial complaints? Why else make the effort to convince women that they are "uncomfortable" with men in almost any circumstances? For that matter, why else bend over backward to make the law enforce "comfort" in the first place? This situation is the result of an ideology that insists on conflating the trivial with the serious.

As Patai points out, this debate presupposes confusion over the difference between social constructionism and essentialism. Many feminists, including the most radical, deny that they are essentialists. They do so for at least two reasons. First, essentialism would mean that heterosexual men have no choice when it comes to their attitudes toward women. And that would mean freeing them from moral responsibility for subordinating or even attacking women. Second, even ideological feminists usually insist on paying lip service to pluralism, the lingua franca of politics. As Alice Echols has pointed out,[72] the difference between essentialism and pluralism might not matter. If heterosexuality is so deeply engrained through culture, after all, it might just as well be imposed by nature.

Deconstruction is the method of choice for all purposes among postmodernists. The aim is to "subvert," or "problematize" disapproved ideas, institutions, behaviours, cultural productions, and so on. Before consciousness raising can take place, after all, false consciousness must first be exposed, challenged, undermined, subverted, or transgressed – that is, deconstructed. In this case, the target is heterosexuality: that which brings men and women together.

Sheila Jeffreys, a British feminist and separatist, believes that heterosexuality as a social construction is based on the "ideology of difference."[73] By this, she means an ideology that sees women as powerless creatures (which is precisely what MacKinnon and her ideological colleagues believe about women). Like MacKinnon, she believes that men eroticize this powerlessness of women and are then attracted to it. "Jeffreys's views," writes Patai, "bring together the two strands I am calling 'heterophobia': the fear of and antagonism toward the Other – that is, male sexuality, especially as manifest in heterosexuality; and the turn toward Sameness, understood as the only kind of authentic relationship possible."[74]

The ideas of Jeffreys would seem to suggest that men cannot be blamed for their evil ways. If you cannot blame people for accepting a biological pattern that was imposed on them as embryos by nature, how can you blame them for accepting a symbolic pattern that was imposed on them as infants and children by culture? Neither Jeffreys nor any other feminist, at least of this school, has raised that question. In any case, we suggest, the facile "insight" of Jeffreys can be expressed concisely as a syllogism. The power differential between men and women is evil. The power differential between men and women is inherent in heterosexuality. Ergo, heterosexuality is inherently evil. There is an irony in all this. Most feminists take pride not only in the "connectedness" they presume to be inherent in femaleness (even though they cast suspicion, to say the least, on the connectedness of women to half of the human race) but also in the diversity or pluralism they presume to be inherent in feminism (even though many are willing to exclude from feminism, depending on circumstances, the "voices" of women who oppose them in one way or another). They often argue that only men are dualistic: troubled by the exotic, the foreign, the alien, the dangerous Other (even though, in doing so, they clearly embrace their own form of dualism). Patai calls this replication of power language the promotion of a "radical feminist agenda," because the utopian project of eliminating all power would involve the elimination of all relationships except those of clones reared exactly alike. There will always be some differences that can translate into hierarchies of power: if not wealth or privilege, then intelligence, artistic sensibility, health, and age. "It is, of course, true that quid pro quo harassment – sexual shakedown – presupposes some imbalance of power. All blackmail does."[75] But, she continues, differences of power need not damage relations.

The logical conclusion of this belief that only men wield power, or that only women are incapable of doing so, is an attack on the notion that women are capable of giving consent to sexual relations with men. And ideological feminists have indeed drawn this conclusion – even though they argue that women are indeed capable of *withholding* consent: "no," they maintain, really does mean "no."

The most common response to this theory of heterophobia is to trivialize it. How many feminists, after all, really want to destroy heterosexuality? Not many. Therefore, why bother with these loonies? And why bring feminism into disrepute just because of a few radicals? But before answering that question, think more carefully about those radicals. Do we really want to declare that straight men are sexist for feeling physically attracted to female bodies or even for merely thinking about them? This question was certainly taken very seriously by feminists in the 1980s and 1990s. Listen to a letter to the editor from one lesbian reader of *Ms*: "We may be your worst nightmare," she states in connection with an article on current trends in feminism, "but we are also your future."[76] Taken to its logical conclusion, ideological feminism really does lead to lesbianism, because only lesbians are ready, willing, and able to do without men altogether and therefore to end "patriarchy." (Because our "patriarchal society" nevertheless permits artificial insemination by donor, they can produce children without having to form even the most fleeting liaisons with men.) But not all women are lesbians. Those women who do want intimate and sexual relationships with men, therefore, will have to rethink some of their assumptions about both sexual orientation and sexual harassment.

It will not do to dismiss Patai's notion of heterophobia just because few women are prepared to go all the way and become lesbians. "The problem is not the 'fringe' feminist that ... is rejected by most women. The problem is the general antagonism toward men that has been part of feminism from its very beginning ... Linked to the very successful movement against sexual harassment, it has brought us to the present heavy-handed and ever-expanding definitions of what even [Jane] Gallop refers to as a 'loathsome crime.'"[77]

At the heart of Patai's theory is not the conspiracy of a few lesbians, who represent neither most feminists nor even most lesbians, but the collusion – direct or indirect, witting or unwitting – of many straight women. Why else would they try to explain away, or even apologize for, their own sexual orientation? And that is precisely what they do in *Heterosexuality: A Feminism and Psychology Reader*.[78] This anthology was edited by two gay women, Sue Wilkinson and Celia Kitzinger, but many of the essays were written by straight women. The authors are clearly troubled by conflict between their sexual orientation and their feminist identity. Listen to Mary Crawford: "I use heterosexual privilege to subvert heterosexism."[79] And Sandra Bartky: "The felt impossibility of changing one's sexual orientation is not an argument for the desirability of this orientation."[80] Sandra Bem explains, in a way that might remind some readers of defendants at the McCarthy hearings, that she has lived and loved a man for twenty-six years but is not and has "never been a 'heterosexual.'"[81] Why not? Because her sexuality is "organized around dimensions other than sex,"[82] whatever that means.

The relation between fringe and mainstream feminists can be seen very easily in connection with mainstream feminists' evaluation of one designated lunatic. Valerie Solanas, as we have already mentioned, was the founder of SCUM (Society for Cutting Up Men) and the author of its manifesto. To be blunt, she hated men. In fact, she advised women to kill men and even tried to kill one – Andy Warhol – by herself. She saw no reason to apologize for anything. Solanas was indeed a radical extremist. She was clearly part of the "lunatic fringe" (and was even committed to a mental institution). But, as Patai observes,

Solanas did not lack feminist champions for her exorbitant gesture, as evidenced by the two representatives of NOW, Ti-Grace Atkinson and attorney Florynce Kennedy, who accompanied her to court. Atkinson said on that occasion that Solanas would go down in history as "the first outstanding champion of women's rights," while Flo Kennedy called her "one of the most important spokeswomen for the feminist movement ... In her long introduction to the 1970 edition of the SCUM *Manifesto*, [Vivian] Gornick called Solanas a "visionary" who "understood the true nature of the struggle" for women's liberation. [Years later, Mary Harron made a movie based on this event: *I Shot Andy Warhol*. Once again, the critics glorified Solanas.] It is revealing that far from expressing alarm at the manifest unity of theory and praxis in Solanas's violence against men, some reviewers of this film have treated Solanas as a free spirit and see this celebrated in the movie.[83]

Sally Miller Gearhart, on the other hand, is not a lunatic. She is a professor of communication, at any rate, and participates fully in mainstream society and mainstream feminism. Nevertheless, she openly advocates the decimation of men. Literally. She would allow no more than 10% of the population to be male. Why? Because she believes that women are innately peaceful and kind and caring and sharing and loving, and so on (explaining away unacceptable female leaders as the dupes, or puppets, of men), and that men are innately violent and evil and horrible. Precisely how would she decimate the male population? Partly by giving women total autonomy in reproduction and allowing men no say in it whatsoever, partly by encouraging "men to participate in their own demise by willingly assisting in a program of reducing their numbers (reassuringly, she makes clear that mass murder is not contemplated, but rather, slow attrition through new reproductive technologies and support from men for feminist goals). And from what I see on some feminist e-mail lists and in the published work of some men ... there are indeed accommodating males who would gladly embrace even this policy for the sake of maintaining their cherished, but never entirely secure, status as 'feminist men.'"[84]

Not all women are enthusiastic about Gearhart's plans. She explains these scoffers away as "male-identified" women who need to be reeducated (along with recalcitrant men, no doubt). It is worth noting here that proposals of this kind are not as farfetched as they might sound. Women have already mobilized for complete control over the use of new reproductive technologies. We have already mentioned the Feminist International Network of Resistance to Reproductive and Genetic Engineering, a very sophisticated and influential organization that draws on the skills and resources of academics in many countries. Although members oppose some technologies, they do not oppose all of them. They want those that would give reproductive autonomy to women, at least theoretically or partially, but not to men.

Marilyn Frye, who teaches women's studies at Michigan State University, is another feminist who buys the separatist line. And she, too, is not exactly beyond the mainstream. "For females to be subordinated and subjugated to males on a global scale, and for males to organize themselves and each other as they do, billions of female individuals, virtually all who see life on the planet, must be reduced to a more-or-less willing toleration of subordination and servitude to men. The primary sites of this reduction are the sites of heterosexual relation and encounter – courtship and marriage-arrangement, romance, sexual liaisons, fucking, marriage, prostitution, the normative family, incest and child sexual abuse."[85]

We have indirect evidence, too, in support of Patai's theory. Even in the 1990s, it was obvious to everyone, including disappointed feminists, that young women were having trouble with the word "feminism." They liked the economic gains made by feminists, to be sure, but disliked something in the mentality of feminists whom they knew or had read about. Few of these young women could articulate precisely how the problem had come about – some might have declined to do so for fear of being attacked as politically incorrect – but they often referred to intolerance in general and occasionally to "man hating" in particular. Outraged feminists denied these charges, of course, just as they deny Patai's charge of heterophobia.

Just as misandry is the sexist counterpart of misogyny, presumably, heterophobia is the sexist counterpart of homophobia. Yet Patai's new word, though clever, is not necessarily helpful, because the word "homophobia," applied as a blanket condemnation of all who oppose homosexuality, denotes irrational fear (which is a psychological problem) even though it almost always *connotes* implacable hatred (a moral problem). Patai disregards this linguistic duplicity. She makes it clear that heterophobia, like homophobia, really is about hatred (in addition, perhaps, to fear). By referring to heterophobia, in any case, she focuses attention beyond misandry itself to its logical conclusion: the ideological goal of "protecting" women from all contact with men: economic, social, physical, and sexual. In other words, Patai shows that those ultimately (but not solely) responsible for misandry are the lesbian *separatists* (the word, as we understand it, refers by no means to all lesbians). Only they, as we have already pointed out, can take ideological feminism to this logical conclusion (unless they make exceptions for their own sons or a few "male feminists," the men we have called "honorary women"). They attack not only men, therefore, but also women who consort with men. In short, they attack heterosexuality. This is not about lesbians per se. It is about an idea that only lesbians, presumably those without sons, are capable of adopting if they want to do so. These women are a tiny minority. But to those who might conclude that they are of no importance in the larger context of feminism, we say, read on. Here is Patai.

At the present moment, "sexual harassment" seems often to be little more than a label for excoriating men. It has become the synecdoche for general male awfulness. Its real function at this moment, in addition to keeping feminist passions at a fever pitch, is to serve as the conduit by which some extreme feminist tenets about the relations between the sexes enter everyday life with minimum challenge. No longer a well-intended effort to gain justice for women, it has been turned into a tool (powered by a legal apparatus and manipulated by a professional cadre of trainers and enforcers) for implementing, and indeed normalizing, what was once merely a marginal and bizarre feminist worldview.[86]

Elsewhere, she adds an important connection between what might be the active or direct misandry of some and the passive or indirect misandry of many others:

Let me therefore be clear that what I am mainly criticizing here is an important – and to me profoundly disturbing – aspect of feminism: its predilection for turning complex human relations into occasions for mobilizing the feminist troops against men. There is within much feminist writing today (as there has been for the past few decades) a pretense that the charge of male bashing is a slanderous mischaracterization motivated by political impulses that are conservative (and thus assumed to be reprehensible). But it is plain and irrefutable that much contemporary feminism is indeed marred by hostility toward men. The virulence of it varies from group to group. But the antagonism is pervasive, and through the attack on "sexual harassment," it has entered society at large.[87]

Taking what some would consider an extreme position, Patai argues that in our time, the whole notion of "women" has been fragmented according to race, sexual orientation, region, class, and so on. Hatred of men is therefore probably the one thing that unifies women today. The result is what she calls the "oppression sweepstakes."[88]

The belief that men as a group are bent on attacking and oppressing women as a group is an idée fixe, a central or even primal obsession seldom questioned even in ideological circles. This became obvious to Patai at a conference held in 1998 to celebrate the twentieth anniversary of MacKinnon's *Sexual Harassment of Working Women*. The conference began with Dworkin emotively calling the audience's attention to the backlash that began when white middle-class men saw that sexual harassment laws were going to affect them.

This reaction, Dworkin thoughtfully suggested, showed us that "millions of men wanted to have a young woman at work to suck their cock." Did anyone rise to contest such outrageous slander directed at all or most men? On the contrary ... MacKinnonite terms were universally accepted as the key to social problems: Battery is "about" male power, control, and domination. So is rape. So is stalking. A tone of urgency was sounded by speaker after speaker, many of them seemingly alarmed that issues of "privacy" were resurfacing, as in the Monica Lewinsky matter, and were fueling a "backlash." [89]

The women present were all supporters of MacKinnon's movement. Patai recalls no mention of any problem such as false accusations, but does recall hearing numerous testimonials by those who had "survived" harassment.

One common way of defending hatred is to "justify" it as the result of fear. Hatred often is the result of fear, true, but even that hardly justifies hatred. It could be argued, after all, that anti-Semites are genuinely afraid of Jews. What makes hatred different from fear, although the two are very closely linked, is the factor of motivation. Fear does not necessarily have a moral dimension. We can be afraid of people without believing that they are motivated by malice. Hatred always has a moral dimension. We hate people, because we believe that they are not only powerful but also evil.

Another common way of defending hatred is to "justify" it as a response to the hatred of others. Once again, it often is. But even that hardly justifies hatred. Not unless it justifies revenge as well. Listen, now, to Patai:

It is astonishing that decades of progress for women, decades of denunciation of misogynist ideas, should have brought us to the point where a mere reversal – misandry instead of misogyny – should count as serious feminist thought and should be taught and promoted in the name of feminism. Although it is not difficult to match crazed feminist pronouncements of our time with crazed masculinist assertions from the past, there are two important differences. The first is that – apart from collections of misogynistic rants across the centuries (the same sorts of material professors like to hand out to their students to shock them into sudden awareness of the long history of male disdain for women) – few of us today, least of all in the academy, are exposed to persistent hysterical denunciations of women. For the writings of feminist extremism, on the other hand, there does seem to be a large and apparently insatiable market, and their authors are without question among the best-known names in contemporary feminism. The second difference is that no one ever believed or claimed that the old misogynistic ravings could pave the way to a better life for humankind, whereas somehow heterophobes have gained acceptance for many of their prejudices precisely because they are being proclaimed in the name of an ideal female future.[90]

Actually, Patai's second point of difference is debatable. Some of the passages often cited were written by theologians, for instance, and their misogynistic points of view did indeed work their way into mainstream theology as ways of producing a "better life for humankind." On the other hand, Patai ignores a third point of difference. The old misogyny was created and disseminated without the knowledge available to us through hindsight. Our ancestors did not know precisely what could happen when hatred was ignored, tolerated, or justified in the name of some theology or ideology. We do. Hatred is never justifiable, not even when it is the result of ignorance or fear. It is even less justifiable, however, when propagated by those who have the benefit not only of historical hindsight and even personal or collective experience as victims of hatred but *also* of sophisticated thinking about the nature of hatred – racial, religious, linguistic, or whatever – and its relation to ideology. This point is very important, because it challenges the common belief that "radical" feminists can be distinguished neatly from mainstream feminists and therefore prevented from discrediting the larger movement. They can be distinguished in some ways, true, but not always neatly.

Feminists like to point out, especially when some aspect of feminism is challenged, that the movement is anything but monolithic; there are many feminist "voices." Most of them feel free enough to raise questions about this or that effect of feminism on women. Others do not. So far, however, very few have felt free enough to raise questions about the effect of its doctrines on men, at least not in connection with any compassion for men. What makes Patai very unusual, even among those who are open to criticism of feminism, is her recognition that feminist extremism is problematic because of its effect on *men*. Yes, feminist extremism creates problems for women (bringing feminism into disrepute, causing squabbles among feminists, or leading to charges of sexual harassment against a few female professors).[91] Yes, it reduces university classes to group therapy sessions (turning college students into fearful and neurotic infants). Yes, it prevents any mature perspective on sexuality (misunderstanding the nature of power). In addition, though, it propagates hatred toward men. Hers is a specifically moral position, not merely a practical one. According to Patai, "the writings of the most notorious and least responsible among heterophobes have enormously contributed to the creation of a 'gotcha' atmosphere in which individual autonomy and its sexual manifestations in particular are under attack."[92] Whether feminists will take this particular critique seriously enough to do anything about misandry remains to be seen. Patai's reviewers, by and large, have not.

Ideological feminists do hold out some hope for men, but only to the extent that men are willing to stop being men. From this it follows that feminists may blame those men who are unwilling to do the right thing. This has become clear in their response to recent developments in medicine. Given the relentless hostility of ideological feminists toward heterosexuality in general and male sexuality in particular, it is not surprising to find that some of them have ridiculed medical treatments for impotence. Whether feminists want to admit it or not, men are as central to their ideology as Jews are to anti-Semitic ideology. It could be argued, in fact, that ideological feminism is itself "phallocentric" because of its preoccupation with male power.

The wonder is not so much that some otherwise sensible women have come to believe this nonsense but that even a few men – the ones that we call "honorary women" and that Patai calls "groveling men" – have come to agree with them. These converts to ideological feminism and thus zealots for the true faith, do whatever they can, short of surgery in most cases, to reject their own maleness. The sort of thing that gives the Uncle Tom, or the "self-hating" Jew a bad name. Patai discusses a few of these guys, the ones with high profiles as friends of famous heterophobes. One is Dworkin's long-term roommate (and eventual husband) John Stoltenberg, who argues that he has eliminated dualism by "refusing to be a man,"[93] one of those "penised humans."[94] Like Dworkin, who is clearly his mentor, Stoltenberg equates maleness with evil. Hence his demand for the "End of Manhood."[95] Another example is Robert Jensen, whose stated goal is to refuse all sexual gratification, including that provided by other men and even by erotic pornography, on the grounds that he could not imagine any sexual act that was not contaminated by "patriarchy" (defined, as usual, in terms of control or power) and thus by evil.

Stoltenberg and Jensen are obviously extremists. But that is not a good enough reason for dismissing their cultural significance, for failing to take them seriously, because they are indeed taken very seriously by ideological feminists, including those who have influenced public opinion and public policy. These men are feminist trophies, or advertisements. They supposedly provide living proof that ideological feminism, if taken to its logical conclusion, is transparently correct. After all, even "they" admit it. However, not many men, feminists surely realize, will go to such lengths in the effort to win medals from feminists.

There is something very pathetic about many of the men who call themselves "male feminists" and who are usually exempted by feminists from the general attack on men. Their response to misandry, at any rate, does sound more than a little neurotic. Although they have not (so far) advocated castration or sex-change operations, and although asceticism, including sexual abstinence, is common both historically and cross-culturally, this particular form of asceticism is disturbing because of its double standard. What makes it unprecedented, however, is its social function (or lack of one). Historically and cross-culturally, asceticism has always been associated with prestige – possibly too much prestige in some cases[96] – not with shame or self-loathing. Ascetics give up worldly pleasures, to be sure, but they see no reason to refuse both spiritual and worldly rewards in return for doing so. The former might include spiritual powers of one kind or another: access to the divine through visions or theophanies, spirit possession, esoteric knowledge, prophetic revelations, telepathy or out-of-body travel, and so on. The latter might include membership in publicly honoured and sometimes politically powerful orders. Stoltenberg and Jensen ask men to embrace asceticism in return neither for spiritual rewards (unless self-righteousness masquerading as altruism counts as a spiritual reward) nor for worldly rewards (unless ideological feminists are willing to offer any, which seems very unlikely).

Quite apart from any decline in the incidence of sexual harassment itself, the debate over sexual harassment has affected society in at least four ways.

It has spawned an industry, [97] for one thing, just as it has spawned similar ones in connection with single parents, domestic violence, and rape. This industry might be good for the economy, but it might not be so good for society. To cope with rapidly multiplying cases of sexual harassment, there must be cadres of trained specialists ready for action: theoreticians, therapists, publicists, lobbyists, lawyers, fundraisers, and so forth. With a whole new field of legal expertise opening up, the opportunities for both legal scholars and legal advocates are virtually infinite. The courts will be clogged with cases for decades to come. As a result, there will be more lawyers, and richer ones, than ever before. Entrepreneurs have already found ways of cashing in on new opportunities for lawyers. Spytech, for instance, produces miniature tape recorders. Its advertisement goes like this: "Sexually harassed? Prove it. Stop it. Sue."[98] A two-page ad in *Harper's Magazine,* beginning on the cover's inside page, addresses employers as follows: " Domestic violence affects 1 in every 4 women. It costs American businesses over $3 billion each year. And your company can be part of the solution. Domestic violence is the leading cause of injury to women in our country, and its impact extends from the home to the workplace. The result? Shattered lives and billions of dollars in business losses annually due to absenteeism, turnover, medical expenses and lower productivity ... If your most valuable assets were at risk, wouldn't you protect them?"[99] The assets at risk are female employees at *home*, however, not at work; the risk is not sexual harassment but domestic violence. The ad implies that these are two forms of the same problem.

Here is a Canadian example of this industry. A company called The Edge uses its website to advertise "training services." It offers "problem solving techniques," "awareness programs introducing employees to the issues of harassment, discrimination and workplace conflict," "detailed, intensive training for management, including introduction and application of step-by-step management procedures – detailed manuals provided during training; practical workshops," and so forth. All are designed to meet "your" particular needs. One bulleted item reveals a close link with the government. Contact us, it advises readers, "[w]hen you need a human rights practitioner with twenty years experience, including six years as Director of Communications and Education at the Ontario Human Rights Commission."[100] It must be comforting to know that there is always a career in private industry after a prestigious government appointment ends.

Second, the debate over sexual harassment has endangered freedom of speech. Long before the advent of political correctness in its current form, legislators knew that freedom of speech always is and always must be limited. We have libel laws to make people think twice before using their own freedom of speech to attack others. We have laws to protect people from those who consider it fun to scream "fire" in crowded theatres. We have laws prohibiting the use of speech to advocate criminal activities. And we have laws to punish those who indulge in blackmail or intimidation – which is exactly what sexual harassment can amount to. Using freedom of speech to intimidate employees is one thing. Using it in ways that merely seem offensive to some people is another thing entirely. American laws to protect people from what is offensive eviscerate the First Amendment and, in doing so, destroy the foundation of a democratic society. Similar comments would apply to Canadian laws.

As many pointed out during the American debate over flag desecration, freedom of speech means nothing at all if it includes the freedom to say only those things considered inoffensive. We might dislike vulgar talk. We might dislike erotica. But the mentality endorsed by MacKinnon and other ideological feminists, the one that is now institutionalized in law, could be infinitely more dangerous to a free society. Should it really be a duty to *look* for anything in the work environment that might be offensive to women in general? If so, then some serious questions must be asked. Do we really want to live in a society that, if this mentality were held up as a model, would inevitably encourage intolerance? (The term "zero tolerance" has an ironic twist; those who insist on it are usually the same people who insist on unlimited tolerance for their own contributions to "diversity," including overtly ideological ones.) Do we really want to work in an atmosphere that, under these circumstances, would inevitably encourage snoopers, spies, and informants? It is true that finding evidence of harassment is hard. But to repeat the old adage once again, some cures can be worse than the diseases.

One aspect of free speech, seldom discussed or even acknowledged, has something to do with fashion. In our society, people are free to express themselves by dressing as they see fit. Well, more or less free. Those who wear jackets or T-shirts with racist slogans, for instance, might have some explaining to do. More to the point here, though, is the power exerted by mainstream fashions. People are legally free to dress up in hoop skirts or togas, but most people would be much too inhibited by the current sartorial standards, informal but nonetheless powerful, to do so in public.[101] Many cultural observers have commented on the current trend for girls and young women to emulate, or at least look like, rock stars or supermodels. These icons – Madonna, say, or Britney Spears – have carefully cultivated the look usually associated with street prostitutes, one that features bare midriffs and tattoos. (Boys and young men, too, follow fashions that glorify life on the "street." Their idols – rockers, rappers, and punkers – set the tone by trying to look and act like pimps or thugs.) And yet not many cultural observers have commented on the specific significance of hairstyles for girls, young women, and middle-aged women. When Jennifer Aniston changes her hairstyle, the event is not exactly ignored by journalists and paparazzi. Commercials for shampoos and related products indicate a definitely sexual subtext to all this. The most obvious, perhaps, are the ones produced by and for Herbal Essences hair products. Like all hair commercials, they feature a woman tossing her head and letting her hair fly freely. But unlike most others, they feature, in addition, the sound of an orgasm.

The implication is clear, and it has been for centuries. Hair fetishism has a long history, after all, the only new development being a reversal of interpretation.[102] Until the 1960s, loose hair symbolized sexually loose women. From the 1960s on, loose hair – the longer and wispier the better – has symbolized sexually *free* women. This brings us to the matter at hand: the relation between current fashions for women and sexual harassment. We are not suggesting that women who dress provocatively deserve to be harassed or that those who harass them may be excused for doing so. We are indeed suggesting, however, that women who present themselves in provocative ways should realize what they are saying to men and decide on whether that is actually what they want to say. If so, then they should welcome, or at least expect, the advances of men. If not, then they should take responsibility for making wiser choices every morning.

Some women have the courage to acknowledge this. Ellen Frankel Paul, deputy director of the Social Philosophy and Policy Center at Bowling Green State University in Ohio, warns of the danger inherent in using the courts as a way of policing behaviour. "Do we really want legislatures and judges delving into our most intimate, private lives," she asks, "deciding when a look is a leer and when a leer is a civil rights offence? Should people have a legally enforceable right not to be offended by others? At some point, the price for this protection is the loss of both liberty and privacy rights."[103] To which we would add another price: the rejection of personal and collective maturity as a goal worth seeking.

Third, the debate over sexual harassment has endangered democracy. Perhaps because of the long utopian tradition in America, many ideological feminists (and others) now argue for the use of legal coercion, rather than moral persuasion, to eliminate speech that they find offensive. As readers of both American and European history know, however, attempting to build utopias often leads to nightmarish dystopias. After all, utopias are based primarily on the urge to escape from human finitude (enforcing conformity to some ideal of perfection) and on the urge to control (forcing others to accept your own ideal). But there is no perfect society or even a perfect workplace. People are flawed. Choices are unavoidable. Risk is everywhere. Part of being an adult, therefore, is the ability to accept these fundamental facts of the human condition. Some forms of pain should be prevented by law, including intimidation and blackmail or quid pro quo cases of sexual harassment. But we should confront other forms of pain on our own (if need be with the help of an ombudsman). These forms of pain would include the use of offensive language. Why? Because people are not like the robots; eventually, they rebel against repression. In short, we can either respect the limits on the urge to control – and freedom of speech surely requires us to limit that urge – or pay the price for refusing to do so.

We have not yet heard from Camille Paglia. As usual, she has a lot to say about feminism (or at least ideological feminism, in our parlance) and its effect on society. For her, the hostile-environment policy, is

grotesquely totalitarian. It offends free-speech rights and is predicated on a reactionary female archetype: the prudish Victorian lady who faints at a sexual innuendo. This isn't feminism; it's Puritanism. The Anita Hill case, far from expanding women's rights, was a disaster for civil liberties. That Hill, an articulate graduate of the Yale Law School, could find no job-preserving way to communicate to her employer her discomfort with mild off-color banter strained credulity. That Thomas could be publicly grilled about trivial lunchtime conversations that occurred 10 years earlier was an outrage worthy of Stalinist Russia ... Feminist excesses have paralyzed and neutered white, upper-middle-class young men as should be obvious to any visitor to the campuses of élite schools ... While men must behave honorably (governors and presidents should not be dropping their pants in front of female employees or secretly preying on buxom young interns), women must also watch how they dress and behave. For every gross male harasser, there are 10 female sycophants who shamelessly use their sexual attractions to get ahead. We don't want a society of surveillance by old maids and snitches. The proper mission of feminism is to encourage women to take personal responsibility without running to parental authority figures for help.[104]

Finally, these developments have legalized misandry. Even if most men could be coerced into outward conformity, that would do nothing to reverse this trend. On the contrary, it would more likely have the opposite effect. Because the new definition of sexual harassment makes it easier to convict people who are guilty of no such thing, we have merely replaced old problems in the workplace with new problems. At one time, women had to worry about sexual or physical intimidation by men. In our time, men have to worry about legal or political intimidation by women. Given the size of many financial settlements, we would have to be either incredibly naive or profoundly ideological to ignore the possibility that some women are motivated to frame men. Life in the workplace is already pervaded by suspicion, resentment, self-righteousness, and hypocrisy.

At issue in the continuing struggle between women and men, no less than that between blacks and whites, is whether to promote separatism or integration. Separatism has been fashionable for the past thirty years of cynicism, but not everyone has abandoned integration.

9

Female Victims v. Male Victims:
The Case of Violence against Women

Rape violates women physically and mentally, humiliates them, devastates their sense of self-respect, undermines their dignity, and often leaves them with a sense of inferior status in the community which may never be undone. Threat of rape makes threat of such violation a permanent feature of the landscape of women's lives.[1]

[P]artner abuse is routinely portrayed and acted upon as though it were almost exclusively about men abusing and victimizing innocent women and, by extention [*sic*], their children – despite the overwhelming sociological evidence that a significant amount of abuse is also suffered by male partners.[2]

On Super Bowl Sunday, 2004, Janet Jackson and Justin Timberlake caused a national furore during their performance for the half-time show. According to their plan, Timberlake tore off part of Jackson's costume and left her breast partially exposed (the rest of it was covered with a "nipple shield"). There was a lot of angry talk about exposing children to sexually explicit behaviour. But some people saw an even deeper problem. According to Don Macpherson, the real problem was not sex but misogyny. Timberlake, presumably a role model for boys, had symbolically committed a sexual assault on Jackson. "It was not Jackson who bared her breast," wrote Macpherson, "but rather her male fellow performer ... And while it was part of a stage act scripted in advance, in the act itself there was no indication Timberlake had Jackson's consent to do so."[3] Yes, but this was indeed a scripted performance. Jackson was at least as responsible for what happened as Timberlake. If we blame him and other male pop stars for legitimating this symbolic act, then surely we should blame Jackson and other female pop stars as well. It can hardly be said, after all, that the latter have presented themselves as modest and innocent or even as naive. On the contrary, as we noted in chapter 8, they have done everything to push the boundaries of female nudity and provocation. And with what purpose in mind? What is the message that they want to give men? Look but don't touch? Of greater importance is the message that some feminists want to give men: that even symbolic acts of sexual violence against women constitute *actual* violence against women.

After an introduction on the term "violence against women," we will review the legislation governing it. We will then discuss the debate over domestic violence, the debate over rape, and the misandric fallout from these debates.

Closely related to pornography, prostitution, and sexual harassment, according to ideological feminists, is something known generically as "violence against women" or "male violence" (the latter never refers, for some reason, to the violence of men against other men). These terms include, at the very least, both domestic violence and rape. They have become feminist trump cards, because everyone agrees that acts of physical aggression are intolerable. Trouble is, that agreement does not go very far in the controversy that has been generated.

Not everyone agrees on precisely what constitutes violence in the first place, for instance, let alone violence against women. Should there be any significant distinction between physical violence and "emotional violence"? What is more important, not everyone agrees that violence against women should be singled out from other forms of violence for special attention. Some ideological feminists do not care about violence against men, whether by women or by other men. Others believe that there is no fundamental difference between violence in general (including violence against men) and violence against women in particular. They believe instead that all forms of violence, like everything else in a patriarchal society, are ultimately derived from the paradigm of violence against women. The only way to end violence of any kind, therefore, is to end the subordination of women. From their point of view, referring to violence in general is therefore tantamount to ignoring or even trivializing the underlying problem of violence against women.

Not everyone agrees, moreover, with another fundamental premise of ideological feminists: that violence against women is merely one end of a continuum that begins with risqué jokes, erotic publications, or heterosexuality itself. In other words, they believe, all men are implicated in all crimes – including everything from kissing to raping – against all women. From this point of view, men are the archetypal oppressors of women, no matter what form the oppression might take. Case closed.

In 1978, Congress passed the Privacy Protection for Rape Victims Act. This legislation included Federal Rule of Evidence (FRE) 412, which was popularly dubbed the "rape shield" law. Rule 412 consists of both evidentiary rules and procedural requirements.[4] It stipulates that evidence of the past sexual behaviour of an alleged victim of rape or assault is not admissible except in three circumstances: first, if the defendant claims that the plaintiff has invented the story of sexual assault to explain awkward facts – a pregnancy, an injury, or an absence – to her husband or boyfriend; second, if the defendant claims that he had a sexual relationship with the alleged victim and therefore understood that she had given her consent on the most recent occasion (although courts usually reject this claim if the reference is to a much earlier phase of the relationship); third, if excluding evidence would violate the constitutional rights of a defendant – such as the right to know the nature and cause of the accusation, the right to a speedy and public trial by an impartial jury, the right to be confronted with the witnesses against him, and so forth (all under the Sixth Amendment) and the right to due process (under the Fifth Amendment). Note the gendered lingo; those who wrote these laws made no attempt to use gender-neutral terminology, even though men can be and sometimes are raped.

Since it is the defendant's burden to show why any of these three exceptions should be allowed, 412 favours the plaintiff, who would prefer to exclude evidence. "Assume that the government's case consists entirely of v's testimony that A raped her. The government's case would be far from overwhelming and v's credibility would be a critical issue in the case. The proffered evidence is directly related to v's motive to lie, and therefore, to her credibility. Furthermore, A's friend will testify about the affair he had with v on the night of the alleged incident. By doing so, this witness will also partially corroborate A's version of the facts. Accordingly, a court is likely to find that the evidence is favorable to the defense."[5]

In the Violent Crime Control and Law Enforcement Act of 1994 (also called the Violence against Women Act), the ante was upped to favour the plaintiff even more strongly in rape cases. Three new federal rules of evidence were introduced. Rule 413, "Evidence of Similar Crimes in Sexual Assault Cases," states that "[i]n a criminal case in which a defendant is accused of an offense of sexual assault, evidence of the defendant's commission of another offense or offenses of sexual assault is admissible."[6] Rule 414, "Evidence of Similar Crimes in Child Molestation Cases," and Rule 415, the "Evidence of Similar Crimes in Civil Cases Concerning Sexual Assault or Child Molestation," provide further definitions of evidence.[7]

According to 413 and 415, the offense of sexual assault includes any conduct proscribed by chapter 109A of Title 18, United States Code, which includes "the intentional touching, either directly or through the clothing, of the genitalia, anus, groin, breast, inner thigh, or buttocks of any person with an intent to abuse, humiliate, harass, degrade, or arouse or gratify the sexual desire of any person."[8] This definition allows a wide range of evidence – for instance, evidence of a pinch on the butt – that had not previously been used in a criminal case against a defendant.

These new rules were by no means unopposed when they were being drafted. The Advisory Committee on Evidence Rules considered responses from judges, lawyers, law professors, and legal organizations. The overwhelming majority opposed 413, 414, and 415, mainly because they would allow biased evidence.[9] They noted also that the problems at issue could be solved by means of existing federal rules of evidence. Furthermore, the committee pointed out, "the new rules, which are not supported by empirical evidence, could diminish significantly the protections that have safeguarded persons accused in criminal cases and parties in civil cases against undue prejudice. These protections form a fundamental part of American jurisprudence and have evolved under long-standing rules and case law. A significant concern identified by the committee was the danger of convicting a criminal defendant for past, as opposed to charged, behavior or for being a bad person."[10] Moreover, the new rules overrode protections such as the hearsay rule or rule 403's balancing test.[11]

The upshot of the committee's review was an almost unanimous vote (except for representatives from the Department of Justice) to oppose the new rules. In view of all this, the committee urged Congress either to dismiss the rules or to make them amendments to rules of evidence 404 and 405.[12] When these recommendations went back to Congress, Representative Susan Molinari, who had sponsored the new rules, reminded Congress of the enormous support that they had within President Bush's violent-crime bill.[13] She then announced that the new rules would take effect within the year and could be repealed or modified only by additional legislation.[14] In defense of her position, she argued that the "enactment of this reform is first and foremost a triumph for the public – for the women who will not be raped and the children who will not be molested because we have strengthened the legal system's tools for bringing the perpetrators of these atrocious crimes to justice."[15] Moreover, she argued, the "proposed reform is critical to the protection of the public from rapists and child molesters, and is justified by the distinctive characteristics of the cases it will affect."[16]

Congress passed several other acts to curb other forms of violence against women and children in the early 1990s: the Victims of Child Abuse Act of 1990, the Equal Justice for Women in the Courts Act of 1994, the Safe Homes for Women Act of 1994, the Violence against Women Act (VAWA) of 1994, and the Family Violence Prevention and Services Act of 1996.[17]

Of particular interest here is the Violence against Women Act, which originated with feminist interest in hate-crime legislation. James Jacobs and Kimberly Potter observe that the Hate Crime Statistics Act of 1990 named eight hate crimes and defined prejudice as "a preformed negative opinion or attitude toward a group of persons based on their race, religion, ethnicity, national origin, or sexual orientation."[18] The political scenario that accompanied the passage of this act is intriguing. It was demanded by a coalition that included B'nai Brith's Anti-Defamation League, the Anti-Klan Network, the International Network for Jewish Holocaust Survivors, the American Arab Anti-Discrimination Committee, the Japanese American Citizens League, and the Organization of Chinese Americans.[19] All declared that hate crimes had reached epidemic proportions. Somehow, they managed to exclude women's groups, although the latter had lobbied very hard for inclusion. Why? Because, said the coalition, statistics on rape and domestic violence were already being collected by the government. However, Jacobs and Potter suggest that the real reason was to avoid being overwhelmed by such a massive lobby group. In any case, feminist advocacy groups replied by calling the exclusion "gender bias" and lobbying Congress either to amend the act or create a separate one for violent crimes against women. And the politicians complied, ever mindful of the fact that most voters are women.[20] The Violence against Women Act was the result. Victims of rape and domestic violence could now use the civil courts, with their low standards of proof and no presumption of innocence, to sue for damages.[21]

In 2000, Congress passed the Victims of Trafficking and Violence Prevention Act. Division A is the Trafficking Victims Protection Act.[22] The word "trafficking" in this document means using fraud or coercion to rape, abuse, torture, starve, imprison, or psychologically abuse girls or women. Citing the findings of Congress, it held that trafficking in the national and international sex trade is a modern form of slavery and the fastest-growing source of profit for organized crime.[23]

Trafficking is very broadly defined here to include psychological abuse, a vague notion that can be exploited easily for political purposes. And despite the claim that there were no laws that acknowledged the gravity of trafficking offenses, except when children were involved, many laws against sexual assault were in place at the state level. Feminists were motivated at least partly by the sheer prestige of federal law, no doubt, along with the gravity of violating it.

Division B is a revision of the Violence against Women Act.[24] Mandating a vast bureaucracy, it requires legal assistance and "advocacy" services; grants to coordinate services and activities at federal, state, and local levels; shelters for battered women and their children; grants to study arrest and antistalking policies; ways to enhance school and campus security; transitional-housing assistance for victims of domestic violence; grants for "training" and "educating" judges, court personnel, and forensic examiners; a national domestic-violence hotline; federal counsellors for victims; a study of state laws regarding insurance discrimination against victims of violence against women; a study of violence against women in the workplace; unemployment compensation for victims of violence against women; a report on the effects of parental-kidnapping laws in domestic violence cases; the development of ways to prevent battered immigrant women and children from remaining locked in abusive relationships; protections for older and disabled women; pilot programs on safe havens for children; "supervised visitation and safe visitation exchange of children by and between parents in situations involving domestic violence, child abuse, sexual assault, or stalking";[25] notice requirements for sexually violent offenders; and a research program, along with its own task force, to oversee implementation and coordination of the recommendations. This revision replaced the words "racial, cultural, ethnic, and language minorities" with "under-served populations."[26] Also, a new category of violence was introduced: "dating violence" by one "who is or has been in a social relationship of a romantic or intimate nature with the victim."[27]

Due to the original VAWA, the federal government has maintained a Violence against Women Office (VAWO). Its publications encourage "victim service agencies and legal service providers to enhance delivery of quality comprehensive legal services to victims of domestic violence, sexual assault, and stalking."[28] Here are some titles: *Understanding DNA Evidence*; *The Sexual Victimization of College Women*; *The Nature, and Consequences of Intimate Partner Violence*; and *The Criminalization of Domestic Violence*. The office provides the *Toolkit to End Violence against Women*, moreover. This was developed by the National Advisory Council on Violence against Women, which was co-chaired by the Departments of Justice and Health and Human Services.

The Federal Bureau of Investigation makes use of several statutes covering crimes against children. We have already discussed the ones on porn and child support. Others protect minors from aggravated sexual abuse, sexual abuse, and prostitution.[29] In 1996, the Pam Lychner Sexual Offender Tracking and Identification Act declared that sex offenders who had two or more convictions or were convicted of aggravated sexual abuse must register as sex offenders, the length of time they spend on this registry depending on the type of offence.[30] The Crimes against Children Unit of the Federal Bureau of Investigation has a National Sex Offender Registry, as does the National Crime Information Center.[31]

Canada has taken similar steps to protect plaintiffs (who are almost always women) in rape cases and make it easier to prosecute defendants (almost always men). In 1982, Parliament amended two sections of its Criminal Code. Section 276 limits cross-examination about sexual history.[32] Section 277 prohibits evidence about sexual reputation.[33] These changes became known as Canadian "rape shield" laws. "Sexual history" now refers to sexual acts known to have been performed, and "sexual reputation" only to alleged proclivities.

Section 276 is very much like its American equivalent, rule 412. "[E]vidence that the complainant has engaged in sexual activity, whether with the accused or with any other person, is not admissible to support an inference that, by reason of the sexual nature of that activity the complainant ... is more likely to have consented to the sexual activity ... or ... is less worthy of belief."[34] Like the American counterpart, it makes an exception if the evidence "is of specific instances of sexual activity ... is relevant to an issue at trial ... [and] has significant probative value that is not substantially outweighed by the danger of prejudice to the proper administration of justice."[35] To make a decision, the judge, provincial court judge, or justice must take into account

the interests of justice, including the right of the accused to make a full answer and defend ... society's interest in encouraging the reporting of sexual assault offences ... whether there is a reasonable prospect that the evidence will assist in arriving at a just determination in the case ... the need to remove from the fact-finding process any discriminatory belief or bias ... the risk that the evidence may unduly arouse sentiments of prejudice, sympathy or hostility in the jury ... the potential prejudice to the complainant's personal dignity and right of privacy ... the right of the complainant and of every individual to personal security and to the full protection and benefit of the law ... and any other factor that the judge, provincial court judge or justice considers relevant.[36]

Section 277 states that "evidence of sexual reputation, whether general or specific, is not admissible for the purpose of challenging or supporting the credibility of the complainant."[37] Moreover, section 666 says that "where, at trial, the accused adduces evidence of his good character, the prosecutor may, in answer thereto, before a verdict is returned, adduce evidence of the previous conviction of the accused for any offences, including any previous conviction by reason of which a greater punishment may be imposed."[38]

The rape-shield laws were challenged in *R. v. Seaboyer; R. v. Gayme*.[39] The two defendants argued that their right to a fair trial under the Charter was infringed by the Criminal Code, which does not allow a defendant (apart from the three exceptions that we have mentioned) to cite the plaintiff's previous sexual history.

According to one of the men, he sincerely believed that the woman had given him consent and also that his credibility would be reinforced by evidence of her sexual history. LEAF argued against him, because his defense would have been "according to the accused's beliefs and not according to the victim's experience."[40] In addition, LEAF argued that men make the following wrong assumptions about women: that they either secretly want to be raped – ironically, MacKinnon herself actually agrees with that because of her own assumption about the "eroticization" of male violence – or are congenitally promiscuous, that women argue coercion to cover their promiscuity, that women cannot be violated if they are no longer virgins, that women consent to sexual activities unless they fight back vigorously, that women are not unduly troubled if they know the men involved, and that women might say yes for fear of being killed after saying no.

The Supreme Court upheld section 277 but struck down section 276, arguing that its legitimacy should be decided in each case by the judge alone. For Christopher Manfredi, nonetheless, "one should not exaggerate the extent to which LEAF lost in *Seaboyer*. Indeed, the government invited representatives of the Canadian feminist movement to participate actively in the drafting of a new sexual assault law that redefines both the nature of consent and the defenses available to defendants in sexual assault proceedings. In this sense, LEAF was able to convert a legal defeat into a political victory."[41]

To encourage the reporting of rape and litigation, LEAF argued in *Canadian Newspapers Co. v. Canada* that it was necessary to prevent newspapers from publishing the names of alleged victims.[42] But in the case of a false complaint, argued the opposition, publishing these names might bring forth witnesses to support the defendant. The opposition argued also that not publishing these names would violate freedom of expression, which is protected by the Charter. A unanimous decision by the Supreme Court supported the ban on publishing names, however, arguing that it did not violate freedom of expression and protected the equality of "women and children."

To deal with the problem of violence against women, Health Canada established several Family Violence Initiatives between 1986 and 1997. These brought federal, provincial, and territorial governments together with Crown corporations, nongovernmental organizations, professional agencies, universities, aboriginal community organizations, and so forth. Beginning in 1995, moreover, Canadian law gave strong support to women in cases of domestic violence. Saskatchewan passed the Victims of Domestic Violence Act that year and other provinces followed suit. The Saskatchewan legislation includes several parts. According to the Emergency Intervention Orders, only alleged victims may occupy their homes; alleged abusers may not live or communicate with either their alleged victims or the families of their alleged victims. According to the Victims' Assistance Orders, convicted abusers must provide financial compensation to their victims. And according to the Warrants of Entry, police officers may enter any home in which domestic violence is suspected.[43] This powerful legislation was challenged in several court cases.[44] As a result, claimants had to show that serious violence had indeed occurred.

In 1995, Bill C-42 amended the Criminal Code as follows: it made protective court orders both easier to get and more effective, increased the maximum penalty for violation of a peace bond (a form of restraining order) from six months to two years, and reclassified "hybrid offenses" (which allowed prosecutors to proceed directly, without requiring victims to testify twice).[45] More amendments were added that year by Bill C-72, which excluded intoxication as a defense in cases of assault and sexual assault. Still more amendments had been added the following year by Bill C-41, which had allowed judges to include offences against spouses and children as aggravating factors for purposes of sentencing and also allowed victims to seek restitution for expenses incurred by moving out to avoid physical harm.

The Firearms Control Act of 1996 introduced several changes: it required Canadians to get licenses for all weapons, established a national registry of these weapons, and raised the mandatory sentence for sexual assault or other violent crimes to at least four years.

In 1997, Bill c-27 introduced several more changes. These made it easier for young victims and victims of sexual exploitation to testify in court, allowed for the prosecution of Canadians who sexually exploit children abroad, increased penalties for those who hire juvenile prostitutes and those who stalk and kill, and made it clear that female circumcision is an offence. That same year, Bill c-46 protected victims of sexual offences by restricting the use of personal records such as those compiled by psychiatrists or counsellors. The federal budget for one year, 1997–98, included not only $30.7 million to deal with domestic violence in particular but also federal subsidies to deal with violence against women in general. In the late 1990s, some provinces set up domestic-violence courts to ensure a specialized response to women, which might involve emotional and financial support for witnesses, cultural interpreters, tapes of emergency calls, photographs of injuries, or speedy trials.

A government report of 1998 addressed to the United Nations Commission on Human Rights reviewed what the Canadian government had done for women since 1994.[46] Measures taken had included inaugurating public-awareness campaigns, developing "gender evaluation tools" for "gender-based analysis," funding shelters, and establishing research centres.[47] In addition, the report covered topics such as federal initiatives, provincial and territorial initiatives, criminal-justice measures, statistics, "training" programs for the criminal-justice system, prevention awareness programs, and support services such as safe houses and crisis interventions. The report is worth a read for anyone who can endure its bureaucratic jargon. Here are the highlights.

The federal government had discussed "training" or "educational" programs for judges. Plans had involved the promotion of feminist legal theories and provided statistical support based on feminist analyses. The discussion had referred to similar programs for the Royal Canadian Mounted Police and the National Parole Board; both programs had been intended to increase "awareness of equality issues affecting various groups who feel disadvantaged or inadequately understood by the Canadian justice system."[48] Both had included tools that would be useful in coping with violence against women. One example is the *Investigative Guide for Sexual Offences*, which describes appropriate ways of investigating sexual assaults and effective ways of creating workshops to "educate" communities.[49]

The report went on about how "to do gender equality analysis in the prosecution of family violence cases."[50] In addition, the federal government had set up "awareness" programs that had been intended for use in schools, to raise consciousness among children, counsel those who had experienced abuse, and "guide" professionals in medical and social work. Canadians had now been granted programs for (male) "abusers," moreover, from short interventions to intensive therapeutic ones for those in prisons or on probation. These programs had received a great deal of publicity in the mass media.

The report linked sexual assault and the economic status of women. Canadians had now been given the benefit of workshops on how to improve women's participation in the economy. One of these, held in 1998, had been called "Women and the Knowledge-Based Economy and Society." Its mandate had been to ensure that "gender-based" (read: feminist) analyses for all "future policies and legislation to determine their implications for women and men."[51] The underlying logic had been distinctly MacKinnonesque: that violence against women occurs primarily because women have a lower economic status than men. In *Seaboyer* the feminist Legal and Education Action Fund (LEAF) used the same argument:

It is submitted that sexual assault is an equality issue ... Women are singled out for sexual assault and their accusations of sexual assault are systematically disbelieved because of their gender, that is, because they are relegated to an inferior social status as female, including being socially defined as appropriate targets for forced sex ... It is submitted that in an equal society, sexual assault on women and children would be exceptional, rather than as common as it is under current conditions of inequality.[52]

In its discussion of violence against women, the report cited fallacious statistics contained in the Violence against Women Survey of 1993 (which we discuss in appendix 3) and called them "a national base of information on the extent of violence against Canadian women in Canadian society."[53]

The debate over domestic violence is very acrimonious and has been for decades. In terms of legislation, though, women have clearly won the debate. They have had enormous success in establishing public awareness and prevention programs, which include "gender-based" evaluation tools and special services for women. The latter, in turn, include hotlines, shelters, counsellors, specialized courts, new police policies (entering homes where violence is suspected), new court policies (preventing contact between violent men and their children or mandating supervised visits or awarding houses to female victims), and so forth. Women needed many of these reforms. Trouble is, ideological feminists have exploited them to empower women in ways that not only foster misandry but also create systemic discrimination against men. The results go beyond reform. Most people, both women and men, still assume that only women need to fear domestic violence.

Before proceeding, please note that this section is about violence *within* the home (although, as Warren Farrell points out, violence is not the only weapon used by men and women against their spouses or partners).[54] Violence outside the home is another matter. Many more men than women resort to violence outside the home, usually against other men. Our point here is only that the story of domestic violence, sometimes known specifically as "abused women," is much more complicated than anyone would guess after a steady diet of ideological rhetoric from feminists.

There is clearly a legitimate link between statistics and laws; the latter should be made in view of the former. But what if the statistics are methodologically flawed or prejudicially interpreted? To place that discussion in its proper context, we turn now from domestic violence against women to domestic violence *by* women. The former is a serious problem, to be sure, but so is the latter. And neither journalists nor feminists have said much about the latter, except in attempts to explain it away as an aberration, one that is usually caused either directly or indirectly by men in any case. Scholars, on the other hand, have been researching this topic for decades. And not only male scholars.

Contrary to conventional wisdom, which is based on the suppression of evidence and even biased statistics, research that began in the 1980s has repeatedly shown that women commit or even initiate domestic violence at least as often as men do. In the research of Murray Straus and Richard Gelles, 53% of the women questioned admitted that they had struck first.[55] Other studies indicate that women are more likely than men to become violent without expecting reprisals.[56] According to Coramae Mann, only around 10% of the self-defense claims are legitimate.[57] Why? For one thing, some women kill men who are incapacitated in wheelchairs, asleep in bed, or not then engaged in violent or threatening behaviour. By making pre-emptive strikes, albeit strikes based on reasonable fear of future violence, these women take the law into their own hands. Since men are often victims of domestic abuse, moreover, some scholars refer now to the Battered Man Syndrome, which is the counterpart of the Battered Woman Syndrome (although not all of the reasons that men stay in abusive relationships are the same as those of women who do so).

Warren Farrell still had to rebut denials that men were often victims of domestic violence. In *Women Can't Hear What Men Don't Say*, he sum-marized all this evidence:

To their credit, despite their assumption that men were the abusers, *every* domes-tic violence survey done of both sexes over the ... [last] quarter century in the United States, Canada, England, New Zealand, and Australia ... found one of two things: Women and men batter each other about *equally*, or women batter men more. In addition, almost all studies found women were more likely to *ini-tiate* violence and much more likely to inflict the *severe* violence. Women them-selves acknowledged they are more likely to be violent and to be initiators of vio-lence. Finally, women were more likely to engage in severe violence that was not reciprocated.[58]

According to both women's support groups and to police reports, men are responsible for approximately 90% of domestic violence. According to men's support groups, on the other hand, women are responsible for 81% of domestic violence.[59] Which to believe? For feminists, the answer is obvi-ous. For researchers, the answer is not so obvious, or should not be. The whole point of research, after all, is to examine the evidence and possibly find something new, not merely to confirm what is already assumed. Some research eventually does confirm earlier assumptions or hypotheses, but not because of any hopes on the part of scholars.

Farrell consulted the National Organization for Women. Were there any two-sex studies of domestic violence, he asked, showing that most batter-ers were men? He was referred to the National Crime Victimization Survey, but this presented him with a problem. The survey asked men and women if they had ever been "hit" or "kicked" in the context of a crime. Men were found to be much more likely than women to answer in terms of violence outside the home. Women were found to be much more likely than men to answer in terms of violence *within* the home, which was and is legally defined as a crime. As a result, more women than men claimed to have been the victims of *domestic* violence. "We have educated women to think of being punched or kicked by a man as a crime, so a crime survey can get women to report that as a crime; we have not yet educated men to think of being bitten, punched, kicked, or hit with a frying pan as a crime, so a crime survey fails to get men to report these behaviors as a crime. A crime survey cannot hear what men do not say."[60]

Besides, Farrell points out, men are more likely than women to be specific in responding to questions. Asked if he has ever been battered, he might say no. Even after being hit repeatedly with a frying pan. Asked if he has ever been hit with a frying pan by his wife, on the other hand, he might say yes. How to explain this difference in perception between the sexes? There might be some biological or evolutionary reason for men to favour specificity, but the most obvious reason in this case is surely that both women and men have been carefully trained over the past twenty-five years to identify even slapping a woman as domestic violence. Neither men nor women, on the other hand, have been trained to identify even stabbing a man specifically as domestic violence.[61]

Moreover, Farrell found evidence that both sexes trivialize injuries done to men. According to a survey by the Department of Justice, 41% of Americans find it "less severe when a wife stabs her husband *to death* as they do when a husband stabs his wife *to death*."[62] The same double standard is applied to nonlethal forms of violence. Both sexes consider it more serious when a man hits, bites, or throws something at a woman than when a woman does precisely the same thing to a man.[63] Nonetheless, most people would say, surely the *effect* of violence is more severe when women are the victims (which would be a matter of practical, but not moral, importance).

It is true that more women than men, 2.9% versus 1.9%, seek medical help as a result of domestic violence.[64] "Is this because a frying pan hurts a man less," asks Farrell, "than a fist hurts a woman ... Or is there something wrong with the way we are measuring who is injured? To measure which sex is injured more by measuring which sex reports to the doctor more is to make the same mistake we made by assuming women were battered more because they reported domestic violence to the police more."[65] The lamentable fact is that men are much less likely than women to seek medical help in *any* circumstances, even for routine checkups. They would have to be much more severely injured than female victims, therefore, to end up in emergency rooms.

Even those who do are not necessarily identified as refugees from troubled homes. Physicians are not trained to ask male patients, unlike female ones, either leading or specific questions about domestic violence. Nor has any government published information to help physicians identify the subtle signs of domestic violence in male patients, unlike female ones. "It is exactly the feeling that men are stronger – usually true – that [ostensibly] gives women permission for hitting them harder and using weapons. This is even true in mothers' attitudes toward their sons vs. their daughters. Sons are more than twice as likely as daughters to be injured when their mothers hit them."[66] As a result, says Farrell, even the statistics on men who do show up in emergency rooms might not adequately reflect the number of victims of domestic violence. According to him, women are more likely than men to use weapons. "The weapons women use are more varied and creative than men's, doubtless in compensation for less muscle strength."[67]

And the women of some other societies are not much different in this respect from those of our own. Farrell examined statistics not only from the United States and Canada but also from the United Kingdom, New Zealand, British Honduras, Puerto Rico, Israel, and Finland. Except in Puerto Rico, he found, women are either just as likely as men to indulge in domestic violence or more so.[68] In addition, Farrell examined the statistics on various subcultures in the United States. He found, for example, that in the case of Quakers, who are pacifists by creed, both men and women indulged in minor forms of violence and at approximately the same rate: 12% for women versus 11% for men, slightly higher in both cases than among the general population. When it came to severe forms of violence, however, the Quakers were much more peaceable: 2.5% for women (versus 4.4% for other women) and 0.8% for men (versus 3% for other men). Culture, in short, can make a difference.[69]

According to one American study conducted by the Department of Justice, observes Jerry Adler, about 2.5 million crimes of all kinds are committed against American women every year.[70] This study was based on interviews rather than police reports, which tend to underestimate the number of domestic assaults. According to the National Clearinghouse for the Defense of Battered Women, nevertheless, 800,000 women are battered every year in Pennsylvania alone![71] Not even the staid American Medical Association, apparently, can be trusted. On one occasion, it reported that family violence killed as many women in five years as the total number of Americans killed in the Vietnam War.[72] This would mean 10,000 women murdered every year, though, which is more than twice the number recorded by the FBI.[73] "Yes, it would be better if journalists were more skeptical of statistics," writes Adler. "But they're not the ones who have turned public-policy debate in America into a tug of war over data. What's important to know about spouse abuse is that it's wrong, whether it kills 1,400 women a year or some other number. Data on sexual molestation even if it were accurate ought to have no bearing on anyone's civil rights. Someday we'll remember that facts are only the shadow cast by truth."[74]

Similarly, Philip Cook observes that there is a "higher or nearly equal rate of domestic violence against men."[75] He devotes the first chapter of *Abused Men* to a critical analysis of statistical sources: police reports and surveys. He asks questions about the many variables. Is the violence trivial (slapping, grabbing, shoving, pushing)? Is it serious (injuries requiring medical attention)? Is it catastrophic (murder)? Is its category underreported or adequately reported? On the question of whether women physically assault their mates at a rate similar to men, he observes that "[t]he answer often depends on who is asking the question, how it is asked, and how the data are analyzed. Statistical results from surveys can vary greatly owing to differences between the populations studied, so it is often best to directly examine results obtained from different reporting groups first in order to piece together an overall picture. It then becomes easier to judge these results fairly as they compare to more generally representative surveys."[76]

But precisely what kinds of violence are involved in these studies? If women really do engage in domestic violence, maybe they are just throwing burned toast around the kitchen or elbowing their husbands out of the way. Maybe men, by contrast, are knocking their wives out cold or shooting them. In that case, the numbers would be lying and should be dismissed. But the studies reported by Farrell – and he reported a lot of them, carefully documenting each – indicate nothing of the kind. One of them makes a clear distinction between minor and severe types of violence. The former includes throwing an object (4.1% by husbands versus 7.4% by wives); pushing, shoving, or grabbing (10.4% versus 10.9%); and slapping (2.6% versus 3.8%). The latter includes kicking, biting, or punching (1.3% versus 3.4%); hitting with an object (1.6% versus 2.8%); beating (0.8% versus 0.6%); choking (0.8% versus 0.6%); threatening with a knife or gun (0.4% versus 0.7%); and using a knife or gun (0.2% versus 0.1%). In all but three categories – beating, choking, and threatening with a knife or gun (though not actually using a knife or gun) – wives outranked husbands.[77]

Following a study of police records by Maureen McLeod, Cook reports that

72 percent of the attacks against women by men involved the use of bodily force (hitting, punching, slapping, kicking, etc.), but for women assaulting men, only 14 percent involved bodily force ... Only 15 percent of the women faced a gun or a knife in a domestic battle. A gun or a knife was used or threatened against a male victim 63 percent of the time ... Owing to the greater use of cutting objects and other weapons, McLeod states, "Offenses against men are significantly more serious in nature than are offenses against women." Her examination of police reports found, "Whereas just over one-fourth of all spouse abuse incidents involving female victims are categorized as aggravated assaults, the corresponding statistic for male victims is demonstrably higher ... 86% are aggravated; over two-thirds of these aggravated events are serious assaults with a weapon." ... The more frequent use of weapons by women (82 percent for women versus 25 percent for men) in spousal assaults results in a greater injury rate for men, according to McLeod: 77 percent of the assaulted men report some injury. These statistics clearly exceed estimates of

the extent of victim injury among female victims, generally documented as between 52 and 57 percent." In fact, McLeod says, 84 percent of the men who were injured by domestic violence required medical attention, with 50 percent of these being hospitalized overnight or longer.[78]

Cook concludes that "males may suffer serious injury more often whereas females likely suffer a greater number of total injuries ranging from minor to serious."[79] After examining a great deal of evidence – police reports, hospital surveys, military surveys, shelter surveys, national surveys – he questions the claim that domestic violence by women can always be explained as self-defense. "Although the data do not indicate what proportion of the violent acts we see in response to violent acts by men, the fact that women had higher mean and median rates for severe violence suggests that female aggression is not merely a response to male aggression."[80]

As for domestic murder, Cook reports that more women than men are indeed killed by their spouses. The difference is 20%.[81] According to Farrell, though, many more wives would be implicated in murder if several hidden factors were taken into account. For one thing, some women use poison or some other method that might be listed in official records as an accident. Other women either persuade their boyfriends (occasionally male students) or hire experienced hit men to murder for them. These murders, if solved, are listed as "multiple-offender killings." They do not show up, therefore, in the statistics on women who murder. "We only know," says Farrell, "that in multiple-offender killings there are four times as many husbands as victims than wives, according to the FBI."[82]

More men who kill their wives than women who kill their husbands, by the way, also kill themselves. Their motivation is not to collect insurance money, or to marry someone else. "In brief," writes Farrell, "a wife's style of killing reflects her motivation, which requires the killing not be detected; a husband's style of killing reflects his motivation and, well, a husband who kills himself is pretty likely to be caught – a dead husband is a dead giveaway. Even if her killing does get detected, it is much more likely to never be recorded as a spouse killing – but as a multiple-offender killing, or an accident or a heart attack. When a woman is murdered, we are more likely to track down the killer than when a man is murdered."[83]

Who are these women who batter and sometimes even kill their husbands? Mainly women who were battered as children: the same variable accounts for many men who batter and sometimes kill their wives. (According to one study, ironically, both boys and girls who were beaten by their fathers grew up to become victims, but those beaten by their mothers grew up to become victimizers.)[84] Women are conditioned to think about men, says Patricia Pearson, in precisely the same way as men themselves do. As a result, many women are not even aware of the damage they can inflict on men. And the shelters seldom teach women how to deal with their own anger and violence. Even in the late 1990s, observes Pearson, 23% of women in one study – a figure that had not changed over the previous twenty years – believed that "slapping the cad" is justifiable.[85] That lesson is taught very effectively through popular culture. In fact, as we observed in *Spreading Misandry*, what we call The Slap is a convention so deeply embedded in popular movies and television shows that few people even wonder about it. Each episode of the sitcom *Men Behaving Badly*, for instance, began with a montage of old movies in which women slap or punch men hard enough to knock them down or even out cold. What makes that convention so interesting is that it does not presume any physical provocation. Women who slap men do so because of something that has been said to them or even implied about them, not something that has been done to them.

Women have learned, moreover, to manipulate the cultural system very effectively to their own advantage. "Donning the feminine mask, they can manipulate the biases of family and community in order to set men up. If he tries to leave, or fight back, a fateful moment comes when she reaches for the phone, dials 911, and has him arrested on the strength of her word: 'Officer, he hit me.' With mounting pressure on North American police forces to disavow misogynistic attitudes and take the word of a woman over a man, female psychopaths and other hard-core female abusers have an extremely effective means to up the ante and win the game."[86]

If all of this is true, though, why do so few people know about male victims of domestic violence? Who are these men? Farrell explains that academics have suppressed evidence by intimidating their colleagues. Men have been very reluctant to report their own victimization, moreover, and journalists have been reluctant to write about it. Finally, the whole notion of men being battered by women is so counterintuitive that few people even think of the possibility. Having already discussed the first explanation, suppressing evidence, we turn now to the others.

Men are indeed very reluctant to report abuse from their wives or female partners. And Farrell is by no means the only one to say so (although he was among the first). Drawing her information from a support group for battered husbands, Pearson points out that blue-collar men have been conditioned to think of themselves in macho terms as invulnerable. Others refrain from hitting back or reporting damage for less obvious reasons. First, they are conditioned by the notion that "real men" are not supposed to fight women; doing so actually diminishes their status. Second, they are afraid of losing their children in custody suits. Third, they realize that attention would inevitably shift to them on the assumption that only men are violent. Fourth, we would add, men are afraid of public ridicule for being unable to defend themselves from their wives or female partners.

(Similarly, men are afraid not to risk their lives in battle; for men, as for women, there has always been a "fate worse than death.")

Men are much less likely than women to report their domestic tribulations to police officers, journalists, researchers, or physicians in emergency rooms. The most obvious explanation is simply that most men are still ashamed to admit that they are sometimes victims and in need of help. Actually, many men are ashamed to be in need no matter what the circumstances. Even asking for directions to a gas station, as stand-up comedians often point out, can be problematic. "A battered man knows there are no shelters for battered men," in any case, "because no one really believes he exists."[87] Well, some people do believe them. But they are likely, most men still believe, to respond with ridicule. That adds shame to fear and anger.

Even men who do end up in emergency rooms, says Farrell (albeit on the basis of anecdotal evidence from men who speak to him on radio shows), often disguise their injuries as the results of athletic accidents. They are usually successful, he adds, because it is much easier for physicians to believe that healthy men have been tackled by quarterbacks than brained by their own wives. The result of all this is "learned helplessness" au masculin. "Both sexes feel helpless," writes Farrell, "when the love of their life turns into the nightmare of their life. But men ... feel much more helpless about asking for outside help. In brief, women's strength is in knowing when they feel helpless. Men's weakness is not knowing. The fact that we have identified women's 'learned helplessness' but not men's is ... a sign that the women's problem is on its way to being solved, while the men's is as yet unrecognized."[88]

Moreover, Farrell observes, "men learn to call pain 'glory'; women learn to call the police."[89] Men have been conditioned from childhood to accept pain as the measure of their worth as men. This is not masochism. Men do not understand the pain they endure, in general, as deserved punishment or as an end in itself. They understand it as a necessary evil. "Why," asks Farrell, "did virtually every culture reward its men for enduring violence? So it would have a cadre of people available to protect it in war. The people considered the most in need of protection were women and children. The sex considered most disposable was men – or males."[90] To be a man, in short, has been to protect other members of the community even at the cost of one's own life. "Part of the pressure men put on each other to carry out this mandate is ridiculing a man who complains when he is hurt. We often think that when a man insults another man by calling him a 'girl,' the insult reflects a contempt for women. No. It reflects a contempt for any man who is unwilling to make himself strong enough to protect someone as precious as a woman. It is an insult to any man unwilling to endure the pain it takes to save a woman's life – including the pain of losing his own life."[91] This is definitely not to say that we should continue to see men, or any other group of human beings, as an expendable class or race. It is merely to acknowledge a historic reality of immense psychological importance for both men and women.

Feminists have argued that all this talk about men protecting women amounts to nothing more than a patriarchal smokescreen. Far from feeling obliged to protect women and children, they say, men feel justified in assaulting them. How else can you explain the men who do, in fact, assault women? This is a fundamental premise of ideological feminism. It is the fundamental assumption also of many treatment programs for abusive men. But the assumption is false. "Battering a woman," Farrell observes, "is the male role *broken down*. A man who batters a woman is like a cross-dresser: he's out of role."[92]

One obvious explanation in the context of this book is the general breakdown of gender itself, which began (consciously) among men who joined the "beat" and "hippie" movements but was far more effectively institutionalized by women who joined feminist movements. Although Farrell refrains from pointing it out, this is a very serious problem today because of ideological or postmodernist attempts to "deconstruct" all notions of gender, not merely as social constructs but as evil ones. The importance of this knowledge when treating abusive men can hardly be exaggerated. Assuming that they resort to violence because of their patriarchal power is unlikely to produce effective treatment, after all, if the underlying problem is precisely the opposite. This approach will not, therefore, empower women. It will empower only ideological feminists.

But more than the breakdown of gender – a cultural system – is involved here. The term "women and children" is still used routinely by journalists to indicate those who should be off limits in connection with war and violence. And women are still considered immune to conscription for combat.[93] This indicates that men are still considered the protectors, at least in theory, of society. So why do some individual men turn against the very people whom they have been taught to protect? "When a man feels the woman he is supposed to protect is threatening him or verbally chopping him apart, he begins to make a mental transfer from protecting her to protecting himself from her. She begins to lose her status as a woman."[94] Being a protector, Farrell points out, means having the power to protect, but not all men have enough to maintain even the illusion of offering protection. Far from having too much power, he suggests, they have too little. In anger and frustration over a discrepancy between the cultural ideal for men and the economic reality for themselves, they turn against the ideal (a topic that we will discuss much more fully in *Transcending Misandry*).

The relation between power and violence, says Farrell, presents us with an ironic twist. The evidence indicates that "when *women* abuse, they are sometimes in a position of power, sometimes without power, and some-times they are experiencing both simultaneously. When men abuse, they are much more likely to be in a position of power*less*ness – the act of abuse being a momentary act of power designed to compensate for underlying experiences of power*less*ness."[95] As it happens, elderly women are more than four times as likely to abuse their husbands as elderly men are to abuse their wives.[96] The husbands, usually older and in worse physical condition than their wives, are in no position to do any damage. The wives feel powerless in the way that elderly people always do, but they feel pow-erful, too, in relation to their husbands. (Ditto for abusive mothers.)[97]

This strongly supports what common sense has always suggested: people who victimize others pick on those least likely to fight back. "Why are women more likely to abuse men who are powerless while men are more likely to protect women who are powerless? Or, put another way, why, if he feels powerless, is *he* more likely to be abusive *and* she is also more likely to feel abusive? She perceives him as no longer being able to protect her, so she acts on her instincts to get rid of a man who can't protect her. (Remember, she survived for millions of years by selecting protectors, which means knowing how to weed out men who can't protect her.) Put another way, female abuse of men who can't perform is instinctive. She feels powerless when he feels powerless."[98]

It is unnecessary to agree that this phenomenon is instinctive, and we do not. It is enough to see its inner logic. Farrell adds that abused lesbians, too, often suspect that their partners feel dependent rather than powerful. "So among women, feelings of power or powerlessness – or some combination of both – seem in various ways to catalyze abuse."[99] The situation is quite dif-ferent among men. Farrell points to a study of the American Psychological Association, which found that abusive behaviour by men correlated more closely with feelings of powerlessness – having no job or a poorly paid one, being uneducated or poorly educated, receiving emotional support from few friends or other social contacts, using drugs or alcohol, suffering from psy-chological problems such as depression, and so on – than abusive behaviour by women.[100] "Men's greater physical strength would seem to indicate men's violence toward women involves male power ... [But] this is tricky, because men learn to use that strength to protect women and will beat up or even kill a man whose uses it against a woman. It is when the power of his masculin-ity breaks down that he is most likely to be violent toward a woman."[101]

Closely linked with the relation between pain and "glory" is that between pain and love. Farrell's explanation of this phenomenon sounds like masochism.

Men have learned to associate being abused with being loved. For example, becom-ing the football or ice hockey player some woman will love (and men will respect) requires his enduring physical abuse, name-calling, hazing, or emotional humbling. News magazines such as Maclean's help us reinforce our propensity to call men who are physically beaten "heroes," even as we call women who are physically beaten "victims." Taking abuse will get him through boot camp so he can become the officer some woman will adore; and it is part of the territory of "death professions" like firefighting or coal mining, where he hopes to earn enough to afford a wife. By the time he is eligible for love, he has been trained to be humbled, hazed, and abused.[102]

So men have a hard time admitting, first to themselves and then to others, that they are in trouble. Suppose, however, that they do admit to being in trouble. Why not leave? This is the very question asked of women in similar circumstances. Feminists have always insisted that some female victims of domestic violence stay not merely due to economic hardship (even though the low-income women in at least one study were actually more likely than high-income women to leave)[103] but also due to Battered Woman Syndrome. This combination of low self-esteem and fear of being hunted down not only explains why they stay but also, allegedly, justifies them in resorting to murder. As Farrell points out, though, some male victims have either the same or equivalent problems.

Like many women, for instance, many men are economically unprepared to leave. Not all men even have jobs, let alone well-paid jobs. Not even all men with well-paid jobs can afford to maintain *two* homes (which, according to the law, is what they would have to do). And not all men are willing either to leave their children, often their only source of love, or to leave them with violent mothers. "Many men, then, endure the physical hurt of being beaten rather than endure the emotional torture of feeling they've left their own children unprotected, lost love, and lost their home. When these combine with the helplessness that emerges from the fear of asking for help, they create the 'Battered Man Syndrome.'"[104]

Just as men are reluctant to acknowledge their own victimization, argues Farrell, journalists have been reluctant to report it. Both they and their readers or viewers rely on notions that have become conventional wisdom, notions that are actively fostered by some feminists. Men in general batter women, but women in general do not batter men. Men do so out of contempt, but women do so in self-defense. Men can always leave home, but women cannot due to lack of money or fear of revenge. Women try to solve domestic problems through talking, but men try to do so through violence, due to the belief that women are their property and should therefore submissively accept the superior status and privileged position of men.[105] No wonder, as Cook observes, journalists seldom use gender-neutral language when the general topic is domestic violence. The generic culprit is always "he," the generic victim always "she."

And no woman ever complains to the editor about *this* example of sexist language.

We have already noted that much of the evidence collected from surveys indicates that women actually initiate domestic violence at least as often as men do. In *No Angels: Women Who Commit Violence*, a collection of essays, several authors question the assumption that women are innately peaceful, that only exceptional women – that is, only women who could be considered either mad or bad – are capable of violence.[106] But in the end, these authors excuse and even legitimate violent women by suggesting that they merely react in a rational way to the violence of men. Maybe they have not read the studies on domestic violence among lesbians. According to one, rates of abuse were higher among lesbians in their prior relationships with women than in their prior relationships with men: 56% had been subjected to sexual aggression by their female lovers, 45% to physical aggression, and 64.5% to emotional aggression.[107] Another study found that levels of violence were higher among lesbians than among gay men: 55% of gay women reported physical violence but only 44% of gay men.[108] Yet another study found that 47.5% of gay women reported violence in their relationships but only 22% of gay men. Moreover, 38% of the women reported using violence against their partners but only 22% of the men. "Lesbian violence shatters the myth," writes Farrell, "that women abuse only when men drive them to it. It dispels the myth that male power and male privilege create violence against women. Lesbians do not have much male power and privilege."[109] Of course, feminists often "explain" abusive women by claiming that patriarchy causes or even forces women to behave in these ways. (Never mind that this reduces women to the level of passive morons.) But if patriarchy can be blamed for the bad things about women, as Farrell points out, surely it must be lauded also for the good things about men.

Whatever. In *The Battered Woman*, Lenore Walker threw down the ideological gauntlet to lawyers and legislators.[110] This book has become the authoritative defense for killing husbands or male partners who are not immediately engaged in violence. Walker claims that the Battered Woman Syndrome has two defining characteristics. First, women somehow "know" that they are about to be murdered. Second, they are psychologically unable to leave. They are justified in striking first, taking the law into their own hands. (Ideological feminists seldom allow that technicality to stop them from blaming male victims.) By coining the term "Battered Woman Syndrome," Walker directly or indirectly legitimated what would otherwise be called vigilante justice. According to current law in many places, the action of the battered woman qualifies as self-defense. "The problem is," says Farrell, that "the husband is too dead to defend himself. And the court can't hear what men are too dead to say. In contrast, when men claim self-defense, they are often not even believed by their counselors."[111]

The Battered Woman Syndrome has been widely accepted as an explanation for why women remain with violent men. It relies heavily on the idea that women learn helplessness after failed attempts to escape from the cycle of abuse (but also, say feminists, after millennia of cultural conditioning to make women submissive or, as MacKinnon would say, to "eroticize" male brutality). These women, so says the theory, feel trapped and thus ironically refuse help from the outside world. They are especially reluctant to press charges due to economic dependence or fear of physical retaliation. But Grant Brown points out that the figures do not confirm this theory. On the contrary. First, they show "that women are *more* willing to testify against their partners ... the more seriously they have been injured by them. Second, women are more willing than men to testify against their partners, regardless of the level of injury suffered ... All of the evidence indicates that abused men fit the theory of the 'battered woman' better than abused women do!"[112]

One result of these misconceptions about domestic violence, is a difference in the way that men and women are treated by the courts.

As a result of the invisibility of the female methods of killing, women who do kill benefit from the stereotype of women as innocent and are treated very differently by the law: thirteen percent of spousal murder cases with women defendants result in an acquittal vs. 1 percent of murder cases with men defendants. Similarly, the average prison sentence for spousal murder (excluding life sentences and the death penalty) is almost three times longer for men than for women – 17.5 years vs. 6.2 years.[113] And, thus far, a woman has never been executed for killing only a man. When we can only see women as innocent, the law becomes equally blind.[114]

Brown, in an excellent Canadian study of this problem, finds considerable evidence of systemic discrimination against men. His primary goal is to show that prosecutors are the major players in cases of domestic violence. His secondary goal is to examine other players – police officers and judges – in connetion with data that are relatively inaccessible to the public. Brown used two sources, both from Alberta, that had never been studied: databases that track responses by the Edmonton police to domestic violence from 1999 to 2000 and files on domestic violence compiled in 2001 by the crown prosecutor's office in Edmonton.

Given the importance of these findings (and the need to respect every nuance of highly technical language), we find it worthwhile to quote extensively from Brown's own summary.

The results of this investigation indicate that men who are involved in disputes with their partners, whether as alleged victims or as alleged offenders or both, are disadvantaged and treated less favourably than women by the law-enforcement system at almost every step. Men are much less likely to report their victimization to the authorities to begin with, either because they consider it unmanly to do so or because they believe the authorities will not take their complaints very seriously, anyway. When men do report their victimization, or when it is reported for them by third parties, the police are less likely to lay charges against their partners than they would be to lay charges against comparable male suspects. In fact, the police seem reluctant to lay charges against women in partner violence cases unless a relatively serious offence has been committed or other aggravating factors are present. The result is that, even though the charging ratios by the Edmonton police in the period under scrutiny are higher against women than in many other jurisdictions in Canada in the past, they still diverge greatly from what the sociological data on partner violence indicates would reflect reality. The categories of female-only assaults and mutual aggression seem especially under-represented in the police charging data.

After laying charges, police are significantly more likely to take a man into custody than a woman, even when factors such as the level of injury inflicted and prior criminal record are taken into account. Nor do prosecutors tend to mitigate this disparately harsh treatment of men. On the contrary, prosecutors appear to pursue cases involving male suspects more vigorously than those involving female suspects. Thus men are more likely to be found guilty and are less likely to benefit from withdrawn charges, even though they are suspects in proportionately more of the no-injury cases. Men are also less likely to benefit from favourable plea bargains, despite the fact that they have committed, on average, less grievous offences. And men are significantly more likely to receive harsher sentences than women, even when all other relevant factors are taken into account. Indeed, gender is often *the most significant factor* in predicting how the law-enforcement system responds to incidents of partner violence.

This pattern of unfavourable outcomes bears all of the classic signs of a self-reinforcing system of discrimination against men, a system that is supported by ideological myths and stereotypes. Public-awareness campaigns based on information from official sources typically promote the awareness of and remedies for female victims only; so men who are victimized often do not even realize that help (such as it is) is available to them, and many of their cases do not come to the attention of the authorities. Many men have had experience with the law-enforcement system and refuse to engage it when they are themselves the victims of abuse. They can be forgiven for wondering why they should subject themselves to all of the embarrassment associated with pursuing charges against a violent female partner when the justice system does not seem inclined to take it seriously anyway. This reluctance on the part of male victims, in turn, reinforces stereotypical attitudes of police and prosecutors, who figure either that the man can look after himself or that he is not really interested in pursuing his complaint anyway. Since relatively few cases involving violence by women reach the courts, judges acquire the mistaken impression that violence against men is not a serious social problem, and excuse their leniency toward women with the sexist assumption that children should not be punished for the crimes of their mothers. Prosecutors, seeing how judges routinely slap women on the wrist for even fairly major assaults, lose incentive to fight these cases aggressively in the courts, and offer favourable plea-bargains to the women instead. And the police, seeing that prosecutors do not appear to pursue cases against women as vigorously as cases against men, in turn decide not to lay charges against women except in the clearest of cases. Up and down the system, everyone quickly adjusts to the political myth that family violence is only about protecting "women and children" from abusive male partners. Breaking this cycle of bias can only be achieved through system-wide concerted, and conscious efforts.[115]

Brown discusses several other examples of systemic discrimination in the courts against men. Consider the problem of no-contact orders, which prevent suspects from having access to their own property, their own homes. For reasons that Brown explains elsewhere, most of the suspects are men. He sees no justification for their treatment, in view of the fact "that mutual aggression is the most common form of partner violence." Moreover, he suggests that "if the police fear continued violence but do not want to take both the man and the woman into custody, the least they could do by way of mutual accommodation is to allow the man to stay in the home and take the woman to a shelter."[116] Or, we suggest, the reverse. But that would mean creating shelters for men.

Now think of plea bargaining. Brown shows that the most significant factor in that system is the sex of suspects. This, in fact, "is the only variable that is associated, at statistically significant levels, with receiving 'any term' as a penalty for partner violence. In other words, being male is more likely to result in receiving a more severe penalty on a plea-bargain than any other factor ... including the level of injury to the victim ... It seems that prosecutors are driving a much harder bargain with the men who are charged with partner violence than with the women, despite the generally more violent profile of the women in this sample."[117]

There is no reason to assume that similar findings would not be discovered in cities other than Edmonton, whether in Canada or the United States. Indeed, the province of Alberta is generally considered rather less likely than many other places to be guided directly or indirectly by feminist ideology. If even part of Brown's thesis is correct, it would be prudent, let alone conscientious, to call for a systematic and publicly funded study of the problem that he has revealed. No society can function harmoniously if one segment of the population is subjected to intentional or unintentional discrimination by the state. And a quick glance at the Internet indicates that many men, including those not involved personally with domestic violence, believe that they are the targets of systemic discrimination.

Even though ideological feminists have politicized domestic violence, they have turned rape into their ultimate trump card. Whenever they run out of arguments about other matters, they point to the symbolic and political nature of rape as the ultimate crime of men against women (although, as they point out in other contexts, rape is only one end of a single continuum that includes domestic violence, sexual harassment, pornography, and so forth). Thirty years ago, Susan Brownmiller claimed, in effect, that rape is also the *universal* crime of men against women. We live in a "rape culture," she claimed in *Against Our Will*.[118] What she meant was that, the conscious intentions of individual men notwithstanding, all men subjugate all women by the universal female fear of being raped. This claim is still a fundamental – no, *the* fundamental – doctrine of ideological feminism.

Feminists have urged an interpretation of equal protection under the law that involves special legal protection for women against violence by men.[119] Failing to report and punish rape encourages rape. That increases fear among women. And that, in turn, diminishes their freedom of movement. Feminists have sought protection in constitutions (or their amendments) and charters. They have sought them also, when stymied by lack of precise wording or lack of opportunity, to add the necessary wording in reinterpretations of existing legislation. Some Americans, for instance, have tried to interpret the Fourteenth Amendment very broadly – it guarantees equal rights to all citizens – in order to seek redress at the federal level for crimes such as rape. They claim that state courts have been indifferent to sexual offences against women. Others have tried to use the Commerce Clause of the Constitution, arguing, according to Wendy McElroy, for federal regulation of violence against women on the grounds that violence, or even fear of it, interferes with women's productivity and mobility as workers. "The cost of gender violence to the national economy," they say, "was estimated at between $5 billion and $10 billion."[120] Never mind that crimes of violence, including rape, actually declined in the late 1990s.[121] Among the big players in the controversy over rape legislation has been Catharine MacKinnon. As we say, she has been involved in both American and Canadian court cases.[122]

The claim that women sometimes find it necessary to kill men surfaced as the subtext of several critically acclaimed and successful movies: *Thelma and Louise*, *I Shot Andy Warhol*, and *Monster*. In each of these movies, the latter two being based on true stories, the female protagonist is portrayed sympathetically for killing one or more men.[123] Yes, yes, everyone involved with these movies duly acknowledged that killing people – even these gross, vulgar, and brutal men – is wrong. And yes, everyone acknowledged that the protagonists are pathological and therefore unsuitable as role models. But the fact is that these protagonists really do evoke sympathy from viewers. Emotionally, viewers are encouraged to cheer them on. And not only in scenes that actually involve self-defense. By now, it seems self-evident to almost everyone that the male victims are not intended to be seen as real people or at least as realistic characters but as symbolic representatives of patriarchal tyranny.

In *Monster*, serial killer Aileen Wuornos is depicted as someone who had suffered molestation as a child at the hands of her father and continued to suffer as an adult prostitute from rapists. When she finally kills for the first time, it is to defend herself against a john who tries to rape her. No wonder viewers are encouraged to think that her rage eventually spills over into murder. No wonder, she sees all men as rapists (even one who actually offers to help her). Nonetheless, just in case, she weeps and expresses some remorse to the young woman who befriends her (but later betrays her in court). Not many movies explain the behaviour of male serial killers, by contrast, in connection with childhood abuse or lack of love. Nothing in *American Psycho*, for instance, prepares viewers to see Patrick Bateman as someone who had been mentally deformed by an unhappy childhood. He is simply a handsome and charming demon.

Partly as a result of all this ideological baggage, at any rate, discussions of rape involve several serious conceptual problems: defining rape, identifying rape victims, and prosecuting alleged rapists. The very word "rape" is now problematic. Some feminists define it as a subcategory of "sexual assault," which covers a very broad range of offenses. The implication is that all offenses, no matter how innocuous some might seem, are manifestations of a single crime – all are tantamount to rape. The linguistic inflation of MacKinnon and Dworkin is legendary. When MacKinnon can seriously claim that she was raped by a negative book review (a bizarre event that we will come back to in a moment), even though the review merely used her own analogy between words and rape, it is surely time to examine the matter more carefully. Maybe the impact of language actually diminishes as a result of what could be called linguistic inflation. What can the word "sacred" mean, for example, when it is used to describe everything from rites to rights, from encounters with the divine to citizenship in the state or even the security of a friendship? What can the word "awesome" mean, similarly, when it is used in connection with such trivial things as the size of a pizza or the colour of a shirt?

The word "rape" has already been inflated, partly by MacKinnon herself, to include sexual harassment. And that, in turn, has been inflated to include possession of an "offensive" magazine or poster. But MacKinnon has upped the ante by resorting to hyperinflation. Her point in *Only Words* is that porn, including nonviolent erotica, is literally a form of sexual assault.[124] She made the same point in connection with the review of her book by Carlin Romano in *The Nation*.[125] Romano, a former philosophy teacher, began his review with two hypothetical scenarios designed to test MacKinnon's claim: one person thinks about raping MacKinnon; another person does something about it. Is there a difference or not? The first scenario is offensive, at least to MacKinnon, but does it constitute rape? Does it constitute even a provocation to rape?

MacKinnon herself insists that she does make a distinction between what actually happens and what is imagined or stated. For rhetorical (and ideological) purposes, though, she conveniently ignores this distinction. In this way, she herself can be accused of not taking language seriously enough. Those who care about words, after all, care enough to use them carefully and precisely. Actually, MacKinnon does not care about words at all. She cares about the safety of women. This, in itself, is fine. But is she really protecting women by debasing language? That remains to be seen. At stake here is no longer an academic dispute but a legal and political dispute.

Although not all victims of rape are women and although not all rapists are men (according to the very broad definition of rape that, ironically, some feminists now advocate), we are interested here in the majority of cases: women raped by men. The publication in 1994 of a massive study of sexual behaviour in America, *The Social Organization of Sexuality*, was greeted as a milestone, the most important event of its kind since Kinsey's study almost fifty years earlier.[126] Among its findings were that many women (and some, but not as many, men) reported that they had been forced into sexual acts on at least one occasion. This study did not use the word "rape" to describe this phenomenon. That word has been so inflated semantically, so loaded politically, that it would be virtually useless in a scholarly work. But the connection between "sexual act" and "rape" must not be ignored, because it points at the very least to a problem of all statistical studies: they can be used, and often are used, in tendentious ways. Have all these women been raped? The answer depends on how rape is defined, of course, and, unfortunately, on who defines it.

Even though the authors themselves carefully avoid that word, many of their readers probably infer it. Everyone can agree that being forced into sex without consent is rape. Not everyone can agree, though, on what constitutes force. For some people, it refers to physical coercion. For others, it can refer also to psychological intimidation or emotional manipulation. For how many, one wonders, does it refer even to attitudes – a vague sense of duty, say, or a desire to please – that exist only in the minds of women who are "forced" into sexual acts? Nonetheless, for some feminists, men would still be the guilty ones, collectively though not always individually. After all, they explain, men have created a culture that directly or indirectly encourages women to adopt this submissive attitude. Even women who willingly submit to men, in other words, are still innocent victims; the culture (of femininity) *makes* them do it.

This explanation might be more convincing if the same logic were applied to men. Hundreds of thousands of men locked up in prison could use the same defense for shooting neighbours, selling drugs, robbing convenience stores, driving under the influence, and so on. Why not argue that the culture of masculinity, poverty, and racism makes *them* behave in these ways? In both cases, there is some truth. If men were nothing more than the creations of a sinister culture, they could hardly be expected to take responsibility for their own behaviour. And that defense would apply not only to crime in general but also to rape in particular. But individual men really are held responsible for their own behaviour, regardless of their youth in dysfunctional families or their conditioning by dysfunctional subcultures. Why, then, should women be exempt from the same standard? The problem of rape is very serious, but so is the problem of using statistics, whether explicitly or implicitly, to make political statements about rape. Statistical studies are unlikely to clarify the problem of rape unless everyone can agree on what rape is in the first place.

Central to any discussion of rape is its definition, as we have said in chapter 8, which remains a topic of controversy, to say the least. Here we must turn away from statistics and back to the law, because many legal definitions of violence against women, including the definition of rape (and the legal terms that have replaced that word in some jurisdictions) have been directly or indirectly influenced by ideological ones. One obvious example is the Violence against Women Act, in which the definitions of sex crimes are explicitly elided with hate crimes.[127] American legal definitions vary from one state to another but usually include one or more of the following features: sexual intercourse that involves physical coercion; sexual intercourse that occurs without explicit consent, sexual intercourse with someone who is mentally or physically handicapped, sexual intercourse with someone who is under the age of consent.[128]

At the federal level, definitions of rape have been provided for the purpose of collecting statistics. Lawrence Greenfeld, a statistician with the Department of Justice, has compiled a glossary of "sex offenses" found in over two dozen sets of statistical data maintained by the Bureau of Justice Statistics and the Uniform Crime Reporting program of the FBI. Greenfeld points out that the use of terms and definitions is far from uniform. One definition of rape involves "forced sexual intercourse in which the victim may be either male or female and the offender may be of a different sex or the same sex as the victim. Victims [of forcible rape] must be at least 12 years old ..." Another definition involves "forcible intercourse, sodomy, or penetration with a foreign object. Does not include statutory rape or non-forcible acts with a minor or someone unable to give legal consent, nonviolent sexual offenses, or commercialized sex offenses. Includes attempts." Yet another definition involves "forcible intercourse (vaginal, anal, or oral) with a female or male. Includes forcible sodomy or penetration with foreign object. Does not include statutory rape or any other nonforcible sexual acts with a minor or with someone unable to give legal consent. Includes attempts."[129]

All these definitions make a primary distinction between "statutory rape" and "forcible rape." One definition of the former involves "carnal knowledge of a person without force or the threat of force when that person is below the statutory age of consent. The ability of the victim to give consent is a determination by the law enforcement agency." Another definition involves "carnal knowledge of a child without force. Includes attempts."[130] One definition of "forcible rape," on the other hand, involves "the carnal knowledge of a female forcibly and against her will. Assaults or attempts to commit rape by force or threat of force are also included; however, statutory rape (without force) and other sex offenses are excluded."[131] Another definition involves "carnal knowledge of a person forcibly and/or against the person's will; or not forcibly or against the person's will where the victim is incapable of giving consent because of his/her youth or because of his/her temporary or permanent mental or physical capacity. This offense includes both male and female victims and threats and attempts." Yet another definition involves "forcible intercourse with a male or female. Includes attempts and conspiracies to commit rape."[132]

Both types of rape, "forcible" and "statutory," are considered sexual assaults. Under "other sexual assaults," however, are crimes that involve "gross sexual imposition, sexual abuse, aggravated sexual abuse, and other acts such as fondling, molestation, or indecent liberties where the victim is not a child. Include attempts."[133]

Unfortunately, it is impossible to compare American definitions of "rape" with the Canadian one, because the word "rape" is no longer used as an official classification in Canada. Instead, the Criminal Code refers to three types of "sexual assault." In a case of "(simple) sexual assault,"[134] "someone forces any form of sexual activity on another person without that person's consent" and – this is important – the assault includes "kissing, fondling, grabbing, sexual intercourse, etc."[135] In a case of "sexual assault with a weapon,"[136] "someone uses or threatens to use a real or imitation weapon ... [or] threatens to cause bodily harm to a 3rd person" or "more than one person assaults someone in the same incident."[137] In a case of "aggravated sexual assault,"[138] the most serious of all, "someone is wounded, maimed, disfigured, brutally beaten, or in danger of dying, while being sexually assaulted."[139] These three types of sexual assault are listed in order of seriousness and severity of punishment. As a whole, then, "sexual assault" is defined in Canada as an assault of a sexual nature that might or might not involve sexual penetration.[140]

The American system, on the other hand, "contains only one narrow version of sexual assault. The offence of forcible rape is limited to forced sexual intercourse by a male against a female. This crime differs from the Canadian sexual assault offences, which are neither gender-specific nor confined to sexual intercourse ... Therefore, comparing the Canadian sexual assault offence and American offence of forcible rape would not be reliable."[141] Although rape is classified in the United States as one kind of sexual assault, in short, it is not in Canada. There is no separate classification for rape, which, along with other crimes, is classified as sexual assault (under the three classifications listed above). Why is this worth noting here? Because the Canadian system classifies rape in the same category as kissing without consent; rape is just one end of a single continuum. This system allows Canadians to inflate the seriousness of these other sexual assaults. On the other hand, it does acknowledge that men can be raped, not only women (although it probably assumes also, incorrectly, that men can be raped only by other men).

Ideological feminists, both American and Canadian, often claim that sexual assaults are unlike any other crimes. Sexual assault is unique, they sometimes argue, because no other crime is about sex. But you could just as easily say that no other crime but murder is about death (although even that is debatable in view of the fact that several crimes, legally distinguished according to motivation, involve death). Even if it were true, then, this statement would be tautological and therefore almost meaningless. But is it true? The fact is that not one but several crimes are about sex, the most obvious being sexual harassment. Significantly, those who make this claim hide the ideological implication that sexual harassment is just another form of rape. Moreover, they "forget" something that ideological feminists have been insisting on for at least thirty years. Rape, they say, is about power and *not* about sex.

We discuss claims of this kind by Susan Molinari, an American, below. Her Canadian counterpart, Pamela Cross, argues that sexual assault – she refers here specifically to what everyone understands as rape – is a "unique crime."[142] And it surely is, because every form of crime – indeed, every phenomenon – is unique. If it had no distinctive characteristics, how could we describe it or identify it at all? But every phenomenon is also linked with others in a larger, coherent pattern. Cross would never actually deny that sexual assault is one form of assault or that assault is one form of interaction, that interaction is one form of human behaviour, and so on. What she does deny is that sexual assault has anything significant in common with other forms of assault. What she means, of course, is that sexual assault is *uniquely* unique. That is a very problematic claim, because it raises the level of rhetoric from merely ideological to metaphysical. To describe something as uniquely unique would be to describe it in terms that are utterly beyond those used by either scientists or social scientists. Cross believes that sexual assault is so heinous that it requires not only a separate legal standard but also a separate moral standard. The result is to isolate sexual assault from all other forms of assault and thus create a category that is, in effect, sacrilegious. To commit a sexual assault (presumably on a woman) is to commit an act that cannot be defined in purely secular terms and is therefore beyond the scope of any rational discussion.

With this in mind, then, consider Cross's explanations for her claim that sexual assault is a unique crime. First, she claims that it "is the most intimate of offences, in a way that even murder is not."[143] This implicit downgrading of murder would come as a nasty shock to the families of murder victims. But what precisely does Cross mean by "intimate"? We are not nitpicking; precision really is necessary in any discussion of law. Does she mean that sexual assaults occur privately? But so do many other crimes. Suicide bombers kill or injure people on crowded buses or in public buildings, to be sure, but most people – those who intend to get away – do so as stealthily as possible.

Cross claims that "most other crimes do not require privacy in the same way that is required for sexual assault."[144] But she presumes anachronistically things about sex that many people no longer presume. Consider what happens at movie theatres. Although the people ostensibly having sex are actors (some but not all of whom use stunt doubles), the people watching them in public auditoriums – men and women, often on dates – are not. Are they embarrassed by what they see? If so, they certainly do not make that clear to the Hollywood producers. On the contrary, as the producers know very well, explicit sex on the screen is big at the box office and is now making inroads even on television and the Internet. In fact, say the moguls, the more of it the better. This attitude, one aspect of the sexual revolution, marks a significant change for the middle and upper classes.[145] This change is by no means confined to the phenomenon that takes place in theatres. Making out in public, or at least in the crowded context of dorm parties and raves, is not exactly unheard of nowadays.

And it is precisely in this context, fueled by booze and drugs, that sexual assaults are likely to occur.

Or does Cross mean by "privacy" that sexual assaults take place in the context of close emotional relationships? Probably, but so do many other crimes: murders are often committed by people who have very close emotional relationships with their victims. Or does Cross refer merely to physical proximity? Surely not, because she denies the parallel of murder. What could involve closer physical proximity than stabbing someone, say, or strangling someone? Well, what then?

On the same topic, Cross claims that "[v]ictims of most other crimes feel no sense of personal shame that makes them reluctant to inform the authorities that a crime has taken place."[146] But male victims of domestic violence, for instance, find themselves in precisely the same category. And not much has been done to change either their attitudes or those of society and its agents: police officers, lawyers, judges, physicians, and social workers. How many men could convince a court, moreover, that a woman had initiated unwanted sexual behaviour? According to the stereotype, every man wants to engage in sex at all times and in all places. Even though every man knows that this is false, how many male judges or jurors are likely to say so in court? Fewer and fewer women, on the other hand, feel ashamed of themselves or responsible in any way for the immoral and illegal behaviour of those who attack them. On the contrary, more and more of them feel indignant (and with good reason). This means that Cross's claim is, once again, anachronistic.

So is a closely related claim. "Seldom do victims of more 'public' kinds of crimes fear," writes Cross, "that they will be blamed for what has happened to them. For example, a homeowner who has been robbed after leaving a door or window unlocked is unlikely to feel the same sense of responsibility for what has happened as do many sexual assault victims."[147] This almost incredibly facile analogy is based on a false assumption. Is it true that only victims of sexual assault blame themselves for what others do to them? What about the parents – including fathers – of children who are kidnapped while they are busy talking to their friends or doing business on their cell phones? They would almost certainly feel much more guilt. People do often prefer to "blame the victim," but not only the victims of sexual assault. What about all those, not only in Canada and elsewhere but even in the United States, who blamed Americans themselves for the attacks of 11 September 2001? The lamentable fact is that most people use blame for irrational purposes now and then. Blaming either themselves or others provides an explanation for evil. Otherwise, they would have to acknowledge that the world is governed by chance or chaos and is thus meaningless.

Cross claims that sexual assault is unique in that it "often [leaves] no physical injuries and little, if any, forensic evidence."[148] Actually, that has been true until recently of most or even all crimes except physical assault. Living victims of sexual assault have not always had much evidence, it is true, and for a variety of reasons. But that situation is becoming less and less common due to new forensic technologies. Cross's chief aim is to help living victims, moreover, not dead ones. But her claim is about sexual assault in general and is relevant to legal proceedings against those accused of both raping and killing their victims. The fact is, however, that police departments routinely present forensic evidence in court of murder victims who had been sexually assaulted.

According to Cross, moreover, "the perpetrator is often known, and even known very well, to the victim" of sexual assault but not of other crimes.[149] Once again, the same really could be said of many other crimes. To take only one example, most members of rival gangs have known each other all their lives, sometimes very well, but still see no reason not to kill each other. On the other hand, many sexual assaults are perpetrated by strangers on dark streets. If victim and victimizer know each other, Cross points out, that could make alleged victims harder to believe; they could be considered not objective enough.[150] Okay, but the same would be true of alleged victimizers; their testimony, too, could be considered not objective enough.

In connection with one thing, however, Cross does have a point worth taking seriously. "It is not uncommon for women to be unsure themselves," she writes, "about whether or not they are the victims of a crime. This is not necessarily because they have a lack of knowledge about the law, but rather because the context in which the events took place is often complex."[151] But this raises a very serious question. If a crime is so subtle that not even the victim is certain that it took place – or, to put it differently, that the victim must be coached by an ideological cadre to explain it as a crime – then what legitimates the use of law to punish it in the first place? Unwittingly, Cross has actually trivialized sexual assault.

Also problematic is the identification of rape victims. In *The Invisible Boy*, Frederick Mathews presents a great deal of statistical evidence to show that violence against boys and men is indeed very pervasive.[152] It is neither a neurotic delusion brought on by our therapeutically oriented culture nor a political plot to trivialize the victimization of girls and women. Of interest here are not male victims of abuse in general but male victims of sexual abuse in particular – which is to say, of rape.[153] Mathews carefully identifies those who sexually abuse boys and men: men and women, strangers and acquaintances, family members and members of institutions. It is true, he writes, that most of the culprits, including those who select male victims and those who select female ones, are straight men. It is true that serious physical injuries are more often caused by them, especially to male victims, than by women.[154] But he adds something that startled us. "As recently as 10 years ago, it was a common assumption that females did not or could not *sexually* abuse children or youth."[155] Nonetheless, after reviewing the studies, he estimates that anywhere between 3% and 25% of sexual abusers are women. Moreover, he adds, "there is an alarmingly high rate of sexual abuse by females in the backgrounds of rapists, sex offenders and sexually aggressive men ... [156] Male adolescent sex offenders abused by 'females only' chose female victims almost exclusively."[157]

While male perpetrators are more likely to engage in anal intercourse and to have the victim engage in oral-genital contact, females tend to use more foreign objects as part of the abusive act. ... This study also reported that differences were not found in the frequency of vaginal intercourse, fondling by the victim or abuser, genital body contact without penetration or oral contact by the abuser.

Females may be more likely to use verbal coercion than physical force. The most commonly reported types of abuse by female perpetrators include vaginal intercourse, oral sex, fondling and group sex (Faller, 1987; Hunter et al., 1993). However, women also engage in mutual masturbation, oral, anal and genital sex acts, show children pornography and play sex games. ... The research suggests that, overall, female and male perpetrators commit many of the same acts and follow many of the same patterns of abuse against their victims. They also do not tend to differ significantly in terms of their relationship to the victim (most are relatives) or the location of the abuse (Allen, 1990; Kaufman et al., 1995).[158]

In a study by K.L. Wallace and others, adds Mathews, "8% of the female perpetrators were teachers and 23% were babysitters, compared to male perpetrators who were 0% and 8% respectively."[159] Elsewhere, Mathews provides the following statistics: "Forty percent of juvenile homicide victims were killed by family members, mostly parents. Fifty-three percent of boys were killed by their fathers and slightly more than half (51%) of the girls were murdered by their mothers."[160]

Males do appear to be the majority of *sexual* abuse perpetrators, but women are the primary *physical* abusers and *neglecters* of children. Mothers and fathers appear to be equally likely to use corporal punishment. Mothers and fathers can inflict serious and lethal harm on a child. Since more neglect and physical types of violence are perpetrated against children than sexual abuse, we need to take a serious look at how our terms and concepts are blinding us to a large and neglected part of the abuse problem.[161]

Now consider what actually happens in both American and Canadian courtrooms. Rape cases were once very hard to prosecute. For several reasons, not all victims were willing to press charges. They did not want others to know that they had lost their virginity; they were too modest to speak about sexual matters publicly; they were hiding their infidelity; they could seldom expect to win. To solve this problem, feminists adopted several strategies that have been adopted, in turn, by courts and legislatures.

One strategy was to demand that the rules of evidence be rewritten. Thirty years ago, the defense lawyer in a rape case was likely to use what was considered evidence of the alleged victim's promiscuity – her clothing, speech, mannerisms, and so on – to prove that she had given her consent to sexual activity and thus to cast doubt on her credibility as a plaintiff. The assumption was that only a "bad" woman wanted sex and was therefore unlikely to tell the truth – either because she really was bad or because she was afraid to gain a bad reputation. Because her sexual history was featured, she found herself on trial, in effect, and therefore subjected to extensive cross-examination. This mentality was challenged in the 1970s as a result of the sexual revolution and the women's movement. A woman's character, feminists insisted, should not be judged by her sexual activities outside marriage. But if women were sexually liberated and therefore indifferent to what anyone thought about their sexual activities outside marriage, why would they need or even want a law to protect them from being embarrassed about these activities?

Never mind. By the end of that decade, American legislatures and courts were prepared to avoid evidence of the alleged victim's sexual history. That evidence, it was argued, discouraged women from reporting rapes, had only a tenuous connection with the rape being tried, embarrassed the plaintiff, confused the investigation into facts of the case, and wasted time.

Susan Molinari's defense of rape-shield laws, which we have already mentioned in the review of legislation, is an American version of Pamela Cross's argument. For Molinari, rape cases are unique

and often turn on difficult credibility determinations. Alleged consent by the victim is rarely an issue in prosecutions for other violent crimes – the accused mugger does not claim that the victim freely handed over [his] wallet as a gift – but the defendant in a rape case often contends that the victim engaged in consensual sex and then falsely accused him. Knowledge that the defendant has committed rapes on other occasions is frequently critical in assessing the relative plausibility of these claims and accurately deciding cases that would otherwise become unresolvable swearing matches.[162]

Trouble is, Molinari fails to acknowledge the fact that sexual intercourse really is very often – most often – the result of mutual consent, which is why exceptions must be explained. And seduction really is – by definition – clouded by ambivalence, which is why date rape is much harder to define than the kind of rape that occurs in dark alleys. Besides, the two interactions that Molinari compares, sexual intimacies and financial transactions, are inherently dissimilar. Her analogy, no matter how clever it appears on the surface, is therefore not merely facile but false. The former is as complex and subtle and ambiguous as human nature itself, which is why it has been explored by poets, philosophers, and even theologians for time out of mind. The latter, on the other hand, is as simple as the entries in a ledger.[163]

Some feminists go further. Much further. Lawyers find it hard to get male judges to take women's accounts of rape seriously, says Sherene Razack, because they find it hard to establish empirical proof. She suggests replacing factual evidence, therefore, with personal stories "where the social and historical context of the tale is critical to our understanding of it."[164]

Another strategy to avoid the problems faced by alleged victims of rape is to demand victim-impact statements. Even though they are not used to decide on guilt or innocence – they are read at sentencing – the theory behind their use in court is closely related to the replacement of objective evidence with subjective stories. Martha Nussbaum opposed the introduction of these women's stories, often called "empathy narratives," into the courtroom.[165] Contrary to the feminist argument, she pointed out that judges usually do empathize with women who accuse men of raping or assaulting them. In fact, they find it much harder to empathize with men who are accused. The defendants, therefore, not the plaintiffs, need rules and structures. Nussbaum concluded with good reason "that we should admit all evidence about the victim that is relevant to establishing what happened and what the defendant did – and then no more. In the penalty phase, the jury or judge should turn to the difficult task of understanding the character of the criminal, because the penalty phase is about his fate."[166] But victim-impact statements, she added, "function primarily by giving vent to the passion for revenge against such offenders."[167]

Victim-impact statements feed into the ideological notion that all men are rapists, which is the misandric face of gynocentrism.[168] According to Dworkin, every pimp and every rapist – but also every john, pornographer, murderer of women – represents the interests of all men, normal men (a mentality we have already discussed in connection with public response to Marc Lépine). Or, to put it the other way around, all men – including those considered normal – are really pimps and rapists (but also johns, pornographers, and murderers): "Rapists and pimps, representing the interests of normal men, some of whom rape, some of whom buy, seem to have the law of gravity on their side: they reify the status quo, which is what gives them credibility, legitimacy, and authority ... No matter what lie they tell, it passes for truth, because the hatred of women underlying the lie is an accepted hatred, a shared and unchallenged set of prejudiced assumptions."[169] Dworkin considers it perfectly legitimate and even morally appropriate, therefore, for women to *hate* men: "It is fine for her to hate those who ripped into her if hate keeps her willing to talk, unwilling to let silence bury her again."[170]

Dworkin uses the word "hate" in its popular sense: intense dislike or intense anger. But this word has a deeper meaning, one that she might or might not disavow. As we have said, it refers not to a transitory emotional state but to a culturally propagated and institutionalized worldview in which some people are held in contempt by virtue of their group identity. As a result, that very mentality is both popularized and legalized or otherwise institutionalized.

Underlying everything we have said about rape legislation and rape trials is the prevalence of double standards. Instead of favouring defendants, laws and courtroom procedures now favour plaintiffs; they betray systemic bias by favouring women over men. The details of a man's sexual history, unlike those of a woman, are presumed relevant to the case against him and may therefore be discussed in court. If a man committed sexual abuse before, moreover, the law assumes that he probably did it again in the current case. Where there's smoke, in other words, there's fire. Do we really want our laws to be based on questionable proverbs?

Our legal systems are founded not on proverbs but on the moral and philosophical conviction that every defendant must be considered innocent unless proven guilty. But given both the rape-shield laws and the current stereotypes of men as rapists and molesters, that way of thinking is being turned on its legal head. In rape cases nowadays, the defendant is guilty unless proven innocent. The burden of proof is on him rather than his accuser. Sure, it is now easier to bring rape cases to court and easier to bring in convictions. At what cost not only to men, however, but also to society as a whole?

If a man's sexual history may routinely be considered in court, why not that of women? Given the difficulty of proceeding without evidence, let alone witnesses, every source of information should be considered worthy of consideration. It is true that sexual history, whether of the accuser or the accused, is not actually evidence. Just because a woman gave consent on earlier occasions does not mean that she probably did so on the occasion being discussed in court. But just because a man assaulted a women on earlier occasions, according to the new view, somehow *does* mean that he probably did so on the occasion being discussed in court. Just because he once pinched her on the butt does not, in fact, mean that he raped her on the occasion being discussed in court. But in the absence of any other basis on which to decide a case, the sexual histories of *both* might tip the balance.

We have solved some problems, in short, but only by replacing them with new ones. American feminists themselves have noted a double standard in the new rules of evidence used by courts in rape cases. And they have done some fancy verbal footwork to justify it. Discussing the challenges of her job, Jane Aiken, a professor of law at Washington University in St Louis, notes that American students often acknowledge the unfairness to men of this asymmetry. "Rule 415 says that prior sexual misconduct is relevant and probative of behavior on the present occasion. Rule 412's rationale is that a woman's sexual history is not a good predictor of her present behavior."[171] She suggests that teachers can help students overcome what they "perceive" to be unfairness by arguing that both 412 and 415 are needed to reduce the bias that jurors bring to the case in their attempt to find facts. "Both of these rules assist the trier of fact in focusing on the behavior of the alleged perpetrator, rather than indulging in stereotypical beliefs that women cannot be believed when making claims of sexual misconduct. The result is a powerful tool to combat long-held stereotypes that have infected sexual misconduct cases: the victim either invited the treatment, or deserved it, or is not to be believed without sufficient corroboration."[172] She goes on to say that the problem of bias against women is not merely that of jurors but also that of judges.

In earlier times courts were allowed to discuss the sexual history of an alleged victim. In our time, they are allowed to discuss the sexual history only of an alleged victimizer. Courts presume that a women's sexual history is *irrelevant* (although they make a few exceptions, which are defined very narrowly and subjected to strict tests for relevance). But they presume that introducing evidence of a man's sexual history *is* relevant (unless doing so happens to conflict with his constitutional rights under the Fifth or Sixth Amendment). And the evidence need not be narrowly defined or subjected to strict tests for relevance.

Ideological feminists insist on an additional double standard. When a woman says "no," she means "no," even if she either said or implied "yes" moments earlier. (This is why her sexual history is supposedly irrelevant, although some feminists, including MacKinnon and Dworkin, go further by claiming that women are incapable of giving consent to men in *any* circumstances). No matter how a woman behaved until the very moment in question, all that matters is whether she gave consent at this particular moment. These feminists insist also, however, that a man's sexual history really is relevant.

At the heart of all sexual relationships is ambivalence. A woman might want intercourse, for example, but also fear it. Even now, this is often true of intercourse outside the context of marriage, although the use of contraception can mitigate her fear of pregnancy, and condoms her fear of disease. The sexual revolution has largely eliminated her fear of losing her reputation, but it has not eliminated all anxiety. And even men are sometimes unwilling or unable to have sex, although they are seldom willing to admit it. The meaning of "yes" or "no" is not easily sorted out, in short, despite the best efforts of those who campaign on campuses and elsewhere for "sexual correctness." Recognizing ambivalence, in fact, lies at the very heart of sexual activity.

To underline the problems of both ambiguity and ambivalence, consider the behaviour of Adrien Brody. After winning the Academy Award for best actor in 2003, he grabbed Halle Berry and kissed her on the lips.[173] He embraced her so tightly, in fact, that her body swayed under his.[174] Berry looked stunned and uncomfortable (although she later denied that she was).[175] She certainly had not given him permission to kiss her, let alone to embrace her. Did she have grounds for accusing him of sexual assault? The only obvious difference between this event and many others now considered both immoral and illegal is that Brody's behaviour was witnessed by thirty-three million people. The audience cheered. They might have been cheering for his performance in *The Pianist* rather than on stage, to be sure, and they might have refrained had they had time to think about what they had seen. Even later, nonetheless, no one commented on this as a potentially punishable act of sexual assault. No charges were ever laid against Brody. Can all this be explained merely as a matter of people being out of touch with the law? Or is the law out of touch with people? Two things seem clear. Brody's behaviour was ambiguous, to say the least, and Berry's response ambivalent.

Men accused of rape sometimes claim to have received implied consent.[176] The notion of "implied consent" can be problematic, but so can the notion of what we call "implied nonconsent." The problem is accepting one but not the other, the latter but not the former. Defining "lack of consent," Cross writes that it "can be conveyed by words or actions. Even if a victim does not say NO directly, she can communicate it through struggle or body language."[177] In other words, she can struggle to imply *lack* of consent. The court would recognize that but not her use of body language to imply consent. Canada's Criminal Code does allow for something known as an "honest and mistaken belief in consent," and in *R. v. Ewanchuk*,[178] the Canadian Supreme Court rejected implied consent but allowed the defence of an "honest but mistaken belief in consent."[179] But how can that be distinguished from implied consent? Without an explicit agreement, after all, no one could hold the former without believing, honestly but mistakenly, that the latter had been given. An honest and mistaken belief in consent makes no sense, in fact, without the possibility of implied consent.

Ewanchuk exposed a problem of profound importance – one that goes far beyond the rape cases that come up in court. If implied consent is so difficult to argue in court, why would any man have sexual relations with any woman in any circumstances without written proof of her consent? Even that would be legally irrelevant. A woman could change her mind in the few minutes or seconds between signing a consent form and engaging in sexual activity. And "no," of course, means "no." Perhaps unintentionally, this doctrine severely erodes the kind of trust that is necessary for healthy sexual relations. We would have said "destroys" except for the fact that most men and women, ignorant of the law, continue to copulate on the basis of trust that has no legal standing whatsoever.

Legal experts often say, and with good reason, that extreme cases do not generate good laws. And yet Canada's Supreme Court has indeed used an extreme case, rape, as the basis for legislation that will have a profound impact on even healthy sexual encounters between men and women. But some feminists, those at the extreme end of a political continuum, believe that there can be *no* healthy sexual encounters between men and women. At one time, they point out, women were at the mercy of men. They fail to add that men, in our time, are at the mercy of women.

To remove the double standards that we have been discussing would mean to challenge the idea that rape is always more serious than *framing* someone for rape. It certainly is, when it causes death or deadly disease or serious injury. Otherwise, both rape and falsely framing someone for rape, which can lead to a lengthy prison sentence and the lifelong consequences of being a convict, are comparable.

And consider the misandric fallout from all this. If our analysis of contemporary trends in the United States and Canada is correct, then the effects of negative stereotypes about men now rival and possibly surpass those of negative stereotypes about women. For decades, ideological feminists have described most or even all men as rapists and molesters just below the surface. Dozens of laws and policies – those that govern equity, porn, child support, sexual harassment, and so on – are now stacked against men. The rape-shield law is only one example, perhaps the most important one of all.

How can we restore parallelism and therefore justice? On the one hand, it could be argued that the reputations of both men and women are seriously harmed as a result of either adultery or promiscuity. Judging from popular culture, it seems clear that married men, no less than married women, are still attacked for even considering extramarital or extrarelational affairs. In that case, we should prohibit the use of sexual history in the case of both defendants and plaintiffs but then introduce exceptions for both in egregious cases.

On the other hand, it could be argued that the reputations of neither men nor women are seriously harmed today as a result of their sexual activities either inside or outside marriage. Men were once given "permission," supposedly, to have extramarital affairs. How many women these days really worry about their reputations as chaste or virginal beings? Judging from popular culture – think of *Sex and the City* and talk shows – it seems clear that not many women are embarrassed by the intimate details of their sex lives. This, we have been led to believe during the past forty years, is part of what sexual liberation is all about. In that case, we should *allow* the use of sexual history for both defendants and plaintiffs, but with the few exceptions that we have already discussed.

In an ideal world, sexual intercourse would be the venue for neither sexual violence nor sexual politics. In the real world, lamentably, it is the venue for both. What can we do while waiting for the messiah? Here are a few suggestions. Because the second and third are unlikely to be adopted or even taken seriously, we conclude this discussion on a dismal note.

In an ideal world, we would not need legislation to govern sexual relations. In the real world, we obviously do. Therefore, everyone should be carefully taught the legal implications of sex – including the precise legal meaning of "sexual assault," the specific kinds of evidence that may or may not be used in court, the actual penalties for those convicted, and so on. This could be a standard unit of sex education in high schools and repeated in the student guide books distributed at every university.

In an ideal world, no one would rely on alcohol or drugs to overcome social and sexual inhibitions. In the real world, more and more people do. And the consequences can be brutal or even deadly. Just as we legally prohibit drinking or shooting up before driving, we should socially discourage drinking or shooting up before copulating. It would take a colossal cultural effort to make this the norm in our intensely hedonistic society, but it would be worth a try.

In an ideal world, finally, no one would try to justify double standards. In the real world, many people do. We once had a double standard that favoured men. Thanks to ideological feminists, we now have one that favours women. Like the old one, it has both moral and legal implications. No intelligent man, given these circumstances, would have sexual relations with women at all. Any man whose need for sex trumps his need for legal security should take at least one simple precaution: carrying written consent forms along with his condoms. It takes only a moment to put on a condom for physiological protection. Why not take an additional moment for legal protection? Even that would not satisfy all women – as we say, ideological feminists believe that women are incapable of giving their consent to sexual relations with men and thus refuse to acknowledge that women should have some moral or legal responsibility for their own behaviour – because a woman might always change her mind after signing. Still, having written consent from her, with date and time, might be of some use to a man in court. It might be better, at any rate, than nothing at all.

Small measures of this kind might help a few men, but they would do little to solve the problems created for men by the shift to a gynocentric worldview.

Much of the current thinking and discourse, both public and professional, about abuse and interpersonal violence is based on a woman-centred point of view. This is neither right nor wrong, good nor bad, but rather the result of who has been doing the advocacy. However, as a result of this history, victims have a female face, perpetrators a male face. Because of this image of perpetrators as having a male face, violence in our society has become "masculinized" and is blamed exclusively on "men" and "male socialization." Although there is without question a male gender dimension to many forms of violence, especially sexual violence, simple theories of male socialization are inadequate to explain why the vast majority of males are *not* violent.[180]

Not only are most men not violent, some of them are the victims of violence. What about the effects on male victims of sexual abuse? "Compared to non-abused men," writes Mathews, "adult male survivors of sexual abuse experience a greater degree of psychiatric problems, such as depression, anxiety, dissociation, suicidality and sleep disturbance."[181] In these ways, they are just like female victims. And why would anyone expect it to be otherwise? The answer is obvious: "Most of the literature on the impact of abuse has been written about female victims and thus tends to reflect a female-centred perspective. There has been, in Fran Sepler's words, a 'feminization of victimization.'"[182] But the effects of ignoring boys and men as victims of violence go beyond the academy.

Our minimization and denial of male victimization so permeates our culture that it is in evidence everywhere from nursery rhymes, comic strips, comedy films, television programs and newspaper stories to academic research. We give male victims a message every day of their lives that they risk much by complaining. Stated succinctly, if a male is victimized he deserved it, asked for it, or is lying. If he is injured, it is his own fault. If he cries or complains, we will not take him seriously or condone his "whining" because he is supposed to "take it like a man." We will laugh at him. We will support him in the minimization or its impact. We will encourage him to accept responsibility for being victimized and teach him to ignore any feelings associated with his abuse. We will guilt and shame him to keep a stiff upper lip so he can "get on with it."[183]

We discussed the messages of popular culture in *Spreading Misandry* and will do so again, from a slightly different perspective in *Transcending Misandry*. Listen to Mathews:

When we give a message to boys and young men in any shape or form that their experience of violence and victimization is less important than that of girls and young women, we are teaching them a lesson about their value as persons. We also teach them that the use of violence toward males is legitimate. When we dismiss their pain, we do little to encourage boys and young men to listen to, and take seriously, women's concerns about violence and victimization. When we diminish their experience or fail to hold their male and female abusers fully accountable, we support their continued victimization.[184]

Elsewhere, Mathews discusses the implications of all this not only for research but also for the assessment of male victims and the development of programs to help them. In addition, he discusses the direct and indirect messages given to male victims and comes to an assessment similar to our own: that Canada is ignoring the problems of boys and men. "Many questions remain unanswered. Why is it that Canada, a country that prides itself on being a compassionate and just society, lags behind other countries in advocacy for male victims? Why has the media refused to give equal coverage to male victimization issues? Why do we consistently fail to support adult male victims? Why do we support a double standard when it comes to the care and treatment of male victims?"[185] Similarly, he opines that "when trying to determine the prevalence of sexual harassment toward males, we are faced with the same problem of Canada lagging behind other western democracies ... virtually no research has been undertaken in Canada that documents the prevalence of sexual harassment of males."[186] If our thesis is correct, then Canada's lack of attention on this problem could be related to Canada's gynocentrism.

Clearly, we do not live in an ideal world and never will, but that is no excuse for complacency or cynicism. Doing the best we can to reverse polarization between men and women, however, surely means more than merely replacing misogyny with misandry or confusing justice with revenge.

PART FOUR

Society on Trial:
From Classroom to Legislature

Although feminist ideologues continue to talk about having a "long way to go," they have in fact been remarkably successful. In only a few decades, they have generated a social, intellectual, and economic revolution. In this part of the book, we examine the origins of that revolution, the ways in which ideological feminists have "reinterpreted," "renegotiated," "reinscribed," "relocated," "resituated," or "repositioned" academic standards of truth in research to suit themselves. Using postmodernism as their front, they have colonized fields as diverse as the humanities, the law, and the social sciences. It is primarily because of this revolution at the upper levels of academia, propagated not only in countless classrooms but also in countless chatrooms on the Internet, that our society is becoming just as gynocentric as the androcentric one that feminists were supposed to correct in the name of equality between the sexes. It is primarily because of this "engaged scholarship," in other words, that the "advocacy journalism" we discussed in part 1 was possible in the first place.

The mentality discussed so far amounts to what we have described as a quiet revolution. We have all but replaced the old androcentric worldview with a gynocentric one. But the main topic of this trilogy is misandry, not gynocentrism. The two are closely linked, of course, though not necessarily identical. In the concluding chapter of this book, we discuss the ways in which gynocentrism can lead to misandry and misandry to serious problems for any democratic society.

Democracy can take at least two forms in the modern world: the liberal democracy and the welfare state (although these overlap considerably). Among the defining features of democracy in either of these forms, at least in theory, are two of particular importance here. One of them is political transparency: proposed laws are debated openly in legislative assemblies that represent the voters and then either approved or not approved. The other is the give and take between majority and minority interest groups (albeit within the limits established to prevent any tyranny of the majority): each group is expected to lobby for its own political interests. But the introduction of ideology – we refer here not only to its content but also to favoured strategies such as the use of fronts to avoid debate, infiltration to achieve hegemony within institutions, deconstruction to eliminate rivals, and political correctness to silence adversaries – perverts both features and thus endangers the democratic polity.

In chapter 10, we discuss the function of women's studies, a field in which ideology often takes precedence over scholarship. In chapter 11, we conclude with a discussion of the results.

10

Ideological Feminism v. Scholarship: Women's Studies as a Front

The Women's Studies Program at McGill university provides students with the opportunity to examine how the intersections of gender, race, ethnicity, sexuality, religion, class and culture shape identity and inform power relationships. The program emphasizes feminist theoretical and empirical scholarship and fosters understanding of historical, multicultural and contemporary social and intellectual issues.[1]

Women's studies is quite explicitly feminism in action in an academic setting. Many courses in women's studies, especially the lower-level introduction to women's studies sorts of courses (which, by the way, fulfill general-education requirements in many universities), are issues oriented. They are far too often talking not about women's contributions but about women's victimization. Thus, they typically have a roster of issues such as violence against women, pornography, abortion, homophobia, white privilege, and so on that the class goes through one by one. These issues typically are not presented as problems to be studied from many points of view but rather as problems to be exposed by feminist ideology. The bottom line to me is that far too often women's studies classrooms convey attitudes to be endorsed by the students rather than substantive knowledge.[2]

Misandry has not unified all feminists, to be sure, but it has certainly unified enough of them – explicitly or implicitly, directly or indirectly, consciously or subconsciously – to create a powerful movement. Their headquarters is the college classroom, and, thanks to the Internet, it now includes countless electronic venues devoted to women's studies. In addition, it includes countless others that are either more overtly political or less academically respectable (which we discuss in appendix 11).

In this chapter, we consider ideological feminism in the university by examining three closely related topics: its version of epistemology, its notion of "engaged scholarship," and what links it with women's studies but also with women's networks and the professions – especially law.

Even though many other ideologies have been discredited by history and therefore abandoned, feminist ideology has been remarkably successful because of its postmodern matrix. In *Spreading Misandry* and earlier in this book we discussed the features of ideology in general and of feminist ideology in particular, linking the latter with other ideologies on both sides of the political spectrum. Although we discussed postmodernism, too, a few additional comments are necessary here (and especially in appendix 1). Postmodernism is not, per se, an ideology. In theory, it opposes all ideologies. In practice, though, nothing could be further from the truth, not only because of the intellectual dishonesty among postmodernists, who "deconstruct" all ideologies except the ones that they like, but also because of their epistemology. How do we know about the world? On what intellectual authority can we discuss the world and act in it? Modernism offers one model, which is usually identified as science, but the same basic principles – they add up to the disciplined use of reason – apply also to other forms of scholarship. Postmodernism offers another model. And ideological feminism offers a variation on that.

The epistemology of modernism, its theory of knowledge, is hardly esoteric, although some authors warn that current hostility toward science, not only from the religious right but also – and especially – from the political left, might change that.[3] Scientists claim that they can describe the world accurately enough for all practical purposes. To do this, they observe the world, propose hypotheses to explain what they observe, collect empirical evidence or conduct experiments to test their hypotheses, and then draw conclusions that can be either verified or falsified by the observations or experiments of other scientists. At the heart of all this is an epistemological principle: that the human mind really can encounter reality, mediated by the senses, and thus really know something about it. Scientists do acknowledge that various factors can limit this ability. Both the senses and the mind are notoriously subject to illusion,[4] which is why scientists insist on the cultivation of logic, skepticism (refusal to accept the ultimate authority of casual observation, anecdotal evidence, conventional wisdom, or even of what passes for common sense), and – above all – objectivity. By that, they mean the ability to sift through evidence and draw conclusions without regard to vested interests, whether collective or personal – that is, without regard to financial support from institutions or emotional support from colleagues and without regard to theological beliefs, ideological doctrines, political goals, and so on.

At the beginning of this third millennium, most people in our society have come to value science, especially in connection with medicine and technology (even though many of them value religion, too, which often takes the form of a worldview in conflict with that of science). But a growing number of people, so far confined mainly to ideologues or religious fundamentalists, have come to negate the value of science in general and objectivity in particular – not merely the lamentable ways in which science is sometimes used, by the way, but also the intellectual foundations on which it is built. Among these critics of modernism, of course, are postmodernists. Along for the ride are ideologues of one kind or another, including feminist ideologues. And the consequences of their "paradigm shift" can be felt not only in research labs and college classrooms, where scientists seldom take them seriously, but also in courts of law and even government bureaucracies, where legal authorities and political leaders take them very seriously indeed.[5] Although other ideologies have used the umbrella of postmodernism to attack modernism, we confine ourselves here to feminist ideology and its use of the postmodernist umbrella.[6]

For postmodernists in general, the chief problem with science – or, indeed, with modern scholarship of any kind – is its origin in one particular culture at one particular time: the culture of Western Europe in the seventeenth century. From this origin, they deduce that science is just one cultural construction among many, one that is inextricably tied to the beliefs of particular people and therefore worthy of no privileged position in relation to the ways of thinking produced in other cultures at other times. That is the theory. The fact is that postmodernists almost always *do* privilege particular ways of thinking: marginal Western ones and non-Western ones. This practice accounts for the growing status of both Western folk medicine and non-Western medicine. Many postmodernists claim that these forms are just as effective as scientific medicine. Many of them might indeed turn out to be effective, but postmodernists make this claim on political grounds, not scientific ones.

For ideological feminists, the problem is more specific. They believe that Western culture in the seventeenth century was fatally contaminated by the ultimate poison of patriarchy, which could be the result of either maleness itself or a form of masculinity so deeply embedded that it might as well be maleness. And if this claim fails to convince political adversaries, they simply "re-situate" or "re-contextualize" their point of view in some other "discourse" that will.

After decades of complacency, scientists have begun to respond. They acknowledge that their way of thinking took shape in Western Europe during the seventeenth century, due to an unrepeatable chain of ideas and events but see no logical connection between that historical fact and the intellectual value of science. What their critics see as something particular, in other words, scientists see as something universal. That view might not be politically correct, they say, but it is true nonetheless. Whatever its cultural and historical origin, science now belongs to everyone (which is why some non-Western feminists see it as their best hope).[7] Adopting the scientific method might not be easy for non-Western societies, although the Japanese have shown that it can be done effectively enough, but it was not easy for Western societies either. It took almost three hundred years of conflict for science to become firmly embedded in the West, and it is under attack even now for both theological and secular – which is to say, ideological – reasons. Scientists acknowledge, moreover, that the full implications of their findings have sometimes been missed or even deliberately ignored. It is true, for instance, that women should have been encouraged long ago to take up careers in science, but that seldom happened, because of human fallibility and not because of anything inherently wrong with science.

Most of those who attack science know little or nothing about it. Nonetheless, postmodernists now question either the existence of objective reality or the ability of anyone to see it. This presents a very attractive opportunity for some advocates of women or other "subaltern" groups being oppressed by the lingering academic shades of "dead white males." Why would feminists, in particular, want to undermine the search for objective reality? Some of them do not, of course, because they rely on the search for objective truth to prove their claims about the victimization of women. Others do, though, in order to bypass messy disputes over those claims. If they can show inherent bias against women in research under the established rules, which are based on the possibility of knowing at least something objective about the external world, then they can dismiss politically or ideologically inconvenient complexity and ambiguity without further ado. At the same time, they can fill the void with research based on rules of their own. Not rules that openly foster objectivity, to be sure, but ones that openly foster subjectivity. Once the subjective "voice" of women (or minorities) has been established as a new standard, of course, no dissonant "voices" need to be taken seriously; women can presumably "know" things by virtue of being women and affirming their own subjectivity, things that men cannot know by insisting on the ostensibly universal standard of objectivity.

This point of view has put feminists (and other postmodernists) on a collision course with science itself, the ultimate expression of the search for objective knowledge. How to "deconstruct" science or at least to undermine its credibility? Partly by colonizing one of its newest frontiers: chaos theory. Chaos theory is a legitimate field within science, of course, so feminists (and other postmodernists) revel in the spectacle of scientists apparently deconstructing their own fields and thus, wittingly or otherwise, contributing to the feminist project. Chaos theory reveals a profound "paradigm shift," they believe, which will destroy the "hegemony" or "privilege" of objectivity and replace it with the "pluralism" or "diversity" of "multiple subjectivities."

Paul Gross and Norman Levitt have responded to this challenge in *Higher Superstition*.[8] Despite its name, they argue, chaos theory does not support the notion that scientific laws are obsolete. It repeals neither Newtonian physics (which scientists continue to use for many practical purposes) nor rational thinking (which remains the basis not only of science but also of logic). It has not, in fact, inaugurated a revolution. This field developed in order to account for a neglected class of behaviour. "Chaos" occurs because every form of measurement is inherently flawed; "chaos theory" simply recognizes that the resulting errors grow exponentially in some systems. Even chaotic behaviour, in other words, is a rule-governed process. To put all this in a very simple form, think of playing roulette. The wheel is simple and has a structure, but the outcome of any spin is virtually impossible to predict. Or think of flipping a coin. We can calculate the probability for either heads or tails, but we cannot predict the outcome for any one flip.[9]

Given postmodernist distortions of scientific theory in connection with chaos theory, why be surprised at the postmodernist distortions of scientific theory in connection with rational thinking itself? Feminists who rely on postmodernism – not all of them do – tend to equate rational thinking with linear thinking, classifying both as patriarchal, without the faintest notion of what scientists actually mean by linear thinking. Their aim is to promote "lateral thinking" or other "alternative ways of knowing." Edward de Bono introduced the former term decades ago, in the nonscientific context of education, merely to connote creativity and problem solving "outside the box."[10]

The problem is due, say Gross and Levitt, to distortions of what scientists mean by both "chaos theory" and "linear thinking." As a result, postmodernists (and creationists) feel free to make extravagant claims that are based not on science but on pseudo-scientific metaphors – a habit that Gross and Levitt call "metaphor mongering."

Because these critics work in fields such as literature and "cultural studies," their attacks focus on the linguistic or rhetorical imagery associated correctly or incorrectly with science, not its content. Why did scientists once talk about the human egg as "passive" and the sperm as "active," for instance? Was it really because men were either unwilling or unable to see what women would presumably have seen immediately, even before scientists – male scientists – discovered the egg's active role in selecting and absorbing the sperm? Why do scientists still talk about "attacking" a problem? Is it really because they are just brutal "warriors" dressed up in lab coats?

At issue here is not so much science per se (modernism versus postmodernism, for instance, or "traditional science" versus "feminist science") but extending the epistemological rhetoric used against both science and modernism to undermine the legal position of men. To explore that problem, we must first discuss the epistemology of ideological feminists in general

and its impact on women's studies – which is the breeding ground of ideological lawyers and bureaucrats.

In one way or another, feminist epistemologies are radically subjective.
They refer to "women's ways of knowing" as distinct from and opposed to
those of men. Why the difference? Why do men and women see the world
differently? One ideological answer is that women are victims and men
oppressors. Another is that women are innately different from (read: superior to) men. Yet Janet Radcliffe Richards and Mary Beth Ruskai argue that
there can be no such thing as feminist epistemology.[11] Richards begins by
illustrating the rhetoric and jargon characteristic of feminist appeals for a
new epistemology with the following passage from Elizabeth Grosz:

[Luce] Irigaray's work thus remains indifferent to such traditional values as "truth"
and "falsity" (where these are conceived as correspondence between propositions
and reality), Aristotelian logic (the logic of the syllogism), and accounts of reason
based upon them. This does not mean her work could be described as "irrational,"
"illogical," or "false." On the contrary, her work is quite logical, rational, and true
in terms of quite *different criteria*, perspectives, and values than those dominant
now. She both combats and constructs, strategically questioning phallocentric
knowledges without trying to replace them with more neutral or more inclusive
truths. Instead, she attempts to reveal a politics of truth, logic and reason.[12]

In other words, anything goes in the battle to discredit an adversary.

At the heart of this essay by Richards is her claim that a feminist epistemology would be both self-contradictory and self-defeating. To make her
point, she uses a hypothetical scenario: convincing an intelligent and educated woman, a nonideological feminist, to reject science in favour of "feminist science." To do so, this woman would have to be convinced that there
is something wrong with the way things are in the world. In that case,

she must obviously have a view about the way things are, or she could not think
there was anything wrong with it; and she must also have some ideas about what
possibilities there are for change, or she would not be able to say that things should
be otherwise. She must, in other words, have a range of first-order beliefs about the
world: the kind of belief that is supported by empirical, often scientific, investigation. Beliefs of this kind also imply that she has other beliefs about second-order
questions of epistemology and scientific method, since in reaching conclusions
about what to believe about what the world is like and how it works she has, however unconsciously, depended on assumptions about how these things can be found
out, and how to distinguish knowledge from lesser things. These assumptions will
become more explicit if any part of her feminism involves (as it is pretty well bound
to) accusing the traditional opposition of prejudice, or of perpetrating or perpetuating false beliefs about women. Similar points apply to questions of value. In order

to make any complaint whatever about the way things are, a feminist must at least implicitly appeal to standards that determine when one state of affairs or kind of conduct is better or worse than another; and if her complaint takes a moral form rather than a simply self-interested one – if, like virtually all feminists, she expresses her complaints in terms of such things as injustice and oppression and entitlements to equality – she must be appealing to moral standards of good and bad or right and wrong, of which she thinks the present state of things falls short. And if she has such normative, first-order standards, that in turn will imply something about her attitudes to the higher-order questions of meta-ethics, whether or not she thinks of them as such.[13]

The argument continues, at length, in this carefully reasoned vein. At each point, Richards says something like this: "So the arguments through which traditional feminism reached its first conclusions involved no departure from familiar standards of evidence and argument in ethics, epistemology, and science, but actually presupposed them. It was *by appeal* to these very standards that the position of women was first claimed to be wrong. And notice that all arguments of this kind depend on absolutely ordinary logic. It is *because* the traditional beliefs are incompatible with traditional standards of assessment, that the challenge to the received view in its own terms is possible."[14]

And even if some feminist claims were true, adds Richards, that would be due to something other than feminism (or any other ideology). Given their interests, it is hardly surprising that feminists have pointed out facts that scientists have missed. But those facts would have been "there" no matter who pointed them out or why.

Richards concludes that feminist attempts to establish their own epistemology are likely to have the most negative effect on women themselves:

It is hard to imagine anything better calculated to delight the soul of patriarchal man than the sight of women's most vociferous leaders taking an approach to feminism that continues so much of his own work: luring women off into a special area of their own where they will remain screened from the detailed study of philosophy and science to which he always said they were unsuited, teaching them indignation instead of argument, fantasy and metaphor instead of science, and doing all this by continuing his very own technique of persuading women that their true interests lie elsewhere than in the areas colonized by men. And, furthermore, outdoing even his own contrivances, in equipping them with a sophisticated, oppression-loaded, all-purpose rhetoric that actually obstructs any serious attempt at analysis.[15]

Daphne Patai and Noretta Koertge, too, describe what passes for feminist epistemology and subject it to a withering critique.[16] In an article of her own, Koertge shows why feminist "paradisciplines" or feminist "correctives" within established disciplines have been so successful in universities and why feminist ideology is no longer confined to women's studies.[17] "Paradisciplinary initiatives are even taking root within the sciences. Psychology of women, black psychology and biology of women have now been joined by feminist economics and feminist geography. Opposition to the most central methods and tools of science is fostered in the paradisciplines of ethnomathematics, Afrocentric science, and feminist methodology. We thus are faced with a profusion of new academic specialties that not only claim to complement traditional scholarship but also to replace or "reinvent" it in radical ways."[18] There are two reasons, she says: academic separatism and affirmative action.

By the former, Koertge refers to the "founder effect" explained by evolutionary biologists. Once a small group of organisms is isolated, inbreeding will cause the dominance of its idiosyncrasies and, given enough time, a new species. And so it is, she says, with feminists in women's studies. From the beginning,

there was a deliberate attempt to isolate feminist scholarship from the rest of the academy [at least partly to avoid subjecting feminists to the same standards of criticism as other academics]. Some authors would cite only women in their footnotes; since men were thought to be biased, only women were considered competent to referee articles for publication; men were sometimes even excluded from attending conferences and were rarely invited to speak. The policy of restricting participation in allegedly academic discussions to people of the appropriate "identity" was sometimes also used to filter out people on the basis of race, ethnicity, and sexual orientation [that is, whites and heterosexuals]. By severely limiting the influence of outside commentary and by aggressively promoting each others' work, the seminal (ovular?) works within these various alternative disciplines quickly gained the trappings of scholarly success. To be blunt, how can one deny tenure to someone whose book receives rave reviews in (feminist) journals and whose book jacket sports blurbs from (feminist) professors at Berkeley, Columbia, or M.I.T.[19]

Affirmative action did the rest, because the influx of women tended to favour fields in what became a "pink collar ghetto." But how could it have been otherwise? Those already established in academia explicitly and vehemently denied the most fundamental principles of scholarship.

None of [Talcott] Parsons's norms are acceptable: logic is a patriarchal device for browbeating nonlinear thinking; since all knowledge is contextual, the search for generality is a form of imperialism; empirical validity must be tempered by moral and political appraisals.

Communality of a nonhierarchical sort is acceptable, but the rest of [Robert] Merton's norms must go: a humane community would be based on trust, not skepticism;

universalism should be replaced by standpoint theory, which says that reports are always to be understood as a product of the culture, gender, ethnicity, class of the observer who made them; no activity can be or should be disinterested. Quite the contrary, a commitment to correct political and social goals is to be encouraged.[20]

As for academic objectivity, Koertge adds, ideological feminists believe that "observers should always remain emotionally connected to what they are studying; the richness of subjective experience should not be stripped away in the vain search for a lowest common denominator of objectivity; intuition should not play second-fiddle to abstract, cold rationality/objectivity; knowledge is always perspectival and tied to local context, and the attempt to find an objective or 'God's eye' point of view always ends up privileging the powerful. Thus the playful curiosity so characteristic of so-called pure science must be replaced by an attitude of caring and commitment."[21]

These strictures make no scientific sense. Nor, adds Koertge, do they make political sense for women and their allies. "What a pity, if in the name of liberating women, feminists should now encourage women and members of various ethnic groups to stay comfortably within the habits of thought that conform to traditional gender and cultural stereotypes. One of the joys of liberal education in either the arts or sciences is the challenge to learn how to think differently. How patronizing to tell young women that the ways of logic, statistics, and mathematics are not women's ways – that all they need to do is stay connected."[22]

Of great interest here is the foundation of feminist epistemology: the authority of experience – the experience of women, that is, whether understood in the personal sense or the collective. Knowledge is said to be "located" or "situated" or "positioned" according to either biology (innate faculties that allow women to "know" what men cannot) or history (powerlessness, which somehow allows women to "know" what men cannot). According to the biological notion, men and women are innately different for more than reproductive reasons. Students learn about a distinctive "female way of knowing," "female logic," "female voice," and so on. According to the historical notion, men and women are conditioned to be different. This idea is considered easier to "prove," and it is thus more popular among ideological feminists. Either way, the word "difference" can be morally problematic. Experts in women's studies often use it politely and indirectly in connection with some innate *superiority* of women over men (even though almost every feminist claims to oppose both essentialism and dualism).[23] Patai and Koertge see this emphasis on difference as the cornerstone of both pedagogical orthodoxy in women's studies and ideological separatism among feminists.

Donna Haraway, for example, describes the "dominant" epistemology – presumably that of men alone – in terms of objectivity, value neutrality, and pure inquiry.[24] She describes feminist epistemology – that of women – as subjective, value laden, and (in effect) purely political. Like good post-modernists, she keeps asking questions that begin with "whose." Whose knowledge have we accepted so far? Whose evidence? Whose interpretation? Whose interests are at stake? These, say many academics in women's studies, are the most important epistemological (and therefore political) questions that feminists can ask. And the answer is always the same cynical one: that of whatever group has the most power. For ideological feminists, that answer is a euphemistic reference to men (or at least white men).

Objectivity implies universality. If something is objectively true, after all, it must be true for all people. Subjectivity, on the other hand, implies particularity. Something might be true for some people but not for others, say, or true in some circumstances but not others. But feminist ideologues, despite their lip service to postmodernist relativism, identify universality objectively with men and particularity objectively with women. Never mind that this confirms the old misogynistic stereotype of women as irrational beings or that it contradicts the ostensible disdain of women for objectivity. Unlike women, who revel in "diversity" (except for those who step out of line ideologically), men speak with one "dominant voice" (except for those, if any, who can somehow be converted to feminism and adopt a female "voice"). This "voice" of men is usually known as "the male model" or "the male standard." And the word "male" indicates something biological, something innate, unlike the word "masculine."

Although there are many "feminisms," each one is a collectivist movement; an "individualist movement," in fact, would be a contradiction in terms. And most feminists, no matter how marginal or how liberal, claim to speak for women in general. When they refer to knowledge, not surprisingly, they refer primarily to women's knowledge. Like other "knowledges," it is "socially constructed" within the community of women and its "webs of belief."[25] (The word "web," presumably referring to the web of a spider, is a ubiquitous but puzzling and even ironic metaphor. Feminists use it to connote "connectedness" or "interconnectedness," something allegedly unique to women. Zoologists, on the other hand, tell us only that spiders use webs to trap insects for food.)

Epistemology is not nearly as impersonal or dry as it sounds, at least not in women's studies. It has both therapeutic and political implications, which are, in fact, closely interrelated. After all, "empowering" women is supposed not only to improve their economic potential and political status but also to transform their personal and collective identities.

Academics are not the only ones to have participated in the "social construction" of women's knowledge. Think of pop psychologists and their role in creating a culture of therapy movements. Think in particular of their ultimate creation: the daytime talk show. This genre is intended to "empower" viewers – and most are women – by making them feel better about themselves. Remember that the rise of therapism and feminism were simultaneous. Coincidence? Hardly.[26] The two are now interconnected, at any rate, on many levels. In line with the therapeutic model now prevalent in popular culture, say Patai and Koertge, students in women's studies are often asked to provide "testimonies" about their own experiences in order to "get in touch with their feelings" – that is, with their anger toward men. To facilitate this, teachers use small group discussions or, better still, role-playing in which women "experience" their abuse by men.[27] Students are then required to record their emotional reactions in journals and analyze them according to feminist criteria. They learn that knowledge is based on experience, in other words, and that it is personal in nature. Growth is measured by progress toward feminist analysis. By the time that they have internalized feminist perspectives, students have become "empowered" by "voicing" their feminist ideas and being "affirmed" by other women. They have been transformed. Consciousness has been raised.

In the popular teach-yourself book called *Women's Studies*, Joy Magezis asks what prospective students can hope to get from this field.[28] She emphasizes the personal dimension of women's studies: the field helps students understand the ways in which society has shaped and limited them in connection with race, ethnicity, class, sexuality, and so forth. This understanding builds their self-confidence and gives them a sense of control. In other words, once again, the field "empowers" them. Moreover, it helps women to connect with each other through courses and networking. Next, she discusses the history of feminism, indicating a clear link between that history and women's studies. Finally, she presents an exercise called "your views." Students are asked to examine their own views on what it means to be women and on what they have in common with other women. With this in mind, students begin writing journals or making videos or creating other forms of self-expression. Exercises of this kind appear everywhere, so students are always aware that the political is personal and the personal political. In effect, teachers say the following: here is the correct theory; document it with your own experiences. This exercise places a premium on emotion rather than reason, and emotion, in turn, is closely related to collectivism, although this relationship is often disguised by appeals to "pluralism." Magezis mentions feminists from various perspectives: socialist, radical, psychoanalytic, black, and liberal. An exercise called "Looking at different feminist views" asks readers to describe which *feels* closest to the truth and why. She tells them that they need not find one, though, because women come together when necessary – even when they disagree (which would be news to Camille Paglia, Christina Hoff Sommers, Katie Roiphe, Daphne Patai, and other dissident feminists).

But ideological feminists in women's studies place most emphasis on group therapy, not individual therapy, which is hardly surprising in view of the fact that collectivism is a primary feature of every political ideology. Teachers praise collaborative and "connected" learning. Because they identify hierarchy with patriarchy, "the male model," and because hierarchy is latent in the very concept of the teacher-student relationship, they hope to remove it to whatever degree is possible in a patriarchal institution. Profs can always give an A to every student and thus foster "equality." One contributor to an e-mail list argued for the elimination of all traditional academic notions: grading, deadlines, facts, specializations, disciplines, objectivity, logic, rules of any kind, or whatever.[29] In line with this collectivist focus, many teachers encourage students to gain credits given for internships done in women's organizations and "mentored" by the feminists they find there.

By now, it should be clear that the collectivist approach is not only therapeutic, or personal, but also political. Patai and Koertge surveyed 150 women's studies students at two universities with very different profiles.[30] Students at both, presumably female, defined the goals of women's studies primarily in gynocentric and activist terms: to increase women's self-esteem, to empower women, to help women develop careers focused on eliminating patriarchy and sexism, and so on. (These students were careful to contrast their own goals with those of feminist "male-bashers" and militants, or radicals).[31]

This result raises two important questions: Is there any significant difference between women's studies and ideological feminism? Or is the former merely an academic arm of the latter? Based on both interviews and their own extensive experience as professors of women's studies, Patai and Koertge say yes to both and go on to expose the political, or ideological, dimensions of many women's studies programs. Using the analogy of religious studies or Chinese studies, it could be argued that women's studies is simply an interdisciplinary approach to the study of women. But this field, say Patai and Koertge, almost always has a political orientation. It is linked with the needs and problems of women, which are almost always said to be caused by men, and with the goal of improving women's status. With all this in mind academics have made formal attempts to define women's studies. Teachers and researchers, they argue, should use feminist principles.[32] And courses should be about the evils of patriarchy such as sexual harassment, molestation, domestic violence, rape, inadequate reproductive rights, and attempts to prevent women's "agency."

Magezis begins her book with a telling observation: "Women's studies is putting women centre-stage ... It's about giving women a fair chance to live up to their potential. Women's studies brings together our personal experiences and the study of ideas. It is a way of examining the world from women's points of view, coming to understand it and then making changes. Into the twenty-first century, we women need to take hold of our future."[33] By "we," she refers exclusively to women (as if men could be neither interested in nor affected by anything under discussion). This definition is clearly gynocentric. Given the topic of women's studies, which is women, gynocentrism is an occupational hazard in the field. Worse, this definition of women's studies fuses the academic study of ideas with the nonacademic experiences of political identity and political mission. No wonder Simon Fraser University's Department of Women's Studies advertised for a professor with the following qualifications: "extensive experience in academia, the professions, or as an *activist*."[34]

Worth noting here is the fact that Magezis defines feminism in much the same way:

Feminism is based on the idea that society is not treating women fairly. It looks at why this is so and how women are oppressed. It works for women's liberation ... [F]eminism means different things to different women. For example, some would say it is working for equality with men in our society, while others say it is out to change the whole way society is set up. Feminism is a broad social movement which allows different points of views under the umbrella of working for women's rights and against female oppression. Whether or not you want to call yourself a feminist is something that only you can decide. But don't feel that you have to use the title in order to find out about women's studies.[35]

Note that word "feel," once more, presumably a synonym for "think."

Magezis admits that "feminism" is a controversial word, although she argues that this problem amounts to nothing more than public relations, and therefore prefers "women's studies." It makes no difference to her, because both words mean much the same thing. But the latter does sound more respectable, certainly in academic circles, and is more likely to attract new recruits (along with more funding). In short, women's studies operates as a front, in the old Marxist sense, for feminism.

Many code words and phrases are used to disguise the fact that women's studies is a front for feminism. The classroom devoted to women's studies, for example, is supposed to create a friendly "environment" in which women not only learn but also feel "affirmed" or "empowered." Academic journals refer to the need for a climate in which women feel fully integrated and fully valued within the academic community. Unfortunately, they often fail to specify precisely what doing so would actually entail. Universal and uncritical acceptance of feminist ideology? If so, that in turn would entail orthodoxy and censorship – both of which should be intolerable in any community, particularly in an academic one, but also in one that ostensibly values "diversity." An academic community exists mainly to encourage the free exchange of ideas and development of new knowledge. If this is undesirable in the university, then the university has ceased to *be* a university.

The same problem emerges in connection with another proposal about "valuing" and "developing" academic fields of particular interest to women. This sounds benign, but it could be a thinly veiled reference to some requirement that the university actively *promote* feminism, even ideological feminism. Universities are no more obliged to promote feminism than they are to promote capitalism, nationalism, communism or any other ism. On the contrary, secular universities exist primarily to collect data, describe phenomena, test hypotheses, and *question* ideas whether they originate in the most established orthodoxies, the most radical ideologies, or anywhere in between. Universities should be places where scholars can discuss ideas openly and freely but not necessarily where they do so comfortably. Decorum is one thing, a good way to facilitate the exchange of ideas, therapy another. If you believe that emotional comfort is more important than intellectual energy, then you need a therapeutic community rather than a scholarly one.

But Patai goes much further in her critique of women's studies, arguing that women's studies is not an academic discipline at all but the academic arm of an political movement – what we, once again, call a respectably academic front for ideological feminism. Not surprisingly, many reviewers in women's studies have attacked her. In responding to them, she has been required to repeat her initial premise over and over again.

Women's studies is quite explicitly feminism in action in an academic setting ... [Courses] are far too often ... not about women's contributions but about women's victimization ... These issues typically are not presented as problems to be studied from many points of view but rather as problems to be exposed by feminist ideology. The bottom line to me is that far too often women's studies classrooms convey attitudes to be endorsed by the students rather than substantive knowledge.[36]

Academic disciplines are supposed to be objective and therefore apolitical. They maintain the ideal of scholarship, in other words, even though individual teachers and authors sometimes insist on promoting their own perspectives at the expense of free inquiry. Ideologies, on the other hand, are supposed to be political. And because every ideology has a point of view, one that gives adherents a sense of purpose both individually and collectively, ideologies are to that extent also subjective. In this case, Patai argues, that point of view includes hatred both of men and, either implicitly or explicitly, of heterosexuality. She must have expected feminist advocates of women's studies to keep on trivializing or attacking her point of view. And indeed they have.[37] But by doing so en masse, ironically, they undermine their own counterclaim: that those in women's studies welcome, or at least tolerate, criticism.

Opening what feminists consider an infamous colloquy on the state of women's studies, hosted online by the *Chronicle of Higher Education*,

Patai made her claim very clear: "It's an unusual opportunity, in my experience, for in fact one of my fundamental criticisms of women's studies is that it has not been open to discussion with critics but has instead too often maligned their motives, which makes it impossible for substantive debate to take place."[38] In any case, we suggest, Patai's critics adopted six basic strategies (usually combined): who, me?; everyone's doin' it; reversal; necessary evil; much ado about nothing; and shifting the blame.

Most of the arguments against Patai include tiresome variations, by both teachers and students, on the theme of "who, me?" "But *I* don't proselytize in *my* courses," they protest. "*I* don't turn *my* classes into group therapy sessions. *I* don't teach *my* students to hate men."[39] Patai is a malicious turncoat, they say, who cites a few preposterous exceptions in order to defame women's studies or even women themselves. Besides, they add, feminists are such a diverse lot. Why take Patai's criticism seriously? Listen to Jenea Tallentire, a graduate student at the University of British Columbia: "I noticed that young men especially were interested in hearing me out, though I had a few heated discussions with some. I sensed their bewilderment because they had 'heard of' that mythical fire-breathing feminist and [instead] got me – I kept my 'fires' to a minimum. I tried to stress the varied opinions in feminist studies (also news to most people), and the fact that many who say they are feminists are nothing of the kind, or at least do not 'represent' even a good number of feminists."[40] Notice that she refers to feminist studies, not women's studies, something that might be more significant than she realizes. On the one hand, she argues that feminism has room for "varied opinions." On the other hand, she continues the same sentence by declaring that those who hold undesirable opinions are either not really feminists at all or too marginal to be worth taking seriously! Well, *that* must have helped those bewildered young men.

Listen now to Christine Littleton, whose specialty at the University of California, Los Angeles, is feminist law: "SHI [the Sexual Harassment Industry] is, of course, a construct of Professor Patai's."[41] In other words, Patai has set up a woman of straw only to illustrate her own point by torching it. Later on, Littleton says that "It is possible that particular party lines 'own' the sexual harassment issue at Amherst in a way that most institutions have outgrown, discarded, or never experienced. Whether or not Patai has mistaken her small corner of the world for the world itself, however, this book does not admit of any more modesty in its claims than its title [*Heterophobia*]."[42] Or listen to Beatrice Kachuck at the City University of New York: "I have never encountered anything like a 'therapy' class."[43] Or Heather Kleiner, a retired professor from the University of Georgia: "The women's studies scholars I was associated with for over twelve years were engaged in the same activities as all good academics:

analyzing and critiquing the 'givens' of their respective fields and of society, guiding students to awareness, understanding and action."[44] Or Adrienne McCormick at the State University of New York, Fredonia: "I have always taught the pro-sex and anti-porn positions on pornography; I have students[45] preparing a presentation right now on abortion that will take into account women who are pro-choice and pro-life; I have men in my classes and encourage them to take more courses. These approaches to key women's studies issues are mirrored in many of my colleagues' classrooms in women's studies as well." In short, Patai is said to be misrepresenting the field "by imposing a homogeneity upon them that does not exist."[46] Here is Patai's response:

It's interesting to me that to make criticisms gets one cast as imposing "homogeneity." Let us suppose that Adrienne is perfectly accurate in her description of her own teaching and [that] of colleagues. That in no way contradicts my claim and that of other critics that there are serious problems of ideological browbeating and indoctrination passing as teaching going in women's-studies classrooms. This is an old question. What percentage of programs and classes have to reveal problems before women's-studies faculty take these problems seriously and address them instead of saying as I have been repeatedly told, "It doesn't happen here"? My experience is that even at schools where the women's-studies people are making this claim the problems do indeed exist, as I hear behind the scenes from students and other faculty at these institutions and as is even confirmed by the fact that some of these institutions, which claim there are no such problems in women's studies, that at some of these institutions women's-studies people have actually attempted to have rescinded invitations that I have gotten from other groups to speak there. This hardly shows the openmindedness and tolerance and nondoctrinaire attitudes that these same feminists characteristically claim.[47]

Those who claim, in effect, that "everyone's doin' it" rely implicitly on two highly questionable notions, one traditional (that two wrongs can indeed make a right) and the other postmodern (that there is no such thing as apolitical scholarship in the first place). "Given the inevitably political nature of deciding what ideas to disseminate," says Diana Blaine, at the University of Southern California, "how would you describe the political agenda of non-women's studies courses? And why are you more comfortable with the propagation of these unacknowledged agendas than you are with the ideas overtly being articulated in women's-studies courses?"[48] Kristin Rusch, at the University of Maryland, asks a very similar question: "Isn't a specifically feminist viewpoint (and variations thereof) a legit perspective to study on the issues you [Patai] mentioned? Certainly Marxists have something important to say about these issues, as do Freudians, theologians, and others. What's wrong with looking at feminist views on these issues?"[49] According to Lisa Jadwin of St John Fisher College, the field "may simply be trying to bring the study of gender into systematic focus, and to ensure that the contributions of women to human history are acknowledged and studied with the same consistency as the contributions of men."[50]

Responding to arguments of this kind, Patai challenges the double standard of those who make them. "My Spanish and Portuguese department does not have a mission statement that involves political transformation. Most women's studies programs do. Women's Studies *is* feminism, by definition, in most programs/departments, and feminism is a political program. (Have a look at the National Women's Studies Association's mission statement. It makes absolutely clear that Women's Studies is providing feminist/womanist education in the service of a political mission – to free the world of a variety of isms.)"[51] She adds that the "idea that leading scholars [in those other fields] are forcing their graduate students to toe a particular line is more parody than reality – and wherever it does happen, it's unfortunate and should be resisted. However, that sounds like a very peculiar defense of women's studies. 'We force our students to toe the line, but so does everyone else' is hardly a recipe for change or improvement."[52] Of course, both Patai and her critics use the argument of "more parody than reality." Even so, Patai's point is well taken. Many advocates of women's studies do indeed reject a double standard (in this case), but they do so by actively promoting bias instead of challenging it and then, either implicitly or explicitly, justifying it on postmodernist grounds.[53]

In response to a question about whom she would consider fit to teach women's studies, Patai notes that this field

was created to be the "academic arm of the women's movement," and this phrase is still repeated again and again in the mission statements of various programs. I don't believe it's appropriate for a secular university to have a program committed to a particular ideology. To the extent that women's studies *is* feminism [as distinct from being about feminism], it is, in my view, academically illegitimate. The study of women, our history, gender roles, etc., on the other hand, are all entirely legitimate and important subjects. One can be a feminist, as I am, and not a supporter of women's studies or of feminist activism [specifically] in education.[54]

Other critics focus on reversal. Because Patai accuses women's studies of promoting a double standard, they find it convenient to accuse her of the same thing. Littleton admits, for example, that the stories of those accused falsely of sexual harassment do need to be told. "It is troubling, however, in a book that takes other feminists to task for telling the story from only one side, that Patai makes little or no effort to be fair to the accusers [in harassment cases]."[55] But Patai has documented a mountain of literature about the experiences of victims or alleged victims of sexual harassment. "By contrast, there is a mere handful of books questioning the legal arguments for treating sexual harassment as discrimination, and casting doubt on the claims of uniquely grievous harm done to women ("survivors") by men's sexual or gender-related words or gestures. Given this imbalance, it hardly seems excessive for me to have devoted two hundred pages or so to a challenge to the prevailing views."[56] She could have underscored the word "prevailing."

Still other critics acknowledge some excesses in women's studies but claim that the field is (in effect, because they never use these words) a necessary evil. They point to the lack of a better alternative, suggesting that the end might justify the means: "Isn't it possible to teach women's studies," asks Jane Elza of Valdosta State University, "without going to extremes? Imagine the world without women's studies – would it be better off?"[57] This is an important question, and we will return to it at the end of this chapter.

Some critics argue that Patai has been guilty of much ado about nothing. She admits that some individual teachers in women's studies "are committed to education and not to replicating in their students their own attitudes and trajectory. The question, of course, is what happens to those teachers in the institutional framework of women's studies. And there the news isn't so great. What you [Jane Elza] call not going to extremes, many women's studies faculty would call caving in to discredited liberal ideas. An entire analysis of the world and of education – a very flawed analysis – underlies women's studies and is used in defense of its orthodoxies and 'extremes.'"[58]

The troublesome relation between women's studies and feminism has not gone unnoticed in the academic world. In some places, the problem is resolved by calling a spade a spade – "feminist studies" – although that hardly settles the question of why any political movement should have its own department in a university. In other places, it is resolved by resorting to a euphemism: "gender studies."[59] Even when the word "gender" is used in the United States and Canada, it is almost always associated either directly or indirectly with women and, more recently, with gay people. Because "gender" originated as a linguistic term, referring to both feminine and masculine nouns, you would expect gender studies to include the study of both women and men, both straight and gay. But you would almost always be wrong. Men are hardly ever studied or even mentioned – except, of course, insofar as they are said to oppress women (a topic that we discuss in appendix 10).

Knowledge, we conclude, is truly on trial. Yes, there have been some debates over freedom of expression and even some critiques of women's studies. But these have not halted the advance of "engaged scholarship." By the late twentieth century, it had been established, institutionalized, and even bureaucratized. It had come, therefore, to have a life of its own. The university had become a laboratory for experiments in the larger world that resulted in social revolution on an unprecedented scale and, given the lack of accountability to either scholars or legislators, in unprecedented secrecy. Through the back door, as it were, ideological feminists had institutionalized gynocentrism at best and misandry at worst.

Programs in women's studies proliferated at universities during the last quarter of the century. According to Joan Korenman, there are approximately 650 women's studies programs, departments, and research centres. In 2001 most Canadian universities were offering women's studies courses: 35 out of 45 had minors programs; 29 had majors programs; some had honours or joint honours programs (no statistics were provided for that category), and 16 had graduate programs as well.[60]

One function of women's studies is to create a lobby group. And one way of achieving that is to, well, lobby for its own expansion. A Canadian academic bulletin advocated that universities hire more tenured feminists and more people to work on their support staffs, enlarging their quarters, promoting their field by all levels of the administration, and even "outing" any feminists who might remain "closeted."[61] The bulletin triumphantly announced that a thousand undergrads and eighty grads would be promoting feminist networks in every major profession.

In addition, teachers in women's studies have increased their influence at the professorial level through books and articles. Feminism has become institutionalized not only in the university, therefore, but also in the publishing industry. Ideologically oriented feminists have generated an enormous literature over the past few decades. You might think that their works are published only by university presses, but many are in fact published by trade houses, which explains why the academic jargon of feminism has become part of popular parlance.[62] Publishing houses now hire feminists, thereby succumbing to pressure from those who want major works to include contributions from women. Think, for instance, of the *Routledge Encyclopedia of Philosophy*.[63] Writing for the *New York Times Book Review*, George Steiner mentions a "disturbing feature" of this project:

Known to be a lucid ironist with a sharp nose for the fraudulent, chief editor Edward Craig confesses that the encyclopedia has had to cater to "devotees" of current French feminist incantations. Why so? Whence this modish obligation? Whatever the motives, the consequences are regrettable. The most fanatic and self-advertising of post-structuralist, post-modernist, deconstructionist and feminist French gesturing are accorded space and regard. A special editor shepherds their bacchanalia. Yet there is every likelihood that sanity will be regained before too long and that these illegible outpourings and their begetters will be seen to have risen without any lasting trace.[64]

All these books, no matter who publishes them, are used as texts in countless university courses and promoted on the Internet in countless lists of core books for those interested in feminism, "women's studies," "gender studies," "cultural studies," and so on.

This brings us to the important topic of feminist networks, which link elite members of university departments with their grassroots counterparts, on the one hand, and with professions, on the other. Networking begins in the universities themselves. Departments of women's studies increase their power base within the university by networking with campus groups such as women's resource centres and women's unions.

Networking is easy these days because of the Internet. By now most or all women's studies programs have their own websites that contain information on courses, research centres, archives, libraries, databases, archived files, chatrooms, correspondence courses, and other resources. Surfers can find both national and international guides on using the Internet to locate and assess these resources.[65] Academic websites are often linked, in turn, to nonacademic sites on women's studies (an oxymoron, but never mind that for the moment).

At one site, *Women's Studies Programs in North America*, visitors can find alphabetical listings by state and university, that were compiled not by an academic but by a musician, Gerri Gribi, "who strives to bring the diverse 'unsung' history of women and minorities to life" with a show called *A Musical Romp through Women's History*.[66] Besides promoting both the show and her album, *The Womansong Collection*, she sells mailing labels for the women's studies list as well as for her list of women's centres. Clearly, academic and nonacademic networks overlap, and the term "women's studies" is popular enough among women to be appropriated for advertising.

Joan Korenman has linked her list of women's studies programs, departments, and research centres to syllabus collections and film reviews. Commenting on this site, which had been visited by 4,400 people in 47 countries when she checked, Korenman says, "When I need information, I have an international body of well-informed virtual colleagues to whom I can turn."[67] She presented her research about online resources for women, what she calls "cyber-feminism," at the United Nations Conference on Women held in Beijing, as well as at numerous other conferences and workshops.

Our only point in discussing feminist sites on the Internet, however, is to illustrate the remarkable growth of women's studies (or whatever academics call this field) over the past few decades. Its influence radiates from the classroom to both the university as a whole (through students who learn what to demand from academic and administrative officials) and the larger society (through countless graduates who have gone on to work in private and public institutions). Its influence radiates also from academic networks (such as the American Association of University Women or the Canadian Federation of University Women) to professional societies representing many academic disciplines (each of which has its women's caucus or women's wing). These networks are linked, in turn, with both government bureaucracies (the Department of Education and the Violence against Women Office, say, or Status of Women Canada) and nonacademic groups (such as "grassroots" websites on women in popular music, women in the arts, and so forth).

Established in 1966, the National Organization for Women (NOW) currently has a membership of over 500,000 in 550 chapters throughout the United States. Its mission statement claims that NOW "advances women's rights and promotes the goal of equality in the United States and around the world through education, litigation, advocacy, networking, conferences, publications, training and leadership development."[68] An affiliate, the National Organization for Women Foundation, raises money for its projects.[69] NOW produces a steady stream of press releases on topics of interest to women that focus heavily on abortion but also on rape and other forms of assault, the "feminization of poverty," affirmative action, pay equity, the "glass ceiling," misogyny in movies and ads, women's rights in countries such as Afghanistan, women's health, and lesbian interests (adoptions, hate-crime legislation, and same sex marriage). NOW runs workshops and conferences for young women to encourage them to call themselves feminists and act accordingly. This organization pays particular attention to the legal and political processes that affect women. It mobilizes women for causes, urges them to sign petitions, to lobby, to march, to vote. In 1998 the cause was lobbying against the impeachment of President Clinton (who might have cheated on his wife but nonetheless supported women's causes). In 1999 it warned Congress against those who were supporting the rights of fathers (even though women were simultaneously urging men to take fatherhood seriously). In 2000 it promoted presidential debates on matters of interest to women. In 2001 it prevented conservative John Ashcroft from becoming the attorney general. In 2002 it organized a national conference on "gender" and a Gender Lobby Day in Washington, a national conference on domestic violence, the fifth annual Love Your Body Day, and a forum for disabled women. In every case, the word "gender" really did refer specifically and exclusively to women. One mantra keeps recurring in NOW's publicity: "Turn anger into activism."[70]

Of particular interest to us, having discussed negative stereotypes of men in *Spreading Misandry* and the fact that so few people are willing to acknowledge that problem, is NOW's annual report card on the state of radio and television programming. Its campaign is called "Watch Out, Listen Up!" Topics for assessment include the number and severity of violent, threatening, or hostile acts against women; sexual exploitation; social irresponsibility; and inadequate sexual ratios on shows. The latter problem is defined as the percentage of women or girls in the cast, with deductions for negative stereotypes and bonus points for positive ones, or "role models" (especially for minority women and lesbians). NOW encourages women who are offended by programs to contact radio stations, television channels, broadcasting networks, production companies, newspaper editors, and other public figures; to organize house parties so that participants can listen to or watch shows, discuss them, and plan letter-writing campaigns or other events; form local task forces; demonstrate at stations or channels with low marks; and, ultimately, to lobby in Congress.[71] A website provides all the names and addresses. In its survey for 2000, NOW named Fox a "network of shame" for its routinely shabby presentation of women (even though its presentation of men was, arguably, no better). The publicity around this designation and related picketing led to a discussion between Patricia Ireland, president of NOW, and the incoming president of Fox Entertainment. A subsequent press release by Ireland indicated that more "woman-positive" shows would be in the works. Staged for publicity? You bet.

The Ms. Foundation emerged from *Ms.*, the magazine founded in 1972 by Gloria Steinem and Dorothy Pitman Hughes.[72] Every year, the foundation honours five "women of vision," each of whom receives the Gloria Steinem Award. Its mission statement refers to its support of measures to help women and girls govern their own lives and to break down "barriers based on class, age, disability, sexual orientation and culture" by changing public awareness, promoting law reform, and establishing social programs on abortion, violence, pay, and health.[73] It provides funds to local, regional, and national organizations for improving women's economic opportunities, education, advocacy skills, and leadership training. One of the foundation's main projects was Take Our Daughters to Work Day, the premise of which was that consciousness raising must start early (although the event is now called Take Our Daughters and Sons to Work Day). The foundation gets endorsements for this event from famous women, especially those who choose nontraditional careers and those who become politicians. Moreover, it sells gifts to mark the occasion: hats, T-shirts, tote bags, calculators, buttons, and stickers.

A close ally is the Feminist Majority Foundation, another American advocacy group working to improve women's lives through economic, social, and political policies. Here is its mission statement: "Our organization believes that feminists – both women and men, girls and boys – are the majority, but this majority must be empowered."[74] Despite the inclusive language, the exclusive focus on women is quickly apparent with talk of "countering the backlash to women's advancement, and recruiting and training young feminists to encourage future leadership for the feminist movement in the United States."[75] Its sister organization, the Feminist Majority, lobbies on causes such as preventing the Supreme Court from being stacked with conservative judges and recruiting young feminists by sponsoring rock concerts. This foundation has a feminist canon posted on its web site. To ensure dissemination of its point of view, the site includes lists of feminist bookstores, electronic versions of books, publishers, reviews, and specialized bibliographies.[76]

Even though feminism began at the elite level,[77] especially in the universities, its influence spread rapidly to the popular level through networking, and it now has a life of its own.[78] Many of the organizations accessible over the Internet are big – remember that NOW has 500,000 members – and politically savvy enough to link elite feminists, especially members of the academic elite, with grassroots feminists.

Canada, too, has many feminist advocacy groups. The largest is the National Action Committee on the Status of Women: "A Coalition of over 700 member groups, NAC is the largest feminist organization in Canada, respected around the world for its ability to shape public opinion, influence decision makers and mobilize its membership and the Canadian public to work for equality and justice for all women."[79] All Canadian taxpayers, including male ones, fund a feminist advocacy group *within the government itself*. Called Status of Women Canada, it "is the federal government agency which promotes gender equality, and the full participation of women in the economic, social, cultural and political life of the country ... It promotes women's equality in collaboration with organizations from the non-governmental, voluntary and private sectors. In promoting women's equality globally, s.w.c. works with other countries and international organizations."[80] Its specific goals are

to promote policies and programs within key institutions that take account of gender implications, the diversity of women's perspectives and enable women to take part in decision-making processes; to facilitate the involvement of women's organizations in the public policy process; to increase public understanding in order to encourage action on women's equality issues; and to enhance the effectiveness of actions undertaken by women's organizations to improve the situation of women ... The principles, objectives and activities or organizations receiving funding from the Women's Program should support the attainment of women's equality as defined in the United Nations Convention on the Elimination of Discrimination Against Women, the Federal Plan for Gender Equality, the Canadian Charter of Rights and Freedoms and the Beijing Platform for Action.[81]

Status of Women Canada organizes the annual International Women's Day, which always focuses on a specific theme. The theme of 2002, only a few months after the terrorist attacks on New York and Washington, was how to replace a global culture of violence with one of peace. In addition, Status of Women Canada provides tool kits for every occasion that include questions and answers about events, suggested videos about women, and background information on women. They encourage women to e-mail their friends and to put special messages on fax cover sheets, voice mail, web sites, and computer screensavers, or in the pay envelopes of employees. They urge women to put up posters, show videos, and hold brown-bag lunches, so that women of all ages and backgrounds can discuss their experiences in the battle for equality. In addition, the kits encourage women to set up information fairs with displays about local or national organizations and resources for women, and to interview women, present shows or concerts, organize conferences or panel discussions, set up photo or art exhibits, and, of course, raise funds. They ask teachers to lead student discussions and organize projects about women. They ... well, the list goes on and on. The point is for women not only to copy and distribute these kits but also, if possible, to come up with their own ideas. A list of coming events across the country is always posted on the Internet. These events are sponsored by government groups but also by local groups (mobilizing against sexual assault, say, or domestic violence), universities, arts centres, museums, political parties, religious organizations (notably the United and Unitarian Churches), and so on.

Status of Women Canada provides tool kits, with posters, for an additional annual event, the National Day of Remembrance and Action on Violence against Women, which is held every year on 6 December. This event was established by Parliament in 1991 to commemorate the day that Marc Lépine, whom we discussed in chapter 4, murdered fourteen women in Montreal. According to the website, it "represents a time to pause and reflect on the phenomenon of violence against women in our society. It is also a time to have a special thought for all the women and girls who live daily with the threat of violence or who have died as a result of deliberate acts of gender-based violence. Last but not least, it is a day for communities and individuals to reflect on concrete actions that each of us can take to prevent and eliminate all forms of violence against women."[82] The site notes that members of Parliament will observe a minute of silence and urges all Canadians to do the same and to signify their support for women by wearing a white ribbon. The white-ribbon campaign, as we noted in chapter 4, provides an opportunity for male feminists to pledge their help in educating other men about violence against women. As it does for International Women's Day, this site posts a schedule of activities occurring across the country. Many of the same groups sponsor this event, but those dealing with violence have a more prominent role than other groups. Also, these events are more overtly religious than those associated with International Women's Day: candlelight vigils, memorial services, and even pilgrimages to shrines such as the one on Decelles and Queen Mary Road in Montreal and the one at Hawthorne Park in Vancouver. Some groups show videos such as *After the Montreal Massacre* and *Waking Up to Violence*.[83] Others encourage testimonials by women who have been abused.

No opportunity for political or ideological advocacy is lost. On its website, Status of Women Canada tells academics doing studies on women how to promote their research. It offers to disseminate results throughout the federal government, distribute them to cabinet ministers, send them to hundreds of libraries, develop fact sheets, and post everything on its web site. The site tells visitors how to be "proactive" in communicating with those who run the mass media and how to write a press release that everyone will notice. Women should "dress it up to look and sound like news," make it appear urgent by faxing instead of mailing, and use a "grabber headline."[84] The site explains how women can use advocacy groups, the public relations departments of universities, and friends to review their reports in policy journals. And it provides an extensive list of publishers, web sites, research networks, and academic journals. Remember, this group operates *within* the government and is funded by tax dollars.

In appendix 12, we discuss a report titled "School Success by Gender: A Catalyst for the Masculinist Discourse," by Pierrette Bouchard, the primary author, along with Isabelle Boily and Marie-Claude Proulx, that was sponsored by and has been promoted by Status of Women Canada.[85] It describes the baneful effect of "masculinist discourse" on "progressive" theories of education. (As we explain in a moment, "masculinism" is an evil reversal of feminism.) Here now are a few comments on the status of the report in strictly academic terms.

The report began as an investigation into the education of boys and girls, but for a report that purports to represent the best of current scholarship in the social sciences, this one is notable for its lack of methodological rigour. It does have an academically respectable veneer, true, but as the authors describe it, their method[86] presents at least three problems. As we say in appendix 12, the research question is overtly politicized. It assumes that concern for the education of boys is tantamount to lack of concern (or worse) for the education of girls. Moreover, the authors admit that they expanded the scope of their research at some point from the education of boys and girls to the more general topic of "the backlash against feminism."[87] That might explain why their list of keywords for content analysis includes not only "education," "boy," "girl," "gender difference, "academic success," "men," "male," and "fatherhood" but also "violence" and "suicide."

Although this project began as research on the print media, it was expanded at some point to include websites. The authors do mention this at the end of a section on method,[88] but they say nothing at all about the method used for these websites. Compared to the authors' rigorous (but tendentious) analyses of print material, their analyses of the websites seem highly impressionistic. The authors merely present readers with a few misogynistic quotations, a few misogynistic cartoons, and then launch into a discussion of using hate legislation to ban them. Although these items are important,[89] because expressions of hatred are always important, the process by which they were selected is unacknowledged. The authors offer no evidence that these items are pervasive or even common. Nor do they make any attempt to distinguish between crankiness or rudeness and hatred. And there is a difference. A big one.

Nor, of course, do they refer to feminist sites that use misandric quotations and jokes. (We discuss some of those in appendix 9, but they are by no means the nastiest; we chose them for subject matter rather than style.) There is no reason to blame Bouchard and her colleagues for confining their search to what men are saying about themselves or even to what hostile things some of these men are saying about women in general and feminists in particular. These are phenomena like all others and thus worthy of research.[90] There *is* a reason, however, to blame them for deliberately creating the impression – they could hardly have done so accidentally – that women are not doing precisely the same things on their own websites: saying hostile things about the opposite sex. At no point, not even once, do the authors either say or imply that women routinely engage in the equivalents of everything that they scold the men in question for doing: blaming them for every conceivable human problem; either stating or insinuating that most (sometimes all) of them are guilty and deserve to be ignored, ridiculed, or punished; and spreading theories developed by others (without explaining why that would be problematic in the first place).

The report contains so many passages that betray double standards that we must be content with one example here (and refer to others in appendix 12).

Toward the middle of the decade [the 1990s], we begin to see in the media discourses that cast suspicion on female elementary teachers, single mothers and feminists, blaming them for the problems experienced by boys. A key element seen in this period is the emergence of a victimization theme, in which boys are portrayed as being discriminated against by an education system that has become a feminist environment. Co-educational schools are challenged and, toward the end of the decade, we see systematic links established to the male suicide rate, boys on Ritalin, fathers gaining custody of their children, the suffering of male abusers, the loss of male identity, false allegations of violence against men, etc.[91]

The information here is correct (except for the part about the suffering of male abusers, which is made out to look like sympathy for people whose behaviour is unacceptable but is actually nothing more than an explanation for the origin of their behaviour). Yet readers would never know from this passage that feminists were at that very moment developing an ideology based on a conspiracy theory of history. It was in this climate that we plunged into something approaching mass hysteria over satanic-ritual abuse and recovered-memory syndrome. And, apart from anything else, that left a cloud of suspicion over all male teachers, daycare workers, and fathers (whether divorced or not).

According to many feminists, not only ideological ones, girls are the victims of discrimination by an education system that has ignored them. Some feminists have defended the continued existence of separate colleges for women and separate schools for girls. Other feminists have advocated separate sports teams for girls (even though they have refused to accept separate teams for boys).[92]

The report's failure to define its central concept undermines its academic credibility. The word "masculinism" does not appear in its glossary of technical terms, although it is explained in a note according to the usage of Martin Dufresne, a feminist who writes in French.[93] Readers are expected to know that "masculinism" signifies an evil reversal of feminism, which is why its main product is described invariably as a "backlash" against feminism.[94] The implication is that the only possible reason for anyone to question feminist positions, or even merely to discuss the problems of schoolboys, would have to be a nefarious one, which makes it clear that "masculinism" has been created largely by feminists themselves. A useful analogy would be the mediaeval Christian notion that witchcraft must have been a sinister parody of Christianity and its "black sabbath" of the eucharist, say, or the Christian notion of Judaism as a religion that revolves around the blasphemous rejection of Christ. What could better illustrate the close relation that we have identified in both this volume and in *Spreading Misandry* between gynocentrism and misandry?

The "masculinism" discussed by Bouchard and her colleagues could be described as an ideology,[95] actually, in the Marxist sense: it involves hidden assumptions about the way things are that allow a ruling class to perpetuate its hegemony over other classes. By tacitly encouraging readers to assume that "masculinism" is an ideology in the Marxist sense, the report tacitly discourages readers from wondering if feminism is also an ideology in some sense. That is why it refers over and over again to the "masculinist discourse"[96] (the latter word being postmodernist jargon, most often, for the absence of any relation to reality at best and the presence of a sinister conspiracy at worst).[97] Using this word for the opposing position implies also that it has no legitimacy whatsoever, that it is intended only to hood-wink people and thus oppose the truth of feminism. This is ironic in view of the fact that postmodernism claims to have exposed the folly of all claims to objective truth. In theory, all of these claims can be – and should be – "deconstructed."[98] In practice, there are exceptions. Postmodernists use deconstruction only on whatever they dislike and want to destroy. Conse-quently, the authors of this report refer to "masculinist discourse" but "fem-inist knowledge."[99] Masculinism is by definition based on either illusions or lies; feminism, on the contrary, is by definition based on truth. (Just in case anyone fails to get the message, however, they often add words such as "alleged," or "seems" to the claims of their adversaries.)[100]

Like other ideologues, Bouchard, Boily, and Proulx do not consider themselves bound by any requirement for either intellectual or moral integrity. Otherwise, how could we explain a contradiction that is repeated over and over again in their report? On the one hand, they insist on aggre-gated data, on generalizations. On the other hand, they actually use disag-gregated data, which are broken down into categories that are defined by context. Women benefit either way, as we explained in chapter 5, because the disaggregated data show the specific contexts where men dominate and therefore where affirmative action for women would be helpful; the con-texts where women dominate, though, are usually ignored. At the same time, aggregated data generally show that women as a class are behind men as a class; this provokes the demand for change.

Bouchard and her colleagues are very explicit about the "limitations of the masculinist discourse on education," one of the primary ones being "generalization to an entire gender."[101] They claim that the "issue should be framed in terms of gaps between the sexes, taking into account such facts as social origin and family and cultural environment. Generalizations must be avoided. It is also important to differentiate between school suc-cess, educational achievement and social success, because they are not all the same thing."[102] Even so, they continue in the very next sentence by contradicting themselves. "The data ... show that girls are still confined to traditional areas of schooling, although they now graduate from university in greater numbers."[103] Well, which girls? Girls with which origin, which type of family, which cultural environment? They refrain from offering any answers. The entire feminist project, after all, is based on precisely the idea that generalizations can and should be made. Otherwise, how could they argue that women are an oppressed *class* (one that transcends the economic or other criteria that apply to some women but not others) and that men are an oppressor *class* (one that likewise transcends economic or other cri-teria that apply to some men but not others)?

Examples of this contradiction and the double standard on which it is based occur not once or twice, please note, but throughout the report.[104] It is a fundamental feature of the method, not a careless lapse. The authors try to make two points: that boys in general have no serious problems and that girls in general do. Sometimes, they bring out statistics to support these claims. Failing that, they resort to what could be called "globalization," even though they explicitly condemn that phenomenon in its economic sense. Okay, so girls in the industrialized world are doing well in school. But girls in other parts of the world are not! Ergo, considering the entire world's female population, *Canadian* girls need all – not some or even a great deal but *all* – of our compassion, research, and funding. This tactic is out of place, to say the least, in a document that is intended to advise and is paid for by the government of one heavily industrialized country. Given this situation, no one should be surprised to find that the authors of this report attack men's groups for having the audacity to demand government funding for research on men and projects that would help men but demand it for themselves alone over and over again.

Even though this report began, as we have said, as an investigation into the education of boys and girls, a very specific topic, its authors use all the arguments that we have identified in this book as the all-purpose trump cards of ideological feminists. Women have less power (whatever that is)[105] than men. Women are paid less than men for the same or similar work. Women do more unpaid work than men do. Women are more likely than men to be poor. Whatever. It came as no surprise to us that this report on education includes a long discussion of violence against women (even though the statistics presented are contradicted by a study conducted by another agency of the federal government, Health Canada)[106] and ends with a proposal for more censorship and more hate legislation.

At the heart of this mentality is what we call "comparative suffering" (which we will discuss more fully, in connection with *competitive* suffering, toward the end of *Transcending Misandry*): the pervasive belief that human suffering (apart, perhaps, from purely physical suffering) can and even should be quantified. As a result, segments of the population – segments usually defined in connection with "identity politics" – come to be pitted against each other in a relentless contest over which one suffers most and thus deserves all of society's compassion (let alone its tax dollars). So, who suffered more? Jews who endured twelve years under National Socialism and ended up in death camps? Or Africans who endured three hundred years of slavery in America and another hundred of segregation? If you believe that a morally acceptable answer can be given, then you believe in comparative suffering. Although they never actually define "suffering," Bouchard and her colleagues clearly believe that women suffer more than men and therefore feel entitled to demand a monopoly on sympathy (and funding). Even so, their position is based on a nonsequitur. The fact that one group suffers more than another, after all, does not mean that it should enjoy a monopoly on public sympathy (or funding). They know this, and even say so, but with the kind of disclaimer that is so out of sync with everything else they say as to have no meaning. "We must resist attempts to place male and female victims into a competition for resources or credibility," Frederick Mathews observed several years earlier. "We can no longer afford the divisiveness along gender lines that permeates discussions about male and female victims' experiences. If we are to advance the anti-violence movement at all in Canada, we have to move more toward 'gender reconciliation' and away from the bullying of one another that passes for advocacy in many public discussions."[107] Sure.

Throughout "School Success by Gender," from cover to cover, is a belief that the authors consider beyond question: that only girls and women are victims. Many readers of the report, we hope, will ask why the authors find it impossible to take the needs and problems of boys as seriously as they do for girls. The thought does occur to them at one point, when they ask the following questions: "[S]ocially, should attempting or committing suicide create some hierarchy of concern? Can death or the desire to take one's life – man or woman – be ranked on a scale of importance?" But without actually answering their own questions, they continue directly as follows: "Masculinists stress this aspect to create a picture of the discrimination/victimization of men in society without any ethical consideration."[108] Throughout the report, in fact, these authors either ridicule or condemn the very idea that boys or men might be victims in *any* way. Moreover, they accuse those who assert it of perpetuating the pernicious cult of victimization.[109] (Never mind that women themselves have been playing that very game, effectively, for decades and that women were actually the pioneers.) Giving any consideration to the idea that boys and men might be victims, even lesser victims, would be to ignore the notion of male hegemony and its expression in a "masculinist discourse" (which is to say, a patriarchal conspiracy). This belief had already been challenged by Mathews in his report for Health Canada, *The Invisible Boy*. Given the heavy rhetoric from Bouchard and her colleagues, it is worth quoting Mathews at length – remembering that he wrote his report no fewer than seven years *earlier*.

Male victims, like female victims before them, have encountered their share of critics and detractors, people who refuse to believe them, ignore prevalence statistics, minimize the impact of abuse, appropriate and deny males a voice, or dismiss male victimization as a "red herring." When prevalence statistics are given for male victimization, it is common to hear the response that the vast majority of abusers of males are other males, a belief which is simply not true. This comment is usually intended to frame male victimization as a "male problem."[110]

Here is a serious moral problem. The fact that one man is injured by another man does not mean that the former should be held responsible for his own injury. That would be what feminists call "blaming the victim," when the victim is female.

In many respects, male victims are where female victims were 25 years ago. Most of us forget the enormous opposition the women's movement encountered as women began to organize and claim a voice to speak against violence and name their abusers/offenders. The services and supports that exist presently for women were hard won and yet are still constantly at risk of losing their funding. By comparison, there really is no organized male victims "movement" per se. Males, generally, are not socialized to group together the way women do, to be intimate in communication or see themselves as caregivers for other males. In short, much of what male victims need to do to organize a "movement" requires them to overcome many common elements of male socialization, all of which work against such a reality ever happening."[111]

That was several years ago. Despite the psychological problem for men of acknowledging vulnerability, more and more of them are willing to do so. Some of them – not all of them, not even most of them, but some of them – do so by expressing hatred toward feminists or even toward women in general. Bouchard, Boily, and Proulx surely are correct about that. Unfortunately, they do not understand the main reason for that hatred: women who refuse to take them seriously as people. This does not mean that women deserve hatred in return – hatred is inherently evil no matter what the circumstances – but it does mean that women, the ones who ridicule or ignore the claims of men, are part of the problem and that feminists should clean up their own house.

Male victims walk a fine line between wanting to be heard and validated, to be supportive of female victims and to be pro-woman, while challenging assumptions they feel are biased stereotypes. Their challenges to some of these stereotypes are often met with accusations that they are misogynists, part of a "backlash" against feminism, or have a hidden agenda to undermine women's gains. If any of these accusations are true, they must be confronted by all of us. But if they are based only on the fear that recognition of males as victims will threaten women's gains, then that is the issue we should be discussing right up front, not minimizing male victims' experiences in a competition to prove who has been harmed the most. Nonetheless, it is important for all of us to recognize that it may be difficult for many women to listen to male victims' stories until they feel safe in this regard.[112]

We have established in this chapter that ideological feminism, usually in the guise of "women's studies" (but sometimes in that of "gender studies" or even "queer studies"), has had a profound impact on education and, in turn, on those who are educated. Through many networks, ideological feminists have contributed heavily to the gynocentric worldview that is now prevalent in our society. Based on a feminist epistemology, it is preoccupied exclusively with the needs and problems of women. In theory, gynocentrism need not be misandric (just as androcentrism need not be misogynistic). In practice, that is seldom the case. To the extent that this worldview encourages citizens to ignore the distinctive needs and problems of men, even if it refrains from overtly attacking them, we must consider it a misandric one. The inevitable result is gynocentrism at best or misandry at worst. Either way, scholarship is compromised by advocacy. What feminists call "engaged scholarship," in other words, is nothing more than feminist ideology masquerading as scholarship.

Among the most troubling aspects of all this is the pervasive influence of ideological feminism on law. In *The Charter Revolution and the Court Party*, F.L. Morton and Rainer Knopff[113] write that in the United States during the 1960s,

the heyday of the Warren Court, there was a popular joke in American universities about where to locate sovereignty in the U.S. The American people seized sovereignty from King George III in 1776 and transferred it to the Constitution in 1787. But since the Constitution has come to mean only what the judges say it means, and since the judges say only what they read in the *Harvard Law Review*, sovereignty in the U.S. now rests with the faculty at the Harvard Law School. As recently as 1994, Mary Ann Glendon (of Harvard Law School) confirmed the underlying truth of this joke. Writing about the "powerful synergy [that] links the appellate judiciary and the legal academy," Glendon maintained that just as "[m]any professors strive mightily to influence the course of judicial opinions, [so] many judges reach out in their opinions to 'constituents' in the professoriate."[114]

Postmodernism, as everyone knows by now, has had as great an impact on law schools as it has on departments of philosophy, religious studies, literature, and so forth. In this particular field, it is often called "critical literary studies" (CLS, an offshoot of Marxist Critical Theory).

The postmodernist contention that all knowledge is constructed found a receptive audience among lawyers trained in the adversarial method of argument. Constructing one-sided and self-serving accounts of conflicts is what common-law lawyers are trained to do. Under the CLS banner minority, multi-cultural, native, feminist, and gay-rights advocates have deconstructed such traditional legal norms as judicial independence, judicial impartiality, and the rule of law as nothing but disguises for class privilege, racism, sexism, and heterosexism. By the 1980s, the 'Crits,' as they are known, had become the dominant faction at the most prestigious American law schools.[115]

We are not talking about isolated radical institutions, by the way, but about truly mainstream ones. Morton and Knopff report that

[t]he prestigious *Yale Law Journal* recently published an article by Paul Butler, a black law professor, who defended the right of black jurors to ignore evidence and to acquit black defendants in non-violent cases as a way of protesting racism in the criminal justice system.[116] Patricia Williams, a black law professor at Columbia University, has defended a young black woman who made up a story about being raped by a gang of white men. This lie was justified, Professor Williams argues, because "her condition was clearly the expression of some crime against her, some tremendous violence, some great violation that challenges comprehension." The lie was justifiable, the Columbia University professor continued, because it "has every black woman's worst fears and experiences wrapped into it."[117]

It would be hard to imagine a law school in the United States or Canada that does not yet offer courses in feminist legal theory. Some publish journals devoted exclusively to feminist law: *Harvard Women's Law Journal*; *Women and Rights Law Reporter*; *Yale Journal of Law and Feminism*; *Yale Journal of Law and Liberation*; *Berkeley Women's Law Journal*; *Cardozo Women's Law Journal*; *Duke Journal of Gender Law and Policy*; *Hastings Women's Law Journal* (from the University of California); UCLA *Women's Law Journal*; *William and Mary Journal of Women and the Law*; *Wisconsin Women's Law Journal*; *New York University Review of Law and Social Change*; *Women's Law Journal of Legal Theory and Practice* (from the University of Pennsylvania); and *University of Michigan Journal of Law Reform*. Some idea of the content can be gleaned from the mandate of the *Women's Law Journal of Legal Theory and Practice*, which is

to provide a meaningful forum for women's and men's voices on a variety of issues surrounding women's relationship to jurisprudence generally, and to the practice of law specifically. Topics that will be addressed by the Journal will include, but will not be limited to, the following: women attorney's experience in the workplace, in the courtroom, and in other professional settings; how race, ethnicity, sexual orientation, disability and spirituality affect women practitioners and their clients; balancing a legal career with family; feminist lawyering; feminist legal theory; the history and evolution of women lawyers and litigants in American jurisprudence; and women's narrative and creative expression of their experience in and around the legal system.[118]

Writing in the *Harvard Women's Law Journal* are feminist legal luminaries such as Martha Minow, Catharine MacKinnon, and Andrea Dworkin (even though she is not a lawyer). Here are the titles of some articles: "Against the Male Flood: Censorship, Pornography and Equality"; "'To Give Them Countenance': The Case for a Women's Law School"; "A

Reasonable Battered Mother?: Redefining, Reconstructing, and Recreating the Battered Mother in Child Protective Proceedings"; "Public Women and the Feminist State"; "Race, Gender, and Social Class in the Thomas Sexual Harassment Hearing: The Hidden Fault Lines in Political Discourse"; "Anti-Stalking Laws: Do They Adequately Protect Stalking Victims?"; "Single-Sex Public Education after VMI: The Case for Women's Schools"; "Rape, Genocide, and Women's Human Rights"; "Comparable Worth in Ontario: Lessons the United States Can Learn"; "Rape and Women's Credibility: Problems of Recantations and False Accusations Echoed in the Case of Cathleen Crowell Webb and Gary Dotson"; "Melodrama and Law: Feminizing the Juridical Gaze"; "Gender in Evidence: Masculine Norms v. Feminist Reforms"; "Recognizing Violence against Women: Gender and the Hate Crimes Statistics Act"; "Perspectives on Our Progress: Twenty Years of Feminist Thought"; "Legal Limbo of the Student Intern: The Responsibility of Colleges and Universities to Protect Student Interns against Sexual Harassment"; "Feminism, Epistemology, and the Rhetoric of Law: Reading *Bowen v. Gilliard*"; "Criminalizing the Exposure of Children to Domestic Violence: Breaking the Cycle of Abuse." Some issues even have poetry with titles such as "I said, 'No.'"[119]

Feminism in Harvard Law School, according to John Sedgwick, has created a veritable war zone. In "Beirut on the Charles" he describes – no, reveals – the rampant politics at one of the nation's most prestigious institutions that have

pitted faculty members against faculty members, faculty members against students and, perhaps most viciously of all, students against students. Relations have broken down so completely that Dean Clark recently appointed Professor Emeritus Roger Fisher, the famed negotiator who has attempted to reconcile Kuwait and Iraq, to act as a kind of marriage counselor for the law school "community." Few expect that he and the faculty members working with him will succeed. "It's a shark tank here," one student said. Harvard Law School is not the only law school that suffers from such political tensions. "Diversity issues are in the air at all leading law schools and all leading universities," said Harvard Law's Dean Clark ... But at Harvard, even if you don't take a side, you are given one. Everyone is typecast by his or her race, gender, sexual orientation and political perspective, be it Left, Right or center. Such details are like being a Virgo or a Gemini to an astrologer. They tell Harvardians everything they need to know about someone. The personal is political at Harvard Law, and the political is personal. Both can get nasty.[120]

Sedgwick traces the trouble, correctly, to CLS.

The current troubles may have drifted down to the students, but they started with the faculty, back in the Seventies, with the battles over the Crits, or Critical Legal

Studies movement, led by lanky, boot-wearing Professor Duncan "Funky Dunk" Kennedy. The Crits made the fairly strict Marxist argument that, for all its attempts at justice, the law merely perpetuated the interests of the ruling class. Kennedy laid out the philosophy in a small, privately printed volume called *Legal Education and the Reproduction of Hierarchy*, which was quickly nicknamed "Duncan's Little Red Book" ... But even bad movies occasionally get remade, and, to many observers, those issues of the current PC era that are uppermost in the minds of the students are simply restylings of CLS's neo-Marxism. Now, instead of directly decrying the ruling class, the students pick at its racism, sexism and homophobia. In fact, they invoke those terms so often and so loudly that that troika might stand as Harvard Law's holy trinity ... Through an organization called the Coalition for Civil Rights, the students went so far as to sue the university for discrimination in faculty hiring, claiming that their education has suffered due to the lack of minority and women professors. The suit got as far as the Massachusetts Supreme Judicial Court."[121]

Here is Sedwick's parting shot at Beirut on the Charles: "Many things are distorted at Harvard Law, not the least of them gender relations. As I looked around the Bow, it seemed to me that the women, for all their talk of victimization, were the sexual predators in this ecosystem, and the men the prey."[122]

Much the same thing has happened in Canada. Canadian law schools began to grow most rapidly, during the 1960s and 1970s, at the very moment when political and ideological movements were becoming prevalent in universities. "CLS was carried back to Canadian law schools by the increasing number of law graduates choosing to do their LL.M's at Harvard and Yale rather than Cambridge or Oxford."[123]

The new autonomy of Canadian legal education coincided with the triumph of postmodernism among university-based intellectuals. Postmodernism rejects the possibility of scientific or objective knowledge, claiming that all knowledge is self-interested and reflects (and supports) unequal power relationships based on class, gender, race, and so forth. It portrays the political, legal, and cultural traditions of western civilization as the corrupt legacies of "dead, white, heterosexual, male" privilege. For example, deductive logic and concepts of evidence are often dismissed as phallocentric modes of reasoning. Convinced of their own unique virtue and the corruption of all who disagree or question, postmodernists fuel the new reign of political correctness that has stifled intellectual freedom at Canadian universities over the past decade ... In Canada, the postmodern angst has focused more on gender and sexual orientation than race. Recently, however, the Canadian Bar Association released a report alleging wide-spread racism throughout the legal system. A subsequent inquiry revealed that the CBA's finding was based not on reliable data, but on the committee's embrace of "critical race theory."[124]

All of this has been supported by what Morton and Knopff call advocacy scholarship (what ideologues call engaged scholarship and what we call ideology). "While the simple view is that interpreting the Charter is the responsibility of the judges," they write, "the interpretive community is in fact much broader and clearly includes legal academics ... The burst of advocacy scholarship that followed the adoption of the Charter was a calculated component of Court Party strategy to maximize the political utility of Charter litigation."[125] By 2002, 60% of the students in most law schools were women. That in itself, given the heavily politicized orientation of many, should be a good indication of things to come for men.

University-based intellectuals are at the heart of the postmaterialist left in all Western democracies. They diagnose our social ills – racism, sexism, heterosexism, etc. – and prescribe the cures. What distinguishes American and now Canadian politics is the extent to which this new knowledge class successfully pursues its agendas through litigation and the courts. The consequent politicization of legal scholarship in Canada parallels – indeed, emulates – post-war American practice ... The process has not been spontaneous and happenstance. In the U.S., "flooding the law review" with favourable articles has been an established tactic of movement interest groups ... In Canada, it became part of an explicit strategy of influencing the influencers adopted at the outset of the Charter era. It has been an astoundingly successful strategy, in large part because it has been largely unopposed. The legal commentators are all singing from the same hymn book.[126]

Law schools are closely linked to advocacy legal groups. One major player in feminist legal politics in the United States since 1972 has been the National Women's Law Center, a nonprofit organization based in Washington, DC. It defines itself as follows: "The Center uses the law in all its forms: getting new laws on the books and enforced; litigating groundbreaking cases in state and federal courts all the way to the Supreme Court ... educating the public," and so on.[127] It has worked to improve conditions for women in terms of money (enforced child-support programs, social security), employment (high-quality child care, anti-harassment legislation, affirmative action, equal pay, military jobs), education (educational and athletic opportunities, anti-harassment policies, affirmative action), and health (women's-health report cards, family-planning programs, reproductive-health services).

The National Women's Law Center is supported by the Department of Health and Human Services, foundations, corporations, unions, law firms, and professional associations (such as the National Association for Public Interest Law and the National Education Association). Its interest-group orientation is clearly indicated on its web site, which invites women to become informed about current debates and legislation, become involved by contacting members of Congress, and join its e-mail alert network. The National Women's Law Center has litigated in several important cases. One of these was *Brentwood Academy v. Tennessee Secondary School Athletic Association* (2001),[128] the result of which makes state athletic associations provide equal opportunities for girls and boys. It monitors judgments in the Supreme Court and warns women of their political implications. In 2001, for instance, it noted that some protections for women were being cut back and some challenges to women-friendly legislation were being defeated only by slim margins. Women were told to get politically active and prevent another conservative judge from being appointed to the Supreme Court, because even one more could have a critical impact on "women's constitutional rights to privacy and equal protection, and the federal statutory protection of women's rights in employment, education, and health, safety and welfare."[129]

In Canada, the major feminist legal advocacy group since 1985 has been the Legal Education and Action Fund (LEAF). Even though LEAF is a non-governmental and nonprofit organization, it was inspired by a report issued by the Canadian Advisory Council on the Status of Women. This report told feminists how they "could take advantage of the unique opportunity provided by this forum [the Charter] to pursue social change through litigation" and recommended "the establishment of a single national fund, the direct sponsorship of (preferably winnable) cases, and a complementary strategy of education and lobbying."[130] LEAF's official website defines its mission this way:

LEAF is a national, non-profit organization working to promote equality for women and girls in Canada. Using the equality provisions from Section 15 of The Canadian Charter of Rights and Freedoms as a basis to advance women's rights, LEAF presents arguments, or intervenes, in cases where women's rights are at risk in Canadian courts...

At LEAF, we recognize the complex issues related to women's rights, and we know that, in an ever-changing society, the importance of these rights must not be overlooked. That is why we believe strongly in working, through the courts, to protect the rights of *all* women, of *all* ages, in Canada, and in communicating to Canadians the scope of these Charter equality rights.[131]

Because LEAF is a women's organization, there is no reason for any reference to the rights of men. Still, we should at least ask questions about the rights of men. Christopher Manfredi argues that LEAF's objective is

not merely to defend women's legal rights, but to use legal action as a way of advancing a favorable policy agenda. In the micro-constitutional political arena of charter litigation, this meant occupying the equality rights field and pursuing a secondary constitutional rule that equality must be given a substantive, rather than purely formal, meaning. The problem with formal equality, LEAF argued, is that its emphasis on equality of opportunity and the neutral application of the law does nothing to compensate women for the accumulated disadvantages of past exclusion. In order to be "truly" equal, the law must be sensitive to the substantive differences in the economic, social and political status of various groups.[132]

He goes on to note that LEAF's strategy included the generation of "respected theory," or "engaged scholarship," to ground the notion of substantive equality. This was created by feminist law professors, including LEAF founders such as Beth Atcheson, Marilou McPhedran, Elizabeth Symes, Shelagh Day, Gwen Brodsky, Mary Eberts, and Lynn Smith. Together, they produced more than thirty books and articles between 1981 and 1992.

Manfredi observes that "this literature tended to be proscriptive and prescriptive rather than retrospective and descriptive, suggesting that the feminist movement's use of 'legal literature is part of a long-run approach, in which indirect influence in the form of shaping the climate of opinion' is the key objective."[133] The *Canadian Journal of Women and the Law*, established by the National Association of Women and the Law in 1985, greatly facilitated the publication of this legal literature. In the 1960s and 1970s, according to Manfredi, there were only fifty entries on the subject of equality in the *Index to Canadian Legal Periodical Literature*. Between 1981 and 1992, there were 283.[134]

More than anything else, LEAF has been aided by the Court Challenges Program. It began in the mid-1970s as a government agency to provide financial assistance for important court cases, those that tested language and equality rights guaranteed in the Charter, and thus to develop principles for deciding when discrimination has occurred.[135] Funding was provided for research and consultation before cases went to court, for the actual process of litigation, for research on the possible effects of court decisions, and for strategic meetings to promote equality and facilitate access to it.[136] Between "1982 and 1991, LEAF received $1.4 million in general funding and at least $84,400 to finance its intervener participation in six cases."[137] In fact, federal and provincial sources amounted to about half of LEAF's entire budget.[138]

LEAF's position has been adopted on 37 of 52 issues in the 31 Supreme Court cases in which it has participated since 1988 ... it has been the most frequent non-government intervener in Charter cases, intervening in almost ten percent of the Supreme Court's Charter cases decided since 1988. LEAF also accounts for about fifteen percent of all non-government interventions, and appears in approximately one of every five Charter cases that attract at least one intervener. Moreover, its success rate (71.2%) has been more than twice as high as that of Charter claimants in general (30%).[139]

Manfredi concludes by discussing the reasons for feminist success in Canada. First, a set of general interpretive principles that can be exploited for specific litigation has been introduced. This makes it possible to bring about policy changes and to develop strategic alliances with other groups. (The Canadian Civil Liberties Association and REAL Women, a right-to-life group, have been its only serious opponents.) Second, there are extremely close ties with the Court Challenges Program (members sitting on its board of directors, its advisory committee, and its equality panel), various human rights tribunals with similar interests, university law schools, and women's organizations.[140] Third, there is government support from both the Court Challenges Program and Status of Women Canada (its own lobby group within the federal government and provincial counterparts). Finally, strategies have been developed by the United Nations. Canada, in turn, has ratified documents produced by the United Nations. "Once LEAF was established, it adopted a self-styled campaign of influencing the influencers that included fostering supportive legal scholarship. LEAF organizers clearly considered this to be much more than an academic exercise. 'The shaping of the Charter will be an intensely political process,' Sheila McIntyre explained to fellow feminists, [one that is] 'far more responsive to public pressure than [to] constitutional law.'"[141]

Throughout this analysis of equality legislation in Canada, we have pointed out the judicial activism on the part of feminist interest groups. We are now in a position to put their role in broader perspective. Morton and Knopff define the "Court Party" as a coalition of groups that have promoted judicial power over legislative power.

In addition to litigating on behalf of their respective policy agendas, Court Party groups use the Charter in a variety of other ways. They employ the Charter and its judicial glosses as symbolic resources in the normal course of political lobbying. In an ongoing campaign of influencing the influencers, they attempt to affect Charter interpretation through Charter scholarship, the politics of judicial appointment, and judicial education seminars after appointment. A well-organized group pursues the judicial protection and expansion of its Charter turf on all of these fronts simultaneously.[142]

The authors add that

In addition to legislative and financial resources, the Canadian state provides the Court Party with a rapidly expanding rights bureaucracy. This resource is what Les Pal describes as "positional support": "access for some groups and not others to information or to decision-makers or to a formal or quasi-formal role in decision making ... This new rights bureaucracy includes courts themselves, of course, but also administrative tribunals, human rights commissions, legal departments, law reform commissions, law schools, and judicial education programs. Together, these constitute a web of bureaucratic nodes for initiating, funding, legitimating, and implementing the rights claims of Court Party interests.[143]

They note also that these equality players have affiliations with many agencies. Ultimately, they accuse the universities.

In this chapter, we have argued that something has gone seriously wrong with women's studies. With respect to the history of women, a profound change in scholarship has taken place over the last few decades. Information on women was once much less widely available than it is now, either because scholars were not interested in women, or because they lacked access to women. Female informants might have been off limits to male anthropologists. Or female accounts might not have been written down. This history has now been reclaimed and the problems faced by women exposed, thanks largely to the interest and tenacity of female scholars. As a result of this scholarship, much of which is now done by and taught by those in the field of women's studies or by women in other fields, our view of the world is more complex and nuanced.

But this field has been infiltrated – we dislike using that word but have found no adequate alternative – by ideological feminists. They have tried out several excuses for doing so: the alleged invisibility of women, the alleged need for a social revolution, and even the allegedly flawed notion of scholarship itself. They were cautious for a while but gradually realized that they had no need for caution. They referred openly to "engaged scholarship" and the need for partisan politics within the university or even within the classroom. To the degree that female scholars considered themselves a women's political movement and wanted to improve women's role in society, they approved of this new dimension of women's studies. More recently, some have decided that scholarship and politics are incompatible. A few have taken the risk of acknowledging that to be in women's studies means to accept not only gynocentric orthodoxy but also ideological misandry.

Clearly, women's studies has been turned into a front for feminist ideology. How could there really be a front in the old Marxist sense? Because gender has replaced class as the all-purpose explanation. And because that change has coincided with the rhetoric of pluralism. And because this ideological worldview has become so firmly entrenched in popular culture that it is hard to stand back far enough to see the problem. This takes us to the topic of our final chapter: a quiet revolution.

11

Misandry v. Equality:
A Quiet Revolution

This is no simple reform. It really is a revolution. Sex and race because they are easy and visible differences have been the primary ways of organizing human beings into superior and inferior groups and into the cheap labour on which this system still depends.[1]

God knows, in the last twenty-five years, man as "the enemy" has certainly emerged [within feminism].[2]

The title of this book, like the first and third volumes of this trilogy, includes the word "misandry." We define "misandry" as hatred of men. It is therefore the counterpart of misogyny, hatred of women. We showed in part 1 of this book that misandry has become acceptable in public debates mediated by journalists, talk show hosts, academics, and other shapers of public opinion. In the court of public opinion during the 1990s, men were routinely stereotyped in connection with high-profile cases. They were routinely attacked by feminist ideologues as a class of demons ("satanic ritual abusers"), sexual abusers, sexual harassers, and mass murderers. Even Karen DeCrow, former president of the National Organization for Women, noticed the phenomeon. Hence the second epigraph for this chapter.

We shifted attention in part 2, though, from misandry to gynocentrism. The latter, we said, is a worldview based on the implicit or explicit belief that the world revolves around women. It is therefore the counterpart of androcentrism, a worldview based on the implicit or explicit belief that the world revolves around men. Our point was that gynocentrism has become de rigueur behind the scenes in law courts and government bureaucracies, which has resulted in systemic discrimination against men. This focus on gynocentrism continued into part 3, where we examined the role of academics in creating the new worldview.

In this brief concluding chapter, we tie up some loose ends by discussing the relation between misandry and gynocentrism, the underlying premises

of ideological feminism with those things in mind, the strategies that ideological feminists have used, ideological feminism as a revolutionary worldview, and the link between this "quiet revolution" and earlier revolutions.

Misandry and gynocentrism are not necessarily linked at all. People can be
preoccupied with their own needs and interests without denying those of
other people, much less hating them. And so it is, no doubt, for many feminists. They want sexual equality, period. Other feminists are more preoccupied with the problems faced by women, some devoting their lives to the
cause. These women are clearly gynocentric. But even they are not necessarily misandric (just as androcentric men are not necessarily misogynistic
or, for that matter, just as Christians are not necessarily anti-Jewish).[3] But
some women do become misandric (just as some men become misogynistic
and some Christians anti-Semitic). What transforms a nonideological
worldview into an ideological one is the presence of not only essentialism
(the focus on "us" and "our" virtues or needs) but also dualism (the focus
on "them" and "their" vices or just deserts). There is nothing subtle about
ideology, but there is something subtle about the ways in which people
adopt it. Dualism involves hatred, after all, and who believes in that? No
one. Certainly not consciously. Those who do hate, therefore, must find
ways not merely of justifying it or even excusing it but of denying it even
to themselves.

But wait. Even though misandry is not an inherent feature of gynocentrism, it is an inherent *possibility* (just as misogyny is an inherent possibility of androcentrism). If the world revolves around women, then it follows
that nonwomen – which is to say, men – are irrelevant except for purposes
of sexual pleasure (something that even some heterosexual women are willing to forego on ideological grounds) or reproduction (which requires
nothing more than a "teaspoonful of sperm"). All it takes to produce
misandry is the ideological proposition that "they" are not merely irrelevant but inadequate or evil. Women, including egalitarian feminists, find it
easy to scoff at those prissy critics who insist on pointing this out. Unfortunately, they do so by ignoring history and what it reveals about the
human tendency to simplify problems by resorting to ideologies. That tendency was present even among those who produced the biblical tradition.[4]
Not everything in that tradition is as lofty as the Book of Hosea, say, or the
Sermon on the Mount. Some sections are not so easily admired, at least not
today. According to the Old Testament, many ancient Israelites had nothing but loathing for their "heathen" neighbours.[5] According to the New
Testament, some early Christians had nothing but hostility for "the Jews."[6]

In theory, as we say, only gay women can take feminist ideology to its
logical conclusion: separation of women from men. Most women, especially those with sons, are more willing to compromise. But, as we say also,

in connection with Daphne Patai's theory of "heterophobia," even straight women sometimes find it expedient to support or at least tolerate the latent separatism of feminist ideology. Implicitly or explicitly, directly or indirectly, consciously or subconsciously, many women – not merely a tiny minority of lesbians – either support or tolerate a movement that deliberately fosters excessive fear of men (and fear of life in general)[7] and therefore the development of policies and laws intended to make the world safe for women by discouraging contact with men. Even though misandry is generated by an elite stratum of gynocentric academics, therefore, its institutionalization presents all women (and therefore men) with serious legal and moral problems. It is easy to recognize overt hatred and condemn it but not so easy to recognize covert hatred and, given political conditions, condemn it. Feminist ideologues have found ways of embedding misandry in culture, ultimately in the form of law, without calling it that. Even men find it hard to see systemic discrimination against themselves, although that situation is changing, just as women once found it hard to see systemic discrimination against themselves.

This book has identified one fundamental feature of the laws, American and Canadian, that now govern relations between men and women: systemic discrimination against men. By "systemic discrimination," we refer to several things.

First, legal discrimination against men is part of a pattern with deep roots in culturally transmitted beliefs, not merely an isolated phenomenon. Anyone who looks can see this pattern in laws governing affirmative action, pay equity, maternal custody, child support, pornography, prostitution, sexual harassment, and violence against women. In all cases, directly or indirectly, men are identified exclusively as the villains (even though that sometimes amounts, as in the case of affirmative action, to the villainy of their ancestors).

Second, legal discrimination against men is pervasive, not merely a collection of anomalies. The same arguments are used over and over again, differing just slightly from one context to another. The most obvious example is provided by those who believe that rape is only one extreme point along a continuum, which begins with the mildest expression of heterosexual interest and ends with murder.

Third, legal discrimination against men is the result of both conscious and subconscious motivations. This is more complicated than it sounds. Ideological feminists are certainly prejudiced against men, and they are certainly aware that men are paying the price for legal changes that benefit women. Some of them believe that men deserve to pay that price. Others merely do not care. But most of the people involved in passing or administering laws are not ideological feminists. They are not directly (or even indirectly in some cases) motivated by hostility or indifference. Egalitarian feminists care about society as a whole, at least in theory. Some might genuinely care about men but not see any other way of achieving their goals for women. Others might believe that men, given their godlike power, cannot be seriously harmed in any case. And what about men themselves, or at least those who have some say in what goes on? Some male politicians care about nothing more than getting votes; if more women vote than men, they might think, then so be it. Not very different are some male academics or journalists and other public figures; for whatever personal or professional reason, whether cynical or altruistic, they want the approval of women and look the other way when considering the cost for men. The result is a mentality that accepts systemic discrimination against men. Almost anything can be said about men or done to men, in short, without the expectation of a public outcry. Only now is that mentality being questioned and even challenged.

The premise that underlies systemic discrimination against men is that women need to be protected from the power of men in every aspect of daily life. And underlying that premise are the various characteristic features of feminist ideology. We have discussed them several times in this book but find it worthwhile to summarize them now in connection with the specific topics under discussion here.

Essentialism and dualism are really two sides of the same coin; each implies the other. Essentialism is about "us," dualism about "them." In other words, "we" as a class are good (victims), and "they" as a class are evil (oppressors). Both are most clearly revealed, simultaneously, in ideological discussions about child custody. Ideological feminists classify fathers routinely as people who should not be trusted with children (and are not needed by children in any case, except for support payments). At the same time, they classify mothers routinely as people who should be. Forced to choose in the interest of children, they claim, the law should side with mothers and against fathers. Even when they do not feature essentialism, though, ideological feminists do feature dualism. Every topic that we have discussed in this book is founded on the premise that women are innocent victims who must use legal measures to curb the oppressive and overwhelming power of men. In every case, according to ideological feminists, the problem is not merely a legal anomaly but a legal principle that is rooted ultimately in a clash between two irreconcilable worldviews. And the worldview of women (along with political allies), they claim, must destroy that of men. They make this point most dramatically in connection with violence against women, of course, but they make precisely the same point in connection with sexual harassment and even pornography.

The other characteristic features of ideology follow from those two and are all closely interrelated. Hierarchy, for instance, is a logical result. If "we" are good and "they" are evil, after all, then it follows that the former rank higher in a moral hierarchy than the latter do. In a democracy, especially one that is based increasingly on opinion polls, that gives "us" an enormous political advantage over "them." One likely result, as we have already suggested with regard to identity politics in general and affirmative action in particular, is the development of a caste system (or, if you prefer, the replacement of one caste system with another). One result of dualism is selective cynicism: adopting a cynical attitude toward "them" (but not toward people like "us"). Even though the most ideological of feminists would admit that not all men are likely to beat their wives and molest or abandon their children, they have shifted the burden of proof. Men are guilty, in this moral universe, unless proven innocent. In that case, why not try to change divorce and custody laws accordingly?

Ideological feminism is a collectivist movement, which is why adherents make claims about women (or men) as a class. They must explain away individual women who disagree with this or that claim – and there are many in some cases – as the victims of "false consciousness" and thus the dupes of men. This is certainly what happens in connection with pornography. Ideological feminists make it clear that women who tolerate or even approve of it are beneath contempt, female Uncle Toms. Because collectivist movements care about classes of people, not about the fate of any individual, they embrace an ethic of consequentialism. And because the end justifies the means in connection with the fate of individuals, it does so in connection with the fate of classes as well. Consider the arguments in favour of affirmative action or pay equity. Sure, say feminists (and not only ideological ones), these programs discriminate against men. But that means is justified, they add, by its noble end: creating a "level playing field." They use the same rationale, at least privately, to justify the scams that we have discussed in connection with statistics abuse. Okay, they might admit when cornered, so lying to the public and even to government officials is wrong. Sort of. But, they might add to themselves and their supporters, doing so is justified in light of the struggle to improve things for women. And once the deed is done, it can never be undone; phony statistics continue to do their job, still cited repeatedly and still embedded in public consciousness, no matter how hard anyone tries to challenge them. When repeated like mantras, they create their own reality.

Three more characteristic features of ideological feminism (or any other ideology) should be discussed together, because they are three aspects of the same thing. Revolutionism is about using power, whether physical or legal, to force society into radically new directions. This characteristic explains the impatience of ideological feminists with reform, which they regard as an obstacle in the way of revolution. In universities, they campaign not merely for the admission of new ideas about women (and men) but also for the replacement of one epistemology with another. Without that, they believe, women will be confined to tinkering with this or that reform; the new world will never be born. And utopianism is the belief that humans can remake this world to such an extent that the result really would be, in effect, a new world. In this new world, women would no longer be faced with violence from men. Moreover – and this is the sine qua non of utopianism – they would no longer be faced with any limits at all to personal freedom or fulfillment. (We say "personal," because collectivism would no longer be necessary; having achieved their class goals, women could end the class struggle against men.) Women would no longer have to choose between children and careers, for instance, and no longer have to endure the slightest emotional discomfort in the presence of men. In fact, they would no longer have to live with men at all; this would be a utopia for women, not for women and men. Knowingly or unknowingly, this is why some feminists have pushed for laws and policies that separate the sexes by making heterosexual interactions, including the most harmless words or gestures, increasingly perilous for men. As for quasi-religiosity, this is the ultimate context of "heterophobia." It is surely no accident that some of the phenomena associated with ideological feminism are strongly reminiscent of overtly religious ones. Consider only some of the most obvious ones that we have discussed in this book: Take Back the Night parades, for instance, and memorials for the victims of Marc Lépine. These events are overtly secular, at least in most cases, but they are covertly religious in several important ways. For one thing, they draw heavily on religious prototypes (liturgies, say, or pilgrimage shrines). Moreover, they focus on collective identity and collective mission. In short, they generate an emotional intensity that can be compared legitimately only with overtly religious events.

Theory is one thing, reality another. How have feminists, especially those of the ideological kind, actually achieved their goals so effectively? What have their characteristic strategies been? To produce the pattern of systemic discrimination against men (even as a by-product) and to represent its underlying premise (along with the premises that underlie that), ideological feminists have had to invent or refine several specifically legal strategies. We can identify at least five distinct types.

One type of strategy involves defining or redefining a problem so that it has ideological significance and political power. It is true that some of the legal changes demanded by feminists over the past several decades originated in problems that they faced by entering both higher education and the work force in massive numbers for the first time. But some of them originated in the emotional confusion of heterosexual relations at a time of rapid change. To establish these legal changes as legitimate solutions to bona fide problems, feminists have exploited ambiguity in their definitions.

Even when quantitative information is available, though, it can be manipulated. Some feminists have used aggregated statistics, for instance, which have skewed the results to support their claims. Others have fabricated statistics. Even academic feminists have indulged in statistics abuse by publishing false statistics in professional journals, often specialized ones that are accountable only to feminist editorial boards.

Having defined or redefined problems ideologically, these feminists have had to get them onto the agendas of justices and legislators. This goal has always involved the mobilization of resentment. Like all other activists, they have made effective use of the mass media. They have appeared on talk shows, for instance, and written for popular magazines. Almost made to order for this purpose have been highly sensationalized trials about child abuse (the McMartins), domestic violence (Lorena Bobbit and O.J. Simpson), sexual harassment (Clarence Thomas), mass murder (Marc Lépine), and so on. Public debate over cases of this kind has not only raised the consciousness of women (and many men) but also politicized the legal process more than ever.[8]

This strategy would have been inconceivable without the prevalence of identity politics. Ideological feminists have usually relied on public perceptions about the vaunted power of men and therefore on the rhetoric of either victimology (defining women as a victim class) or demonology (defining men as an oppressor class) – or both. They have sometimes relied, however, on the distinctive vulnerability of men. Because men have traditionally seen themselves – and have been seen by society – as protectors of women (and children), feminists have found it easy to shame men into accepting whatever is allegedly necessary to protect women (and children). Moreover, most men are still adept at maintaining a "stoical" attitude: not complaining when attacked, especially by women. Feminists have found, not surprisingly, that most men would at least keep quiet about their own victimization by "gendered analysis."

To be successful, these feminists have had to expand their networks on a continuing basis. A few radical activists can do very little, but an army of angry citizens can do a great deal. Elected officials cannot afford to ignore them. Even appointed officials, in many cases, must be confirmed by government bodies that are responsive to political movements (a fact that Clarence Thomas learned the hard way). With all that in mind, feminist ideologues have taught women how to be politically savvy, how to "get things done" in legislatures, how to initiate e-mail campaigns, how to contact journalists and political representatives, how to arrange press conferences, how to organize boycotts or petitions, how to raise money for worthy causes, how to shame or intimidate the men who run legal or political institutions, and so forth. Among the most important way of expanding feminist networks, however, has been to infiltrate institutions.

Working within the political system, ideological feminists have managed to create special bureaucracies for women that have functioned as advocacy organizations operating within the government itself. In addition, they have fostered the appointment of feminist lawyers to human rights tribunals at various levels of government. These tribunals can now force government departments to create laws that suit women or to implement them more effectively.

Not all women vote for feminist or feminist-influenced candidates. Ideological feminists would still have had a hard time, therefore, without cultivating other segments of the population. To ensure that they will always have a majority, feminists have made alliances with minority groups under the banner of "diversity" or "multiculturalism" (even though the main beneficiaries have always been women). As a result, the process of legalizing gynocentrism (with its shadow of misandry) has taken on a life of its own in city councils, state or provincial legislatures, federal governments, and international organizations such as the United Nations.

Ironically, some feminist ideologues have probably been disappointed to find that women are not always losers and men not always winners (although not one would ever admit that). When women at home are doing well, therefore, feminists often emphasize the deplorable condition of women in other parts of the world. Who would care about what happens to American or Canadian men in universities, after all, when the women of Afghanistan or Iran are excluded even from elementary schools? Never mind that elected officials here are responsible for making laws that affect their own citizens, including men, and not for laws that affect the citizens of other countries.

Ideological feminists have become major players in our legal systems as researchers, lawyers, judges, and bureaucrats. Not surprisingly, they have come up with several specifically legal strategies: ways of using the law to serve the interests of women.

One obvious strategy is to create new laws. To do this, they have sometimes referred proposed legislation from lower to higher administrative levels, federal laws having more status than state or provincial ones and criminal laws having more status than civil ones. Sometimes, though, they have referred proposed legislation from higher administrative levels to lower ones, national governments having more clout at home than international organizations. They have done that surreptitiously by coaxing their governments to sign international treaties with conservative riders, or opt-out clauses, but later coaxing them to abandon those riders and join the "progressive" world. Recently, the World Court gave feminists a "vagina dentata." No, not the Freudian metaphor about neurotic fear of an imaginary threat. This is a real threat, one with "teeth": taking legal action against recalcitrant governments.

Another strategy is to change constitutions or reinterpret existing ones. Ideological feminists in Canada have managed to get protections for women written into the nation's Charter of Human Rights and Freedoms, which is attached to the Constitution. American feminists have lobbied hard for the Equal Rights Amendment but have not yet been successful. Even so, they have been able to reinterpret constitutional amendments through court challenges, reinterpreting the Fourteenth Amendment to include special protections for women, say, or the Commerce Clause to regulate child support and pornography.

These feminists have used several additional legal strategies, including biding their time by lobbying for incremental changes (creating very broad and ambiguous definitions and then adding greater specificity for women by means of court challenges or linguistic inflation); shifting negative rights to positive ones (from equality of opportunity, based on the negative right to freedom from discrimination, to equality of result); changing strict standards for legal tests, which assess the constitutionality of laws, to moderate ones; creating new standards (replacing the "reasonable person" with the "reasonable woman," objectivity with subjectivity, reason with feeling, damage with discomfort); exploiting emergency situations to give women the benefit of any doubt (police interventions, for instance, before charges are laid); bypassing due process in the interest of quick processing (establishing special courts, for example, that lack the usual safeguards); exploiting exceptions to establish new norms, even though doing so creates double standards (creating modified equality of opportunity, with special protections for pregnant women, and then expanding it to argue for equality of result); and encouraging change by establishing bureaucracies and industries to implement, reinterpret, and extend the law or its quasi-legal version of codes and policies into all institutions (universities, corporations, government departments – you name it – which are either bribed with financial "incentives" or intimidated with specific penalties).

Yet another strategy is returning to the barricades. When people do notice and protest the legal revolution – those who do are often men, because gynocentric legislation discriminates against them – they are immediately attacked as "masculinists," shamed into conformity, or sent for "reeducation," "sensitivity training," or whatever it might be called. When all other strategies fail, ideological feminists have pulled out their trump cards: "violence against women," the "glass ceiling," and "backlash." They have always realized that few people would be willing to challenge what has long been presented as conventional wisdom, even though the statistics that support them are sometimes skewed or even fabricated.

Although these strategies have not always worked the first time, they have gradually had a massive effect on the legal systems of both the United States and Canada.

Why do many people still find it hard to see the magnitude of these changes? Because they have been disguised. Ideological feminists have hidden behind various fronts. Some of these fronts have been linguistic, mainly euphemisms: human rights, parental rights, or even children's rights fronting for women's rights; equality for superiority; gender balance or equity for affirmative action; gender-based analysis for feminist analysis; gender studies for women's studies; women's studies for feminism; targets for quotas; diversity for uniformity; and reform for revolution. Other fronts are more than linguistic (postmodernism being a front for ideologies, for instance, and pluralism for essentialism). These fronts cannot, actually, be separated so easily. They all rely heavily on rhetoric, which takes on a life of its own; euphemisms become integrated in a worldview that presupposes them. Ideological feminists have hidden also as insiders. They have infiltrated institutions such as government bureaus, human right's tribunals (which can trump government departments), the mass media, and professional societies by demanding that more women – that is, feminists – be appointed.

All of this amounts to a cultural revolution, we suggest, not merely the inevitable drift caused by "change." It might be tempting to dismiss us as alarmists and thus not so different from the ideologues we are attacking were it not for the fact that feminists themselves often discuss their movement in overtly revolutionary terms. Hence this chapter's first epigraph, by Gloria Steinem. For ideological feminists, "revolution" has exclusively positive connotations. You need not actually join a Goddess cult, after all, to believe that the most important historical change since the origin of patriarchy has been the advent of a movement to overthrow it. That idea could be accepted by liberal feminists (who believe that the elimination of gender distinctions will make true equality possible for the first time in history) almost as easily as by ideological feminists (who believe that the destruction of patriarchy will initiate a return to paradise). Even the nineteenth-century suffragists, most of them very respectable members of society, considered their movement the harbinger of a new era. They argued that giving women the vote would provoke a radical break with the past and usher in a new golden age of peace, harmony, justice, connectedness, or whatever.

On this, at least, we agree with ideological feminists. Their movement has indeed been revolutionary. We disagree only on our evaluation of that revolution. If equality had remained the chief goal of feminists, it would have continued and enhanced the liberal revolution that began, falteringly, more than two hundred years ago. But equality has not remained the goal of all feminists. Some of them, fewer in number than egalitarian feminists but greater in influence by the late twentieth century, have moved considerably beyond political equality in connection with "life, liberty, and the pursuit of happiness" or, in the Canadian version, "peace, order, and good government." What they want, and what they are in the process of achieving with the support of their allies and under the protection of postmodernism, is either utopian or dystopian, depending on your point of view: a radical reorganization of society, one that requires either writing new constitutions or reinterpreting current ones in ways that would have seemed not merely dangerous but unintelligible to their original authors, certainly those of the eighteenth century.

There is something quasi-religious about secular, political, ideologies, as Mircea Eliade observed decades ago. Mark Cimini argues that ideological feminism functions as a religion, as the functional equivalent of Christianity or any other traditional religion. He argues in addition, however, that the American government supports this religion – it not only legislates but also taxes citizens on that basis – and therefore breaches the wall of separation between church and state.[9]

Ideological feminism must therefore be discussed as a revolutionary movement in the same sense as the movements that produced other radical revolutions – in France, Russia, Germany, China, and so on. How did we get here? No revolution comes out of the blue or for any one reason. We all passed history tests in high school by writing about the many causes of this or that revolution and how they converged at a particular moment in circumstances that might otherwise have had no importance. And so it is in this case.

Like many revolutions, this one originated not with those who had the most to gain economically but with those who had most to contribute intellectually. In short, it originated among the members of an educated elite. They were in college during the 1960s, absorbed the Marxist tradition, and then modified it to suit their own needs. Even though women were dissatisfied with the lack of respect they found in neo-Marxist, or New Left, circles, they found that this environment provided them with valuable tools. Among the most valuable were literary and critical techniques, known collectively as "critical theory," established by the Frankfurt School of Marxism. Out went old-style rabble rousing among the workers (who were growing fewer due to economic changes, in any case, and played hardly any role in the new movement). In came clever, sophisticated, hermeneutical critiques of bourgeois and especially of patriarchal culture. The movement prevailed only among students, at first, because only they could understand the critiques (or had time to study them). By the 1980s, though, many of those students had become "tenured radicals."[10] Eventually, they became heads of departments or lawyers, judges, and politicians.

By the 1990s, this revolution had entered a new phase that was made possible by the Internet. No longer were ideological points of view on either side of the political spectrum limited to a few initiates at universities and their immediate social or professional networks. Websites welcomed everyone. And just as ordinary people began investing eagerly and heavily in the stock market, ordinary people began reading and responding to what they found on the Internet. Many observers warned of websites produced by right-wing ideologues, who were obviously dangerous because of their ignorance, and the population at large. Few warned of websites produced by left-wing ideologues who were anything but ignorant. Some feminist websites spread information that all women (and many men) found useful in their quest for reform in the interest of equality. Others spread information that ideologues found useful in their quest for revolution in the interest of something other than equality (though usually in the name of equality). A public debate emerged over the government's role in monitoring the Internet, true, but only in connection with pornography and right-wing hate literature; no one ever went after sites purveying the hate literature of ideological feminists.

After the collapse of communism in Eastern Europe (and its unofficial collapse in China), Marxism per se declined. But neo-Marxism morphed directly into postmodernism. Many aspects – its focus on the problem of "hegemony," say, and the need for "unmasking," "exposing," "deconstructing," and other forms of "subversion" – remained unchanged. It could be argued in addition that neo-Marxism morphed indirectly into ideological feminism and several closely related ideologies on the political left. It took very little imagination to replace the word "bourgeoisie" with "patriarchy" and "class" with "gender."

Despite all the rhetoric and techniques derived from neo-Marxism, not all ideological feminists make the connection with neo-Marxism. And with good reason. Another factor sometimes hides it. Marxism, both old-style and new-style, can be traced back to the Enlightenment and its dream of creating a utopia based on reason. But some feminists rejected the part about reason, which, they argued, was inherently "male." Their search for a female essence led them to neo-Romanticism and its dream, when applied to the collectivity and taken to its logical conclusion, of creating a utopia based on nation or race. In one notorious case, this was called "blood and soil." Ideological feminists replaced both "class" *and* "race" with "gender." The result is thus an ironic marriage (you should pardon the patriarchal expression) of both the Enlightenment and Romanticism.

Long before the turn of the century, ideological feminists were earning graduate degrees and becoming university professors. But just as the civil rights movement had been overtaken by the black power movement slightly earlier, egalitarian feminism was overtaken in the universities by ideological feminism. Integration was definitely not the goal. It was separatism of one kind and degree or another. With that in mind, new programs were established within old departments and, best of all, new departments or even new "disciplines" were established. The most important were women's studies, gender studies, or queer studies (fronts, as we say, for feminist ideology or closely allied gay ideology) and cultural studies (a front for closely allied postmodernist doctrine). For various reasons, mainly political ones – no university wanted to be seen as anti-women, for instance, because so many women were entering as students – these new disciplines were left largely immune to academic criticism. Even as other feminists have rejoiced in the successful entry of women into every sphere of life, ironically, ideological feminists in universities have nursed grievances and mobilized resentment. And they have taken their revolution to the streets, as it were, by training ideologically motivated cadres of lawyers, journalists, social workers, social scientists, statisticians, bureaucrats, psychologists, and therapists who have created the industries that focus on child support, sexual harassment, and so on – with their vested interests.

As we have said repeatedly, not all feminists are ideologically oriented, not necessarily even in universities. Most women surely prefer integration to separation, in fact, and reform to revolution. So how can we explain the success of ideological feminists? And they have been astonishingly successful, by the way, if success is measured in terms of legislation and bureaucratic sleight of hand.

For one thing, most citizens – both women and men – are likely to support what is clearly in their own interest. And this is appropriate, by and large, in any modern democracy. Legislation to mandate affirmative action or prevent sexual harassment, for instance, is seemingly in the interest of all women (although the latter will increasingly be in the interest also of men who work for women). The fact that this legislation can be motivated by something other than the desire for justice or belief in egalitarianism, that it can have either unintended or undesirable effects, is not disturbing enough to prevent most women from supporting it anyway. In numbers and solidarity, after all, there is strength. And if the drive for new legislation comes from ideologues, even those who sometimes say or write loony things, so be it. What matters, many believe, is that all women stand to benefit in the long run from anyone who expands public perceptions of what women can do. Very few women or even feminists would agree with much of what Andrea Dworkin says, but even fewer would be willing to denounce her promotion of hatred. On the contrary, most would rather apologize for her as someone who nonetheless "pushes the boundaries" for women.

Moreover, modern democracies are governed largely according to public opinion. And public opinion in our society supports altruistic rhetoric, at least in theory. Even though democracies explicitly encourage citizens to vote on the basis of their own needs, after all, they also implicitly encourage citizens to consider the needs of society as a whole. Many are swayed by the ideals of justice and tolerance – today, these ideals are often known as "pluralism," "diversity," and "multiculturalism" – which might or might not coincide with personal or group self-interest. And feminists have been very effective in causing citizens, except for those who overtly oppose feminism, to equate their movement with justice and tolerance (an equation that is usually correct in the case of egalitarian feminism). Not surprisingly, they equate opposition to these ideals with tyranny. Feminist policies are explained in ways that promote, or seem to promote, both justice (even though that is often confused with revenge) and tolerance. Many women sincerely identify themselves with these ideals. So do many men, for that matter, including white men.

Who is going to argue, in public at any rate, that there could be anything wrong with "equity," a term derived from the exalted rhetoric of human rights and used in connection with civil rights for women, black people, gay people, and all other people who have experienced prejudice or discrimination? The ability to examine it in connection with specific claims and specific proposals by specific political organizations or leaders, unfortunately, is not one that our society has cultivated. Even universities now encourage the deconstruction only of "traditional" ideas or institutions; others are granted privileged status and thus immunity to challenge.

This brings up the strategic alliance between ideological feminists and ideological gay people. The alliance was hardly inevitable for gay men. They could have tried to ally themselves with other men. Not all men's movements were receptive to gay men, true. But not all women's movements were open to gay women – in fact, not even all gay women were open to gay men or any other men – and that never discouraged lesbian feminists. Nonetheless, many gay men found it politically expedient to ride on the coattails of ideological feminists. Because feminists had already argued that women suffered under the gender system of patriarchy, all they had to do was show that gay men (and gay women) suffered just as much or even more under the same system. The alliance with feminism was almost inevitable for gay women. Much more easily than other women, they could take feminism to its ideological conclusion: separation from men.

Of importance here, though, is the mere fact that this alliance has made political sense. Two or more groups making the same arguments and demanding the same measures, after all, greatly strengthen the position of each. This is how "identity politics" works. Although any one group might have little in common with the others, all have at least one important thing in common: hostility toward whatever is considered the "dominant" or "traditional" culture. As the ironically traditional proverb has it, the enemy of my enemy is my friend.

In some ways, our society really is more tolerant than it once was. Very few people today would actually want to restore institutionalized discrimination against black people, gay people, or women. (In other ways, as we have shown in this book, our society tolerates and even demands institutionalized discrimination.) But more than tolerance is involved in the success of ideological feminism. The political lingua franca of our time is spoken only by those who claim to be victims. And this language, in turn, is tied up inextricably with emotionalism – that is, the glorification of emotion at the expense of reason.

Emotionalism, no less than nationalism and ethnocentrism, is clearly the direct descendant of Romanticism (although emotionalism, unlike nationalism and ethnocentrism, derives also from evangelical Protestantism).[11] But the current popularity of emotionalism cannot be explained entirely in that way. For one thing, it has been aggressively marketed by a consortium, as it were, of therapeutic industries. Pop psychology both dominates and permeates many fields, most obviously the field of entertainment. Daytime talk shows focus explicitly on therapy. "Reality shows" reward contestants for screaming about their emotional pain, weeping over their abuse, and revealing their most intimate feelings. Crime shows provoke unrealistic fear. Like sitcoms, most pop songs rely exclusively on sentimentality. Other songs satisfy the desire for "empowerment" by expressing rage and fostering resentment. Think of journalism. "In your face" news shows dominate the ratings. Advocacy replaces objectivity as the goal. And what about the courts? Victims give dramatic speeches in court to influence sentencing. Crusading ideologues argue that angry or fearful victims of domestic abuse are not guilty if they resort to murder. Others have reversed the principle of "innocent unless proven guilty" in connection with charges of sexual harassment. And the legislatures? They redefined marriage to bolster the self-esteem of gay people. Education? Reformers institute regulations designed to promote both personal and collective self-esteem at the expense of scholarship. Public life? People demand extravagant mourning for celebrities. Political correctness becomes a way of bolstering collective self-esteem. Officials give public apologies for brutal events or institutions that ended decades or even centuries earlier. Lobby groups define themselves in connection with collective victimization. Politicians claim to "feel your pain." Officials base policies on public opinion, rather than any coherent philosophy. And ecclesiastical authorities revise or reinterpret liturgies that function primarily to provide group therapy or "build community."

At the same time, as we say, feminist ideologues have promoted essentialism – especially the idea that women are innately guided more by feelings or intuitions, not ideas, and are therefore superior to men – by using the front of pluralism. Whether emotionalism in our time originated in the personal self-indulgence fostered by popular culture or the collective self-indulgence fostered by elite culture is debatable. The point is that these two phenomena are interdependent; each feeds on the other (and both on the anti-intellectual legacy of Romanticism). They make it easy and even necessary to couch all political claims in the rhetoric of victims (who deserve sympathy for their current or historic suffering) and victimizers (who deserve contempt).

All these things are happening at the same time, moreover, as unusually rapid social, economic, and technological change. Which came first, the chicken or the egg? It makes no difference for our purposes here. What does matter is the resulting stress, which leads directly, as it often has throughout history, to scapegoating and moral panics. People not only want but also need to identify the source of their anxiety and thus regain a sense of being in control over what would otherwise have to be understood as the random forces of a chaotic universe. The source of severe problems is seldom easy to identify correctly, though, because it is usually complex and ambiguous. These problems often have many causes, not just one. And some of them originate within ourselves as individuals or communities, not among those who can be considered outsiders. Western societies, like many others, have inherited a long tradition of dualism: seeing life in terms of good versus evil and, not coincidentally, "us" versus "them." Once "they" have been identified with evil and threat, a process backed up these days by ambiguous or even bogus statistics, it makes sense to use the law accordingly. And if constitutions get in the way of new legislation, having been written in naive or misguided times, then existing laws can be reinterpreted or implemented in appropriate ways by judges and bureaucrats on the advice of experts in the social sciences. It could be argued cynically, in fact, that these experts are produced by professional industries with vested interests in continuing social problems. The more problems that remain unsolved, after all, the more jobs for experts.

But in what sense is this a *quiet* revolution? The term "quiet revolution" originated in Quebec during the 1960s. After centuries of rural passivity and docility under the Roman Catholic Church, people decided to create a modern, dynamic, urban, and industrial society. Within a decade, life in Quebec had changed almost beyond recognition. People abandoned the old religion en masse. Convents and monasteries emptied. Cities and suburbs grew. Women entered the workforce. The birth rate fell dramatically. As for the ancien régime, a quasi-fascist one, it was quickly voted out of office for the first time in decades. The new regime, a liberal one, emphasized education, business, and bureaucracy (which took over many functions formerly given to the church). This quiet revolution was soon accompanied by a not-so-quiet one fueled by nationalism, which, in many ways, replaced Catholicism. Despite a few violent incidents, however, this revolution never turned into a rerun of the French Revolution. Politicians reorganized society from top to bottom, democratically, by changing public opinion in favour of reform and enacting legislation accordingly. The same strategy was used, slightly later, elsewhere in Canada and the United States. Although neither Marxists nor feminists in those places were aware of it, the quiet revolution in Quebec was a prototype for their movements.

Have all those movements, or even the one in Quebec, been entirely benign? The answer clearly depends on who is answering. Many people are better off, but others are worse off. Some problems have been solved, but new ones have been created. Even though democracy has been preserved, surely a good thing, an inherent problem of democracy – one that was well known to the founders of American democracy as the potential for mob rule – has been revealed. Democracy is a political system, albeit the safest one that we know, not a moral principle. Whether it promotes the good or not depends almost entirely on the moral awareness of voters – not on their moral sensitivity in any sentimental sense but on their ability to think analytically and critically about moral problems.

To the extent that feminism has endorsed egalitarianism, then, we are surely better off than we would have been without it. Every movement that supports equality, after all, strengthens the moral fabric of democracy. To the extent that feminism has endorsed ideology, on the other hand, we are surely worse off (although we should add, in fairness, that the feminist version of ideology is only one form among several and by no means the original one). What will happen in the future is beyond knowing, of course, but the fragmenting legacy of identity politics is not encouraging. We still face instititionalized polarization not only between men and women but also between blacks and whites and many other groups. In addition, we face the institutionalization of a group hierarchy analogous to caste (which we discuss in appendix 7).

The new century has produced a few signs of reversal. The most obvious one, for men and women, was public response to the events of 11 September 2001. For the first time in many years, it was widely and publicly intuited that *men* – those who tried to rescue people trapped in the World Trade Center, say, and those who fought the hijackers over Pennsylvania – could make a distinctive, valued, and necessary contribution to society. If those images of specifically masculine heroism remain fresh, then men can still hope to establish a healthy identity and thus help create a healthy society. But it would be unwise to see this, yet, as a decisive turning point. For one thing, the terrorists themselves were all men. Also, very different images of men have been purveyed for many years. Egalitarian feminists have argued that women can do everything that men can do, which leaves men with no possible source of identity. And ideological feminists have argued that women are better than men, which leaves men who believe them with a highly negative identity. The damage will not be undone in a day, a year, even a decade. Besides, an identity based exclusively on physical courage and physical aggression might prove no different from earlier forms of masculinity – the very situation that gave rise to problems for both women and men in the first place.

It is with this in mind that we will turn in the final volume, *Transcending Misandry*, to a discussion of men themselves – of men, that is, as distinct from public perceptions of men in popular culture and the effects of those perceptions on legislation. There, we will devote much more attention to men as seen through scholarship than through ideology. Meanwhile, our main points are that gynocentrism has entailed misandry and that misandry has been institutionalized as systemic discrimination in the laws of our countries and the policies of our institutions. This is not merely a matter of perception, even perception filtered through the mass media, but of the fundamental social, economic, and political forces that shape our lives. In some ways, changes over the past thirty years have been beneficial. They have made women full participants in society. In other ways, however, old problems have merely been replaced with newer ones.

We conclude this book on a note of pessimism. Like many other segments of our increasingly fragmented society, women now have a very heavy investment in the rhetoric of victimhood. Not all women, therefore, want to correct or even acknowledge the problems we have examined here. One way of perpetuating the struggle of women no matter how many gains are made is to identify the underlying problem as maleness itself, which can never be corrected (except by eliminating men in some way). Another is to make the standard of correction utopian, which can never be satisfied (except by establishing a totalitarian regime).

Appendices

Responding to Our Critics:
Spreading Misandry Revisited

Spreading Misandry, the first volume of this trilogy, sold well enough. Within a few months, in fact, it was reprinted. It sold so well, though, in part because of its controversial topic. Critics – we include here reviewers and talk show hosts, along with their guests and callers – either liked the book intensely or disliked it intensely. Only two reviewers occupied something like the middle ground. They said, in effect, ho hum. Though clearly irritated by the topic of our book, one reviewer was prepared to tolerate it as almost inevitable in a world preoccupied by gender. Because our point of view was necessary for academic balance, at least in theory, he admitted that this book was possibly useful for university libraries.

Those who liked the book deluged us with calls and letters to thank us for going public with this long-suppressed topic. A few offered to help us publicize the book. One was planning to make a documentary film on the topic. Among these supportive responses, the most poignant were from men who had personally encountered institutionalized bias against men. Most of these men, trying to make sense of things in the aftermath of divorce and custody battles, understood that the double standards they faced in court were closely related to the patterns of misandry we had discussed in connection with popular culture.

Those who disliked the book, on the other hand, were either contemptuously or ferociously hostile. A few resorted even to ad hominem attacks on us. One reviewer, for example, called us "Beavis and Butthead." Another called us "Robin Hood and Maid Marion" – but could not decide which of us was which! Yet some of these hostile critics raised interesting questions, and we would do well to answer them.

Some critics praised us for providing such relentless documentation of misandry in popular culture, but others scolded us for not being relentless enough. Even though we did not attempt a scientific study – we admitted that, although one critic accused us of "bragging" about not doing so – we did what we could with the resources available to us, enough to indicate the existence of a phenomenon worthy of more study.

A truly scientific study would have required much more money for personnel and travelling. For one thing, we would have required a sociologist to supervise the collection of data. To collect the data, moreover, we would have required people in randomly selected regions of the United States and Canada – urban, suburban, and rural – at randomly selected times over a decade, merely to monitor television viewing. We would have required additional people to monitor movies released in those regions at randomly selected venues – both cineplexes and "art houses" – during the same period. Other media would have required equivalent methods. Finding money to support this politically incorrect project was very hard in any case, but finding money to support it on a larger scale would have been impossible. Our stated aim was not to have the last word on this topic, in any case, but to establish the existence of a major problem and open it up for discussion – that is, to stimulate more research. The decade that we studied has now passed, but we would like very much to see some social-scientific microstudies of current popular culture.

Other critics ridiculed us for wasting time on popular culture, supposedly a trivial topic, in the first place. All of the productions we examined were, well, nothing more than entertainment. Why make a big fuss, they asked, over productions that no one takes seriously in the first place? But there are people who do, in fact, take popular culture seriously. And many of them, ironically, are feminists. They have never tolerated the trivialization of popular culture in connection with its characteristic portrayals of women. Negative portrayals, they say over and over again, indicate nothing less than rampant misogyny: hatred of women. It is worth noting one critic, therefore, who actually denied that the admittedly negative portrayals of men in popular culture have anything to do with hatred. According to this academic – she is the director of a feminist institute – these portrayals are merely innocent and amusing comments on the "foibles" of men. But would she say the same thing about the negative portrayals of women in popular culture – including rap, the one musical genre in which misogyny is still tolerated? If she did, she would be ostracized immediately by every feminist of her generation.

In this sense, the feminists – like the Marxists before them – have been correct. Entertainment really is never just entertainment, although it is nonetheless also that.[1] No matter how innocuous, it always reveals something about the society that produces it and – more importantly – about the society that consumes it. At the very least, it reveals familiar notions about the way things are – what could be called the prevalent worldview. Why do we need scholars to reveal these familiar notions? Precisely because they are so familiar. The more obvious something seems, after all, the easier it is to escape notice. To put it another way, entertainment must always be intelligible – and thus reasonably familiar – to those who experience it. Otherwise, there could be no suspension of disbelief.

Consider what actually happens when viewers watch a movie, say, or a television show. For an hour or two, they enter a world that is clearly not real but is nevertheless realistic enough to allow for the suspension of disbelief. All they know of the world being presented to them, however, is what they actually see on the screen and hear from the speakers. For all intents and purposes, during that one or two hours, this *is* the real world. In connection with portrayals of men and women during the 1990s, lamentably, movies and television shows were often characterized by extreme polarization: evil or inadequate men versus virtuous or victimized women.

If this were merely a theory about sexual polarization in mass entertainment, it might make very little difference to anyone except a few academics in fields such as popular culture and film studies. But we gathered a great deal of corroborating evidence from highly publicized events in real life during that same period – evidence that was not presented in the first volume but is presented in this second one. Was it purely a coincidence that men and women were sharply polarized in mass entertainment, after all, even as they were sharply polarized in the public square – even as one wing of a major political movement explicitly justified this polarization in ideological terms? Not likely.

But did misandry in popular culture have any effect on either men or women? Did it actually cause misandry in real life? Some reviewers, referring to misandric jokes and sitcoms, asked a few of their male friends or colleagues if they felt threatened by misandry. Not surprisingly, some of these men admitted nothing of the kind. Our immediate goal in *Spreading Misandry*, however, was to discuss not the psychological damage potentially done by misandry to boys and men (a topic that we will discuss in the final volume of this trilogy) but the moral damage done to society as a whole. To put it bluntly, double standards – hatred is verboten when directed toward women or minorities, in this case, but acceptable or even amusing when directed toward men – must undermine the moral fabric of any society. It is impossible to teach children effectively that hatred or revenge is wrong, in short, if they learn directly or indirectly that either is apparently right in some cases. It makes no moral sense. Given the facile arguments put forward in all seriousness by our *adult* critics, arguments that either ignore moral thinking altogether or distort it in the interest of political expediency, the future of our society looks bleak indeed. In that case, then, we should surely use this discussion of misandry as one way of fostering a larger discussion about the nature of society, democracy, civic virtue, ideology, political correctness, and so on.

There is no point in rehashing the old chicken-and-egg question. Movies do reflect cultural trends, to be sure, but they also create those trends. And that is not considered a controversial statement among scholars in film studies. If the world is presented in polarized terms often enough – and we presented enough evidence to indicate that this was indeed the case during the 1990s – it surely makes sense to suggest that viewers bring back something of that experience into the real world. Just as simulated violence probably desensitizes viewers to real violence, simulated polarization between men and women (or any other segments of the population) probably desensitizes viewers to real polarization. In other words, any discrepancy between the reel world and the real world becomes blurred; viewers come to take for granted that the gender stereotypes presented are just as realistic – not only familiar but also expected and acceptable – as the cars and clothing presented.

It will not do, therefore, to trivialize popular culture. Nor will it do to adopt a double standard, trivializing entertainment in connection with portrayals of men but not in connection with portrayals of women. And judging from the public response to *Spreading Misandry*, that is precisely what some feminists, including male feminists, continue to do, even though this double standard inherently undermines their own point of view about women in popular culture.

Some critics argued that we had ignored inconvenient features of popular culture. Not all movies and television shows, for instance, present viewers with negative stereotypes of men. Some actually glorify men. And we agree. But there is more to this glorification than meets the eye.

In *Spreading Misandry*, we showed that pop cultural misandry in the 1990s could be arranged along a continuum from the relatively trivial mockery of men to the much more disturbing dehumanization or even demonization of men. It is true that not all productions could be placed legitimately along this continuum. Some had nothing much to do with gender at all. Others were called misogynistic merely because they were *about* misogyny – and one of these, *In the Company of Men* (Neil LaBute, 1996), was really misanthropic rather than misogynistic. But still others did indeed glorify men.

How were men, as such, glorified in popular culture? Almost always in connection with combat of one kind or another. After a lull in the 1960s and 1970s the popularity of movies such as *Rambo: First Blood II* (George Cosmatos, 1985) and *Top Gun* (Tony Scott, 1986) indicated a revival of machismo during the next decade. Suddenly, soldiers and other fighters (often human-robotic hybrids) were "in" again. Arnold Schwarzenegger and Sylvester Stallone, to name only two action stars, were big hits at the box office in films that were often addressed directly and primarily to adolescent boys. But several new trends emerged in the 1990s and have continued into the new century.

For one thing, the old machismo now has a rival. The new machismo, as presented by Hollywood, is based on a rejection of mature manhood as defined by some *distinctive*, *necessary*, and *valued* contribution made to society by adult men. Even though the warrior archetype is a very dangerous one when other archetypes are either absent or marginalized, warriors of one kind or another – soldiers, say, or policemen – have often served society well. An earlier generation understood this. Gary Cooper is emotionally remote in *High Noon* (Fred Zinnemann, 1952), for instance, but he does what has to be done. He exemplifies both moral and physical courage. That much can hardly be said of the grotesquely vulgar and socially inadequate male protagonists of recent movies such as *Dumb and Dumber* (Peter Farrelli, 1994), *Dude, Where's My Car?* (Danny Leiner, 2000), *Freddy Got Fin-*

gered (Tom Green, 2001), *Deuce Bigalow, Male Gigolo* (Mike Mitchell, 1999), *The Animal* (Luke Greenfield, 2001), *Jay and Silent Bob Strike Back* (Kevin Smith, 2001), and so on.

Also, more and more of the action stars have been female. This is particularly true of fantasy and science fiction (genres that give them supernatural or genetically enhanced powers) and action pictures (in which Asian martial arts even out the anatomical difference between men and women). The most obvious examples on television, recently, have been Sarah Michelle Geller in *Buffy, the Vampire Slayer*, Jessica Alba in *Dark Angel*, and Jennifer Garner in *Alias*. In film, we have had Drew Barrymore, Lucy Liu, and Cameron Diaz in *Charlie's Angels* (Joseph McGinty Nichol, 2000). These productions focus directly or indirectly on the future. At the same time, productions that feature male fighters often focus directly or indirectly on the past.

World War II, for instance, has become more popular than ever as the venue for male action stars. Cinematic examples would include *The Thin Red Line* (Terrence Malik, 1998), *Saving Private Ryan* (Steven Spielberg, 1998), *Pearl Harbor* (Michael Bay, 2001), and *Hart's War* (Gregory Hoblit, 2002). The male characters in these movies are clearly glorified as self-sacrificing contributors to the common good of society, not ridiculed as buffoons or attacked as maniacal fiends. This should be good news for men, right? Not so fast. World War II, like Vietnam, was fundamentally different from more recent wars in one way of particular importance here. It was sexually segregated. Only young men engaged in combat, and only young men came home in body bags. Unlike Vietnam, however, World War II can still be considered morally acceptable (and militarily effective). In short, movies or shows about it encourage male viewers to feel nostalgic for a time when it was still possible to have a healthy masculine identity *as men*. In the real world of everyday life, that situation no longer exists. Sexual segregation is no longer acceptable. Even combat, the final frontier, is now in the process of being sexually desegregated, although the process will not be complete until a generation of young women has grown up with the expectation of being *drafted* into combat – and the rest of society has accepted the fact that young men will no longer be the only ones to come home from war in body bags.

Although these movies cannot be classified as misandric, therefore, they are just as disturbing from our point of view as misandric ones. They present men, consciously or subconsciously, with a central question: What can it possibly mean to be a man – not an individual, not a citizen, not a Christian or a Jew, not an athlete or an intellectual, but a *man* – in our society? And they provide no obvious answer. Any notion of masculinity based heavily or even exclusively on the heroism of young men during World War II is easily reduced to the level of nostalgic and atavistic fantasy in our time – just as the jousting tournament became a ceremonial vestige of aristocratic identity at a time of rapid military, economic, and social change. And as we say, combat is in the process of being sexually desegregated.

References to soldiers killed in World War II and Vietnam, say, are now routinely neutered on days of remembrance. Politicians and commentators – even advertisers – refer piously to the "men and women who fought for their country," even though all of those who actually fought were (by law) men. The same is true in connection with other forms of combat. Most people hailed the hundreds of New York "firefighters" who risked or even lost their lives while trying to rescue others on 11 September 2001 – even though all of them were men, not women. The mere fact of this anomaly, which prompted a few men to argue that we still need specifically male heroes (partly to offset all the specifically male villains presented in popular culture), indicates that political correctness will not solve the underlying problem of masculine identity and that the events of 11 September 2001 have not yet resulted in a renewed appreciation of men per se. Everyone appreciates the people who risked their lives, to be sure, but not everyone appreciates them specifically as men. The sexual desegregation of combat would surely be a good thing for providing an ultimate symbol of sexual equality, thus supporting all other forms of equality (and preventing the state from sacrificing citizens who happen to be male), but it would also be a bad thing to the extent that it would diminish the possibilities for establishing a specifically masculine identity. We will discuss the implications of that situation in *Transcending Misandry*.

Over and over again, critics asked rhetorically how so many misandric productions could have been created by men themselves? That question is based, however, on several unwarranted assumptions.

For one thing, these critics assumed that only men were (or are) involved in the entertainment industry, which was (and is) not the case. Despite its male director, for instance, the screenplay of *Thelma and Louise* (Ridley Scott, 1991) was written by Callie Khourie. And *He Said, She Said* (Marisa Silver; Ken Kwapis, 1990) had a female director as well as a male one. But at least two other unwarranted assumptions, much more important ones, are involved.

These critics assumed that those who create popular culture restrict themselves to productions that they personally consider virtuous or educational or edifying or whatever. In fact, nothing could be further from the truth. These folks are in business. They want to make money. They produce and sell, therefore, whatever they believe people will buy. And if misandry sells, as misogyny once did, then so be it.

Not many studio executives would be able to identify or even define misandry, of course, much less either to approve of it or disapprove of it. But their approval or disapproval is beside the point here. We have learned in connection with other forms of hatred that those who purvey it often do so unwittingly. Few in the 1920s deliberately fostered hatred on the vaudeville stage, but the ethnic jokes enjoyed by audiences then would now be considered racist and thus intolerable. Why, then, does misandry still sell? The quick answer is that misandry, unlike any other form of hatred, is still considered politically correct; no one is considered righteous for protesting against something that is generally considered acceptable. The long answer is more complicated.

In a very few cases, this phenomenon might be explained in connection with "self-hatred" (a phenomenon long known to Jews who worry about other Jews assimilating anti-Semitic stereotypes.) There are male converts to feminism, especially among academics. What they lose in self-esteem by being ashamed to be men they hope to gain in gratitude or admiration from women. But most men do not fit that description and strongly resent men who do. Why do *they* not protest against misandric productions? One quick answer is that they do, in fact, protest. Warren Farrell, for instance, has been doing so for years. [2] Another quick answer is that many men are afraid to protest. Some are afraid of losing their jobs, others their respect from their female colleagues (or wives and daughters), and still others their own identity as liberals. The long answer, once again, is more complicated.

Most men are still either unable to recognize misandry (although that situation, judging from public response to our book, is changing very quickly) or unwilling to do so. Why unwilling? Because acknowledging that men have a serious problem is tantamount to acknowledging that they are not in control of their own lives – that they are not, in other words, real men, especially if the problem confronting them is presented by women. On one radio talk show after another about *Spreading Misandry*, at least one man would call in to say that *he* felt perfectly secure about *his* masculinity and could not see why these so-called men were whining about misandry. One man said that he took pride in being oafish or piggish and thus deserved to be ridiculed by women (even though that makes no sense). Were they trying to convince women to pin medals on them? Were they trying to convince themselves that they had nothing to worry about? Or were they simply agreeing that men are oafish or piggish and – because they have no urge to change their own behaviour – so be it?

The same critics assumed that our primary purpose in *Spreading Misandry* was to examine the motivations of those who produce popular culture. Nothing could be further from the truth. Our primary purpose was to understand not the individual psychology of those who produce it but the collective psychology of those who do so and – more important – those who enjoy it. Our first task, therefore, was to document the existence of misandry in popular culture during one decade. As scholars, after all, we realized that no phenomenon can be explained before it has been carefully documented and described. We offered an explanation for this phenomenon in chapter 8: that the origin of misandry in popular culture is a top-down phenomenon, not a grass-roots phenomenon, and has its ultimate source in the ideological branch of feminism. We expected critics to argue with us over that. We expected them to raise questions, moreover, about our interpretation of this or that production. We did not, however, expect them to deny the very existence of misandry. And, in fact, very few have done so. What some have indeed denied is that anyone should *care* about it. Since that lies at the very heart not only of controversy over *Spreading Misandry* (and, no doubt, over the second and third volumes of this trilogy) but also of our own purpose in writing, it is worthy of a very careful response here.

To ask why anyone should care about the highly negative portrayal of men in popular culture is to deny that one segment of society is worthy of respect, let alone common decency. Nevertheless, many reviewers of *Spreading Misandry* – including some men – did so. How could they argue, in an allegedly egalitarian society, against the fundamental premise of equality? Possibly because they were either unable or unwilling to think carefully about the meaning and implications of equality. They had come to believe that only victim classes should have a right to speak in the public square and that men may not be considered a victim class (although they make exceptions for minority men).

Many feminists, moreover, had come to believe a self-serving fantasy. Men, they had become convinced, have such godlike power that they are incapable of being damaged. Therefore, anything goes (especially for ideological feminists, who believe that the end can justify the means). That, we suggest, is probably the single most serious mistake ever made by feminists. In both this volume and *Spreading Misandry*, we have shown that men are indeed the targets of hatred (and, in the third volume of this trilogy, we will argue that men can be seriously damaged by that hatred).

In any case, our underlying aim was not to add yet one more class to the long list of society's official victims, although we were obliged to use the current lingua franca of victimization. Our underlying aim, in fact, was to move beyond the polarizing and paralyzing rhetoric of victim class versus oppressor class toward what we call "intersexual dialogue" (which we will discuss in the third volume of this trilogy). If even men can be victims of hatred, after all, then all people can be. And if even feminists can propagate hatred, then all people can do so. Therefore, it would surely make sense to frame public debates in terms other than the facile notion, which originated in Marxism but has been used routinely by movements on both the left and the right, that every significant human conflict can be explained in terms of a victim class versus an oppressor class.

Some critics claimed that we were attacking all feminists, not merely ideological ones. How could they make that claim in the face of our countless – and often very tiresome – qualifying words such as "some feminists," "in some feminist circles," "ideological feminists," and so on?

Many feminists brag about the "multivocality" of their movement, claiming to respect "diversity," "pluralism," and so on (although they often rely on those words to hide conflict, thus defending even aspects of feminism that they, personally, dislike.) We were extremely careful, therefore, to specify precisely which type of feminism we were attacking. In fact, we identified no fewer than nine criteria, all or most of which must be present for a movement of any kind to qualify as ideological. Even so, we were accused over and over again of attacking feminism in general rather than one school of feminism in particular.

This would seem hard to explain at first glance, at least in connection with those critics who had actually read the book, except for two possibilities. Some feminists might have *liked* these nine characteristic features of ideology and agreed that all or most of them are indeed essential to feminism. In that case, it would have made sense to believe that we had attacked all feminists worthy of the name. But others might have disliked those same features of ideology and been either embarrassed that any feminists had adopted them or ashamed that they themselves had done so. In that case, it would have made sense to defend all feminists and thus close ranks against an external threat.

Directly or indirectly, the critics we have just mentioned challenged our use of analogies. One guest on a talk show, for instance, found our analogy between ideological feminists and Nazis "very disturbing." The analogy *is* very disturbing, of course, but not for the reason she had in mind: How dare anyone make such an ugly and extreme comparison. For one thing, as we say, our analogy was not between feminists and Nazis. It was between ideological feminists and Nazis, and not only Nazis, or ideologues on the right, but also ideologues on the left.

But her main point was that the content of feminism, presumably in any form, is benevolent and thus has nothing in common with that of malevolent National Socialism. And that is true of feminism in general, though not of ideological feminism. But our analogy was not about the content of these ideologies. Moreover, our analogy was not about the results of these ideologies. It was about the *mentality* of those who produced them.

Given the horrific results of Nazi ideology, it is worth pausing here to examine the nature of any analogy. There is no such thing as a perfect analogy. A perfect analogy would not be an analogy at all, by definition, but an equation. Why use analogies? Because many fields of scholarship would be impossible without them. History is certainly one example. Those who ignore history, according to the old saying, are doomed to repeat it. The truth is a little more complex. Historical events do not recur in precisely the same way, ever,[3] but general patterns often do. If enough characteristics of an earlier situation are similar to those of a current one, it surely makes sense for historians and others to ask if the likely results will be similar. But historians are by no means the only ones to examine historical patterns. Of interest to us in the historical record of ideological movements is the moral (or immoral) perspective that all have in common. It is very unlikely, to say the least, that ideological feminists, if given enough political power, would ever produce extermination camps for men. (Apart from anything else, exterminating men would be counterproductive unless women could reproduce themselves.) But that does not excuse ideological feminists, on moral grounds, for hating men. Even if the Nazis had never murdered a single Jew, likewise, that would still not have

excused them, on moral grounds, for hating Jews. The importance of our conviction that hatred is inherently evil (although no person or community can be
innately evil, which would leave them with no choices) is profound. It comes up
over and over again, in one way or another, throughout this trilogy. The absence
of that conviction, unfortunately, underlies many comments by our critics.

Some critics actually tried to *justify* misandry in popular culture by arguing that it
represents nothing more than payback time after years of misogyny in popular culture. So what if men were ridiculed in the 1990s or even if they are still ridiculed?
(Most of these people had fixated on the first one or two chapters of *Spreading
Misandry*, which were about misandric humour, but had ignored later chapters
about more disturbing forms of imagery.) This way of "thinking" reveals a frightening inability or unwillingness in our democracy to think clearly about fundamental moral principles.

Justice is not the same, after all, as revenge. Justice leads to healing and reconciliation; revenge, on the other hand, leads to hatred and polarization. How could
such a basic distinction be ignored even by journalists, who supposedly encourage
people to think about what goes on in the public square? The answer, we suggested
in *Spreading Misandry*, was to be found not among the ignorant masses but among
the intellectual, artistic, and political elites – whose mentality slowly filters down
through the mass media of popular culture and develops a life of its own.

For at least thirty years, the dominant worldview in those circles has been postmodernism. As the name indicates, postmodernism originated as a reaction against
modernism. And modernism was (still is in some circles) characterized by its glorification not only of progress in general but also of reason in particular. Modernism can be considered the most recent version of a worldview that goes back to
the eighteenth-century Enlightenment (or even to the Renaissance). Postmodernism, on the other hand, can be considered the most recent version of a worldview that goes back to late eighteenth-century romanticism (and, indirectly, to the
Reformation).[4] Deconstruction is the favourite analytical technique of postmodernists: casting doubt on every premise held or hidden by their adversaries. They
characteristically ask two questions: What is truth? And whose truth? And their
answer to both is simple: There is no such thing as truth, only "our truth" versus
"their truth" (or, as they like to say, "our discourses" versus "their discourses.")
If there is no such thing as truth, of course, there can be no such thing as justice
either – only "our justice" versus "their justice." Postmodernist academics are usually careful not to draw that conclusion (even though it is the only logical conclusion). Why? Because they actually do believe in the existence of truth – that is,
truth according to their own ideologies. (An ideology is not merely any set of ideas
or any philosophy. It is a worldview or, as we define it, a systematic re-presenta-
tion of reality in order to attain specific social, economic, and political goals.)
When popularized, however, postmodernism fosters moral relativism and thus dis-

courages people from even thinking carefully about moral problems such as the distinction between justice and revenge.

One result of postmodernism is pervasive – but selective – cynicism. Everything that "they" say is suspect and should therefore be deconstructed but not, of course, what "we" say. And the result of that, in turn, is to legitimate dualism. In other words, "they" are part of a titanic conspiracy against "us."

Of course, this leaves us open to the accusation of being dualistic ourselves. After all, we believe that "they" (ideological feminists) are wrong. But dualism is not about opposition toward this or that idea. It is about hostility toward people – not individuals but groups – who are classified as inherently or even innately evil according to class, race, sex, or whatever. These perpetual enemies, they say, must be destroyed in one way or another – if not killed then at least marginalized – before the dawn of a new golden age becomes possible. To oppose the ideas of some women (or men) is not dualistic, in short, but to hate women (or men) as such really is. To put it another way, we believe in tolerance for everything except intolerance. And intolerance, unfortunately, is one effect of ideological thinking.

Birth of the Bogeyman:
One Subtext of Modern Witch Hunts

According to Judith Levine, the modern pedophile has a "genealogy." It began with his first appearance at the height of industrialization during the nineteenth century. Social tension at that time was brought on by the exploitation of children in factories. Most people were either unable or unwilling to remove children from those satanic mills until reformers made them do so. But they noticed that these children were affected not only by hard work for little pay but also by more opportunities for sexual contact. In fact, many took to the streets and became prostitutes. Parents fixated on this problem, which took on even greater symbolic importance than economic problems. It was in this context that modern notions of the pedophile were born, along with the notion of "white slavery," a racially charged fantasy propagated by both tabloid journalists and idealistic reformers. It was one thing to allow the corruption of innocent children – they were now defined primarily in connection with innocence – by working them to death; many families simply needed the money brought in by their children, and a few powerful families grew rich by employing them for next to nothing. It was another thing to do so by allowing molesters to defile them sexually. The result was law reform on a colossal scale. Apart from any other measures, the age of consent was raised from as low as seven to as high as eighteen[1] and homosexuality was criminalized.

The "sex monster," as Levine calls him, went into hibernation as a result of this crackdown. He reappeared briefly during the Depression, when social tension, particularly in connection with hordes of unemployed and possibly dangerous men, reached a new high. It disappeared promptly, though, when World War II presented people at home with clear external enemies and those on the front (or even at home in countries close to the front) with many more opportunities than usual to indulge in sex on their own. After the war, he returned. The threat of perverts on the loose symbolically expressed widespread anxiety about not only the restoration of normality within the family but also the possibility of communist spies within the community. By now, the moral rhetoric had been heavily infused with clinical jargon, and whole industries had been developed to deal with the problem. The "sexual psychopath," as he was now called, was governed by "uncontrolled and uncontrollable desires."[2] Even though statistics recorded no rise in violent crimes against children, "commissions were empaneled, new laws were passed, and arrests increased. Whereas most of these, like most arrests today, were for minor offenses such as flashing or consensual homosexual sex, a few highly publicized violent crimes drew a clangor of public demand for dragnets, vigilante squads, life imprisonment, indefinite incarceration in mental institutions, castration, and execution of the psycho killers, all of which were revived in the 1980s and 1990s."[3]

Meanwhile, pornography became a major target, due partly to a rare convergence between conservative and radical political forces. From the left came ideological feminism. Even though ideological feminists represent the left in many ways, they have moved far to the right in other ways. Believing in both female essentialism (a kind of sexual nationalism) and feminist dualism (a kind of sexual racism) is characteristic of what Levine calls "sexual conservatives." For them, she says, sexual relations – at least those with men – are inherently evil and must be either surrounded with elaborate (and enforceable) codes or eliminated entirely. Every venue that might bring women together with men is suspected of leading directly to the sexual harassment of women. And that, they believe, includes everything from risqué banter to domestic violence and rape. In fact, they give almost as much attention to symbolic struggles, such as the one against pornography, as they do to more obviously urgent ones against violence itself. From the right, of course, came religious conservatives. These two streams flowed together, we suggest, at a summit meeting in 1986: the Meese Commission on pornography. They agreed

to legitimate a wholesale crackdown on adult porn and, eventually, on an alleged proliferation of "child pornography." The satanic-abuse witch-hunts (which dovetailed with the pornography scare and later became a more general panic over child abuse) also alchemized feminist and right-wing fears. Feminist worries about children's vulnerability to adult sexual desire gradually reified in a therapy industry that taught itself to uncover abuse in every female patient's past. Religious conservatives, mostly middle-class women who felt their "traditional" families threatened by the social-sexual upheavals of the time, translated that concern into the language of their own apprehension. They saw profanity – in the form of abortion, divorce, homosexuality, premarital teen sex, and sex education – everywhere encroaching on sanctity. To them, it made sense that adults, with Satan as chief gangbanger, were conspiring in "rings" to rape innocent children.

Throughout the quarter century, in a complex social chemistry of deliberate political strategy, professional opportunism, and popular suspension of disbelief, sexual discomfort heated to alarm, which boiled to widespread panic; hysteria edged out rational discourse, even in the pressrooms of established news organizations and the chambers of the highest courts. The media reported that children faced sexual dangers more terrible than anything their parents had ever known. Along with lust-crazed Satanists, there were Internet tricksters, scout-leader pornographers, predatory priests – an army of sexual malefactors people the news, allegedly more wily and numerous than ever before.[4]

At any rate, the man who either produced or "consumed" pornography (and this category included Clarence Thomas for those who tried to prevent the confirmation of his nomination to the Supreme Court) became a new version of the old "sex monster."

Within a few years, police testified that child porn had never been more than a boutique business even in its modest heyday in the late 1960s. The first law wiped out what little kiddie porn remained on the street, and by the early 1980s, the head of the New York Police Department's Public Morals Division proclaimed the stuff "as rare as the Dead Sea Scrolls." The 1.2 million figure [for victims], which [child psychiatrist Judianne] Densen-Gerber subsequently doubled, was revealed to be the arbitrarily quadrupled estimate of an unsubstantiated number one author said he'd "thrown out" to get a reaction from the law enforcement community. Densen-Gerber would soon slip from the public eye under suspicions of embezzling public monies and employing coercive and humiliating methods at [New York's drug rehab centre] Odyssey House. [Collaborator Lloyd] Martin would later be removed from his post at the LAPD for harassing witnesses and falsifying evidence.[5]

But, as Levine points out, their work had already been done very effectively. Journalists continued to spread bogus statistics. In the United States, Congress passed the Protection of Children against Sexual Exploitation Act of 1977. In Canada, Parliament established the Meese Commission in 1986 (which are discussed in chapter 7).

Right-wing groups dropped moralistic talk of "decency" and adopted that of "family values." As Levine says, the "wide, fat enemy 'pornography' began to fade from view. Now both antiporn feminist and conservative propaganda aimed at the sleaker [sic], 'hard-core,' the scarier 'child pornography.'"[6] Feminists were not terribly interested in porn featuring boys, partly because that was gay porn – which is to say, something that was politically touchy. "And where was this new pornographer? Densen-Gerber and Martin had been unable to run him down on the urban streets. He'd eluded capture in the suburban childcare centres. Now, said his pursuers, the fugitive had found his way to everywhere and nowhere. He was on the Internet, where he had joined a vast club that zipped pictures of copulating kids among them, sidled up to children in chat rooms, and enticed them into real-world motels and malls. With the family room connected by a mere modem to the wild open cyberspaces, even the home was no longer safe."[7]

Most of those caught by police are caught as a result of sting operations, of entrapment. At one time, undercover cops would solicit their interest in pictures and then arrest them for trying to buy it. Now federal agents pose on the Internet as minors, arrange meetings with children, and then arrest anyone who shows up. Officials claim that they are preventing crimes. But another possibility, suggests Levine, is that "the government, frustrated with the paucity of the crime they claim is epidemic and around which huge networks of enforcement operations have been built, have to stir the action to justify their jobs. The same logic can explain why the volume of antiporn legislation has increased annually. From a relatively simple criminalization of production and distribution, the law eventually went after possession and then even viewing of child-erotic images at somebody else's house."[8]

To understand the witch hunts, though, means more than sifting through the historical evolution of a bogey man. "Our culture fears the pedophile," says Levine, "not because he is a deviant, but because he is ordinary. And I don't mean because he is the ice-cream man or Father Patrick. No, we fear him because he is us."[9] She refers to the fact that what is commonly attributed to the dirty old pedophiles – being sexually attracted to children (especially girls) – is, in fact, something experienced also by "us." To explain that, Levine draws on the work of literary critic James Kincaid, who traced the cultural history of child molesters back to the nineteenth century.

Anglo-American culture conjured childhood innocence, defining it as a desireless subjectivity, at the same time as it constructed a new ideal of the sexually desirable object. The two had identical attributes – softness, cuteness, docility, passivity – and this simultaneous cultural invention has presented us with a wicked psychosocial problem ever since. We relish our erotic attraction to children, says Kincaid (witness the child beauty pageants in which JonBenét Ramsey was entered). But we also find that attraction abhorrent (witness the public shock and disgust at JonBenét's "sexualization" in those pageants). We project that eroticized desire outward, creating a monster to hate, hunt down, and punish.[10]

The problem with Levine's explanation is that she actually refers by "we" and "us" only to "they" and "them" – that is, to men. But because women are at least as anxious about pedophilia as men are, possibly more so, the panic can hardly be attributed to the sexual fantasies that women have about men. After all, not many women are erotically attracted to men who could be described as soft, cute, docile, or passive.

But the story is even more complicated than that. Levine points out that something else was going on, or was widely believed to be going on, at the very moment that all these witch hunts were erupting. And this was hardly coincidental. "The story behind these stories – one that was more plausible and therefore perhaps more frightening to baby boomer parents than tales of baby-rapists in black robes – was that of more teen sex, starting earlier and becoming more sophisticated sooner, with more dire consequences."[11] As we see it, parents are terrified of not being able to help their children become healthy adults, partly because so few have thought carefully enough about what it means to be a healthy adult in the first place. Instead of blaming themselves for creating a self-indulgent and hedonistic society, one that must therefore blur the distinction between childhood and adulthood, they blame some sinister Other or group of Others. In this case, they blame it on male predators – and, either implicitly or explicitly, on males as sexual beings.

What, precisely, was so disturbing about early or frequent sexual activity? This is the question that got Levine herself into so much trouble. The mere fact that she could ask it indicated to some readers that she wanted to promote perversion. As Levine points out, though, the current revulsion toward childhood sexuality is a relatively modern phenomenon. For many centuries, Europeans assumed that children were born in sin – that is, in a state of moral or spiritual corruption – and required conversion to Godfearing adulthood. But then in the late eighteenth century, that paradigm was reversed. Europeans and Americans began to believe that children were born innocent and gradually corrupted by the sinful world of adults. (The same paradigm was applied to remote places, which were inhabited by "noble savages" and thus uncontaminated by "civilization.")

> As the cultural critic James Kincaid has shown, the English and French philosophers of the Romantic Era conjured the Child as a radically distinct creature, endowed with purity and "innocence" – Rousseau's unspoiled nature boy, Locke's clean slate. This being, born outside history, was spoiled by entering it: the child's innocence was threatened by the very act of growing up in the world, which entailed partaking in adult rationality and politics. In the late nineteenth century, that innocence came to be figured as we see it today: the child was clean not just of adult political or social corruption, but ignorant specifically of sexual knowledge and desire. Ironically, as children's plight as workers worsened, adults sought to save them from sex.[12]

In the early twentieth century, the notion of childhood innocence was challenged. This time, innovation took the form of psychoanalysis. For Freud, children were indeed born with sexual desires, although he added that these desires lay dormant, or subconscious, until puberty. For him, moreover, sexual desire was not inherently problematic; it was problematic only because of the ambivalence generated by "civilization." But G. Stanley Hall, who brought Freudian theory to America, painted a somewhat darker picture. Adolescence – he coined that word – was fraught with danger, especially sexual desire.

All this history lives on in us: zeitgeists do not displace each other like weather

systems on a computerized map. We still invest the child with Romantic innocence: witness John Gray's cherub-bedecked *Children Are from Heaven*. The Victorian fear of the poisonous knowledge of worldly sexuality is still with us; lately
it's remembered in the demonic power we invest in the Internet. Hall's image of
teen sexuality as a normal pathology informs child psychology, pedagogy, and
parenting: think of "risk behaviors" and "raging hormones."

Since Freud, the sexuality of children and adolescents is officially
"natural" and "normal," yet the meanings of these terms are ever in dispute, and
the expert advice dispensed in self-help books and parenting columns serves only
to lubricate anxiety: Is the child engaging in sex too soon, too much? Is it sex of
the wrong kind, with the wrong person, the wrong meaning?[13]

Levine discusses the implications of all this in chapters on the censorship of material addressed to children, our perceptions of "deviant" children, statutory rape
(and the implication that girls, like women, do not really want sexual activity), the
rejection of sex education, and so on. Of particular interest here, however, is her
chapter on the "pedophile panic."

By now, we are all familiar with what countless television journalists and government officials have said about the problem of rampant sexual activity and violence among students in high schools or even some elementary schools (along with
their use of drugs). We are all familiar, in addition, with what they have said about
the legions of pedophiles waiting to abduct and rape those same students. "I believe
that we're dealing with a conspiracy," said Kee MacFarlane, director of the Children's Institute International in Los Angeles and central figure in "satanic-ritual
abuse" (being among those who fomented hysteria), "an organized operation of
child predators designed to prevent detection. If such an operation involves child
pornography or the selling of children, as is frequently alleged, it may have greater
financial, legal, and community resources at its disposal than those attempting to
expose it."[14] But is the rhetoric overstated? Levine thinks that it is. "The problem
with all this information about pedophiles is that most of it is not true or is so qualified as to be useless as generalization."[15]

One problem is how to define "pedophilia" in the first place. "That's because a
'pedophile,' depending on the legal statute, the perception of the psychologist, or
the biases of the journalist, can be anything from a college freshman who has once
masturbated with a fantasy of a ten-year-old in mind to an adult who has had sexual contact with an infant."[16] The resulting confusion and hysteria are due at least
partly to those who practise linguistic inflation: blurring the distinctions between
trivial and truly dangerous behaviours – not to make the latter seem harmless but
to make the former seem harmful.

Another problem is the association between pedophilia and violence.
"Pedophiles are not generally violent," says Levine, "unless you are using the term
sexual violence against children in a moral, rather than a literal, way. Its perpetrators very rarely use force or cause physical injury in a youngster ... Bringing them-

selves down to the maturity level of children rather than trying to drag the child up toward an adult level, many men who engage in sex with children tend toward kissing, mutual masturbation, or 'hands-off' encounters such as voyeurism and exhibitionism."[17]

It is worth noting here, by the way, that the very things said by some people about sexual relations between children and pedophiles – that is, between girls and men – is said by some feminists about sexual relations between women and men: that these behaviours by men are inherently evil and can therefore be morally evaluated without regard to actual physical or even psychological harm to women and that women are incapable of giving their consent due to an eternal and universal "power imbalance" between the sexes.

Levine stresses the fact that children are sexual beings. All children explore their bodies and seek physical pleasure by touching, fondling, flashing, mooning, masturbating, playing "doctor," and so on. These behaviours are not only inevitable features of growing up, she says, but also valuable and even crucial ones. Levine concludes that children should not be "protected" from that basic fact of life and that they cannot be without grave consequences for them, their families, and society in general. Her critics notwithstanding – they tried to prevent the book's publication on the grounds that it is "evil," "blasphemous," "vile," and "subversive" – Levine does not advocate juvenile intercourse, rape, or pedophilia. What she advocates is common sense in the face of yet another witch hunt. To put it another way, Levine warns us against pathologizing (and criminalizing) behaviours that would seem perverted or dangerous in very few societies (if any) except our own. This might sound strange at a time when promiscuity has become prevalent among adults recently liberated from the repressive restrictions of Victorianism – we discuss these restrictions in chapter 8 – until you realize that many feminists have reacted against the sexual revolution and established new codes of "sexual correctness," ones that strongly reinforce the Victorian notion that sex is inherently bad – not only dangerous but also wrong – for women.

Levine concludes that the cure (convincing parents that sexual activity in their children is inherently dangerous or evil, warning children that sexual predators are everywhere, and creating legislation that undermines both privacy and democracy) can be worse than the disease (a very small number of truly dangerous people). She examines "the policies and practices that affect children's and teens' quotidian sexual lives – censorship, psychology, sex education, family, criminal, and reproductive law, and the journalism and parenting advice that begs for 'solutions' while exciting more terror, like those trick birthday candles that reignite each time you blow them out."[18]

Misleading the Public: Statistics Abuse

One of our problems in writing this book has been to find reliable statistics that would either support or undermine our hypotheses, not because we have so few statistical studies but partly because statistical studies are so often ambiguous and partly because of what we call "statistics abuse." This problem has surfaced in almost every topic under discussion here.

We are not social scientists. Our book is based primarily on moral arguments, not statistical ones. Nonetheless, we cannot easily avoid referring to statistics. We need to know something about the facts before we can come to moral conclusions about them. Our point in this appendix is not that statistics are useless. Clearly, scholars need to work with *some* figures, but they need also to be cautious in doing so and to be suspicious of figures that sound shocking, especially if they either confirm or undermine politically charged arguments.

This appendix begins with a look at statistics in connection with ethics and democracy and continues with a look at statistical scams in connection with two topics: standards of living after divorce and violence against women.

This could be described as a golden age of statistics. Most people in our society, having acknowledged the supremacy of science as a way of knowing about the world, demand hard evidence (or at least what seems like hard evidence) to support their points of view on public policy. Not surprisingly, most books on relations between men and women rely heavily on statistics.

Why do so many people, both scholars and laypeople, now take it for granted that positions on moral problems can be legitimated or even proven by statistical evidence? At least four reasons should be considered. One reason is simply the prevalence of utilitarianism summed up in Jeremy Bentham's famous dictum: "The greatest happiness of the greatest number is the foundation of morals and legislation." How can we know what would make the greatest number of people happy? In our time, through statistics. Most advocates of this approach are probably unaware that their way of thinking is rooted in a particular school of philosophy, believing instead that it is rooted in common sense. The fact remains that the world-view of any commercial and industrial society is based fundamentally on the closely related principles of efficiency and cost-effectiveness, which depend on the effective use of statistical analysis.

For decades, moreover, prominent psychiatrists propagated the notion that being healthy meant primarily "fitting in," being "well-adjusted," conforming happily to some standard. Because their goal was to turn "deviant" people into "normal" ones, they used words such as "norm" and "normal" not merely to describe statistical patterns but to prescribe moral ones. But is the statistical norm always desirable? Is a majority opinion always ethical? History certainly provides no reason, in either case, to assume that the answer is yes.

Also the rise of welfare states has encouraged our reliance on "hard facts" when making moral choices. Armies of social scientists are required to conduct research; legions of bureaucrats, social workers, and other professionals are required to implement their findings and proposals. The lingua franca of government and, therefore, of newspapers, classrooms, and talk shows is a numerical one: statistics. Many people have come to believe that almost any social problem can be reduced to quantifiable terms. Even now, though, some people maintain that a few forms of behaviour are inherently right or wrong, regardless of how convenient, practical, or popular that conclusion might either be or seem at the moment.

Finally, there is something about democracy itself that encourages "groupthink." Although modern democracies are founded on the principle of individual rights matched by individual responsibilities, they are founded also on the principle of majority rule. Policies are established by counting heads (although most democracies have found ways of avoiding tyrannies of the majority).[1] Those who think for themselves – those who depart, in other words, from the consensus – are unlikely to see their positions upheld by the state, unless they can convert a large enough group to their position. But modern democracies are founded also on the assumption that elected representatives are better informed and thus more competent than ordinary citizens to make decisions. What does it mean, therefore, when public policy is established more and more often on the ephemeral basis of public opinion polls or popular demonstrations? What does it mean when elections themselves are subverted time after time by broadcasting the results of exit polls on television? It means that positions, even moral positions, are considered legitimate to the extent that most people seem to agree with them. Consensus is necessary to hold any society together, true, but only if it is based on the consistent application of philosophical, legal, theological, or moral principles.

Part of the problem in any research project is methodological. Which variables should be considered? Which groups of people should be questioned? How should the questions be formulated? How should the results be tabulated? Another part of the problem is implicit bias. Even the most academically responsible researchers make assumptions about men and women that are reflected in both the questions they ask and the answers they supply. Still another part of the problem, however, is explicit bias. Some researchers are more interested in promoting feminist ideology and thus the political and economic interests of women, for instance, than they are in finding out privately, let alone acknowledging publicly, that women not only can but often do resort to domestic violence. Consequently, they overtly denounce studies that make their political or ideological programs more complicated. They have good reason for fearing the results of many studies, actually, because they indicate that the most fundamental assumptions of ideological feminists about both men and women cannot be supported by close scrutiny of the empirical evidence.

In any case, statistics are notoriously unreliable, perhaps because of changes in the methods used by social scientists. From their inception over a hundred years ago, the social sciences have been subject to raging debates over method. Because social scientists themselves have repeatedly raised questions about the validity of various methods, no one should be surprised when "outsiders" raise questions of their own. Consider the words of Frans de Waal, an ethologist:

> I speak from years of frustration with the literature on human behavior. How do people actually behave? Available are answers to questionnaires, which at best reveal how people perceive themselves and at worst how they wish to be perceived. Available, too, are data on the behavior of human subjects in experiments. People who do not know one another are brought together in a laboratory room. All variables supposedly are under tight control in such settings, but the link with real life is lost. The observed social relationships have neither past nor future. We might as well investigate the swimming of fish by taking them out of the water. Where are the basic observations of human conduct within the family, at work, at school, at parties, on the street, and so on? Granted, there are methodological problems, but it should not be too difficult to take notes on people in action – not more difficult, surely, than fieldwork on dolphins or arboreal primates. In the natural sciences, simple descriptive data form the bedrock on which theories are built. Linnaeus preceded Darwin. The social sciences, however, seem to be trying to skip this tedious phase. Studies matching the descriptive detail of ethological work on animals are not easily come by.[2]

Actually, anthropologists do try to provide this kind of descriptive detail. Whether anthropology should be classified within the social sciences or the humanities, however, is still a matter of debate. Depending on the interests of any given anthropologist, it can have affinities with either.

Like the natural sciences, the social sciences are self-correcting. Social scientists continually challenge the findings of their colleagues and revise the findings of their predecessors. This is as it should be. Unfortunately, many laypeople need to be warned against placing undue confidence in the methods and findings of any particular researcher or even those of many at any particular time and place.

The answers are only as revealing, after all, as the questions asked. Sometimes, questions are poorly framed. "After a year of hand-wringing over a Roper poll that seemed to indicate that nearly a quarter of Americans believed the Nazi Holocaust might never have happened," writes Jerry Adler, "the poll was shown to be flawed because many people didn't understand the question. In a new poll with better questions the number of Americans who agreed that it was "possible ... the Nazi extermination of the Jews never happened" went down to 1 percent. But the mere fact that professional researchers could make such a mistake by inadvertence suggests the vast potential of statistics for misleading the public by intention."[3]

And the questions asked, as feminists themselves know well, are often heavily influenced, whether consciously or unconsciously, by the backgrounds and political interests of those who ask them. They might be influenced also, unfortunately, by the conscious or unconscious manipulation of figures by scholars with political or ideological axes to grind. This should come as no surprise to anyone. Scholars in both the social and physical sciences have long been aware – long before the advent of postmodernism – that bias with respect to either the expected or the desired results can present a problem in research.

It is good to be wary also of those who question statistics. Those who dispute this or that figure might have much to lose if it is accepted. Denial, too, is a form of bias. Sometimes denial is based on naivete; at other times, though, it is based on something more sinister. What can we say about those who argue, for instance, that "only" two or three million Jews were murdered by the Nazis? Nazism would have been no less evil had it led to the murder of one million, one hundred thousand, one thousand, or even one hundred innocent victims. Notwithstanding the utilitarian point of view, evil is a function of motivation in strictly moral terms, not of extent. In *emotional* terms, of course, it is otherwise. We are much more disturbed by murder on a colossal scale than murder on a smaller scale. Numbers do count, therefore, when it comes to political action.

Nevertheless, not all challenges to statistical figures should be dismissed or attacked as forms of denial. Sometimes, there really are good reasons for avoiding statistical arguments or questioning them.[4] Statistics are often misused, whether intentionally or not. It is the mandate of scholars to insist on the pursuit of truth, not expediency, but scholarly integrity is not the only thing at stake. In a democratic society public policy, which is intended to correct major social problems, is at stake too. If the facts we use to understand these problems are nothing more than artifacts manipulated by those of this political persuasion or that, then problems can never be solved.[5] "Great issues of public policy," observes Adler, "are being debated by people who have no idea what they're talking about. Estimates of homelessness range from 223,000 to 7 million. A United States senator announced in debate that 50,000 American children were abducted by strangers every year – a figure so striking that it took five years to dislodge from public consciousness, although it exceeded the real number by approximately 45,000."[6]

Almost everyone has been caught off guard by the fact that not all feminists are above bias. After all, ideological feminists have been very, very vocal in condemning the bias of male scholars. (Their general support for postmodernism notwithstanding, few feminists claim that all statistics are biased; making that claim and including figures that support their own positions would be self-defeating.) It is true that not all feminists are taken in by ideologically biased statistics. Admitting in public that figures are biased, though, is another matter entirely. Even to question the figures used by ideological feminists is to invite the accusation of being part of a "backlash." Philip Sullivan has identified this as a major problem in Canadian universities.[7] Feminism has not attained universal respectability, he writes, and for good reason. It is not merely a matter of men feeling threatened by feminism and thus creating a hostile work environment for feminists. It is a matter of distinguishing between rigorous and shoddy – that is, tendentious – scholarship (which we discuss in chapter 10). Moreover, men are not the only ones who question the work of feminist academics.

One example of statistics abuse emerged in connection with divorce and child custody. It began with the publication of *The Divorce Revolution*, by Lenore Weitzman, who provoked a massive uproar by presenting statistics to show that men experienced a much higher standard of living after divorce and women a much lower one.[8] Weitzman claimed that the standard of living for men increased by 73% after divorce and that for women it decreased by 42%. But scholars questioned her approach. "Amid the hosannas for Weitzman's findings that echoed in the nation's courtrooms, lecture halls, and legislative chambers ... critics charged that her sample – 228 people who had been divorced in 1977–78 – was too small to be representative. Furthermore, the respondents were all from Los Angeles, an area which has its own unique culture of divorce and divorce laws. These concerns, however, received little play in the press, and Weitzman shielded her research from further scrutiny."[9] It was Richard Peterson, of the Social Science Research Council, who first discovered that Weitzman had gotten the math wrong.[10] Using Weitzman's own data, he observed, she should have come up with 27% and 10% instead of 73% and 42%. But even his figures were inadequate,[11] as Geoffrey Christopher Rapp and others have pointed out, because they were based on Weitzman's questionable data and failed to account for several significant variables.[12]

A much larger study was conducted by Atlee Stroup and Gene Pollock on the basis of data collected between 1983 and 1987 by sociologists at the National Opinion Research Center, which is affiliated with the University of Chicago. Stroup and Pollock found that both wives and husbands have financial problems after divorce. In the first year, according to their study, the income of women declines by an average of 22% (30% for unskilled women and 12% for professional women), far from the 73% found by Weitzman. What they discovered about the income of divorced men, though, was even more startling. Not only did their income not increase by 42%, it actually decreased by approximately 10% (19% for unskilled men and 8% for professional men). These findings were reported at the National Council on Family Relations in 1992 and then as "Economic Consequences of Marital Dissolution" in the *Journal of Divorce and Remarriage*.[13] Not many academics were interested. "Weitzman's claims having by that time achieved a hammerlock on public opinion," challenges were very politically incorrect.[14]

Meanwhile, her figures were being quoted and used in the most influential venues. The American Sociological Association awarded Weitzman its book award in 1986 for her "distinguished contribution to scholarship." Her statistics were so widely accepted and so tenaciously held at all levels of society, represented by academic journals no less than popular daytime talk shows, that even research from prestigious institutions was ignored or attacked if it conflicted with what Weitzman had found. "It was taken as a given that [the numbers] were correct," says Angela James, a sociologist at the University of Southern California. "I think there were some concerns raised on the part of scholars in that area of research, but they did not get nearly as much attention as the statistics themselves. Almost every article on the subject – and on many related subjects – cited that statistic ... New scholars coming to the arena may not have read the skeptical reviews but they definitely knew of Lenore Weitzman's book."[15] As for Weitzman, she continued testifying in Congress and in state legislatures across the country, influencing fourteen laws in California alone. Eventually, in spite of evidence to the contrary, her figures were cited in President Clinton's budget for 1996. They had "attained the status of received truth" (or, as we would put it in connection with ideology of any kind, revealed truth).[16]

Whatever might be said about the motivation of Weitzman herself – no one can ever know whether she made a stupid mistake or a clever one, although the fact that she stonewalled for ten years before allowing the truth to come out could make anyone suspicious – the motivation of those who *use* her statistics is obvious. How, asks Rapp, did all this happen?

> The answer was that in the increasingly radicalized atmosphere that characterized the debate over the economics of divorce, the 73/42 statistic had the force of an idea whose time had come. The disparity it pretended to uncover was so dramatic that it became the perfect media sound-bite, a shocking factoid which after many repetitions seemed to ring true. Perhaps more importantly, Weitzman's numbers could be used to promote just about any agenda, further ensuring the statistic's popularity. Weitzman herself, for example, said that her study indicated the need for changes within the no-fault system of divorce which by 1986 was in place in 48 states. Others saw the statistics and recommended scrapping no-fault entirely.[17]

Well, not *any* agenda. The numbers precluded any movement that might have taken divorced fathers seriously. Susan Faludi and some other feminists were outraged by public acceptance of Weitzman's findings, sure, but they were outraged only by what they took to be a backlash against the gains already made by divorced *women*. Why interpret the phenomenon in that counterintuitive way? Because they believed that "the media" had conspired to scare women who might consider divorce by convincing them that doing so would leave them on a downward economic spiral.[18] Most feminists, however, realized that the intentional or unintentional scare would ultimately serve the interests of women by provoking demands for law reform. Only Christina Hoff Sommers, as far as we know, understood that these two conflicting interpretations really amounted to the same thing. "Lenore Weitzman's research is used by many groups of feminists to trash men ... no matter what. It's either 'men are monsters,' or 'we don't need them.'"[19] Even now, after Weitzman has recanted and the story has been told many times, her figures are hardly ever challenged. If this book had been written by someone at Harvard, after all, how could it be wrong?

> It is probably impossible to overestimate how influential Weitzman's 73 percent figure was ... A search of databases found that over 175 newspaper and magazine stories have since cited Weitzman's numbers. Even this figure understates enormously the extent to which her findings have invaded popular culture. Like a virus out of control, Wetizman's results have surfaced in an unknown number of reports in which her figures are erroneously attributed to other sources ... When looking at academic sources, however, we are able to get a more accurate count of how widespread Weitzman's influence was. There were citations in 348 social science articles, 250 law review articles, and 24 appeals cases. Her figures were characterized as "ranking among the most cited demographic statistics of the 1980s."[20]

It was precisely with Weitzman's phony statistics in mind that Cathy Young wrote a review of *First Wives Club*. This cinematic comedy, based on a best-selling novel by Olivia Goldsmith, is "about three aging women who are dumped by their husbands and set out to get even, using various sneaky and illegal tactics to bring the men under their thumb and strip them of their property."[21] It was a hit at the box office, so we must assume that it made a lot of women feel good about themselves and reinforced group solidarity. Moreover, it was warmly greeted by critics in such influential publications as *Time*[22] and the *New York Times*.[23] "The movie's feminism is a dubious sort," writes Young. "It is not about women making it on their own but about women taking men's money: 'I don't get mad, I get everything,' says one character."[24] In other words, this movie is about revenge. It feeds the revenge fantasies not only of women whose ex-husbands have mistreated them, moreover, but also of most other women. They "know" from Weitzman and other sources of what passes for conventional wisdom that the game of divorce is usually won by men. On the picketing of this movie by advocates of fathers, Young observes that "[s]ome may chuckle that these men don't have a sense of humor, a charge often made against feminists. But the men have a point. It's only a movie, but the attitudes it promotes – that personal problems between men and women are political, that the man is always to blame and the woman is always the victim – has dangerous consequences in real life."[25] Among these consequences was Weitzman.

Even during the 1980s, a few academics realized that domestic violence was often committed or even initiated by women. In Britain, Erin Pizzey wrote not only about domestic violence against women in *Scream Quietly, or the Neighbours Will Hear*[26] and established the first shelter in London for female victims but also about domestic violence against men in *Prone to Violence*.[27] In the United States, Suzanne Steinmetz wrote an article on "The Battered Husband Syndrome" for *Victimology*.[28] But no research, no matter how scholarly, could be undertaken seriously before the first national survey was conducted by Steinmetz, along with Murray Straus and Richard Gelles. In *Behind Closed Doors*,[29] they reported what they themselves could hardly believe: that 3.8% of husbands beat their wives but 4.6% of wives beat their husbands.[30]

This new evidence was hotly denied by many feminists, who managed for years to suppress any debate about it in the public square. Steinmetz received scathing attacks from academics, more on rhetorical than academic grounds. She received a bomb threat at the University of Delaware and a threatening phone call at home from a woman: "If you don't stop talking about battered men, something's going to happen to your children and it won't be safe for you to go out."[31] No one ever did attack her or her children. Years later, though, Steinmetz found out that some colleagues had tried to ruin her career by urging women on her faculty to lobby against her promotion and tenure.[32] Ironically, given the compassionate and egalitarian rhetoric of feminism, the wonder is not that a few of them have resorted to intimidation in the name of women but that *any* of them have.

Steinmetz admitted that "wives are injured in greater numbers by their husbands" but also noted that "the average violence scores show wives to be slightly more likely to resort to violence than husbands."[33] This was unacceptable to those who had a vested interest in domestic violence as a woman's problem and an industry based on services to battered women. But wait. The threats continued.

In an attempt to try to keep me from speaking, I had thinly veiled threats put on me. I was speaking at an American Civil Liberties Union conference [which championed free speech] and they received threats. They were told if they allowed me to speak, the place would be bombed ... I was told before giving an address at a Canadian university I would have major problems by one group of radical women. They wrote to the college president and said I should be stopped from coming to speak ... What happened to me was nothing, trust me, compared to what Murray Straus has gone through. He always says I had it worse, but I

don't think so ... He's had women academics come up to him and almost physically accost him in the hall because they've been so angry.[34]

Even though Murray Straus, one of her co-authors, had been the president of
academic associations and had received awards for research on families, he was
heckled, booed, and picketed and targeted by a telephone campaign accusing him
of misogyny, sexual harassment, and even beating his former wife.

It is almost beyond belief that some critics can ignore or dismiss these studies.
Perhaps even more serious is the implied excusing of assaults by women
because they result from frustration and anger at being dominated. This is parallel to the excuses men give to justify hitting their wives, such as a woman's
being unfaithful ... In my opinion, [these] are not feminist critiques, but justifications of violence by women in the guise of feminism. This is the betrayal of
the feminist ideal of a nonviolent world. In addition, excusing violence by
women and denying overwhelming research evidence may have serious side
effects. It may undermine the credibility of feminist scholarship and contribute
to a backlash that can also undermine progress toward the goal of equality
between men and women.[35]

As for Richard Gelles, Steinmetz's other co-author, he faced similar hostility from
professional colleagues: no longer being elected to office in professional associations, no longer being asked to speak at conferences, and so on.

The same thing happened to R.L. McNeely, an attorney and a professor of
social welfare at the University of Wisconsin at Milwaukee. He, too, wrote on the
topic of domestic violence against men and had his career threatened by ideological adversaries as a result. McNeely observed that these feminists "are not about
the search for truth. What this is about is a search for political power. That is power
based upon a concept of a defenseless group of people being victimized by a larger,
stronger aggressor. When people start recognizing that, indeed, domestic violence
seems to occur both ways, that undercuts the whole concept of weakness, out of
which comes power. It's based on a concept of being an exclusive victim. That's why
some people react so strongly. A lot of these people are absolutely convinced that
they are on the 'correct' side."[36]

Americans set the precedent for censorship of politically incorrect information in
1979. Published evidence from a survey conducted for the Kentucky Commission
on Women included statistics only on the abuse *of* women.[37] Someone suppressed
the ones on abuse *by* women. How do we know, then, that 38% of the women
acknowledged attacking men without physical provocation? Because some professors eventually managed to get hold of the original computer files.[38] It is unnecessary to assume that everyone involved in this scandal was motivated directly by
feminist ideology. Some might have been motivated by fear of losing research

grants, academic tenure, publishing contracts, or even common courtesy in public from colleagues. This story was not new, but the context must have seemed new to anyone who had believed that only men would stoop so low.

Because *Behind Closed Doors* had raised more questions than it could answer, and despite the pious denials and condescending dismissals, at least a hundred projects on domestic violence against men were begun over the next twenty-five years. Approximately half the researchers were women, and most of these women were feminists who expected to refute Straus, Gelles, and Steinmetz.

The statistics on domestic violence against men might surprise many readers, just as they did the early researchers. Nevertheless, these statistics were found by reputable social scientists throughout the 1980s and 1990s.

People working on the subject of family violence now had a choice: they could expand the field to include male victims – establishing that abused men were not the same men that were abusing, and vice versa for women – or they could do what they did: devote an extraordinary amount of energy to shouting the data down. For feminists, the idea that men could be victimized was nonsensical. It didn't square with their fundamental analysis of wife assault – that it was an extension of male political, economic, and ideological dominance over women. If women were so clearly subjugated in the public domain, how could there be a different reality behind closed doors? Activists anticipated, moreover, that the ... data might be used to devalue female victims, in the manner of male lawyers, judges, and politicians saying, "See? She does it too"; case dismissed.[39]

The same thing was happening in Canada. In 1989, a study found that 39.1% of the women questioned had assaulted their husbands, and 16.2% of those who had been assaulted defined these assaults as severe. In fact, 90% of the women who had asssaulted their husbands said that they had not acted in self-defense. "They had been furious or jealous, or they were high, or frustrated. Rational or irrational, impulsive or controlling, they had hit, kicked, thrown, and bitten. Fourteen percent of the men went to the hospital."[40] Another Canadian study conducted that very year at the University of Alberta found that 12% of husbands and 11% of wives were victims of domestic violence. Its findings on women were published, of course, but not those on men.[41]

The debate over domestic violence was reaching a crescendo by the mid-1990s, especially after the arrest in 1994 of O.J. Simpson for the murder of his wife and her friend. Journalists came up with staggering figures. But not everyone fomented hysteria.

How many battered wives are too many?
That's an easy one: in an ideal world, even one is too many. But we live in a glaringly imperfect world, in which battered wives are only one exhibit in a

panorama of human misery clamoring for our attention. So when O.J. Simpson's history of wife-beating came to light after his arrest, women's advocacy groups were quick to point out that what was really shocking was how often this happens among ordinary families. Undoubtedly many Americans were shocked to read in Time magazine that 4 *million* American women are assaulted by a "domestic partner" each year. It must have been especially shocking to those who read in Newsweek that the number of women beaten by "husbands, ex-husbands and boyfriends" was 2 *million* a year.

This is terrible. Not because of the implication that either Time or Newsweek is wrong by a factor of 2, but because the divergence reflects society's actual state of ignorance on such an important and theoretically verifiable statistic.[42]

Even today, these numbers are cited at least in the context of informal discussions.

According to John Fekete, quantitative studies, with their presumably scientific basis, have helped to create the view that all men are violent. "Specifically, it turns out that the numbers look more alarming if research subjects check off micro-actions from a list of event-descriptions, rather than describe their interpretation of their own experience."[43] He goes on to show how the set of scales created by Straus and Gelles (the Conflict Tactics Scales) have been modified and then misused by other researchers in the field (such as Mary Koss and her colleagues who did the Sexual Experiences Survey reported by *Ms.* in 1987).[44] The scales are misused when research subjects are not allowed to interpret their own experiences, when these are defined as abuse rather than conflict, or when rape is placed "on a continuum with normal male behaviour within the culture."[45]

Among the serious effects of ideological takes on violence against women is the inflation of definitions. As a result, all men are stereotyped as violent. Even in 1979, Lenore Walker, a psychologist and author of *The Battered Woman*, had extended the definition of "violence" to include other forms of intimidation. "A battered woman," she writes, "is a woman who is repeatedly subjected to any forceful physical *or psychological* behavior by a man in order to coerce her to do something he wants her to do without any concern for her rights."[46] Walker writes that in one case, "it is clear that there was a good deal of provocation. There is no doubt that she began to assault Paul physically before he assaulted her. However, it is also clear from the rest of her story that Paul had been battering her by ignoring her and by working late, in order to move up the corporate ladder, for the entire five years of their marriage."[47] Walker referred even to professional women whose husbands do not accompany them to social events! "Those women who attempt to have some kind of social life never know whether their batterer will be charming company, leave the party, become inattentive or bored, or verbally humiliate them."[48]

In view of this definition, Walker concluded that no fewer than one out of every two wives can be classified as a victim and thus should not be considered responsible for her own behaviour, including, apparently, premeditated murder. This definition is an integral part of Walker's larger theory of violence – a profoundly ideological one, by the way, which has been used extensively and effectively by Catharine MacKinnon and other feminists in their efforts to rewrite existing laws. According to Walker, who identifies herself as a feminist,[49] violence against women (the only kind of violence that troubles her) is "the misuse of power by men who have been socialized into believing they have the right to control the women in their lives, even through violent means."[50] Walker admits that "[u]fortunately ... I tend to place all men in an especially negative light, instead of just those men who do commit such crimes. Perhaps when more is known about batterers, we will need to view them also as victims."[51] In the meantime, however, the presupposition of her psychotherapeutic approach is that "the man is a batterer and the woman is a battered woman."[52]

Many women (and even a few men) have moved step by step from the belief that every man is a potential abuser to the belief that every man *is* an abuser and also from the belief that every man is a potential rapist to the belief that every man *is* a rapist. In other words, all men are evil. At one time, rape was defined as something that strangers sometimes did to girls or women. Nowadays, rape is defined as something that husbands or boyfriends routinely do to women or girlfriends. Here is the ideological trump card par excellence. What better way could there be to make women afraid of men and thus feel the need of feminist measures to protect themselves? Ideologues are quite willing to foster panic. Ironically, that strategy has not generated new stereotypes, which would have been bad enough, but given new life to old ones: women are passive and nonviolent, according to both misogynists *and* feminists, men aggressive and violent. These stereotypes not only allow misogynists to excuse their own behaviour but also allow feminists to avoid the disturbing fact that women are capable of violence.

According to Sommers, "the idea that a high percentage of American men are brutes is promoted in three illegitimate ways":[53] first, by generalizing from high-risk populations; second, by classifying pushes and shoves and slaps as "battery"; third, by referring to studies that do not even exist.[54] Fortunately, women as well as men have begun to question the use of statistics to manipulate the political process. Sommers is among those who have discussed the hoax about Super Bowl Sunday. Here is the story. On Thursday, 27 January 1993, a coalition of women's groups met in Pasadena to hold a press conference. They told journalists that the number of women battered during or after the Super Bowl game on Sunday would be 40% higher than on a normal day. To support that figure was Sheila Kuehl of the California Women's Law Center, who cited a study that had been produced three years earlier at Old Dominion University in Virginia. Also present, to add authority, was Linda Mitchell of Fairness and Accuracy in Reporting (FAIR). Next day, Lenore Walker told viewers of *Good Morning America* that she had come to the same conclusion after monitoring police reports on these occasions for ten years. On the show with Walker was Laura Flanders, another representative of FAIR. On Saturday, Lynda Gorov wrote up the story for a major newspaper.[55] What was the point of all this? Even though violence against women occurs at all times, Americans were told, it increases dramatically when fostered by the brutality of football, which is emblematic of masculine culture. Cheering for the home team, therefore, was tantamount to cheering for local rapists.

Where did these statistics originate? Could any reputable scholar vouch for their legitimacy? Were other interpretations possible? Ken Ringle, at the *Washington Post*, was among the very few journalists who even bothered to ask these questions – risky ones, in fact, because anyone could accuse him of misogyny for trying to defend men. Ringle got the runaround, in fact, when he tried to follow the story's trail. Janet Katz, one author of the study cited by Kuehl, told him that her findings had nothing to do with Walker's. On the contrary, she and her colleagues had found no correlation at all between admissions to emergency rooms and the occurrence of football games. So that was a blind alley. Gorov admitted to Ringle that she had never actually seen the study and advised him to consult her source at FAIR. Mitchell, at FAIR, told him to consult Walker. Her office told him to consult psychologist Michael Lindsey, a leading authority on battered women. And Lindsay admitted that he could see no basis for Walker's conclusions. When other reporters later on contacted Walker, who was clearly at the epicentre of this controversy, she replied that her findings were not for "public consumption" (even though she had personally announced them on national television) but only for "guidance" among advocates in women's groups. "It would have been more honest for the feminists who initiated the campaign," writes Sommers, "to admit that there was no basis for saying that football fans are more brutal to women than are chess players or Democrats nor any basis for saying that there was a significant rise in domestic violence on Super Bowl Sunday."[56]

On 31 January, Ringle's story was published in the *Washington Post*, and Robert Lipsyte warned readers of the *New York Times* that the Super Bowl had turned into an "Abuse Bowl."[57] On 2 February, Gorov's newspaper published what amounted to a retraction of her earlier story, along with a withdrawal by Steven Rendell of support for FAIR.[58] Later on, Mitchell admitted to Ringle that she had known during the original press conference that Kuehl was distorting the Old Dominion study. In one sense, the story was over. In another sense, however, the story had taken on a life of its own. Sommers observes that "despite Ken Ringle's exposé, the Super Bowl 'statistic' will be with us for a while, doing its divisive work of generating fear and resentment."[59]

During an interview as president of the National Organization for Women, Patricia Ireland once told Charlie Rose about a study by the March of Dimes which showed that battery of pregnant women was the number one cause of birth defects. Sommers observes that to repudiate ... victimology statistics is to open oneself to recrimination even from some dedicated and sincere feminists. "What is so wrong," they say, "with exaggerating and overstating when trying to cope with an epidemic of wife abuse? Women are suffering. In casting doubt on activists' claims, you are doing far more harm than good." To this, [the] response must be that even well-meaning untruths inevitably undermine the good-faith efforts to help the victims of real abuse and discrimination. The acts that constitute severe domestic violence are crimes that shatter lives; those who suffer must be cared for and those who cause their suffering must be prevented from doing further harm. But in all we do to help, the most loyal ally to compassion is truth ... Divisive falsehoods like these are fueling resentments that blight male/female relations in this country. Finally, phony feminist statistics make for bad social policy. If Ms. Ireland, Ms. Quindlen, Ms. Pollitt and their sisters-in-arms are right that the average male is a serious threat to women, then a massive make-over of American society would indeed be called for. If, however, 2%–3% of men are abusive, then we need to target that group and leave the remaining 97%–98% of men alone.[60]

Yet another major hoax is repeated relentlessly by journalists, academics, and politicians. This one involves at least two feminist icons. In *The Beauty Myth*, Naomi Wolf claims that no fewer than 150,000 women die in the United States every year from anorexia. In *Revolution from Within*,[61] Gloria Steinem repeats that claim. The point in both cases is to make an ideological claim: that men cause this "holocaust" of women. But the claim is preposterous. Sommers learned from the Centers for Disease Control that 101 American women died of anorexia in 1983, 67 in 1988, and 54 in 1991. Tragic on moral grounds, yes, but not on emotional – and therefore political – grounds that were even remotely comparable to a "holocaust."

Caused by men? That claim, too, is highly questionable. Women participate actively and eagerly in the culture that produces anorectic standards of feminine beauty, after all, and female stars in Hollywood – Calista Flockhart and Lara Flynn Boyle come to mind – react angrily when told that they are too thin and thus set bad examples for girls and young women. Besides, men have historically – except for a very brief interval in the 1920s and once again since the 1960s – preferred buxom women over thin ones for the obvious reason, at least in earlier centuries, that the former look as if they are healthy enough to bear healthy children. (During the late mediaeval period, it is true, fashionable women were portrayed by artists as very thin. But so were fashionable men.) Finally, neither Wolf nor Steinem bothers to note the parallel between young women who starve themselves to look beautiful and young men who consume dangerous anabolic steroids – side effects include organ damage and even death – to look athletic or macho.

At any rate, Sommers challenged Wolf's and Steinem's figure in *Who Stole Feminism?* That was enough for Flanders, who attacked her in FAIR's newsletter.[62]

Although Flanders admitted that the 150,000 American women did not die of anorexia every year, she accused Sommers (and, presumably, the Centers for Disease Control) of using "highly dubious" figures all the same. Many who die of anorexia, she averred, are mistakenly reported in the statistics for heart failure or suicide.

> Ms. Flanders should have called the CDC's National Center for Health Statistics ... to learn just how many women between 15 and 24 (the prime anorexia years) are dying of heart failure. For 1991 the figure is 19. As for suicide, the 1991 figure is 649. Of these young women, how many are likely to have been dangerously emaciated and have had doctors who mistakenly reported the cause of death as suicide rather than anorexia? It would be astonishing if the number were as much as ten percent of the total. That would add about 70 fatalities to the official CDC figure.[63]

Our point here is not that feminists are unique in faking research for political ends. That is clearly untrue. Our point is only that journalists and politicians – and all citizens – should be careful before accepting at face value bizarre statistics that just happen to support their own political positions. At the very least, we should all refer to statistics that both support and do not support our positions, especially when controversies have erupted over the statistics on both sides. The harm done by hiding these controversies can never be repaired, after all, because every article or book that repeats tendentious claims is reproduced countless times by publishers, cited in countless footnotes, and so on.

The same crescendo occurred in Canada at the same time. This was partly local fallout from the American story of O.J. Simpson and partly fallout from the local one of Marc Lépine. In *Moral Panic*, John Fekete observes that a problem exists even at the governmental level. Statistics Canada is a highly respectable and even venerable institution that has a direct impact on public opinion and thus both direct and indirect influence on legislation. But when it comes to gender, Fekete argues, Statistics Canada produces documentation that is sloppy at best and deceitful at worst. It is guilty, in short, of succumbing to the tyranny of political correctness. Fekete indicts the growing industry of dubious research that is intended to promote panic and rage among women, one result being to manipulate the political process. Politicians should be influenced by public opinion, yes, but what if public opinion is based on ignorance? Not many politicians have the moral integrity or even the intellectual curiosity to question statistics gathered by academics, let alone by government officials.

A 1993 study by Statistics Canada had the cooperation of six federal departments, as well as police officers, some academics – Fekete calls them "advocacy experts" – along with activists from transition houses, sexual assault crisis centres, and ethno-cultural and refugee services, as well as feminists.[64] "[T]his whole project was developed during the height of the post-Lépine 'war-against-women' panic,

and in a way that guaranteed that the survey would belong to the clinical population of violence victims and to its biofeminist advocates."[65] The survey investigated
the extent of violence only against women and sought information only from
women. It ignored the possibility that women themselves might perpetrate violence
either against men or against other women.

> What is scandalous is that this study, which purports to provide pioneering
> national information about relationship interaction in Canada, is a single-sex
> survey. In my view, the decision to ask only women about acts of violence per-
> petrated against them is highly partisan. The inflammatory figure, which is
> this survey's claim to fame, is that 51% of Canadian women have experienced
> at least one incident of violence since the age of 16 ... [T]he question that was
> one of the two main staples for generating the survey's physical-assault data is
> a yes/no question: "Now, I'm going to ask you some questions about physical
> attacks you may have had since the age of 16. By this I mean any use of
> force such as being hit, slapped, kicked, or grabbed to being beaten, knifed or
> shot."[66]

According to the results, one third of the victims complained of threats so severe
that they feared for their lives. But, points out Fekete, "Statistics Canada is misre-
porting its own data: the figures here refer to perpetrators, not to victims. It is not
that 34% of *women* fear for their lives; nor that 45% of *women* feared for their
lives in a past marriage. It is that 34% of those *partners* who were complained
about made the women fear for their lives, including 45% of the allegedly violent
partners in past marriages."[67] The study not only misinterpreted its own data but
actually double-counted figures to get these data. In addition, Fekete challenges the
basic premise that misunderstanding in connection with casual fondling can be
included legitimately with intimidation in connection with the most shattering
transgressions. Women were asked if they had ever received unwanted attention
from male strangers, say, or if they had ever been made to feel "uncomfortable" by
men who commented on their beauty or "blew kisses" at them. The implication
was that there is no moral difference between the expression of heterosexual interest in a woman, albeit unwanted, and rape (a topic that we discuss in chapters 8
and 9).

Not all statistics used by politicians are produced by academic or governmental
bodies. Among the most notorious examples of statistical engineering cited by
Fekete is a study produced by an overtly partisan group: the Canadian Panel on
Violence against Women.[68] This study – funded by the government, it cost taxpayers $10 million – claimed that 98% of Canadian women are sexually violated. This
conclusion is self-defeating, in a way, because it looks too much like the "electoral
victories" of 98% in totalitarian countries. Why not simply claim, as some feminists do, that all women are sexually violated or even that all men subject all
women to sexual violation? These claims require no statistical "evidence." They are

supposedly self-evident on ideological grounds. As David Thomas points out, these claims involve "an elementary error of logic: All buttercups are yellow flowers, but not all yellow flowers are buttercups. Similarly, all rapists are men, but that does not mean that all men are rapists. This is, of course, part of an attempt to induce guilt by association ... The notion that all men are "capable" of rape is either ... absurdly prejudicial, or meaningless."[69] The Canadian study was considered necessary to convince women who prefer not to think of themselves as ideologues. (An interesting analogy could be made with religious people who prefer to believe that science "proves" their theory of creation.) But who is going to take this problem seriously, especially since most of those concerned about it (for the time being) are men? And men, unlike women, are supposedly incapable of honest scholarship when their own interests are at stake.

In 1995, Earl Silverman got the data on men from a research assistant and wrote it up himself. No one would publish it.[70] In 1997 a Canadian study about abused men was suppressed. It found that 46% of the women questioned and only 18% of the men had resorted to violence. Only the data on men, in this case, were published. Someone found out, asked to see the original research, and was refused. "It was only when he exposed the refusal in his next book, combined with another three more years of pressure, that the 46 percent female violence was released and published. By that time, Canadian policy giving government support for abused women but not abused men had been entrenched. As were the bureaucracies; as were the private funding sources like United Way."[71] In 1999, the United Way of Greater Toronto increased its grant to services for abused women and children by $1 million, the annual total then reaching $3.3 million. This mainstream benevolent organization gave not one cent for abused men.

Grant Brown writes that systemic discrimination against men is the direct result of these biased statistics.

> [P]artner abuse is routinely portrayed and acted upon as though it were almost exclusively about men abusing and victimizing innocent women and, by extention [sic], their children – despite the overwhelming sociological evidence that a significant amount of abuse is also suffered by male partners. The prevailing orientation to the problem is typically supported by little more than speculative, ideological rationalizations of the sociological evidence, if not outright suppression or denial of that evidence. Genuinely gender-inclusive research is needed to test the validity of this orientation, and to determine whether it has had a beneficial or detrimental effect on the administration of justice.[72]

Brown explains that research on this topic can be flawed in at least two important ways. In some cases, it is based on sources that are incomplete and hard to analyze. In other cases, it is focused on the work of judges or police officials but not prosecutors.

Some feminists make no pretense of relying on statistics, even when statistics might be used to serve their cause. Andrea Dworkin, for instance, claims that her own intuition or insight supersedes any other form of evidence. Her argument is based on what she calls "experience," something that is ultimately, by definition, beyond the grasp of anyone who has not had her experience, something that transcends, in other words, the need for discussion or research.

Silencing Men:
The Trouble with Political Correctness

Contrary to the protestations of those now called "politically correct" by their adversaries, this term was once used by the former themselves without the slightest trace of irony. The first to do so, according to William Safire, were on the left.[1] The notion of "correct ideas," or "correct thinking," originated in 1963 with Chairman Mao. It gained massive popularity among his followers in the Western world with the publication of his Little Red Book of ideological platitudes and slogans. For dedicated communists, Safire continues, correct thinking was "the disciplined inculcation of a party line expressed in all forms of social and political intercourse."[2] To those on both left and the right, "correct" came to mean anything that reflected the group's opinions, doctrinal orthodoxy, conventional wisdom, and so on. In the late 1980s more people (though still a minority) began attacking conformity on the left, especially at universities. The term "politically correct" thus became an insult.

Political correctness operates on the right, too. During the war in Iraq, for instance, many dissenters claimed that they had been "censored." (This was ad hoc behaviour by individuals rather than censorship per se, however, which is established by law.) The most famous examples, not surprisingly, were in the entertainment industry. Consider only two of the most notorious examples. Bill Maher, host of *Politically Incorrect*, observed on the air that terrorists who crash into office towers, unlike American soldiers sending missiles from a distance, were not cowards, whatever else they were. Soon after that attack on conventional wisdom, his show was cancelled. Singer Natalie Maines, of the Dixie Chicks, observed that she was ashamed that the president, who was about to invade Iraq, came from Texas. This led to public demonstrations of anger and an "apology" from Maines. Given our ideological topic in this book and its primary venue at the university, however, we focus attention here on the left.

Advocates of political correctness seldom even pay lip service to freedom of expression, except, when pressed, as some abstract and remote ideal. On the contrary, they often explicitly deny the value of free speech. Consider one debate over precisely this in the pages of a Canadian academic journal, bearing in mind that precisely the same arguments would be used in the United States and many other Western countries. Supreme Court justice John Sopinka wrote an article in *University Affairs* to support freedom of speech as an essential requirement for scholarly debate, one that should be protected by the law.[3] In the next issue, an academic reader protested vehemently. With beguiling rhetoric, Allan Hutchinson chastised those, such as Sopinka, who want to appropriate freedom of expression to serve their own political interests – that is, according to Hutchinson, to maintain the status quo.[4] Hutchinson opined that freedom of expression is never above partisan politics and must be kept that way. But much of his argument was facile. Yes, the debate over free speech does have a political dimension. It does not follow that this is the only dimension, however, or even the most important one. In fact, it has intellectual and moral dimensions as well. By "privileging" the political, to use deconstructive jargon, Hutchinson not only "problematized" the latter but also trivialized it.

Hutchinson accused Sopinka, and others like him, of refusing to acknowledge the political implications of supporting free speech. He believed that merely admitting his own "political agenda," moreover, legitimated his position. Any possibility of evaluating either position, therefore, surely lies in our ability to examine both in terms of some criterion other than politics. In fact, Hutchinson's political position was no more innocent than Sopinka's. If Sopinka could be accused of using a moral or intellectual argument to bypass a political one, after all, Hutchinson could be accused of using a political argument to bypass a moral or intellectual one. In any case, Hutchinson's political point was shot through with questionable moral and intellectual assumptions.

Supporters of political correctness usually rely on the conspiracy theory of history. "The problem is not so much to do with who favours freedom of expression," Hutchinson wrote, "but who benefits most from elevating it above other values. Put crudely, it is those who have the power to speak, not those without it. Established interests – white, male, straight, etc. – have more to gain from prioritizing free speech over equality; it serves to preserve the status quo rather than to change it."[5] Quite apart from any political connotations, this cynical passage has obvious moral connotations. Hutchinson was accusing those who oppose political correctness of doing so for sinister motives. He was accusing them, in effect, of evil. Because he chose to argue on political grounds rather than moral grounds, however, he felt no need to say so directly, much less to back up this assertion. It was enough, for him, merely to use a verbal weapon in the political struggle.

Hutchinson claimed that equality and free speech are merely "competing values." In any case, from his point of view, free speech is an illusion. It is fostered by those who actually have the "power to speak" instead of those who do not. But this is questionable for at least three reasons. For one thing, precisely who are those with this "power to speak"? By now, it could easily be argued that straight white men are the only citizens *without* it. Whether political correctness is actually enforced by law and policies or not, after all, it is enforced by public opinion and always has been. To argue that even the most scholarly critique of a feminist claim can be taken seriously in the current atmosphere as the focus of intellectual debate rather than ideological ranting is, relying on the most charitable interpretation, to be incredibly naive.

Moreover, the opposition between equality and free speech is inherently false. Free speech ensures that theory and practice coincide. To eliminate it in the name of "equality and dignity" is, as we learned during the Vietnam War, like destroying a village in order to save it.

Finally, free speech is precisely what guarantees the "power to speak," and not only for those with "established interests." No one is arguing for the opposite of political correctness, after all, in which only those with established interests may say what they want. By suggesting that some people are, Hutchinson skewed the debate. At issue for his adversaries, to judge by the arguments they put forward, is not whether free speech should be confined to themselves, either directly or indirectly, but how to extend it more effectively to include everyone. As one observer put it, the notion of respecting minority points of view by protecting them from other points of view does nothing except "suppress free expression of the kind of strong, distinctive beliefs and values that people will stand up for. So-called respect for opposing views readily devolves into a sterile, paralysing kind of political correctness."[6] If free speech is deliberately restricted to the few, it is meaningless in the context of a democracy, let alone a university.

Opportunism can work both ways. It is true that straight white men now have the most to gain from free speech. At the moment, how could it be otherwise? They (and religious people) are the only ones now threatened, explicitly and directly, with the loss of it. On the other hand, it is true also that those who classify themselves as victims of free speech have the most to gain from *denying* it to others. Advocates of political correctness confuse justice with a dubious combination of expediency and revenge. Their position is based not only on opportunism, moreover, but also on cynicism. Instead of acknowledging the fear that new ideas *might* not compete successfully with older ones, even in the university, they argue conveniently that new interests *cannot* compete with older ones. In doing so, they affirm the belief that scholarship is ultimately nothing more than a clever way of seeking class privileges (whether old or new) rather than seeking truth (no matter how haltingly). Consequently, the voices of those who defend older ideas, or "interests," must be drowned out and freedom of speech eliminated – which is to say, offered only to those who claim some unique need for it.

Hutchinson accused Sopinka of hypocrisy, too: arguing for freedom of expression but then denying it in unpalatable cases. To make the point, he presented a syllogism. Sopinka, he wrote, had advocated constitutional protection for freedom of expression; murder, rape and violence are forms of expression; ergo, Sopinka should advocate constitutional protection for these physical forms of expression no less diligently than for verbal ones. But the syllogism is foolish. There is a difference, a big difference, between murder, rape, or any other kind of violence and unkind words or even – and this is really what matters in the debate over free speech in the university – opposing ideas. At this point, Hutchinson revealed his own hypocrisy by claiming to fight for those who need protection from unkind words. His own words, however, could have been profoundly offensive to the victims of murder, rape, and other forms of violence.

But something else is involved in this debate. It is often argued that unkind words can lead to violence. And so they can. But banning them, too, can lead to violence. One reason people resort to violence, after all, is precisely their sense of having no legitimate outlet to express their fear, frustration, or anger. For decades, the communist countries of Eastern Europe did everything they could to oppose expressions of nationalism, individualism, and everything else considered bourgeois, reactionary, or antisocial. The results in, say, the former Yugoslavia, hardly justify their efforts. What every democratic society must do, what every university exists to do, is encourage people to think for themselves. Of course this involves risk. But nothing worthwhile – not maturity, not democracy, not scholarship – is without risk. Hutchinson used the rhetoric of equality to undermine freedom of speech and, in doing so, transformed old inequalities into new ones.

Less aggressive or sophisticated advocates of political correctness often base their claim on what sounds irrefutable: the need for sensitivity. But they, too, are hypocritical. On closer examination, they invariably argue for *selective* sensitivity – that is, sensitivity to some groups of people but not others. This is not sensitivity to others as a general moral principle. People are always more sensitive to some people than to others. They are more sensitive to those of their own kind, whether defined by race or sex or anything else, than to those they consider threatening. But selective sensitivity is a lamentable fact of life, not a worthy moral goal.

What goes around, as they say, comes around. There is a perfectly good reason to use "politically correct" in a pejorative sense, especially when applied ironically to the heirs of those who first used it in describing themselves and to the leaders of our own time who purport to represent diversity! It focuses attention, legitimately, on the belief that their own way of thinking is correct and all other ways incorrect (or, among the more cynical, that some ideas are expedient for promoting the cause and others inexpedient). This belief in "our truth" versus "their truth" makes sense in terms of divine revelation, it is true, but divine revelation is hardly an authority that could or would ever be claimed by those who believe that Western religions are really insidious "superstructures" designed to generate "false consciousness" and thus maintain bourgeois or patriarchal hegemony.

The problem with those who insist on political correctness has nothing at all to do with the causes that they promote. It has everything to do with the self-righteous, anti-intellectual, and even totalitarian way that they go about doing so (stifling debate by censoring free speech through laws or behaviour codes) and the opportunistic use that they make of a double standard (ignoring or even assaulting the feelings of those who are excluded from their list of society's official victims – which is to say, those who had done the same thing to them).

The politically correct, among others, ostensibly have one main goal: eradicating prejudice. And who could argue with that? There have indeed been serious cases of prejudice against minorities in modern Western societies (though no more than in other societies). Hindus in Britain protested when Matchbox Toys produced a series of figures called Monster in My Pocket, which included the following: werewolves, hobgoblins, zombies, ogres, vampires, ghouls, witches, hunchbacks and two popular Hindu deities: Ganesh and Kali.[7] Muslims have long pointed to prejudice directed against them in press coverage of Islamic fundamentalism and terrorism. This problem was addressed directly by President Bush after 11 September 2001. In the 1970s, however, cartoons often showed Arab sheiks, sinister with their exaggerated Semitic features, standing behind gas pumps and leering. Arab stereotypes of oversexed degenerates, shrewd scoundrels, bloated slave traders, and so forth had long been featured in popular movies.[8] The same problem can be found even in academic circles. Jews have discovered, for example, that Christian feminists sometimes succumb to traditional anti-Semitic polemic. In this case, Christians present Jesus as someone who had come to liberate women from their enslavement under the patriarchal laws of Judaism.[9] The fact is that identity, whatever its basis, is not always respected. The complexity of reality as minorities have experienced it is not always acknowledged. Due to the imbalance of power, moreover, it is seldom easy for members of minority communities (and women in the past) to speak out. As a result, they feel "silenced."

At the very least, an effort should be made to avoid language that excludes whole groups of people. Linguistic history notwithstanding, it is obvious to most people by now that the generic "he" no longer refers to both men and women. Fortunately, the English language is easily adapted, both grammatically and aesthetically, in most situations. Simply by using the plural instead of the singular, for example, speakers and writers can avoid constructions that are either clumsy ("he or she," and "his/her"), ungrammatical ("their" when referring to a single person), or unpronounceable, legalistic, and, well, barbaric ("s/he").

No doubt aware of this, some people nevertheless prefer more pretentious solutions. They do not want merely to avoid inappropriate language. They want to demonstrate their own rectitude. Sometimes, therefore, they make a point of alternating between the generic "he" and the generic "she." Sometimes, they do not even bother with that self-conscious declaration of their commitment to equality. In an article for the august and venerable *Journal of the American Academy of Religion*, for example, Mark Cladis uses the generic "she" throughout. "A reasonable person," he writes, "is someone who, among other things, desires to justify her beliefs when confronted with sensible doubts or questions. She will ask herself..."[10] In this heavy-handed way, Cladis preaches as well as teaches. Quite apart from presenting ideas or theories about the subject at hand, he treats his righteous feminist readers to moral edification even as he exposes his ignorant sexist readers

– for their own good, presumably – to moral chastisement. After reading the article, some readers might conclude that the subtext establishing his own moral, political, and ideological credentials is more important to Cladis than the essay itself. In another essay in the same issue, James Wiggins, president of the Academy, indignantly and pretentiously uses "*sic*" to correct the generic "he" in a quotation by Albert Einstein![11]

Well, what is the solution to the problem of previously ignored groups? To take revenge by silencing others? To claim the need for protection from the pressures of public or academic debate? To ignore scholarship as an excuse for promoting political expediency? Unfortunately, the desire to control what others say, even if initiated with good intentions, has a profoundly destructive impact on any free society. This brings us to some egregious cases of prejudice against *majorities*. Does that sound preposterous? If it does, our society is in big trouble. By definition, after all, a democracy must allow the majority to dominate (though not persecute). Discrimination against the majority, therefore, must not be dismissed as irrelevant. It has serious moral and legal implications.

Participants in the interfaith memorial service for victims of a Swissair disaster, for instance, represented several religions. Included were Christians, Jews, and Muslims. The service was supposed to be ecumenical, of course, but it was not. Jewish and Islamic but not Christian scriptures were read. Agreeing to this, in fact, was a condition for the participation of Christians at all.[12]

Political correctness is always linked closely with deconstruction, both being tools used together by postmodernists. Deconstruction involves the "destabilizing" or "subversion" of institutions, beliefs, and so on. Which ones? Those that are politically incorrect. Which ones are politically incorrect? Those that have been deconstructed. That the aim of deconstruction is to destroy one thing and replace it with another, not merely to add "diversity," is made surprisingly clear. In an essay for the *New York Times Magazine*, Bob Morris discusses a brochure depicting a model family. On the surface, every member seems to be healthy, happy, and wholesome. But Morris finds out that the truth is less attractive.

> It all seemed pretty seamless. Model son played sweetly. Model dad watched lovingly. Model mom remained upstairs in makeup. For this they were earning a couple thousand dollars each. So how would I unravel them? It turned out I didn't have to. Because as soon as I asked about their home life, model dad got testy. Then, when I asked him how long he and model mom had been married, he became belligerent. Why? Because *they're not married*. They don't even live together. And of course it would be very bad for their image were I to report such a thing. After meeting model mom (who seemed to have almost nothing to say to model dad) I left them in the Rockwellian world of art-directed hugs and turkey, relieved to know that the model family is only a model family when it's paid to be one.[13]

At one level, Morris takes justifiable pleasure in the unmasking of self-righteous hypocrisy. We all know that those who present themselves as ideal types seldom live up to expectations. At another level, though, Morris suggests that there is something wrong with having ideals in the first place. For him, the paintings by Norman Rockwell that represent an ideal America are not merely sentimental but dangerous. They give people the shocking impression, he believes, that "traditional" families (which most people understand as one in which both mother and father live with their children) is better than other forms of family life. In fact, he suggests, it is worse. Hence his relief at discovering the sinister reality that underlies the glossy facade.

This way of thinking, however, is not just selectively cynical and self-righteous but self-defeating as well. No society can exist unless it presents people with some ideals to emulate. Of course no one ever attains the ideal totally or perfectly. Is that any reason to abandon the ideal itself? According to the more politically expedient postmodernists, it is indeed. They believe in the legitimacy, even the necessity, of blurring the distinctions among fact, opinion, and interpretation. "[It] is a measure of how far we have gone, or how far we are, in the belief that any social reality is an arbitrary construction that could just as easily have been any other social reality, and that knowledge is only, or mainly, a form of power, and that power is domination of the kind that pits the simple and unevolving dominator, with his reality against a simple and unevolving dominatee, with hers."[14]

Moreover, political correctness always involves some form of opportunism. In their massive effort to bring women back into history, politically correct feminists often feel free to turn historical figures into modern feminists or proto-feminists. This is obviously the case in popular culture, which has always treated history as a source to be ransacked for the stories of people who can be transformed into heroic icons or at least adjusted to suit the needs and tastes of later generations. The same is true, though, of elite culture. Whether they call it revisionism or not, for example, historians have always revised history in view not only of new facts that come to light but of new theories or ideologies that come into fashion. But few historians, until recently, did so *intentionally*. Nowadays, some academics believe that doing so is an appropriate way of "deconstructing" history, of giving a "voice" to marginalized groups. But they do not always listen carefully to those being studied. As a result, they fall into the same trap as their adversaries: reading into the past what they think should have been there.

Consider the case of Carolyn Karcher, author of *The First Woman in the Republic: A Cultural Biography of Lydia Maria Child*.[15] In a review of this book, Drew Gilpin Faust discusses the ahistorical result of politically correct and deconstructive historiography.

The author demonstrates her ahistoricism [by observing] that Child's work seems to have a "startlingly modern ring." Throughout her book, Ms. Karcher views

Child within the context of her own 20th-century concerns and standards, rather than offering a textured portrait of the way Child herself viewed her world. Ms. Karcher hails her for variously "anticipating" the 20th-century historians Richard Slotkin, Richard Drinnon and Sara Evans; "recent trends in feminist scholarship"; "the revolutionary 20th-century educator Paulo Freire" and even Freud.

Ms. Karcher is then discomforted when Child, quite naturally, shows herself [to be] a daughter of her own age: demonstrating a distressingly tenacious ethnocentrism; a "tinge of racism"; an unfortunate paternalism; anti-Catholic, anti-French and anti-Irish bias; and an inability, late in life, to comprehend the class and labor conflicts that were emerging around her. Although Ms. Karcher struggles to construct Child as a proponent of a "truly egalitarian, multicultural society," she is ultimately disappointed, admitting that Child "would never succeed in formulating an ideal of human brotherhood that did not involve the absorption of other cultures into her own."[16]

At least Karcher is able to admit defeat in this respect. Not everyone is that honest. Faust's concluding observation is extremely interesting: "Making a historical case from present knowledge is an ethnocentrism operating over time instead of over social or geographical space."[17]

Respectable Porn:
The Debate over Romance Novels

Romance novels present a problem for feminists. On the one hand, they are formulaic books of little or no literary value. And worse, the formula reinforces stereotypes of women. On the other hand, they are written both by and for women.[1] Obviously, much hangs in the balance when their cultural function is discussed. Why do women write them? Why do women read them? So far, most feminists have condemned these novels as anachronisms even as they have defended their authors and readers as unwitting dupes of a patriarchal society that prevents women from understanding their own oppression. More recently, though, feminists have begun to defend both the books and their readers.

The romance genre, addressed to women, is often compared to one or more genres addressed to men. These are usually said to include not only science fiction, adventure, and war but also porn. Feminists have noted that the female characters are either crudely stereotyped and "objectified" (as in porn) or almost non-existent (in the other genres).[2] Although these productions clearly serve some need of the men who buy them, therefore, they are not considered respectable. Neither were romance novels until very recently, although they clearly serve some need of the women who buy them. Apart from anything else, these books present women as victims who are saved by strong men – that is, naive young women who end up happily and safely married to powerful men. Why would any feminists approve of that scenario? For several reasons, actually. One thing is certain: these books have been reevaluated, reclassified, and sometimes rewritten as the literature of female "empowerment." The male characters are just as stereotypical as ever, of course, but no one cares about them. To the extent that male characters are stereotyped and "objectified" in the interest of female ones (and female readers), though, these stories could be called "respectable porn."

Angela Miles has produced a most ingenious and elaborate defence. Far from being embarrassed by romance novels, she uses them as evidence for (among other things) the theory of comparative suffering so useful in promoting feminist ideology. Fantasies of an ideal lover who is both strong and sensitive are so popular among women, she claims, because women – unlike men, presumably – are emotionally deprived. We can see that women suffer more than men, she argues, because otherwise men would produce romantic fantasies for themselves. Instead, they produce emotionally empty pornographic fantasies. In what follows, we examine romance novels and the debate that they have provoked in more detail, bearing in mind this underlying assumption.

According to Sarah Bird, approximately "600,000 readers belong to Harlequin's book club and buy, sight unseen, month in, month out, every book in their favourite series. Readers' letters, focus groups, surveys, and sales enable the editors to keep their fingers on the pulse of their audience. This information in turn is passed along to writers as guidelines. Looking at the these tip sheets after being absent for more than five years, I'm convinced that if you want to know what is up with women in the land, you could do worse than consult the rules of the romance-writing game."[3]

Well, what precisely is up with women in the land of Harlequin? This is what Miles tries to answer in "Confessions of a Harlequin Reader: Romance and the Myth of Male Mothers."[4] Because feminists have frowned on romance novels for allowing women to escape into reactionary fantasies in which women are swept off their feet and rescued by strong men and because literary critics look down on them for pandering to unsophisticated low-brows who are satisfied with formulaic plots and verbal clichés, Miles feels the need to spend her first four pages merely explaining her desire to defend them in the first place. Some of her attempts to do so are, to be charitable, naive. "Readers of westerns," she avers, "are not commonly supposed to live in expectation of a stage coach at the door but Harlequin readers are presumed to believe in the Harlequin world and to live in daily expectation of the hero's arrival."[5] Not so fast. Readers or viewers of westerns are not expected to believe in the literal reality of stage coaches, to be sure, but they are often expected to believe in the metaphorical and psychological reality that underlies the mentality of gunslingers. It was for precisely this reason that many Americans were dismayed when George W. Bush, from Texas, became president. It could be, as Miles argues, that Harlequin readers "have as good a grasp on reality as any other formulae readers,"[6] but is that anything to celebrate? From what she herself writes elsewhere in her article, we would say no.

Although Miles presents her discovery of Harlequin romances as a "coming out" story, that genre is derived from a much older narrative genre with deep roots in Western culture. Several terms used by Miles, including one in the title itself, "confessions," indicate a connection, consciously or unconsciously made, with an earlier phase of this older genre. We are referring to the Protestant conversion story. Like so many of the testimonials by evangelicals, hers is marked by the characteristic movement from confession of shame and guilt, to repentance, on to the "born again" experience, and, finally, to "sharing."

Like most women, I think, I read one or two Harlequins over the years when nothing else was available. All I saw, at first, were sexist, predictable, often poorly written stories with boorish heroes and embarrassingly childish heroines. They have a rigid formula which, unlike many other aspects, has remained unchanged over the years ... Imagine my surprise when I first found myself actually enjoying a Harlequin. It was one summer when I stayed at a friend's cottage and it rained for days and days. I lay on a comfortable sofa ... After I returned to the city and the pressures of thesis writing, I continued to read the occasional Harlequin; but I sometimes *chose* to read them when other books were available. At the time, I explained my pleasure in them by the fact that I was very, very busy and tired and needed a break ... Gradually, I began to read more and more Harlequins, until one day, when I found myself about to buy one, I began to suspect I was hooked ... As soon as I realized this, I "came out." As a feminist I know that the personal is political and that we must struggle individually to change ourselves as well as collectively to change society. Yet I didn't want to lose the strange comfort I found in Harlequins and I didn't feel they were terribly destructive or sinful. I could justify making Harlequins a non-struggle area of my life only if I genuinely felt they weren't so bad. And if they weren't so bad I had to be able to tell my friends that I read them. In any case, skeletons in the closet leave you awfully vulnerable, if not to blackmail then to terrible embarrassment, and I wasn't up to living with the risk. I didn't make a public announcement or send cards but I did drop it into conversations whenever I could.[7]

Once Miles discovers the hidden key that unlocks the mystery of why women like romance novels, she reveals it to other women with the zeal of a missionary. They, too, can now indulge in their secret passion without guilt or shame. Not only are these novels not politically anachronistic or artistically worthless, according to Miles, they are also psychologically or even spiritually redemptive. "When a reader knows the Harlequin formula, she can identify the hero figure immediately, anticipate the pattern of events, and is involuntarily caught up in an extremely active and demanding psychological interaction with the text, one that has been called, without irony or exaggeration, 'the Harlequin experience.'"[8] Just as religious experience usually precedes theology (which is an attempt to explain the ineffable experience in cognitive terms), this introduction precedes analysis (which is her attempt to explain the subjective in objective terms). "My experience as a feminist and Harlequin reader starkly raised the question "What do they offer me?" I began reading Harlequins before they were even slightly influenced by the values of the women's movement ... and as a feminist I often found their message/story offensive. I had to suspend or censor these judgement/feelings in order to enjoy the book. The fact that I could do this suggested that there was another level of meaning for me."[9]

The explanation offered by Miles is really very simple. The romance novel is not as childish as it seems. In fact, it is really a roman à clef. Or, to pursue the religious analogy in her title, it is a myth: a story that is told in symbolic language and that reveals some truth about the human condition. As such, it consists not of idiosyncratic individuals in complex situations but of archetypal characters in idealized situations. Miles describes the essential and archetypal attributes of the heroine, the "other man," the "other woman," and the hero. A brief description of each should explain a great deal about Miles and her political perspective, even if it does not explain a great deal about the Harlequin romance itself.

The heroine is generally a waif-like creature. She might be an orphan, penniless, far from home, or inherently vulnerable in some way. She has some psychological problems, too. Very often, she is accident-prone. Sometimes, she is just plain silly. She is almost always unsure of herself in some basic way. For this very reason, feminists have attacked the genre. Why, they argue, should women be infantilized? Why should heroines be women who cannot make it on their own but depend, instead, on men? If the heroine is ultimately looking for fulfilment in heterosexual love, though, she gives in (to what Miles apparently considers a weakness) only at the last moment.

> It ... has been suggested that the uppity, reactive, foot-stamping behaviour of the heroine may give women readers pleasure because they like to see heroines who can talk back to men and give them a hard time. Readers like heroines who do not try to please and impress men, who are, at least at first, indifferent to male opinion. Certainly, the heroine is *never* looking for a man or thinking of marriage. If she is not indifferent to men and marriage, she has an absolute aversion. Early on she isn't interested enough to use feminine wiles; later she disdains their use. One explanation put forward for this is that the heroine's lack of interest in the hero is required by a traditional code that forbids "good" women to take an active part in initiating sexual relationships. But when I first began to ponder the heroine's unvarying initial indifference or aversion to the hero, it seemed to me that the heroine's lack of initiative is important not primarily because we are bound by an internalized patriarchal morality but because it indicates *genuine love* (whatever that is).[10]

Miles claims to know precisely, however, what is meant by "genuine love." The heroine wants to be "loved for herself, warts, tantrums and all."[11] In short, she yearns for the kind of unconditional love she had, or wanted, as a child.

The "other man" is, of course, an inadequate man. He is the one *not* chosen by the heroine. In fact, he is the foil against which the hero is measured. He is the stereotypical wimp. "These 'other men' are weak, childish, dependent, sullen, and needy. They whine and pout and constantly demand attention and mothering from the heroine."[12] Not surprisingly, the heroine rejects him in no uncertain terms. "Harlequins," observes Miles, "are about *not* having to mother men."[13] In fact, the heroine wants a man to take care of her. There is a double standard here. Men who want someone to take care of them are contemptible wimps, but women who want the same thing are sympathetic heroines.

Corresponding to the "other man," is the "other woman." She is the heroine's rival for the hero's love. Unlike the heroine, according to Miles, she is aggressive and domineering. "In earlier Harlequins, these [characters] are a whole species of extremely beautiful, manipulative women who pretend to be all heart and warmth to men but don't bother to hide their coldness, indifference, and cunning from other women. Your quintessential male-identified woman."[14] But in the Harlequin world, as in the real world, things are changing. "In more recent Harlequins, the other woman is much less likely to be a nasty, male-identified, woman-hating manipulator. She may be kind and friendly, warm, generous, and gifted, but still breath-takingly beautiful and a feared potential rival for the hero's love." Being up to date and politically correct in a feminist age, we surmise, means that no woman – not even the "other woman," – may be portrayed in a negative way. Though idealized, the new "other woman" remains a rival in relation to the heroine. No longer "bad," she is nevertheless envied and feared by the heroine.

Of primary importance for Miles, though, is the hero. He, too, stands in symbolic opposition to the "other man." Not only does he not depend on the heroine, he also remains indifferent to her until the very last page. Moreover, he is often patronizing, boorish, arrogant, or even sinister. In fact, he often bullies the heroine. On the other hand, he has many admirable qualities. He is strong, for instance, and self-sufficient.

In view of all this, the archetypal romance novel is surely *Gone with the Wind*, by Margaret Mitchell. After more than sixty years, the book remains popular. (Even more popular, though, is the filmed version.)[15] The story has always appealed primarily to women. It can be seen, in fact, as the romance novel's direct prototype.[16] Its major characters certainly correspond to the types characteristic of this genre. Scarlett O'Hara is the sheltered but determined heroine. Melanie Wilkes is the perfect but resented "other woman." Ashley Wilkes is the chivalrous but wimpy "other man." And what of Rhett Butler?

Consider what Helen Taylor says of him in *Scarlett's Women: Gone With the Wind and Its Female Fans*: "Swashbuckler and tough guy; entrepreneur and war hero; enigmatic stranger and relaxing confidant; sexual wizard and tender parent; wanderer and home-lover; iconoclast and visionary. Is it any wonder he is the stuff female heterosexual fantasy is made of, or that so many women find his final parting so profoundly tear-jerking?"[17] Of particular interest here is Taylor's assertion that Rhett "must surely be the twentieth-century prototype of the hero of postwar mass-produced romance fiction, he who combines a restrained violence with gentle nurturant loving, and who remains (until the end) a sexually magnetic enigma."[18] As the characteristically idealized but ambiguous hero, in short, he is warm, generous and protective, but also dark, aggressive, and vaguely sinister.[19]

Vaguely sinister? Even though Rhett is considered disreputable in elite circles, readers or viewers are expected to sympathize with this honest and straightforward man rather than the smug or outdated leaders of polite society. Even though he has acquired considerable wealth through gambling and piracy, moreover, viewers are expected to admire his enterprise and ambition. All the same, as Taylor points out, they are expected also to be thrilled by his more threatening characteristics, especially those conventionally and stereotypically associated with maleness. Even his physical appearance is big, muscular, predatory, and animalistic – unlike Ashley, who is elegant, aesthetic, reserved, refined, sensitive, moralistic, civilized – and thus associated stereotypically with femaleness. In the book, Rhett "is associated with the forces of evil, mystery and male sexuality, with his black eyes, hair, face and clothes and his wild stallion. His darkness allies him with other legendary and fictional figures, too, from the pirate and villain of melodrama to the swarthy Victorian hero and the gangster. Attractive but sinister, sexually irrepressible but morally repulsive, all these are connotations of the dark and inscrutable Rhett Butler."[20]

Because these qualities are far less obvious in the movie than in the book, very few female viewers have consciously thought of Rhett as sinister. On the contrary, they have admired his virile and handsome appearance, his sophisticated way with women, his shrewd approach to life in general and pragmatic approach to politics in particular, his insight into human nature, his gentleness with Bonnie, his appreciation of Melanie and – most of all – his patient devotion to Scarlett. He understands her. He woos her. He pampers her. And yet he, well, rapes her.

It is possible, at any rate, to interpret his behaviour in one scene with that in mind. The most famous scene in the movie, the one featured on countless posters and lobby-cards, the one that suggests a reason for the movie's extraordinary popularity among women, shows Rhett carrying Scarlett to the bedroom upstairs – against her stated will. Although the women of earlier generations seldom interpreted this as a rape scene, some do now. The controversy is not exactly trivial. It has enormous symbolic, and thus political, significance. It is notorious enough, in fact, to have been discussed in a column of the *New York Times*: "Word for Word: A Scholarly Debate."

The particular debate began after Christina Hoff Sommers told an audience that "[m]any women continue to enjoy the sight of Rhett Butler carrying Scarlett O'Hara up the stairs in a fate undreamt of in feminist philosophy."[21] Incensed, Marilyn Friedman told another audience that the behaviour of Sommers could be described as "treasonable to women."[22] Friedman declares that only someone ignorant of feminism could claim that rape is "a fate undreamt of in feminist philosophy." But Sommers said precisely the reverse. She argued not that Scarlett's fate was rape but that it was something far more complex and ambiguous than rape. "I have read quite a lot of what the gender [ideological] feminists write," replied Sommers. "And I have learned that they almost always interpret a text in a way that puts the most *humiliating* construction on women's experiences with men. The gender [ideological] feminist ... 'subtext' of almost everything written about men and women in the patriarchy is rape, prostitution, debasement."[23]

Well, was it rape or not?[24] Even Friedman admits that the case for rape is debatable, at least theoretically. "By the time Butler gets to genital penetration, O'Hara is sexually aroused."[25] Presumably, she becomes an automaton; totally controlled by Rhett – or, better still, by ways of thinking and feeling engrained in her mind by men in general – Scarlett cannot be held responsible for behaviour that she herself later regrets. But Friedman ignores the larger context of this scene. When Scarlett wakes up the next morning, after all, she is happy with whatever fate had befallen her the night before. Because this is so obvious in the movie, Friedman turns instead to the book. "In her own words of recollection the next morning, as written by Margaret Mitchell, O'Hara had been 'humbled,' 'hurt' and 'used' ... brutally.'"[26] But the words quoted have been taken out of context. Friedman has forgotten, apparently, to quote the entire passage: "And now, though she tried to make herself hate him, tried to be indignant, she could not. He had humbled her, hurt her, used her brutally through a wild mad night and she had gloried in it."[27] Ignoring this little technicality, Friedman continues: "O'Hara, it seems to me, has a more credible understanding of her own experience than does Sommers."[28] Actually, it is Sommers, not Friedman, who finds Scarlett's own understanding credible. And not only Scarlett's understanding, we might add, but that of all the women who, for whatever reason, find this episode so delightful.

Friedman admits that "the narrow definition of rape" might not be applicable. "However, I use the term 'rape' in a wider sense, in which it refers to any very intimate sexual contact which is initiated forcibly or against the will of the recipient. Perhaps ... we should refer to this wider notion as 'sexual domination.'" In other words, as Sommers points out, "Friedman insists that even when 'no' turns to 'yes,' a rape has occurred ... She now finds herself in the position of conceding to the macho male the sexist thesis that women like the idea of being raped (in the 'wider sense')."[29]

Friedman argues that "this scene arouses the sexual desire of some men."[30] In other words, it is pornography. Actually, there is no evidence whatsoever that men like this scene. In fact, the entire movie has never been particularly popular among men. According to the evidence, it is and always has been popular mainly among women. This is a problem that Friedman never even addresses. Whether the scene actually depicts a rape or something else, after all, is irrelevant. Whether the fictional Scarlett actually enjoys it or not is irrelevant. Very relevant, though, is the fact that millions of real women identify themselves strongly with Scarlett and clearly do enjoy it. What this fantasy actually means, of course, is another matter entirely. Both women and men need to find out what it means.

Ambivalence toward the hero in romance novels is nothing new. Helen Taylor points out that these stories have a long history, one that goes back to the eighteenth century. The hero of that tradition was not only handsome, charming, and aristocratic or wealthy. He was also someone "with an enigmatic, shady past history, a reputation for sexual excess and scandal, exquisite taste and perfect self-control, a proud and determined ability to keep his distance and appear cruel to the woman he eventually overwhelms with passion."[31] One writer of romance novels echoes this. Of the hero's advances toward the heroine, she observes that "he overpowers her [so that] she shouldn't look as though she absolutely hates this."[32] The implications of this ambivalence, though, have yet to be fully understood.

The debate over this famous, or infamous, scene from *Gone with the Wind* highlights the current debate over sexual relations between men and women. It says something about the ambivalence women have always felt toward men. In everyday life, ordinary men can seldom, if ever, satisfy the contradictory needs or desires of women. Therefore, women must choose between, say, adventurous sailors and steady accountants. Men have always been aware that women want to be considered attractive by men or, at the very least, to be noticed by men. But men have recently become aware also that openly acknowledging their sexual interest in women, openly enjoying the beauty of a female body, is considered vulgar, disreputable, or even oppressive by many women. The latter say that they find it degrading and insulting rather than flattering, for example, when men whistle at them on the street. Feminists are very explicit about it: wolf whistles, they say, are sexist. This is the premise, in fact, on which countless situation comedies and even more serious television programs are based. Moreover, it is the basic premise of all romance novels. Heroines must be sensuous or even sensual but not overtly sexual. They must remain chaste to the end – that is, until the marriage ceremony. Readers accept sexual intercourse after marriage, because (even if for no other reason) they accept the desirability of children, but they do not want their escapist pleasure disturbed by frank talk of sexual intercourse.[33] Not surprisingly, male heterosexuality is now referred to contemptuously, in some feminist and lesbian circles, as "phallocentrism" or "phallocracy."

What interests Miles most are the hero's admirable qualities, not his sinister ones. Unlike the "other man," the hero offers the heroine protection, security, and tenderness under the right circumstances. In short, according to Miles he offers her the kind of love associated with mothers. The hero is a mother! "True love, as unconditional love which comes unsought and unearned, without the heroine actively seeking it and regardless of what she does to antagonize the hero, is like our dream of mother-love. The hero's nurturing and domineering behaviour, two aspects of the childhood experience of mothering, are presented as two constant and interacting themes, often evoked with symbols of mother and child in scenes which echo mother/child images, and involve explicit references to the male as caretaker/mother and the female as a motherless child."[34]

Miles devotes most of her essay to this ingenious but facile analogy. It is, in fact, the heart of her argument. She does acknowledge a need to answer "the complex question of why women would fantasize a mother figure as male."[35] After twenty-seven pages, though, she admits that she can offer only "initial observations" on this problem. According to Miles, "one obvious reason [for arguing that the hero is a mother] may be that in a patriarchy only men have enough social power to represent the powerful mother figure. Paradoxically, female figures other than mythical ones do not have the necessary power and resources to stand for the mother."[36]

This is obvious? Miles would have to provide some evidence for what would otherwise seem, at the very least, contrived. What has "social power" to do with symbolism? How, for example, would Miles explain the rise of Christianity? The earliest Christians, after all, were a bunch of despised sectarians, destitute peasants, and illiterate slaves. They had no social power. Their god was an executed criminal, their symbol the cross on which he had been tortured! By the late Middle Ages, on the other hand, Mary had indeed become a powerful symbol of motherhood. So powerful that devotion to her had almost eclipsed devotion to Christ. Besides, the social power that supposedly enables men to represent mothers is the very kind of power that Miles considers antithetical to "women's consciousness."

Undaunted, Miles provides another possible answer to the vexing problem, this one based on warmed-over Freudianism. If the hero is male, she avers, the psychological threat of fusion with Mother is mitigated. By the same token, though, the threat of fusion with Father is augmented. Incestuous feelings toward the latter are surely not so very much more acceptable than incestuous or regressive feelings toward the former. Besides, why should symbolic fantasies of marrying Father be experienced as threatening? The whole point of a fantasy, after all, is precisely to indulge in thoughts and feelings that would otherwise be condemned as foolish or immoral.

Miles comments on her lesbian friends, finally, who read Harlequin romances. For Miles this clearly shows that the novels are not merely about love and sex between straight people. The implication is that lesbians would be unable to find any value in books about straight love, in which case they would be cut off from most of the world's great literature. But this is utter nonsense. Human identity transcends sexual identity. Gay people are not a separate race or species. They are as capable as any others of seeing their own humanity reflected in the fictional characters (no matter how seemingly different from themselves) of straight authors. And they are as capable as any others of creating these characters themselves. In books valued by all people, gay authors – Somerset Maugham, E.M. Forster, and Tennessee Williams, to name a few – have written movingly, compassionately, insightfully, and convincingly about straight love.

According to Miles, romance novels commonly focus on themes such as the ambivalent feelings of the heroine toward the "lover/mother," her joy at being noticed and despair at being unnoticed, her problem of "sibling" rivalry for love and attention, her intense longing for security through fusion, and so forth. Yet she points to hardly anything about her relationship with an idealized mother that could not be said equally of her relationship with an idealized father. "Certain types of activities, commonly shared by mother and child, appear frequently enough in different Harlequins to earn the status of themes. The hero and heroine shop for clothes for the heroine together; he comforts her when she has bad dreams; he scolds her for risking illness; he tucks her into bed and gives her medicine; he leads her by the hand; restrains her physically from running away, having tantrums and so on."[37]

With the possible exception of shopping for clothes, these activities are all associated with the ideal parent whether mother *or* father. Having quoted a Harlequin
passage in which the hero saves the heroine's life, Miles concludes as follows: "It is
not incidental ... that the hero has ... like the mother, actually given the heroine
life."[38] The analogy is forced. It is true that mothers alone gestate. And it is true
that mothers alone are associated also with activities that sustain new life. But
fathers are associated with saving or protecting new life from perils outside the
womb and beyond the home (in addition, of course, to providing the material
resources that enable mothers to nourish the young). It could be argued that very
few real fathers are as tender and loving as Rhett Butler, sure, but it could be argued
as well that very few real mothers are as tender and loving as Rhett – or Ellen
O'Hara or even Mammy.

Now consider the reality of parenting more closely. It is safe to say that we would
all like the kind of unconditional love under discussion here. But those fortunate
enough to receive it as children are precisely those least likely to go on seeking it
through fantasy as adults. If so many women are addicted to romance novels, therefore, it would be logical to conclude that they were not given enough love as children in real life. Because Miles associates this kind of love only with mothers,
though, it would be logical to conclude in addition that the problem has been
caused by a widespread inadequacy of real mothers. For Miles, no doubt, this conclusion would be unacceptable. But the same logic could be used to argue for the
hero as father. That women do, in fact, feel strongly about fathers can be seen not
only in the productions of popular culture (which often portray fathers doing the
very things described by Miles, albeit clumsily) but also in the findings of psychiatrists (who note that girls seek a distinctive kind of love and guidance from their
fathers, which later enables them not only to succeed in achieving personal goals
but also in establishing healthy heterosexual relationships) and even, ironically, in
the works of some feminists (who argue that children – presumably this includes
girls – need fathers who are fully integrated into the emotional structure of family
life). It could be argued that real fathers seldom express their love adequately, in
short, but not that daughters feel no powerful need for this love. On the contrary,
many feel the need precisely because their own fathers did not express their love
adequately. That would be a more attractive hypothesis to Miles, but the same logic
would refute her own hypothesis about mothers.

Miles has devoted a great deal of energy to legitimating the fantasies of women.
As we say, her theory is both cumbersome (relying heavily on the misandry of ideological feminism) and counter-intuitive (denying the obvious maleness of heroes).
But she has proposed it for a reason. In her introduction, she gives as her reason
the need to explain the embarrassing fact that many intelligent women like sim-
plistic, stereotypical, and standardized romance novels. (Others have tried to
explain the equally embarrassing problem of soap operas, which are produced primarily by and for women.) Even in the introduction, though, she makes it clear

that the topic is of far more than scholarly interest to her. At stake is her identity as a feminist. This "suggested that there was another level of meaning for me; something less explicit that appealed to me and presumably to other readers; something that could help to explain why this simple and threadbare formula should so attract women, and how women, who know it to be false, can lose themselves in it; in other words, something that could begin to answer the question 'What is the myth of romance for women?'"[39] Not surprisingly, perhaps, the answers provided by Miles are both explicit and implicit. Explicitly, she argues merely that the romantic fantasies of women are superior to the pornographic ones of men. Underlying the entire article, though, are two implicit arguments: that (female) homosexuality is superior to heterosexuality, and that women are superior to men. We will now examine each of these three arguments in more detail.

Miles argues explicitly that the romantic fantasies of women are superior to the violent ones of men. First, she admits that Harlequin romances provide women with an escape from reality but adds that women need to escape. Okay, they do. Everyone does at one time or another. That is part of being human. But Miles implies that men do not. Her way of thinking could be expressed as a syllogism. Romance novels provide an escape from emotional deprivation; romance novels are written by and for women alone; ergo, emotional deprivation is suffered only by women – which is to say, only women have a legitimate reason for escapist fantasies. If men do not need an escape, though, why do they turn to their own forms of fantasy, which include pornography, science fiction, westerns, stories about sports and survival in the wilderness, and so on? Pornography itself, moreover, consists of at least two genres: the kind that stimulates erotic fantasies and the kind that stimulates violent ones. Because Miles fails to mention the distinction, it could be assumed that she acknowledges none. In that case, she would take the common position that erotic images, because they objectify women, are no more innocent than violent ones. On the contrary, she would say, both are inherently sexist. It is true that Harlequins do not lead women to acts of violence (although even violent porn does not necessarily lead men to acts of violence). All the same, they can lead to serious social problems.

Taken at face value, they encourage women to expect the impossible from men. Publicly, women demand gentleness and sensitivity from men. In itself, that demand is unambiguous and at least theoretically possible for most men to meet. But privately, if romance novels are any indication of their fantasies, women long in addition for aggressiveness and challenge from men. That presents men with a double message. Their ideal is inherently ambiguous and thus very hard for most men to attain. Even if boys were taught the emotional and relational skills women admire in the Harlequin hero, after all, these skills would still conflict in the real world directly with what boys are taught of the hero's competitive and combative skills. As it happens, boys are seldom taught the former and often taught the latter.

Hardly ever are they taught how these skills might be combined in a healthy personality. The result of this confusion is a kind of intrasexual polarization among men. At one end of the continuum is the inadequate wimp. At the other end is the macho barbarian.

Not taken at face value, on the other hand, these novels encourage the withdrawal of women from men. If Miles were correct, if the hero were a mother, then the message to men would be that women need them either as replacements for mothers or not at all. To paraphrase a familiar racist cliché, "the only good Indian is a dead one," Miles would have us believe that the only good man is a woman – that is, a man who no longer exists as such. Why should men not respond with anger to the charge that they are inherently either inadequate or irrelevant? Women are dehumanized by men in some ways, it is true, but men are dehumanized by women in others. One kind of masculine pornography could be associated with violence, but feminine pornography could be associated with self-righteousness. The former might be even worse than the latter, but neither is any good. Feminist separatism (on which Miles bases her argument) is, along with male violence, directly involved in generating the kind of conditions that would bring about the dissolution of our society – or any society. Just as romance novels can lead to intrasexual polarization, then, they can lead also to intersexual polarization.

The second argument, like the third, is implicit. Miles does not actually say that female homosexuality is superior to heterosexuality, but no other conclusion can be drawn from what she does say. Following Nancy Chodorow and many other currently popular feminists, Miles argues that women are erotically self-sufficient.[40] The bond between women and men is secondary; the bond between mother and child – especially, as Miles argues, between mother and daughter – is primary. "The erotic power of the hero," she writes, "is achieved because he is the mother; he offers the complete gratification of safe total, passive surrender."[41] If this new twist on the old Freudian Elektra complex were correct, of course, then heterosexual intimacy would be nothing more in this age of sperm banks than a primitive way of conceiving children, preferably daughters. Heterosexual love would be a luxury that many women could do without. Their primary emotional needs would be served, presumably, by their mothers and other women. Heterosexuality would be the "root cause" of suffering for women, in fact, because "the emotional deprivation almost all women suffer in a heterosexually structure[d] society where women are care providers, rarely receivers, and where most women can expect no mothering or nurture after early adolescence, all combine to explain why the fantasy of mothering in the guise of a romantic hero is the predominant form of escape for women."[42] Permeating this essay, then, is what amounts to lesbian separatism. If the primary bonds for women are with other women – mothers, daughters, friends, and presumably lovers – why should women maintain contact with men at all? No wonder Miles refers to her realization of the value in romance novels, a redemptive experience that legitimated her identity as a reader of them, in terms of "coming out." The problem here is not homosexuality itself but the way in which Miles chooses to legitimate it: by delegitimating heterosexuality – which is to say, the kind of intimacy and interdependence that link women and men in enduring relationships.

Discussing her coming out experience, she observes that "it got easier as I developed arguments defending women's romantic fantasies as harmless (to others at least), human, and relatively innocent, especially when compared to the pornographic fantasies of men."[43] If Miles refers here to the kind of pornography that is based on sadomasochistic fantasies, we would agree. But if she refers to erotica in general (on the assumption that the mere enjoyment men find in looking at beautiful women is immoral), we would have to disagree with her. The implication of this attitude is that male heterosexuality as such is immoral.[44]

There is a parallel, as we have already indicated, between romance novels and erotica. The former are less vulgar, to be sure, but can nevertheless be defined with the latter as pornography. In the first place, both genres exploit images of the opposite sex by using them as screens onto which their own fantasies, representing their own needs, are conveniently projected. Although it is now common for feminists to discuss masculine pornography from the perspective of women, it is very uncommon for anyone to discuss feminine pornography from the perspective of men. How does Miles think men might feel about the way they are presented in Harlequins? She never asks this question. Nevertheless, the answer is not difficult to guess. Men would feel the same way any other group of people feel about being stereotyped. In this case, as we have said, men are stereotyped either as substandard (wimps) or superhuman (heroes who are both macho and, paradoxically, nonmacho). This would be true, moreover, even if Miles were correct in arguing that the men in the latter category really appear to women as mothers in drag. In that case, after all, the only men left, as such, would be those in the former category.

Besides, romance novels really are about the manipulation of power. Miles grudgingly admits that it is not quite unheard of for women to have fantasies of power over men (in which case she disagrees with Marilyn French and her colleagues).[45] "Some of us do," she says, "some of the time."[46] Think of the sadomasochistic fantasies that please some women just as they do some men. Nevertheless, she quickly exonerates Harlequin novels from this patriarchal taint. "The popularity of Harlequin Romances," she argues, "suggests that most women are not primarily interested in and do not gain satisfaction from power over others or the power to aggress."[47] But if readers do not fantasize about attaining power over men, how can we explain the fact that heroines always *do* attain power over their heroes? How can we explain the fact that so many female viewers applauded the heroines in *Thelma and Louise* for attaining power over men? Unlike recent movies, romance novels urge women to dream of attaining only emotional power over men. Even so, it is indeed power over men. After all, the heroes are so sick with love by the last page that their earlier indifference to the heroines melts away like ice on a spring day. The heroines themselves do not actively, or at least consciously, seek this hold over them, true. But readers obviously hope and know that they will attain it; otherwise, they would not read these formulaic books. To be sure, power is not an end in itself. Heroines do not relish this emotional power for its own sake. It is a means to another end. What they really want is "security" – that is, emotional and physical safety, along with (if we take the hero's social or economic position seriously) wealth, pleasure, and status. Not only is power over men the means to an end, though, but also men themselves are the means to an end. They supply women with what Miles herself defines as the goal of fantasy: "what is desirable but unattainable or non-existent."[48]

It will not do, therefore, to eulogize women by declaring "that most women's erotic pleasure, desire, and potential does not find itself primarily in phallic focused intercourse outside of intimacy, nurture, care, and security; and most women's sense of self and fulfilment requires a rich world of interrelationship and interdependence."[49] No doubt, many women want these very things (as do men). But if the erotic or quasi-mystical experience of childbirth and nursing makes women so "interrelated" and "interdependent,"[50] how can they be so unrelated to and independent of *men*? Miles makes it very clear, after all, that the autonomy of women is innate and not merely some response to negative experiences with men. And if the traumatizing experience of forming identity makes men so rooted in "discontinuity," why is there no equivalent to the lesbian separatist movement among gay men? Ironically, then, the very assertion that only women are truly integrated and connected to other people or other living things is refuted by her own claim that the emotional lives of women are self-contained, that their emotional needs are best satisfied by other women, that they simply do not need men. Whatever reasons lesbians use to legitimate separatism, the vaunted "permeable boundaries" that supposedly enable women to feel at one with all living things of the natural order cannot be counted among them – unless, of course, men are conveniently excluded from the natural order.

The third argument, too – that women, as such, are superior to men – is implicit. Unlike the second one, though, it is implicit not only in specific statements made by Miles but also – and this is extremely important – in her whole way of thinking. The comparisons made are highly moralistic. In each case, one term is identified as superior to the other. The former is then identified as good (which is the essence, as it were, of essentialism) and the latter with evil (which indicates the presence of dualism, too). Two things must be said about this way of thinking. In the first place, it is illogical. Just because one thing is better in some way than another does not mean that it is actually good; both, in fact, might be bad in other ways. For this reason, it is possible to choose one course of action as "the lesser of two evils." Similarly, just because one thing is worse in some way than another does not mean that it is actually evil; both, in fact, might be good in other ways. But logic has little or nothing to do with this third and ultimate argument of Miles. Dualism, on the other hand, has everything to do with it.

Without a trace of irony, she refers approvingly to Mary O'Brien, who "has argued that women's integrated experience of birth as a continuity of mediated labour provides the material basis for a female consciousness, which is more integrated and less dualistic than male consciousness rooted in a discontinuous experience of reproduction through the alienation of their seed."[51] Miles draws an almost inevitable conclusion from the similar opinions not only of Chodorow but also of Dorothy Dinnerstein and Jane Flax.[52] They have written of a "continuous identification with the mother which gives women the basis for a less separative, more relationally defined and connected sense of self than men. Thus women's experience of self and the world is very different from the competitive and dualistic male sense which has been called the 'human condition' and which shapes all patriarchal cultures and values."[53] True, the origin of these patriarchal cultures and values – what she obviously considers evil – is existential rather than genetic. But that distinction is irrelevant, because the former is as universal as the latter. Ironically, in any case, it does not occur to Miles that making invidious ontological comparisons of this kind – identifying "us" with what amounts to innate virtue and "them" with what amounts to innate vice (even though neither virtue nor vice, by definition, can be innate) – lies at the very heart of dualism!

Elsewhere, Miles agrees with Adrienne Rich, who has written that "to accept and integrate and strengthen both the mother and the daughter in ourselves is no easy matter because patriarchal attitudes have encouraged us to split, to polarize, these images, and to project all unwanted guilt, anger, shame, power, freedom, onto the 'other' woman."[54] Once again, it does not occur to Miles (or Rich) that by projecting guilt, anger, shame, power, and freedom onto men, instead of the "other woman," they are reversing the sexual hierarchy rather than moving beyond it. In fact, they are perpetuating dualism, not breaking away from it. Implicit is the notion that men and women may legitimately be considered, like blacks and whites in the days before integrated schools, both separate (if women have no emotional or sexual need for men) and unequal (if the fantasies of women are superior to those of men).

Ostensibly, Miles has adopted an apologetic approach: defending women who like romance novels. Actually, though, she has adopted a polemical one: attacking men for making romance novels necessary, as it were, in the first place. "Not only are Harlequin heroes grown up (rare birds in women's experience)," she writes, but in addition "they are sensitive and considerate and take care of the heroine – something so unexpected that the heroine frequently marvels about it."[55] When men write things like this about women, they are denounced for sexism. But Miles has a very specific point to make. As we say, she argues that the hero (male and good) is really a woman and that the heroine's rival (female and bad) is really a man! The wimp (male and bad) is, of course, still a man. By overtly contradicting the plain literary statements, Miles has managed to link femaleness with all that is good and maleness with all that is evil. When men are good, it is because they are really women (mothers). When women are bad, on the other hand, it is because they are really men (male-identified women)! Nothing could better illustrate the inherent misandric dualism in ideological forms of feminism.

Miles draws heavily on the work of those feminists who make biological or psychoanalytical claims for "interrelatedness" as a uniquely female quality. Mary O'Brien, Carol Gilligan, Nancy Chodorow, and many others discuss this notion in far more sophisticated but no less superficial ways than Miles. To have any meaning, this word must refer not only to empathy but also to responsibility. But what is responsibility? The authors we have been discussing use it in the sense of taking responsibility for others. In that future-oriented sense, it means willingness to act on their behalf. The same word, on the other hand, can be used also in the sense of taking responsibility for ourselves. In that past-oriented sense, it means willingness to accept guilt for the destructive things we have done to others. Ideological feminists claim that the former is a quality uniquely or innately female and the latter a quality uniquely or innately male. It would be difficult indeed to think of any ideological feminist who explicitly acknowledges that women share the burden of guilt with men for any social problem and not much easier to think of an egalitarian feminist who does. Even obvious examples of complicity are generally explained away as things that women have been "forced" to think or do by the men who dominate society. When women support war, for example, it is only because they have been manipulated cynically by the patriarchal institutions that promote violence and nationalism. When men do so, of course, it is because their "impermeable boundaries" inevitably lead them to love killing others.[56] When men support peace, on the other hand, it is only because they have been influenced by feminists or protofeminists. When women do so, it is because of some innate oneness with the "web of life" that leads them to love caring for others.[57]

In a less dramatic way, Miles does the same thing. Why do so many female readers see nothing peculiar about the "uppity, reactive, foot-stamping behaviour" of their heroines? Because men have made them that way! "Ann Snitow and others read the hero's bullying and the heroine's infantilization as a part of the general patriarchal message that women are not full people, are not to be taken seriously, are not responsible and are necessarily dependent on men."[58] (Why this should be reflected in the secret fantasies of women is not explained.) It is precisely this unacknowledged but pervasive dualism of ideological feminists that diminishes the credibility of their own claim to being uniquely "interrelated" (and, by implication, superior to men). At any rate, Miles herself can hardly claim to be an exemplar of this quality. Considering the topic of this particular essay, for example, she fails even to consider the possibility that romance novels send double messages to both women and men (who seldom read them but often find out about them in one way or another, especially when they see the cinematic versions with their girlfriends or wives). As a result, the women who write and read romance novels are morally implicated in the confusion and conflict between men and women.

But even if Miles were correct, even if this "interrelatedness" were some uniquely or innately female characteristic, that would *still* not make women morally superior to men. There is nothing inherently good, after all, about being interrelated or even interdependent. That is a fact of life for all living beings, male and female. Relationships take on moral overtones only when they are defined in terms of a larger philosophical or theological context. As long as people are valued only for what they can provide or do and not for what they are, words such as "nurture," "care," and even "love" can be used only in the most superficial sense. Consider this matter in more detail.

It is very easy to love those who provide us with what we want, whether we seek physical and emotional security or property, prestige, and pleasure. It is not wrong to want any of these things. What is wrong, though, is to pretend that there is some moral gulf that divides those who want the former from those who want the latter – or women who use men from men who use women. With regard to people, exploitation is defined by the act of using others (sometimes by intimidation and sometimes by manipulation) to serve our own needs or satisfy our own desires, not by the type of need or desire. In short, Harlequin heroes are used by Harlequin heroines. When men do that to women through fantasy, it is called "pornography." And when they do so in real life, it is called "objectification" or "exploitation."

It is very hard, on the other hand, to love with the expectation of nothing in return. Not even the gratitude and solicitude of children. That is the specifically moral dimension of love. Romance novels are said to be about fantasies of love. And love, in turn, is linked in these novels to marriage. It is generally assumed that marriage, or the path toward it, begins with the desire not only for physical intimacy but for emotional intimacy as well. Unfortunately, it is seldom assumed – by men or women – that marriage could or should lead to something deeper than either physical or emotional intimacy. Considering love in a moral sense, therefore, there is no significant difference between the readers of feminine pornography and those of masculine (erotic) pornography.

We have made three main points. First, romance novels say something disturbing about the fantasies women have of men, not something laudable about the fantasies they have of other women. Second, when romance novels are interpreted by ideological feminists, the result reveals more about the latter than the former. Third, that an ideological mechanism, what we call "comparative suffering," allows these interpreters to justify not only the unfair stereotypes of men explicitly presented in the novels (if women alone are deprived, then they alone need compensatory fantasies) but also their own polemical arguments about the superiority of women (if women alone produce and consume these fantasies, they alone are interested in caring or "nurturing").

So far, however, we have discussed only traditional romance novels, which appeal to women with positive but confused attitudes toward men. They want men, to be sure, but they want men unlike any that they could possibly meet in everyday life. Is that still true of more contemporary romance novels? In a way, it is. The hero is still impossibly unattainable. Otherwise, his value as a fantasy would be diminished and the genre would disappear. Still, there has been a major change in the Harlequin world.

As it happens, one of the most lucrative markets in our time is for romance novels that reflect specifically feminist (though not necessarily ideological) perspectives. Those who write romance novels these days, in other words, explicitly legitimate their work in terms of feminism. Kelli Pryor makes this much perfectly clear in the opening line of her article on a convention of the Romance Writers of America: "Think of a weekend with Thelma and Louise – but without the guns."[59] This metaphor of combat is very appropriate in view of that old proverb about the pen being mightier than the sword. Listen to Pryor's description of what she saw and heard at the convention. "In a chandeliered hall with floral carpets, best-selling author Susan Elizabeth Phillips ... is wearing an elaborate open work-embroidery blouse and describing the romance novel as an expression of female empowerment: The heroine takes on a domineering hero and by the end of the book she has turned him into a sensitive human being. 'In other words, she has turned him into a *woman*,' Phillips says. The audience cheers."[60] This is the kind of "empowerment" now being promoted among women by romance novels. Once again, the only good man is a woman. Miles might have distorted the meaning of traditional romance novels – the ones, no doubt, that continue to embarrass her as a feminist – but she might have some insight into contemporary ones. It could be that they no longer have the function of escapist fantasies but have instead the function of *political* fantasies. Our main point here, though, is that the dualistic perspective on gender is no longer just the expression of academics. It is the expression of a mass-market industry purveyed at the check-out stands of countless supermarkets throughout the country.

Romance novels are not misandric – they do not promote hatred toward men – which is why we did not discuss them in *Spreading Misandry*. We discuss them here, especially in connection with our discussion of pornography, to illustrate the double standard according to which stereotyping and objectifying men is considered respectable, or at least acceptable, but not stereotyping and objectifying women.

Bargaining at Beijing:
United Nations or United Women?

Among the many goals of the United Nations is improving the status of women. To that end, it has called many conferences, established many organizations or offices, and produced many documents. Being about women, they are all gyno-centric. In itself, that is perfectly legitimate. The problem is that this gynocentrism has become more than a focus to be adopted for specific practical purposes. It has become a worldview in its own right, a particularistic worldview in conflict with the universalistic one that is expressed in founding documents of the United Nations. Among those promoting it are, of course, ideological feminists. They use the rhetoric of gender, human rights, and equality. But they do so in ways that give a tendentious meaning to each. "Gender" usually refers only to women, as if it were never problematic for men. "Human rights" usually refers only to women's rights, as if these were never conflict with those of men or even of children. "Equality" usually refers to a goal that only women need to attain, as if special "corrective" programs for women were never the cause of new problems for men, at least in Western countries. And we are interested here only in two Western coun-tries: the United States and Canada.

In 1946, the United Nations created its Division for the Advancement of Women. After being renamed, relocated, and restructured several times since the 1970s, it is now part of the Department of Economic and Social Affairs and located in New York. It works closely with the United Nations Commission on the Status of Women, which has representatives from forty-five countries on a four-year rotation. They meet annually to set global standards on women's rights, refer specific women's problems to other United Nations agencies, and make policy recommen-dations to improve the status of women. In 1975, Mexico City was the venue for its first World Conference on Women.

During its Decade for Women, 1976–1985, the United Nations established many institutions to improve the status of women, including the International Research and Training Institute for the Advancement of Women and the United Nations

Development Fund for Women. In 1979 the General Assembly adopted the Convention on the Elimination of All Forms of Discrimination against Women (abbreviated here as "the Convention"). This Convention is the major document on sexual discrimination. Some passages use cautious language, which suggests equality of opportunity. Other passages permit affirmative action on a temporary basis. Still others endorse equality of result. More about this document in a moment.

Two more world conferences on women were held during the 1980s: those of Copenhagen and Nairobi. The most recent was held in 1995: that of Beijing. Two major documents were drafted for this conference, then debated and ratified: the Beijing Declaration[1] (abbreviated here as "the Declaration") and the Beijing Platform for Action ("the Platform").[2] The wording of both reflected a consensus of participating women. Those who ratified them went back to their own countries with the goal of instituting the recommendations.

Political bargaining is not as easy when the rights of all citizens must be taken into account, though, as it is when only those of women need be taken into account. Delegates have not always been successful in convincing their governments to change. Periodically, therefore, the General Assembly reviews their progress. In its report on the twenty-third special session, of 2000, it adopted "further actions and initiatives to implement the Beijing Declaration and Platform for Action, annexed to the present resolution" (abbreviated here as "the Annex").[3]

Because many people understand the Convention of 1979 as a purely political document, those who signed it being bound by few obligations and therefore lacking clout, the United Nations introduced its Optional Protocol in 2000.[4] It contains procedures that allow "individual women, or groups of women, to submit claims of violations of rights, as protected under the Convention, to the Committee on the Elimination of Discrimination against Women" if they have exhausted all remedies in their own countries. One procedure allows the committee itself "to initiate inquiries into situations of grave or systematic violations of women's rights," although countries may make use of an opt-out clause.[5] At one time there were few legal means of enforcement by the United Nations itself, although there were once member countries that changed their laws accordingly. Recently, though, the International Court of Justice, an arm of the United Nations that is popularly known as the World Court, created procedures to deal specifically with member countries that do not measure up to their treaty obligations in connection with women. To the extent that symbolism matters, countries with bad report cards lose status in the international community.

With this historical background in mind, consider several themes found in the Declaration, the Platform, and the Annex. First, human rights.

Among the most ubiquitous and seemingly harmless terms is "human rights" (even though the people who use this term have no coherent philosophy on which to support human rights). And what could possibly be wrong with human rights? Not a thing. Not unless the term is used as a euphemism for the rights of any specific group. The aim of some feminists is to reinterpret human rights by giving primacy to the rights of women. We say "primacy," because women's rights and human rights are not identical and do not necessarily even converge. Human rights are universal; they apply by definition to all human beings. Women's rights, by definition, apply only to women. And these sometimes conflict with those not only of men and boys, or even children of either sex, but also with those of various religious communities. More about that in due course.

As delegates at Beijing from around the world commented on two draft documents that had been prepared earlier, the discussion of women's needs and problems was subtly transformed into a discussion of women's rights. According to Mary Glendon, a professor of law at Harvard who observed the proceedings, this focus on women's rights presented a serious challenge to *human* rights as understood by another document of the United Nations: the Universal Declaration of Human Rights (abbreviated here as the "Universal Declaration"). Leading the onslaught on human rights, she points out, were European and Canadian delegates. They attacked several things that were supposedly protected by the Universal Declaration: marriage (by article 16), the family (article 16), mothers and children (article 25), and freedoms of thought, conscience, and religion (article 18). The new mentality could be summed up in connection with several presuppositions. First, claimed the Europeans and Canadians, people are autonomous and self-sufficient; they and their rights exist apart from any references to their families or communities. Second, rights are entitlements; they have no corresponding responsibilities. Third, many new rights should be added specifically for women; this would make them something other, though, than human rights.

More disturbing still, according to Glendon, was that these delegations actually tried to *remove* references in the drafts to human dignity. Why? Possibly because human dignity would include the rights of both women and men. "Recognition of inherent human dignity and of the equal and inalienable rights," according to the Universal Declaration's preamble, is intended for the protection "of *all* members of the human family." Article 1 adds that "*all* human beings are born equal in human dignity." This is amplified in article 2, which says that human beings deserve "the rights and freedoms set forth in this Declaration, without distinction of any kind, such as race ... sex ... religion." According to article 6, "*everyone* has the right to recognition everywhere as a person before the law." Article 7 says that "all are equal before the law." And article 12 says that "*no one* shall be subjected to arbitrary interference with his privacy, family, home or correspondence, nor to attacks upon his honour and reputation."[6]

Some delegates at Beijing refused to allow direct quotations from the Convention on the Rights of the Child, possibly because those rights could be interpreted in a way that would conflict with the rights of women: the right to abortion, say, or the right not to acknowledge a biological father in any way. With that in mind, we suggest, they campaigned for inclusion of the term "sexual rights" (presumably those of women) wherever possible.

The strategy of Beijing's Western coalition (minus the Americans) was to get new wording on women's rights into the two documents that emerged: the Declaration and the Platform. Once that was done, it would be possible to proclaim international norms and therefore shame countries into shaping up to the new reality. Incremental change, after all, has always been their strategy of choice. But what about the Universal Declaration? From one point of view, that document was written in "sexist" language and could therefore be considered passé. From another point of view, these delegates were merely trying to expand human rights by conferring new ones on women. From yet another point of view, however, they were clearly trying to *change* human rights. This would have been news to their own governments. In fact, it was news. Bad news. After the Catholic contingent gave a press release about what was going on, European legislatures began to debate the changes proposed by their representatives in Beijing. This provoked enough dismay at home to require last-minute changes in Beijing (although the Canadian government was quiet, because these new proposals were actually close to its current policy). But a great deal of damage had already been done and not all of it could be undone.

Glendon adds that European and Canadian delegates wanted the rights of girls to be independent, not related to those of their parents. In fact, they tried to eliminate even "mother" from the draft – except, of course, in connection with the right of women to reproductive autonomy. For these delegates, after all, motherhood is a lifestyle choice, one that they will not allow to define or even constrain women. In this postmodern age, they referred not to "the family" but to "families." Using the plural meant that families headed by single women, or even by two women, would have the same status as families headed by married women and their husbands. In fact, says Glendon, these delegates tried to eliminate any recognition at all of parental rights and duties.

The Canadian delegation, in line with political developments at home, campaigned for rights based on sexual orientation. Even the Europeans rejected that for some reason. Maybe the European Union, as distinct from any particular European country, was divided on that topic. Canada, too, was divided. But gay activists had already made a great deal of progress. Only a few years later, they were campaigning for the legalization of gay marriage.

Amartya Sen, an expert on development, observed that something else was missing in the rhetoric coming from Europeans and Canadians: any reference to the fact that educating women leads to the use of contraception, which leads in turn to lower birthrates. Why would women want to gloss over that? Possibly because it would deflect attention from the real interest of both the Europeans and the Canadians: the replacement of human rights by women's reproductive rights and autonomy.

Not surprisingly, in view of all these implicitly ideological maneuvers, European and Canadian delegates explained women's poverty as the inevitable result of inequality between men and women – that is, as the inevitable result of male power over women. They made not one reference to any other possible cause of poverty among women (and men): economic, social, political, or whatever.

So much for the demands of Western feminists at Beijing. What about delegates from other parts of the world? According to Glendon, they sat silently in the face of all this pressure. They seldom spoke at negotiating sessions. In the end, though, they signed on the dotted lines. She believes, not without reason, that they had been intimidated. Many non-Western feminists openly resent what they consider the newest form of Western imperialism. They want to improve the condition of women but also to remain Hindus, Muslims, Buddhists, and so on. The extent to which they can reform their traditions without reducing them to window dressing is another matter. The Western experience of reforming religion in conformity with modernity has not been particularly or unambiguously successful in that regard, because modernity itself is inherently secular. Some Jews and Christians resort to compartmentalization; they isolate religion from the secular world. Others retain only those aspects of religious tradition that can be reconciled with modernity, at least metaphorically; they discard the rest as primitive or embarrassing anachronisms. But if ideological feminism were to prevail – like all political ideologies, it functions as a secular religion and thus as a rival of traditional religions – that would make the disappearance of distinctive religions, and thus of distinctive cultures as well, almost a certainty.

In any case, the Europeans and Canadians at Beijing tried to eliminate all references to religious ethics or spirituality. When they did refer to religion, it was to religious intolerance or extremism. Never mind that article 18 of the Universal Declaration strongly implies that religion is a positive feature of human existence: "Everyone has the right to freedom of thought, conscience and religion; this right includes freedom to change his religion or belief." So much, then, for all the jive talk about "diversity," "pluralism," and "multiculturalism."

The Declaration and the Platform might well represent the apogee of interest-group influence. And both documents assume that influence will be used to mobilize women in their own countries. "The active support and participation of a broad and diverse range of other institutional actors should be encouraged, including legislative bodies, academic and research institutions, professional associations, trade unions, cooperatives, local community groups, non-governmental organizations, including women's organizations and feminist groups, the media, religious groups, youth organizations and cultural groups, as well as financial and non-profit organizations."[7] These documents refer repeatedly to the need for networks that encourage "the growing strength of the non-governmental sector, particularly women's organizations and feminist groups ... [which have] become a driving force for change ... [and have] an important advocacy role in advancing legislation or mechanisms to ensure the promotion of women."[8] According to the Platform, the United Nations International Research and Training Institute for the Advancement of Women "should identify those types of research and research methodologies to be given priority, strengthen national capacities to carry out women's studies and gender research, including that on the status of the girl child, and develop networks of research institutions that can be mobilized for that purpose."[9] (In chapter 10 and

appendix 11, we discuss women's studies and gender research in relation to ideological feminism.)

In both the Declaration and the Platform, euphemisms abound. One is the word
"gender" itself. For some reason, it is never defined.[10] Nonetheless, it is ubiquitous:
"gender issues," "gender focal points," "gender equality," "gender sensitivity,"
"gender balance," "gender analysis," "gender impact analysis," "gender perspectives," or whatever. Despite occasional references to the "equality of women and
men," this term is obviously intended to disguise the fact that these documents are
designed for women, not men. Presumably, only men must change if we are to create a "full and equal partnership"[11] between the sexes, whether at home or in the
workplace. The corollary is that men are either personally guilty (for not approv-
ing these measures) or vicariously guilty (for reaping the benefits of their patriarchal ancestors). According to these documents, "equality" is really about affirmative action – known as "mainstreaming of gender perspectives," "targets and
goals," or "special mechanisms" – to improve the lives and increase the power of
women. They reveal no interest whatsoever in the possibility that results might go
beyond sexual equality and discriminate against men or boys.

The Annex uses similar rhetorical strategies. Readers, at least those who count,
have already been converted to the true faith of ideological feminism, which is why
no attempt is made even to acknowledge moral ambiguity or complexity. Every
section in the main body begins with a list of "achievements" to date, in any case,
and concludes with a list of "obstacles" to be overcome. The former builds morale,
and the latter motivates continued efforts for the cause. Throughout the document,
moreover, words are used as mantras. Repeated over and over again, these not
only become self-legitimating but also discourage careful thought about their
implications.

Sometimes, it is true, the Annex refers explicitly to both women and men:
"Ensure universal and equal access for women and men throughout the life-cycle,
to social services related to health care."[12] The term "boys and men," too, appears
here and there. On one occasion, the Annex says that the problems of women "can
only be addressed by working together and in partnership with men towards the
common goal of gender equality around the world."[13] On another occasion, the
Annex admits that "customary practices and negative stereotyping of women and
men still persist"[14] (although the perfunctory nature of that admission about men
becomes clear almost everywhere else).[15] In a document that explicitly focuses
attention on women, however, why mention men at all? These passages are
intended to suggest some underlying inclusiveness. But that is an illusion. They create a front for the underlying lack of any practical interest whatsoever in the needs
and problems of either boys or men.

References to the latter almost always have negative connotations, in fact, referring to something that makes them evil or to something that they owe to girls and
women. "Research into and specialized studies on gender roles are increasing,"

advises the Annex, "in particular on men's and boys' roles, and all forms of violence against women, as well as on the situation of and impact on children growing up in families where violence occurs."[16] Research has *begun* on boys and men, it is true, but the Annex does not refer to that. It refers instead to the decades of research, some of it highly questionable, on "violence against women." Elsewhere, the Annex urges readers to develop "policies and implement programmes, particularly for men and boys, on changing stereotypical attitudes and behaviours concerning gender roles and responsibilities to promote gender equality and positive attitudes and behaviour."[17] It refrains from adding that women might need to change their own "stereotypical attitudes and behaviours." In our own society, even to judge only on the basis of popular culture and public opinion, women clearly hold negative stereotypes of men. And these, as we show throughout this book, are becoming heavily institutionalized in law.

Similarly, "gender perspective," "gender balance," "gender equality," and "gender-sensitive research" are almost always used in gynocentric ways – which is to say, in connection with the needs and problems only of women – even though the word "gender" should refer to the cultural traditions associated with both sexes. "Develop and support the capacity of universities, national research and training institutes and other relevant research institutes," advises the Annex, "to undertake gender-related and policy-oriented research in order to inform policymakers and to promote full implementation of the Platform for Action and the follow-up thereto."[18] It would be naive to imagine that those who wrote this Annex would be open to any research not in conformity with feminism, especially ideological forms of feminism. It calls for "engaged scholarship" – information and analysis to support preconceived feminist views. As for "political will and commitment," which occurs over and over again throughout the Annex, that is a euphemism for ideological resolve. The only thing preventing progress, apparently, is political pressure from unreformed misogynists. Nowhere does this Annex acknowledge the possibility that anyone could disagree in good faith with its underlying premises.

The most ludicrous word used in the Annex, however, is "herstory," which is defined right there as a "widely used term denoting the recounting of events, both historical and contemporary, from a woman's point of view."[19] It is widely used, to be sure, but only as a polemical gesture among feminists; no one actually claims that the etymology of "history" is sexist. The feminists who use "herstory" are the same people, including those who prepared a website for Canada's National Action Committee for the Status of Women, who use "womyn" or "wimyn" to avoid the linguistic contamination of any word that includes "man" or "men."[20]

The ubiquitous word "empowerment" is used almost exclusively in connection with women. The implications are that only men hold power (or that power can be defined only in connection with those forms of it that are usually associated with men) and that only women lack power. As we argue throughout this book, however, that notion of power is inadequate to describe conditions even in our own "patriarchal," or "phallocentric," society.

Several words represent what could be described as the feminist colonization of virtue. Because the Annex is about women, not men, "peace," "justice," and "development" are linked over and over again with women. Comparable references to men, being both few and ambiguous, underscore this link. The unavoidable implication is that only women want these good things or that only women have the innate skills to produce and sustain them. The Annex urges implementation of the Beijing Platform "to ensure that commitments for gender equality, development and peace are fully realized."[21] Elsewhere, we read the following passage: "Peace is inextricably linked to equality between women and men and development."[22] But why, precisely, is inequality between the sexes a cause of war (unless one country attacks another at least partly to eliminate that form of inequality, which is what Americans did in Taliban-ruled Afghanistan)?

The same applies to "holistic," a word used relentlessly, and other terms associated with the traditional lore of non-Western societies. These societies are allegedly oppressed by the men, but not the women (except in some indirect sense) of our own society. For instance, the Annex urges readers to take a "holistic approach to women's physical and mental health throughout the life cycle."[23] The implication is that only women know, value, or need those things. Elsewhere, it advises readers to "protect the knowledge, innovations, and practices of women in indigenous and local communities relating to traditional medicines, biodiversity and indigenous technologies."[24] On several occasions, it refers more explicitly to "women's knowledge." There are "traditional" cultures that explicitly link women with some forms of knowledge, but those societies also explicitly link men with other forms. Are we to assume that outsiders have a moral responsibility to protect only the former? Apparently so. Otherwise, the United Nations would have created equally elaborate international mechanisms to protect the latter. The United Nations has not done so, despite local campaigns against "cultural genocide," because of the link made by feminists between specifically masculine traditions and "patriarchy," or "phallocracy." That is something to be attacked, they believe, not protected. As a result, feminists either consign these traditions to the dustbin of history or open them up to women. The second approach sounds more respectful and useful, and in some ways it is both. On the other hand, it destroys the value of those traditions for the formation of masculine identity, which would allow men to make distinctive contributions, and thus undermines the foundations of these societies.

Some terms are deliberate obfuscations and are intended for readers who do not count but might object if they understood them in the larger context of this document. The Annex defends "freedom of religion" in one or two passages, for instance, but makes it clear elsewhere that this defense applies only to the extent that religious communities accept the principles being promoted by the United Nations. If they reform themselves accordingly, fine; otherwise, they must be discarded. This is an intrusion not merely into the personal realm but also into the public, because traditional forms of religion never confine their activities to the personal. Religion governs attitudes toward family life, at the very least, which is a kind of bridge between the private realm and the public.[25]

On the one hand, this Annex admits that in some "cultural, political and social systems, various forms of the family exist and the rights, capabilities and responsibilities of family members must be respected. Women's social and economic contributions to the welfare of the family and the social significance of maternity and paternity continue to be inadequately addressed. Motherhood and fatherhood and the role of parents and legal guardians ... are also acknowledged and must not be a basis for discrimination."[26] But that statement is prefaced by one that compromises its gender neutrality: "The inadequate support to women and insufficient protection and support to their respective families affect society as a whole and undermine efforts to achieve gender equality."[27] One implication here is that families depend primarily on mothers; fathers are helpful at best and expendable or even dangerous at worst. Another implication is that families headed by single mothers or by lesbian couples are just as beneficial to children as families headed by both mothers and fathers.

Finally, we come to "root causes." This term appears on almost every page of the Annex, three or four times on some pages. As many people have pointed out in connection with anti-Americanism after September 11, this is an ideological euphemism. Terrorism is caused by poverty and tyranny, some argue, but those are caused in turn by American foreign policy. Ergo, America is the "root cause" of terrorism. Something very similar is at work in this Annex. It calls for "research to develop a better understanding of the root causes of all forms of violence against women in order to design programmes and take measures towards eliminating those forms of violence"[28] and for research on the "root causes, factors and trends in violence against women, in particular trafficking."[29] These "root causes" could not be poverty and tyranny, because the latter are treated throughout the document as symptoms rather than causes of suffering for women. "Inadequate understanding of the root causes of all forms of violence against women and girls hinders efforts to eliminate violence against women and girls."[30] Only three sentences later, readers are asked to examine "sociocultural attitudes." That is a euphemism for misogyny: a male pathology that presumably crosses the boundaries of both space and time. The real "root cause," therefore, would be the power of men over women. Or, to put it more bluntly, men.

The process of transforming human rights into women's rights, too, continues in the Annex. A massive but repetitive progress report, it uses the rhetoric that is characteristic of all documents produced by the United Nations and, indeed, of those produced by many feminist organizations. Trying to have things both ways, it advises readers to collaborate for the "promotion and protection of all human rights and fundamental freedoms of women and girls, the dignity and worth of the human person and equal rights for women and men."[31] Either women are not covered by human rights (and therefore need specific rights as women), or the fundamental freedoms of men and boys are unimportant.

Women have organized at both the national and the international levels to replace equality of opportunity with equality of result. They have been very successful in doing so at the United Nations and also in countries that have come under the influence of its worldview, especially Europe and Canada but increasingly the United States as well.

Given the gynocentrism of these documents, it is hardly surprising to find that the United Nations has promoted affirmative action for women. The Commission on the Status of Women commented in 1991 that article 4(1) of the Convention refers to positive action – that is, affirmative action to create equality of result – "as a temporary measure necessary to permit the implementation of equal rights"[32] and to create equal representation of men and women (also called "gender balance") in political parties and political life in general.[33] Member countries were allowed to define affirmative action. They were bound by few obligations, and no mechanisms were set up for enforcement. Therefore, notes Anne Peters, the Convention was seen by many as a purely political document.

The Annex explicitly endorses affirmative action in the sense of "equal pay for work of equal value."[34] In addition, it endorses proportional representation based on "the goal of 50/50 gender balance in all posts, including at the Professional level and above in particular at the higher levels in their secretariats, including in peace-keeping missions, peace negotiations and in all activities."[35] It recommends that governments "[s]et and encourage the use of explicit short- and long-term time-bound targets or measurable goals, including, where appropriate, quotas, to promote progress towards gender balances ... on a basis of equality with men in all areas and at all levels of public life, especially in decision- and policy-making positions, in political parties and political activities, in all government ministries and at key policy-making institutions, as well as in local development bodies and authorities."[36] The Annex promotes new "national machineries" to achieve gender balance and "to play an advocacy role and to ensure equal access to all institutions and resources."[37]

Gynocentrism, like androcentrism, relies on double standards. If the world revolves around "us," after all, then what happens to "them" is either unimportant or justifiable as retribution. We permit ourselves to say or do, therefore, what we would never permit others to say or do. The Annex is littered with double standards. It calls for "strong national machineries ... to promote the advancement of women and mainstream a gender perspective in policies and programmes in all areas."[38] For some reason, though, it fails even to mention laws that force men, but not women, into combat. This omission would be okay in a document that focuses on women, actually, if conscription were nonetheless denounced in a document that focused on men. Unfortunately, no such document exists. "Given the gap between male and female life expectancy," the Annex says elsewhere, "the number of widows and older single women has increased considerably, often leading to their social isolation and other social challenges."[39] Despite the legitimate focus on women, it might have included an aside or at least a footnote on the need for research to help men improve their health. Or it could have mentioned that need in a document specifically on the needs and problems of men. Once again, no such document exists. The social isolation of women is more important, apparently, than the biological vulnerability of men. The Annex urges readers "to examine the decline in enrolment rates and the increase in the drop-out rates of girls and boys at the primary and secondary education levels in some countries ... and ... design appropriate national programmes to eliminate the root causes and support lifelong learning for women and girls."[40] This reference is presumably to non-Western countries, where the problem is serious. In many Western countries, after all, the "decline in enrolment rates and the increase in the drop-out rates" applies to boys, not girls. Why ignore that problem? Could it be due to lack of interest in boys? Or the belief that boys do not deserve any consideration?

The broad scope of these documents is striking: from the home to the workplace, from the local to the national or international, from the private to the governmental. Everywhere, they refer to testing or monitoring for harm done to women. Nowhere, though, do they refer to testing or monitoring for harm done to men or even children (except, of course, for girls). Nowhere, in fact, do they refer to limits of any kind.

Although the current wave of feminism began as a political movement with the limited goal of integrating women into the workplace and other areas of public life, some feminists have turned it into an ideological movement with a global mandate. How does its proselytizing mentality fit in with that of the United Nations? After all, the latter is a fountainhead of rhetoric about "diversity," "pluralism," "tolerance," and "multiculturalism." The reason is not hard to find when you consider that it is the fountainhead also of postcolonialism (or postmodernism in the industrialized world). What postcolonialism (or postmodernism) seldom acknowledges are the support that it provides to ideologies, by "deconstructing" other ways of thinking and the fact that those ideologies function as secular religions. Like many other religions, secular religions proselytize. Many Westerners once believed that the spread of Christianity was a positive feature of their colonial empires. More recently, many have come to believe that it was a negative one. But secular religions have replaced Christian proselytism with ideological proselytism. First Marxism and then feminism, both Western ideologies. They have turned the United Nations, which began with the limited goal of preventing wars, into the global headquarters of feminist missionaries.

No one who takes seriously from an impartial point of view the documents that we discuss here could imagine that they actually promote diversity or even tolerance. They refer over and over again to the dignity of "indigenous" cultures, but the fact is that they would utterly destroy those cultures if implemented fully. And the destruction this time would be complete, not partial, due to the political, economic, bureaucratic, and technological resources available to feminists through the United Nations. The new religion is implacably opposed to tolerance of anything that conflicts with feminist ideology. It insists on one model for social change (ironically, given postcolonial rhetoric, a Western one). With that in mind, every aspect of daily life – education, marriage, reproduction, work, entertainment, religion – would be forced into conformity with an ideological vision of utopia.

If these documents were fully implemented here, in the United States and Canada, the prognosis for democracy would be far from hopeful. The required targets – they amount to quotas – are to be imposed in most countries by government fiat, after all, not by majority opinion. But even in democratic countries, ideologues have found ways to get around that thorny problem. Instead of trying to convince the public and working through elected representatives, they often bypass the legislatures and work instead, behind closed doors – which is to say, through the courts and within the bureaucracies. And this is happening today not only in Canada but also in the United States. Many American feminists have lost hope that the required number of states will ratify the Equal Rights Amendment (although the campaign continues), but they have found hope in the United Nations. Ratifying documents of the kind discussed here would do as much or more to support ideological feminism than any constitutional amendment. Better yet, very few Americans would even be aware of what was happening. The revolution could be achieved quietly, in committee chambers, and without resistance.

Paved with Entitlements: The Road to Caste

A website of the Canada's federal government distinguishes between equality of opportunity (known at this site as "formal equality") and equality of result (known as "substantive equality"). The former is defined in connection with people "getting the exact same treatment as other people." The latter is defined as "full participation in society by everyone, regardless of personal characteristics or group membership ... [which] requires challenging common stereotypes about group characteristics that may underlie law or government action as well as ensuring that important differences in life experience, as viewed by the equality seeker, are taken into account."[1] This site makes it clear that fostering substantive equality is Canada's official method of ending systemic discrimination, in short, but neglects to mention that formal equality had already been modified in connection with pregnancy and other matters of interest specifically to women. It attributes those modifications to substantive equality, which makes it seem that formal equality is inherently misguided or even a sinister product of patriarchy.

Of great importance here is the reference to "full participation," which sounds innocuous enough. Who would argue against that? But terms of precisely that kind have been used over and over again to justify the additional demand for equality of result. This prepares the way for the government's endorsement of "substantive equality," which is defined as a broader view. It recognizes "that patterns of disadvantage and oppression exist in society and requires that law makers and government officials take this into account in their actions. It examines the impact of law within its surrounding social context to make sure that laws and policies promote full participation in society by everyone, regardless of personal characteristics or group membership." The paragraph goes on to say that "[s]ubstantive equality requires challenging common stereotypes about group characteristics that may underlie law or government action as well as ensuring that important differences in life experience, as viewed by the equality seeker, are taken into account. The Supreme Court of Canada recently affirmed its commitment to a substantive approach to equality in its unanimous decision in *Law v Canada*."[2]

This is modified equality of opportunity, so far, except that words such as "promote" and "ameliorate" are more proactive. This suggests that the term "substantive equality" is being introduced via the middle ground, where there is a high degree of consensus. Here is an example with which few would disagree. Citing the case of *Eldridge v. British Columbia*,[3] the site opines as follows: "If a Deaf patient cannot understand or communicate effectively with his/her doctor s/he is simply not receiving the full and equal benefit of free medical care. To ensure substantive equality for Deaf patients, sign language interpretation must also be funded."[4] Not doing so would provide merely formal equality, in other words, but doing so would provide substantive equality. That would not follow from equality of opportunity or even from a modified form of it.

Many people have commented on "identity politics" and the institutionalization of group identities that are based on innate, or biological, characteristics. Of particular interest here is sex: maleness and femaleness. (Other examples would include ethnicity, race, or sexual orientation). The groups in question have always existed, true, and most (though not all, unfortunately) have been acknowledged respectfully in democratic societies. But they have not always been given legal encouragement. This new approach is called "diversity" (or "multiculturalism" in connection with factors other than biology) and justified in connection with "pluralism." In fact, however, these words hide a problem. To understand it, consider an analogy with one country that has a much longer history of diversity than any Western one: India.

For most Westerners, "caste" is a dirty word because of its common association with the hereditary, exclusive, and hierarchical assignment of group status in India. That system has become notorious in modern times for entrenched inequality and therefore injustice. It connotes both elite Brahmins (think of an analogous elite, the "Boston Brahmins") and outcastes (so low that they are considered beyond, or beneath, the hierarchy).

Caste in India was originally based on occupation and allowed some mobility. By the fifth century A.D., however, the system had hardened; caste membership had become fixed by birth. The system had also fragmented into many groups, sometimes called "subcastes." Among the many rules governing caste were two of particular importance in maintaining exclusivity: members may marry only within the caste and eat only among those of their caste. Caste became "the primary subject of social classification and knowledge."[5] Nonetheless, whole castes could still rise in the hierarchy, and personal identity could still be described in connection with overlapping criteria. In *Castes of Mind*, Nicholas Dirks describes that system very fully. Indians recognized many forms of identity, which were

> part of a complex ... [and] constantly changing political world. The references of social identity were not only heterogeneous; they were also determined by context. Temple communities, territorial groups, lineage segments, family units,

royal retinues, warrior subcastes, "little" [or minor] kings, occupational reference groups, agricultural or trading associations, devotionally conceived networks and sectarian communities, even priestly cabals ... Caste, or rather some
of the things that seem most easily to come under the name of caste, was just one
category among many others, one way of organizing and representing identity ...
Regional, village, or residential communities, kinship groups, factional parties,
chiefly contingents, political affiliations, and so on could both supersede caste as
a rubric for identity and reconstitute the ways caste was organized.[6]

This system was still somewhat fluid until the late nineteenth century. Rigidity
intensified, Dirks explains, when the British introduced caste as an administrative
category for the census,[7] although they did so on what were believed to be empirical grounds: how Indians defined themselves. He adds that "it was under the British
that 'caste' became a single term capable of expressing, organizing, and above all
'systematizing' India's diverse forms of social identity, community, and organization. This was achieved through an identifiable (if contested) ideological canon as
the result of a concrete encounter with colonial modernity during two hundred
years of British domination. In short, colonialism made caste what it is today."[8]
Elsewhere, he writes that caste was "made out to be far more – far more pervasive, far more totalizing, and far more uniform – than it had even been before ...
What we take now as caste is, in fact the precipitate of a history that selected caste
as the single and systematic category to name, and thereby contain, the Indian
social order."[9]
Because caste became even more important than it already had been, it is hardly
surprising that many Indians were even more dissatisfied with their assigned level
than they had been. In fact, it created "extreme sensitivity" to social status in general and social precedence in particular. This led to a deluge of petitions in protest.
And this, in turn, led to intense competition. Castes began to organize politically to
improve their status in the hierarchy, which led to unprecedented caste conflict and
many protests to the government. As a result, notes Dirks, the British stopped using
caste before the census of 1931. But the organization of society based on fixed
group identities arranged in a hierarchy did not go away.
During the fight for independence, the outcastes (also known as "untouchables,"
"scheduled castes," or "backward castes") began to mobilize for their own emancipation, as part of an anti-Brahmin movement.[10] One of its leaders was B.R.
Ambedkar, who advocated proportional representation and a form of affirmative
action in the emerging electoral bodies of late-colonial India. Though an untouch-
able, Ambedkar was educated abroad – he got a PHD from Columbia – and after
independence became a founding father of India's new constitution. He believed
that caste was the main impediment to equality and thus to social justice. His argument, summarized by Dirks, was that their status could be improved only by using
the constitution to establish "reservations" – what we know as affirmative action –
at universities and in the civil service for outcaste and tribal communities.[11] But this

meant that belonging to these groups – by definition, the lowest – suddenly conferred *opportunities* and *benefits* that were tempting enough to cause the envy and
resentment of groups that were actually lower in economic status. In other words,
prestige alone was no longer the only game in town. At stake also was economic
advancement. Reservations, or affirmative action, proved so attractive that even
groups with higher status than those eligible for government help still wanted to
qualify. Advocates argued for the inclusion of other backward castes, which led to
the Backward Classes Commission of 1953.

Although the category of backwardness was nebulous, continues Dirks, the
commission decided that 2,399 groups deserved help from the government. This
did not prevent a deluge of claims by other groups that they, too, deserved the status of "backward." Because of political agitation and worry about entrenching
caste, the report was eventually dropped. Interest in it was revived before the election of 1977, however, by the Janata Party. After coming to power, it appointed
the Mandal Commission to study the matter. By the time its report was ready, the
Janata Party was out of power. Returning to power in 1989, it once again took
up its mandate to reform the system by increasing the number of groups eligible
for reservations. Reforms announced in 1990 were accompanied by a flurry of
attempted suicides on the part of young people who had been declared ineligible,
by virtue of caste, for government help.[12] They would not get into universities or
get government jobs, while those under them in the caste hierarchy would. A
furore led to the Janata Party's defeat in yet another election. By associating caste
with reservations, Indian state governments ensured that caste would become
even more entrenched than ever. Caste now conferred real benefits, after all, and
who would want to give up benefits?

Despite protests, reservations have come to stay in India. The system has
become deeply embedded in popular consciousness. So deeply embedded, says
Dirks, that there is "no simple way of wishing it away, no easy way to imagine
social forms that would transcend the languages of caste that have become so
inscribed in ritual, familial, communal, socioeconomic, political, and public the-
aters of quotidian life."[13] The Supreme Court has ruled that only 50% of civil-
service positions may be reserved for specific groups, but even this qualification
is not fixed in stone. Because of a loophole, some state governments have pushed
the figure to 80%. (A bill to reserve 30% of the seats in Parliament for women,
however, has not yet succeeded.)

At first, the analogy between India and our societies – between a caste and any
group offered special status – seems very remote. India is not the United States or
Canada. A Hindu caste is much more rigidly defined, for instance, than any group
in our society except the Amish and the Hasidim (who are not lobbying in Washington or Ottawa). Intermarriage, to take only one example, has traditionally
been (until recently) very uncommon in India but very common here. In this
sense, the interest groups under discussion in this chapter are not equivalent to
the castes of India. Nevertheless, the analogy is worth examining more closely

because of what it reveals about the underlying assumptions of those who favour affirmative-action programs – and also because of what it reveals about our prospects for social harmony.

Gathering data makes it possible to establish social-engineering projects such as affirmative action and pay equity, which makes it possible, in turn, to institutionalize the rivalry of groups based for the most part on innate characteristics: sex, race, ethnicity, and so on. The information supplied by those belonging to preferred groups, after all, is rewarded. This could indeed be understood as the making of a caste system.

Critics of proportional representation and affirmative action have noted that identity politics can be especially fractious in countries with many competing groups. But, you might ask, in the United States or Canada? Well, why not? Consider the current emphasis on political identity according to sex and skin colour. Or the current use of those very categories on census forms. Or the link between data collected and government policies. Or the fact that additional groups – gays, for instance, and transsexuals – have lobbied for official status as victim classes, which might well lead to demands for affirmative action. Many other groups, no doubt, will do the same thing. And why not? The logic is inescapable.

Once groups are assigned "reservations" with better economic opportunities, it is very hard to change the system.[14] Established groups will always struggle to retain their benefits, and new ones will always struggle for their own – even though most calls for affirmative action are called "temporary measures." The system perpetuates itself and expands. It becomes far more rigid than social structures based on class – which, not being based on innate characteristics, provide at least some opportunities for mobility.

Consider the case of Canada. On one page of a government website for the Court Challenges Program,[15] the key words for those who take their causes to court in Canada are "a group which has experienced and/or is now experiencing social, legal and/or economic disadvantage."[16] One important factor is whether a group "already experiences disadvantage in society."[17] Elsewhere, we read: "Aboriginal women, same-sex couples, and newcomers to Canada from developing countries already experience disadvantage as groups in society."[18] In addition, the website refers to groups that are currently "vulnerable to prejudice, or stereotyping," groups that are currently being "mistreated or having [their] needs/conditions overlooked," groups that are currently "being prevented from participating fully in society," and "minority communities within the broader society."[19] Sometimes, the site uses another abbreviated list, or formula. It refers to "women, members of visible minorities, persons with disabilities, and Aboriginal peoples. As well, employers must move towards a representative workforce."[20]

But not all these groups can claim to have been victims of discrimination in Canada. Some have just immigrated. Others were elites in their original societies and, it could be argued, discriminated against others. In any case, Grant Brown points out that they have generally been better educated than other Canadians:

With respect to visible minorities, note that Canadian immigration law has for decades favoured relatively wealthy, well-educated, and skilled applicants. Consequently, this group is not, on the whole, disadvantaged relative to native-born Canadians by any objective measure. There is, for example, no correlation between designated-group membership and educational attainment in Canada. Even as long ago as 1981, the national census showed that Filipino-Canadians had the highest percentage of members who had attained some post-secondary education (59%). They were followed by Jews (53%), East Indians (46%), Koreans (43%), Japanese and blacks (both 41%), Scandinavians (40%), and Dutch (39%). On this scale, Chinese-Canadians were tied in ninth place with Canadians of British ancestry (38%). Below them ranked persons of German (37%), Polish (35%), Ukrainian (32%), and French (29%) descent. Italian Canadians had the same rate of attainment of post-secondary education as did aboriginal Canadians (23%) – and yet are deemed to be advantaged members of Canadian society. Data from Statistics Canada based on the 1991 census show that 18% of Canada's 1.9 million visible-minority adults held a university degree, compared with only 11% of other Canadians. The employment picture for visible minorities in Canada is more mixed [although this differed by just a few percentage points].[21]

Why confer special protection on visible minorities now? Because government officials assume that their colour makes them liable to discrimination in the present or future. But something similar could be said about men. They were not victims of discrimination in the past – unless, of course, you remember that young men have often been forced by law to risk their lives in military combat – but they certainly are now (although feminists try to legitimate discrimination as a necessary evil or the means to some higher end). Denial leads to a moral quagmire. What would it mean in moral terms, after all, if we were to say that historic forms of discrimination were wrong but current ones are okay as remedial measures? Apart from anything else, it would mean belief in the (secularized) Christian doctrines of vicarious guilt and even vicarious atonement.[22]

   In short, the United States and Canada could indeed develop versions of the caste system. They have recognized precisely the same basis (though not necessarily the same language) for identity ("us" versus "them") and precisely the same political strategies ("deconstruction" of the "dominant" culture, affirmative-action programs, and so on) as the government of modern India. As in India before the British, people have formed identity in connection with many groups: religious, social, political, ethnic, linguistic, and so forth. As in India, group conflicts have made it necessary for them to seek solutions for urgent political problems with social and economic aspects. And as in India, the process has led to severe problems: racial tension in the United States and linguistic conflict in Canada. Like India, but unlike the United States, Canada has tried to solve those problems in the context of writing a constitution (although the United States has done similar things in more indirect ways). Like India, the United States and Canada officially require affirmative-action programs in connection with federal contractors programs (although "reservations" are actually embedded in India's constitution and only supported by Canada's Charter). Like India, Canada has produced an official list of groups considered worthy of these programs – a list that keeps growing. And like India's interest groups, American and Canadian ones have learned to use the rhetoric of democracy, with its focus on rights, in ways that raise fundamental questions about democracy itself.

By definition, democracies involve minorities and majorities. And women are sometimes treated as if they were a minority. We have heard a great deal about what rights a minority should have. And with good reason, because every society is tempted to allow a tyranny of the majority. But what rights should a majority have? And what happens if a majority is consistently thwarted?

APPENDIX EIGHT

Here Come the Feds:
Case Studies of Affirmative Action
and Pay Equity

When it comes to hiring professors, affirmative action is sponsored by "federal contractors" programs in both the United States and Canada. In Canada both the Federal Contractors Program and the Employment Equity Act have been championed by the Canadian Association of University Teachers (CAUT). Its explicit goal has been to hire women and members of "visible minorities" in direct proportion to their numbers in the general population.

One of the more problematic aspects of [Canadian] employment equity concerns defining the categories "visible minority," "aboriginal ..." and "disabled." Given that human racial classifications are highly disputable sociological constructs that have no basis in objective biological fact, who is to count as a visible minority, or an aboriginal? Where along the continuum from (e.g.) Greece through Turkey and Iran to Pakistan does one draw the line at becoming "visibly" non-white? What about Latin-American descendants of the conquistadors – are they disadvantaged or not? (Official answer: No.) What about wearing a yarmulke, or other distinctive ethnic dress? (Official answer: Arabs count as visible minorities but not Jews, however each might dress.) How many of one's grandparents or great-grandparents have to be aboriginal, or otherwise non-white, for one to qualify? (Official answer: only one, as far back in the family tree as one cares to go.) Exactly how blind or feeble-minded does one have to be to count as disabled for employment equity purposes? (Official answer: we accept whatever you tell us.) Given the mixed heritage and mixed health of a large proportion of the ... population, these are pressing questions.[1]

To that end, the government has intimidated universities by forcing them to establish numerical "targets." Failing to do so means trying to get along without the federal grants on which almost all universities depend. But by agreeing to comply, universities have abandoned some fundamental aspects of both intellectual and moral integrity. Nonetheless, even these measures have failed to satisfy CAUT and other advocates of both affirmative-action programs and pay-equity programs. Consider a submission by CAUT to a review of the Employment Equity Act.

It was clear that universities had still not met their "targets" under the Federal Contractors Program. Rather than ask hard questions about its own ideological presuppositions and methods, CAUT explained the failure conveniently in connection with "the practical reality that enforcement of the criteria and other requirements of the [Federal Contractors Program] have [sic] been revealed to be problematic."[2] After all, no university had yet been found guilty of any infraction and punished accordingly. Besides, the submission observed, universities had found sinister ways of avoiding punishment for not complying with the rules. One example would be double counting a single employee who fits two classifications for preferment. Clearly, more punitive action would be required. "We recommend a review of the status of these groups [women and minorities] and the development of stronger initiatives to make Canadian universities inclusive."[3] By "initiatives," they meant penalties. At issue was enforcement. CAUT wanted to amend both the Federal Contractors Program and the Employment Equity Act with that in mind. A tribunal would be added to the Employment Equity Act, for instance, and this tribunal would be accessible at every stage and not only as a last resort.[4] Moreover, new demands would have to be met.

CAUT recommended, although "demanded" would be a more accurate word, "gender-based analysis" to establish precisely why universities had failed to comply with the program (or, from our point of view, why the program itself had actually made things worse). "The effect of such an analysis," said the submission, "is likely to reveal that the program has an adverse effect on the representation (and hence participation) of women (for example, women of colour, aboriginal women, women with disabilities)."[5] Producing a gender-based analysis – that is, a feminist analysis – would be in accordance with Canada's official policy under the Equal Employment Act of doing so for all federal programs, policies, and laws. And by specifying the type of analysis, the findings would be predetermined. As feminists have always said, research is inadequate for the needs of women unless researchers are trained to ask the "right questions." They must know the *answer*, in other words, before beginning their research.

Notably absent from this list of the university's (or the program's) victims were white women. Why? Because white women were already being hired preferentially by universities; focusing on other women provided a reason for continuing the ideological struggle for a feminist utopia and, of course, for maintaining or even expanding the new bureaucracies. Why expand? Because more and more groups are demanding privileged treatment. If "they" got preferential treatment, after all, why shouldn't "we"? The logic, once set in motion, was hard to set aside. "CAUT is aware that there is considerable concern among equity committees within Canadian universities that lesbian[s], gays, bisexuals and [the] transgendered are not presently included as designated groups under the Employment Equity Act and FCP."[6]

Pay equity has legal status under Canada's Employment Equity Act, which was passed in 1995. CAUT recommended also that the Federal Contractors Program be enforced, ultimately, by the Canadian Human Rights Commission's Employment Equity Program.[7] By removing pay equity from the realm of ordinary legislation and placing it in that of human rights legislation, endorsed not merely by Canada but also by the United Nations, the stakes would be raised significantly. Failure to comply would lead not merely to the loss of government funding but to much more serious consequences. Moreover, the focus would shift from the complaints of individuals to those of the groups considered Canada's official victim classes as defined in accordance with guidelines established by both the Charter and the United Nations. "As the Employment Equity Act together with the Canadian Human Rights Act constitute quasi-constitutional fundamental rights legislation," moreover, "the funding mechanism [for pay-equity programs] must be directed through Parliament rather than through the bureaucratic and limiting route of a Treasury Board submission process."[8]

Because Canada now officially rejects even modified formal equality and officially endorses substantive equality, it is hardly surprising to find the latter explicitly mentioned by CAUT: "The goal of the [Employment Equality] Act must include emphasis on the achievement of substantive equality, not just procedural equality. If this were achieved then the emphasis on participation rates (numbers) would not permit an employer to rely upon the global numbers as evidence of equality of participation and opportunity for members of the designated groups."[9] But this idea took on a new and ironic twist. "Increasing numbers," added the submission, "can lead to increased hostile environments where ignorance and inadequate support structures, training, awareness building programs do not exist. [sic; the text must have been intended to read as follows: Increasing numbers can lead to increasingly hostile environments, where knowledge, adequate support structures, training, and awareness-building programs do not exist.] Equality of treatment, participation and opportunity goes [sic] far beyond representation." Even substantive equality, in short, was no longer good enough! In this utopian and ideological world, every conceivable problem – including the slightest sign of dissent, interpreted as a "chilly environment"[10] – would have to be eliminated by regulation.

Finally, it is worth noting that CAUT preferred to make changes behind the scenes rather than through public debate. The submission referred, for instance, to someone who was about to challenge the Federal Contractors Program in court by means of another program that funds Charter challenges. "While CAUT is not involved in this effort, we support the comments made in the Application and look forward to the results of their research." But the very next sentence revealed an anti-democratic approach, because CAUT added that "litigation could be averted by the adoption of amendments to the program and the Act." Litigation takes place in public; arguments, both pro and con, are submitted for approval in court. An amendment to the Federal Contractors Program would be made in private, on the other hand, not in court. And not in Parliament. How convenient for those who want to create a revolution but by generating as little fuss and encountering as few objections as possible.

Listed on the website for Canada's Pay Equity Review are many organizations representing the interests of women, including departments or agencies of both the federal government (such as Status of Women Canada) and provincial governments (such as the Manitoba Women's Advisory Council and the Quebec Pay Equity Commission), as well as nongovernmental organizations (such as the National Action Committee on the Status of Women and the National Association of Women and the Law).

This website lists not a single organization representing the interests of men. Is the assumption that men have none, that they deserve none, that all other organizations represent men by default, or what? This state of affairs reflects the fact that "gender," though ostensibly a category that includes both women and men, almost always refers exclusively to women; most people assume that a "gender" problem is by definition a women's problem. (We discuss various aspects of this assumption in chapter 10 and appendix 11.)

Here is one example from the task force's own website. The task force, viewers read, will "undertake consultations with relevant individuals and organizations, including but not limited to employer and employee organizations, groups representing the interests of women workers and experts in the pay equity field."[11] Why establish a task force? Because of a gap in pay between women and men, which "increased to 30.1 percent in 1999 ... A 1999 Statistics Canada report ... indicates that although the male-female wage gap has narrowed over the past few decades, a persistent unexplainable male-female wage gap continues to exist. After accounting for gender differences in work history and other factors, the study concludes that approximately one half to three-quarters of the gender wage gap cannot be explained. This unexplained portion of the gender wage gap is commonly referred to as the pay equity wage gap."[12]

Documents submitted to the task force "must demonstrate how the proposed research paper will contribute to the overall objective of the Pay Equity Review, which is to develop options which may ensure greater clarity and effectiveness in the way pay equity is implemented in the modern workplace."[13]

According to the same website, various "options" are being proposed. Among these is some sort of "oversight agency," possibly one with authority for public "education." Who would set the tone? Feminists, whether female or male, who are ideologically committed to the notion that only the needs of women deserve to be taken seriously? If so, the agency's moral legitimacy would be questionable. And how would the word "education" be interpreted? If this agency were to use its authority and resources to convince the public that only women have needs and problems worthy of consideration by the state, it would be interpreted as indoctrination.

Dissing Dads: The Debate over Custody and Child Support

For two reasons, we have focused most attention on problems underlying the rhetoric of women: of those feminist groups, in particular, that directly or indirectly put their own interests before the interests not only of men but also of children. First, this is a book about men and the rhetoric of ideological feminism about men. Fatherhood is a very significant feature of manhood even for men who do not themselves become fathers, just as motherhood is even for women who do not themselves become mothers. Second, women threw down the gauntlet. Some men have responded in kind, true, by refusing to acknowledge even the possibility that women might have some legitimate problems with advocates of fathers. But some women have responded, in turn, by refusing to acknowledge even the possibility that men might have some legitimate problems with advocates of mothers. Canada's National Association of Women and the Law, for instance, uses its website to complain of "criminal sanctions against women who make 'false allegations'"[1] of violence or molestation. Can this organization seriously believe that women should be *allowed* to make false allegations – note the use of ironic quotation marks, as if these allegations were self-evidently either trivial or nonexistent – with impunity? Our goal is not to defend extreme positions taken by men, at any rate, but merely to warn readers that fathers must be taken seriously in connection with the needs of children and that fatherhood must be taken seriously in connection with the needs of society. At the moment, that is not the case for either of these needs.

Feminists in both the United States and Canada have reached a consensus on custody and child support. They want exclusive control over custody and as much money as they can get from the courts. By the turn of the century, the debate had heated up. Professional legal organizations and departments of justice were reviewing the controversies over custody and child support. In this appendix, we will discuss the current debates in both the United States and Canada. Representing the American scene are a report of 2002 by the American Law Institute called "Principles of the Law of Family Dissolution" and some feminist websites. Representing the Canadian scene are a parliamentary report of 1998 called "For the Sake of the Children," a government report of 2002 called "Putting Children's Interests First," and some feminist websites (responding to those reports).

In 2002 a professional organization called the American Law Institute produced its revised "Principles of the Law of Family Dissolution." On the surface, this report seems fair enough. In other words, it does not seem to belong with "dissing" documents. Below the surface, though, it does. The document begins with a look at the various problems that are inherent in any discussion of custody and goes on to propose a new legal system that would prevent, or at least mitigate, those problems.[2]

One conflict is between predictability and individuality. Guidelines and formulas are useful to the extent that one size, as it were, fits all. Most people conform to one classification or another, which reduces the likelihood of litigation and of manipulative behaviour by one or both parents. The rules are simple and easy to apply. The result is efficiency. On the other hand, not every family fits conveniently into bureaucratic schemes. Outcomes are predictable for them, to be sure, but they might not be appropriate to their particular circumstances. Far better in these cases, therefore, to allow judges more leeway in making their decisions. The result is flexibility.

Throughout the twentieth century, custody legislation focused on the best interest of the child. That was the test, or standard, according to which all considerations were measured. From the middle of the nineteenth century to the last quarter of the twentieth, everyone assumed that it was in the best interest of all children to live with their mothers. The principle affirmed, therefore, was predictability. Once people stopped assuming that, however, the test became very vague. The principle affirmed now was individuality. Decisions could be based on almost anything. "Critics charge that the unpredictability of results encourages parents to engage in strategic behavior, take their chances in litigation, and hire expensive experts to highlight each other's shortcomings rather than work together to make the best of the inevitable. The test is also condemned because of the room it allows for those who apply it to express biases based on gender, race, religion, unconventional behaviors and life choices, and economic circumstances."[3] Other critics point out that the test now sets unrealistic expectations. "The standard tells courts to do what is best for a child, as if what is best can be determined and is within their power to achieve. In fact, what is best for children depends upon values and norms upon which reasonable people sometimes differ. Even when consensus exists, there are substantial limits on the ability of courts to predict outcomes for children and to compel individuals to act in ways most beneficial to children."[4]

To solve these problems, most jurisdictions now try to make the test more concrete than it has been by specifying precisely which factors should be considered and which should not be. But this approach can be helpful only if these factors are arranged according to priority. Some states explicitly prefer one form of custody, therefore, over another. In Oregon, for instance, joint custody is preferred over sole custody. Yet the institute observes that these preferences are based on "factual and normative assumptions about families and children" that are not made by all families or communities.[5] This "runs counter to the commitment this society avows toward family diversity."[6] We wonder if that statement is accurate even in this age of political correctness. Do most Americans truly believe that there is no such thing as an ideal family and therefore of a best alternative in the event of family dissolution? And would that be a truly legitimate assumption even if most Americans were to make it?

Another conflict is between the principle of finality and that of flexibility. At some point, parents must accept an arrangement and do the best they can with it. This offers stability to children. On the other hand, parents must be ready to adapt when circumstances change. At the moment, finality trumps flexibility. "Once a decision is reached, it is expected to be final; relitigation is considered a failure of adjudication and often is limited by a strict modification standard."[7]

As for the conflict between judicial supervision and private ordering, priority has usually been given to the latter – that is, to the parents – because of several assumptions. In ordinary circumstances, parents are the most likely adults to love their children, this love inspires them to act responsibly, and parental autonomy makes them more committed to the care of their children than they would be if supervised by the state. These assumptions are tested, of course, in connection with divorce.

Closely related is the conflict between biological and de facto parents. So far, biological parents are given priority over de facto ones. In theory, this reinforces parental commitment. In fact, though, many children are cared for by other people: grandparents, stepparents, or parental partners who function as co-parents. Giving rights to the latter might undermine the commitment of society to parents, which is why children are removed only from demonstrably unfit parents. But not doing so might undermine the valuable and stable relationships that they have with children. "Yet states have carved out an exception for one group of nonparents – grandparents – who may be given rights sometimes without regard to their prior contact with the child."[8] The prevailing priority still operates, because grandparents are still biologically related to their grandchildren.

Finally, we come to conflict between the protection of children from harm and the privacy of family life. Everyone wants to make sure that children are not beaten or molested, but no one wants to create an Orwellian dystopia run by the state. To avoid these problems a new system is proposed. Its cornerstone would be a parenting plan – that is, "an individualized and customized set of custodial and decision-making arrangements for a child whose parents do not live together."[9] This plan would be mandatory for any parent seeking either custody of or access to a child. Ideally, it would be a joint plan. "A parenting plan is not simply a recital of who 'wins' custody and who has to settle for visitation. The assumption ... is that each parent ordinarily will play an important ongoing role in the child's life... The parenting plan must also contain provisions that respond to anticipated changes and can resolve future disputes as to matters that may not have been anticipated."[10]

Neither "custody" nor "visitation" would be a relevant word; both would be replaced by "custodial responsibility," which would refer to a wide range of functions and would therefore be used in connection with both parents. "Once planning for the child at divorce is viewed as a more dynamic and complex process, terms that imply one form of custody over another are inadequate."[11] This arrangement would be legitimated partly on the basis of "diversity," or not relying on one preferred model (even though diversity itself is a preferred model, one that not all families or communities would accept as legitimate). Even so, it would be better than the adversarial, winner-takes-all, approach that is currently used.

The new system would prefer voluntary agreements, parenting plans, rather than reliance on decisions imposed by the courts. The courts would intervene only to resolve disputes or to prevent domestic violence. In some cases, the courts might facilitate negotiations between the parents by requiring them to attend parenting classes, or they might provide them with information about mediators (but they would not require mutually hostile parents to engage in face-to-face mediations).

The system would rely on "structured yet individualized"[12] decision-making principles. "The principal rule for allocating custodial responsibility when parents do not otherwise agree is that custodial time between parents approximate the share of caretaking each parent performed for the child before the parents separated. By focusing on how the child was cared for previously, the past caretaking rule anchors the determination of the child's best interests not in generalizations about what post-divorce arrangements work best for children, but in the individual history of each family."[13]

This sounds fair on the surface. But it all depends on how we understand caring. According to the proposed system, providing financial support is *not* a form of caring. If one parent works full time (presumably the father) and the other stays home, then the former must do his full-time job *and* do half of all the childcare if he is to have a chance of being considered the primary caretaker in the event of divorce. Even if the mother works part-time, the cards are still stacked against a father who works full-time. The same argument could be made for mothers who work full-time and fathers who stay at home or for fathers who work part-time while mothers work full-time, of course, but these arrangements are far more rare than the others. The fact is that women as a class would come out ahead with this "principal rule." Because most mothers would be the primary caregivers according to the system's definition, that would almost always make them the custodial parents – even though the term "custody" would be dropped.

A lack of sincerity is obvious in the double-talk that follows: "This does not mean that caretaking arrangements are expected to remain the same after the divorce. What it means is that a parent who has been the primary caretaker of the child should remain so, and that parents who had co-equal roles before their separation should also retain those roles afterwards, if possible."[14] What does that mean? If the second sentence is taken seriously, then it does mean that caretaking arrangements are expected to remain the same. Besides, what was done before divorce might or might not indicate the best that could be done in new circumstances.

Moreover, according to the proposed system, "unless circumstances exist warranting access limitations ... each parent should be allocated an amount of custodial responsibility that will enable the parent to maintain a relationship with the child, even if this level of responsibility is not supported by the parent's past level of involvement in the child's care. In the case of a parent who has contributed in other ways to the child's welfare, such as by providing financial support, the amount of responsibility to be allocated should not go below a certain presumptive amount of time."[15] But that ignores the intrinsic merits of a father's relationship with his children, allowing only a patronizing concession to the fact that he should have some contact – the amount of contact is not specified, but "should not go below" refers only to a minimum – if his main contribution is financial. This is very different from the assumption of shared parenting and maintains the proverbial notion that fathers are nothing more than ambulatory wallets.

The new system would allow exceptions for several additional reasons: the preferences of older children, keeping siblings together, earlier arrangements that might harm the child due to "a gross disparity in the quality of the emotional attachments between the child and each parent,"[16] and so on. But look at these exceptions more carefully. The preferences of older children could favour fathers, as could the quality of emotional attachment, true, but either consideration could easily be countered by the need to keep siblings together. In any case, how could anyone ever establish "emotional quality"? Instead of protecting children, this approach might merely encourage one parent to turn children emotionally against the other.

The new system appears to stand for fairness. It would prohibit consideration of race, ethnicity, sex, and sexual orientation. It would limit consideration of religion and sexual conduct in connection with possible harm to the child. It would allow consideration of economic circumstances only in connection with practical arrangements. On the other hand, it stacks the cards in women's favour by elevating emotional care over financial care. More important, it fails to acknowledge that fathers are especially important for helping their sons and daughters to achieve healthy sexual identities. (More about that in *Transcending Misandry*.)

It gets worse. The new system would allow for the inclusion of someone who has paid for child support without being the legal parent, lived with a child for two years and believed that he is the biological father, lived with a child since its birth on the basis of a co-parenting agreement with the legal parent or parents, and so on. But when a man has lived for two years with a woman and her children by *another* man (whether he knows the situation or not), he is required by law to provide child support in the event of separation or divorce. Once again, is he a real parent or merely a wallet?

The new inclusiveness might apply to a grandparent, stepparent, or the nonmarital partner of a legal parent; these de facto parents have "lived with the child and ... regularly performed at least half of the caretaking functions ... with the consent of at least one of the child's parents and without expectation of financial compensation."[17] Here, again, the amount of care – and that is defined in exclusively emotional terms – trumps all other considerations. The criterion, however, is more explicit than in other circumstances: it must be *half* the amount of care.

We do agree with one aspect of the new system. Once cases come before the courts, it would provide safeguards at every step of the process against child abuse or domestic violence. No criterion would take precedence over safety. That is as it should be.

Because women have become accustomed to sole custody – and most feminists now consider motherhood an essential feature of female identity – many women dislike the idea of joint parenting. To protest joint-parenting legislation in Michigan, Gloria Woods, president of that state's branch of NOW, wrote and published on the Internet an article called "'Father's Rights' Groups: Beware Their Real Agenda."[18] Knowing that women today win sole custody in most cases, and that they benefit economically from child-support payments, mothers are aware of the high stakes and therefore support the status quo. Woods argues that enforced joint custody is useless for parents who cannot work together, because this arrangement places the children in psychological war zones. Instead of demanding that parents, including mothers, either act responsibly or pay the consequences, she implies that fathers are more responsible than mothers for creating psychological war zones. Worse, she argues, violent fathers might place their children in what amounts to *physical* war zones (even though the evidence does not indicate that fathers are more likely than mothers to assault their children).

These feminists rely on two additional arguments. One goes like this: advocates of fathers' rights ignore "the diverse, complicated needs of divorced families," which can have "serious, unintended consequences on child support."[19] That argument is nothing if not vague. Besides, it can work both ways. Maybe feminists, given their own preoccupation with the rights of adult women, are just as guilty of ignoring all these complications. Another argument goes like this: everything would be fine "if only fathers would share the parental responsibility."[20] But why on earth would they do so when so much feminist rhetoric tells men that fathers are either assistant mothers at best (and thus of no real importance in family life) or potential molesters at worst? In other words, they are either unnecessary luxuries (because women can do anything that men can do) or dangerous liabilities.[21]

Ideological feminists have collected or produced social-scientific studies to back up their position on what is best for children. "Joining Michigan NOW in opposing this [joint parenting] legislation," says Woods with pride, "are: antiviolence/women's shelter groups, the bar association, child psychologists, social workers, family law experts, judges, lawyers, and even the Family Forum."[22] But these are the very same groups that have vested interests in the child-support industry. The statistical war is far from over. On the contrary, it is just heating up.

Similar points of view advocating the interests of mothers and children have shown up on Canadian websites. These are often more sophisticated than those of their counterparts advocating the interests of fathers and children but not more honest or fair. Many are overtly hostile to fathers, in fact, and some resort to outright lies.

In Canada, fathers have a better chance, at least in theory, to make radical changes in the legal system, partly because the laws governing marriage and divorce are federal, not provincial (although provincial governments usually amend their own legislation on closely related matters accordingly). Advocates of both mothers and fathers have lobbied for changes to the Divorce Act. In late 2002 the federal government recommended some changes and caused a furore in doing so. But the story begins several years earlier.

In a report of 1998, *For the Sake of the Children*, an all-party parliamentary committee examined shared parenting and decided to recommend it. The terms "custody" and "access" would be replaced by the term "shared parenting," and the "tender-years doctrine" (which had almost automatically given custody to mothers) by decisions based on individual cases. The basic criteria would include not only "the best interest of the child" but also the following: the stability of family relationships, the "ability and willingness of each applicant to provide the child with guidance and education, the necessaries of life and any special needs of the child," "the child's cultural ties and religious affiliation," "the importance and benefit to the child of shared parenting," "both parents' active involvement in his or her life after separation," and so forth.[23] The report recommended better programs to prevent divorce in the first place or to improve the process of divorce from the perspective of children, including better conflict-resolution mechanisms. It stated explicitly that "there shall be no preference in favour of either parent solely on the basis of that parent's gender."[24] Cases that involved proven violence would be treated differently to account for this important variable. In addition, it recommended improving the guidelines and formula to fix the amount of child support by considering the effect of taxes, the income of each parent, and so on. In addition, the following measures would be included: "recognition of the expenses incurred by support payors while caring for their children; recognition of the additional expenses incurred by a parent following a relocation of the other parent with the children; parental contributions to the financial support of adult children attending post-secondary institutions; the ability of parties to contract out of the Federal Child Support Guidelines; [and] the impact of the Guidelines on the income of parties receiving public assistance."[25]

These changes would be accompanied by a unified family-court system across the country and the accreditation of family mediators, social workers, and psychologists who work in shared-parenting assessments.

Among those testifying to the parliamentary committee were lawyers claiming that some of their colleagues "make a practice of escalating the fight between divorcing parents. These practices include encouraging their clients to make false claims of abuse and encouraging women to invoke violence as a way to ensure an advantage in parenting and property disputes."[26] Still others noted that charges of violence are entered in the affidavits of lawyers for ex-wives, even though these charges have never been verified by professional agencies. Finally, some people testified that family courts operate in secrecy, without transcripts and due process, let alone standards of proof that would be demanded in criminal and civil law. Clearly, they said, the system was corrupt.

Men, mainly fathers, presented their own arguments to the parliamentary committee. They referred to "gender bias in the courts, unethical practices by lawyers, flaws in the legal system, false allegations of abuse, parental alienation, and inadequate enforcement of access orders and agreements."[27] As for gender bias, fathers noted that the "tender age" doctrine in common law once applied only up to the age of seven but now applies to all of childhood and even beyond. No social-science evidence indicates that mothers are innately superior to fathers. Besides, the pattern of mothers staying at home with their children is usually the result of agreement between both parents. Why use that against fathers when the marriage breaks down?

Individual women, local and national women's groups, social service agencies, and women's shelters testified as well. Their comments, in fact, were included in the report. First and foremost, they opposed shared parenting. Why oppose it when so many married women want their husbands to become more involved in family life? Some said that they feared domestic violence, which they equated with the violence of men against women and children. They quoted a study conducted by Statistics Canada, the *Violence against Women Survey*, which claimed that 29% of Canadian women experience violence in their marriages or common-law relationships.[28] These women made several additional claims. Women are the primary caregivers for children during marriage and should continue in that capacity after divorce, they claimed, because the moment of divorce is an inappropriate time to assess gender equality. Men want shared parenting only to exercise control over their former wives, they claimed, or to decrease their financial obligations in child support. Fathers often renege on their parenting commitments, they claimed, disappointing the children.

The report was ignored not only by Justice Minister Anne McLellan but also by her successor Martin Cauchon. Meanwhile, behind the scenes, feminists had already taken action.[29] In late 2002, after much dithering, the Liberal Party presented a bill in Parliament[30] that ostensibly would reform the Divorce Act in accordance with recommendations from the parliamentary committee but actually would preserve women's control (although no politician would ever admit to caving into pressure from a lobby group of any kind).

One change was highly publicized: the use of "parenting order" and "contact order" instead of "custody" and "access." Fathers had lobbied hard to replace "custody" and "access" with the language of "shared parenting." Since "parenting order" and "contact order" mean the same thing as "custody" and "access," they have denounced the change as nothing more than window dressing.

Another change was deliberately suppressed. By this time, though, critics were no longer asleep at the wheel. Advocates of strengthening the relationships between fathers and children noticed that one passage of the old Divorce Act was now absent. The repealed passage, section 16(10), had required judges to give children "maximum contact" with both parents (except, of course, for parents likely to indulge in violence or molestation).[31] This change "was not mentioned in the Justice Department's news releases or media briefings when the contentious Divorce Act amendments were introduced."[32] Virginia McRae, a lawyer for the Department of Justice, offered an official explanation for the "de-emphasis" on contact with both parents. "We did not want people to get bogged down on the quantity of time a child spends with a parent. It really is about the nature of the ongoing, continuing beneficial relationship between parents and children, and to focus on a 'maximum' gave people something more to fight about. It's about what the needs of the children are."[33] Are we to believe that this furtive move, which happened to coincide precisely with the demands of a powerful group that lobbied specifically to eliminate the notion of "maximum contact," was motivated merely by the urge to prevent unnecessary squabbling? The amount of time parents spend with their children really is important, after all, despite all the jive talk about "quality time," especially when one parent is denied much or even any time by the other. Besides, as we have already shown, the amount of time is directly related to the amount of money that changes hands. Senator Anne Cools was characteristically blunt in her appraisal of McRae's attempt at political damage control: "It's an attempt to shift back to the earlier position ... of 'mother gets all.'"[34] And she was not the only critic. "It's going to perpetuate the gender bias that already exists in the court system;" said Jay Hill of the Canadian Alliance Party; "that's my great fear."[35]

In 2002 the Department of Justice produced a new report, this one called *Putting Children's Interests First*.[36] Some feminists were clearly involved in its production, even though other feminists denounced it. Despite the title, in fact, we find evidence that this report did place the interests of women above the interests of children by discouraging fathers from being actively involved in parenting and indirectly discouraging men from marrying or having children in the first place. This report was presented to Parliament as part of the government's mandatory review of child support. The apologetic for the formula continued. As Alar Soever points out, "no fewer than seven reasons [were] given why the costs relating to access time should not be recognized. Conversely, not one positive attribute of recognising these costs, such as affording the children a comparable standard of living in both their homes, is even mentioned."[37]

According to *Putting Children's Interests First*, says Soever, "the paying parent's costs related to access are offset by the paying [*sic*: he must mean the receiving] parent's direct and hidden costs" and "the guidelines already recognize that a paying parent will spend time with the children."[38] When Soever wrote about this problem to Virginia McRae, co-chair of the Family Law Committee, she explained that the "hidden costs" were "diminished career advancement opportunities and reduced ability to earn overtime pay."[39] The irony was not lost on Soever, who noted that the receiving parent (usually the woman) has already argued in the divorce settlement against the paying parent's desire for greater access to the children. Besides, the hidden cost of diminished career opportunities falls under the category of spousal support in the Divorce Act, not child support.[40]

At the end of the day, then, it is the children of separation or divorce who are most harmed by the child-support Formula (which has now become, by fiat, the domestic-support formula). It financially rewards fathers who pay their mandatory child support, says Soever, but ignores their children and financially punishes fathers who are actively involved with them. Never mind. A new government came in. All bets are off. Irwin Cotler, the minister of justice, has declared that the Divorce Act will not be revised until the Supreme Court has ruled on gay marriage (assuming that divorcing gay couples would have to be given due consideration).

Even as we were finalizing this book, in 2004, one case was being prepared to challenge the constitutionality of Canada's laws governing custody and child support.[41] Gerald Chipeur is the lawyer for three unrelated plaintiffs: a mother married to a man with children of his own, a divorced father with joint custody, and a boy who was separated – against his will – from his father after his parents divorced. Chipeur argues primarily that current divorce and custody laws violate section 15 of the Charter, which guarantees equal rights to all Canadians. Current laws make it much easier for mothers than fathers to gain custody; mothers are ten times as likely as fathers to be awarded sole custody. This amounts to systemic discrimination against fathers. And because fathers are men, by definition, this contradicts the Charter's guarantee of freedom from discrimination by sex. Moreover, he argues, current laws allow courts to withdraw the right of fathers to communicate and interact with their children, which violates their freedom of association. Losing legal status as a parent is tantamount, moreover, to being stigmatized as an unfit parent. And the result, finally, "can be emotionally as painful as any other loss of a child, such as the experience of a death of a child or a missing child."[42]

But this case is not about the rights only of fathers. It is about the rights of children, too, as defined by the United Nations in its Convention on the Rights of the Child – a document signed by Canada. "The child is subjected to the same cruel treatment when deprived of the full benefit of a child-parent relationship."[43] The suit argues that custody should not be awarded in an adversarial context and that children should have some say in the matter. Some fundamental legal problems, moreover, should be solved, including the use of "hearsay and unsworn evidence from people such as child psychologists and the over-reliance on independent child assessors who vary widely in skill, personal preferences, prejudices and sensitivities."[44] This suit claims that the law should "require a showing of harm or likelihood of harm to a child before a court may deprive a parent of equal custody of the child."[45]

Despite the real problems faced by fathers as a result of divorce and child-support legislation since the 1980s, feminist groups complain that this very body of legislation has either already harmed women or will do so. It is worth reviewing their comments for what they reveal about both the overt and the covert aims of these groups (in connection with changes proposed in 2001 and 2002).

One Canadian website, produced by the National Association for Women and the Law, resorts to the very attack that feminists have rightly deplored when used against women: "This Committee was swayed by the emotional – at times hysterical – presentations from the 'fathers' rights' lobby."[46] The author, Pamela Cross, blames all proposed changes on upstart fathers.

> Men's rights lobby groups rose up in protest against these new guidelines. Fathers who were resistant to paying decent levels of support for their children insisted that many of them wanted to be custodial rather than access dads, thus eliminating the need for them to pay support. Many more fathers claimed that they were routinely being denied access to their children by vengeful mums who were out to take them for as much money as possible.[47] These men's groups found a sympathetic audience in the Senate, which stated it would only lend its support to the new child support legislation if then-Minster of Justice Alan Rock would establish a joint House of Commons/Senate committee to look at custody and access. Thus the Special Joint Committee on Child Custody and Access was created as a direct byproduct of men's rights opposition to the new child support guidelines introduced by the federal government in 1997... Unfortunately, the committee's anti-woman perspective was apparent throughout this process. Hearings were dominated by men's and grandparent's rights activists whose comments always focussed on the alleged pro-woman bias in the law. Organizations working with women – especially anti-violence organizations – attempted to ensure that women's voices and experiences were heard by the Joint Committee. Unfortunately, they were treated unfairly in the process. Heckling by men's groups was not stopped by the committee members, and in many cases, feminist presenters were physically intimidated and threatened by men's groups.[48]

Everything was just fine and dandy, thank you very much, until selfish fathers joined selfless mothers among the lobby groups in Ottawa. If it is true that feminists were heckled or even intimidated, then Cross justly rebukes the men's groups in response. To be honest, however, she would have to admit that women have been running the show for a long time and deliberately used their influence to silence men, or that the lobbying of women, unlike that of men (or grandparents), was supported by tax dollars. Since Cross admits nothing of the kind, we must conclude that she is part of the problem rather than its solution. And children, of course, are the chief victims of self-interest and self-righteousness on the part of adults whether male or female.

So much for the tone. Two arguments appear over and over and over again on this website (and other feminist sources). One is that the men involved have no interest in either being fair to their former wives or taking care of their children;

they want only to control them. The other is that these men are violent; giving them joint custody or even merely visiting rights puts women and children at risk. Neither argument is supported on these sites by authoritative sources or by documentation that would lead visitors to them. (This is true even of a page aimed specifically at journalists and lawyers, which primes them with fragmentary and undocumented statistics on everything from time spent by fathers with their children to the violence unleashed by fathers.)[49] Even if the statistics were presented in full and documented, however, they would still be contentious. Some can be interpreted in various ways, for instance, and others are contradicted by other statistics.

These trump cards are based on ideological claims about men in general, claims that have been accepted as fact by many people – including many men – merely because of their constant repetition. The most obvious ones are that men (unlike women) are innately unsuited to child care and that men (unlike women) are innately given to controlling or abusing others. The implications of these claims extend far beyond the immediate source of conflict, divorce and custody, calling into question the whole idea of a society in which men and women can live together peacefully and effectively in families. We will examine those in due course. For the time being, listen to what feminists are saying about proposals for legislative change.

These proposals are based partly on the idea that divorced women need economic security and partly on the idea that children need contact with their fathers. It is worth noting here that, ideological rants notwithstanding, none of these proposed legislative changes has ever ignored the fact that exceptions require special treatment. No legislative change has ever ignored the fact that demonstrably violent men, for instance, should not have the same rights as other men. At stake here, therefore, is not what the legislation says about individual men but what it says – or, from the perspective of some feminist sites, what it fails to say – about all men. The belief that violence by men is the rule, not the exception, underlies these sites, one could argue, not the welfare of children. If women claim to be acting responsibly in the name of children by accusing men of bad faith, after all, why should men not claim to be acting responsibly in the name of children by accusing women of bad faith?

Now, consider a site set up in 2001 by the Ontario Women's Network on Custody and Access, consisting of representatives from seven presumably mainstream organizations.[50] Its aim is "to respond to federal law reform initiatives on the Divorce Act and family law legislation."[51] This mission statement is expanded elsewhere at the site. "The Network is insisting that any changes to the federal Divorce Act take into account women's ongoing inequality in the family and in society, particularly as it pertains to their role as the primary care-givers of children, their experiences of woman abuse perpetuated by their partners, and their limited access to the legal system. Any reforms ... must also include an explicit recognition of violence against women and its impact on women's autonomy and the security of themselves and their children."[52] Many others, including Cross, have repeated that mantra: "Women have a right to live independently and to enjoy their autonomy."[53]

Everywhere you turn at this site, you encounter preposterous double standards, deliberate obfuscations, and even outright lies. To take only one example for the moment, the site rails passionately against "the emotional and anti-woman backlash of the well-financed minority of men who claim to speak for the rights of fathers."[54] That one fragment of a sentence contains enough material for an extensive analysis. As for the charge of emotionalism, there is some truth in it. Some fathers find themselves in outrageously unfair positions. Why would anyone expect them not to respond emotionally? But if women can claim to be both emotional and objective – and feminist academics claim precisely that – why should the same not be true of men? (We are not convinced that either claim is well-founded, actually, but that is another matter.) As for the charge of an "anti-woman backlash," it is true also in some cases. Some sites do indeed refer to "feminazis" and promote misogyny. But we have found few sites advocating fairness to fathers that display more misogyny than this site and others like it display misandry. And finally, what about this "well-financed minority"? The fact is that advocacy groups for women are infinitely better financed (and better organized) than those for men. Much of the money used by women's groups comes from the government – which is to say, from taxpayers both female and male. Classified with visible minorities, for instance, women benefit from the Court Challenges Program. When they go to court over discrimination against female citizens, the government pays them to challenge its own laws. When men go to court over discrimination against male citizens, they pay their own way.[55] Moreover, women's groups are heavily funded by government agencies such as Status of Women Canada and its provincial equivalents. Even with the cutbacks that come to all government projects now and then, women's groups still retain access to tax dollars and influence that no men's group even dreams about. Groups representing grandparents, too, receive no government funding. In addition, of course, women solicit donations from members of their own organizations.

One page at this site focuses attention on inequality within the family. Women, visitors are told, do most or all of the housework without pay. When they do work for pay, they suffer from "systemic racial and sexual discrimination" and therefore earn only 72% of what men do. Once divorced, 60% live in poverty – and up to 80% when they have children under seven. "Despite changes in the law, many men still refuse to pay child support and spousal support, and welfare rates are too low to meet the actual shelter and basic needs of women and their children."[56] (Note the site's reference to "women and their children," by the way, as if they belong to women exclusively.) These claims are tendentious, to say the least. The first claim is by no means uncontested.[57] As for the oft-quoted global figure of 72%, it does sound very disturbing, true, unless you remember two things. First, it includes all the women who choose either not to work or to work part-time, rather than full-time, and it includes older women with inadequate education or training. Second, the wage gap narrows considerably among younger women and men.

But economic equality is not the only, or even the primary, problem discussed at this site. "One striking example of the impact of this inequality is woman abuse: poverty reduces a woman's capacity to leave an abusive spouse, and a controlling man will use his social and economic power to maintain his dominant position in the family. As the United Nations has recognized, 'violence against women is a manifestation of the historically unequal power relations between men and women.'"[58] On another page at this site, we read that "custody has become such a hot topic for many men because it is about money and power, as well as about who is looking after the children,"[59] as if precisely the same thing were not true of many women. Poverty does indeed reduce a woman's ability to leave an abusive man, but the same thing applies to a man, especially in a society that would expect him to maintain two households.

Refraining from any mention of the fact that some women abuse men and others children (or both), the site claims that men abuse women precisely because men have more money or power of any other kind than women. Once again, this reduction to "power relations" indicates a classic ideological claim: that men abuse women merely because they can – that is, because they are men. The experience of daily life should be enough to teach everyone that people (of both sexes) abuse others (of both sexes) for a very wide range of reasons, some of which have nothing to do with either economic or physical power. One example of unequal power relations between men and women, of course, can be seen in the way that women have come to dominate all current discussions of the family and society, including this one. At another website, Cross warns readers: "Do not think this does not matter to you. Whether or not you will ever have to deal with custody and access law yourself, almost without question someone you know and care about will, and the anticipated proposals for changes to the Divorce Act will have significant implications for *her*."[60]

In appendix 7, we discuss the ideological slant characteristic of the United Nations. It is no accident that that this site and many other feminist sites – another example is that of the National Association of Women and the Law[61] – refer to that organization. It refers also, not coincidentally, to section 15 of the Charter and legal cases germane to it. "The Supreme Court wrote," notes the site in connection with *Willick v. Willick*,[62] "that the Divorce Act must be interpreted in a way that is 'sensitive to equality of result as between the spouses.'" And, who would oppose equality? In this case, though, "equality" is a misleading word. As we keep saying, the term "equality of result" expresses a particular interpretation of equality, one that is preferred by those who believe that their political interests are not served by modified equality of opportunity. The result is not even an interpretation of equality, in fact, but a perversion of it. Equality of result does not require equal treatment under the law. On the contrary, it requires preferential treatment (presumably in order to achieve equality in the future). Similarly, in connection with B.C. *Government and*

Service Employees' Union v. B.C. Public Service Employees' Relations Commission,[63] also known as the Meiorin case, this site adds another quotation from the Supreme Court: "Interpreting human rights primarily in terms of formal equality [that is, equality of opportunity] undermines its promise of substantive equality and prevents consideration of the effects of systemic discrimination."[64] Ironically but not coincidentally, the very call for preferential treatment of women (implicit in equality of result) is nothing other than a call for systemic discrimination in favour of women.

Finally, this section exhibits open hostility toward any encroachment of fathers into family life after divorce – and, by implication, before divorce or even in the absence of divorce. "Mandatory shared parenting, and mandatory mediation are examples of what the government MUST NOT DO." No proposed or enacted legislation ever "mandated" shared parenting (also known as "joint custody"). What has been proposed is the presumption of shared parenting *unless* it can be shown that children are in danger of physical harm or some other severe harm. (Some websites comment on other forms of harm.) But the reference here is only to "violence against women," as if that could be discussed adequately in isolation from violence of any other kind. "It is in the children's best interests that women's security, liberty and dignity be respected and promoted by laws and policies in Canada."[65] To be sure, although that in itself says nothing about the security, liberty and dignity of children. Overlooked is the possibility that it would also be in the best interests of children – especially of boys – to respect and promote, in addition, the security, liberty, and dignity of men.

Another page at the same site is organized more specifically around "the best interests of the child." The main goal is to reject any form of shared parenting that might be established by law reformers. In a diatribe, the site informs visitors that men seldom take their share of the responsibility for childcare either during or after marriage. "Even when there are joint custody orders, or agreements between parents to 'share parenting,' children usually continue to live with their mothers, and it is women who take care of their day-to-day needs and support them financially."[66] In that case, though, why would it make any difference what the law says?

On yet another page, visitors read that "many men become 'disappearing fathers.' They do not fulfill their parental responsibilities, including the task of taking the minimal amount of time agreed to visit their children, and begrudging or disregarding the financial support they have to pay to meet their share of the child's needs."[67] Well, some divorced or separated fathers do follow that pattern. But given the circumstances – included are self-righteous and hostile former partners (who might well encourage the children to become equally hostile); police officers, social workers, psychologists, and even judges carefully "reeducated" to have immediate sympathy for mothers but not fathers; indifferent bureaucrats; politically correct legislators; and avaricious or corrupt collection agencies – it is surely a wonder that so many do not.

It would take a major research project to find out precisely why many fathers move heaven and earth, at great emotional expense, to retain contact with their children. That research will not be done as long as social scientists are satisfied that ideological feminists already have an answer to the claim that is seldom even made – which is to say, that most fathers in crisis have nothing better to do with their time and energy than seek revenge against their former wives or girlfriends (thus demonstrating, conveniently for ideologues, that the world revolves around women). Like mothers – and like all human beings – fathers are probably motivated by conflicting urges. Even those fathers and mothers who do want to punish former spouses, after all, might nevertheless also want sincerely to stand by their children. If we as individuals cannot tolerate or even acknowledge ambivalence and ambiguity, which are characteristic and universal features of human existence, then we have lapsed into terminal cynicism. What, then, can be said of a whole society that has institutionalized cynicism in the law?

Elsewhere at this site we read about the importance of "embracing diversity," which means that a "white, middle-class standard must not be used to determine what kinds of parenting are appropriate or to evaluate 'parenting plans' of all families."[68] Yes, but that flies in the face of what this site demands: a single *feminist* standard. Very few of the women who created this site would even consider the possibility that fathers have parenting skills or styles that, though very different from their own, might nevertheless be "interpreted in a manner that is respectful of the diverse realities of families in Canada."[69]

On the contrary, they acknowledge not a single distinctive or necessary thing that fathers might be able to contribute to family life. They show nothing but contempt, in other words, for fathers who fail to accept the superiority of mothers (and, in effect, leave parenting to them). They imply on every page that fathers want only to exploit their children in order to harass or attack the mothers. "The standard must take into account the specific Aboriginal, as well as diverse racial, ethnoculural communities, and immigrant experiences" in relation to parenting.[70] Are we to believe that these women would accept cultural practices that do not measure up to the standard of feminism (let alone ideological feminism)? Anyone who does believe that is naive to the max. After all, many are cultures that feminists either have condemned or would have to condemn as patriarchal. The site includes that passage in order to add the respectability conferred by political correctness. When it comes to custody and child support, diversity is the very last thing that the folks who created this site would tolerate. For good measure in connection with "diversity," the site warns against continuing "discrimination on the basis of ... sexual orientation in custody and access cases."[71] Given its exclusive concern for women, this warning probably refers mainly to lesbians (but with the understanding that some gay men, especially those most likely to want children within the context of gay relationships, find it politically expedient to adopt feminism in one form or another).

Another page at the same site is about parenting after separation. "Claims by Father's Rights groups that men receive unfair treatment by the courts in custody decisions are simply untrue. Courts often award custody to women because they recognize that the mother was the primary caregiver when the relationship was intact. In such cases, they recognize that children will suffer the least upset in a separation if they remain in the care of the parent who has been the primary caregiver."[72] This passage begins with a facile observation: claims that men receive unfair treatment are "simply untrue." In other words, no father has ever been shafted by the system. Almost as facile is what follows. It is true that women are usually the primary caregivers, but at least one reason for that is the a priori message to men in our society, including the one conveyed effectively at this site, that fathers have no necessary or even significant function in family life. That being the case, why be surprised when fathers leave childcare to mothers?

One part of the solution to this problem would be to give men (and boys) a different message by taking them seriously, in law, as parents or potential parents. Another part of the solution would be to acknowledge that fathers and mothers characteristically provide children with different *kinds* of primary care. And even if young children do not suffer by being left with their mothers, older children might. And even younger ones might not in the long run. To deny that possibility, once again, is to deny the need of children for fathers in *any* situation, not merely in one of separation or divorce. That is a very radical claim, one that is supported with evidence neither at this site nor anywhere else. It is a belief, an assumption, an ideological claim, that few visitors are likely to question.

Elsewhere at this site, we learn that "when men do apply for custody of the children, they often get it despite the fact that they had not exercised their fair share of parental responsibilities during the relationship."[73] Actually, this accusation is disingenuous. Fathers usually get custody in these cases, after all, only because the mothers are even less responsible than they are. If this accusation were true, though, it would still disregard the fact that custody is not about the past – a reward, say, for services rendered – but about the present and future. Separation or divorce is a radical change in the lives of all concerned: children, mothers, and fathers. What fathers once did or did not do, for a wide range of reasons, is not necessarily what they *would* do in these new circumstances. If they can adjust to so many other changes when required to do so – and most of these men, by far, do find ways of carrying on with their lives – why assume that they either cannot or will not adjust to this one? Here again is the old stereotype that only women are fit to become parents (as long as they are supplied with money either by the fathers or by the state). Even male gorillas have been known to care effectively for their infants, especially when the females are either dead or reject their infants for one reason or another; the task is not one that these animals have learned from infancy, but it is one that they can do and will do.[74]

According to this site, moreover, the principle of "maximum contact" between both parents and their children, enacted in the Divorce Act, was a step in the wrong direction. Why oppose that? Because it was accompanied by the "friendly parent rule," these feminists claim, which gave custody to the parent most likely to grant visitation rights to the other parent. "Mothers who seek to protect their children from abusive or controlling fathers are often labeled 'unfriendly,' and they may lose custody of the children because the courts find them 'uncooperative.'"[75]

Visitors read elsewhere that "[m]aximum contact with both parents is supposed to be in the best interest of children, but it often is not. When a father is violent, abusive or controlling it is not in the best interest of the child to have extensive contacts with him."[76] The ante has been upped. Fathers are demonized for being not only violent and "abusive" but also "controlling." Psychological control, in fact, is the rhetorical counterpart to physical violence. The implication is that only men like to control others. Presumably, women never do so unless they are either insane or somehow driven to it by men. In fact, as anyone should realize from the experience of daily life, women can be just as controlling, manipulative, and domineering as men. As those who have read the politically "controversial" studies of domestic violence should know, moreover, women can be just as violent toward children as men are. You can argue forever about the precise statistics on female violence toward children, either as mothers or as babysitters, but it is clear by now that it makes no sense to assume either the innate "nurturance" of mothers or the innate violence of fathers. Law reform – joint custody – has been designed to take precisely this ambiguity into account, presuming that both parents truly care about their children unless one (or both) of them clearly does not. That is the equivalent of presuming that people on trial are innocent unless proven guilty. This site, on the other hand, would have us succumb to cynicism – selective cynicism, of course, in that only men would fall collectively under suspicion.

But wait. More accusations. "In addition, the maximum contact rule is regularly used by vindictive men to harass ex-partners, by allowing them to take mothers back to court for any allegation of access denial. Father's Rights groups say that unfair denial of access by mothers is a big problem, but it actually happens in a very small percentage of cases."[77] Without documentation, of course, visitors to the site have no way of checking either contention. Besides, arguments of this kind, based on politically motivated generalizations, are self-defeating. Reality is more complex than advocates of any position like to admit. Precisely the same kind of argument, after all, has been made by women's-rights groups. They complain about fathers who fail to show up for visits with their children. It could be argued that this, too, actually happens in a very small percentage of cases. When it does, moreover, the explanation could be either circumstances beyond their control or overt hostility from their wives and even from the children living with their mothers.

Visitors to the site are told that joint custody is acceptable in theory but that "problems appear when the courts impose joint custody on parents against their will." What can that possibly mean? No court would ever award joint custody to a father (or mother) who wants nothing to do with parenthood. The site's deceptively simple statement must refer, therefore, to cases in which the court gives joint custody against the will of *mothers*. Which problems appear? One might be that "women are often left with the burden of physical and financial responsibility for their children." But you can hardly blame the courts for the failure of fathers to honour the legal obligations assigned by it. And besides, the burden of physical and financial responsibility is what these mothers would have under *sole* custody – which is presumably what this site advocates. "And in the process," the section adds, "they will lose the autonomy necessary to raise their children."[78]

But why should any parent (except a widow or widower) have that kind of autonomy in the first place? Since when is the autonomy of either parent "necessary" for children? The section continues with what amounts to an answer. "Joint custody can also significantly lower child support awards, and women often end up living in poverty." This argument would make more sense, morally, if sole custody (or "60%" custody) by mothers – the solution advocated by this very site – did not leave so many fathers living in poverty after duly making their child-support payments. "Finally," this section warns, "joint custody is a tool that can be used by violent or manipulative men to continue to exercise control over their children and ex-partners for many years after separation or divorce."[79] Once again, what is sauce for the gander should be sauce for the goose as well. If joint custody allows that kind of behaviour by men to continue, it allows the same kind of behaviour by women to continue. No one has ever claimed that joint custody is a solution to human stupidity, malice, spite, selfishness, or neuroticism – traits that are obviously shared by both men and women. It is merely the lesser of two evils (assuming the absence of violence): maintaining the relationships of children with both parents, though not under the ideal conditions of a happy marriage, or severing their relationships with either mothers or fathers.

In a section on "mandatory shared parenting," the site mentions similar approaches in other countries and concludes that "more women have to deal with husbands who try to control the way they raise the children but don't actually share in the caregiving work. More children are placed in the care of abusive and violent fathers, and more parents spend more time in courts litigating the meaning of the different clauses in their parenting plans. Shared parenting can work: but it must never be imposed on parents, and it [must] not be allowed in cases of woman abuse or child abuse."[80] Since no documentation is provided, once again, no one can check the international statistics. The rest of these claims can be questioned more easily.

Some fathers, having been awarded joint custody, do try to "control" the way their children are brought up. So do some mothers. In fact, so does everyone at one time or another. We all need to have some control over the world around us. And we all want at least some control over whatever is most important to us. The site refers to total or exclusive control, of course, and implies that only men want it. Some do. So do some women (something made clear inadvertently, as we will show, by this very site). That is what can happen in cases of separation or divorce. These are bad situations. No legal system can ever change that, but any legal system can try to mitigate the damage. As for fathers who fail to share in the "caregiving" work, that might depend on precisely what care is thought to entail. If we assume that it can be defined in exclusively emotional terms, we are being not only naive but also ahistorical.

At all times, most fathers have cared for their children as "providers." Not so long ago, that involved introducing sons to the exciting but hazardous outside world, instilling self-discipline, teaching them trades, and teaching them how to compete with others or setting them up in businesses. Nowadays, single mothers try to do all those things with help from the state instead of husbands. But not even the most successful single mother can teach her sons how to be healthy *men*. And not even the most successful single mother, alone, can teach her daughters how to experience men in healthy ways. Not all fathers live up to the ideal, of course, but neither do all mothers.

We do not need to discuss the standard charge of violence yet again, but we might need to reiterate one thing. The Special Committee on Custody and Access did not recommend that "shared parenting become mandatory."[81] It recommended only that shared parenting be presumed in the absence of compelling reasons for a different arrangement.

Many of these arguments are rehashed yet again in the section on "parental responsibility," the term proposed to replace "joint custody" or "shared parenting" (although all three are very similar). This approach has already been tried in Britain, Australia, and the state of Maine. "Reports indicate," visitors learn without being given any reference to the research, "that the reforms in the UK and in Australia have not been successful. No report has yet been done on the Maine model."[82] But successful for whom? For children? For fathers? For men? For mothers? For women? For society? For the short term? For the long term? If the goal in each case was to give mothers what amounts to exclusive ownership of children or to give women ultimate control over family life, of course, then this solution probably has failed. But questions about motivation and underlying ideological assumptions are not what anyone responsible for this site would want to discuss.

"Like joint custody," this section continues, "its success will depend on the good will of the parents involved. Women already complain that there is no mechanism to enforce or monitor fathers who do not exercise scheduled access and disappoint their children."[83] Yes, but *every* plan depends on the good will of the parents involved. How could it be otherwise except in a totalitarian state? And men already complain that there is no mechanism to enforce or monitor mothers who find excuses to prevent children from seeing their fathers. This passage, like many others, indicates a strong urge to control children, to control men, and therefore to control society as a whole. It is hard to avoid the conclusion that the problem for these women with "parental responsibility" is not so much that it might prove harmful to children as that it would prevent them from having exclusive control over children.

That becomes even more obvious in the passage's conclusion: "As with mediation, there may [that is, might] be no public record, no right of appeal and no constitutional guarantees. Like mediation, it's a service that would likely be privatized, without national standards."[84] Of course, no one at this site ever complains about the lack of accountability, from the perspective of fathers, in the family-court system, with its psychologists and social workers and bureaucrats working behind the scenes. Besides, the same problems could just as easily affect fathers. And what "constitutional guarantees" are we talking about? Some fundamental "right" of women to have exclusive control over family life? It would take some fancy footwork, to say the least, for feminists to interpret section 15 of the Charter – which guarantees sexual equality – in that way.

Like almost every other page at the site, this one concludes with the shibboleth of violence. The usual trump card. "In family law disputes, women are often fighting for the safety of themselves and their children, while some men are fighting to maintain power and control."[85] But the same argument could be used in reverse. And this kind of comparison, the best of one with the worst of another, is not legitimate. The bad news is that some men and some women really are interested primarily in themselves and their need for control, revenge, identity, political virtue, or whatever. The good news, on the other hand, is that some women and some men really are interested primarily in their children. No system is ever going to change human nature, once again, not even that of a totalitarian state. People are complex beings with ambivalent attitudes and contradictory needs. All any system can do is try to treat every litigated case individually and not on the basis of preconceived ideas, whether cultural stereotypes or ideological beliefs, about what men or women in general are all about. Will that always work out for the benefit of children? No, but the alternative, the one implied but never actually stated on this website, would be infinitely more dangerous.

At the site's page on women's access to justice, visitors learn that men often manipulate the family-law system in order "to punish the women and children who leave them ... as a way to continue holding power and control over their former wives and girlfriends."[86] Some men do, no doubt. But are we to believe that women are somehow above using the system for the same reasons? The only people who have seldom or never come across vindictive women are infants (and even some children are abused by their mothers). Stalking is probably more characteristic of abusive men than it is of abusive women. But the latter have much more effective ways of harassing their former partners. More effective, because they are perfectly legal. Besides, stalking is already illegal, not only in the context of separation or divorce, by the way, but in any context. No alteration to the Divorce Act will change that.

In another section, the site lists all the ways in which abusive men misuse contacts with their children. They ask for information about the doings of their former partners, say nasty things about them, threaten to withhold child-support payments, try to gain sympathy, and so on. This is indeed an ugly side of human nature, partly because it puts children in an extremely difficult position. As usual, though, visitors to the site are implicitly asked to believe that women refrain from doing and saying precisely the same things. No one who has lived in this world for more than a few years (except feminist ideologues) could honestly claim to believe that.

In the following section, this site explains how abusive men can misuse contacts with their children. It is because the law allows them to do so, apparently, or even encourages them to do so. "Family Courts often do not believe women or their children when they say they are abused or exposed to violence. Most family lawyers are not adequately trained to work with or represent the interests of abused women and their children in court."[87] Once upon a time, this was true. Not only is it no longer true, on the other hand, but the reverse is probably true. Beginning in the 1980s and picking up steam in the 1990s, federal and provincial governments established extensive "reeducation" programs (either mandated or demanded by public pressure) for police officers, social workers, emergency-room physicians, lawyers, judges, legislators, and so on. Men may now be forced out of their homes on the mere say-so of women – that is, without evidence.

This site laments that law reformers recommend "only taking into account incidents of 'proven' violence when determining custody: in many cases women cannot prove violence enacted against them because of insufficient evidence."[88] Women and children, according to this site, need access to a "legal system that recognizes woman abuse and children's exposure to violence, and believes women and children when they say that they are abused/exposed to violence."[89] In that case, what they really need is something other than a democracy in which all citizens are treated equally under the law and no citizen may be arrested, tried, or convicted, on the basis of an unsubstantiated accusation. Otherwise, we might as well return to the Salem of 1692. If insisting on evidence and due process indicates a survival of patriarchy, in short, then even that would be preferable to the current status quo in which "women don't lie" has become an article of faith in politically correct circles – that is, the circles that run our legal and other bureaucracies. But once again, no system is perfect. People must choose, now as always, between a system that allows a relatively few guilty people to go free, possibly to strike again, and one that allows many innocent people to be destroyed. By refusing to acknowledge a massive cultural change in the latter direction, at any rate, this site indulges in outright dishonesty. Visitors read that women need access also to a "legal system that holds abusive men accountable for their actions,"[90] for instance, as if that were not already the case and were not part of any reformed version of the Divorce Act.

Every section of this site concludes with instructions under the headings "Act Now!" or "What You Can Do!" One page includes a sample letter addressed to the minister of justice. The writer expects "that any changes to the federal Divorce Act will acknowledge the prevalence of violence against women and put provisions in place to ensure that child custody and access arrangements protect women and children from exposure to violence and abuse on the part of former partners. These provisions are entirely in keeping with the federal government's national and international commitments to end violence against women, including its support of the United Nations Declaration on the Elimination of Violence against Women."[91]

Note the word "prevalence," as in "prevail." Violence against women not only occurs often, according to this letter (which conveniently forgets about all other forms of violence, including domestic violence, that targets men), it is the *prevailing* pattern. It is the norm of a society still languishing under the tyranny of patriarchy. It is the major factor to be considered in any revision to the Divorce Act. And just in case the minister is not convinced by the questionable statistics that underlie this statement, he – it was a he, by the way, Martin Cauchon – is intimidated by the threat of exposure to ridicule or contempt by the world community. The letter continues with a demand for "gender-based analysis," a euphemism for feminist analysis. This too, after all, is mandated by documents of the United Nations – the Beijing Platform is mentioned – that have been signed by Canada. (At its site, too, the National Association of Women and the Law refers to Beijing.)[92] The letter then asks for the minister to "hold a consultation with equality-seeking women's organizations that work on the issue of violence against women and are familiar with how family law, including its impact on child custody and access arrangements affects women."[93] "Equality" has become a peculiar word, as we have already observed, denoting one thing but connoting the opposite.

The worldview of this website is a separatist one. It is based on the notion of female "autonomy," understood not in the relative sense of psychology or sociology (because no human being can ever be, or should ever be, completely autonomous) but in the political sense of ideological feminism. What the latter requires, ultimately, is a utopia in which women have as little as possible to do with men (except for a few gay men, perhaps, or a few converts to ideological feminism). This would mean not only complete maternal autonomy (exclusive jurisdiction over children) but also complete reproductive autonomy (a project that has been the goal of agitation for several decades by groups such as the Feminist International Network of Resistance to Reproductive and Genetic Engineering).

In this political and ideological context, the urgent demand for a legal system that presumes or even mandates custody by mothers alone makes sense. What better way to build a feminist utopia, after all, than to create a male generation reared from infancy to young manhood on the edifying feminist doctrines of their mothers and untainted by the corrupt patriarchal doctrines of their fathers – and a female generation, reared from infancy to young womanhood on the same basis, that wants and needs little or no contact with men? This is surely one reason for the site's explicit rejection of proposals for mandatory mediation and parenting programs.

As for the former, we read on one page that "[e]ven in the absence of violence, many women who enter into mediation compromise too much, sometimes jeopardizing their own and their children's welfare."[94] To be sure. But so do many men. Some believe – not surprisingly, given what society tells them – that they cannot be as effective at parenting as women. Others are afraid of conflict. Still others worry about the effect of conflict on their children.

And as for the latter, we read that "[f]orcing parents to take parenting classes assumes that divorce/separation is bad for children."[95] So divorce is good for children? Because "[s]tudies show that children are often stressed and anxious when living in a home where their father hurts their mother. When their mothers leave the abusive relationship, they are able to heal, and feel safe and secure. Mediation, parenting plans, and parenting classes only work when no abuse or power imbalance is present, and where parents have shared the responsibility and care for their children during the marriage relationship."[96] Well, children are indeed stressed in those circumstances, although we have no reason to assume that most children do live in those circumstances. But children are stressed also by the crisis of divorce or separation, unfortunately, especially if that means separation from one of the parents – and particularly, though not only, for boys separated from their fathers. A breakup is sometimes the lesser of two evils, yes, but that does not make it good for children. The best solution for them would be for both parents to remain with their children and conduct themselves like adults with each other. But that would require more maturity than most adults can be expected to attain and also – this is important – more maturity than our self-oriented society is willing even to recommend.[97]

The ultimate good as defined at this website is not to repair marriages (because the only reason that they need repair in the first place, apparently, is due to the wicked ways of men) or to learn new parenting skills (because the only parents who need new ones, supposedly, are fathers) or even to establish working relationships for practical purposes (because that would require women to remain in contact with men) but to limit or end the presence of men in families. This is implied, not stated. We cannot prove that our interpretation is correct, of course, because we cannot get into the minds of those who established these sites. But we are interested in the *effects* of what they write, not their inner motivations or whether these have been conveyed adequately or inadequately. Visitors to this site or similar ones are likely, we believe, to draw the same conclusion that we have drawn. Some will like the message of separatism, and others (including many feminists) will not. But not very many – certainly no one who is familiar with the literature of ideological feminism – will fail to see it.

Our approach here has been, admittedly, impressionistic. It would require a full-scale research project to gather a large enough sample of websites for inspection. Someone in the social sciences should do this research.

APPENDIX TEN

Gynotopia:
Feminism at Academic Conferences

In *Dinotopia*,[1] by James Gurney, a professor and his son find themselves on a lost island where humans coexist peacefully with dinosaurs. But Dinotopia is truly neither a lost paradise nor even a longed-for utopia. Conflict does arise; otherwise, there could be no story. This fantasy is delightful, in any case, because readers (or viewers of the television series) know that real dinosaurs once prevailed over all other forms of life; had any humans been around sixty-five million years ago, they would surely have been prey for at least some of those powerful beasts. A similar fantasy is played out every year, at least in theory, in the context of academic conferences. On the surface, a kind of politically correct harmony reigns. Everyone knows, however, that this is illusory; beneath the surface, one species prevails – the one that uses postmodern rhetoric to disguise or legitimate ideological claims. Advocates of several ideologies have done this successfully in the past. At the moment, those of ideological feminism are most successful.

Even a cursory examination of papers presented at annual conferences of the Modern Language Association during the last decade of the twentieth century makes it clear that gynocentrism prevailed. (The same could be said of many other academic organizations, let alone the many feminist academic and nonacademic organizations.) Not everything said or done at the conferences discussed here was either directly or indirectly about women, of course, but so many things were – papers at almost every panel – that visitors from another planet might well have called this world a "gynotopia."

During the 1990s, gender was among the most common topics, along with race, postcolonialism, canon, and so on.[2] By "gender," presenters almost always referred to the distinctive problems of women as represented in literature – problems due almost invariably to the oppressive "social constructions" created by men. The word "gender," in short, almost always indicated a specifically feminist approach. Only a few papers, on the other hand, referred to the distinctive problems of men as represented in literature. Even papers that did, however, often adopted feminist approaches. So did those on the problems of gay men and women, for that matter, although feminism in

that context was known as "queer theory." As a result, these conferences were profoundly gynocentric (and, to some extent depending on content, misandric as well).

Feminist theory, queer theory, and postcolonial theory – sometimes combined as
"cultural studies" – are all products of postmodernism. Most of the papers presented
at these conferences are easily identifiable as postmodern from their titles and subti-
tles alone – that is, from their use, or overuse, of deconstructive jargon. Code words
– "intertextuality," "strategies," "voices," "construction" – for instance, appear
over and over again. Because postmodernists claim that there is no such thing as
truth (except, presumably, for the truth of what they themselves are saying), their
chosen titles acknowledge only shifting "discourses" about it. But some words clarify their intentions. They refer over and over again to "contested sites" of "resistance," "subversion," and "transgression." These words strongly suggest political
motivations. The titles listed below are littered, moreover, with words indicating that
the authors' goals can be attained merely by focusing on one (politically expedient)
aspect or even one perception of an amorphous reality rather than some other one:
re-presenting, re-forming, re-formulating, re-positioning, re-situating, re-locating,
re-inventing, re-negotiating, re-thinking, re-imagining, re-inscribing, re-stating, refiguring, re-assessing, re-articulating, re-constructing, re-visiting, re-considering, re-
conceptualizing, re-contextualizing, re-drawing (boundaries), and so on.

We turn now to two conferences, one held at the beginning of the decade and one
held at the end. The conference of 1990 included several papers about men in literature.[3] These papers do not necessarily represent the perspective of men, certainly not
that of straight men. Indeed, they usually represent the deconstructive perspective of
feminists and queer theorists. Here is the list: Gender and Genre ("As I Am a Man":
The Structure and Stakes of Masculinity in "The Thorn"); Margins of Masculinity:
Discourses of Male Subjectivity in Nineteenth-Century Anglo-America (Bachelor-
hood, Reverie, and the Odor of Male Solitude; The Detective as Pervert; Marginally
Criminal: Male Subjectivity in *Sister Carrie*); After Atwood: Feminist Utopias in the
1980s (Nonessentialist Versions of Male Violence); Showing the Boys How: Staël
Rewrites Masculinity (Suicide as Self-Construction; "Let's Do It after the High
Roman Fashion": Staël's Critique of Revolutionary Heroism; What's Wrong with Mr.
Right? The Melancholy Face of Patriarchy in *Corinne*); The Turn of the Century in
the Twentieth Century II: Feminist Perspectives – Feminist Reform Meets Modernist
Form (Real Womanhood versus Conventional Manhood: Marie Stopes Backstage);
The "Voice" of David Mamet: Plays and Screenplays (Phallus in Wonderland:
Machismo and Business in *American Buffalo* and *Glengarry Glen Ross*); The Fiction
of Dorothy L. Sayers: A Symposium on the Centenary of Lord Peter Wimsey (Lord
Peter Wimsey: A Member of the Neighboring Sex); Wang Wen-Hsing: Postmod-
ernism and the Contemporary Chinese Text (Male Happiness: Wang Wen-hsing);
Shaping Masculinities: Victorian Writers, Artists, and Their Careers (The Pre-
Raphaelite Brotherhood and the Problematic of Manliness; Muscular Aestheticism:
Pater's Discipline; Policing Swinburne's Desire: Reshaping the Male Writer's Mas-
culinity); Men in Women's Places: Exploring Masculinity in Hollywood Film (John

Wayne, the Western, and the Ideal of the Family on the Land; Masculinity in Crisis: The Dialectic of Female Power and Male Hysteria in *Play Misty for Me*; Hometown as Male Domestic Space in *It's a Wonderful Life*; "Don't Ever Rub Another Man's Rhubarb": The Homoerotics and Homophobia of *Batman*); The Fiction of Masculinity: Images of Men in Modern Literature (The Ideal Friend: Gay Representatives of the Heterosexual Male; Man among Men: David Mamet's Homosocial Order; Tang Ao in America: Male Subject Positions in Maxine Hong Kingston's *China Men*; Unveiling the Prick: The (De)Construction of (Western) Masculinity in David Henry Wang's *M. Butterfly*); Humor of the American Family (Playing House: The "New" Masculinity in 1980s Situation Comedy); Spectacular Bodies (The Castrato, Spectacle, and Gender in the Eighteenth Century); Composition, Context, and Gender (Composition Theory and the Myth of the Self-Made Man: Authentic Voice and the Rhetoric of Masculinity); Gender and Generation in Frances Burney's Novels (Relating Families: Brotherly Love, Brotherly Hatred in Frances Burney's Fiction); 1980s Chicano Literature: A Cornucopia of Prizes (Women and Men: Villanueva's Ultraviolet Sky); The Ties That Bound: Homophobia and Relations among Males in Early America (Sodomy in the New World; The Prurient Origins of the American Self; New English Sodom; The Sodomitical Tourist); The Concept of the Male Child in Children's Literature (The Image of the Male Child in Literature: Or, Why I've Stopped Teaching C.S. Lewis's *The Lion, the Witch and the Wardrobe*; Growing Up Male in the Nuclear Wasteland: *Danger Quotient, Fiskadoro, Riddley Walker*, and the Failure of the Campbellian Monomyth; Generic Archetypes? Universality and Maleness in LeGuin's Earthsea Trilogy; Reluctant Lords and Lame Princes: Engendering the Male Child in Nineteenth-Century Juvenile Fiction).

The same conference included eighty-eight papers about women (but also, albeit indirectly in some cases, about men) in literature. Once again, the dominant perspective is the deconstructive one of ideological feminism and queer theory. Here is the list: Gender and Genre (Mourning, Masochism, and Mothers: Felicia Hemans on the Origins of Poetry); Dante, Petrarca, Boccaccio: Intertextual Perspectives (Tamed Amazons and Tearful Virgins: Narrative Strategies and Feminine Authority in Boccaccio's *Teseida*); "New Behns, New Durfeys Yet Remain in Store": New Views of Restoration and Early Eighteenth-Century Drama (Woman's Wit: Some Successful Female Tricksters in Restoration Comedy); Emily Dickinson in the New Century: Publication, Critical Reception, Influence ("Vinnie's Garden": Emily Dickinson and the Women's Nature Poetry Tradition, 1880–1925); Black Chicago Renaissance: Old and New (Women and Agency in Marita Bonner's *Frye Street and Environs*); Netherlandic Language and Literature (Van Deyssel's *Een liefde*: Art, Passion and the Construction of Sexuality); Sexual-Textual Poetics: Mary Wroth and the Sidney Family Men (In My Father's House: Mary Wroth and Robert Sidney; "All Arcadia on Fire": Mary Wroth Reads Philip Sidney; The Sidney Family Romance: Mary Wroth and William Herbert); Theorizing "Third World" Literature (The Problematics of the Western Feminist Model in Israeli Literature); Le Déshabillé dans la *Recherche* de Proust (The Art of Undress(ing): The Déshabillé in Proust's *Recherche*; Discursive

Sexuality: Veiling and Undressing in Proust; Elaborate Négligée: Reading Proust with Blanchot); Chicano Folk Drama: Issues and Approaches (The Defiant Voice: Feminist Rhetoric in the Luxican-Chicago Pastorela; *Pastoras* and *Matachines*: A Feminist Look at Chicano Folk Drama); Thinking through the Body: Cultural Differences and Women's Bodies (Writing the (Lesbian) Body; Between Western Feminist Theory and Third World Women's Literature: Reexamining the Mother-Daughter Relationship in Wansuh Park's *Mother Roots*; A Question of Power: The Psychotic Body in a Work by Bessie Head; The Dead Feminine Bodies of *Frankenstein*); After Atwood: Feminist Utopias in the 1980s (Renewed Subversions: Gender and Power in Recent Feminist Utopias; Nonessentialist Versions of Male Violence; Wordplay and Revolution); Problems of Affirmation in Cultural Theory I (Critical Theory and the New Mestiza: A Deconstructuralism for the Nineties); Toward a Political Pedagogy in Hispanic Literatures and Cultures: A Workshop (Strategies for Teaching the Other "Other": The Black Woman in Latin America; Strategies for Feminist Team Teaching of Hispanic Women Writers; Strategies for Teaching us Hispanic Women Writers; Strategies for Teaching a Feminist Political Latin American Culture Course); Fictions of Feminine Compliance (Pudeur among the Pigeons and Other Rousseauistic Fictions; Slaves, Masters, and the Sexual Contract: Prévost's *Histoire d'une Grecque moderne*; Fictions of Feminine Compliance in Kant's Third *Critique*; Beyond the Heart of Women: Postrevolutionary Sentiment); Revolting Acts: Gay Performance in the Sixties ("Pop Comes from the Outside": Absorption, Theatricality, and Gender in Sixties Performance; Gay Vanguardism; The Critic as Performance Artist: Susan Sontag's Writing and Gay Subcultures); Issues of Sexuality and Subjectivity in Old French Literature I (The Feminization of Law in the *Advocacie nostre dame sainte Marie*; Sex Change and Subjectivity in *La mutacion de fortune*; To Speak or Not to Speak: Silence, Sexuality, and the Representation of Subjectivity); Perceptions of Otherness: Gender, Sex, Race, Religion, Nation I (Wilhelm von Humboldt and the Difference between the Sexes; Taking a Woman's Word for It: The Memoirs of the Jewish Salonière, Henriette Herz); The "New Woman" as Poet: American Women's Poetry, 1910–1930 ("You Are Not Male or Female": Moore's "Octopus" and the American Sublime; "We Women Who Write Poetry": The Plural Subject in Amy Lowell and Louise Bogan; Women's Poetry in *The Masses*; The Repulsive Woman as Poet: Djuna Barnes and the Politics of Sexual Deviance); Margaret Oliphant: Gendered and Subversive Strategies in Her Fiction (Victorian Seamstresses, Victorian Goddesses: Images of Aggrandized Womanhood in Margaret Oliphant's Fiction; Scandalous Women and Changing Mores: Margaret Oliphant's *The Sorceress*; Independent Women in Margaret Oliphant's Fiction: Gentle, Gendered Subversion); Renegotiating Marxism and Pragmatism (Ideology: Or, Feminist Discourse, Practically Speaking); Doris Lessing: Feminist Critical Contexts (The Riddle of Doris Lessing's Feminism; New Sites of Power: Lessing's Antiessentialism); Third World Literature and the Biblical Call for Justice (Unbinding Literary Feet: Twentieth-Century Chinese Women Writers); Unread Texts (Femmes sauvages, femmes civilisées: Marie de l'Incarnation entre la clôture et les bois; The Heroine at War: Gender Deviation and Self-Division in the

Mémoires of Madame de la Guette); Social Theory and Social Fiction I (Women and Marriage in Gyp and James); Medieval and Renaissance Italian Literature (Gender and Cultural Literacy in the Improvisation of the Sixteenth-Century Commedia del l'Arte); Representing Modernist Texts: Editing as Interpretation (H.D.: Text, Canon, and Gender); Feminist Composition, Feminine Composition (Composition, Gender, and the Uses of Texts; What Is Feminine Composition, and Why Should We Teach It; How Composition Anthologies En-gender Subjectivity: Or, "Once More to the Lake"); "All Generations Shall Call Me Blessed": Female Saints in Medieval England (*Crystis Wyfe*: Saint Faith in England; *Ourse*, "Maide of Noble Fame": Saint Ursula in Middle English History and Hagiography; Torture as Appropriation: Saints and Their Public in Middle English Hagiography); The Turn of the Century in the Twentieth Century II: Feminist Perspectives – Feminist Reform Meets Modernist Form (Real Womanhood versus Conventional Manhood: Marie Stopes Backstage; "My Buried Life": The Lady in T.S. Eliot's "Portrait"; Voyaging Out: Modernist Primitivism and the Discourse on the New Woman; Rewriting the Domestic Novel as Political Critique); Editing H.D.: Female Texts and the Meaning of Silence (H.D. and Richard Aldington: In and out of Silence; Another Life Relived: The Challenges of Editing the H.D.-Pearson Correspondence; Gender Politics in Editing H.D.); The Figure of the Preacher in Twentieth-Century American Literature (A Woman in the Pulpit: Gender and the Structures of Power in *Elmer Gantry*); John Milton: A General Session (Saying No to Freud: Milton's *A Mask* and Sexual Assault); Joyce & His Life (Joyce and Women: Challenge and Discovery); Women's Studies Programs in the Rocky Mountain Region (The Women's Studies Program at the University of Wyoming; Women's Studies at Wichita State University); Romance Epic I (Women and Their Sexuality in *Ami et Amile*: An Occasion to Deconstruct?); Women's Studies, Cultural Studies (Reading against the Grain: 2,600 Years of Women Writing in India; I Won't Always Be a Penniless Subaltern; A Cultural Agenda for the Next Millennium; Metathesis: Reading the Future, Future Reading; Going Public: Latin American Feminism in the 1980s; Othering: Heterogeneity and Discourse); Lesbianism, Heterosexuality, and Feminist Theory (Mapping the Frontier of the Black Hole: Toward a Black Feminist Theory; The Lesbian Phallus: Or, Does Heterosexuality Exist? Perverse Desire, the Lure of the Mannish Lesbian); Sexual Encounters and Dramatic Performance (Anxieties of Intimacy in *Twelfth Night* and Other Plays; Restoration Shakespeare, the Male Gaze, and the Woman Actor; Rehearsing Sexual Encounters); The Material Book in the Seventeenth Century (Isabella Whitney and the Female Legacy); Victorian Science and Literature (Sex and the Science of Political Economy in the *Edinburgh Review*); Afro-Hispanic Literature and Contemporary Critical Theories (Feminist Criticism and Black (Fe)Male Hispanic Texts); The Discipline of History and Its Discontents in Narratives of Late Eighteenth- and Early Nineteenth-Century England (The Discipline of History: Genre Theory and Female Paranoia in *Northanger Abbey*); The Fiction of Dorothy L. Sayers: A Symposium on the Centenary of Lord Peter Wimsey (Lord Peter Wimsey: A Member of the Neighboring Sex); Jean Genet's *Un captif amoureux* (Writing Gender in Resistance: Jean Genet and Leia Khalid); Cultural Criticism on Henry James (Degeneration and Feminism: Cultural Determinations Shaping Character in Henry James's *The Bostonians*); John Milton: Construction of the Self and Problems of Agency (When God Proposes: Agency, Marriage, and Gender in *Tetrachordon*; Eve in Eden and Other Beauty Spots); Voices of Silence (Behind the Arras: Editing Renaissance Letters; Editing the Letters of Lady Anne Southwell; Problems in Editing Margaret Cavendish); Feminine Voices in Hispanic Literatures; New Approaches to Literature and Socialization in Eighteenth-Century Germany (Die fehlende Mutter: Sozialpsychologische Überlegungen zur Ödipus-Problematik in der Literatur des 18. Jahrhunderts; Unterdrückung oder vernachlässige Aufsicht? Väter und Töchter bei Lessing und im Sturm und Drang; The Mystery of Mignon: Object Relations, Abandonment, Abuse, and Narrative Structure); Historical Determinations in Renaissance Texts (Gender, Power, and the Female Reader: Boccaccio's *Decameron* and Marguerite de Navarre's *Heptameron*); Wang Wen-hsing: Postmodernism and the Contemporary Chinese Text (Working on Chia-pien (Family Matters): Presenting Some Problems and Solutions); Anne More Donne: Reading Her Present Absences in the Verse of John Donne (Woman as Mortal Sacrament: Ambivalent Mourning in the Sonnet on Anne's Death); Autobiographical Writing: The Question of the Canon (Autobiography as Suicide: Women and the Forms of Confession); Heroism at Home: Women's Struggles in Domestic Life in Early Twentieth-Century American Fiction (Charlotte Perkins Gilman's Paradoxical Domesticity; Reconstructing a Home: The Emergence of an African American Female Identity; Dorothy Canfield's Domestic Novels); Margaret Atwood in International Contexts (The Moral Geography of *The Handmaid's Tale* – and *Uncle Tom's Cabin* and *Nineteen Eighty-Four*); Mark Twain's Female Coterie: New Perspectives in Twain Biography ("I Am Woman's Rights: Olivia Langdon Clemens and Her Feminist Circle); Women's Responses to Shakespeare Today: Gender, Race, and Colonialism (Miranda's Canadian Metamorphoses: A Study in Postcolonial Resistance; Contemporary Indian Uses of Shakespeare: Issues of Gender and Race); Reading Valle-Inclán: In a Feminine Mode? (Mari Gaila: Un personaje androgino de Valle-Inclán; Translating Valle-Inclán's *Salida* in an English (Sub)Version of *La lampara maravillosa*); Shaping Female Subjectivity in Hispanic Narrative (Woman as Subject: Violation and Volition in Cervantes and Zayas; Bearing Motherhood: Issues of Maternity and Degradation in the Novels of Emilia Pardo Bazán; The Shape of Things to Come: The Female Nude and Narrative Voice in Vargas Llosa's *Elogio de la madrastra*; "La nena terrible": Directions of Desire in the Stories of Sivina Ocampo); Women's Studies, Cultural Studies Workshop I (Crisscrossing: A Theory of Black Feminist Dialogics; Rehistoricizing the 1920s: Gender, Race, and Modernism; Epistemological Intersections for Women's Studies and Cultural Studies); Comparative Approaches to Ethnic Literature (Representing Women: Critical Approaches to Ethnic Literature; Feminist Concepts of "Eros and Power" among Asian American Writers); The Embodied Voice: Feminine Figures of Song (Music and Maternal Voice in *Purgatorio* 19; Ophelia Sings the Blues; The Poet's Song and the Prostitute's Cry; Her Mother's Voice: Madonna's "Like a Prayer"); The 1590 Faerie

Queene: Four Hundredth Anniversary of the First Publication (Spenser's Women's Book); The Uses of Popular Culture in the Study of Literature (Inscribing the Female in the American Dream: Updike's *S* and Popular Culture); Crises on the Left: Dominance, Competition, and Uncertainty in Contemporary Italy (*Sputiamo se Hegel*: Feminism, Autonomy, Dialectics); Representations of Women in the Eighteenth Century (La mujer prudente en Ramón de la Cruz; An Enlightenment Premiere: Feminism and Innovation in the Theater of María Rosa Gálvez); Eve, Ham, and Their Colonial Contexts: Race and Gender in the Seventeenth Century ("What Strange New Courses": Aphra Behn's *Abdelezar* and the Reconstruction of Difference); The Turn of the Century in the Twentieth Century III: Enculturation and Canon in Modern Literature (Pornography and the Professional Author: The Sexuality of Modernism); American Literature and Social Resistance (The Goods of Historical Change: The Place of Black Feminist Criticism "In Theory"); Disruptive Discourse of Southern Women Writers ("A Good Mother Is Hard to Find": Flannery O'Connor's Rhetoric of Violence and Suffering; The Politics of Finding a Voice in Walker's *The Color Purple*); *H* Is for Hero(ine): The New Woman Detectives (Sisters in the City: V.I. and Lotty in Paretsky's Chicago; More than Murder: Moral Agency in Lesbian Detective Fiction; Probing the Territory: P.D. James and Liza Cody as Social Critics; Murders Academic: The Professor as Detective and Detected); Psychoanalytical Approaches to Jane Austen (Sexual Identity in *Mansfield Park*: A Freudian Approach; Maternal Empathy in *Pride and Prejudice*: From the Perspective of Object-Relations Theory; Kohut, *Emma*, and Humiliation); Women in Ethnic Writing (Authorizing Female Voice and Experience: Ghosts and Spirits in Kingston's *The Woman Warrior* and Allende's *The House of the Spirits*; Marxism, Feminism, Ethnicity: Questions of Definition and Difference in Kingston's *Tripmaster Monkey* and Amy Tan's *Joy Luck Club*; Confirming the Place of the Other: Ethnicity and Gender in Paula Gunn Allen's *The Woman Who Owned the Shadows* and Paule Marshall's *Brown Girl, Brown Stones*; The Unbearable Looking Glass: An Approach to Reading Contemporary Black American Women Writers); Aesthetics and Politics: South Africa (Sex and Politics: Challenge to Racism in Nadine Gordimer's *Occasion for Loving* and *A Sport of Nature*); Rebellion, Reform, Rereading: Female Authority in Early Modern England (Constructions of the Woman Reader in Mary Wroth's *The Countess of Mountgomerie's Urania*; Gender and the Subject of Sovereignty: Elizabeth Cary's Edward II; Margaret Cavendish and the Science of Reform); Witchcraft and Sexology (The Second Sarah and Further Wonders of the Invisible World; The Misgovernment of Woman's Tongue: Gender, Language, and Authority in the Worlds of Ann Hibbens and Anne Hutchinson; Revolutionary Virtue and the Federal Family: Or, Good Sex Makes Good Politics); Materializing Culture I: Commodifications, Conversation, Combat (Between Public Culture and Private Lives: Women's Reading Groups and the Making of the Middle Classes; The Militarization of Feminism); Early Women Writers in English: Integrating the Curriculum; Gender and Power in Yeats (Kathleen's Cracked Looking Glass: Yeats, Gender, and National Identity; Among the Dragon Rings: Concentric Structure in "A Woman Young and Old"; Looking for

Georgie; Crazy Jane and the Irish Episcopate: The Politics of Sexuality in the Late
Yeats); Teaching with and against the *Norton* (Pope and Feminist Pedagogy); Toward
a Theory of the Mystic's Autobiography (A Genre of Their Own: The Autohagiogra-
phies of Medieval Women Mystics; Autobiography as Cultural Text: The *Book* of
Margery Kempe); Catalan Language and Literature (Gender in Exile: Forms of Alle-
gory in Mercé Rodoreda's "The Salamander"); Gender, Politics, and Literature
(Freud, Race, and Gender; The Violence of Gender; Sexual Politics: Twenty Years
Later); Screening of *Hamlet Comes to Mizoram*, arranged in conjunction with the
special session Women's Responses to Shakespeare Today: Gender, Race, and Colo-
nialism; New Directions in French Studies: The Impact of Feminism (The Power of
the Repressed Feminine: Nathalie Sarraute and Autobiography; Women Writers and
History; The New French Feminism: Ten Years Later); Medieval Literature (Lam-
precht and the Perfect Woman); Popular Culture and the Arts ("Wild Beasts" and
"Excellent Friends": Romance, Class, and the Popular Female Warrior); Joyce Cary's
Women (A Feminist Looks at Joyce Cary; The Eclipse of Romance in *The Moonlight*;
A Woman's World, *A Fearful Joy*, and the Human Condition; Art and Reality: The
Women in Cary's Life); Melancholia and the Question of Feminine Subjectivity (Kris-
teva's Mother and the Gender of Depression; The Tears of Narcissus: Modern The-
ory, Early Modern Texts; Melancholia and *Jouissance*: Reopening the Case of the
Missing Penis); Spenser, Milton, and Pornography (Gross Feeders and Flowing Cups:
Is Naked Ministering Pornographic in Book 5 of *Paradise Lost?*; Discourse and Intercourse: The Ludlow Mask as Intellectual Pornography; *Areopagitica*, Censorship,
and Pornography; At What Cost Heroism? The Female Body in Book 2 of *The Faerie
Queene*); Women in the Theater of Judgment: Gender and the Law in Shakespeare
and Webster ("It Shall Teach All Ladies the Right Path to Rectifie Their Issue": Bas-
tardy Law in Webster's *The Devil's Law-Case*; Right Recourse: Female Inheritance
and Shakespeare's *Henry V*; The Authorizing (M)Other: Witchcraft, Gender, and
Inheritance in Shakespeare's First Tetralogy); Barrio, Ghetto, Chinatown, and Urban
Rez (Barrios and Cities in Chicana Writing and Selected Readings); Learning and
Teaching a Foreign Language: Contributions from Left Field (Desire and Language:
Selon Lacan and Kristeva); The Rhetoric of Ethnic Criticism: Ducking the Issues of
Controversial Texts (Unrecognized Feminist Subversion in Hurston's *Seraph on the
Suwanee*); Contemporary Austrian Women Writers (Wiener Frauenverlag: Stimmen
aus der Tiefe; Women Writers and the Austrian Past; Das Erbe der Töchter: Vergan-
genheitsbewaltigung und Selbsterfahrung in Elisabeth Reicharts Prosa); In Celebra-
tion I: Twenty Years of the Women's Caucus; Problems in Cultural Studies I: Nonelite
Women (Poet and *Politica*? The Role of the Poet in a Pluralist Society; Chicanas Writ-
ing across Borders; From Literacy of Differentiation to Feminist Literacy); The Three
Asian Nobel Prize Winners: Tagore, Kawabata, and Mahfuz (Gender Construction in
the Fiction of Naguib Mahfuz); Relations between Old English Poetry and Prose
(Anxieties of Female Governance: Reading Social Formations in Prose and Poetry);
Historicizing the New Censorship (Sexwork, Power, and the Law); Laura Riding at
Ninety: Most Modernist or Postmodernist (The Plotting of the Truth: Women, Lan-

guage, and Laura Riding's Renunciation of Poetry); Subject and Subjection in Renaissance Rhetoric (Sexual-Textual Politics in Puttenham's *Arte of English Poesie*); The Flesh Made Word: Figuring Women's Bodies in Victorian Fiction (Interiority in Fictions of the Fall; Moralizing Hunger; Majestic Bodies: Figuring the Mythic in Oliphant's Fiction); *La Sonrisa Vertical* and Approaches to Literary Erotica by Spanish Women (Whose Masochism, Whose Submission? Critical Nurturing and the Disappearing Subject in Almudena Grande's *Las edades de Lulú*; Detecting the Erotic in Mercedes Abad's Ligeros libertinajes sabaticos); Women's Studies, Cultural Studies Workshop II (Postmodernity, Feminism, Theory, Cultural Critique; The Edges That Blur: Women's Studies, Cultural Studies, and the Politics of Analogy; Who's Calling Whom Subaltern? US Academics and Third World Women: Is Ethical Research Possible?); Winnicott in Literary Studies (J.D. Salinger and the Myth of Maternal Return); Women and the Divine (Whose Eyes Are Watching God? The Theology of Zora Neale Hurston; Women's Prophecy, Women's Prayer: Barrett Browning, Dickinson, Rossetti, and God; The Road to Rome: Muriel Spark and the "Nevertheless Principle"); Postcolonial Subjectivity II (Female Subjectivity and Bodily Consciousness: A Reading of Rawiri's *G'Amérakano-Au carrefour* and *Fureurs et cris de femmes*; Representations of the Self in A. Djebar's *L'amour, la fantasia*); The Slavic Challenge to Poststructuralist Theory (Sexual Revolutions: Blok and Yeats); Eroticism, Asceticism in Golden Age Poetry (The Magdalenic Figure in Representative Poetic Texts); Sexual Encounters and Dramatic Theory (Getting Desire: Sexuality, Representation, and Williams's *Streetcar*; Lesbian Sexual Encounters; Abject Relations: (En)Gendering Pain in *The Conduct of Life*); Attitudes toward Change in Contemporary English (Women, Men, and Speaking Strategies); Tactical Shakespeare: Resistance and The Economy of the Early Modern Subject (The English History Play and the Problem of Female Resistance; Erotic Resistances in Shakespearean Drama: Boundaries, Apertures, Matrices; Early Modern Characters and Postmodern Subjects: Counterhegemonic Discourse in *The Comedy of Errors* and *The Winter's Tale*); Africa in the Romantic Imagination: Rethinking Exoticism (Wordsworth's "White-Robed Negro": Race and Gender in 1802; "Black" Rage and White Women: Charlotte Brontë's African Juvenilia; Why Cultural Studies? Reexaminations, Theoretical Questions, Alternative Models (Feminist Literary Criticism and Cultural Studies); A Sense of Distinction: Taste in Seventeenth-Century France (Gender and the Politics of Taste); Italian Women Writers: The Revision of the Canon (Double Marginality: Matilde Serao and the Betrayal of the Canon; Narrative Voice and the Female Experience: Redefining Images in the Regional Worlds of Grazia Deledda and Maria Messina; "L'invasione smisurata": The Themes of Neurological Disease and Madness in Elsa Morante's Novels; "Caring Voices" in Clara Sereni's Narrative: A World of "Differences"); In Celebration II: Twenty Years of Feminist Publishing – The Book(s) That Changed My Life; Louise Erdrich's Fiction: Marginality, Centrality, Madness, and Mothers (Marginality in *Love Medicine*; Fleur, "The Funnel of Our History": The Centrality of Women in Louise Erdrich's Chippewa Landscape; Madness and Myth: Constituting the Constitutive Subject, the Representation of Native American

Experience and Women as Other; Adoptive Mothers and Throwaway Children in the Novels of Louise Erdrich); Teaching Literature and Other Arts: Reflections on Recent Theoretical Issues (Gender Issues in Teaching Literature and Other Arts); Art, Power, and Politics in the Modern South (The Spunky Little Woman: You Can't Be One in the South If You're White); Reiseliteratur und utopische Perspektiven (Sisters and Pilgrims: Women as Religious Travelers and Exiles, 1600–1750); Women's Studies, Cultural Studies (An Account of the Struggle at Rutgers; Crossing (Out) the Disciplines; Women's Studies, Gay Studies, Transitional Cultural Studies; Women's Studies, Cultural Studies: Some Problems); The Family as Fictional Construct in Children's Literature (The Politics of Representation: The Family as Ideological Construct in the Fiction of Arthur Ransome; Changing Faces: Pictures of Women in Fairy Tales; Performing Family); Renaissance Heroic Fictions: Text and Theory (Pillars of Virtue, Yokes of Oppression: The Ambivalent Foundation and Function of Philogynist Discourse in Ariosto's *Orlando furioso*); Exoticism and Colonialism (Vis-à-vis the Other: German Women Writers Describe the Orient); Materializing Culture III: Poetry, Politics, History (Women/Woman: Modern Poetry, Gender, Ideologies, and Feminist Cultural Studies); Avant-Gardes: Past and Present, Theory and/versus Practice (Women, the Avant-Garde, and Contemporary Writing Practice); Dorothy Richardson, Dissenting Feminist (The Foreword to *Pilgrimage* as a Feminist Manifesto; Dorothy Richardson's Theory of Gender Difference; The Woman behind *Pilgrimage*); Emily Dickinson, 1890–1990: Rereading Her "Letter" after One Hundred Years (Containing the Phallus: Overturning the "Worm" in Poem 1,670 and Beyond; "Who Goes to Dine Must Take His Feast": Toward a Feminist Code of Language Exchange); Language in Contemporary Art (The Image, the Word, and the Unmarked Woman); Property, Propriety, and Virtue in British Literature, 1770–1820 (Bankrupt Heroines: The Economics of Self-Effacement in Frances Burney's *Evelina* and *Camilla*; Sermons and Strictures: Conduct-Book Propriety and Middle-Class Women; *Mansfield Park*, Hannah More, and the Evangelical Redefinition of Virtue); Scott and His Contemporaries: Formations of Cultural Identity (Folk Voices and Female Enthusiasts: Scott, Hogg, and the Culture of Calvinism); The Gay Nineties I: Bodies as Texts (Unmediated Lust: The Impossibility of Lesbian Desire); Graduate Students: Beginning Professionals, Beginning Pedagogy (Writing and the Politics of Difference; Undergraduate Resistance to Feminist Concerns); Sexualities and Textual Markers (Play)Wrights of Passage: Women and Games-Playing on the Stage; Sight and Sexuality in *La última niebla*); Female Autobiography: Tradition and Innovation (Writing "Femystic" Space: In the Margins of the *Castillo interior*; Toward a Poetics of Martyrdom: Luisa de Carvajal y Mendoza's Escritos autogiográficos; Elementos autobiográficos en una comedia desconocida de Sor Juana, *La Segunda Celestina*); Sexual Encounters and the Dramatic Text (A Transcendental Infidelity: Kleist, Lacan, and *Amphitryon*; Sex, Class, and Stage Space in *Miss Julie*); Chaos Theory and Cultural Analysis (Gender, Chaos, and Science: Subtexts in Complex Dynamics); Continuing the Quest: The Poetry and Prose of James Wright (Women and James Wright); English Romantic Women Writers (Mary Robinson and the Poetic Marketplace of the 1790s; Felicia

Hemans and the Effacement of Women; What We Say, Not What We Do: *Franken-stein* and the Woman Writer's Predicament); Habeas Corpus Feminae: Theories of Women's Representation in Literature and Law ("Home-Rebels and House-Trai-tors": Gender, Class, and Petty Treason in Early Modern England; Criminalized Bod-ies, Sexualized Crimes: Legal and Literary Representations of Women in Twentieth-Century America; Typist, Housewife, Mother, Spy: The Role(s) of Ethel Rosenberg in Legal Documents and Postmodern Literature); Staging Alternative Shakespeares: His-tories and Hypotheses (Straw Lances – Performance as Weapon: Or, Untaming the Shrew; "She's Good, Being Gone": Or, Everything I've Got Belongs to You; The Way-ward Sisters Go on Tour); Women Writers on World War II: Shifting Frontiers in Global War ("Too Naked and Uncivilized": Women and Jews in World War II Fic-tion by British Women; Scrambling the Language of Authority: Revolutionary Humor on the Homefronts; Underground Lives: Women's Personal Narratives; Vio-lence in Female *Bildung*: Hisako Matsubara and Ella Leffland); Contemporary Span-ish Theater, 1985–90 (New Works by Women Playwrights); Women's Studies, Cul-tural Studies Workshop III (Always Take Measurements, Miss Kingsley, and Always Take Them from the Adult Male; Plantocratic Paradigms and Otherness: Jane Austen and Mary Wollstonecraft; Kalpana Dutt and the Discourse of Indian Nationalist "Terrorists"; Translating Gender); From Novel to Film: The Problematics of Trans-forming Multicultural Texts (Traducing Race, Gender, and Class Identity: The Hol-lywoodization of *The Color Purple*); The James-Hawthorne Relationship (James's Portrait of Female Skepticism); Kafka's Rhetoric I (The Erotic Couple in "The Cas-tle": Women as Connectors); Spectacular Bodies (The Spectacle of Sensibility: Bodily Diagnostics in Diderot's *La religieuse*); Problems in Cultural Studies II: American Minorities ("When Boys Collide": Gender Negotiations in African American Cul-tural Studies); The Uses of Popular Culture in Gender and Ethnic Studies (Gender Differences in Reading Popular Narratives; Victorian Underwear and Representa-tions of the Female Body); New Directions in French Studies: Literature and Film (Eric Rohmer: Gender, Culture, Camsea); Body (Politics): Theory and Representation (The (Body) Politics of Feminist Theory; Metonymy and Androgyny: The Figure of Woman in Renaissance Rhetoric); *Beowulf* (The Body of the Mother in *Beowulf*); Edith Wharton: Issues of Class, Race, and Ethnicity (In Nettie's Kitchen: Edith Whar-ton and Working-Class Women; Class and Gender in *The Custom of the Country*; Anti-Semitism, Misogyny, and the Anxiety of Authorship); In Celebration III: Navi-gating into the Feminist Future(s) (Institutional Constraints to a Radical Vision; ... or Hang Separately?; The Black Studies Movement and the Ladies; Roads to and from Eressos); In Celebration IV: Twenty Years Together – The Commission on the Status of Women, the Women's Caucus, the Gay and Lesbian Caucus, and the Division on Women's Studies in Language and Literature; Feminist Theories and Old French Studies: Problematic Intersection (Reading the Female Body: Essentialism and His-torical Differences; Scopophilia and Linguaphilia: Film Theory, Psychoanalytic The-ory, and *Erec et Enide*; Medieval Studies and the Ideology of Gender: The Women Trouvères); Composition, Context, and Gender (The Feminization of Composition;

Composition Theory and the Myth of the Self-Made Man: Authentic Voice and the Rhetoric of Masculinity; Academic Preparation, Academic Discourse, and the Doctrine of Separate Spheres); On Teaching Swift (Swift among the Feminists: An Approach to Teaching); Gender and Generation in Frances Burney's Novels ("Oh Dear Resemblance of Thy Murdered Mother": Female Authorship in *Evelina*; Family Circles, Female Circles in *The Wanderer*); Chaucer and Rape (Chaucer and the Discourse of Misogyny; Rape as Literary Transgression; Chaucer, Chaucerians, Rape, and Indifference); Radical Heterogeneities: Theory, Gender, and Language (For a Postmodern Solution to the Impasses of Feminist Theory; Feminism, Gay Theory, and Male Subjectivity; "Normative" Feminism and Experimental Writing by Women); Testing the Limits of Liberty: Nonfiction Writings of Early American Women (The Captivity Narrative as Female Text; From Anxiety to Authority: Bathsheba Bowers's *An Alarm Sounded* (1709); Signing the Republican Daughter: The Letters of Eliza Southgate, 1783–1809; "Ambitious to Be Free": Self-Empowerment in *Silvia Dubois's Biography of the Slav Who Whipt Her Mistres and Gand Her Fredom*); Vietnam and the Postmodern Moment ("Rambo's a Pussy": Seduction, Rape, and Subjectivity in Vietnam Films); American Indian Literatures: Old Traditions and New Forms (Modern and Traditional Women's Issues in the Poetry of Luci Tapahonso); Tennyson and Women (Suppressing Suicide: Tennyson's Elaine – Text/Image; Emily Tennyson's Deathbed: Another View of Tennyson and Women; Gender and Sexual Relationships in the Great Beyond); Virginia Woolf and Humor (Patriarchy through the Looking Glass: Or, Woolf's Reflections on the Lords of Misrule; The Sense of Humor in *Jacob's Room*; Carnivalesque Comedy in *Between the Acts*; Potsherds from a Woolfen Archaeology: Potshots at the Patriarchs); Surrealism and the Other (The Lesbian Other: Surrealism as Disguise); The Return of the Suppressed: Other Voices in the Hebrew Bible (Adultery in the House of David; Poetic Silence: En-gendered Suffering in the Book of Job; Zipporah and the Struggle for Deliverance; Out of My Sight: The Buried Woman in Biblical Narrative); Portuguese Literature: Poetry and Drama (Sabina Freire: First "Modern" Female Character in Portuguese Drama? What Does Woman Want? *Cantigas de Amigo* as Strategies of Containment); Feminism, History, and Cultural Studies ("Savage" Mothers: Feminism, Race, and the Enlightenment; Literature, History, and the Organization of Knowledge); Feminist Theory and Linguistic Theory in the 1990s (Escaping the Prison-House of Silence: Women, Power, and Cognitive Linguistics; When Hetero- Becomes Homoglossia: Language and Gender in the Short Fiction of Margaret Atwood; When "He" Means "She": Verbal Cross-Dressing in Women-Identified Writers); Encyclopedias as a Literary Genre (The "Poetry" and Feminist Ethics of Anna Jameson's *Sacred and Legendary Art*); Investing (in) the Body: Postmodernity, Practice, and Social Theory (Circulating Femininity on the Free Market: Helen Gurley Brown's *Sex and the Single Girl*); Reading Diseases: Literary Texts and Medical Contexts (Female Masochism, Feminist Aesthetics: Elfriede Jelinek's "Lust"; Classical Heroines in Modern Eastern European Texts: The Western Reader Responds (Bitov's "Penelope": Women's Space in the Male-Centered Narrative; The Archetypal Alien: Göncz's *Hungarian Medea*;

Wolf's *Cassandra*: Myth as Medium against the "Male Reality Principle"); 1980s Chicano Literature: A Cornucopia of Prizes (Women and Men: Villanueva's Ultraviolet Sky; The Female Voice in Rios); Social Theory and Social Fiction II: The Inscription of Gender (Utopian Socialism and the Feminine Origins of the Social Novel; Flora Tristan's Ways of Knowing; Reading Women: The Novel's Place in Hysteria's Text); Women in Russian Literature (The Feminine Subject in Russian Poetry: Lisnianskaya and Petrovykh; Whimsey and the Daughters of Echo: Marko Vovchok and Political Writing); Gender and Politics in Recent Film and Television (Gender and Genre: The Politics of Representation); Reinventing Gender (A Diva's Confessions: Homosexuality and the Art of Personality; Ghostly Instructors: Women's Visions of Yeats, Yeats's Visions of Women; Otto Weininger and the Modernist Woman); Feminism and Postcolonial English Literatures (Caught in the Act: Sexuality, Liberation, and Entrapment in the Fiction of Nadine Gordimer; Politics, Gender, and Growing into Womanhood: Jamaica Kincaid, Zee Edgel, and Michelle Cliff; Thresholds of Difference: Feminism, Decolonization, and Native Women's Writing in Canada; Literacy and Orature: A Tension in Black South African Women's Writing); Race, Gender, and Fictional Form in American Literature, 1880–1925 (Rape, Racial Violence, and Black Female Heroism in Pauline E. Hopkins's Contending Forces); Literature and Politics in the Era of the English Revolution (Class, Gender, and Literacy: Some English Printers and Readers of the 1650s); Patterns of Male and Female Discourse in Early Iberian Literature (Patterns of Male and Female Discourse in the Traditional *Romancero*; "Amigo fals e desleal": Discursive Strategies in the *Cantigas de Amigo*; Mediadoras del deseo en el Corbacho: El discurso feminino segun el predicador; The Language of Love in Montemayor's *Diana*); Women Writing Letters across the Genres in Sixteenth- and Early Seventeenth-Century France (From Writing to Its Absence: Epistolary Silence and the Closure of Happiness in *L'astrée*; Duplicité narrative chez Hélisenne de Crenne: Des *Angoysses douloureuses* aux *Epistres familieres et inventives*; Le roman familial comme alibi à la production de l'écriture chez Marie de l'Incarnation; Functions of Tragic and Comic Love Letters in Marguerite de Navarre and Several Seventeenth-Century Comedies); Women of Color (Letting Go of the Thread: The Lesson of Gloria Naylor's *The Women of Brewster Place*; The Black Woman as Urban Exotic: Exportation and Exploitation of Afro-American Beauty; City as Circe: The Locus of Endless Desiring in Gwen Brooks's and Toni Morrison's Works); Colonial Baroque Culture: The Arising Consciousness of Spanish American Identity (Feminine Portraiture and the Baroque: The Challenge of Sor Juana); Conceptos medievales en la empresa de Indias (Silent Women in the Chronicles of New Spain); Noncanonical Pedagogies: Gender and Class; Gender, Reading, and Writing in Late Medieval England (Female Literacy and Early Middle English Religious Writing; "Bokes to Hem Assigned": The Gendering of Literacy in Late Medieval England; "Book-Mad" Women and Margery Kempe); Exploring Race (The Women in the Works, Life, and Career of Phillis Wheatley); Issues in Gender, Race, Ethnicity, and Class in the Two-Year College (Transforming the Curriculum to Include the Scholarship on Women: A Multicollege Plan; Integrating Women into Humanities Courses;

Teaching Issues of Class, Race, and Gender in an Introductory English Course: Triumphs and Pitfalls); American Dramatic Realism (Feminism and Dramatic Realism: Possibilities and Limitations); Feminism, Theory, and Cultural Criticism: Transforming the Scholarly Journal (The Advent of Theory and the Transformation of Journal Editing; The Politics of History: Publishing Dialogically; The Politics of Independent Journal Publication; Radical Paradoxes: Networking and the Fate of Scholarly Publishing); Iris Murdoch's Fiction: The New Directions (The Changes in Murdoch's Women); Hedda at One Hundred: *Hedda Gabler*, 1890–1990 (*Hedda Gabler*, Sex, and Class in Early Modern Drama); Women's Studies, Cultural Studies Workshop IV (Christina Serad and the Politics of Cultural Critique; Alice Walker: Writing beyond the Blues; Can the Subaltern Speak in English? Studying Middle Eastern Women); The Tropicalization of North American Discourse (In the Heat of the Night: The Tropicalization of Language and Women in *Palm Latitudes*); Reading the Bible: Cultural Perspectives in Seventeenth-Century England and America ("Fair Idolatresses": Idolatry and Gender in Milton's Republican Discourse); The Dark Side of Enlightenment (Unenlightened Bodies: Rationality and Gender in Philosophical Medicine); German Baroque Literature ("Dirnen-Barock": Das misogyne Frauenbild im Barockroman und seine sozialen Grundlagen in der gesellschaftlichen Wirklichkeit); Chicana and Chicano Literature in the 1990s: A Forum of Position Papers (The Woman Question and Noncanonical Texts; New Directions in Chicana Writing); Advances in Slavic Philology (Women's Studies and Slavic Philology); Cultural Studies and Hispanism (Gender and Ideology in Caribbean Narrative); Gender, Writing, and Violence in the Recent Texts of the French New Novelists (Sadism and the Nouveau Roman; Figuring Violence: Postmodern Meanings of Robbe-Grillet's Metalepsis; La violence et la subversion féminine dans "Manne" d'Hélène Cixous); In Celebration V: Troublemakers in the 1990s – Feminist Interventions in Politics and Culture (Christa Wolf's Cassandra and Accident: A Model for Women's Troublemaking in the 1990s; Feminism Here and There: Academic Politics and Political Art, 1990; Fracturing Meanings: Making Space for a Poem); Problems of Affirmation in Cultural Theory II (Affirmation and Agency in Ecofeminist Dialogics); Christopher Marlowe Workshop: Marlowe's History – Textual, Personal, National (*Dido Queen of Carthage* and the Discourses of Rulership and Romance); Dickens and the Everyday II: The Body and the Domestic (*Bleak House* and the Body; Gender Difference and the Everyday: Dickens's and Eliot's Responses to *Mary Barton*); *For Whom the Bell Tolls* II: Literary Aspects ("Something in It for You": Female Relationships in *For Whom the Bell Tolls*); Indian Influence in Eighteenth-Century English Literature (Women Good and Bad: Ethnopolitical Dynamics and the Language of Gendering in Dryden's *Aureng-Zebe*); Joyce's Alternative Semiologies ("He Read the Meaning of Her Movements in Her Frank Uplifted Eyes": Semerotics – Or, Feminine Body Language and Masculine Desire in Portrait; "In the Beginning Was the Gest ... for the End Is with Woman": The Language of Gesture and the Language of Women); New Directions in Irish American Literature (Responses to Oppression in Irish American Fiction by Women); The Texts of Southern Food (Agrarianism, Female Style; Black

Women, White Women: The Dining Room Door Swings Both Ways; Sweeping the
Kitchen: Revelation and Revolution in Contemporary Southern Women's Writing);
Transcendentalists and Society (Theodore Parker's "American Church": Race, Gen-
der, Class, and the Logic of Intuition; Theodore Parker and Women); Virginia Woolf
and the Tradition of the Essay (Virginia Woolf's Essay Form: Paradigm for a Feminist
Poetics; Virginia Woolf's "Truths" as Sleight of Hand; A Voice of One's Own: Implications of Impersonality in the Essays of Virginia Woolf and Alice Walker; Between
Writing and Life: Woolf and de Beauvoir's Uses of the Essay); Feminine Voices in
Francophone Literature; Gender, Race, and "Othering" in the Narrative Arts (The
Necessary Subversion of Ana Lydia Vega); In Search of a Liberated Female Charac-
ter (Concha Méndez: A Feminist Voice among the Vanguard; La mujer nueva lati-
noamericana en Yo Vendo unos ojos negros de Alicia Yánez Cossío; Writing the Sub-
ject: Female Protagonists in Narratives by Diamela Eltit, Paulina Mutta, and Reina
Roffé; Poetics of Hope: Gioconda Belli's Línea de fuego); La representación del
cuerpo humano en las novelas de Galdós (Writing of the Feminine Body in Galdós);
The Gay Nineties II: Politics, Texts, Strategies (Women's Studies, Gay Studies,
Transnational Cultural Studies); Toward a Definition of Sand's Feminism (Consuelo:
The Fictions of Feminism; The Limits of Sand's Feminism: Marriage in the Novels of
Her Maturity (1857–76); Un idéal mythique de la femme; Textual Feminism in
George Sand's Early Fiction; Women Writing Men: Female Authors and Male Pro-
tagonists (Ich war verkleidet als Poet ... Ich bin Poetin! The Masquerade of Gender
in Else Lasker-Schüler's Prose; Bild (zer)störung: Zu Brigitte Burmeester, Anders oder
Vom Aufenthalt in der Fremde; Karin Struck's Indictment of the Addictive Society;
Women Writing Men: Christa Wolf's Kein Ort Nigends – Kleist as a New Male Identity); Women's Spiritual Narrative (Kristeva on Jeanne Guyon; The "Devout Solilo-
quies" of Elizabeth Singer Rowe; Dorothy Day's Conversion Narratives).

The annual conference of 2000[4] included thirty-three papers about men in litera-
ture. These papers do not necessarily, once again, represent the perspective of men.
On the contrary, they usually represent the deconstructive perspective of feminists
and queer theorists. Here is the list: Region and Transnation (Rural Spaces and
Differences among White Men); Recent Trends in Latin American Theater (The
Impotence/Importance of the Male Intellectual in Mexican Theater Written by
Women); Re-forming Southern Literature, Reforming the South (Race, Masculin-
ity, and the South: Lessons from Thomas Dixon and D.W. Griffith to The Klans-
man, O.J. Simpson's First Movie); Eros and Pain in the Middle Ages (Cutting and
Eros: Castration, Knighthood, and Composite Genders); Queer Approaches to the
Spanish Comedia (The Unmasculine Activities Committee and the Golden Age
Stage); Classy Writing: George Gissing and the Complexities of the Late-Victorian
English Class System (Money and Manhood: Gissing's Redefinition of Lower-Mid-
dle-Class Man); The Family in Medieval Courtly Romance (Fathers and Sons in
the Chevalier as deus espees); Realists and the Romance of Street Credentials (Vio-
lating the Ultimate Taboo: White Men's Property, White Women, and Street Cre-

dentials in Richard Wright's *Native Son*); Violent Desires: Sexuality and Literature in World Wars I and II (Peg Legs and Roses: Sex and the Wounded Soldier in Henry Green's *Back*); Women, Writing, Community: The Language of Reform (Foreign Bodies: Representations of the Male Other in George Sand's Fiction; Language and Gender: Sex as Work/Labor in the Discourse of Male Bonding); Sex, Pornography, Marriage (Viagra Vice: Philip Roth's *The Human Stain* and J.M. Coetzee's *Disgrace*); Resisting Gender (The Illogics of Masculine Identification in Christopher Lee's Transvideos); Feeling Things: Race, Sex, and the Politics of Objects (The Faux Father's Compass: Living History, Reenacting Objects); Masculinity Studies and Feminist Theory: Backlash and Advances (Masculinities and Superordinate Studies; Queer Theory and Masculine Reempowerment; Stiffed and Punch Drunk: W(h)ither Masculinity; Reenfleshing the Bright Boys; or, How Male Bodies Matter to Feminist Theory); Queering the Family (Daddy's Boys; Papadada: Reinventing the Paternal); Comparative United States Literatures I: Turn-of-the-Century Sexualities (The Clubfoot and the Peg Leg: The Male Body in the Postbellum American South); Incorporations: Child-Adolescent Issues (Re)Forming Disability (Fathers and Sons: Family Incorporations of Disability); Feminist Ethics and Epistemologies/Éthiques et épistémologies féministes (Make Room for Daddy? Do "Masculinities" Have a Place in Feminist Epistemology?); Language, Literature, and Politics in the Twentieth-Century United States (Dismantling Booker T.: Or, What Happened to My Modernism and My Black Maleness When I Took a Job at Duke); The Function of the Courtroom at the Present Time: Law and Literature, 1837–1910 (A National Trial: The Expert Witness, the Common Man, and Mid-Century Stagings of Masculinity); Ethnographic Fictions (Dangerous Languor: Medical Ethnography and the Exotic Male in Confessions of a Thug); Native Sons, Cultural Kings: Harry Belafonte and Performances of Citizenship (Madmen in the Kitchen: Harry Belafonte and Elvis Presley in the Contact Zones of the 1950s; Calypso Harry and the Performance of Black Manhood; James Baldwin on Film: The Black Male Matinee Idol as Artist and Activist, 1955–85); Australia and Sport: Physicality, Image, and Text (Running Addiction and Masculinity in David Foster's "Eye of the Bull"); Presenting the Environment: Film, TV, and Popular Culture (Jungle Jims: Extreme Sports, Eroticism, and Nature as Personal Trainer for Men in Disney's *George of the Jungle* and *Tarzan*); New Approaches to Hawthorne (The Man behind the Veil: Hawthorne and the Writing of Masculinity; The Homosocial Homosexual in *The Blithedale Romance*); Democracy, Citizenship, and the State in American Literary Studies (Bo-Zhoo, Brudders: The Politics of Fraternity in *Nick of the Woods*); Ethnic Communities and Urban Spaces ("If the City Was a Man": Founders and Fathers, Cities and Sons in John Edgar Wideman's *Philadelphia Fire*).

The same conference included (once again) eighty-eight papers about women (but also, albeit indirectly in some cases, about men) in literature. Here is the list: Feminism against Time (Why Feminism Is Not a Historicism (and It's a Good Thing Too); Third World Women's Time against Western Time; Refusing History);

The Other Britain I: Late Victorian and Early Modernist Orientalism (Female Orientalist Fantasy: E.M. Hull's *The Shiek* and D.H. Lawrence's *The Plumed Serpent*); The Ethics of Postcolonial Writing (Violence, Love, and the Fictional Imagination: The Ethics of Reading Incest in Arudhati Roy's *The God of Small Things*; Locational Hand-Wringing: The Ethics of Postcolonial Feminisms); Genres, Genes, and Geography in Feminist Perspective (The Gendering of Public Spaces in Early Modern Drama; Language, Genetics, and Geography: The Case of "African Eve"); Epic I: Epic Sexualities (A Tragic Fall from a Trojan Horse: Sex and the Perilous Cliché; Sex and Epic Epiphany: Desiring the Goddess in Sidney, Spenser, and Cervantes); Sex: Alternative Positions (Through the Courtesan's Eyes: Liane de Pougy's *Idylle Saphique*; "Sugar Daddies" and "Chicken Hawks": The Homosexual as Pedophile in Nineteenth-Century French Prose Poetry); Italian and Italian American Women Wringing (Amelia Rosselli e la poesia della differenza: *La Libellula*; Stories of Sicilian Girls: Italian and Italian American Women's Mythological Visitations; Obsession: Francesca Mazzucato's *Hot Line*; Fulfillments of Rimbaudian Prophecies? From European Feminists to Italian American *Poete*); Body and Violence (The Victim's Body: Reading Violent Narratives in Contemporary Brazilian Women's Fiction); Writing from Prison I: International Perspectives (Gender and Representation in Two Women's Prison Memoirs from El Salvador); Narrative Contaminations I: Sexuality and Contamination (Eroticizing German Fascism in France: Sartre, Doubrovsky, Genet; Contaminating the Scene: Lesbian Litter in an Otherwise Beautiful Landscape); Pluralizing Early American Literature: New World Experience through a Comparatist Lens (Anxious Spirits and Deviant Bodies: Witchcraft and Treason in the Late Seventeenth Century); Commercial Seductions: Popular Women Writers and the Literary Market of the 1920s (Loose Women and Frivolous Publics: The Serialization of *Gentlemen Prefer Blondes* in *Harper's Bazaar*; "An Unwonted Coquetry": The Commercial Seductions of Jessie Fauset's *The Chinaberry Tree*; Zona Gale's Serious Popular Fiction); African Prison Literature (From the Womb of the Prison: A Rereading of Saadawi's *Woman at Point Zero*); Images of Teachers and Teaching (The Lady Professor); Female Modernists and Film Culture (Visualizing National Culture: Dorothy Richardson and the Politics of *Close Up*; HD's Distractions; Nancy Cunard in Black and White); The Other Britain II: Passing in Britain, 1880–1930 (Crazy Women Drivers: The Borderline Woman in Great War Fiction); Disrupting the Center: Contemporary British and Irish Women Poets (Disturbances of the Other: Conflicts between Class and Gender Power in the Poetry of Carol Ann Duffy); Mapping Trajectories of British Slave Narratives ("Me Know No Law, Me Know No Sin": Who Speaks for the Morality of Slave Women?); Marriage and Modernity (White Turkeys, White Zombies, White Weddings: The Personal Erotics of Laboring under Modernity; Properties of Marriage; Love and Political Commerce in the 1910s); Rethinking Resistance in Early-Twentieth-Century Working-Class Literature (Maternity and (the) Work: Edith Summers Kelly's *Weeds*); Cervantes's Women: Bodies That Materialize (Speaking in Tones: Cervantes's Translator Transila; Redressing Dorotea; The Body in Pieces: Imagining the Female Body in Cervantes's *Novelas ejemplares*); Recent Trends in Latin American Theater (Marx, Villa, Martín Luis Guzmán: Fantasmas y fantoches en entre villa y una mujer desnuda de Sabina Berman; The Impotence/Importance of the Male Intellectual in Mexican Theater Written by Women); Uwe Timm and the Ethnographic Gaze (Dangerous Liaisons: The Sexual Politics of Colonialism in Uwe Timm's *Morenga*); Nineteenth-Century Literary Onomastics ("Not Much of an Explanation": Victorian Onomastics and the (Mis)Naming of the Middle-Class Woman in Gaskell's *Wives and Daughters*); Online Discourse: Theoretical Perspectives (Cyborg Feminist Networks and Productions); Signed Language and Literature (Gender Linguistics in American Sign Language); The Vicissitudes of Narcissism (School Subjects: Gender and Narcissistic Entitlement in the Classroom); The Powers of Horror: Trauma and Testimony (Talking Heads: Orpheus and Medusa in Contemporary Women's Posttraumatic Poetry); Figuring the *Morisco* in Golden Age Spain (Jarifa's Choice: The Representation of Moorish Women in Golden Age Spanish Literature); Pietism Reconsidered (Women's Religious Speech in Halle and Herrnhut: The Sermons of Anna Nitschmann); Representing the Seventeenth Century in Anthologies, Syllabi, and Curricula (Representing Gender in the Seventeenth Century); Functions of Victorian Culture at the Present Time I: A Roundtable (Exhibiting Victorian Women); Textualizing the Self: The Genres of Early America (Where the Literary Meets the Didactic: Early American Women's Travel Narratives); Women's Reading Practices in England, 1580–1700 (Reading and Gender in Early Modern England; How Can We Know What Women Read in Early Modern England?; Women Reading Shakespeare in Early Modern England); Gender and Genre: The Picaresque in Contemporary Women's Narrative (The Ironies of Discourse in the Feminine Picaresque; The Pícara and the Flâneur: Modes of Transformation in Angela Carter's *Nights at the Circus*; The Pícara in Brief(s): Underwear as Narrative Manipulation in Two Contemporary Picaresque Novels by Women); Whose Standards? II (Who's the Reader? Who's the Writer? Electronic Versions of Early Women's Texts); Shifting the Image, Shifting the Story: Traditions, Allusions, and Intertexts in Margaret Atwood's Works (Feminist Intertextuality: Atwood Uses Bluebeard's Key); Eros and Pain in the Middle Ages (Sadism and Submission in Fin Amors: Perverse Punishments for Unwilling Women; Sweet Suffering Transformed: Eros and Pain in the Works of Christine de Pisan; Cutting and Eros: Castration, Knighthood, and Composite Genders); Pirandello's World: A Psychological Perspective I (As He Desired Her: A Girardian Reading of Pirandello's Obsession with Martas Abba); Epic II: Epic Historiographies (Meddling Women and Biblical Histories in Renaissance Florence); Feminism in Time (Feminism out of Time; Found Footage: Feminist Histories Lost in Time; Nationalist Time and the Politics of Everyday Space); Historicizing Queer Subcultures ("What's That Smell?" Queer Dyke Subcultures Now and Then); Theorizing Multiculturalism and Children's Literature (Wetbacks, Funny Boys, and Herb Women: Multicultural Gender in Children's Literature); Red, White, and "Blue"?

Contemporary American Independents ("Bitches'll Fuck Your Shit Up": Indie Films, Hip-Hop, and Women); Fictions of Peace: The "Great War" of Jane Addams, Zona Gale, and Dorothy Canfield Fisher (Playing with the Big Boys: Jane Addams and William James; "Knowing Nothing of Nations": The Feminist Pacifism of Zona Gale and the Women's Peace Party); "Hispanic" Women, Politics, and Social Justice: Historical and Cultural Perspectives (Gestiones para el nuevo milenio: Movimientos femininos, organizaciones feministas, y la política en Argentina; Re-presentaciones de la represión: Pedagogía y lucha armada; "Una historia para comprender lo que nos pasó": Biografía, justicia política-social, y la mujer en Hispano-américa; *Mujeres de abril*: Representaciones de mujeres combatientes en la República Dominica); Formal Session of the South Asian Literary Association (At a Loss for Words: Reading the Silence in Women Writers' Partition Narratives; Abducted Bodies, Partitioned Souls: Women's Lives in Amrita Pritam, Urvashi Butalia, and Veena Das; The Gendered Rape of the National Body and the Partition Fiction of Attia Hosain, Suraiya Qasim, and Bapsi Sidhwa); The Family in Medieval Courtly Romance (Family Relationship in Chrétien's Romances; Mother-Child Relationships in the Roman d'Enéas); African Cinema (Woubi Cheri: Negotiating Subjectivity, Gender, and Power); Women, Labor, and Radical Literature in East Asia (Chinese Empress as Exemplar: The Dramatic Portrayal of Wu Zetian and the Cultural Revolutionary Struggle for Women's and Laborer's Rights; To Write or Not to Write: Narrative Permutation and Political Allegiance in Ding Ling's *Miss Sophia's Diary* and *Sophia's Diary, II*; Diverging Discourses in Two Korean Comfort Women Plays); National Identity in the Italian Ottocento (The Rhetoric of the "Virtuous Woman" during the Risorgimento and Postunitary Era); After Oxford: Reassessing the Somerville Novelists (The Costs of Culture: Dorothy Sayers, Margaret Kennedy, and the Gender of Snobbery; Writing the Feminist Home Front: Great War Fictions of Vera Brittain and Winifred Holtby; An Intellectual Tradition: The Influence of the Somerville Novelists on Contemporary British Women Writers); Brain Work: Representations of Postindustrial Labor in American Literature (The Gendering of Postindustrial Labor from Riesman to Coupland); Psychoanalysis and the Victorians: Critical Legacies and Their Discontents (Fantasies of Female Symbolic Reproduction in *Bleak House*); Realists and the Romance of Street Credentials (Violating the Ultimate Taboo: White Men's Property, White Women, and Street Credentials in Richard Wright's *Native Son*); There and Back Again: Gender, Discourse, and Transatlantic Circulations to 1750 (Anne Bradstreet and the Circulation of Poetic Authority; Specimen Muse; An Amerindian Princess in Paris: Imagining Paraguaçu in Colonial Brazil); Violent Desires: Sexuality and Literature in World Wars I and II (Captive Sexuality: Women's Holocaust Narratives; Peg Legs and Roses: Sex and the Wounded Soldier in Henry Green's *Back*; Depraved and Corrupted: Sexuality and Censorship after the Great War); Mothers' Memoirs (Mothers of Suicides; Did Your Mama Take Them Dreadful Drugs? Responding to Blame through the Memoir of "Disabled" Motherhood; "A Mother's Love": The Burden of Devotion in Recent Memoirs of

Mental Disability); Social and Moral Responsibility ("Knowledge for What?" Academic Feminism and Distributive Justice; The Ethical Responsibilities of Feminist Educators in a Globalizing Economy; What's Wrong with Building the Discourse of Solidarity in Academia? Reflections on Teaching and *Testimonio*); "Nothing Else Is": John Donne in the History of Sexuality ("Uritur et Loquitur": Donne, Catullus, and "Desire of More"; "Nothing Else Is" – and That's the Problem: Donne, Cixous, and the History of Failure; Glimpsing Nothing: Reading between the Lines in the Book of the Flesh); Academic Careers and the Family (The Two-Career Job Search? A Veteran's Perspective); The Transgressive Impulse in Doris Lessing, Margaret Atwood, and Mary Shelley (Mary Shelley and Literary Women's History; Stuck in the Ice: Apocalypse and Transgression in Shelley, Atwood, and Lessing; Transgressive Spaces: Postcolonial Scenes in Lessing's "Old Chief Mshlanga" and Atwood's "Death by Landscape"); Victorian Writing, Victorian Art (Following the Threat: Women, Needlework, and Publication in the Arts and Crafts Movement); Women, Writing, Community: The Language of Reform ("It May Be That Female Petitioners Can Lawfully Be Heard": Constituting Women Reformers during the United States Indian Removal Debates, 1830–31; "The Blessed Education into a Tolerant Spirit Goes Swiftly On": Frances Willard and the Maintenance of the Women's Reform Community, 1887–92; "The Tragedy of Women's Emancipation": Emma Goldman's Critique of First Wave Feminism, 1905–20); Foreign Bodies: Representations of the Male Other in George Sand's Fiction; Presqu'il, Presque Femme: Hybrid Identities in Sand's *Tamaris*; L'altérité de l'artiste improvisateur dans quelques romans de George Sand); Mixed Subjects: Women Read Latin America (Women, Guerillas, and Love: Understanding War in Central America; After Exile: Writing the Latin American Diaspora; Easy Women: Sex and Gender in Modern Mexican Fiction; The Fence and the River: Culture and Politics at the United States-Mexico Border); Manifesto Writing and Cultural Critique (A Challenge to Death: Women's Manifesto for Peace in the Face of War); Language and Gender (We Don't Speak the Same as We Did Five Years Ago: Diachronic Analysis of Japanese Women's Language Use; Negotiating Religion: The Construction of Gender in Personal Ads; Sex as Work/Labor in the Discourse of Male Bonding); Romantic-Era Science II: Sex and Gender (Romantic Science and the Perversification of Sexual Pleasure; Dissecting for Metaphor: Joanna Southcott, or, Poetry on the Brain; Peacock, Mary Somerville, and the Woman of Science); Functions of Victorian Culture at the Present Time II ("Nurs'd Up amongst the Scenes I have Described": Political Resonances in the Poetry of Working-Class Women); Comparative Cultural Studies and post-1989 Central European Culture (Petrarchan Patriarchal: Allegorical Femininity in Hungarian "Postmodernist" Literature and Film); Open Forum: Part-Time and Non-Tenure-Track Faculty Members (Discourse of Victimization); Sex, Pornography, Marriage (The Discourse of Intimacy and the Crisis of Marriage; Pornography, Erotica, and Repression); Theoretical Approaches to Teaching Tudor and Stuart Women Writers (Teaching the Writings of Early Modern Women from and with a Theoretical Perspective; Theory in the Teaching of Early Modern Women Writers; Early Modern Women Writing Race); Refiguring the Latino and Latina Studies Canon: Genres, Population, Approaches (Chicana Ecofeminism: Gloria Anzaldúa and Judy Baca); Edith Wharton as Transnational (Wharton's *In Morocco*: Feminism and Orientalism); Feminist Philanthropy and Women's Foundations (Women Philanthropists: Myths and Reality; Encouraging Responsive Philanthropy; Are Women the Philanthropic Leaders of the Future?); John Milton: A General Session I (The Troublesome Helpmate, or, How Pandora Got Her Box); Movies as Paradigmatic Narratives (Visual Pleasure and Narratological Cinefeminism); Resisting Gender (Constructing the Transgender Subject: Sexuality, Gender, and the Female-Bodied Man in Diane Wood Middlebrook's *Suits Me* and Jackie Kay's *Trumpet*; Genetic Counter-memory and the Genealogy of the Transsexual); Virginia Woolf on Religious Texts and Traditions (Virginia Woolf's "Reoccupation" of Christian Territory; Mrs. Ramsay's Last Supper: *To the Lighthouse* and the Passion of the Female Christ); Beauty: Now and Then (The Female Artist as Hercules: Angelica Kauffman's Revisionary Aesthetics); Romancing Women: "Gender and Popular Literature in Medieval and Early Modern Europe (Retrieving the Female Voice in European "Women's Song"; Textual Sex and Sexual Tests: The "Doncella Guerrera" in Iberian Romance; Romancing the News: Mme de Scudéry as Journalist); Jewish Cultural Studies and the Question of Religion (Queer Theory and the Invention of Religion); Late Nineteenth-Century American Brotherhoods (Female "Body Snatching Will Out": The American Protective Association's Tales of "Convent Horrors"); Lesbian Disidentifications ("I'm Not a Lesbian, I Just Loved Thelma": Djuna Barnes's Lesbian Disavowal; Against Melancholy: Women Disidentifying Women; "In the Hard and Painful Life": Queer Disidentification and Lesbian Ambivalence); Modernity in Reflux: Modernism, Feminism, and Failed Fictions of Progress (Mothers: Eugenic Feminism and Charlotte Perkins Gilman's Regeneration Narratives; Past Time as Pastime? Sapphic Modernity and the Abandonment of Feminism; Female Peristalsis; Backlash of Fitness Landscape? Feminism and Multiple Modernities); Resituating Glasgow (Black Labor and the New Southern Woman); Contexts of Early Modern German Literature (Reading the Visual Context of Sociability in G.P. Harsdörffer's *Frauenzimmer Gesprächspiele*); Performance and Culture in Contemporary Latin America (Performing Motherhood in Argentina and Mexico: Griselda Gambaro and Hugo Argüelles; Sex in the City: Striptease and the Performance of Style in Cortázar and Peri-Rossi); Medieval Spanish Language and Literature (Medieval Medical Views of Women in the *Lapidario* of Alfonso X); Topics in Earlier German Literature (Female Pain, Female Eroticism: The Eroticization of the Female Body in Pain in Hartman von Aue's Courtly Epics); Medical Knowledge and Cultural Study (Generative Debt: Liberal Politics and the Placenta; Reading Abortion: Medicine and Politics in an Age of Revolution); Ma(Donna): The Image of Italian American Women in Literature, Film, and Television (Rescuing the Fallen Woman: The Issue of Female Representation in Martin Scorsese's Cinema; Anything but Italian:

Madonna's Synthetic Ethnicity; Italian American Women as Comic Foils: Exploding the Stereotype in *My Cousin Vinny, Moonstruck,* and *Married to the Mob*; Transgressive Italian American Women in Carole Maso's *Ghost Dance,* Nancy Savoca's *Household Saints,* and David Chase's *The Sopranos*); Feeling Things: Race, Sex, and the Politics of Objects (Bad Sex Objects; Object and Home Erotics in Dickinson and Gilman); Grief and Gender in Early Modern England ("I Might Againe Have Been the Sepulcure": Paternal and Maternal Mourning in Early Modern England; Ghost Stories in *The Winter's Tale*: Grief in Leones, Aggression in Hermione; Mamillius); Masculinity Studies and Feminist Theory: Backlash and Advances (Masculinities and Superordinate Studies; Queer Theory and Masculine Reempowerment; Stiffed and Punch Drunk: W(h)ither Masculinity; Reenfleshing the Bright Boys, or, How Male Bodies Matter to Feminist Theory); Race and the Subject of Marriage in Late-Nineteenth- and Twentieth-Century America (Captive Wives); Construing Halperin: Acts, Identities, and the History of Sexuality (Theorizing Desire: Acts and Identities in Pre- and Early Modernity; Against Forgetfulness: David Halperin, "pseudo-Foucauldian Doctrine," and the Practice of Lesbian and Gay History; Friendship, Love, and the Discursive Prehistory of Homosexuality); Constituting Ethnic Americans (Radical Black Femininity: The Idealization of Social Progress); Queering the Family (Tardy Epithalamia: Queer Love, the Family, and the Poetry of Marriage); New Perspectives on the *Heptaméron* (Her Story: Social and Sexual Structures of Desire in *Heptaméron* 12); *Liberté, Egalité, Fraternité*: Human Rights and Nineteenth-Century French Literature ("Les droits de l'homme" in 1848: Women of Color and Emancipation); Women in the Colonial Latin American Inquisition (Santa Rose de Lima and the Inquisition; Witches in the Tribunal de la Inquisicion de Cartagena de Indias; And for the Defense, Sor Juana Summons the Inquisition); Re-inventing the Peabody Sisters (Desire, Transgression, and Sophia Hawthorne's *Notes in England and Italy*; Subtle, Shifting, and Subverted Power: Mary Peabody Mann's Innovative Model for the True Woman; Declaration and Deference: Elizabeth Palmer Peabody, Mary Peabody Mann, and Their Complex Rhetoric of Mediation; Elizabeth Palmer Peabody's Problematic Feminism and the Feminization of Transcendentalism); Rethinking Violence, Agency, and Aesthetics: Feminist and Cross-Cultural Perspectives (Documenting Rape Warfare: Feminist Criticism and Translational Epistemologies; The Aesthetics of Romance and the Ethics of Ethnic Violence in Postcolonial Film; "Handing Back Shame": Survivor Discourse and Political Agency in Sapphire's *Push*); Madness, Melancholia, and Mourning: Austrian States of Mind (Inspired Insanity: Women and Madness in Contemporary Austrian Literature); Annual Meeting of the American Boccaccio Association (The Ideology of Love in *Corbaccio*); Racialization, Dangerous Bodies, and the (En)Gendering of Space/Place (Writing on the Social Body: Dresses and Body Ornamentation in Contemporary Chicana Art); The Brown Women Writers Project Online: "New" Texts, New Questions (Searching for Women's Work: Literary and Cultural Analysis of Online Texts; Medieval Women's Manuscripts: Authorship and Encoding Challenges; The

Role of the WWP in the Development of Literary Encoding in the 1990s; Mary Car-
leton's Conditional Moods: A Discourse Analysis of a WWO Text); The Other
Britain III: Modernist Migrations and Topographies – People, Places, and Spaces
in the British Imaginary ("Inconsequent Lives": Anglo-Indian Fictions of Female
Voyaging and Domesticity); Transgressive Sexualities in the Postcolony (Patricia
Powell's *A Small Gathering of Bones* and *The Pagoda*: Articulating Transgressive
Sexualities through the Disjunctures of the Caribbean Diaspora; Nasty "Colored
Girls": The Revenge of the Native Woman Informant; "There Are No Lesbians
Here": Political Definitions in the Age of Human Rights Activisms); Comparative
United States Literatures I: Turn-of-the-Century Sexualities (Wired Love: Sex,
Media, and American Modernity); Boswell's London Journal 1762–1763,
1950–2000: New Approaches ("An I Not Then a Man?" Importance and Autho-
rial Anxiety in Boswell's *London Journal*); Political Trollope (Social Issues and
Political Contexts: Domestic Violence and Trollope's *The Prime Minister*);
Ta(i)lling the Dog: Power, Politics, and Play in the Works of David Mamet (The
Politics of the Deal: The Prisoner's Dilemma, Logical Paradox, and the Lacanian
Gaze in David Mamet's *Oleanna*; David Mamet, Film-acher: Assault on/with Narrative); W. H. Auden's Musical Collaborations (Queer Identities and Musical Collaborations); In Their Own Words: Understanding Chinese and Indian Rhetoric
from Within (The Problem of Global Feminism: An enthymematic Perspective on
Post-Mao Chinese Women's Writing); Teaching Boccaccio's *Decameron* (Women
in the *Decameron*; Anatomizing Boccaccio's Sexual Festivity); The Arts of Joyce
(Whorehouse/Playhouse: The Brothel as the Setting for "Circe"); Feminist Ethics
and Epistemologies/Éthiques et épistémologies féministes (Fémininité et négativité
dans la pensée contemporaine; From "Femme Juive" to "JuiFemme": What Do
French Jewish Women Writers Know?; Make Room for Daddy? Do "Masculini-
ties" Have a Place in Feminist Epistemology?); Public Spectacles (War with Words:
Nineteenth-Century Literary Women in Public); Foreign Languages, Foreign Cul-
tures (Cultural Studies and Sexual Ideologies); Comparative Turns of Centuries
("The Rational Spiritual Part": Gender and Transformation in Late-Century
Music Dramas of Dryden and Purcell); Feminism on Time (Feminist Futures?
Telling Time in Feminist Theory; International Feminism: Timekeeping for the
Nation?); Writing from Prison (Temporality as Queer History: Genet and the Time
of Capital); History and Future of Rhetorics outside the Paradigm (Rhetoric as a
Feminist Project); How We Feel about Bodies: A Roundtable Discussion (Feeling
Differently: Conjugal Reorientation and the Victorian Honeymoon; Much Butter,
Fewer Eggs: Mary Chesnut's Infertility; Gender, Not Sex – and Not Sexuality,
Either); Reading Women I: Nineteenth-Century Women and the Social Work of
Reading ((Im)Proper Reading for Women: Mary Elizabeth Braddon's *Belgravia
Magazine* and the Defense of the Sensation Novel; Reading Mothers, Reading
Daughters; Social Reading, Social Work, and the Social Function of Art in Louisa
May Alcott's "May Flowers"); Interarts Excursions: Italian Poets on Painting in
the Twentieth Century (Women, Futurism, and Visual Writing); Irish Gothic and

Modernity (The Female Collaborator: Property and Authorship in Stoker's *Dracula* and Yeats's *A Vision*); Poe's Unseemly Passions (Poe in Bed: Sex, Biographical Speculation, and Tales of Dying Women); Music, Gender, and Representation (Moll Cutpurse and the Understanding Public: The Dreams of a Roaring Girl; The Importance of Being Greek: Classical Affect and Gender Anxiety in Eighteenth-Century British Musical Aesthetics; "That Blood Can't Be Contained": (Re)Constructing Body, Genre, and Lyric in Black Feminist Hip-Hop); The Invisible Canon: Forgotten Names, Marginalized Texts (La sabiduría de la mujer en la obra de Nemesio R. Canales; Queer Family as Edge: Erica López's Flaming Iguanas: *An Illustrated All-Girl Road Novel Thing*); Opera and Sexuality, Revisited (Balloons and Guillotines: Ethics of Mutilation in Poulenc's Operas; Rescuing Vere from Melville; Forster, Britten, and *Billy Budd*; Romancing the Opera); Acts of Reading and Print Culture in Early Modern Spain (Eve's Apple: Early Modern Hispanic Women Writers on Storytelling and Knowledge); Music and Gender in Twentieth-Century French Literature (Nancy Huston: Music and Feminine Identity; Siren of the Opera, or, Gender Afloat; Vinteuil, Music, and Musical Aesthetics); Women Collecting Poetry in Mid-Seventeenth Century England: The HM904 Miscellany and Open Business Meeting; Family, Gender, and Politics in the Works of Simone de Beauvoir (A Mother-Daughter Link: Four Critics Look at *Une mort très douce*; Gender Instability in *Le sang des autres and Tous les hommes son mortels*; Beauvoir's Fosca: Faustian Overreacher or Product of the Medieval Italian Republics; Le jeu de "je" ou "elle" dans *Les belles images*); Volatile Values (Gender, Sexuality, and the Literary Market in Spain at the End of the Millennium); Gender and Language Learning (Effects of Gender Differences on Students' Motivation in Foreign Language Learning; Gender and Language-Learner Socialization; Language Learning and Gender Differences in Pronunciation); American Picturesques: Visual Culture in the Nineteenth-Century United States (Tourists and Settlers: Gendered Uses of the Picturesque in Antebellum Travel Sketches); On the Uses of Perversity (Economics, Sexuality, and the Perverse Desires of the Nineteenth-Century Novel); The Nineteenth-Century French Heroine Revisited: Amazons, Dandies, and Hysterics (Heroines à Cheval: The Amazon in *Indiana, Les lys dans la vallée*, and *Dominique*; Le dandysme par procuration dans *Illusions perdues*; Folie à Deux: Hysterical Contagion in *Thérèse Raquin*); Brilliance and Schlock I: Brilliance in Twentieth-Century United States Drama (Race and Sexuality in the Modern American Mystery Play); Reading Women II: Twentieth-Century Women and the Production of the Self as Reader (Hall of Mirrors: The Woman Reading and/in Radclyffe Hall's *The Well of Loneliness*; Diverting the Reader: Seriously Reading the Dumb Blonde Seriously Reading; "One of Those People like Anne Sexton or Sylvia Plath": The Pathologized Woman Reader as Literary and Cultural Icon); Teaching America Abroad (Fast Food, Fast Cars, and Fast Women: Confronting Clichés of America in Turkey); Film and History (Historicizing Ida Lupino: A Female Production Code in 1950s Hollywood); New Perspectives in Twentieth-Century English Literature (Unnatural Passions: Sex and Spirituality in Women's Writing);

Comic Scapegoating: Laugher, Identity, and Community in Late-Twentieth-Century American Novels (Sticky Evidence: Masculinity as Scapegoat in *Portnoy's Complaint*); Victorian Freaks! (The Bear Woman and the Lady: Julia Pastrana and the Politics of Spectacle); Images of Maternity in Elsa Morante, Natalia Ginzburg, and Dacia Maraini (The Tigress in the Show: Motherhood in Elsa Morante; Matrophobia and Maternal Ambivalence in Ginzburg's Daughters; The Pregnant Nun: Suor Attanasia and the Metaphor of Arrested Maternity in Dacia Maraini); Modernity, Gender, Aesthetics: Pardo Bazán beyond Naturalism (Transgendered and Transgenred; Incipient Modernism in Pardo Bazán's Short Fiction; Thoroughly Modern Men: Crime, Sex, and Adventure in *La gota de sangre* and *La aventura de Isidro*); Cervantes and Cultural Studies (El *Quijote* y la construcción cultural de masculinidades en la España aurisecular); El Teatro español des Siglo de Oro y las Indias (Seeds of An American Baroque Aesthetic: Gender, Ethnicity, Sustenance, and Theology in Sor Juana's Version of the Conquest; "En Distintas Cuadras": Engendering the Americas in Sor Juana's *Los empeños de una casa*); Cognition and Ideology (Define Cognition: Be Sure to Distinguish Ontological Problems from Both Epistemological Concerns and Feminist-Materialist Accounts of Ideology); Public Appearances: Modernist Women and Social Space ("Street Haunting": Shopping and Public Selving in *Mrs. Dalloway*; "Among the Furnitures": Laura Riding's Leisure Time; "In These Secluded Districts": The Case for Privacy in the Work of HD); Revisions or New Visions? Contextualizing New Woman Literature of the Fin de Siècle (Re-viewing the Pats: New Woman Writing and the Victorian Women's Novel; Painting the New Woman; Progress, Development, and Individualism in New Woman Fiction of the Fin de Siècle); The Transubstantiation of Rhetoric in the Discipline of English Studies (Oratory and the Construction of Gender in Postbellum America); American Humor in the Twenty-First Century (Ludicrous Courtship in Rose Terry Cooke's Short Stories: "I Am What I Seem to Men. Need I Be Any More?"); Brilliance and Schlock II: Schlock in Nineteenth- and Twentieth-Century United States Theater (The First "Miss California": Ramona Pageants and the Romance of the American Southwest); Genre in Children's Literature (The Journey Within and Without: The Female Bildungsroman in Children's Literature); John Milton: A General Session II ("To Set a Foot Forward with Manly Confidence": Milton and the Gender of Liberty); The "New Negro" away from Harlem (Southern Sisters of the New Negro Renaissance); André Gide's Politics (André Gide: From a Politics of Sexuality to a Politics of Commitment); Pressure Points: Spanish Women Writers and the Canon, 1898–1939 (Women Writers Imagine a New Political Order, 1923–31; Couples, Creativity, and the Suppression of Women's Writing: The Case of Concha Méndez; Women Playwrights in the Early Decades of the Twentieth Century); Modern Women Writers Editing Sociology (Figuring Beatrice Webb and the "Serious Artist"; Refusing Middle Age); Reading and Writing Margaret Cavendish in the Context of Print Culture (Gender and the Monumental Book in Cavendish's *Poems and Fancies*); "The Words Continue Their Journey": Atwood's Language,

Style, and Form (Historian or Hysteric? Revising the History of the Canadian Frontier in Margaret Atwood's *Journals of Susanna Moodie*); Edith Wharton and Mass Culture (Misreading *The House of Mirth*: Middle-Class Readers and Upwardly Mobile Desire); Images of Byron (The Female Gaze: Some Women's Portraits of Byron); Mark Twain's Literary Daughters and Sisters (Mark Twain's Debt to Women's Humor Tradition; Mutual Influences: Mark Twain's Correspondence with Nineteenth-Century Women Writers); The Imprisonment of American Culture (Women's Prisons, Women's Lives); Gender and Sexuality in the Cultures of Medieval Iberia (Cultural Assimilation and Gender in *Minhat Yehuda, Sone hanashim (The Gift of Yehuda, Enemy of Women)*; Engendering Trouble in the *Libro de buen amor*; "Dones que feyan d'homens": The Construction of Gender in the Writing of Medieval Catalan History); Pirandello's World: A Psychological Perspective II (Women on the Verge: Tozzi, Pirandello, and Sexual Sympathy); Simone de Beauvoir and the World around Her (Courtesans, Libertines, and Demimondaines in *Le deuxième sexe*; Women Intellectuals and the Canon: Recent Readings of Simone de Beauvoir and Hannah Arendt); *Lord Jim* at One Hundred (Dreams of Grandeur, Fears of Engulfment: Gender and Landscape in Conrad's *Lord Jim*); Dickinson and the Victorians (Finding Herself Alone: Emily Dickinson, Victorian Women Novelists, and the Female Subject); Feminism, Policy, and Politics in the New Millennium; Rhetoric, Technical Communication, and Theory (Situated Knowledges, Embodied Information: Haraway's Cyborg Rhetoric in Feminist Technical Communication Research); Your Tax Dollars at Work (for and against You): Public Policy and Gay and Lesbian Studies (Public Policy and Gay and Lesbian Studies; They Didn't Ask, So We Didn't Tell: Public Policy and the Construction of Federal Homosexuality; Mass Media and Queer Studies; The Impact of Homophobic Media Coverage on Queer Subjectivity); Cronicas: Tales from the Academy – A Workshop (Why Do Women Enter the "Network" So Late, If Ever?); Dreams and Sitings/Citings in Courtly Literature (The Female Gaze and the Spec(tac)ular Male; Female Citings/Sitings in the Dream in Medieval French Narrative; Charles d'Orléans's Dream of Freedom from Women and Grief); East German Women in United Germany: Ten Years Later ("Geboren in frauenbewegter östlicher Nachwendezeit": Looking Back at Eight Years of *Weibblick*; Changing and Maintaining Identity: An East German's Quest for Answers); Les françaises: Etat des lieux / The Status of French Women Today: An Assessment (The Debate over Feminine Terminology; Women in the Media in France; Réussité scolaire et insertion professionnelle des femmes en France); The Mother-Daughter Syndrome (The Triad of the Mother, the Daughter, and Poland in Maria Kunuwiz's *The Stranger*; Exploring and Exploding the Discourse on Motherhood and Creativity: Kristeva and Drakulic's "Marble Stein").

A Front by Any Other Name: Ideology, Gender Studies, and Women's Studies

We have come a long way since the days of Shakespeare, who observed, "That which we call a rose, By any other name would smell as sweet."[1] What must have been heard as common sense to most people in the seventeenth century, however, is clearly no such thing to most people in our time. What we now call a "rose," for instance, might *not* actually smell sweet. Although the powerful have probably always used euphemisms to disguise their intentions, doing so has become more widely known and more widely accepted than ever. And we can think of at least three reasons.

For one thing, consider the influence of advertising, a necessary feature of commerce in every market economy. No longer considered an art, it is taught systematically on the basis of psychological research. Something very similar has happened in the world of politics – and not only, to judge from the euphemisms and slogans of communist countries, in market economies. Elected officials often prefer to follow rather than lead. To do that, they must rely on opinion polls. And to do that successfully, they must say what people want to hear, even if that means distorting the truth. Finally, academics – those with ideological goals – have actively sought and effectively promoted ways of legitimating all this, even though many of them disapprove of advertising, in particular, as the capitalist way of creating "false consciousness." What was once derided as "groupthink," in short, is now acclaimed as "sensitivity" (or satirized by dissidents as political correctness).

In *Spreading Misandry*, we introduced the word "front" with regard to ideological feminists (the term originated among Marxists and is used also in organized crime). The ideological rhetoric of feminism is not palatable to all women, so a front is required – that is, rhetoric that really is considered respectable and can therefore be used to conceal ideas and goals that would otherwise be considered unacceptable. "Ideologues routinely use fashionable rhetoric but without following through on its inner logic ... [T]hey fill old wineskins with new wine. The words are familiar to almost everyone, yes, but not the implications or interpretations intended by this or that ideologue."[2] Some apparently innocent phenomenon or institution is used, in other words, to disguise what would otherwise seem much more disturbing or even sinister.

One front, popular not only among ideologues but also among politicians of all stripes and advertisers of all products, is language. We suggest that the term "gender studies" originated as a euphemism for "women's studies." It has come to include "gay studies" and "queer theory." It functions as a front for ideologies – that is, for feminism and its gay derivative. A study with statistical significance would be an enormous research project in itself, because so many colleges and universities teach either gender studies or women's studies. But, as a quick glance at academic sites on the Internet will reveal to anyone, the following examples are by no means eccentric.

Consider the Center for Gender Studies at University of Chicago. Its website lists forty-six graduate and undergraduate courses offered in 2002–2003. Visitors to this site learn that the center coordinates courses and activities on gender and sexuality. Many courses are, at least ostensibly, about both women and men. Many others are specifically about women or gay people. Not one, however, is specifically about men (although that varies from year to year, at least three – out of almost fifty – having been offered at one time or another). Even when the word "gender" does include men, moreover, it often refers specifically to gay men, bisexual men, and so on. Given the prevalence of courses on feminist or gay theory (along with Marxist, postmodern, and postcolonial theory), the focus of this program is clearly "to locate knowledge in previously suppressed or understudied places and modes of thought."[3] In other words, profs and students interested in the needs and problems of straight white men need not apply.

The website for "gender studies" at Indiana University, Bloomington, starts off inclusively enough. The program, for graduates and undergraduates, offers twenty-two "exciting, interdisciplinary and rigorous courses that concentrate on the position of women and men across many cultures. Masculinity and femininity, often referred to as gender, have evolved throughout history and are still evolving."[4] Most courses are, at least ostensibly, about both women and men – that is, both femininity and masculinity. One is clearly not: Women, Gender, and Culture. Not even one course is specifically about men. But this tally is deceptive.

For one thing, two additional courses are specifically about feminism: Two Centuries of Feminist Thought and International Feminist Debates. In fact, almost every course description refers directly to feminism. Many of the courses listed could be on either women or men, true, depending on demand in any particular year. But when the topics of previous years are listed, the focus is on women: Topics in the Study of Gender; Survey of Contemporary Research in Gender Studies: The Social and Behavioral Sciences (which in earlier years included topics such as "Women, Sexuality and Health: Research Issues and Policy Implications"; "Feminist Social Science"; and "Feminism: Histories, Theories, and Methods"); and Themes in the Study of Gender (such as "Victorian Women and Gender"; "Gender and Sports Journalism"; "Sex Discrimination and the Law"; "Native American

Women and Welfare Policies"; "Women's Health Issues"; "Women Composers"; and "Gender and Military Service").

The teacher of that last course is possibly, though not necessarily, interested in men. The teacher of another course, Sexual Politics, probably is: "Why," asks the course description, "are men expected to be soldiers but women are not (in most societies)?" On the other hand, consider this description of the course on Gender, Sexuality, and Popular Culture: topics include "gender and the power of the image; sex and spectatorship; melodrama, film noire and 'the women's film'; rock music women; Madonna and MTV; race, age and representation; as well as violence, masculinity and pornography." Men are not only placed last on the list but also linked with two inarguably negative topics.

The University of Southern California offers seventy-five courses to its students in gender studies. Some of the courses are cross-listed from other programs or departments. Many are, at least ostensibly, about both women and men. No fewer than twenty-three, though, are specifically about women: Racial and Ethnic Women in America; Woman, Nature, Culture: The Behavioral Ecology of Women; Overcoming Prejudice (on "the most effective strategies and techniques for minorities, women, gays and lesbians, and others subjected to stigma");[5] Women in Antiquity; Women and Global Issues; Women in Judaism; Women in the European Middle Ages; Women, Religion and Sexuality; French Women Writers; Women in Society; Women Writers in Europe and America; Women and Gender in China: Past and Present; Women in Contemporary Literature and the Arts; Women in Music; Women's Literature in Germany; Women in English Literature before 1800; Women In English and American Literature after 1800; Women's Spaces in History: 'Hussies,' 'Harems,' and 'Housewives'; Women in International Development; Images of Women in Contemporary Culture; Studies in Women's and Family History; and Woman [sic] as Writers in World Literature. In addition, eight courses are specifically about feminism: Introduction to Feminist Theory and the Women's and Men's Movements (which nonetheless considers only "men's roles in the feminist movement");[6] Gender Studies and the Community: Internship (including "men's roles in the feminist movement"); Ecofeminism; Special Topics: Seminar in Selected Topics Relating to Gender and Feminism; Feminist Theory; Studies in Gender and Feminism; and Studies in Feminist Theory and Art History.

Only one course is specifically about men: Men and Masculinity. The obsequious description of that course is very revealing.

Why a course about masculinity? After all, academia is infused with *de facto* male biases. Much of the subject matter, theoretical constructs and thematic foci were constructed in a time when men controlled education and women often had scarce access to it. Ironically, the answer to this question can be found in women's studies.

In the generations since feminist examinations of gender began, the mining of the social terrain yielded veins of strata, patterns of formation and rich resources that construct social architectures favoring men. Still, these excavations also unearthed a series of conflicts within the production and performance of masculinities. This course will explore social class, race and ethnicity, sexual orientation and age. The course also looks at the antecedents of today's men's movements. Particular scrutiny will be given to the costs of rigid definitions of masculinity as well as the costs of the power and privilege men exercise over women.[7]

Clearly, an apology is considered necessary for this course even to be offered. At any rate, it assumes the legitimacy of studying men through the eyes of women – that is, of feminism. In fact, its legitimacy as a course is predicated on the extent to which it builds on (read: does not challenge) feminism. Otherwise, how could we explain the reference to "social architectures" favouring men without any direct reference to those favouring women? Although this description acknowledges the costs – presumably psychological – of the "power and privilege men exercise over women," therefore, the implication is that these are of no *moral* importance. For some reason, the description of another course, Introduction to Feminist Theory and the Women's and Men's Movements, mentions only the roles of *men* in feminism. Go figure.

Finally, consider "gender studies" at Northwestern University. The introduction to its website begins by noting a recent change of name from the "women's studies program" to the more inclusive "gender studies program." This change "recognizes the ways in which the field of women's studies has outstripped its original designation and ... implies a greatly expanded reach for our program." [8] In other words, women's studies has expanded to include several other fields: specifically, "queer studies" and "critical race studies." This mission statement makes it clear that the new field "is properly building on the strong foundations established by over twenty years of women's studies scholarship."[9]

Northwestern, which offers eight courses on gender, has been more careful than other universities to use the word "gender" consistently – that is, to make sure that all references to it include both women and men. Nonetheless, many course descriptions make it clear that only women are of interest. Topics in Gender Studies: Gender and Health, for instance, does so immediately. The word "gender" in its title notwithstanding, it begins with the following questions:

How do the biological category "female" and the cultural category "woman" affect patterns of health and disease for both individuals and populations? How do different cultural constructions of gender, sex, and sexuality shape public policies concerning the inequitable distribution of health and disease within the United States, Africa, Japan, South America, and Europe? How do the intersections of gender, biology, sexuality, class, race, and racism produce health inequities. What is the contribution of anthropologists to improving women's health worldwide? To address these questions, this course explores case studies of breast cancer, sexual and reproductive health, mental health, violence, substance abuse, physician-patient interactions, infectious diseases, and access to health resources. Special health issues in the lesbian community in the USA are also discussed.[10]

These questions are not without merit. But many questions are unasked. Why is so little research being done to find out why women live so much longer than men in our society? What measures might be considered to reduce this gap in longevity? And why are men so much more reluctant than women to consult physicians? So much for the alleged inclusiveness of "gender."

The bias at Northwestern is not so much toward feminism itself, however, as to the larger context of political movements such as environmentalism, antiglobalization, postcolonialism, and so forth. Without actually saying so, every course description implies that women are both the primary victims of social or political injustice and the primary creators of social and political justice. Consider the course on Gender Studies for a Small Planet: "What does it mean to understand cross-cultural, transnational, and international processes through the lens of gender and sexuality? Conversely, why are contemporary gender, class, and ethnic/racial identities inextricably bound to these transnational processes[?] Organized around the theme of commodification, this course examines how production, marketing, and consumption of key products (textiles/clothing, tourism, service industries, and world music) link regions and peoples in relations of domination, mutual benefit, solidarity, and resistance."[11]

Despite its rhetorical questions, this description is characteristic not of the academic environment – that is, one in which the answers are not obvious from the get-go – but of a political movement. Hence the rhetoric of "domination," "solidarity," and "resistance." Here is part of the outline for Topics in Gender Studies: Gender and Representation: "We will further examine the issue of representation in relation to cultural hegemony, gender and class hierarchies and postcoloniality: how has 'the Other' (in terms of race, class, ethnicity, sexuality) been represented, what are the implications of representing 'the Other'? What happens when members of groups who have been represented as 'Other' represent themselves?"[12] Significantly, some questions remain unasked: What happens when they turn the tables? In this case, what happens when women represent men as the "Other"? What happens to men when popular culture represents them as the new and only legitimate "Other" (which is what we discussed in *Spreading Misandry*)? Nothing on the website indicates that these questions would ever be taken seriously as topics for scholarly research.

The Canadian situation is very similar. In the *Status of Women Supplement* for 2001, sent out with the *CAUT Bulletin*, Edith Zorychta defines women's studies in connection with a focus on "gender."[13] According to her, this field "provides a scholarly critique of the conventional ideas of what it means to be human and a woman, a critique that is of interest to all scholars and students, male and female."[14] Once again, the word "gender" should refer to both femininity and masculinity. The fact that it seldom does in these circles, that "gender studies" has become a euphemism for "women's studies," reveals a widespread belief that gender creates problems only for women or that only women have distinctive needs and problems. Zorychta claims that just about all students – male students, too, presumably – now take courses in women's studies (surely a claim that would require statistical evidence). And these courses should be of interest to both women and men, she claims, because they involve "the study of constructions of masculinity."[15] Unfortunately, she does not tell us how we can learn anything about men if the perspective applied is that of women – what could be called the "female gaze."[16] Thus, even though academics sometimes pay lip service to the goal of women and men exploring "gender" together, the fact remains that "gender studies" is a field that caters primarily to women. Which is why most departments that teach courses on gender are actually called "women's studies," not "gender studies."

In short, the experts in "gender studies" (let alone women's studies) see no need to study or teach anything about men except the ways in which they create problems for women or sexual minorities. Men appear primarily as evidence to support theories such as social constructionism (according to which all social roles are socially constructed and therefore can be deconstructed to facilitate social change). This should lead to the suspicion that something other than scholarship is involved.

What's Sauce for the Goose: Double Standards in a Government Report

On 30 May 2003 a highly revealing story broke in Canada, but it was not a distinctively Canadian story. Americans who consider themselves immune to the political and ideological forces involved in this story are deluding themselves. When it comes to feminist ideology, as we say, the United States and Canada are not separate societies. When it comes to feminist ideology, in fact, their cultural unity applies even to Quebec. What happens in one country could easily happen in the other – and often does, albeit in slightly different form or to a slightly different extent. Which is why American feminists not only influence Canadian legislation but sometimes intervene directly (by invitation) in the legal or legislative process. More about that later. Here is the story.

It began in 1999. Status of Women Canada, a federal agency, commissioned research on the dangers faced by feminists in their struggle on behalf of women in general and schoolgirls in particular. The title and (redundant) subtitle of the original call for proposals make its political orientation – ideological feminism under the guise of postmodernism – very clear: "Where Have All the Women Gone? Changing Shifts in Policy Discourses."[1] Among those who responded with a proposal were Pierrette Bouchard, Isabelle Boily, and Marie-Claude Proulx. "How specifically," they asked, "was it possible to develop in discourse and thinking, over a period of less than ten years, such unprecedented opposition to girls' achievement at school?"[2] Even at this early stage, the basic premise – widespread and increasing misogyny – had already been established on political grounds; research was required only to provide a suitably political explanation and back it up with evidence. What the question calls "unprecedented opposition to girls' achievement," after all, could have been much less tendentiously called an unprecedented concern for boys' achievement. Why assume from the get-go that concern for boys is synonymous with lack of it for girls or even active opposition to them?

At any rate, three authors – Pierrette Bouchard and her two research assistants, Isabelle Boily and Marie-Claude Proulx – were given a grant, from the pockets of taxpayers, to find out why women were once again under attack. Their report was called "School Success by Gender: A Catalyst for the Masculinist Discourse." Even though Bouchard is a professor of education at the University of Laval, therefore, her specifically academic credentials did not take her very far; she was being paid by a government agency with an overtly political (and covertly ideological) mission, not an academic institution or a neutral government agency.[3]

Interviewed for the *National Post*, Bouchard defended herself as follows: "I have a feminist perspective, but just because I am a feminist, does not mean that I am incapable of seeing that boys are having certain difficulties. Nor do I put all men in the same basket. Not all men are like those I identified in the report."[4] Unfortunately, the report does not support that statement.

For one thing, nowhere does the report actually acknowledge that schoolboys have any problems. Not once, not ever, not even in the most perfunctory or condescending way. Bouchard acknowledges every *claim* to that effect, sure. But on every occasion, without a single exception, she trivializes or even ridicules it, often resorting to the age-old strategy of manipulating men by shaming those who see themselves as helpless or victimized.[5] If the problem that a claim represents is real at all, in other words, it is not worth taking seriously; only the problems of schoolgirls are worth taking seriously. And yet evidence indicates that schoolboys do have problems that are worth taking seriously in the interest not only of the boys themselves but also of society as a whole. This is the conclusion drawn by Jon Bradley, at any rate, of McGill University's Department of Education. The proportion of male teachers in elementary and secondary schools (of the English sector in Quebec) is very low, he points out, and getting even lower. The dropout rate for boys, on the other hand, is higher than that for girls and getting even higher. "Boys do not suddenly decide to drop out in Grade 9; there is not some mysterious gene that kicks in and 'rebellion' and 'stupidity' strike. Rather, boys are gradually turned off school and the pursuit of learning through a long process that commences in pre-kindergarten and moves up throughout the whole school system. This model demands female learning styles, female-selected books and a classroom environment that might do wonders for girls but is academically killing the boys.[6] Bouchard's lack of even the most basic generosity toward boys, let alone compassion for them, is ironic in view of the fact that she calls repeatedly for "egalitarian" approaches to education and even for "equality of opportunity" (by which, to judge from the fact that her recommendations to the government – more programs for girls alone, more research on them alone, more money spent on them alone – amount to an exclusive focus on girls).

Although Bouchard does not claim that all men are misogynists, moreover, she does indeed claim, albeit implicitly, something very similar: that all men are misogynists *except* those who adopt feminism – that is, those who agree with her own brand of feminism. The only good man, for her, is a male feminist. In *Spreading Misandry* we classified male feminists as "honorary women," because the price that they pay for becoming feminists – ideological feminists – is to deny the value of anything distinctive in men, including themselves. They maintain their self-respect as individuals *in spite* of the fact that they are men, not because of it. Being unlike "those others," they expect to gain respect from women (and enmity from men, which confirms their original assumption).

One of the recommendations of this report is that those who express opinions dubbed "masculinist" – by the way, this word is hardly ever used by men (except, perhaps, for those who call themselves "male feminists") and is therefore not some perverse counterpart to "feminist" – should be prosecuted under Canada's legislation against expressions of hate directed toward "identifiable groups." In other words, Bouchard wants to silence those who disagree with her (which is precisely, of course, what once happened to women). She claims that this "masculinist discourse" is tantamount to the promotion of hatred toward women. Although she never actually defines "masculinist," she clearly refers to any position that challenges or even questions a feminist one. Opposing this or that aspect of feminism, she implies, is the same as opposing women. Opposing women is the same as hating women. And hating women is the same as hating Jews, say, or gay people. This turns all of her adversaries into Nazis.

Why all of them? It is true that Bouchard makes her recommendation in connection specifically with hostile websites on the Internet. You might assume, therefore, that she wants the government to prosecute only male rednecks, those who do indeed use websites to incite hatred against women (although she says nothing whatsoever about female rednecks – zillions of them – who use their own websites to incite hatred against men). But wait. Appended to the report is a hit list that names not only male (and some female) individuals, including academics, who have written books or articles that challenge ideological feminist positions but also organizations that promote the interests of boys or men: boys with problems at school or at home, divorced men, fathers (including those without custody), and therapeutic support groups of various kinds. (It does not, of course, include individual men or men's organizations that support feminism.)

This report presents us with the startling fact that we still live in a time of hostility between the sexes. And in war, according to conventional wisdom (which we reject), all is permitted. Or, according to the more sophisticated version, ends can justify means. Bouchard unwittingly illustrates the reason why some people, especially in the United States, have always opposed censorship – that is, legislation that bans obscenity and even legislation that bans literary or other expressions of hatred. They do not approve of obscenity or hatred, but they do realize what can happen when unpopular forms of expression are criminalized. Who decides, after all, where to draw the line between what may be expressed and what may not be expressed? The fact that a respectable academic, hired by a government agency, could recommend to any government in 2003 that only one political point of view be accepted as legitimate – that one ideology be installed, in effect, as the country's official philosophy – should be a wake-up call to anyone who believes that the phenomenon described in *Spreading Misandry* is, or even was, superficial.

Bouchard's report contains so many examples of the feminist double standard – attacking men for doing precisely what feminists have always done – that we can provide only a summary of the more obvious ones here.

"A more detailed look at the groups behind the media discourse reveals an extensive network using the Internet to become established and entrenched and express its ideas. We have found a discourse of hate, often violent and unchecked, directed at women and feminists. Far from being an isolated case, this second level of discourse, which could be called 'underground' discourse, focusses on the same issues as the public discourse, specifically fathers' rights, but without any of the restraint shown in the public discourse."[7] And feminists have not made similar use of the Internet – even showcasing the violent screed of Valerie Solanas and her Society for Cutting Up Men – for their own purposes?

"[T]he ... authors of these articles tended to lump several male issues together."[8] And feminists have *not* done so? It would make no sense for feminists to do otherwise, because one thing that binds all feminists together is the belief that all their problems, specifically as women, are the result of patriarchy (and, for some, of something innate in maleness itself).

"Masculinists are also attacking traditionally female employment sectors, including health care and education, claiming that there are not enough men in those sectors to serve as role models to understand male issues. Their solution is to obtain jobs for men by hiring them in these sectors."[9] And feminists do not make precisely the same claim: that women need "role models," or "mentors," and must therefore be hired preferentially in "male dominated" sectors?

"In this section," according to the report, "we discuss the arguments on which masculinists based their advocacy discourse and how they try to convince the public, through the media, that the women's movement has made men victims of a new social system dominated by feminist values." Elsewhere, the authors complain that "masculinist groups know how to derive maximum benefit from media coverage."[10] And feminists do not use "the media" in their own attempts at "advocacy discourse"? They do not know how to derive maximum benefit from media coverage – even when they present mistaken statistics to the press?

"[M]asculinists are choosing to use political language and jump at any opportunity to have their views published. Hey et al. ... report that there could be no movement in favour of boys before in Britain 'because earlier work had failed to construct a political language – and an activism – around equity beyond competing claims about oppression.'"[11] And feminists have not jumped at every chance to publish their views? They have not developed a "political" language in order to promote those views?

Elsewhere, we read about the "masculinist groups that are increasingly forming national and international networks and feeding journalists information related to recurring events, such as the release of marks on national tests (here or abroad) and Suicide Prevention Week, or current events, such as cases of spousal violence or spousal murders involving child custody and fathers' rights."[12] And feminists do not feed journalists stories that promote their causes – and even feed them phony statistics occasionally?

"But even worse than 'women' are feminists whom masculinists ruthlessly attack. In particular, they denounce the 'plot' that feminists, working in complicity with governments, judges, police officers and the media, have supposedly hatched against fathers and men accused of violence."[13] And feminists have not attacked men as the authors of a prehistoric plot to overthrow a paradisal society under the benign aegis of a Great Goddess and replace it with the oppression of patriarchy?[14] We will discuss this topic in a separate book, tentatively called "Beyond the Fall of Man." For the time being, consider the work of two well-known feminist academics: Marija Gimbutas and Gerda Lerner, along with several "documentaries" widely shown on television that were produced by the explicitly feminist wing of Canada's National Film Board.[15] All these productions are explicitly based on the conspiracy theory of history.

Here are more examples of a double standard. "[The president of the Groupe d'entraide aux pères et de soutien à l'enfant] ... speaking as though he represented all men, stated, 'We are the feminists of the 1990s. We are the ones who are calling for gender equality.'"[16] And the authors – Bouchard, Boily, and Proulx – do not claim to speak as though they represent all women? If not, how could they advise the government to pursue a policy intended to benefit all women?

"These comments [advocating single-sex schools] reveal a narrow, traditional view of gender relations in which girls are temptresses and boys subject to their sexual impulses."[17] And feminists have not used this strategy, arguing that boys are governed by their biological impulses (to be either destructive or "aggressive") and girls by their cultural conditioning (to be either submissive or "nurturing")? They certainly do, according to the study done by Frederick Mathews for Health Canada.

It is not uncommon to hear male students express resentment toward high school anti-violence curricula that presumes [sic] them to be abusers, harassers, rapists and sexual assaulters in waiting. Indeed, it is difficult to feel part of a collective social movement against violence when one's own experiences are dismissed, excluded or minimized. It is evident from even a casual review of this material that much of it contains biased stereotypes and unchallenged assumptions about "male anger," "male aggression" and "male sexuality." All too often, these writers take as a starting point a caricature of the worst imaginable elements of "masculinity" and assume it applies to all male persons ... If we want males to engage in true dialogue, then we have to be open to hearing *their* criticisms, *their* experiences, *their* pain."[18]

"[A]mong other things [concern over the fate of boys in schools] translates into the creation of 'affirmative action' programs."[19] And women have not advocated affirmative action, relentlessly, for their own purposes?

Elsewhere, the authors add that masculinists

argue in particular for gender-based intervention (thereby denying any diversity within each gender group), a return to single-sex classes or schools, and the creation of new programs, or the improvement of existing ones, in order to meet boys' needs as they see them. They want to increase the number of male teachers in order to promote male identification. These solutions also promote a return to traditional male values and the establishment of quotas for admission to certain programs. The same criticism levelled at the way the problem is identified can be made of the solutions proposed. Why treat boys and girls differently, or separate them, if one third of them at the most are having problems at school while three fifths [?] are successful?[20]

And feminists have not advocated precisely the same measures for girls (although feminists, at least those in Canada, usually prefer the euphemism of "targets" instead of "quotas")? Why treat the sexes differently? Because, according to the standard feminist reply, the two are "differently situated." Besides, since when is one-third a trivial measure? If one-third of all girls or women were having difficulty, or even one-quarter, all hell would break loose.

"Therapy groups are interested in personal growth. Much of the masculinist intervention scene involves their peer counselling activities, '12–step' of this or that, healing groups, and ideas from the mythopoetic movement of Robert Bly."[21] And feminists have not exploited, even invented, the mania for pop psychology? Oprah Winfrey is not the role model for millions of women? They did not glorify Princess Diana as a royal guru of self-help therapy?

"Other sites maintained by men's groups display direct threats to feminists and their allies, and contain vicious comments." Elsewhere, the authors complain about a website that names Martin Dufresne, "specifically, encourages people to harass him, and gives out his personal contact information."[22] And feminists do not name names? This very report includes a hit list of both individuals and groups. Although it does not urge readers to intimidate them directly, it does urge the government to take action against them.

Discussing men's groups that write about home life, the report also states that "[i]n this way men become the experts on analyzing the situation in the private domain." And feminists do not claim to be experts on both the private domain (traditionally associated with women) and the public one (traditionally associated with men)? Given the report's hostility to any claims of "traditional" society, we find it surprising, to say the least, that they do indeed want to preserve expertise in the domestic domain for women – even as they claim greater expertise than men in the public domain (because feminism is primarily about the deconstruction of patriarchy and thus relies on insights that originate with women). Not surprisingly, we read on the next page that when "they [masculinists] compare themselves to their female counterparts, they usually fail to provide relevant data about women's real situation."[23] And feminists are in the habit of providing relevant – and correct – information about men's real situation? In that case, why is the "information" about men in this report so dubious?

"Masculinists claim that there is far more research on breast cancer than on prostate cancer (and therefore conclude that this is another example of discrimination against men) because society allocates more resources to breast cancer. In making this claim they turn cancer into a gendered illness by reducing it to only two of its dimensions." And feminists have not turned some illnesses – heart disease, for one – into "gendered diseases"? The passage continues as follows: "The reasons given by masculinists for men's shorter life expectancy are the stress, demands and responsibilities associated with their role, factors that take their toll on men from their earliest years. In their view, the past will inevitably be repeated in the future. If we apply that hypothesis to the status of elderly women, it would appear that a great many of them have experienced extremely trying times during their lives." Actually, it would do nothing of the kind. Because the number of elderly women in relation to that of elderly men is so high, it would appear that these women have *not* experienced extremely trying times. The report recommends that "a network of experts in fields targeted by masculinists should be formed to react to the misinformation campaign, especially since the trigger events for this discourse are known."[24] Okay, but how about a network of experts in fields targeted by feminists? The trigger events – an obvious one being 6 December, a day set aside every year in Canada to commemorate the women killed by Marc Lépine – are certainly well known.

"The publication of gendered data must always be supported by analyses that provide the context, since without it the data only fuel the masculinist discourses."[25] Sure, but disaggregation works – or should work – both ways. If so, it would certainly cause problems for feminists, whose work is usually based on the premise that women are first and foremost a class, an oppressed class, not merely parts of other classes.

"This network [monitoring expressions of hate against women] could also be responsible for gaining a better understanding of how masculinist groups are influencing policy makers, in order to make them aware of the limitations and shortcomings of these discourses."[26] Yes, but the same network should be responsible for gaining a better understanding of how feminist groups – including those of Bouchard and her colleagues – are influencing policymakers.

Take That!
Comparative Victimology

One case study should illustrate the atmosphere in which the ideological "discourse" on domestic violence, discussed in chapter 2, took place. We refer to an issue of *Victimology* from the 1980s that was devoted specifically to that problem.[1] Almost every argument used by two debaters, who were reacting to an article by a third, is used to this day by ideological feminists. In this respect, nothing has changed over the past twenty years.

The original article was written by Peter Neidig, who was director of Behavioral Science Associates. He presented a view of domestic violence based on his clinical experience as a family counsellor and identified several assumptions that he considered not only unwarranted but also counterproductive. His explicit aim was to promote professional "dialogue" about domestic violence. Ellen Pence, of the Domestic Abuse Intervention Project in Duluth, and Jeffrey Edleson, coordinator of research and evaluation for the Domestic Abuse Project in Minneapolis, responded to his article. Both were extremely hostile to Neidig and resorted to personal attacks on his moral integrity. Clearly, dialogue was out of the question then (and probably still is). These people were not able to "hear" each other any more than Protestants and Catholics in Ireland were able to do so, Anglophones and Francophones in Quebec, or Israelis and Palestinians in the Middle East. For Pence and Edleson, Neidig was not merely mistaken. He was sinister. He was the enemy.[2]

Neidig described current research as "highly politicized in that those providing the services are activists, deeply committed to a particular analysis of the causes and means for redressing the social inequities presumed to lie at the root of spouse abuse."[3] Most research focused attention, he claimed, solely on one half of the troubled relationship: researchers blamed only the men involved and even studied only the men. "The typical research publications report the results of interview and/or assessment data on women. This has led to an understanding of the abusive relationship which is by definition biased and incomplete, and is at least subject to limitations which occur when one attempts, no matter how sincerely, to reconstruct from a one-sided account [what are] essentially transactional phenomena."[4] Moreover, the reports used were almost entirely anecdotal; there were very few empirical studies.

The main purpose of Neidig's paper was to discuss what he identified as four underlying assumptions of researchers. "One of our own biases," he wrote, "is that individuals working in this field should attempt to articulate as clearly as possible, both to themselves and to their clients, the principles which guide their interventions."[5] This consideration was not merely academic; it had very practical implications for evaluating treatment programs, since we need to know which are value-based and which empirically based. The latter are not completely objective, he admitted, but they are at least relatively objective.

His differentiation exposed a raw nerve. In this field more than most, researchers often have very heavy emotional investments at stake. "It seems to us inescapable that therapists working in the field of spouse abuse will adopt positions influenced largely by moral and political considerations."[6] These certainly influence the ways in which problems are conceptualized, strategies developed, solutions defined, and so on. As Perry London pointed out elsewhere,[7] the extent to which therapists are confronted with moral problems depends on the significance of the problems with which they choose to involve themselves. He found it hard to imagine more significant and more value laden ones than those involved in the treatment of domestic violence.[8]

At any rate, Neidig identified four assumptions that should be challenged. The first, which was adopted by the National Coalition against Domestic Violence, is that the highest priority should be given to the establishment of shelters for women and children, even though these had already multiplied in the previous few years. "There can be little doubt," Neidig wrote, "that shelters do and should continue to play a vitally important role in a comprehensive response to spouse abuse."[9] They play not one role, however, but several. They have a symbolic function, for instance, their mere existence making it clear to the entire community that something is radically wrong. "Although there has been some question about whether the continuation of sexual inequality contributes to spouse abuse ... or whether the recent increase in power realized by women through the accomplishments of the feminist movement increases the likelihood of wife abuse ... we have taken the position that violence is most likely to persist when the wife possesses significantly less power and fewer resources than her husband."[10] But the most obvious function of the shelters is providing emergency refuge. Most women stay only temporarily and then return to their husbands. Nevertheless, Neidig claimed, a major aim of those running the shelters is to promote separation of husband and wife. "It would seem that this is the primary function as it is conceptualized by those in the shelter movement. In fact, anything less than a total and permanent termination of the marriage seems to be viewed as a failure."[11]

The second common assumption challenged by Neidig is that marriage and family therapies do more harm than good. Some experts believe that marriage counselling, or any other therapy based on participation by both husband and wife, is

ineffective at best and dangerous at worst. Although he maintained that therapies of
this kind are potentially useful and should not be abandoned out of hand, he admitted that they can sometimes be dangerous. As Lenore Walker had pointed out on
Nightline, for example, professional therapists often have such a high commitment
to preserving the family unit that they will try to avoid a breakup even when that is
the best solution. As D. Adams and I. Penn had pointed out, moreover, husbands
might seek revenge if their wives divulge the intimate details of their married lives.[12]

Other experts accuse male therapists of being ideologically and politically dangerous, of harbouring sexist notions of female inferiority or innate female
masochism and promoting patriarchy merely by supporting institutions such as
marriage and the family. Walker and others have consequently claimed that only
women should treat women, and Zak Mettger has consequently argued that only
women should treat violent men.[13]

Still other experts, wrote Neidig, attack marriage or family counselling for giving the impression that women as well as men are involved in generating violence
or that abuse is an interactional problem. This impression, they believe, would
allow abusive men to imagine that the guilt is not entirely their own. Behind this
attack is the third common assumption identified by Neidig: that spousal abuse is
always the man's fault, that the source of all conflict resides within him alone. He
is the only one, therefore, who should change. Ideologues believe that the primary
cause of any man's violent behaviour is the internalization of sexist notions prevalent in society – the belief that women are inferior to men, say, or that hitting
women is acceptable. Many psychologists, on the other hand, believe that the primary cause is a man's inability to deal with his own psychopathological problems:
impulsiveness, low self-esteem, poor communication, poor stress management, and
so on. Neidig identified two reasons why treatment programs for violent men
almost always make this assumption.

First, they need to reject the idea of blaming the victim by suggesting that abused
wives somehow "ask for it."[14] As long as this approach is taken, domestic violence
can be seen as a rare phenomenon that results from a neurotic relationship and be
given over to psychiatrists who would uncover the "real" meaning.

Second, most of the research on domestic violence has been based solely on interviews with victimized women. "At the risk of belaboring the obvious," wrote Neidig, "spouse abuse is by definition an interpersonal transaction. It is violence that
occurs in the context of an ongoing relationship (marriage). The behaviour of each
individual within a marriage is dependent upon the behaviour of the other and each
behavior can be thought of as both a cause and an effect depending on how the
interactional sequence is 'punctuated.'" Because sympathy should be with the victim, it might be difficult to acknowledge that every abusive event is experienced and
interpreted in two ways. "It would seem reasonable to assume," wrote Neidig,
"that women, in their effort to organize, understand and communicate their experiences in an abusive situation would tend to 'punctuate' the sequence of events in
such a way as to introduce a bias into the narration. Again, regardless of how sin-

cere the interviewer and the subject are, the portrayal would at best be incomplete." Neidig noted that there were striking linguistic similarities in reports from abused women and that after a while the interviewers could finish sentences for them. "It of course has enormous therapeutic significance whether these characterizations are a valid description of the violence sequence itself or are rather a valid description of one way of experiencing or punctuating the violence sequence."[15]

Finally, the fourth common assumption – and the most important – identified by Neidig is the obvious but almost always ignored fact that "from a political stand-point, it makes much more sense to define the issue rather narrowly and to present it in terms of 'victims and villains.' To talk about domestic violence which includes child abuse (which is frequently engaged in by mothers), or to belabor the fact that women act violently toward men about as frequently as men act violently toward women ... is to dull the sharp focus required for an effective political movement. However, what might be a good basis for a political strategy is not necessarily a good basis for therapeutic intervention." The assumption that the causes of domes-tic violence reside only in the husband's mind has had several negative effects on treatment programs. If the actors are assigned "fixed roles variously labelled as the 'victim and the batterer' or the 'victim and the perpetrator,'" the former might be tempted to seek revenge and the latter might be tempted to identify themselves with the label assigned to them.[16] Neidig's own bias

> when conceptualizing spouse abuse is to define it as a relationship issue with both parties participating (although not necessarily participating equally) in the violence sequence. We tend to reject labels "abuser" and "victim," believing that neither partner has an exclusive right to either term. In fact, it seems perfectly reasonable although incomplete, that both parties could punctuate the sequence in such a way as to feel victimized. We define abusiveness as learned behavior which is frequently a desperate but ineffective (in the long run) way of effecting behavior change. In our analysis ... violence does not occur instantaneously or unpredictably, but rather it is an interpersonal behavior pattern which couples can learn to control once they learn to discriminate certain "cues" and acquire relevant skills.[17]

Nevertheless, it is often assumed that changes in a man's attitude lead to changes in his behaviour. Neidig claimed that this was an assumption of Emerge, a men's counselling group in Boston, and of virtually every other therapy program designed for abusive men. Following the work of Russell Dobash and Rebecca Dobash, most therapy programs assumed that domestic violence would not be eliminated either until the patriarchal structure of the family and the conditions that kept women subordinate were destroyed or, following the work of Andrew McCormack, until the belief by individual men in male supremacy was corrected.[18] But Neidig found more evidence to support the reverse argument: that changes in a man's behaviour lead to changes in his attitude. He referred to the work not only of Albert Bandura,

E.G. Blanchard, and R. Ritter but also of Leon Festinger. "Our own experience suggests that a skill building approach which attempts primarily to change behaviours
results in a marked reduction of violent episodes and significant change as reflected
in pre- and post-program administrations of measures of locus of control and marital adjustment."[19]

Neidig was more interested in the cause of change than in the chronology of
change, which led to his interest in the ideology of these men's groups.

> The basic premise of their approach is that men are socialized to adopt the atti-
> tude that abuse is an acceptable and normal male behaviour engaged in to main-
> tain dominance over females. It is this attitude which must be changed in order
> to eliminate violence. There are three conditions (attitudes) "that lead directly to
> woman abuse": a man must believe that he has the right to beat a woman,
> believe that it is a legitimate way of solving problems, and believe that he needs
> to maintain his dominant position vis-à-vis a woman ... If it is true that abusive
> men do in fact subscribe to these attitudes, then one would be inclined to agree
> with the men's collectives that the process of eliminating violence is going to be
> slow going and that the prognosis would have to be considered guarded at
> best.[20]

But in fact, Neidig observed, research had failed to support these assumptions.

> Measures of dogmatism and rigidity (The D Scale), attitudes toward self (The
> Coopersmith Self-Esteem Inventory), attitudes towards others (The Generalized
> Expectations of Others Questionnaire) have all failed to discriminate [between
> men and women] or at best have resulted only in statistically significant differ-
> ences with little or no practical, predictive application. Only those measures
> which are more closely related to behavior as opposed to attitudinal variables
> seem to be very promising (measures of stress, assertiveness, and marital adjust-
> ment). The one measure on which both males and females engaged in domestic
> violence consistently differ from non-violent controls is that of the locus of con-
> trol. Thus, if the presumed differences in attitudes exist, we have failed thus far
> to detect them, and in our review of the literature we can find no reports of any-
> one else having empirically verified these attitude differences. Additionally, in
> screening something over one hundred couples who have engaged in domestic
> violence for our spouse abuse rehabilitation program ... we have yet to encounter
> a single individual who believes that "he has a right to beat a woman." That is
> not to say that we have not heard a vast array of excuses, denials, rationaliza-
> tions and other defensive maneuvers. However, at least as we interpret it, the
> extent of the defensiveness supports the view that abusive males generally ascribe
> [sic] to the prevailing norm which defines violence against family members as
> unacceptable. These men continue to engage in abusive behavior not because
> they believe it is right but because they lack the skills to do otherwise and are

subsequently able to avoid responsibility, maintain a sense of being victimized, and neutralize the inhibiting effect of disapproval by self and others through the extensive use of various defense mechanisms.[21]

In other words, precisely because they know that beating women is *not* morally acceptable, they must find excuses to justify their behaviour.

In their response to Neidig, both Pence and Edleson challenged his claim that "shelters serve as a resource for effecting a permanent break from the spouse ... anything less than a total and permanent termination of the marriage seems to be viewed as a failure."[22] This approach, according to Neidig, left many questions that participants in the shelter movement could not answer.

> The unpredictability and seemingly self-defeating behaviour of many battered wives "has produced both cynicism and frustration among the professionals dealing with them" ... An indirect measure of how distressing it may be when women choose to employ the shelter as a temporary refuge rather than as a means to establish their independence from the marriage is suggested by the number of theoretical explanations offered for this [phenomenon]. Learned help-lessness ... exchange theory ... attribution theory ... locus of control ... and the "complex pushes and pulls of numerous forces" ... have all been cited in the literature.[23]

For Neidig, the explanation was much simpler: the goal of those seeking help (temporary refuge) is often inconsistent with those of the people who run shelters (permanent independence).

Although Neidig immediately went on to say that this inconsistency "does not diminish in any way the value of shelters," he had probably oversimplified the matter. In the first place, as Pence observed, the gulf between those who find refuge in the shelters and those who run them can easily be exaggerated. The latter are very often drawn from the ranks of the former and are not merely professionals acting on the basis of abstract ideological positions. Furthermore,

> it is important to acknowledge that we are in the business of rescuing. Neidig says that we set up shelters to rescue women from their marriages. We say that we rescue women from violence. We live in a society which decorates policemen, firemen and concerned citizens for rescuing people from burning buildings or raging floods. But when women rescue other women from life-threatening vio-lent situations at the hands of their husbands or lovers, suddenly rescuing is equated to home wrecking. To separate is also not a negative term to those in the battered women's movement. The function of battering is to dominate and con-trol. We offer women a space, separate and safe. We offer a space separate from violence, from threats, from intimidation, a separate place of self-definition ... Not all shelters measure success in the same ways, but none of those people

contributing to this response knew of a single shelter which ensured success in terms of a permanent break in the marriage. Shelters are in the business of helping women end violence against them, not ending marriages.[24]

Edleson objected also to the way that Neidig had polarized those who work in the field of domestic violence.[25] "He seems to classify the thousands of practitioners and hundreds of researchers in this area of work into two groups: family therapists and 'others.'" But no position, wrote Edleson, was common to everyone in either category. Neidig had succumbed to reductionism. Multiplicity had been reduced to duality. There were those, such as Dobash and Dobash, who took an ideological and activist approach. There were also those, such as Neidig, who saw violence as one element among others. And there were those, such as Edleson himself, who took a "social learning" approach and tried to resocialize violent men. Moreover, there were those who combined all three approaches. "The important point here is that Neidig presents this widely divergent group of researchers and practitioners as one group united in its opposition to family therapy. It is a misrepresentation of the field to do so. This area of clinical practice and research is, contrary to what Neidig states, full of greatly varied and hotly contested issues."[26]

But Edleson overstated his case in the opposite direction. Are there really *no* general assumptions to link those working in the field? Is every women's shelter and every men's therapy group unique in its approach? If so, how could we even refer to a women's shelter "movement" or a men's therapy "movement"? How could we explain the fact that many of the men's groups explicitly acknowledge their ideological debt to pioneering efforts such as Emerge?[27] Having recognized that Neidig ignored the diversity in this field, we should still be able to recognize that some generalizations are necessary for us to say anything at all. The fact that Neidig had tried to identify trends, moreover, does not imply that he had been consciously or unconsciously trying to distort reality.

Edleson made an effort to downplay the influence of the ideologues who really do see marriage and the family as inherently oppressive for women.

A few individual shelter staff members may seek to permanently separate every battered woman from her male partner. It is a gross misinterpretation to attribute such goals to all of the thousands of shelter workers in the United States. The major goals of most shelters in this country are to provide safe refuges to the victims of family violence and to help insure that such violence ends or that, at a minimum, the victims need no longer to be subjected to such violence. In many cases, this may mean helping a woman fight for a legal separation and divorce. In other cases – probably the majority – it means helping the woman bring community pressure to bear on the man in order to persuade him to end his violent behaviour. In any event, the goal of most interventions in families where violence occurs is to bring about the permanent cessation of violence.[28]

His point is well taken. Even if shelter workers believed that divorce is preferable to reconciliation, after all, they would not necessarily foist their opinions on women who come to them seeking temporary refuge. And even if Neidig had been correct in arguing that most shelter workers are predisposed on ideological grounds to breaking up marriages that could be saved, Pence and Edleson would be correct in replying that he was predisposed on professional grounds to saving marriages that should be ended. Although he had noted that shelters perform several other extremely useful functions, he had also given the impression that their value is severely limited by the ideological convictions of those who run them.

If Pence and Edleson were correct in observing an underlying hostility toward the shelters, then Neidig was justly rebuked. But they, no less than he, contributed to the polarization. Both Pence and Edelson consistently chose to interpret his words in the worst possible light. Occasionally, they even ignored evidence to the contrary. Pence referred, for example, to Neidig's claim that "prior to 1970, there was almost no literature to be found on the subject [of domestic violence] 'except for psychiatrically oriented discussions on sadomasochistic marital relationships.'"[29] On the contrary, she argued, "a review of history books would certainly yield a more consistent reference to this historical practice used by men against their wives. In fact, literally hundreds of references to the function of 'wife beating' as a link between the institution of marriage and property laws in Western civilization can be easily documented."[30] Neidig had referred only, of course, to the *social science* literature. Consider the line immediately preceding the one quoted by Pence: "The development of the 'field' of spouse abuse has occurred rapidly."[31] By accusing Neidig of ignoring history itself, Pence tried to establish an image of him as someone who deliberately distorted truth. Moreover, the facts contained in history books do not prove her claim that wife beating has been "part of a systematic use of violence against women to maintain male privilege and status."[32] That was her interpretation of history.

Pence accused Neidig of hypocrisy, too, arguing that he had denied the need for political analysis but was himself "political" (which is to say, politically opportunistic).

> Mr. Neidig states that the current literature is politicized in that those providing services to battered women and batterers are "activists." Since battering is seen by many activists not as a transactional phenomenon as Mr. Neidig maintains, but as an "act of power and dominance," it is reasonable to assume that much of the literature would have some suggestion of "political analysis." It is political for Mr. Neidig to choose phrases such as "violent couples," "abusive relationships," "spouse abuse" and "domestic conflict" rather than to name the person using the violence as the assailant or batterer.[33]

Yes, but it was surely just as politically opportunistic to do what she did in her own essay. By using labels such as "batterer," for example, she reduced the husband from a human being, albeit a seriously flawed and dangerous one, to a demon like an enemy in wartime. The Americans did not fight against the Japanese or the Vietnamese, after all; they fought against "Japs" and "Gooks." Dehumanizing an enemy might be practical, but is it morally acceptable? Pence added that "it is political to ignore that the gender of the person injured is almost always female." It is surely just as politically expedient, though, to ignore studies of domestic violence in which the injured party is male.[34] Pence would have known about them, even in 1984, had she not been blinded by her own ideology.

Pence argued that Neidig was cynical for suggesting that men were stereotyped for reasons of political expediency.[35] But what if the problem goes much deeper than that? Far from being too cynical, Neidig might have been too naive. People who insist on discussing domestic violence in dualistic terms, after all, are not necessarily opportunists. They might sincerely believe that domestic violence is, apart from anything else, a symbolic statement about the relation between men and women in general and, indeed, about history itself. In that case, women are the paradigmatic innocent victims and men the paradigmatic evil oppressors. To question this belief, as Neidig did, is not merely to challenge a political strategy but to challenge the *identity* of those feminists who define themselves in opposition to men (or of male feminists, for that matter, who define themselves in opposition to "those other" men.) If women are implicated in any way with evil, then they are not really so very different from men.

According to Pence, Neidig had argued that "many of those working on the issue of battering have been duped by reading too many anecdotal accounts of battering by women who tend to 'punctuate the event' in an understandably biased way. The age-old woman hating declaration rears its ugly head: women are not physically and sexually oppressed in this country; women lie."[36] But Neidig had said nothing of the kind. He had never suggested, either directly or indirectly, that they lie, at least not more often than men do. What he had claimed was merely that women (like all human beings at all times and in all places) interpret reality. Pence herself was clearly adept at interpreting things, reading into Neidig's words what she, as a feminist, believed he must have had in mind. With her, in fact, it was the age-old polarization of ideology that had reared its ugly head.

Those who believe that they can provide effective therapies for violent men, assuming that the latter are seriously disturbed and not normal, want every piece of information they can find. But those who believe, as Pence did, that domestic violence can be explained in ideological and moralistic terms have less interest in therapy (except insofar as it is necessary for a woman's safety). The model is crime, then, not biology. Pence argued that violent husbands should be locked up like any other criminals. Arrest with no treatment of any kind, she believed, had proven to be at least a short-term deterrent. Likewise, Edleson wrote that "violence by a man against his wife is a crime and the perpetrator of this violence should be treated as such. To speak of 'transactions' is to ignore that a crime has been committed by one person against another. Such a position seems to perpetuate long held beliefs and social norms ... that somehow violence by a man towards his spouse is exempt from current laws concerning interpersonal violence."[37] Like Neidig, however, Edleson worked as a therapist with men convicted of domestic violence. He surely believed that this criminal behaviour was linked in some way with psychopathology. Otherwise, the treatment he offered could have been reduced to lessons in morality or sociological analysis.

Besides, Neidig had never suggested, either directly or indirectly, that wife beaters should be considered innocent and protected from the law. The topic under discussion by Neidig had been neither morality nor legality, after all, but therapy. Domestic violence does involve crime, and incarceration might be necessary. But what about a long-term solution? To prevent violence, it would be necessary to understand what causes it. Because Pence believed in a gynocentric ideology, however, the possibility that she could ever understand men was extremely remote.

But – and this is very important – it was not enough for Pence to observe that men afflict women. She was convinced that they *want* to do so, that doing so seems to men an end in itself. According to her, "the battered women's movement has always asserted that assailants choose to batter – that they are very much in control of the target, the timing, the extent of injuries and the psychological terrorism accompanying the assault."[38] But if men are so much in control, why are so many who engage in these activities either drunk or stoned at the time?[39] Pence did not ask this question, but from her perspective only one answer would have been possible: that they deliberately *choose* to become drunk or stoned in order to have a convenient excuse for their behaviour. But if they are so convinced by the cultural norms of our society that attacking women is perfectly acceptable behaviour, why would they *need* this excuse in the first place? That question presupposes complexity and ambiguity in the attitudes toward women of both society in general and men in particular. Are men really so preoccupied with women that they would drink themselves into oblivion or become addicted to drugs merely to provide themselves with a cover for experiencing the secret joy of assaulting women – even though, according to the very people who take this position, men are openly encouraged to do so? Pence believed that these men are evil, not sick. And because their behaviour is not idiosyncratic but actively promoted by patriarchal institutions, she believed that all men are evil unless they repent and convert to feminism. She believed that they deserve punishment, consequently, not therapy.

Concerning the treatment groups designed for violent men, as exemplified by Emerge, Neidig wrote that "the concept of attitude change has been the hallmark." "The basic premise of their approach," according to Neidig, "is that men are socialized to adopt the attitude that abuse is an acceptable and normal male behaviour engaged in to maintain dominance over females. It is this attitude which must be changed in order to eliminate violence."[40] Although it is obvious that boys and men are socialized in many ways to be violent – standard examples are what they see at the movies or on television, what kind of toys are sold to them, and what they know of their potential role as soldiers – it is by no means obvious that they are socialized to be violent *in order* to persecute women. That is a gynocentric and ideological assumption that Neidig correctly questioned.

As for Emerge, Edleson dismissed its influence by arguing that "this is another example of Neidig's gross over-generalizations about a diverse group of practitioners and researchers." It is true that there are many programs, that these are organized by many agencies, and that they are based on many approaches. "To hypothesize that a unitary set of assumptions are held by an entire field made up of such diverse elements is, to say the least, a superficial treatment of the subject."[41] Yes, but to ignore widely held assumptions on the grounds that they are not actually universal must lead to an equally superficial treatment of any topic.

Instead of dealing with the problem identified by Neidig, Edleson went on to criticize his second assumption: that a psychological (as distinct from a philosophical) "attitude change must precede behaviour change."[42] On this matter, Neidig had probably erred. Edleson pointed out that "contrary to what Neidig has stated ... the first goal of most programs for men who batter is to take steps to help the men change their violent behaviour."[43] This would indeed be more consistent with the primary aim of closely allied women's shelters: providing safety.

Both Pence and Edleson attacked Neidig for suggesting that a man's use of violence against a woman is "interpersonal" or "transactional," that both the male and female "shared responsibility."[44] The real question for both Pence and Edleson, as it still is for ideological feminists, was, Who is to blame? For Pence and Edleson, Neidig seemed to suggest not only that husbands are somehow innocent when hitting their wives but also that wives are somehow guilty for being hit. Neidig did write about "responsibility," but this word can be used in connection with both moral agency and causality. No one can legitimately be held morally responsible for the act of another. Moral responsibility is governed by at least three factors: freedom of choice, motivation, and knowledge of the consequences. A husband *is* morally responsible for hitting his wife, to be sure, if he is free to refrain from doing so, if he consciously intends to injure her, and if he knows what could happen to her (and himself) if he does. He is *not* morally responsible to the extent that he is pathologically deranged,[45] morally incompetent, or mentally incompetent. A wife, on the other hand, could be held morally responsible for the violence of her husband only if she somehow forced him to strike her, a most unlikely scenario. But the situation is more complicated than that. If a husband does something evil for which he alone is morally responsible, why must we assume that his wife is a paragon of virtue? Even though a wife cannot be legitimately held morally responsible for the behaviour of her husband, she surely can be legitimately held morally responsible for her *own* behaviour. If her husband hits her, he alone is guilty for that. But if she has humiliated him or shamed him in some other way, then she is guilty for *that*. Unless we assume that wives are incapable of malice, greed, manipulation, hypocrisy, selfishness, or any other human failing – and this is contrary to the observation of everyday life by virtually everyone – it makes no sense to rule out this possibility. That would create a false dichotomy. Thus, it is at least possible that the acrimonious debate in *Victimology* was caused by ideological thinking on the part of Pence (projecting a generalized dichotomy between good and evil onto women and men respectively) and not by sexist perversity on the part of Neidig.

It is worth pausing here, briefly, to note a double standard that was, and is, common in our society. When men hurt women, it is sometimes said, no account whatever need be taken of mitigating circumstances; no matter how provocative the woman's behaviour, she is an innocent victim. Apparently, though, the reverse does not hold. This was made clear in one segment of the ABC program *20/20*, aired in March 1993.[46] When Jean Harris went to prison for shooting her lover, Herman Tarnower, she received widespread support as "a woman wronged." Tarnower, you see, was an unpleasant fellow. Moreover, he had thrown her aside for another woman. According to Harris's supporters, her behaviour was morally, though not legally, acceptable. Shortly after Harris's release from prison, Barbara Walters reminded viewers that "hundreds of [women had] rallied to her defense, repeatedly petitioning the governor of New York for her release." In fact, Walters noted, Harris had told her parole board that "Tarnower could have prevented this if he had just been a little different that night."[47] In other words, the (male) victim *deserved* to be killed.

At any rate, Pence went on to dismiss Neidig's finding that the attitude of abusive men toward women might not be a crucial factor in domestic violence. "It is not surprising," she wrote, "that Neidig's tests on batterers would show no appreciable difference in negative attitudes towards women by batterers compared to the general population. We live in a culture which is hostile and negative toward women. Few would agree that batterers can be singled out as having any kind of monopoly on woman hating."[48] This, too, was an ideological assumption on her part. To be sure, this culture is hostile and negative to women in many ways. But in other ways, it has placed women on the proverbial pedestal. And in still other ways, as we discussed in *Spreading Misandry*, it is hostile and negative to men as well. Pence believed, on the other hand, that women have a monopoly on suffering (and, by implication, on innocence).

Feminists have clearly learned a great deal about the needs and problems of women. But it could be argued also that they have concealed the fact that men have their own needs and problems. This has led at one extreme to a gynocentric ideology, in which the universe revolves around women. On that basis, it is easy to assume that men, too, must be gynocentric. If men hurt women, it must be because they hate women. And if they hate women, it must be because their universe revolves around revulsion for women. It never occurred to Pence that men might have needs and problems having little or nothing to do with women. Given her ideological perspective, it is not surprising that Pence discounted any evidence that contradicted her own beliefs. That is because ideology, like religion, is self-validating.

Pence concluded by pointing out that

above all else, Mr. Neidig's article is a precious piece of male privilege. Through casual observation, he presumes to define the assumptions and politics of essentially a women's movement which is constantly growing and changing. Under the guise of professional neutrality and scientific rigor, he pretends fiction to be truth. The poverty of his arguments are [sic] a measure of his lack of responsibility to his readers and battered women; calling it an invitation to dialogue in an international journal committed to improving the problems facing victims of crime is evidence of his privilege."[49]

The same arguments, however, could have been used against Pence herself. The moral authority of her movement, too, confers privilege. She believed that disagreement is tantamount to misogyny, after all, which amounted to an implicit form of intimidation. Neidig had presumed to define the assumptions and politics of the women's shelter movement (but more specifically those of the men's collectives associated with it), to be sure, but Pence presumed to define the assumptions and politics of all men throughout history! There is no evidence whatsoever to indicate that Neidig had been irresponsible toward either his professional readers or battered women. He had suggested ways of treating more effectively the men who batter them. Ideological compromise would be a small price to pay for any improvement in the situation, especially for a movement that, according to Pence, is constantly growing and changing. Given her implicit belief that men are evil and women good, it is difficult to feel sympathy for her complaint about this or that oversimplified belief held by Neidig. In fact, it is her belief that looks like speculative fiction, not Neidig's belief that domestic violence is a complex problem requiring an attempt to move beyond self-righteousness.

In that spirit, Neidig had called for dialogue rather than monologue. "As is often the case when treatment efforts are applied to a recently discovered condition, good intentions and the desire to be of help have outdistanced our thorough understanding of the problem and how it may most effectively be ameliorated. This situation is inevitable given our current state of ignorance and does not suggest that intervention efforts should cease. Rather, an attitude of modesty and the avoidance of doctrinaire positions should prevail. At this point, we have more to fear from an unwarranted sense of unanimity and closure than we do from open dialogue and disagreement."[50] Edleson responded as follows:

Neidig has done a disservice to those practitioners and researchers he has stereotyped. He has distorted the positions of many and generalized the positions of few to an entire group. He has attributed certain beliefs to all of the many perspectives represented when there is often great disagreement among the groups. Far from creating open dialogue, he has attacked those who legitimately question the placement of preserving relationships before physical safety and the cessation of violence. Neidig's allusion to family therapists as the white knights fighting the misled is only self-aggrandizing fantasy. His article reflects the opposite of the "modesty and the avoidance of doctrinaire positions" that he calls for in his conclusion. Let us hope that the rich and varied debate that has marked this field from the start continues on a more scholarly level than that represented in the work by Neidig.[51]

The fact is, however, that Edleson was in no position to accuse Neidig of attacking those who disagree with him. His response to Neidig's article hardly welcomed scholarly inquiry. On the contrary, it was one of contemptuous dismissal. The aim of both Pence and Edleson was simply to attack Neidig, not to take his challenge seriously. Instead of trying to answer the questions he raised, they attacked his scholarly and moral integrity. As a result, the level of discussion never moved beyond defensiveness and self-righteousness. If dialogue between men and women is ever to take place, let alone reconciliation, we will have to discard the model of two competing monologues.

By definition, dialogue is a conversation. In the context of everyday life and in literature, it is usually conversation between two people. In other contexts however, it is conversation between two communities that are divided by conflict but interested in reconciliation as well or, at the very least, negotiation. The aim is not to erase differences, to convert the other, but to build mutual respect in spite of differences. Unlike debate, dialogue assumes the continuing presence of two voices, not one. It assumes at least the possibility of reconciliation, not the necessity of submission by one side to the other. Although, as Pence and Edleson showed, Neidig had not always "heard" what was being done by others in the field, they themselves did not always "hear" what he was saying. And Pence was either unable or unwilling even to listen. Patricia Pearson sums up the larger gender debate as follows:

By the late 1980s, activists and scholars within the battered women's movement had grown markedly more militant about the inherent distinctions between men and women ... If women were inherently blameless, it followed with mounting conviction that men were inherently blameworthy, to the point where any investigation of their motives was denounced as providing them with "an excuse." Childhood abuse wasn't relevant, because it was an excuse. So were individual pathologies, marital dynamics, and personal circumstances until the whole field of inquiry was blocked. In Canada, the final report of a multimillion-dollar government panel on violence against women, which canvassed experts from across the nation for several years, concluded in 1993: "If [a man] abuses his wife, it is because he has the privilege and the means to do so." Ten million dollars to cough up a cliché. Those who advise policy makers in the United States had their views summed up in Ms magazine's 1994 special issue on wife beating: "Researchers are now beginning to examine the batterers," wrote Ann Jones.

"It's the same old crap. Nobody wants to admit that men do this because they like to. What began as a nuanced discussion of one of the most volatile arenas of human relating had been reduced to a bigoted creed. Men are evil. Women are good. Domestic violence is wife beating, and any man who finds himself at the receiving end of a woman's fist is a liar or a freak."[52]

Notes

1 At the age of 20, Canadian dropout rates were much higher for men than for women. This gender difference remained at the age of 22: 15% for men and only 8% for women ("Youth in Transition Survey: Education and Labour Market Pathways of Young Adults," [dated] 2002, *Statistics Canada: The Daily*, [visited] 16 June 2004, <http://www.statcanca/Daily/English/today/d04061b.htm>: 3. The American dropout rate in 2001 for those 16 to 24 years old was 12.2% for men and 9.3% for women ("Dropout Rates," [dated] 2003, *National Center for Education Statistics*, [visited] 16 June 2004, <http://nces.ed.gov/fastfacts/display/asp?id=15>: 1.

2 Consider these American sex ratios based on the census of 2000: 3 males for every female between the ages of 10 and 14 commit suicide; 5 males for every female between 15 and 19; and 7 males for every female between 20 and 24 ("Resources for Researchers and Program Evaluators," [undated], *National Strategy for Suicide Prevention*, [visited] 16 March 2004, <http://www.mentalhealth.samhsa.gov/suicideprevention/colltoaction.asp>: 3). In Canada, the suicide rate for young men has been increasing more rapidly than the rate for other age groups and more than the rate for young women (Antoon A. Leenaars, and others, *Suicide in Canada* [Toronto: University of Toronto Press, 1998], 38). In the United States, suicide "was the 8th leading cause of death for males and 19th leading cause of death for females ... More men than women die by suicide. The gender ratio is 4:1; 73% of all suicide deaths are white males" ("Suicide Facts," [updated] 23 December 2003, *National Institute of Mental Health*, [visited] 12 March 2004, <http://www.nimh.nih.gov/research/suifact.cfm>: 1). "From their pattern of ebb and flow, Canada's suicide rates can be seen to shadow those of its neighbour to the south, but since the 1970s Canadian rates have surpassed those of the United States ...

[although] their rates are not far apart."(Leenaars and others, 37). For more details on suicide, see chapter 6, note 52.

3 Canadian Bar Association, Task Force on Gender Equality in the Legal Profession, *Touchstones for Change: Equality, Diversity, and Accountability: The Report on Gender Equality in the Legal Profession* (Ottawa: Canadian Bar Association, 1993) 270–1.

CHAPTER ONE

1 Ellen Bass and Laura Davis, *The Courage to Heal: A Guide for Women Survivors of Child Sexual Abuse* (New York: Harper and Row, 1988) 21.

2 Carol Tavris, "Pursued by Fashionable Furies," review of *Hystories*, by Elaine Showalter, *New York Times Book Review*, 4 May 1997: 28.

3 Mary deYoung, "The Devil Goes to Day Care: McMartin and the Making of a Moral Panic," *Journal of American Culture* 20.1 (spring 1997): 19.

4 DeYoung 21.

5 N. Brozan; quoted in deYoung 23.

6 Carol Milstone, "Sybil Minds," *Saturday Night*, September 1997: 35–42.

7 Elizabeth Gleick, "All in the Head," review of *Memory Wars*, by Frederick Crews, and *Hystories: Hysterical Epidemics and Modern Culture*, by Elaine Showalter, *Time* (Canadian edition), 7 July 1997: 44–6.

8 Milstone 38.

9 Milstone 40.

10 Judith Levine, *Harmful to Minors: The Perils of Protecting Children from Sex* (Minneapolis: University of Minnesota Press, 2002).

11 Kevin Cullen, "More than 80 Percent of Victims Since 1950 Were Male, Report Says," [dated] 28 February 2004, *Boston Globe*, [visited] 9 March 2004, <http://www.boston.com/blobe/spotlight/abuse/stories5/022804_victims.htm>.

12 According to a study completed in 2004, 4,392 clergymen (almost all of them priests) were accused of abusing 10,667 people. Even though pedophilia is often said to have been rampant among the clergy, no more than 4% of Catholic priests, most of them multiple offenders, were involved, according to this study. Commissioned by the National Review Board of American Bishops, it was released on 27 February 2004. Agostino Bono, "John Jay Study Reveals Extent of Abuse Problem," [undated], *American Catholic.org*, [visited] 9 March 2004, <http://www.americancatholic.org/default.asp>.

13 Elaine Showalter, *Hystories: Hysterical Epidemics and Modern Culture* (New York: Columbia University Press, 1997) 12; Stephen Rae, "John Mack," *New York Times Magazine* 20 March 1994: 30–3. Parallels between stories of sexual molestation and alien abductions have been noted by Thomas M. Disch in *The Dreams Our Stuff Is Made Of: How Science Fiction Conquered the World* (New York: Free Press 1998).

14 Rae 33–4.

15 Carl Sagan; quoted in Rae 33.

16 "Are We Alone?" *48 Hours*, CBS, WCAX-TV, Burlington, VT, 20 April 1994.

17 At first Freud took seriously the idea that some of his patients had actually been the victims of incest. Later he changed his mind and argued that most cases of incest occur only in the imagination and not in real life. This is one reason for current feminist hostility to Freud.

18 Tavris 28. The author does acknowledge that some symptoms can look like hysteria but nonetheless have organic causes.

19 DeYoung 23.

20 Richard M. Gardner, *Sex Abuse Hysteria: The Salem Witch Trials Revisited* (Cresskill, NJ: Creative Therapeutics, 1991).

21 Levine 20–44.

22 See Bass and Davis.

23 Showalter; quoted in Gleick 43.

24 DeYoung 23.

25 Gleick 45.

26 Frederick Crews is not so moderate. In *The Memory Wars* (New York: New York Review of Books, 1995) this lapsed Freudian and his colleagues attack the credulity fostered by psychiatry. Had it not been for Freudian "demonology," he argues, its "hyperactive young successor" would never have occurred. In the last analysis, millions of people were perfectly prepared to believe the most bizarre and shocking stories that had no basis in fact. Where, he asks, is the evidence backing up psychoanalytical theory? "But if Freud was a charlatan, psychoanalysis pure babble, and repression nonexistent," writes Gleick, "then Crews must dismiss the more interesting questions: What do our society's obsessions with child abuse, or satanic rituals, or aliens, *really* mean?" (Gleick 46).

27 DeYoung 22. In Canada, the situation is even worse. Canadian officials have still not acknowledged the enormity of professional complicity in a witch hunt. The Saskatchewan government said on 8 January 2004 that "it would not apologize to 12 people who were falsely accused of sadistically abusing foster children and were found to have been victims of malicious prosecution" (Gerry Klein, "Saskatchewan Not Sorry for Malicious Prosecution," *National Post*, 9 January 2004: A-1).

28 Gardner 127–40.

29 There were already a few critics by the early 1990s. See Eleanor Goldstein, *Confabulations: Creating False Memories, Destroying Families* (Boca Raton, FL: Sirs, 1992); Richard Ofshe and Ethan Watters, *Making Monsters: False Memories, Psychotherapy, and Sexual Hysteria* (New York: Simon and Schuster, 1994). By the late 1990s, there were many works on this topic. Here are a few examples: Debbi Nathan and Michael Snedecker, *Satan's Silence: Ritual Abuse and the Making of a Modern American Witch-Hunt* (New York: Basic

Books, 1995); Arlys N. McDonald, *Repressed Memories: Can You Trust Them?* (Ada, MI: Revell, 1995); Claudette Wassil-Grimm, *Diagnosis for Disaster: The Devastating Truth about False Memory Syndrome and Its Impact on American Families* (New York: Overlook Press, 1995); Andrew Meacham, *Selling Serenity: Life among the Recovery Stars* (Boca Raton, FL: Sirs, 1996); Robert Baker, *Childhood Sexual Abuse and False Memory Syndrome* (Amherst, NY: Prometheus Books, 1996); Ronald L. Stephens, *Hypnotism and False Memories: How False Memories Are Created* (Freeport, PA: Ziotech International, 1996); Moira Johnston, *Spectral Evidence, The Ramon Case: Incest, Memory and Truth on Trial in Napa Valley* (Boston: Houghton Mifflin, 1997); C. Brooks Brenneis, *Transferring the Present to the Past* (Independence, MO: International Universities Press, 1997); Harrison G. Pope, *Psychology Astray: Fallacies in Studies of "Repressed Memory" and Childhood Trauma* (Boca Raton, FL: Sirs, 1997); Dean Tong, *Ashes to Ashes ... Families to Dust: False Accusations of Childhood Abuse, A Roadmap for Survivors* (Tampa, FL: Family Rights, 1997).

30 Steven Reiner, "Devilish Deeds," *Prime-Time Live*, ABC, WVNY-TV, Burlington, VT, 7 January 1993.

31 Elizabeth Loftus and Katherine Ketcham, *The Myth of Repressed Memories: False Memories and the Accusations of Sexual Abuse* (New York: St Martin's Press, 1996).

32 Jill Neimark, "The Diva of Disclosure," *Psychology Today* 29.1 (January-February 1996) 78; quoting Loftus.

33 Michael D. Yapko, *Suggestions of Abuse: True and False Memories of Childhood Sexual Trauma* (New York: Simon and Schuster, 1994).

34 Mark Pendergrast, *Victims of Memory: Incest Accusations and Shattered Lives* (Hinesburg, VT: Upper Access, 1995). A review by Ann Diamond noted the atmosphere in which Pendergrast's book had appeared: "This is explosive material, all the more so because of the number of women who now testify to having experienced flashbacks and memories of abuse in early childhood. Who, after all, would doubt what, for so many, is now incontrovertible fact? Incest is everywhere. Faced with so many survivors' stories, most of us feel like passive spectators at a massive tragedy that is engulfing what we used to call 'Western civilization.'" (Ann Diamond, "Exhaustive Look at Victims of Memory: Father Accused of Abuse Looks into Mystery," *Montreal Gazette*, 1 April 1995: H-3).

35 Lawrence Wright, *Remembering Satan: A Case of Recovered Memory and the Shattering of an American Family* (New York: Knopf, 1994).

36 John Goddard, "How Satanic-Abuse Charges Wrecked Family," review of *Remembering Satan*, by Lawrence Wright, *Montreal Gazette*, 25 June 1994: H-2.

37 This argument has been made also by Judith Levine. Despite cross-cultural variation, adult notions of sexuality include the recognition that children must

be physically and emotionally mature enough to engage in sexual behaviour, the outcome of which might be pregnancy. See Suzanne G. Frayser, *Varieties of Sexual Experience: An Anthropological Perspective on Human Sexuality* (New Haven, CT: HRAF Press, 1985).

38 As Levine puts it, "dire assessments of a morally anarchic world are not new. But they tend to crop up in times of social transformation, when the economy trembles or when social institutions crumble and many people feel they're losing control of their jobs, their futures, or their children's lives. At times like these, the child-molesting monster can be counted on to creep from the rubble" (Levine 29).

39 Historians can agree on one thing: that modernity not only ushered in unprecedented levels of both change and stress but did so with unprecedented and increasing rapidity. For our purposes here, we will say that modernity began with the Industrial Revolution in the nineteenth century, though slightly earlier in Britain, and continued into the twentieth. (During that period of approximately 150 years, it spawned new revolutions such as the ones associated with electricity and electronics). Stress intensified occasionally due to specific crises. Of interest here are not the ones brought on by external threats, such as wars, but the ones brought on by internal threats. Stress intensified in the 1930s, for instance, when economic and social structures seemed to be on the verge of collapse due to the Great Depression.

As Levine points out, stress at this deep level often took the form of anxiety about children. But not necessarily – or not directly – about the most obvious perils, the ones that parents themselves inflicted on their own children. At the beginning of this period, for instance, the poor sent their young children to work in mills or mines. Parents worried about what would happen to them without protection from the sexual depravity of adult men who worked there. During the Depression, even middle-class parents worried about the safety of their children. What would happen to them with millions of unemployed men, possibly predators, loitering on the streets? More recently, even rich parents had to worry about the safety of their children. What would happen to them at the hands of workers, especially male workers, in daycare centres? (We discuss the historical background in appendix 2.)

40 Jeffrey Victor; quoted in deYoung 22.

41 According to Gleick, the hysteria spread quickly to Britain and Europe ("All in the Head," *Time*, 7 July 1997: 44–6).

42 John Demos, *Entertaining Satan: Witchcraft and the Culture of Early New England.* Rev. ed. (Oxford: Oxford University Press, 2004).

43 This taboo is found in all cultures, although anthropologists still do not agree on why that should be the case.

44 This molestation is widely condemned, of course, but concepts of childhood and permissible ages for sexual activity vary widely from one society to another.

45 The locus classicus for this theory is Susan Brownmiller's *Against Our Will: Men, Women and Rape* (New York: Simon and Schuster, 1975). More recently, this approach was taken by Bernard Lefkowitz in *Our Guys: The Glen Ridge Rape and the Secret Life of the Perfect Suburb* (Berkeley: University of California Press, 1997).

46 Tavris 28.

47 DeYoung 24.

48 Gleick 46.

49 Neimark 49.

CHAPTER TWO

1 Barbara Ehrenreich, "Feminism Confronts Bobbittry," *Time*, 24 January 1994: 52 (her emphasis).

2 Warren Farrell, *Women Can't Hear What Men Don't Say: Destroying Myths, Creating Love* (New York: Jeremy Tarcher/Putnam, 1999) 126.

3 Alan Dershowitz, Lenore Walker, Lisa Kemler, Jeff Greenfield, Charles Sykes, and Lynn Tipper, interviewed by Ted Koppel on *Nightline*, ABC, WVNY-TV, Burlington, VT, 4 February 1994;

4 Alan Dershowtiz, *Nightline*.

5 Lenore E.A. Walker, *The Battered Woman* (New York: Harper and Row, 1979) xi.

6 Lenore E.A. Walker, *Nightline*.

7 Lisa Kemler, *Nightline*.

8 Jeff Greenfield, *Nightline*.

9 Greenfield, *Nightline*.

10 Charles Sykes, *Nightline*.

11 Lynn Tepper, *Nightline*.

12 Tepper, *Nightline*.

13 This solution would mean, at the very least, taking steps to make dialing 911 an effective measure: ensuring that police intervene quickly to stop domestic violence (but with a responsibility to take seriously both the woman's and the man's account of any conflict), making shelters available to women and men who need them, and so forth. But no one pointed out that the ultimate solution would be to prevent domestic violence in the first place. That would require far more than legal or social reform. It would require genuine dialogue between men and women (which we will discuss in *Transcending Misandry*). In this case, it would have required something other than the ranting of Lorena's supporters. Even more problematic than the verdict itself, in other words, was public sentiment both before and after it was announced.

On the problem of police intervention in cases of domestic violence, see Grant Brown, "Gender as a Factor in the Response of the Law-Enforcement System to Violence against Partners," 20–2, unpublished manuscript; for more information on this Canadian study, contact the author at grant.brown@shaw.ca. Brown refers to earlier studies as well. "In one major partner-abuse survey in the U.S. in 1985, when women called police about abusive husbands, the husbands were arrested or threatened with arrest over 50% of the time; when men called police about abusive wives, the wives were never arrested or threatened with arrest" (Brown 22; referring to Richard J. Gelles and Murray A. Straus, *Intimate Violence* [New York: Simon and Schuster, 1988] 262).

14 A few similar cases did occur, however. On the night of 20 September 1992, for example, Aurelia Macias took a pair of scissors and cut off the testicles of her husband, Jaime Macias. The latter, she contended, had tried earlier that evening to force her to have sex with him. Like Lorena, moreover, she was acquitted; the jury found her not guilty of mayhem and assault with a deadly weapon and could not even agree on the lesser charge of battery. According to Claudia Marshall, who spoke for the jury, Macias had been "verbally and emotionally abused throughout the marriage" and was probably in mortal fear on the night in question. The fact that Jaime, like John Bobbitt, had been fast asleep at the time made no difference to these jurors ("Woman Acquitted in Castration Case," *Montreal Gazette*, 19 March 1994: C-11). A closer parallel to the case of Lorena Bobbitt could hardly be imagined. And Macias took the law into her own hands *before* learning about Lorena. Moreover, as the prosecution pointed out, "the defense had decided to employ the battered-wife defense *after* seeing its effectiveness in the case of Lorena L. Bobbitt." ("Woman Acquitted of Charges in Castration," *New York Times*, 20 March 1994: 27).

15 Susan Estrich, interviewed on *Now*, NBC, WPTZ, Plattsburgh, NY, 22 December 1993.

16 Jamie Lee Evans, interviewed on *Now*.

17 Clay Cogalis thought "the prior abuse made it easier to believe that someone could snap after four years of being, you know, terribly abused, and then ... savagely raped."

18 Evans.

19 Ehrenreich 52.

20 Ehrenreich 52.

21 Wolf had already done a great deal of whining about the beauty myth allegedly foisted on women by men (Naomi Wolf, *The Beauty Myth: How Images of Beauty Are Used against Women* [New York: Morrow, 1991]).

22 Ehrenreich 52.

23 Ehrenreich 52.

24 "The Men's Issues Page" and "Men and Domestic Violence Index" [undated], *World Wide Web Virtual Library*, [visited] 22 September 2002, <http://www.vix.com/men/index.html.>

25 See Molly Dragiewicz's bibliography called "Gender Asymmetry in Domestic Violence," [dated] 5 September 2002, *George Mason University*, [visited] 22

September 2002, <http://mason.gmu.edu/~mdragiew/gender%20asymmetry
%20DV.html>.

CHAPTER THREE

1 Anita Hill *Speaking Truth to Power* (New York: Doubleday, 1997) 345.

2 Clarence Thomas, "Eloquent Lies, [dated] March 2001, *Yale Alumni Magazine*, [visited] 8 March 2004,
<http://www.yalealumnimagazine.com/issues/01_03/ quotes.html>: 7; Thomas
uttered these famous lines at the Senate confirmation hearing in October
1991.

3 Jean Bethke Elshtain, "Trial by Fury," *New Republic* 209 (6 September
1993): 35.

4 We cannot find the origin of that expression, but we did find on the Internet
that it is in common use among American blacks, women, gays, and Arabs.
See Julianne Malveaux, *Sex, Lies, and Stereotypes: Perspectives of a Mad
Economist* (Los Angeles: Pines Ones, 1994), for instance, or Kim Ficera, *Sex,
Lies, and Stereotypes* (New York: Kensington Books, 2003). In any case,
things really have changed in popular culture. By the late 1990s, *Ally McBeal*
had begun to foster a much more tolerant attitude toward workplace flirtations, albeit in the context of situation comedy. Almost all the characters have
had affairs with each other, and this is not presented as something sinister.
Moreover, workplace romances are often "explored" on NYPD *Blue*. By 2002,
detectives Connie McDowell and Andy Sipowicz were moving toward some
sort of "relationship" going beyond work. In this case, a woman takes the initiative. She is not presented, however, as a sexual predator. The same is true
of two lawyer shows that began with the new century: *Philly* and *The Associates*. On *Philly*, Kathleen Maguire and Judge Jack Ripley fall in love with
each other. Although their relationship poses potential problems in court, no
attempt is made to paint Ripley as a sexual predator and Kathleen as a victim
of sexual harassment. On *The Associates*, a Canadian show, everyone flirts
with everyone else no matter what ranks are involved. On all these shows,
and many more, it is taken for granted that men and women who work
together, no matter what their positions in the corporate or bureaucratic hierarchy, are often attracted to each other – and that there is nothing wrong with
this in normal circumstances.

5 Linda Bloodworth-Thomason, "The Strange Case of Clarence and Anita,"
Designing Women, CBS, WCAX-TV, Burlington, VT, 4 November 1991.

6 Elshtain 32.

7 Elshtain 36.

8 Hill claims in *Speaking Truth to Power* that she left the University of Oklahoma because of harassment, partly motivated by racism, including threats on
her life. Politicians outside the university tried to sabotage an endowed profes-

sorship that was to be established in her name, for example, and even to close the law school as a way of getting rid of her. According to Hill, the chair was intended to encourage public debate. But that argument could work both ways. Giving an endowed chair to someone with such a high political profile would inevitably pose a problem for any university committed to scholarship unencumbered by political or ideological affiliations. Was this chair reserved for Hill and her successors, who support one point of view? Or would critics be welcome as well? By this time, Hill was travelling around the world and earning as much as $30,000 for public appearances.

9 Hill has gained some enemies, yes, but this happens to every significant figure in academic, legal, and political circles. "No one can claim that Anita Hill is an unsung heroine," writes Katie Roiphe. "It makes sense that teenagers get caught up in the Anita Hill fury; they are particularly susceptible to feeling uncomfortable about sexuality, and sexual harassment offers an ideology that explains 'uncomfortable' in political terms. The idea of sexual harassment displaces adolescent uneasiness onto the environment, onto professors, onto older men" (*The Morning After: Sex, Fear, and Feminism* [Boston: Little Brown, 1993] 92).

10 Joe Klein; quoted on *Edge*, PBS, WETK, Burlington, VT, 6 November 1991.

11 Nancy Gibbs, "Office Crimes," *Time*, 21 October 1991: 30. Considering the confusion, why be surprised that *Playboy* came up with a cartoon about the much more serious crime of rape. A bunch of prostitutes listen to one of their number, who has just received a telephone call: "That guy who said he was a Peruvian diplomat used a phony credit card? My God, girls, we've been raped" (Charles Rodriguez, cartoon, *Playboy*, April 1995: 146).

12 There was much discussion about this in connection with Michael Crichton's novel and the movie version of it. In *Disclosure*, as we will show, the male protagonist is sexually harassed by his female boss. No one in the movie suggests that he quit his job, so why suggest that Hill should have left her job?

13 No constitution can guarantee that, because happiness is a state of mind and not a legally definable opportunity or a physically quantifiable commodity.

14 It is true that women have developed some distinctive characteristics but not necessarily true that these are "better" than those of men. Moreover, they are usually characteristics that have been carefully fostered by the very society feminists condemn as patriarchal. Women whose self-esteem is undermined when their distinctive contributions are ignored or trivialized by men should expect men to feel precisely the same way when women do that to them. At stake for men is not merely their power (to which their claim is no stronger than that of women), by the way, but their *identity* (for which their need is no weaker than that of women). It seems unlikely that any improvement in relations between men and women will be possible until that problem – and masculine identity is a problem and has been for centuries – is addressed. And men might have as much difficulty as women in doing so (though for quite different reasons).

15 Elshtain 32.
16 Elshtain 32–3.
17 Elshtain 33–4.
18 Elshtain 34 (our emphasis).
19 John Cloud, "Sex and the Law," *Time*, 23 March 1998: 49.
20 Jane Mayer and Jill Abramson, *Strange Justice* (Boston: Houghton Mifflin, 1994).
21 Hill 345, 346.
22 Hill 346, 352.
23 Hill 352, 347.
24 Hill 348, 349, 350.
25 Hill 349–50.
26 Hill 353.
27 Elshtain 34.
28 Mako Nonaka, "Letters," *Time*, 25 May 1998: 11.
29 Wendy Kaminer, "Below the Beltway," review of *Scorpion Tongues*, by Gail Collins, *No Island of Sanity*, by Vincent Bugliosi, and *Spin Cycle*, by Howard Kurtz, in the *New York Times Book Review*, 22 March 1998: 14.
30 June Prentice, "Letters," *Time*, 25 May 1998: 11.
31 Michael Crichton, *Disclosure* (New York: Knopf, 1994).
32 Eve McBride, "Sex in the Workplace Might Be Something from the Past," *Montreal Gazette*, 2 June 1994: A-2.
33 Holly Doan, during a discussion of *Disclosure* and *Oleanna* with reviewer Geoff Pevere (who agreed with her), *Canada AM*, CTV, CFCF-TV, Montreal, 21 December 1994.
34 Ian Katz, "Male Student Seeks Cash after Lecture by Lesbian," *Montreal Gazette*, 9 March 1995: B-10.
35 Katz B-10.
36 To some extent, the discussion of Prevette's and Dearinge's behaviour was based on reason. There were those who argued, for example, that these kissing incidents were trivial. Their point was not that sexual harassment is trivial, to be sure, but that the uproar over these incidents trivialized it. The real problem, they argued, was much more serious. They were referring to little boys who show little girls pictures in *Playboy*, for example, and dare the girls to show how they measure up. "From younger and younger ages," writes Dorothy Nixon, "yes, even in elementary school, insecure boys who are very often being outperformed by girls at school, are learning that sex is a weapon – a weapon handed to them on a velvet cushion by the culture. The pendulum has not swung too far on this issue; it's never too early to educate children about the meaning of respect and self-respect" ("Sexual Harassment: Playing Field Still Not Level," *Montreal Gazette*, 13 October 1996: A-8).
37 Donna Laframboise, "Rules Trivialize Sexual Harassment and Hurt Girls," *Montreal Gazette*, 7 October 1996: B-3. The title of this article might not

have been chosen by Laframboise herself. She actively opposes the kind of double standard it reflects. After all, the *boys* in this case got hurt, being singled out for national attention as proto-criminals, not the girls.

38 Another show of this kind is *Ally McBeal*, which is about the sex lives of male and female lawyers in Boston. Interestingly, it is much more popular among women, than men.

39 People often assume that heterosexuality can be taken for granted, that most men and most women will always get together in one way or another. In fact, this is an oversimplification. Nature itself brings men and women together, sure, but only for brief liaisons. So a major cultural project of all human societies has always been to keep them together on a more enduring basis. That is necessary for several reasons. Some division of labour, whether fair from our perspective or unfair, has provided for the benefit of both children and society as a whole.

40 John Leo, "Harassment's Murky Edges," U.S. *News and World Report*, 21 October 1991: 26.

CHAPTER FOUR

1 Erin Graham; quoted in Brian Bergman and others, "Sisterhood of Fear and Fury: Intimations That 'Marc Was Not Alone,'" *Maclean's*, 18 December 1989: 18.

2 Helen Morrison; quoted in Bergman 18–19.

3 Among the more notorious were the shootings at Columbine High School in Littleton, Colorado (20 April 1999), where fifteen were killed; Springfield, Oregon (21 May 1998), where two were killed; Fayetteville, Tennessee (19 May 1998), where one was killed; Jonesboro, Arkansas (24 March 1998), where five were killed; Pomona, California (28 April 1998), where two were killed; Pearl Mississippi (1 October 1997), where nine were killed; and Moses Lake, Washington (2 February 1996), where two were killed. At other schools, students opened fire but did not succeed in killing anyone: West Paducah, Kentucky; Conyers, Georgia; and Richmond, Virginia. Something similar occurred at W.R. Myers Public High School in Taber, Alberta.

4 Barry Came and others, "Montreal Massacre," *Maclean's*, 18 December 1989:, 14.

5 Greg Weston and Jack Aubry, "The Making of a Mass-Killer," *Montreal Gazette*, 11 February 1990: A-4, A-5.

6 Greg Weston and Jack Aubry, "The Making of a Massacre," *Montreal Gazette*, 10 February 1990: B-4.

7 Weston and Aubry, "Mass-Killer": A-5.

8 Jean Bélanger; quoted in Weston and Aubry, "Massacre": B-4.

9 Weston and Aubry, "Massacre": B-4.

10 Weston and Aubry, "Massacre": B-1.

11 Andrew McIntosh, "Couple's Evening to Celebrate Turns into Nightmare," *Montreal Gazette*, 7 December 1989, A-3.

12 Weston and Aubry, "Mass-Killer": A-4.

13 Morrison; quoted in Bergman 18–19.

14 Eriksen; quoted in Bergman 18.

15 Graham; quoted in Bergman 18.

16 Jennifer Bankier, "Vigil Saddens and Reminds Us Inequities Persist," CAUT *Bulletin*, November 1995: 7.

17 The urge to blame "ordinary" members of alien groups resurfaced more recently in the wake of Daniel Goldhagen's book *Hitler's Willing Executioners: Ordinary Germans and the Holocaust* (New York: Knopf, 1996). According to Goldhagen, mass murder in Germany was produced not by obviously insane or obviously evil people but by "ordinary Germans" (although he never defines "ordinary" in a way that accounts for factors such as class, education, region, and so on). The direct implication is that we may condemn *all* Germans (or at least those of that time) as murderers.

18 Bankier 7.

19 Larry Finkelman; quoted in Graham Good, "White Males Don't Share Lépine's Guilt," CAUT *Bulletin*, 2 March 1996: 2.

20 Edward Renner, Christine Alksnis, and Laura Park, "Sexual Injustice," *Montreal Gazette*, 23 June 1997: B-3.

21 According to a study by the National Coalition of Anti-Violence Programs, gay men and women in four out of six American cities are more often victims of domestic violence than they are of anti-gay violence, although they are much less likely than straight people to report it (Vicki Haddock, "Gay Domestic Violence," *Montreal Gazette*, 23 October 1996: F-10).

22 F.L. Morton and Rainer Knopff, *The Charter Revolution and the Court Party* (Peterborough, ON: Broadview Press, 2000) 184.

23 Graham Good, "Letters," CAUT *Bulletin*, 2 March 1996: 2.

24 Bergman 18.

25 Rosemary Gartner; quoted in Bergman 18.

26 Bergman 19.

27 Brian Gable, [untitled cartoon] *Globe and Mail*, 9 December 1989: D-6.

28 Morrison; quoted in Bergman 19.

29 Bergman 18.

30 See Heidi Rathjen and Charles Montpetit, *December 6: From the Montreal Massacre to Gun Control, The Inside Story* (Toronto: McLelland and Stewart, 1999). Nathalie Provost was one of the female students. Having survived three shots, she said that "there are guys who are feeling very bad about what happened. They keep thinking that they were guilty of something, and it's not true. There is only one criminal in all of this, and he's already dead. Everybody else did everything they could." This attitude was unusual, to say the least. "A girl defending the *guys*? Many people had trouble understanding

that one: in the media and on the street, there were plenty of ignorant people who blamed the male students for not having protected their classmates. With comfortable hindsight, anyone could rewrite the scene and have the guys overpower the attacker. But the truth is, it was perfectly normal to have felt helpless in this situation" (Rathjen and Montpetit 21 [their emphasis]). Blaming or not blaming individual male students was one thing, though, and blaming or not blaming the collectivity of male citizens was something else.

31 It was a moment of masculine heroism, at least among the first-class passengers, who paid honourably in death for their privileges in life. Ironically, this movie ignored the quiet heroism of a real woman on board, Mrs Isidore Strauss, who refused to be separated from her husband of many years.

32 This is true not only in the United States, where all eighteen-year-old boys must register for the draft, but also in countries such as Canada, which are heavily influenced by American popular culture.

33 Aside from Rathjen and Montpetit, cited above, see Gabrielle Mercier-Leblond and Robert De Coster, *Les Interventions psychosociales: La Tragédie du 6 décembre 1989 a l'École polytechnique de Montréal* (Quebec: Groupe de travail De Coster, 1991); *The Montreal Massacre*, ed. Marie Chalouh and Louise Malette (Charlottetown: Gynergy Books, 1991); Wendy Hui Kyong Chun, "Unbearable Witness: Toward a Politics of Listening, *Differences*, 11.1 (spring 1999): 112–49; Julie Brickman, "Female Lives, Feminist Deaths: The Relationship of the Montreal Massacre to Dissociation, Incest, and Violence against Women," *Canadian Psychology* 33.2 (April 1992): 128–43; Daniel Sansfacon and others, "Rapports de sexe et violence contre les femmes: Essai de réconstruction sociale du sens de la tragédie de la polytechnique," *Revue Sexologique* 2.2 (autumn 1994): 107–28; Illah Patricia Wilson, "Metanarrative and Media: Retrospective on the Montreal Massacre," master's thesis, McMaster University, 1992; Pauline Fahmy, *Les évènements de Polytechnique: Analyses et propositions d'actions* (Ottawa: Institut canadien de recherches sur les femmes, 1994); Maureen Bradley, *Reframing the Montreal Massacre: A Media Interrogation* [videorecording] (Vancouver: Mediawise, 1995).

34 Pascoe; quoted in Bergman 18.

35 Gartner; quoted in Bergman 19.

36 Except, of course, when economic support from fathers is required by mothers or when political support is required from male voters and public officials.

37 Civil religion is known also as "public religion." Though never identified closely or directly with any traditional religious institution, it is based on the forms of traditional religion. In this part of the world, that usually means Judaism or Christianity. Like traditional religion, civil religion consists of formalized behaviour associated with special days, sites, rituals, parades, books, and so on, that give symbolic expression to communal worldviews. Even communities associated with traditional religions often have civil religions that

transcend denominational boundaries. The civil religion of diaspora Jews focuses not on Torah, which is considered irrelevant by secular Jews, but on the Nazi nightmare and the Israeli dream.

38 The correct title is Minister of Justice and Attorney General of Canada, who works for the Department of Justice (also known as Justice Canada).

39 This ministry is the wishful thinking of a utopian. There is no such ministry. Not yet, anyway. The closest equivalent so far is British Columbia's Ministry of Community, Aboriginal and Women's Services.

40 Christie Blatchford, "Half Mast, Double Standard: Homage to Montreal Victims Outweighs That Paid to Fallen Soldiers of Three Wars," *National Post*, 7 December 2001: A-1.

41 "Remember Them Well," editorial in *Montreal Gazette*, 11 November 2001: A-16 (our emphasis).

42 Consider a book by someone who can hardly be called a militant feminist: Tanya Melich, *The Republican War against Women: An Insider's Report from Behind the Lines* (New York: Bantam, 1996).

43 Canada, House of Commons, Standing Committee on Health and Welfare, Social Affairs, Seniors, and the Status of Women, *The War against Women: A Report of the Standing Committee on Health and Welfare, Social Affairs, Seniors, and the Status of Women* (Hull, QC: Supply and Services Canada, 1991).

44 Until recently, we would have assumed that their assailants were almost always other men. In chapter 9, however, we discuss recent studies that indicate a quite different state of affairs.

45 Not everyone who approved of the report did so because of a gynocentric perspective, but that did not necessarily prevent them from endorsing it.

46 This is not the first use of military rhetoric. The Feminist International Network of Resistance to Reproductive and Genetic Engineering, for example, used this rhetoric explicitly in its manifesto: "For us women, for nature, and for the exploited peoples of the world, this is a declaration of war" (from the "Resolution from the FINRRAGE Conference, 3–8 July 1985, Vällinge, Sweden; quoted in *Made to Order: The Myth of Reproductive and Genetic Progress* [New York: Pergamon Press, 1987] 211).

47 Andrea Dworkin, "Terror, Torture, and Resistance," [dated] 1991, *Canadian Mental Health Association*, [visited] 7 September 2002 <www.nostatusquo. com/ACLU/dworkin/TerrorTortureandResistance.html>:7 (keynote speech delivered at the Canadian Mental Health Association's "Women and Mental Health Conference – Women in a Violent Society," held in Banff, Alberta, May 1991); cited in "Kill Wife Beaters Who Go Free, Feminist-Rights Activist Urges," *Montreal Gazette*, 13 June 1991: A-7; first published in *Canadian Woman Studies/Les Cahiers de la femme*, 12.1 (fall 1991): 37–42.

48 "For Women Only! The Lioness Method of Rape Prevention," [dated] August

2002, *National Firearms Association*, [visited] 19 September 2002,
<www.nfa.ca>.

49 Vigilantism continues to exist in virtually every nation, of course, but usually
by default rather than by design. No state, no matter how inadequate by alien
standards, can afford to tolerate the idea of citizens taking the law into their
own hands.

50 "Battered Woman Acquitted of Killing," *Montreal Gazette*, 25 June 1991:
A-8.

51 Many people believe that revenge is an acceptable basis for legal or even
moral discourse. Everyone feels the desire for revenge now and then. It is perfectly comprehensible in situations of this kind. But that does not make it
acceptable. In moral terms, after all, revenge and justice are *not* synonymous.
Even in strictly legal terms, it is the need to keep dangerous people off the
streets (possibly to rehabilitate them) and the need to deter others from crime,
not the desire for personal or collective revenge, that society acknowledges.
Locking up those who threaten society is considered their just reward.

The assumption that justice and revenge really are synonymous is becoming
increasingly prevalent at every level of society. In one article, a professor of
law and philosophy argued that the time had come to question the traditional
primacy given to love and reconciliation, to rethink our traditional avoidance
of revenge and hatred (Jeffrie G. Murphy, "Getting Even: The Role of the Victim," *Social Philosophy and Policy* 7.2 [spring 1990]: 209-25). This way of
thinking has long been prevalent among ideologues, who rely on the postmodern belief that nothing can have any intrinsic value and who believe that
ends such as the elimination of crime can justify even an unedifying means,
such as revenge by victims. Do we really want to live in a society that institutionalizes revenge even as a principle of law? Do Canadians, in particular,
really want to retain capital punishment after all? (Ironically, capital punishment was abolished at least partly because, at that time, it was considered
ineffective as a deterrent.) Once ideological thinking is endorsed by society,
especially by the state that represents it, all other ways of thinking are threatened, including those on which the collective notion of justice is based.

52 Any attempt to redefine the mandate of this government study would have
resulted in fierce opposition from those who believe that women have no
responsibility whatsoever for the polarization between men and women (let
alone for the rate of violence against women). Yes, it is true that victims cannot legitimately be held morally responsible for the actions of their victimizers. But one factor complicates this discussion. Just as not all victims are
women, not all women are victims. Apart from the innocent bystanders in this
conflict are those actively involved in fostering hostility. They take control of
their own destiny – and are thus not passive victims – by deliberately promoting the kind of polarization between men and women that perpetuates

conflict. They are not innocent victims. They know what they are doing. They know that they are advocating misandry. In doing so, they are either almost incredibly naive (not realizing that hatred is a very powerful force and cannot be contained easily once it has been let loose) or almost incredibly cynical (believing that more female victims of men will at least provide additional evidence for their theory and thus ultimately advance their cause). Consequently, they must take some responsibility for their own behaviour. This does not mitigate the guilt of men who respond to women with violence, whether provoked or unprovoked. Individual men must pay for their own crimes. But should individual women be encouraged to imagine that they or those they permit to speak in their name can unleash powerful and dangerous forces without accepting some responsibility for the likely consequences?

53 The word "propaganda" is no longer very useful, though, because it is now invariably defined subjectively. It has come to mean promoting a way of thinking that "we" dislike. Using the same methods to promote a way of thinking that "we" do like is hardly ever called "propaganda" (except by the Vatican, which uses the word in the earlier sense of "propagating" the faith).

54 Helen Branswell, "Canadian Men's Suicide Rate Soaring," *Montreal Gazette*, 27 March 1991: B-1.

55 Pierrette Venne; quoted in Branswell B-1.

CHAPTER FIVE

1 Catharine A. MacKinnon, "Making Sex Equality Real," in *Righting the Balance: Canada's New Equality Rights*, ed. L. Smith and others (Saskatoon: Canadian Human Rights Reporter, 1986) 37–8.

2 Lee Dembart, "Letters," *Atlantic Monthly*, February 1994: 11.

3 Michael Ignatieff, *Human Rights as Politics and Idolatry*, ed. Amy Gutman (Princeton: Princeton University Press, 2001).

4 This is true, now, even though section 2 refers only to "male" citizens in connection with the electorate.

5 Roberta W. Francis, "History," [updated] 23 July 2002, *Equal Rights Amendment*, [visited] 4 August 2002,
<http://www.equalrightsamendment.org/era.htm>: 2.

6 Ann Douglas, *Terrible Honesty: Mongrel Manhattan in the 1920s* (New York: Farrar, Straus and Giroux, 1995).

7 Francis 3

8 Anne Peters, *Women, Quotas and Constitutions: A Comparative Study of Affirmative Action for Women under American, German, European Community and International Law* (The Hague: Kluwer Law International, 2000) 94.

9 Peters 95.

10 Other modifications have accommodated the fact that female employees, as a

group, are smaller and weaker than men. To hire more women (especially in fire departments, police departments, and the armed forces), job qualifications are modified.

11 Peters 95; see also *Michael M. v. Superior Court of Sonoma County*, 450 U.S. 464, 469 (1981); quoted in Peters 95. See also *Schlesinger v. Ballard*, 419 U.S. 498 [1975]; cited in Peters 96.

12 In 1992, with the ERA still not ratified, that number was used for the Madison Amendment.

13 Francis 1.

14 For the latest information, see "What's New," [updated] 5 November 2003, *The Equal Rights Amendment*, [visited] 28 December 2003, <http://members. aol.com/ERACampaignWeb/new.html>.

15 See Peters 281, 286–287, 290, 294.

16 Executive Order Establishing the President's Committee on Equal Employment Opportunity, Exec. Order No. 10,925, 3 C.F.R. 1959–1963 Comp. 448 (6 March 1961), Part 3, Section 301, Subsection 1, quoted in Peters 32; *U.S. Equal Employment Opportunity Commission*, [visited] 18 January 2004 <http://www.eeoc.gov/abouteeoc/35th/thelaw/eo-10925.html>.

17 Executive order – Equal Employment Opportunity, As Amended, Exec. Order No. 11,246, 3 C.F.R. 1964–1965 Comp. 339 (24 September 1965) Subpart B, Section 202, Subsection 1; *This Nation*, [visited] 18 January 2004, <http://www.thisnation.com/library/print/eo-affirmative2.html>; quoted in Peters 32.

18 Exec. order 36, Fed. Reg. 17,444 and 23,152 (1971); the four groups were "Blacks, Native Americans, Latinos/as, and Asian Americans."

19 U.S.C. Title 29, Chapter 8, Section 206, (D)(1) (2000), *Legal Information Institute*, [visited] 18 January 2004, <http://www.thecre.com/fedlaw/legal6/uscode29-206.htm>.

20 Here are two important American cases that went before the Supreme Court: *United Steelworkers v. Weber*, 443 U.S. 193 (1979), and *Adarand Constructors v. Pena*, 513 U.S. 200 (1995).

21 Peters 287.

22 See *Adarand Constructors v. Pena*, 513 U.S. 1108 (1995).

23 Civil Rights Act of 1964, Pub. L. No. 88-352, Title VII (1997) (codified as amended in 42 U.S.C., *U.S. Equal Opportunity Commission*, [visited] 18 January 2004, <http://www.eeoc.gov/policy/vii.html>.

24 *Regents of University of California v. Bakke* 438 U.S. 265 (1978).

25 *Grutter v. Bollinger* (2003); *Gratz v. Bollinger* (2003).

26 Another test is called "intermediate scrutiny." In this case, the government interest must be merely "important," not "compelling." The means must be merely "substantially related" to the government interest, not narrowly defined.

27 "Government Publications: U.S. Government Information by Agency and

Department," [dated] 13 June 2001, *Northwestern University Library*, [visited] 5 October 2002, <http://www/library.northwestern.edu/index.html>.

28 "Violence against Women Office," [dated]10 September 2002, *Northwestern University Library* [visited] 5 October 2002, <http://www.ojp.usdoj.gov/vawo/>.

29 "U.S. Department of Labor, Women's Bureau," [dated] 5 October 2002, *Northwestern University Library*, [visited] 5 October 2002, <http://www.do.gov/wb/welcome.html>.

30 The Legal Education and Action Fund was established by feminist lawyers in 1985 and supported partly by Status of Women Canada – which is to say, by Canadian taxpayers. Its main function is to fund and organize feminist interventions before the Supreme Court. According to its website, LEAF is "a national, non-profit organization committed to using the provisions of the Canadian Charter of Rights and Freedoms to promote equality for women ... LEAF undertakes legal action by intervening at the Canadian appellate courts on significant cases that will establish important principles of equality for women. LEAF's cases are selected by its National Legal Committee ... LEAF has ... intervened in over 140 cases and has helped establish landmark legal victories for women on a wide range of issues from violence against women, sexual harassment, pregnancy discrimination, sex bias in the employment standards, spousal support and reproductive freedoms" ("About LEAF," [undated], *LEAF: Women's Legal Education and Action Fund*, [visited] 2 November 2004, <http://www/leaf.ca/about-mandate.html>: 1).

Some feminists have criticized LEAF as a liberal organization that promotes the interests of middle-class white women. See *Women's Legal Strategies in Canada*, ed. Radha Jhappan (Toronto: University of Toronto press, 2002). In her review of that book, Lauren Bowen notes that it "is situated in legal literature rather than political science scholarship. More specifically, the intended audience ... seems to be the Canadian legal left ... The most frequently cited illustration of the flaws in feminist legal strategies utilized in litigation since 1985 is LEAF ... The primary criticisms – much like criticism leveled against the National Organization for Women's Legal Defense and Education Fund in the U.S. context – is that rights discourse is used to reinforce power and privilege. Because rights are universal, those with privilege can claim them as well. The tendency among LEAF lawyers to proceed form fundamental assumptions about women's shared experiences and subjugation abstracts the reality of oppression for most women and tends to render the quest for equality an attempt to acquire the same privileges that too many men enjoy. To argue that point, several of the authors use as an illustration the case of *Symes v. Canada* (1993) where one of the founding LEAF members argued that the cost of her full-time nanny should be a business deduction when filing her income tax return. The situation and exploitation of the nanny was not relevant to the case, suggesting ... that gender equality was to be understood in largely white and middle class terms" ("Women's Legal Strategies in Canada," [dated]

2003, *Law and Politics Book Review*, [visited] 25 November 2004, <http//
www.bsos.umd.edu/gvpt/lpbr/subpages/reviews/jhappan-radha.htm>: 1-2).

Not all critics of LEAF are feminists, of course. See Christopher Manfredi,
*Feminist Activism in the Supreme Court: Legal Mobilization and the Women's
Legal Education and Action Fund* (Vancouver: UBC Press, 2004). Manfredi
makes it clear that LEAF has institutionalized the perspective of ideological
feminism. "There is no doubt," he writes, "that the [ideological feminist]
movement succeeded completely in one respect: it established the constitutional and jurisprudential basis for a comprehensive theory of substantive
equality in Canadian law. Unlike its counterpart in the United States, LEAF
never viewed its objective as the attainment of 'same treatment' for women
and men. Although it obviously sought to eliminate gender-based distinctions
that disadvantage women, it also sought to preserve or establish such distinctions where they benefited women. Consequently LEAF did not intervene to
support just *any* equality rights or sex discrimination claim. Nowhere is this
more apparent than in Brodsky and Day's 1989 study for the Canadian Advisory Council on the Status of Women and LEAF's intervention in *Weatherall*.
In the former, Brodsky and Day lamented the number of sex discrimination
claims then being brought on behalf of men; in the latter, LEAF intervened
specifically to avoid a formal equality outcome that would extend the same
privacy rights to male inmates as female inmates enjoyed" (Manfredi 193; his
emphasis).

31 This phrase, "recognition as persons," makes it sound worse than it was.
Canadians had always recognized that women were human beings and therefore "persons" in the broad sense of that word. The reference here is to a
strictly legal sense. Were women persons – that is, legally competent – for the
specific purpose of this or that law?

32 In 2004, word got out that the National Action Committee was mired in
financial turmoil, partly because an earlier government had cut its funding to
the committee, but also because the NAC had failed to pay its taxes and was
therefore required to pay for both the interest and penalties. Not everyone –
not all women or even all feminists – received this news with dismay.
(Michael Friscolanti, "Women's Group Wants Bailout," *National Post*, 9
March 2004: A-1, A-5). Whatever happens to this particular lobby group,
though, Status of Women Canada will remain a well-funded and influential
organ of the Canadian government.

33 Christopher P. Manfredi, *The Canadian Feminist Movement, Constitutional
Politics, and the Strategic Use of Legal Resources* (Vancouver: Simon Fraser
University: University of British Columbia Centre for the Study of Government and Business, 2000), 19. Manfredi says that this council is not unique;
there is also the Ministry for Small Business, which acts like an advocacy
group within the government.

34 *Lavell v. Canada (A.G.)*, [1974] S.C.R. 1349.

35 Manfredi 23; quoting *Lavell.*
36 *Bliss v. Canada (A.G.),* [1979] 1 S.C.R. 183; this decision was overturned in *Brooks v. Canada Safeway Ltd.,* [1989] 1 S.C.R. 1219.
37 Manfredi 27.
38 In the end, this flexibility was somewhat limited by the interpretive rules of sections 1 and 33. "Under Section 1," for instance, "Charter guarantees are subject to reasonable limits, provided these can be shown to be justified within the parameters of a free and democratic society. Thus, when a court agrees that a government law infringes on the Charter, it must determine whether that law, nonetheless, should stand because the infringement is reasonable and demonstrably justified in the name of a competing right, value or principle. This can be especially controversial because it requires judges to interpret what is or is not a 'reasonable' infringement of Charter rights, and what rights are more important to society than others" (Centre for Research and Information on Canada, *The Charter: Dividing or Uniting Canadians?* CRIC Papers, no. 5 (Ottawa: Center for Research and Information on Canada, 2002) 17.
39 Michael Mandel, *The Charter of Rights and the Legalization of Politics in Canada* (Toronto: Thompson Educational Publishing, 1994) 377–8. See also Rainer Knopff and F.L. Morton, *Charter Politics* (Toronto: Nelson Canada, 1992) 252.
40 Eugene Meehan and others, *The 2000 Annotated Canadian Charter of Rights and Freedoms* (Toronto: Carswell, 1999) 839.
41 "Our Equality Rights in the Charter," [undated], *Court Challenges Program of Canada,* [visited] 28 September 2004, <http://www.ccppcj.ca/e/i-charter.html>:6.
42 "Our Equality Rights" 6.
43 "Our Equality Rights" 6–7.
44 During the 1990s, feminism became deeply rooted in Canadian institutions. The Court Challenges program was disbanded in 1992 but resurrected in 1994, under great pressure from interest groups, as an independent and non-profit organization (even though it receives much of its budget from Heritage Canada, a federal agency supported by taxpayers). The Court Challenges Program was to have a budget of $2.75 million annually between 1998 and 2003. Each court challenge was to be allotted $60,000 from taxpayers, along with $35,000 for any subsequent appeal or intervention. "Finally," according to an annual report, "the Program was granted status as a charitable organization in May 2000. While the focus of our efforts will be on fundraising from government sources, the program can now raise funds from the private sector" (Yvan Beaubien and others, *Court Challenges Program of Canada: Annual Report [for] 1999–2000* [Winnipeg, 2000] 20). This is most unusual: a federal program set up to expedite challenges to federal law. It solicits private funds, presumably from the groups that have something to gain by a court challenge under the Charter. Once again, this is an arm of the government acting as a lobby group.

45 Beaubien 11.
46 *Law Society of British Columbia v. Andrews*, [1989] 1 S.C.R. 143. Other cases in which LEAF has been involved include *Boston v. Boston*, [2002] 2 S.C.R. 413 (which supported "double dipping" from an ex-husband's income, that is, accessing his pension twice); *Irshad (Litigation guardian of) v. Ontario (Ministry of Health)* (2001) 55 O.R. (3d) 43 (C.A.), application for leave to appeal dismissed 13 September 2001, [2001] S.C.C.A. No. 218 (Q.L.) (which was about access to medicare for disabled female immigrants); *R. v. Darrach*, [2000] 2 S.C.R. 443 (which upheld the "rape shield" law: see chapter 9); and *Blencoe v. British Columbia (Human Rights Commission)*, [2000] 2 S.C.R. 307 (which concerned excessive delays in the investigation of a complaint against someone accused of sexual harassment). Other cases include the following: *New Brunswick (Minister of Health and Community Services) v. G.(J.) [J.G.]*, [1999] 3 S.C.R. 46 (about access to legal aid in custody suits brought by unmarried women); *British Columbia (Public Service Employee Relations Commission) v. British Columbia Government and Service Employees' Union*, [1999] 3 S.C.R. 3 (about work standards that favour men); and *R. v. Ewanchuk*, [1999] 1 S.C.R. 330 (about the definition of "no" in cases of rape).
47 Manfredi, "Canadian Feminist" 32; quoting *Law Society of British Columbia*, note 46 at 174.
48 Manfredi, "Canadian Feminist" 33; quoting *R. v. Turpin*, [1989] 1 S.C.R. 1296 at 1332.
49 Manfredi, "Canadian Feminist" 33.
50 *Convention on the Elimination of All Forms of Discrimination against Women (CEDAW): Reference Document* (Ottawa: Department of Justice, 1985), 7 (our emphasis).
51 Canadian Association of University Teachers, "CAUT's Policy Statement on Positive Action to Improve the Status of Women in Canadian Universities: Preamble," *CAUT Bulletin* (March 1991): 12.
   Several years later, Maureen Webb distinguished three types of discrimination in Canadian law. First, direct discrimination exists "where an employer adopts a practice or rule which on its face discriminates on a prohibited ground. For example: 'No Catholics or no women or no blacks employed here.'" Second, adverse effect discrimination "arises where an employer for genuine business reasons adopts a rule or standard which is on its face neutral, and which will apply equally to all employees, but which has a discriminatory effect upon a prohibited ground on one employee or groups of employees in that it imposes, because of some special characteristic of the employee or group, obligations, penalties, or restrictive conditions not imposed on other members of the work force." Third, systemic discrimination is "institutionalized discrimination or discrimination which pertains to a system. It is often used interchangeably with the term 'adverse effect

discrimination,' although the two are not really synonymous ... Certainly, systemic discrimination often includes adverse effect discrimination, but it can also include direct discrimination, such as action taken by the employer on the basis of racial or gender stereotypes. Indeed, systemic discrimination often includes subtle unconscious forms of direct discrimination which may be difficult to prove but which disadvantage minorities in cumulative ways through 'chilly environments' or lack of mentorship" (Maureen Webb, "The Law: What is Discrimination and How Can It be Proved?" in CAUT *Bulletin: Status of Women Supplement* (April 1996): 3; quoting the Supreme Court case *Ontario Human Rights Commission v. Simpson-Sears*, [1985], 2 S.C.R. 536 at para. 18.

52 *A Guide to the Court Challenges Program of Canada* (Winnipeg, MB, 2002) 4.

53 Canada, Department of Justice, *Toward Equality* (Ottawa: Ministry of Supply and Services, 1986) 3–4, 13, 49–56; quoted in Knopff and Morton, *Charter Politics*, 192n55.)

54 F.L. Morton and Rainer Knopff, *The Charter Revolution and the Court Party* (Toronto: Broadview Press, 2000) 122.

55 Recommendation 5 in *National Symposium on Women, Law and the Administration of Justice Department of Justice: Proceedings of the Symposium* (Ottawa: Department of Justice, 1992).

56 *National Symposium* 3: 3.

57 Canadian Bar Association, Task Force on Gender Equality in the Legal Profession, *Touchstones for Change: Equality, Diversity, and Accountability: The Report on Gender Equality in the Legal Profession* (Ottawa: Canadian Bar Association, 1993).

58 *Touchstones* 13. Apart from any other reason, for its optimism was a demographic one: 50% of all law students, even then, were women. The march of progress, says the report, "requires a focus on systemic and group-based inequalities" and "encompasses the right to have one's differences acknowledged and accommodated both by the law and by appropriate social and institutional policies and practices" (*Touchstones* 13). The process had already begun, when the Supreme Court "rejected the so-called 'similarly-situated test' applied in the Courts below in favour of an approach focusing on the remedying of disadvantage. The Court defined the purpose of equality guarantees as promoting the equality of historically and socially disadvantaged groups in a proactive and systematic way" (*Touchstones* 14). On sexual equality in the legal profession, *Touchstones* defines "gender bias" as "the predisposition or tendency to think about and behave toward people primarily on the basis of their sex. Gender bias also refers to the greater value society places on men" (*Touchstones* 12). The gynocentrism of this definition was even more evident in its elaboration. The barriers of gender bias were said to "have an adverse impact on women, attitudes and behaviours ... which are based on stereotypi-

cal beliefs about the nature and roles of the sexes, myths and misconceptions about the economic and social problems encountered by women, and the treatment of real differences between men and women in a manner which disadvantages women, by ignoring or devaluing the female difference. Gender bias links the individual biased behaviour to its systemic origins" (*Touchstones* 12; quoting *Gender Equality in the Canadian Justice System: Summary Document and Proposals for Action* [Ottawa: Department of Justice, 1992] 17.) Finally, *Touchstones* makes a distinction between direct and indirect discrimination.

59 *Touchstones* 13.
60 "Employment Equity Act, R.S.C. 1995, c. 44, s. 2: "Purpose of Act," *Department of Justice Canada*, [visited] 28 January 2004, <http://laws.justice.gc.ca/en/E-5.401/49263.html>.
61 Status of Women Canada, *Setting the Stage for the Next Century: The Federal Plan for Gender Equality* (Ottawa: Status of Women Canada, 1995).
62 *Report by the Government of Canada to the U.N. Commission on Human Rights Special Rapporteur on Violence Against Women* (Ottawa: Status of Women Canada, 1998), *Status of Women Canada*, [visited] 27 October 2004, <http://www.swc-cfc.gc.ca/pubs/unreport/unreport_e.html>.
63 *Canadian Experience in Gender Mainstreaming* (Ottawa: Status of Women Canada, December 2001), *Status of Women Canada*, [visited] 27 October 2004, <http://www.swc.gc.ca/pubs/0662667352/200112_0662667352_4_e.html>.
64 "Canadian Experience" 1.
65 "Canadian Experience" 2.
66 Note here that section 15 of the Charter does not list groups; it lists only the "enumerated" *grounds* of illegal discrimination: race, national or ethnic origin, colour, religion, sex, age, and mental or physical disability. These exclude sexual orientation and other grounds, so lawyers have used analogies to support the claims of some groups. See *A Guide to the Court Challenges Program of Canada* (Winnipeg, 2002) 3.
67 F.L. Knopff and Rainer Morton, *Charter Politics* (Scarborough, ON: Nelson Canada 1992) 253, 255.
68 Manfredi, "Canadian Feminist" 40–1.
69 Manfredi, "Canadian Feminist" 47.
70 Bertha Wilson, untitled paper, in *Gender Equality: A Challenge for the Legal Profession/ La profession juridique face aux defies de l'égalité des sexes* (Ottawa: Canadian Bar Association, 1992) [unpaged manuscript]; papers presented at Conference of the Canadian Bar Association Continuing Legal Education Committee and Task Force on Gender Equality, Toronto, 29–30 October 1992. (The passage appears on page 5 of her speech, but the pagination is not continuous.) For a biography of Bertha Wilson, see Mary Ellen Anderson and Bertha Wilson, *Judging Bertha Wilson: Law as Large as Life* (Toronto: Published by the Osgoode Society for Canadian Legal History by the University of Toronto Press, 2001).

71 Catharine A. MacKinnon, "Making Sex Equality Real," in *Righting the Balance: Canada's New Equality Rights*, ed. Lynn Smith and others (Saskatoon: Canadian Human Rights Reporter, 1986) 37–8.

72 MacKinnon 40–1.

73 See *R. v. Bernardo* (1994), 121 D.L.R. (4th) (Ont. C.A.), leave to appeal to s.c.c. refused; [1995] S.C.C.A. 113; *French Estate v. Ontario (A.G.)*, [*R. v. Bernardo*] (1996), 134 D.L.R. (4th) 587 (Ont. Gen. Div.), affirmed: (1988), 38 O.R. (3d) 347 (C.A.), leave to appeal to s.c.c. refused [1998] S.C.C.A. No. 139; *Kane v. Church of Jesus Christ Christian Aryan Nations*, [1992] No. 3, 1992, 18 C.H.R.R.D./1268; *R. v. Butler*, [1992] 1 S.C.R. 452; *R. v. Keegstra*, [1996] 1 S.C.R. 458; *R. v. Seaboyer; R. v. Gayme*, [1991] 2 S.C.R. 577; *R. v. Sullivan*, [1991] 1 S.C.R. 489; *Law Society of British Columbia v. Andrews*, [1989] 1 S.C.R. 143; *Borowski v. Canada (A.G)*, [1989] 1 S.C.R. 342; Tremblay v. Daigle, [1989] 2 S.C.R. 530; *Tomen v. Ontario School Teachers' Federation*, [1989] S.C.C.A. No. 372; *Brooks v. Canada Safeway Ltd.*, [1989] 1 S.C.R. 1219; and *Canadian Newspapers Co. v. Canada (A.G.)*, [1988] 2 S.C.R. 122.

74 These works include one book, M. Eberts and others, *The Case for Women's Equality: The Federation of Woman Teachers' Associations of Ontario and the Canadian Charter of Rights and Freedoms* (Toronto: The Federation, 1991), and several articles; "Sex Equality and Nation-building in Canada: The Meech Lake Accord," in *Tulsa Law Journal*, 25 (1990): 735–57; "Making Sex Equality Real," in *Righting the Balance: Canada's New Equality Rights*, ed. Lynn Smith and others (Saskatoon: The Canadian Human Rights Reporter, 1986); "Feminist Approaches to Sexual Assault in Canada and the United States: A Brief Retrospective," in *Challenging Times: The Women's Movement in the United States and Canada*, ed. Constance Backhouse and David H. Flaherty (Montreal: McGill-Queen's University Press, 1992) 186–92.

75 Carol Gilligan, *In a Different Voice: Psychological Theory and Women's Development* (Cambridge: Harvard University Press, 1982).

76 Kim Campbell, "The Courage to Listen: How Inclusive Justice Can Bring about Gender Equality and More," in *Gender Equality: A Challenge for the Legal Profession*, ed. Lynn Smith (Ottawa: Secretary of State Women's Program, 1992), 10; bound proceedings of the Conference of the Canadian Bar Association's Continuing Legal Education Committee and Task Force on Gender Equality.

77 Annette Baier, "The Need for More than Justice in Science, Morality and Feminist Theory," in *Science, Morality and Feminist Theory*, ed. Marsha Hanen and Kai Nielsen, *Canadian Journal of Philosophy*, supplement 13 (Calgary: University of Calgary Press, 1987) 56.

78 Faye J. Crosby and others, "Affirmative Action: Psychological Data and the Policy Debates," [dated] 2003, *American Psychological Association Institutional Access: PsycArticles*, [visited] 2 June 2003, <http://http://www.psycinfo.com/library/display.cfm?document=amp/2003/february/amp5829 3.html/>;

published in *American Pyschologist* 58.2 (February 2003): 93–115. Crosby is very influential. See Susan D. Clayton and Faye J. Crosby, *Justice, Gender, and Affirmative Action* (Ann Arbor: University of Michigan Press, 1992); and Faye J. Crosby and Cheryl VanDeVeer, eds., *Sex, Race, and Merit: Debating Affirmative Action in Education and Employment* (Ann Arbor: University of Michigan Press, 2000).

79 Crosby and others 11.

80 Crosby and others 18 (our emphasis).

81 Crosby and others 10.

82 Consider one document from McGill University: *The Annual Report on Full-Time Academic Staffing Changes* (D02–72), which was presented to the Senate on 16 April 2003 by McGill's vice-principal, academic. Table 1 summarizes academic hiring at McGill from 1 January to 31 December 2002. The percentage of women in the pool of applicants can be derived from the table and compared to the number of women hired. All things being equal, fair hiring would be indicated by a percentage of women hired equal to that of women in the pool of applicants. Considering all those hired, in other words, there should be one woman for every four people hired according to the pools of female and male applicants. In fact, however, there is one woman for every three. The rate of hiring women, therefore, is about 30% higher for women than it should be, given their representation in the pool. A breakdown by faculty (those in which enough people were hired to make the analysis statistically significant) shows that women have a 56% advantage over men in engineering, 30% in science, and 27% in arts. Only in medicine were women hired at the rate indicated by the pool.

83 Grant Brown, "The Politics of Preference: A Catalogue of Criticisms of Employment Equity," unpublished draught paper, 11.

84 Stephen Stern, "Jews and Employment Equity: An Unholy Alliance," *Viewpoints*, 23 (March 1995): 5. The author's point, however, is that Jews are now turning away from this tradition.

85 One historical account makes it clear that "there can be no doubt that some of those in authority in the University had become alarmed by the rapid rate of change in its character and that measures were taken in the late 1920s and 1930s to limit the number of Jewish students admitted to McGill. One of those measures was to require a higher percentage in high school leaving examinations from Jewish candidates than from others. The inevitable result was that the Jewish students were on the whole more intelligent, more hardworking, and won more prizes. In response to protests from the Jewish community the measures were abandoned during the Second World War, and the percentage began to rise again. By 1964, the last year statistics concerning religion were gathered, it stood at over 28%" (Stanley Frost and Sheila Rosenberg, "The McGill Student Body: Past and Future Enrolment," *McGill Journal of Education*, 15.1 (winter 1986): 43.

86 Promoting or protecting the gospel of love and truth, for example, has been used repeatedly to justify inquisitions, witch hunts, and wars. But religious ends are not the only ones that can be distorted as justifications for brutality. Both the Marxist "classless society" and the Nazi "organic community" were used in the twentieth century to legitimate mass murder. It will not do to trivialize the problem at hand by arguing that these examples of ends justifying means were extreme. Of course they were. In addition, however, they were the logical results of a mentality that, even under far more benign circumstances, fails to acknowledge a moral bottom line beyond which we cannot move without destroying the lofty ideals we are supposedly pursuing.

It will not do, moreover, to argue that some ends are better than others. Who, after all, is to set the standard? An ideological cadre? Perhaps, for those who sincerely believe that they alone know what is best for everyone else. A survey of public opinion? Perhaps, for those who assume that morality and popularity are synonymous. The point here is that anything at all can be justified by intelligent and sincere people in the name of some ostensibly or even truly noble end. The premise is flawed, inherently flawed.

But could some means not be justified as ends in themselves and not merely in view of other ends? Discrimination against men is perfectly reasonable, many women (and some men) have come to believe, because men supposedly deserve it. They believe that discrimination against men can be justified not only on the grounds of creating more opportunities for women (the means to an end) but also on the grounds of punishing men (the end in itself). Variants of this argument have been used not only by journalists and bureaucrats but also by academics, those who are usually assumed to set the standard for intellectual acuity (though not necessarily for moral insight).

87 Stanley Fish, "How the Pot Got to Call the Kettle Black," *Atlantic Monthly*, November 1993: 128–36.

88 John P. Field, "Letters," *Atlantic Monthly*, February 1994: 8.

89 Stanley Fish, "Stanley Fish Replies," *Atlantic Monthly*, February 1994: 12.

90 Steven Yates, "Letters," *Atlantic Monthly*, February 1994: 10.

91 Fish 12.

92 Lee Dembart, "Letters," *Atlantic Monthly*, February 1994: 11.

93 Fish 12.

94 Some groups do present special problems within any democratic society but not because of any innate characteristics. Included are those who oppose democracy but use its institutions to secure power before destroying it, which is what the Nazis did in Weimar Germany. Almost anything can be tolerated in a democracy except intolerance.

95 Neither is the world of art a microcosm of the larger society. Edward Rothstein has used similar arguments in connection with the controversy of government funding for the National Endowment for the Arts. Rothstein's problem is what he calls the "ideology of democracy." According to this way of

thinking, writes Rothstein, "not only are all people created equal but so are all ideas and all cultures. Even art, an essentially undemocratic achievement by extraordinary gifted individuals, is thrust into a marketplace marked by clamorous demands for democratic distribution" ("Where a Democracy and Its Money Have No Place," *New York Times*, 26 October 1997: 2:1). Once that idea triumphs, Rothstein notes, it follows that rewards are based on politics, not merit.

96 The longer a degree takes, however, the more expensive it is for the university.

97 Consider the following: "Yet, there are many hurdles for those seeking to do research at the MCRTW [McGill Centre for Research and Teaching on Women]. There are, to begin, the challenges faced by younger faculty members who, during the hiring freeze period, were assigned large teaching loads making time for research limited. With many of the women among these faculty members also called upon to take on more than their share of committee work to provide gender representation, time to do research has been at premium" (Shree Mulay, "News from the MCRTW," *Newsletter* (September 2001): 1.

98 Fish 12.

99 In "Politics of Preference," Brown observes that "the debate concerns preferential practices *directly involving employment*, rather than those relating to education, welfare, or other social benefits which might indirectly affect employment opportunities. The distinction is important because job competitions are zero-sum games: an advantage given to one candidate necessarily entails a handicap for the others. In contrast, directing special attention toward certain groups in other areas of social policy does not entail harming anyone else. Thus, to use a standard illustration, segregating girls and boys in high school science and math classes might benefit the girls in some ways without causing the boys' performance to degenerate [although the same principle could be applied in ways, such as sexually segregated schools, that would benefit boys at least as much as girls without harming the latter] ... Education, job training, and other pre-employment equalization policies tend to expand the pool of qualified candidates, whereas employment equity tends to constrict that pool" (Brown 3; his emphasis). By focusing attention on individuals rather than groups, opportunities for improvement would be made available to everyone in need. And if most of the individuals in need were to come from this or that group, then so be it.

100 Pay Equity Review: Introduction," [dated] 21 January 2002, *Government of Canada*, [visited] 20 October 2002, <http://www.payequityreview.gc.ca/1200-e.html.>.

101 "It's Time for Working Women to Earn Equal Pay,"[undated], AFL-CIO, [visited] 17 October 2002, <http://www.aflcio.org/women/equalpay.htm>: 1–2 (our emphasis).

102 Strategy," [undated], *The Men's Health Network*, [visited] 15 March 2003,

<http://www.menshealthnetwork.org/new_goals.html>: 2. Warren Farrell points out that the ratio of work-related accidents is 2.4 men to 1 woman (*Women Can't Hear What Men Don't Say: Destroying Myths, Creating Love* [New York: Penguin Putnam, 1999] 237). American state laws, too, require public jurisdictions to eliminate sex-based wage disparities. In Minnesota, for example, pay equity "is a method of eliminating discrimination against women who are paid less than men for jobs requiring comparable levels of expertise. This goes beyond the familiar idea of 'equal pay for equal work' where men and women with the same jobs must be paid equally. A policy to establish pay equity usually means: 1) that all jobs will be evaluated and given points according to the level of knowledge and responsibility required to do the job; and 2) that salary adjustments will be made if it is discovered that women are consistently paid less than men for jobs with similar points ... Pay equity does not replace collective bargaining." ("Pay Equity/Comparable Worth", [dated] 5 October 2002, *Minnesota North Star, Department of Employee Relations*, [visited] 17 October 2002, <http://www.doer.state.mn.us/lr-peqty/lr-peqty.htm>: 1).

103 Morley Gunderson and Paul Lanoie, "Program Evaluation Criteria Applied to Pay Equity in Ontario," published by Montreal's Centre for International Research and Analysis on Organizations (CIRANO) as Working Paper 99s-38. See "Scientific Papers," [dated] November 1999, CIRANO, [visited] 17 October 2002, <http://www.cirano.qc.ca/en/publications.php?annee=1999&cat=cs&tri=aut&filtrer=Execute>. Gunderson is CIBC Professor of Youth Employment at the University of Toronto and Professor at the Centre for Industrial Relations and the Department of Economics. Lanoie works at CIRANO.

104 Gunderson and Lanoie 1.

105 Gunderson and Lanoie 1 (our emphasis). They add, "The appropriateness of this target could be questioned especially in light of the recent controversial evidence ... indicating that females in Canada (unlike in the U.S. and unlike males in Canada) are not significantly penalized by working in female-dominated jobs" (Gunderson and Lanoie 1).

106 Gunderson and Lanoie 9.

107 Gunderson and Lanoie 13.

108 Morton and Knopff, *Charter Revolution* 125.

109 Morton and Knopff, *Charter Revolution* 126.

110 Martin Loney, "Pay's the Thing: The Federal Government's Huge Pay-Equity Bill Is a Monumental Boondoggle," *Time* (Canadian edition), 24 August 1998, 56. Commenting on the gender war over pay equity in the United States, Loney observes that in marketplace economics, what might "appear to be discriminatory merely reflects the simple laws of supply and demand, rather than any evil, masculine conspiracy" (David Thomas, *Not Guilty:*

The Case in Defense of Men [New York: Morrow, 1993] 73). The same thing would be true of the entertainment industry or any other industry. The fact that more people buy tickets to see a male movie star than a female one (Thomas 74–7), for instance, provides no reason to assume that Hollywood moguls discriminate against the latter.

111 The wage gap might never close, because many women might continue to take time off for their children or prefer to work part-time for many years. As a result, the pool of women at the top might always be smaller than the one for men. In this sense, the "glass ceiling" would remain.

112 "Age discrimination continues to damage our society, reducing both the incomes and the self-confidence of millions of Americans. A Louis Harris survey, conducted in 1989, reported that one million workers aged 50 to 64 believed that they would be forced to retire before they were ready. Most of this group, anticipating an unwanted early retirement, said they would prefer to work for years longer. Another Harris survey, conducted in 1992, found that 5.4 million older Americans – one in seven of those 55 and older who were not working at that time – were willing to work but could not find a suitable job. These discouraging statistics were cited in *The Untapped Resource,* a 1993 report on 'The Americans Over 55 at Work Program,' a 5–year research effort conducted by the Commonwealth Fund to examine the productive potential of older Americans" ("Age Discrimination: A Pervasive and Damaging Influence," [dated] 17 January 2002, *Administration on Aging,* [visited] 15 March 2003, <http://www.aoa.gov/factsheets/ageism.html>: 1). "From 1991 to 1995, an average of 17,000 workers annually brought age discrimination complaints to the Equal Employment Opportunity Commission (EEOC)" ("Age Discrimination" 3).

113 *Weatherall v. Canada (A.G.),* [1993] 2 S.C.R. 872.

114 Meehan 684.

115 Katherine Boo, "The Black Gender Gap," *Atlantic Monthly,* January-February 2003: 107.

116 Boo 107.

117 Boo 107.

118 Boo 108.

119 Paul Offner; quoted in Boo 108.

120 Boo 108.

121 Boo 109.

122 Jean Bethke Elshtain, "Thinking about Women, Christianity, and Rights," in *Religious Human Rights in Global Perspective: Religious Perspectives,* ed. John Witte and Johan D. Van der Ryver (The Hague: Martinus Nijhoff, 1996) 146.

123 Elsthain 147.

124 Elsthain 147.

125   Elshtain 148–9.
126   Elshtain 150.
127   Elshtain 152.

CHAPTER SIX

1   "Parenting after Separation," [undated], *Ontario Women's Network on Child Custody and Access (OWNCCA)*, [visited] 19 December 2002, <http://www.owjn.org/custody/parent.htm>: 3.

2   K.C. Wilson, *The Multiple Scandals of Child Support*, 2nd ed. (Richmond, VA: Harbinger Press, 2003) 6–7; 50.

3   Donna Laframboise, "This Is about Punishing Dad: Myth of the Deadbeat Dad," *National Post*, 28 March 2000: B-1. This is a Canadian case; Americans face similar problems, but their taxes are lower.

4   Robert Seidenberg, *The Father's Emergency Guide to Divorce-Custody Battle: A Tour through the Predatory World of Judges, Lawyers, Psychologists, and Social Workers in the Subculture of Divorce* (Takoma Park, MD: JES Books, 1997) 53–4.

5   What are the actual statistics on custody? Answering that question is more complicated than one might think. American judges, according to Robert Seidenberg, grant paternal custody in approximately 10% of the cases (Seidenberg 11) and only in 3% to 5% of them when custody is contested (Seidenberg 15). Canadian judges, according to Glenn Cheriton, are not much different. They grant paternal custody in 11% of the cases, joint custody in 12%, and maternal custody in 76% (other arrangements being made in 1%). They grant material custody much more often, though, after common-law separations. (Glenn Cheriton, *Child Support, Divorce, Custody, Access and Government Policy* [Ottawa: Commoner's Publication Society, 1998]), 39.

Most divorced or separated parents do settle custody and child support privately and sometimes even amicably. In *Divorced Dads: Shattering the Myths* (New York: Tarcher/Putnam, 1998) Sanford Braver points out that 18% of American divorce-and-custody cases are settled by default (referring to the findings of Eleanor E. Maccoby and Robert H. Mnookin in *Dividing the Child: Social and Legal Dilemmas of Custody* [Cambridge, MA: Harvard University Press, 1992]). This can mean one of three things: the husband and wife agree over custody; one of them does not care enough to dispute the matter; or one of them is "so distraught or otherwise impaired that he or she cannot raise objections" (Braver 89). Another 14% are "self-settled." This means that disputes are settled without resorting to lawyers. Some cases cannot be settled so amicably. Therefore, 9% resort to mediators and 53% to lawyers. That comes to 94%. All of these cases, presumably, end up with the ex-spouses agreeing on custody and other aspects of divorce (although many male ones end up "agreeing" because they believe that they have no hope of winning in the first place). Only 5% end up in adjudication; they are brought before judges, who impose decisions.

Only the relatively few problem cases come to light in newspaper articles or on the websites of advocacy groups. Why worry about them? For three reasons. One is that these cases are settled by the law, and the law has a very powerful symbolic function, in addition to its practical ones. In cases of this kind, it reveals very clearly what society has come to believe about men, women, and children. Another reason is that real people are involved, not merely statistical abstractions. If the law is unfair for even a minority of citizens – in this case, all divorced or separated fathers, including those whose cases never come to light – then its legitimacy must surely be questioned. Of even greater interest here, though, is its moral legitimacy. But perhaps the most important reason is that all men who pay child support are now under continual surveillance by the government, even if they have *never* been in default. We discuss this problem elsewhere.

6 Ideological rhetoric is present occasionally in the claims of advocates for both divorced or separated mothers and divorced or separated fathers; some people, both women and men, are at least partly motivated by self-interest on either the individual level or the group level. Neither side, generally speaking, is entirely altruistic. Neither side is motivated entirely by the interests of children. This does not mean, however, that either side ignores the interests of children – or, for that matter, of society as a whole – because both sides have also campaigned for particular (though often conflicting) interests of children.

7 Wendy McElroy, "Does Rape Violate the Commerce Clause of the Constitution?" [dated] 3 July 2002, *WendyMcElroy.co: A Site for Individualist Feminism and Individualist Anarchism*, [visited] 1 June 2002, <*http://www.zetetics.com/mac/*articles/brzonkala.html>: 4; this article appeared in *Ideas on Liberty*, 50: 1 (2000).

8 Stephen Baskerville, "The Myth of Deadbeat Dad," *Liberty* (June 2002): 27.

9 K.C. Wilson, "Co-parenting and Shared Parenting: Why It Should Almost Always Be Used, and How to Do It," [dated] 2000, *Harbinger Press*, [visited] 3 June 2003, http://wheres-daddy.com/fatherhood/childsupport.htm.; referring to data in Judi Bartfeld and Daniel R. Meyer, "Are There Really Deadbeat Dads? The Relationship between Ability to Pay, Enforcement, and Compliance in Nonmarital Child Support Cases," *Social Service Review*, 68.2 (1994): 219–35; also DP#994–93, Madison, WI: Institute for Research on Poverty, March 1993.

10 Baskerville, "Myth" 28.

11 Baskerville, "Myth" 27.

12 The term "divorce revolution" was coined by Lenore Weitzman in the title of her book and the term "divorce culture" by Barbara Dafoe Whitehead in the title of hers; we have already referred to the former and will refer to the latter in due course.

13 Baskerville, "Myth" 28. The same point is made by Seidenberg, although he
    adds that the whole move to get women off welfare in this particular way was
    provoked by false statistics (which we discuss in appendix 3). "President Clin-
    ton, Secretary of Health and Human Services Donna Shalala, and Attorney
    General Janet Reno, along with a host of senators and representatives, pro-
    claimed there was a '$34 billion child-support gap' and claimed that stronger
    child support enforcement measures could remove 800,000 mothers and chil-
    dren from the welfare roles. But the '$34 billion gap' is a fiction. It has its
    roots in a hypothetical model that occurs in a single paper created by a single
    individual – Elaine Sorensen of the Urban Institute, a liberal think-tank in
    Washington, D.C." (Seidenberg 65; citing *Noncustodial Fathers: Can They
    Afford to Pay More Child Support?*, a report produced in 1994 at the Urban
    Institute, Washington). "According to the statistics of the Census Bureau and
    the Federal Office of Child Support Enforcement, the 'collection gap' for the
    period Ms. Sorensen examined was not $34 billion, but somewhere between
    $3 and $5 billion" (Seidenberg 59; citing *Seventeenth Annual Report to Con-
    gress, for the Period Ending September 30, 1992*, a report from the Depart-
    ment of Health and Human Services, Office of Child Support Enforcement).
       Wilson mentions the same problem, claiming that the figure can be estab-
    lished only if "1. All custodial parents [usually mothers] have orders for child
    support. (Commonly, 44 to 48% do not seek one.) 2. Those without orders
    are getting no child support. (At least 32% say they are.) 3. There is no joint
    custody. (Between 10 to 15% of currently divorced couples use joint custody.)
    4. All cases have their child support amounts set according to the recently
    introduced Wisconsin Guidelines (which less than one-third of all states use).
    5. All obligators (non-custodial parents; fathers) are making average or better
    incomes and able to pay these amounts" (Wilson, *Multiple Scandals* 6–7).
    According to Seidenberg, "[C]hild support enforcement has been ineffective in
    bridging this gap, as the Government Accounting Office ... has reported,
    because 66 percent of unpaid child support is due to the obligor's inability to
    pay. Further, 73 percent of all child support collections comes from non-wel-
    fare cases" (Seidenberg 59; citing *Seventeenth Annual Report*). "Collecting
    more money from these fathers has no effect on the welfare roles. Nonethe-
    less, based on 'Ms. Information,' the 104th Congress passed draconian bills to
    revoke driver's and professional licenses from fathers who fall behind in child
    support" (Seidenberg 59).
       Elsewhere, Seidenberg discusses another contested statistical figure: that
    fathers win half the battles over custody. He traces this figure to a story run
    by the *Washington Post* (Barbara Vobejda and D'Vera Cohn, "As Custody
    Laws Level the Field, Father Often Does Better," *Washington Post*, 14
    November 1994: A-1 ff.). The authors claim that divorced fathers face little or
    no discrimination in court. After observing that "studies suggest" this, they
    fail to identify a single one. Instead, they refer to three isolated cases. "Three

cases from three separate jurisdictions do not a trend make," writes Seidenberg, "much less prove that fathers are winning half the time. Moreover, all
the cited cases had received *national media coverage*, a fact that itself throws
the authors' '50-percent' premise into question. Thousands of fathers lose custody every week, and nobody writes about it. But when a mother loses custody, it is, literally, headline news. The media is its own best evidence that a
father winning custody is still a 'man-bites-dog' story" (Seidenberg 60 [his
emphasis]).

Even government figures can be misleading. "Deadbeat Dad statistics published by the U.S. government include fathers who are only marginally behind
in child support, fathers who are paid up on child support but whose ex-
wives have falsely reported them as not paying, fathers who have moved back
in with the mother and children, and fathers who are literally dead (according
to the Government Accounting Office, 14 percent of 'Deadbeat Dads')"(Seidenberg 112; citing "Mothers Say Fathers Unable to Pay," *Speak Out for
Children*, 8.1 [1992–1993]).

Of more importance here, though, are some other statistics that Seidenberg
gathered. According to him, approximately 90% of what is due for child support is paid voluntarily by divorced fathers who have jobs (Seidenberg 114; citing "Mothers Say"), most failures to pay being due to unemployment. Not
surprisingly, moreover, willingness to pay is directly related to access. Fathers
with joint custody pay 90% of what they owe; those with visitation pay 79%;
and those with neither pay only 45% (Seidenberg 122; citing U.S. Bureau of
the Census, "Child Support and Alimony: 1989," *Current Population Reports*,
Series P-60, no. 173 [Washington, D.C.: Government Printing Office, 1991]).

14 Wilson, *Multiple Scandals*, 25. "Only 4% of the non-custodial parents whose
earnings drop by more than 15% are able to get a reduction in support payments" (Elaine Sorensen, "A Little Help for Some 'Deadbeat Dads,'" *Washington Post*, 15 November 1995, A-25); quoted in Wilson, *Multiple Scandals*
51.

15 "Prior to 1989, non-welfare cases generally were argued on a case-by-case
basis but within parameters established by statute and case law. With the
Family Support Act of 1988, the U.S. Congress established funding incentives
for states to adopt statewide child support guidelines. The states had only one
year to implement statewide presumptive guidelines – but in reality, the deadline was tighter since most state legislatures do not operate year-round. Federal regulations – without requiring any specific guidelines – require that state
guidelines be based on economic data and result in an economically appropriate award. The intent of the new law and regulations was to boost the level of
award 'adequacy,' to create uniformity in application for child support
awards, and to simplify the process of child support determination – all of
which theoretically would reduce the incentive to seek modifications or to
contest the original finding" (R. Mark Rogers and Donald J. Bieniewicz,

Child Cost Economics and Litigation Issues: An Introduction to Applying Cost Shares Child Support Guidelines, [dated] 17 october 2002, [visited] 29 December 2003, <http://www.guidelineeconomics.com/files/LitigationIssues. pdf>: 2. This paper was presented at the Southern Economic Association Annual Meeting, Section for the National Association of Forensic Economics (Alexandria, Virginia, 12 November 2000). See also the published version of this paper: R. Mark Rogers and Donald J. Bieniewicz, "Child Cost Economics and Litigation Issues: An Inroduction to Applying Cost Shares Child Support Guidelines," in *Assessing Damages in Injuries and Deaths of Minor Children* (Tucson, AZ: Lawyers and Judges Publishing Company, 2002).

16 Wilson, *Multiple Scandals* 25–6.

17 "Prosecutive Guidelines and Procedures for the Child Support Recovery Act of 1992," [dated] 25 February 1997, *Office of the Attorney General,* [visited] 21 June 2002 <http://www.usdoj.gov/ag/readingroom/childspt2.htm>: 1.

18 "Prosecutive Guidelines" 2–3.

19 The act had previously been known as Bill HR 1488.

20 "Johnson Announces Hearing on H.R. 1488, the 'Hyde-Woolsey' Child Support Bill," [dated] 8 March 2000, *Advisory from the Committee on Ways and Means Subcommittee on Human Resources,* [visited] 9 December 2002, <http://waysandmeans.house.gov/humres/106cong/hr-18.htm>: 1.

21 Federal Child Support Guidelines: A Technical Report," *Research Report* CSR-1997–IE: 2, 4.

22 "Family Responsibility Office: Introduction," and "Enforcement," [undated], *Ontario: Ministry of Community, Family and Children's Services,* [visited] 22 December 2002, <http://www.gov.on.ca/CSS/page/services/fro/>: 1–3.

23 See Braver.

24 The eight-year study, called Noncustodial Parent: Parents without Children, began in 1985 at Arizona State University. Braver's colleagues were Sharlene Wolchik and Irwin Sandler. In 1996, as a result, Braver served on a panel for the conference called in response to President Clinton's Fatherhood Initiative.

25 Braver 124–45.

26 Braver 87–107.

27 Braver 55–86.

28 Braver 108–23.

29 Braver 16–37.

30 Braver 38–54.

31 Braver 128–9; referring to A. Burns and C. Scott, *Mother-Headed Families and Why They Have Increased* (Hillsdale, NJ: Lawrence Erlbaum Associates, 1994).

32 Braver 124–45. Although this figure shocks the public, as Braver shows, it is accepted by the authors of both academic or popular works on the topic. See,

for example, David Chambers, *Making Fathers Pay* (Chicago: University of Chicago Press, 1979) 29, and Seidenberg 35. Ditto for feminists. See Lenore J. Weitzman, *The Divorce Revolution: The Unexpected Social and Economic Consequences for Women and Children in America* (New York: Free Press, 1985) 460 – although Weitzman's use of some other statistics is highly questionable, to say the least, as we show further on in this chapter and in appendix 3.

33 According to Statistics Canada, the figure is 74.05% for 1992–94. See Cheriton 13; citing catalogue number 84-213.

34 Candis McLean, "Legal Bloodletting: Maintenance-Enforcement Programs Are Ruining Too Many Lives," *The Report*, 15 April 2002: 4.

35 Stephen Baskerville, "Q: Is Court-ordered Child Support Doing More Harm Than Good?" [dated] 2 August 1999, *Insight on the News*, [visited] 1 July 2002, <www.insightmag.com/main.cfm?include=detail&stroyid=215429>: 2.

36 John Tierny, "New Look at Realities of Divorce," *New York Times*, 11 July 2000: B-1; citing Margaret F. Brinig and Douglas W. Allen, "These Boots Are Made for Walking: Why Most Divorce Filers Are Women," *American Law and Economics Review* 2 (2000): 126–69.

37 Tierny B-1.

38 Margaret F. Brinig; quoted in Tierny B-1.

39 Seidenberg 112–113.

40 Our premise in this chapter is that men face severe problems in connection with divorce and custody. But men face severe problems even in connection with separation after cohabiting. And we are not referring only to "palimony." Grant A. Brown has written a brilliant analysis of the Canadian laws that govern "unjust enrichment," for instance (in "Unjust Enrichment in Cohabitation," an unpublished manuscript). This term refers to lawsuits in which one partner, usually a woman, claims to have been denied adequate monetary compensation for services provided within a common-law relationship. Brown analyzes one case that went to the Supreme Court: *Peter v. Beblow* [1993] 1 S.C.R. 90; (1993) 44 F.L.R. (3d) 329. Mrs Peter sued Mr Beblow for unjust enrichment at her expense. Here is what happened. Mrs Peter and her four children came to live with Mr Beblow and his two children. They agreed to pool their resources. His task was to provide room and board, hers to maintain the house and look after the children (her children alone after several years, because the Beblow children had grown up and moved out). When they separated, after twelve years, Mrs Peter claimed that the years at home had deprived her of a college education and higher career expectations (even though the main reason that she had stayed home in the first place was to look after her own children, not Mr Beblow and his children, and the two had agreed on this arrangement from the very beginning). The Court agreed with Mrs Peter, nonetheless, that Mr Beblow had been

unjustly enriched at her expense and therefore made him pay her restitution. Brown shows that the Court's calculations were based on illogical, false, or openly biased principles (such as calculating the monetary value of services provided by Mrs Peter but not of those provided by Mr Beblow). In fact, he shows that the legal system governing cases of this kind reveal systemic discrimination against men (not merely the opinions of these justices but the laws themselves) and for explicitly political reasons (because the Court cited the "feminization of poverty" and the undervaluation of "traditional women's work" in the home as major problems to be solved by using the law in this way). In short, the system is corrupt. Some details of this case – it is taught uncritically and even sympathetically in law schools – are so preposterous, so grotesque, that we encourage readers to contact the author, at grant.brown@shaw.ca, for more information.

41 Braver refers to Martha Fineman, *The Illusion of Equality: Rhetoric and the Reality of Divorce Reform* (Chicago: University of Chicago Press, 1991); Kathleen Mahoney, "Gender Issues in Family Law: Leveling the Playing Field for Women," *Family and Conciliation Courts Review* 34 (1996): 198–218; Lenore J. Weitzman, *The Divorce Revolution: The Unexpected Social and Economic Consequences for Women and Children in America* (New York: Free Press, 1985); Terry Arendell, *Mothers and Divorce: Legal, Economic and Social Dilemmas* (Berkeley: University of California Press, 1986); *Fathers and Divorce* (Thousand Oaks, CA: Sage, 1995); and Mary Ann Mason, *The Equality Trap* (New York: Simon and Schuster, 1988).

42 Seidenberg 7.

43 See Weitzman.

44 Geoffrey Christopher Rapp, "Lies, Damned Lies, and Lenore J. Weitzman," <http://www.acbr.com/biglie.htm>: 1. This website is undated and has no name other than the title of this page.

45 Rapp 1.

46 Braver 119–21.

47 Braver 121–2.

48 Braver 114.

49 Braver 118–19.

50 Braver 116.

51 David Blankenhorn, *Fatherless America: Confronting Our Most Urgent Social Problem* (New York: Basic Books, 1995), 156–7; quoted in Braver 118.

52 The National Institute of Mental Health acknowledges that the number of male suicides per year is on average four times the number of female suicides. They explain this phenomenon in various ways. Men use guns more often than women, for instance, and are therefore successful more often. Or men are more aggressive than women ("Frequently Asked Questions," [updated] 3 January 2000, *National Institute of Mental Health*, [visited] 21 December

2002, <http://www.nimh.nih.gov/research/suicidefaq.cfm>: 1). But scholars have begun to examine variables such as marital status. Both R.G. Rogers ("Marriage, Sex, and Mortality," *Journal of Marriage and the Family* 57 [1995]: 515–26) and A.J. Kposowa ("Marital Status and Suicide in the National Longitudinal Mortality Study," *Journal of Epidemiology and Community Health* 54 [2000]: 254–61) found that divorced or separated men are much more likely than divorced or separated women to commit suicide. Because divorce often separates men from their children, observe J.S. Wallerstein and S. Blakeslee, they often experience depression, failure, and self-hatred (*Second Chances: Men, Women, and Children a Decade after Divorce* [New York: Ticknor and Fields, 1989] 235). See also J.M. Ross, *The Male Paradox* [New York: Simon and Schuster, 1992] 154–7). This topic has not yet been studied adequately, but a great deal of anecdotal evidence links divorce, custody battles, unfair child-support payments, and separation from children with depression and suicide among men. See also Associated Press [David Crary], "Divorced Fathers Snap under Pressure," *Washington Times*, 25 November 2002: A-7).

53 "These results dramatise the terrible consequences of being a divorced man in America, and lead to the question: why are divorced men killing themselves ... As Perrault and Farrell observe, while social, psychological, and even personal problems facing women are readily denounced, societal institutions tend to ignore or minimise male problems as evident in suicide statistics ... As depression and poor mental health are known markers of suicide risk, it may well be that one of the fundamental reasons for the observed association between divorce and suicide in men is the impact of post divorce (court sanctioned) 'arrangements'" (Augustine J. Kposowa, "Divorce and Suicide Risk," *Journal of Epidemiology and Community Health*, 57.12 [December 2003]: 993).

54 Baskerville, "Myth" 30.

55 Wilson, *Multiple Scandals* 20.

56 Margaret F. Brinig; quoted in Tierny B-1.

57 Ronald K. Henry, "Child Support at a Crossroads: When the Real World Intrudes upon Academic Advocates, [dated] 1999, *Alliance for Non-custodial Parents Rights*, [visited] 1 July 2002, <http://www.ancpr.org/ronhenry.htm>, 24, note 26; this article was published in *Family Law Quarterly* 33.1 (1999): 235–58.

58 Braver 23–5.

59 Braver 54.

60 For the statistical profile of an American middle-class family, see Henry.

61 In the United States, according to Rogers and Bieniewicz, there are several basic child-support models. The Wisconsin model is based on a percentage of the noncustodial parent's income; that of the custodial parent is considered irrelevant. The percentage varies according to income but increases with the number of children. Only about a dozen states use this model. The Incomes

Shares model (also known as the Robert Williams model) takes into account the incomes of both parents. It is based on the assumption that a child's standard of living should remain the same after a divorce (Wilson, *Multiple Scandals* 66). Child-support payments rise with income. About thirty-five states use this model. The Delaware-Melson model, a hybrid based on the other two, was created for welfare families. Only a few states use it (Rogers and Bienewicz 2).

62 According to Finance Canada, 99% of the money collected for child support comes from men (Cheriton 15, 23, and 33).

63 Roger Gay observes that child support has been used to prevent the impoverishment of custodial parents, usually wives. This makes it a kind of hidden alimony. Gay, who has testified in Congress, found that "traditional child support law held that to a practical extent, children should be sheltered from the standard of living loss that accompanies divorce. This led to what has been known as a standard of living adjustment or 'add-on' in some models. No one had derived a formula for calculating the amount of the adjustment, and some researchers seemed to believe such derivation impossible" (Roger F. Gay, "Child Support Project Summary," [dated] 25 May 2002, *Project for the Improvement of Child Support Litigation Technology*, [visited] 3 July 2002, <http://www.geocities.com?CapitolHIll/5910/index.html>: 2). He finds that no fair calculation is possible unless it makes a careful distinction between child support and spousal support. Hidden alimony is a very serious moral and legal problem because it involves the government in politically motivated duplicity and thus reinforces public cynicism (Gay 2). Referring to another problem, Gay observes that we need data on how much is actually spent on children, in order to develop a complete theoretical model.

64 In 1999, according to one American study, the average cost of one child was approximately $600 a month. Child tax benefits were approximately $200 a month, however, which meant that the final cost was approximately $400 a month. The average award was between $600 and $1,300 a month, nonetheless, and was paid entirely by the non-custodial parent (Wilson, *Multiple Scandals* 65; he refers to a study by the Family Economics Research Group [Department of Agriculture]. For a household with an annual income of $12,000 to $90,000, the money actually spent on one child ranged from $462 to $995 a month.)

65 According to longitudinal studies on the children of single parents, however, it has become clear that two parents are better than one. It makes sense. After all, sharing the work load and time spent with children, no matter how unequally, is surely better – and easier – than not doing so. But given the political and ideological rhetoric glorifying single mothers, saying so in public had to be supported by statistical research. Among the first to provide evidence of this kind was Barbara Dafoe Whitehead (*The Divorce Culture:*

Rethinking Our Commitments to Marriage and the Family [New York: Random House, 1996]). Here are some recent findings. The children of single parents are less likely to stay in school (Brigitte Berger, "The Social Roots of Prosperity and Liberty," *Society*, 35.3 [March-April 1998]: 44; Linda J. Waite, "Does Marriage Matter?" *Demography*, 32.4 [November 1995]: 483, 494); more likely to live in poverty (Waite 494); less likely to be adequately socialized (Sanford M. Dornbusch and others, "Single Parenthood," *Society* 30:5 (July 1996): 30); more likely to be unmarried when they have children of their own (Waite 494); and so on. According to one authority, the two-parent household is "by far the most emotionally stable and economically secure arrangement for child rearing" (Berger 44). So much for the need of children for two parents, whether biological or adoptive. What about the specific need for fathers? Among the first to discuss that was David Blankenhorn. According to Michael Gurian, at any rate "the single most important factor in determining if a male will end up incarcerated later in life is ... whether or not he has a father in the home" (*The Good Son: Shaping the Moral Development of Our Boys and Young Men* [New York: Jeremy Tarcher, 1999] 182).

66 When American noncustodial parents have their children for 20% of the time, according to Paul Henman and Kyle Mitchell, the cost is 40% of what it would be in an intact middle-income couple household and more than 50% of what it would be in an intact low-income household. This is explained by the cost of maintaining two households and of providing transportation (Paul Henman and Kyle Mitchell, "Estimating the Costs of Contact for Non-resident Parents: A Budget Standards Approach," *Journal of Social Policy* 30.3 [2001]: 495–520). Many Canadian mothers have figured out that the ideal situation is to have their former husbands care for the children 40% of the time. This way, the former remain "receiving parents" and are allowed to collect child-support payments. In addition, they reduce their own expenses. While the children are living with their fathers, after all, the latter must provide for their daily needs. And it does not work that way in reverse (Soever 26)!

67 In the United States, say Rogers and Bieniewicz, "[u]se of gross income for guidelines ignores the advantage that custodial parents receive from preferential tax treatment. This advantage typically is worth several hundred dollars in net income per month. For example, at gross income of $4,000, the custodial parent with two children has about $370 more net income per month than the noncustodial parent to support the children (roughly $4,400 after tax extra income annually). At low-income levels, the difference is quite striking. A little above the poverty level, for equal levels of gross income, the custodial parent has 30 to 50 percent more after-tax income than the non-custodial parent for which to support the children due to favorable tax treatment. On a final note regarding ability to pay near the poverty level, the above

analysis does not include discussion of other potential cost offsets that a custodial parent has that the NCP [non-custodial parent] does not have – or at least the CP has more readily. Food stamps, WIC [Women, Infants, and Children], Medicaid, housing subsidies are generally more available to the CP and are not part of the formula for sharing child costs and cost offsets with the NCP. Because of these tax code changes, for a given level of gross income, the custodial parent has a significantly higher ability to provide the CP's share of child costs compared to the NCP. Use of gross income without adjustments for sharing the child tax benefits between both parents clearly creates an unequal burden for the NCP" (Rogers and Bieniewicz 10–11). They add that "the same standard of living cannot be sustained as in an intact two-parent household. Notably, the maximum standard of living that can be maintained in both households is the average income of both parents (Rogers and Bieniewicz 16).

68 The notion of a "standard case," according to Henry, is based on the assumption that American women earn only approximately 75% of what men earn. (Henry 24, note 21). Guidelines were established on the basis of a hypothetical family consisting of a custodial parent, a noncustodial parent, and two children. Henry refers to several flawed figures. "Twenty-five percent of gross income is used as an average child support guideline amount for two children" (Henry 23, note 20). That 25% was based on the dubious figure – 75% – just mentioned. We showed in chapter 5, however, that the latter was skewed in favour of women. Besides, it would not reflect the situations of actual people involved in particular conflicts. It would surely be more fair to calculate on the basis of each case. If the woman earns more than the average woman, for instance, then that fact would be factored into the amount of child support. In other words, a just system would look at the specific earnings of both the father and the mother. Guidelines could specify amounts as percentages of actual incomes, for instance, rather than as theoretical averages.

69 Roger F. Gay, "A Return to Welfare as We Knew It: The Beginning of the End of Child Support Reform," [dated] 21 March 2002, *Project for the Improvement of Child Support Litigation Technology*, [visited] 1 July 2002; published at *Men's News Daily and Toogood Reports*, <http://www.geocities.com/capitolhill/5910/Georgia_consequences.htm>: 2.

70 Consider the case of Darrin White of Prince George, British Columbia. White "killed himself a month after a judge ordered him to make spousal and child support payments more than double his income ... White was ordered to pay $2,071 a month to support his ex-wife and three children. He was already paying $439 a month to support an older child from a previous marriage, bringing his total monthly obligations to $2,510. But White's after-tax monthly income was only $950 in disability stress pay" (Canadian Press,

"Support Payment Suicide: Man Told to Pay Twice What He Made," *Toronto Sun*, 23 March 2000: 59).

71 McLean 1. Similar things have happened elsewhere. In Britain, the National Association for Child Support Action has noted fifty-five cases of suicide ("The Book of the Dead," [undated] *National Association for Child Support Action*, [visited] 5 December 2002, <http://www.nacsa.org/>; cited in Baskerville, "Myth" 30).

72 Nicholas Riccardi and Greg Krikorion, "Failure to Provide: Los Angeles County's Child Support Crisis," *Los Angeles Times*, 11 October 1998, A-1; cited in Henry, 25, note 29.

73 Wilson, *Multiple Scandals* 44.

74 Wilson, *Multiple Scandals* 28.

75 Wilson, *Multiple Scandals* 44.

76 Baskerville, "Myth" 30.

77 According to Wilson, his company is worth $40 million and has expanded into Canada and Australia (Wilson, *Multiple Scandals*, 57). Other companies include Lockheed Martin and Maximus. "Frequently, all three child-support collection companies will not just act as administrator but adjudicator, issuing administrative child support orders. That is, they set and alter the amounts of support in cases for which they are paid a percentage of what they collect and/or a fee for opening and closing cases" (Wilson, *Multiple Scandals* 58). What about due process?

78 Baskerville, "Myth" 29.

79 "Formula for the Tables of Amounts Contained in the Federal Child Support Guidelines: A Technical Report," *Research Report* CSR-1997–1E.

80 Alar Soever, "The Federal Child Support Guidelines: A Breakdown of Democratic Process and the Canadian Legal System," [dated] 4 April 2002, *Fathers Are Capable Too*, [visited] 17 February 2004, <http://www.fact.on.ca/fathome/header.htm>: 28.

81 Soever 2.

82 Soever 18.

83 Cheriton, personal communication.

84 The English tradition of common law, stretching back five hundred years and recognized today in countries such as Britain, the United States, and Canada, presumes that any child born during a marriage is the husband's. The goal is to prevent children from being branded "illegitimate."

85 "United States Supreme Court Refuses to Hear Case of Paternity Fraud Victim," [dated] 12 June 2002, *PRWeb: The Free Wire Service*, [visited] 10 December 2002, <http://www.prweb.com/releases/2002/6/prweb40284.php>: 1.

86 "Father Takes DNA Paternity Fraud Case to U.S. Supreme Court," [dated] 31 May 2002, *Men's News Daily*, [visited] 1 July 2002, <http://www.mensnewsdaily.com'stories/newswire053102a.htm>: 1.

87 "Father Takes DNA" 1.

88 Legislation varies wildly from one of these states to another. In 1994 Illinois passed the Unlawful Visitation Interference law (Public Act 8896). By late 2002, a bill pending in Vermont would make it a felony for mothers to spread false allegations of this kind, put her in jail for up to two years, and fine her up to $5,000.

89 Martin Kasindorf, "Men Wage Battle on 'Paternity Fraud,'" USA Today, 3 December 2002: A-03.

90 Burt Riddick; quoted in Kasindorf.

91 Mary Ann Sieghart, "Women Behaving Badly," London Times, 28 November 1998: 22.

92 Baskerville, "Q" 4.

93 Baskerville, "Q" 3.

94 There is a debate over the statistics on how many men presumed to be biological fathers are, in fact, biologically unrelated to their presumed children. Carolyn Abraham writes that the lowest figure would be 5% and the highest 30%, with 15% to 18% being commonly accepted (Carolyn Abraham, "Mommy's Little Secret," Globe and Mail, 14 December 2002: F-1).

95 Cristin Schmitz, "Man Cut off from Son at Birth: Must Pay Child Support: Full Amount Owed Even Though Stepfather Also Pays, Ontario Court Orders, National Post, 6 April 2002: A-02.

96 Consider the storm of controversy that followed Vice-President Dan Quayle's comments about Murphy Brown. He was widely ridiculed for criticizing a show that allowed the leading character to bring up a baby without a father. Single mothers have been praised, moreover, on countless talk shows. But support for single motherhood by choice, which does not apply to mothers who are either widowed or abandoned, comes not only from popular culture. See below for a discussion of the Feminist International Network of Resistance to Reproductive and Genetic Engineering.

97 Sarah Schmidt, "Ontario Court Gives Mother Sole Power on Child Surname: Decision Based on Wording of Statute from Peterson Era," [dated] 28 June 2002, [no name for website], [visited] 23 September 2002, <http://www.lapresrupture.qc.ca/cpaJune28_SarahSchmidt.html>: 1; this story actually appeared in the National Post on 21 June. See Kreklewetz v. Scopel (2002) 60 O.R. (3d) 187 (C.A.).

98 Schmidt 1.

99 Schmidt 1.

100 Schmidt 2.

101 Trociuk v. British Columbia (Attorney General) 2003 S.C.C. 34. "On the basis of his sex, the impugned provisions expose the father to the possible arbitrary exclusion of his particulars from his children's birth registration, and, consequently, of his participation in choosing their surname. Moreover, having been so exposed, the father is provided no recourse. The impugned distinctions affect significant interests and do so in a way that the reasonable

claimant in the appellant's circumstances would perceive as harmful to his dignity. A birth registration is not only an instrument of prompt recording. It evidences the biological ties between parent and child, and including one's particulars on the registration is a means of affirming these ties. Contribution to the process of determining a child's surname is another significant mode of participation in the life of a child ... Arbitrary exclusion from these means of participation negatively affects an interest that is significant to a father" (*Trociuk v. British Colmbia (Attorney General)*, [visited] 16 January 2004, <http://www.lexum.unmontreal.ca/csc-scc/en/rec/texte/2003scc034.wpd.txt>. Note, however, that mothers may still refuse to acknowledge the surnames of fathers in specific circumstances – notably rape and incest.

102 Baskerville, "Q" 1–3.
103 Baskerville, "Myth" 30. The increase in the amount of money collected – it doubled between 1992 and 2000 – is accomplished not by "collecting from fathers in welfare-related cases but from increasing the number of employed, middle-class fathers" (Baskerville, "Myth" 30) and increasing the amount that each owes.
104 Robert O'Harrow, "Uncle Sam Has All Your Numbers: Huge Net for Deadbeat Dads Catches Privacy Criticism," *Washington Post*, 27 June 1999: A-01; quoted in Baskerville, "Myth" 30.
105 Steve Dasbach, Libertarian Party press release, 11 February 1998; quoted in Baskerville, "Myth" 30.
106 Baskerville, "Myth" 31.
107 Baskerville, "Q" 2–3.
108 Baskerville, "Myth" 28.
109 Seidenberg 48–9.
110 "About," [undated], *National Child Support Enforcement Association*, [visited] 3 July 2002, <http://www.ncsea.org/about>, quoted in Baskerville, "Myth" 28.
111 Baskerville, "Myth" 28.
112 Baskerville, "Myth" 28–9.
113 F.L. Morton and Rainer Knopff, *The Charter Revolution and the Court Party* (Toronto: Broadview Press, 2000) 107.
114 Seidenberg 11.
115 Gene Colman; cited in "Fathers Lose in Family Court Because of Judicial Interpretation Says Respected Family Law Lawyer," [undated], *Canada Court Watch Report*, [visited] 9 December 2002, <http://www.shareparenting.com>: 1.
116 Carey Linde; quoted in "Fathers Lose" 1.
117 Linde; quoted in "Fathers Lose" 1–2.
118 Edward Greenspan; quoted in "Fathers Lose" 2.
119 Other books include the following: Jeffrey Leving and Kenneth Dachman, *Fathers' Rights: Hard Hitting and Fair Advice for Every Father Involved in a Custody Dispute* (New York: Basic Books, 1997); John Steinbreder and

Richard Kent, *Fighting for Your Children: A Father's Guide to Custody* (Dallas: Taylor, 1998); Douglas Darnall, *Divorce Casualties: Protecting Children from Parental Alienation* (Dallas: Taylor, 1998); Richard Warshak, *Divorce Poison: Protecting the Parent-Child Bond from a Vindictive Ex* (New York: ReganBooks, 2001); Richard Gardner, *The Parental Alienation Syndrome: A Guide For Mental Health and Legal Professionals* (Cresskill, NJ: Creative Therapeutics, 1998); Ashton Applewhite, *Cutting Loose: Why Women Who End Their Marriages Do So Well* (New York: HarperCollins, 1997); and Carleen Brennan and Michael Brennan, *Custody for Fathers: A Practical Guide through the Combat Zone of a Brutal Custody Battle* (Costa Mesa, CA: Brennan, 1994). The latter is a typical how-to manual: how to beat a system, legally, that is stacked against fathers. It includes advice on how to win custody, warnings against procedural errors, definitions of legal jargon, discussions of the psychology of judges, suggestions for clothing to be worn in court, insights on body language, and so on. Unlike some guides, this one avoids a polemical tone and advises readers to work within the system. It compares the problem to a football game, which requires strategies and counterstrategies.

120 "Canadian Families against Abuse by the Legal System," [updated] 23 July 2002, *Surviving the Horrors of Canada's Morally Corrupt Family Court Legal System*, [visited] 9 December 2002, <http://sharedparent.freeyellow.com/SurvivingTheHorrorsOfFamilyCourt.pdf>.

121 "Canadian Families" 1.

122 Paula Roberts, "[An Ounce of Prevention and a Pound of Cure:] Developing State Policy on the Payment of Child Support Arrears [by Low-income Parents]," [dated] May 2001, *Alliance for Non-Custodial Parents Rights*, [visited] 1 July 2002; published by the Charles Stewart Mott Foundation, the Ford Foundation, the Public Welfare Foundation, the Moriah Fund, and the Open Society Institute, <http://www.ancpr.org/developing_state_policy_on_the_p.htm>: 6.

123 *United States v. Timothy Gordon Faase*, 265 F.3d 475 (2001). Glenn Reynolds argues that the framers of the Constitution wanted strict limitations on federal powers and that these were gradually increased by exploiting the Commerce Clause to regulate things other than commerce. This strategy received its first setback in the case of *United States v. Lopez*, 514 U.S. 549 (1995), when the "Court of Appeals for the Fifth Circuit struck down the 1990 Gun-Free School Zones Act, finding it beyond the power of Congress to enact. Such a finding is all but unheard of in the post-New Deal era" (Glenn Harlan Reynolds, "Kids, Guns, and the Commerce Clause: Is the Court Ready for Constitutional Government?" [dated] 10 October 1994, *Cato Institute: Policy Analysis*, 216, [visited] 23 September 2002, <http://www.cato.org/pubs/pas/pa-216.html>: 1.

A second rebuff to the overextension of the Commerce Clause occurred in

United States v. Morrison, 529 U.S. 598 (2000). Christy Brzonkkala alleged "that she was raped by respondents while the three were students at the Virginia Polytechnic Institute and that this attack violated 42 U.S.C.§13981, which provides a federal civil remedy for the victims of gender-motivated violence" ("United States v. Morrison et al.," [undated], *FindLaw*, [visited] 31 December 2002, <http://caselaw.lp.findlaw.com/cgi-bin/getcase.pl?court=US&navby=case&vol=000&invol=99>: 1). This section was part of the Violence against Women Act of 1994. Her case was argued by the government, which intervened to "defend the section's constitutionality." The majority opinion, citing *Lopez* as a precedent, upheld the district court's view that "Congress lacked authority to enact §13981 under either §8 of the Commerce Clause or §5 of the Fourteenth Amendment, which Congress had explicitly identified as the sources of federal authority for §13981" (*Find-Law* 1).

124 *Contino v. Leonelli-Contino* (2003), 67 O.R. (3d) 703 (C.A.).
125 Karen M. Weiler and Marc Rosenberg, "Contino v. Leonelli-Contino," [dated] 28 October 2003, *Court of Appeal for Ontario*, [visited] 16 January 2004, <http://www.ontariocourts.on.ca/decisions/2003/october/continoC39928.htm>.
126 McLean 4.
127 Rogers and Bieniewicz 11.
128 This model uses "actual costs as measured by surveys" rather than indirect estimation and theoretical concepts. It is based on surveys of single-parent households, moreover, and not of intact ones. "Similarly, the appropriate income used in the support tables is average gross income of the two parents instead of combined income. The Cost Shares methodology explicitly shares between the parents both child costs and child cost offsets. An explicit measure of child-related tax benefits is used as a cost offset as an intermediate step in determining the economically appropriate child support award ... The Cost Shares model has components for various major child cost categories. These are housing, food, transportation, clothing, health, child care and education, and 'other.' Each category is based on an average of the expenditures by category from survey data" (Rogers and Bieniewicz 11). This new method of calculating the cost of child support, which avoids many of the problems inherent in earlier ones, establishes basic costs "for a single-parent household using an average of both parents' income as the income factor. The basic child support table has child costs for a single-parent household according to gross income" (Rogers and Bieniewicz 13). It adds other expenses when necessary. The new method deducts from the tax benefit that a custodial parent receives. And it "allocates the net child cost obligation (net of tax benefits) between the two parents based on each parent's share of combined after-tax income that is above a recommended self-support level" (Rogers and Bieniewicz 14). "Families within the survey

varied as to whether they spent specifically on day-care or medical insurance. While the medical insurance likely averaged a small figure, the child care figure is quite significant. With the new category for 'child care and education,' it is easy to exclude this category from the total and to treat child care and education as an 'add-on' in the Cost Shares model ... Importantly, explicit dollar values for a presumptive award by category allow for a specific basis for rebutting the presumption"(Rogers and Bieniewicz 13).

129   "Building Child Support Science from First Principles," [dated] 7 September 1999, *Project for the Improvement of Child Support Litigation Technology*, [visited] 1 July 2002, <http://www.geocities.com/CapitolHill/5910/principles.html>: 1.

130   "Building" 2, 5.

131   In marital relationships, which fall under federal jurisdiction, payments end only when children leave school. This could be many years after they become young men and women. In common-law relationships, which fall under provincial jurisdiction, the obligation for child support ends when children come of age.

132   Soever 26–9.

133   *Francis v. Baker*, [1999] 3 S.C.R. 250; cited in Soever 3.

134   Soever is referring to the Supreme Court's interpretation of section 26.1(2) in the Divorce Act of 1985. This appears in its decision on *Francis v. Baker* (1999). "In some cases," according to section 41, "courts may conclude that the applicable Guideline figure is so in excess of the children's reasonable needs that it must be considered to be a functional wealth transfer to a parent or de facto spousal support. I wholly agree with the sentiment of Abella J.A. that courts should not be too quick to find that the Guideline figures enter the realm of wealth transfers or spousal support." Courts must be flexible about applying the Guidelines, in other words. This is made clear in the summary, too: "A broad interpretation of the word 'inappropriate' in s.4 does not deny children of high income parents any of the intended benefits of the Guidelines because these have not displaced the *Divorce Act*, which clearly dictates that maintenance of the children, rather than household equalization or spousal support, is the objective of child support payments. In order to recognize that objective, as well as to implement the fairness and flexibility components of the Guidelines' objectives, courts must therefore have the discretion to remedy situations where Table amounts are so in excess of the children's reasonable needs that they no longer qualify as child support." Because this case refers to "reasonable support" in the context of wealth, however, the matter is still unclear. What about "reasonable support" in the context of relative poverty? Is it *ever* permissible for child support to be used as spousal support?

135   Seidenberg 182–3.

136 The celebration of Mother's Day is an annual extravaganza in many newspapers. Whole pages are devoted to this secular (and commercial) festival ("Your Moms, Your Muses," *Montreal Gazette*, 5 May 2003: D-1; Lisa Fetterman, "Can't a Breast Be Just a Breast?" *Montreal Gazette*, 5 May 2003: D-2; "Your Mothers, in Your Own Words," *Montreal Gazette*, 5 May 2003: D-3). This is reflected, of course, in the television schedule; many shows feature special episodes for the occasion.

137 Janet Bagnall, "Helping Single Parents," *Montreal Gazette*, 31 January 2003: A-19.

138 Bagnall A-19.

139 Susanne Hiller, "And Baby Makes Two: With the Ticking of Their Biological Clocks Growing Ever Louder, More and More Women Are Deciding to Have Children on Their Own through Insemination from an Anonymous Donor," *National Post*, 17 January 2004: SP1, SP6.

140 Jane Mattes; noted in Hiller SP6.

141 Cathy Ruberto, quoted in Hiller SP6.

142 Hiller SP6.

143 Hiller SP6.

144 On single mothers in particular, for instance, see Jane Mattes, *Single Mothers by Choice: A Guidebook for Single Women Who Are Considering or Have Chosen Motherhood* (New York: Times Books, 1994); Joan Anderson, *The Single Mother's Book: A Practical Guide to Managing Your Children, Career, Home, Finances, and Everything Else* (Atlanta, GA: Peachtree, 1990); Bobbie Reed, *Single Mothers Raising Sons* (Nashville, TN: T. Nelson, 1988); Patrice Karst, *The Single Mother's Survival Guide* (Freedom, CA: Crossing Press, 2000); and Marsha R. Leslie, ed., *Single Mother's Companion: Essays and Stories by Women* (Seattle, WA: Seal Press, 1994). On single parents in general (including single mothers), see Marge M. Kenndy and Janet Spencer, *The Single-Parent Family: Living Happily in a Changing World* (New York: Crown, 1994); Shirley M.H. Hanson, ed., *Single Parent Families: Diversity, Myths, and Realities* (New York: Haworth, 1995); Sharon Yoder, *The Single Parent Guidebook: Up, Up and a Way to Personal Fulfillment* (Georgetown, DE: Fruit-Bearer Publishing, 2000); Marion Peterson and Diane Warner, *Single Parenting for Dummies* (New York: Wiley, 2003); Ruth Bowdoin, *The Single Parent* (Brentwood, TN: Webster's International, 1990); Karin L. Swisher, ed., *Single Parent Families* (San Diego, CA: Greenhaven Press, 1997); Richard Worth, *Single-Parent Families* (New York: F. Watts, 1992); Thomas D. Yawkey and Georgianna M. Cornelius, eds., *The Single Parent Family: For Helping Professionals and Parents* (Lancaster, PA: Technomic, 1990); Timothy Scott, *The Single Parent Family Guide: How to Raise Your Family Strong* (Springfield, MA: Public Information Center, 2001); Brook Noel and Art Klein, *The Single Parent Resource* (Beverly Hills, CA: Champion Press, 1998); Brenda Elwell, *The Single Parent Travel Handbook*

(Seacaucus, NJ: GlobalBrenda, 2002); Saran Pirch, ed., *Single Parents: The Golden Rules for Raising Children Alone* (Los Angeles: General, 1994); Karen L. Kinnear, *Single Parents: A Reference Handbook* (Santa Barbara, CA: ABC-CLIO, 1999); Linda Foust, *The Single Parent Almanac: Real-World Answers to Your Everyday Questions* (Rocklin, CA: Prima, 1996); André Bustanoby, *Single Parenting* (Grand Rapids, MI: Zondervan, 1992); Jane Hannah and Dick Stafford, *Single Parenting with Dick and Jane* (Nashville, TN: Family Touch Press, 1993); and Sara Dulaney, *The Complete Idiot's Guide to Single Parenting* (New York: Alpha Books, 1998).

145 Jane Bock; quoted in Cindy Rodriguez, "Single, Pregnant and Proud of It," *Montreal Gazette*, 10 February 2003: D-3.

146 Bock D-3.

147 Surrogacy sounds like a new idea, and it has not been common in our society for a long time. Nevertheless, women bore children for other women (and their husbands) in ancient Israel, ancient India, and elsewhere. Only one aspect of modern surrogacy is new: using artificial insemination to get the sperm.

148 Gena Corea, *The Mother Machine: Reproductive Technologies from Artificial Insemination to Artificial Wombs* (New York: Harper and Row, 1985).

CHAPTER SEVEN

1 Andrea Dworkin, "Suffering and Speech," in *In Harm's Way: The Pornography Civil Rights Hearings*, ed. Catharine A. MacKinnon and Andrea Dworkin (Cambridge: Harvard University Press, 1997) 25.

2 Helen Fisher, *Why We Love: The Nature and Chemistry of Romantic Love* (New York: Henry Holt, 2004) 110 (her emphasis).

3 Ken Tucker, "Rich Man, Poor SOBs: Donald Trump Lords over a Group of Eager Apprentices, and Viewers Reap the Rewards," *Entertainment Weekly*, 13 February 2004: 63.

4 Andrea Dworkin and Catharine A. MacKinnon, "Pornography and Civil Rights: A New Day for Women's Equality," [dated] 1988, *Andrea Dworkin Web Site*, <http://www.nostatusquo.com?ACLU/dworkin/other/ordinance/ new-day/T2b.htm>: 1.

5 See "Federal Statutes Relating to Crimes Against Children," *Crimes against Children*, [undated] Federal Bureau of Investigation, [visited] 21 June 2002, <http://www.fbi.gov/hq/cid/cac/federal.htm>: 2–8.

6 *United States of America v. David Hilton* no. 98–1513, United States Court of Appeals for the First Circuit.

7 *Ashcroft, (A.G.) v. Free Speech Coalition*, 353 U.S. 234 (2002).

8 "Ashcroft, Attorney General, et al. *v.* Free Speech Coalition et al," [undated] LII [Legal Information Institute][visited] 17 February 2004, <http://supct.law.cornell.edu/supct/html/00–795.LS.html>: 3–4.

9 "Division A – Trafficking Victims Protection Act of 2000," *Violence against Women Office*, 18 June 2002, United States Department of Justice, Office of Justice Programs, 24 June 2002, <http://www.ojp.usdoj.gov/vawo/laws/ vawo2000/stitle_a.htm>.

10 "Division A" 1–2. The Victims of Trafficking and Violence Prevention Act, moreover, held that existing legislation and law enforcement did not acknowledge the gravity of these offenses and were unable either to deter trafficking or to punish traffickers with suitably strong penalties. To improve this situation and make the reduction of trafficking a priority, it mandated the following: an interagency task force, with members appointed by the president and including the secretary of state, to collect and organize data, consult governmental or nongovernmental agencies, and so forth; a special office within the secretary of state; educational and economic opportunities, including programs to promote women's participation in economic decision making, for victims and *potential* victims; assistance, including resettlement, through development agencies to victims in foreign countries; assistance to foreign countries, threatening loss of economic aid to those that fail to comply; special benefits or services to victims – even aliens – in the United States, which could be enhanced by special grants from the attorney general; and special "training" for government personnel.

11 Street prostitution is illegal in Nevada, but brothels are legal (although small counties are allowed to prohibit them). Prostitutes have ninety-day licenses from specific counties and work on three-week shifts (with one week off between each). The Board of Health requires them to use condoms in licensed brothels and to be tested regularly: every week for gonorrhea and every month for syphilis and HIV. Those infected by gonorrhea or syphilis may not work until they have received medical treatment and can show negative test results. Those who still show positive results may no longer work as prostitutes. Various security systems (including proximity to police offices, security fences, and guards) protect them from unwanted customers and violence. The cost of protection, however, is a loss of freedom. They may not leave their brothels without chaperones, for instance. And when they do leave, they may not go just anywhere. Prostitutes pay as much as 40% of their earnings, plus room and board, to brothel owners. In addition, they pay for all medical tests. And they receive no benefits packages. ("Report and Recommendations in Respect of Legislation, Policy and Practices Concerning Prostitution-Related Activities," [updated] 5 February 2004, *Department of Justice Canada*, [visited] 9 February 2004, <http://canada.justice.gc.ca/en/news/nr/ 1998/part3.html>:30). Advocacy groups complain, not surprisingly, that prostitutes are exploited by state interference.

12 *Criminal Code [of Canada]*, R.S.C. 1985, c. C-46, s. 163, Part V: Sexual Offences, Public Morals and Disorderly Conduct," *CanLII* [Canadian Legal Information Institute], [visited] 11 February 2004, <http://www.canlii.org/ca/ sta/c-46/sec163.html>.

13 Bill C-15A.

14 Kirk Makin, "Child-Porn Bill Would Narrow Legal Defence," *Globe and Mail*, 11 February 2004: A-7.

15 *R. v. Sharpe*, [2001] 1 S.C.R. 45; cited in Makin A-7.

16 "Report" 26.

17 John Lowman, *Prostitution Law Reform in Canada* [dated] 1997, [visited] 10 February 2004, <http://mypage.uniserve.ca/~lowman/ProLaw/prolawcan. htm>: 1.

18 Lowman 7.

19 Lowman 22 note 3; he refers to the following: *R. v. Skinner* (1987), 35 C.C.C. (3d) 203, 58 C.R. (3d) 137, 79 N.S.R. (2d) 8; overd); *Stagnitta* (1987), 36 C.C.C. (3d) 105, 43 D.L.R. (4th) 111, 58 C.R. (3d) 164 (Alta. C.A.) and *Reference Re Sections 193 and 195.1(1)(c) of the Criminal Code*, 56 C.C.C. (3d).

20 *Criminal Code [of Canada]*, R.S.C. 1985, c. C-46, s. 210–213, Part VII: Disorderly Houses, Gaming and Betting," [updated] 31 August 2003, *Department of Justice Canada*, [visited] 10 February 2004, <http://laws.justice.gc.ca/en/c-46/41639.html>: 18–20.

21 Indictable offenses, by contrast, are higher offenses and heard by judges and juries.

22 [Federal-Provincial-Territorial Working Group] "Report and Recommendations in Respect of Legislation, Policy and Practices concerning Prostitution-Related Activities," [updated] 5 February 2004, *Department of Justice Canada*, [visited] 10 February 2004, http://canada.justice.gc.ca/en/news/nr/ 1998/part3.html. This document originated in 1998.

23 "Report" 27.

24 "Report" 29.

25 It has always been hard to convict pimps, because most prostitutes are afraid to testify against them.

26 Complicating this discussion is the fact that violence against female prostitutes seems to be rising in British Columbia. According to Lowman, the law marginalizes these women, pushing them "out of residential areas into darkly lit industrial back streets" (Lowman 21) or country roads. But is the number of murders really rising, or has it been inflated because of one horrific series of murders? Police discovered a huge number of bodies buried on a farm near Vancouver, but they were all women who had been murdered by a single person. Robert William Pickton, if convicted, would take his place as the worst serial killer in Canadian history (Philip Saunders and Justin Thompson, "The Missing Women of Vancouver," [dated] 7 February 2004, CBC [Canadian Broadcasting Corporation] *News*, <http://www.cbc.ca/news/ features/bc_missingwomen.html>).

27 "Report" 29.

28 This solution involved a change from the type of offence regulated by 213, from summary to the more serious "hybrid" one, which means a judge must

decide the level of offense. In this case, the police need not catch people in the act of sex or of arranging to have sex; the police would need only "reasonable grounds to believe" that they either have done so or are likely to do so in the immediate future ("Report" 4). Lowman studied the statistics on offences and sentences. At first, despite variation across the country, more prostitutes than customers were charged. But by the 1990s, he adds, the reverse was true. "'The change shows officers now recognize sex workers are actually victims and police resources are better spent pursuing johns and pimps. In the past, prostitutes have been penalized, jailed, fined and shifted from neighborhood to neighborhood, but no concentrated effort was made to go after the customers, and we firmly believe that these men are predators.' Vancouver's Mayor, Philip Owen, agreed: 'I think the whole thing is to rescue the women'" (K. Pemberton, "Policy Not to Arrest Constitutes First in Canada," *Vancouver Sun*, 18 February 1997: B-1; quoted in Lowman 14).

29 "Report" 12.
30 "Report" 13.
31 "Report" 4–5.
32 "Report" 6.
33 "Report" 16.
34 "Report" 23.
35 "Report" 24.
36 "Report" 9.
37 Lowman 13.
38 "Report" 23.
39 "Report" 24.
40 In jurisprudence, MacKinnon has become a feminist icon. With a BA from Smith, a JD from Yale Law School, and a PHD in political science from the University of Michigan, she is the Elizabeth A. Long Professor of Law at the University of Michigan and has taught at other prestigious law schools in the United States and elsewhere: the University of Chicago, Yale, Harvard, Stanford, the University of Minnesota, the University of California at Los Angeles, the University of Toronto, and the University of Basel. In 1978, she was admitted to the Connecticut Bar and in 1986 to that of the Supreme Court. MacKinnon has crafted two major legal doctrines: that sexual harassment is a form of sex discrimination and that porn is a violation of human rights. In 1986 the Supreme Court accepted her theory of sexual harassment. She has been even more successful in Canada, though, where she has worked closely with the feminist Legal Education and Action Fund (LEAF) and has influenced Canada's Supreme Court with her views on equality, porn, and hate speech (Kristin Switala, ed., "Catharine MacKinnon," [dated] 1999, *Feminist Theory Website*, [visited] 23 October 2002, <http://www.cddc.vt.edu/feminism/MacKinnon.html>: 1). She has been active in both countries on behalf of feminists as lead counsel or co-counsel, author of briefs or affidavits, expert witness,

consultant, and so on. MacKinnon has almost single-handedly changed the legal landscape and therefore the cultural landscape as well. Given her predilection for conflating quite different phenomena, her influence extends from porn and sexual harassment to legislation on rape and various other crimes.

In addition, MacKinnon has published a great deal. Her books alone include *In Harm's Way: The Pornography Civil Rights Hearings and Pornography*, ed. with Andrea Dworkin (Cambridge: Harvard University Press, 1997); *Civil Rights: A New Day for Women's Equality*, with Andrea Dworkin (Minneapolis: Organizing against Pornography, 1988); *Only Words* (Cambridge: Harvard University Press, 1993); *Toward a Feminist Theory of the State* (Cambridge: Harvard University Press, 1989); *Feminism Unmodified: Discourses on Life and Law* (Cambridge: Harvard University Press, 1989); *Sexual Harassment of Working Women: A Case of Sex Discrimination*, with Thomas Emerson (New Haven, CT: Yale University Press, 1979); and *The Case for Women's Equality: The Federation of Woman Teachers' Associations of Ontario and the Canadian Charter of Rights and Freedoms*, with M. Eberts and others (Toronto: The Federation, 1991).

41 Dworkin is neither a lawyer nor an academic. Like MacKinnon, however, she is an expert when it comes to rhetoric. She is even better known than MacKinnon, in fact, due to her predilection for highly articulate and quotable rabble rousing. Consider the first epigraph of this chapter, for instance, where she implies (among other dubious things) that "normal men" are "rapists," that "hatred of women" is "accepted" and "unchallenged." Dworkin is often accused of manhating (that is, of misandry), although her followers have tried hard to refute that accusation. On this topic, see Nikki Craft, "The Lie Detector," [undated], *No Status Quo*, [visited] 16 January 2003, <http://www.nostatusquo.com/ACLU/dworkin/LieDetect.html>. Not one of the items refuted, however, is about hatred as such; each is about something that could be linked to hatred. According to one possible lie, Dworkin is "antisex." No, says the site, "her early fiction is especially rich with narration about both lesbian and heterosexual lovemaking (Craft 1). But Craft says nothing about her later work. Besides, fictional accounts do not necessarily imply approval or disapproval. According to another possible lie, Dworkin considers it legitimate for battered women to kill their partners. This, says Craft, is true. Dworkin said precisely that in 1991 at a conference on women and mental health. Craft offers no comment, however, on whether vigilantism is compatible with the rule of law. Consider the following passage: "It is fine for her [the victim of porn, although the context makes it clear that porn and rape are synonymous] to hate those who ripped into her if hate keeps her willing to talk, unwilling to let silence bury her again" (Dworkin, "Suffering and Speech" 34). Dworkin is probably referring directly to anger rather than

hatred. Indirectly, though, it probably amounts to hatred – that is, to the cultural propagation and institutionalization of hostility toward a specific group of people (usually, though by no means always, based on biological characteristics). Hatred for her is merely the political means to an ideological end.

42 Dworkin is MacKinnon's close friend and political ally. Due to their close collaboration, it is very hard to speak of one without the other. Educated during the 1960s at Bennington College in Vermont, known for its leftist politics and bohemianism, Dworkin became a feminist activist and writer. Along with essays and articles, especially on porn, she has written several works of nonfiction, including *Letters from a War Zone* (New York: Lawrence Hill, 1993); *Intercourse* (New York: Simon and Schuster, 1997); *Right-Wing Women* (New York: Perigee Books, 1983); *Pornography: Men Possessing Women* (New York: Dutton, 1989); *Our Blood: Prophecies and Discourses on Sexual Politics* (New York: Harper and Row, 1976); *Woman Hating* (New York: Dutton, 1974); and *Life and Death* (New York: Free Press, 1997). Her point of view, she notes, is based on the personal experience of being "finger-raped" at the age of nine by a stranger; being physically abused by male doctors performing an internal exam on her (when she was jailed during a protest against the Vietnam War), and being a battered wife. Dworkin's nonfiction is based on her personal experiences as a "survivor," she claims, not ideology.

Her fiction goes far beyond the personal, she claims also, because it mixes intellect, imagination, emotion, the collective nature of women's experience, and the literary process itself. Here are some titles: *Mercy* (New York: Four Walls Eight Windows, 1980); *Ice and Fire* (New York: Weidenfeld and Nicolson, 1987); and *The New Womans Broken Heart: Short Stories* (East Palo Alto, CA: Frog in the Well, 1980).

43 MacKinnon, *Toward* 248. See also Wendy McElroy, "Does Rape Violate the Commerce Clause of the Constitution?" [dated] 3 July 2002, *WendyMcElroy.co: A Site for Individualist Feminism and Individualist Anarchism,* [visited] 1 June 2002, <http://www.zetetics.com/mac/articles/brzonkala.html>: 3; this article appeared also in *Ideas on Liberty,* 50.1 (2000).

44 MacKinnon, "The Roar on the Other Side of Silence," in *In Harm's Way: The Pornography Civil Rights Hearings,* ed. Catharine A. MacKinnon and Andrea Dworkin (Cambridge, MA: Harvard University Press, 1997) 18–19.

45 MacKinnon, "Roar," 11–12; see also Andrea Dworkin, "Suffering and Speech," in *In Harm's Way: The Pornography Civil Rights Hearings,* ed. Catharine A. MacKinnon and Andrea Dworkin (Cambridge, MA: Harvard University Press, 1997) 25–6.

46 MacKinnon, "Roar" 20–1.

47 MacKinnon, *Toward* ix–xi; see also 1–80.

48 Dworkin, "Suffering" 35.

49 Dworkin, "Suffering" 28–9.

50 Nonetheless, MacKinnon points out that her legal battles have led to "professional shunning and blacklisting, attacks on employment and publishing, deprivation of research and grant funding, public demonization, litigation and threats of litigation, and physical assault" (MacKinnon, "Roar" 18–19).

51 Martha C. Nussbaum, *Sex and Social Justice* (Oxford: Oxford University Press, 1999) 155.

52 Nussbaum 181.

53 Andrea Dworkin; quoted in Philip Elmer-Dewitt, "On a Screen Near You," *Time*, 3 July 1995: 43.

54 Dworkin, "Suffering" 35.

55 Dworkin, "Suffering" 25.

56 Dworkin, "Suffering" 35–6.

57 Dworkin, "Suffering" 35–6.

58 Andrea Dworkin and Catharine A. MacKinnon, "Findings," [dated] 1988, *Pornography and Civil Rights: A New Day for Women's Equality*, [visited] 8 March 2003, <http://www.nostatusquo.com?ACLU/dworkin/other/ordinance/newday/T2b.htm>: 1.

59 James B. Jacobs and Kimberly Potter, *Hate Crimes: Criminal Law and Identity Politics* (Oxford: Oxford University Press, 1998) 120.

60 *Hudnut v. American Booksellers Assoc.*, 475 U.S. 1001 (1986).

61 Andrea Dworkin and Catharine A. MacKinnon, "The Antipornography Civil Rights Ordinance: A Brief Description,"[dated] 30 September 2001, *No Status Quo*, ed. Nikki Craft, [visited] 8 March 2003, <http://www.nostatusquo.com/ACLU/dworkin/OrdinanceBriefDescription.html>: 1.

62 Andrea Dworkin and Catharine A. MacKinnon, "Causes of Action," [dated] 1988, *Pornography and Civil Rights: A New Day for Women's Equality*, [visited] 8 March 2003, <http://www.nostatusquo.com?ACLU/dworkin/other/ordinance/newday/T2d.htm>: 1.

63 Minneapolis Ordinance, 1983, section 3, subsection 1; quoted in *In Harm's Way* 428, 435.

64 MacKinnon, "Roar" 17–24.

65 Switala 6.

66 *Louis Robinson v. Jacksonville Shipyards Inc.*, 760 F. Supp. 1486 (1991).

67 *R. v. Keegstra* [1990] 3 S.C.R. 697.

68 A factum is a document filed to set out the claim, defense, projection, and so on for either defense or prosecution.

69 Catharine A. MacKinnon and Andrea Dworkin, "Statement by Catharine A. MacKinnon and Andrea Dworkin Regarding Canadian Customs and Legal Approaches to Pornography," in *No Status Quo* 1.

70 Christopher P. Manfredi, *The Canadian Feminist Movement, Constitutional Politics, and the Strategic Use of Legal Resources* (Vancouver: Simon Fraser

University and University of British Columbia, Centre for the Study of Government and Business, 2000) 36.

71 *R. v. Butler*, [1992] 1 S.C.R. 452.

72 Manfredi 37.

73 Manfredi 37.

74 *Butler* at 464.

75 *Butler* at 485. The Supreme Court does not accept all cases, and we have no reason to assume that it would accept one about allegedly harmful effects of pornography on men. Judging from *Butler*, in fact, it probably would not. Sexual equality could remain an abstraction, in other words, unless the entire legal system – including everyone who interprets and enforces the law – chooses to make it a reality. Our contention in this book is that, the Charter notwithstanding, Canadian men face *systemic* discrimination.

76 Manfredi 37–8.

77 MacKinnon and Dworkin, "Statement" 3.

78 Catharine Mackinnon; quoted in Nadine Strossen, *Defending Pornography: Free Speech, Sex, and the Fight for Women's Rights* (Toronto: Scribner, 1995) 229.

79 MacKinnon; quoted in Strossen 229.

80 MacKinnon and Dworkin, "Statement" 1.

81 MacKinnon and Dworkin, "Statement" 2.

82 "There has been a growing recognition in recent cases that material which may be said to exploit sex in a 'degrading or dehumanizing' manner will necessarily fail the community standards test, not because it offends against morals but because it is perceived by public opinion to be harmful to society, particularly women" (*R v. Butler* [1992] 1 S.C.R., [visited] 27 December 2003, <http://www.lexum.umontreal.ca/csc-scc/en/pub/1992/vol1/html/1992scr1_0452.html>:454. We are not sure about the title of this site, which seems to be a transcription from a written document. The page quoted has no title or date.)

83 Gloria Steinem, "Hollywood Cleans Up Hustler," *New York Times*, 7 January 1997: A-17.

84 Steinem A-17.

85 Philip Elmer-Dewitt, "On a Screen near You," *Time*, 3 July 1995: 43. For practical reasons, many feminists have adopted what amounts to an anti-sex or neo-puritanical position (which we discuss in chapter 8). Hence their demands for "sexual correctness." For ideological reasons, however, many feminists have adopted the opposite position. They argue – ironically agreeing with some misogynistic theologians and philosophers, albeit for different reasons – that women have some innate affinity for the material, the carnal, the physical, or the immanent. Only men, they believe, are fixated on the immaterial, the spiritual, the intellectual, or the transcendent. What they mean is that women, supposedly being more concerned than men with the things of this world, are more life-affirming and "nurturing" than men. Among the more

famous advocates of this profoundly dualistic approach is Marilyn French. See her *Beyond Power: On Women, Men, and Morals* (New York: Ballantine, 1985).

86 Although gnosticism influenced Judaism during the Hellenistic period, it never had the massive impact on Judaism that it did on Christianity, because the Hellenistic period was only one period among many in the history of Judaism. It was the founding period, however, of Christianity. The Hebrew Bible (including the Torah) had been orally transmitted, written down, and edited much earlier. Not surprisingly, it evokes a very different attitude toward the material world – including sex, marriage, and the family.

87 Martha C. Nussbaum, *Sex and Social Justice* (Oxford: Oxford University Press, 1999).

88 Catharine A. MacKinnon; quoted in Nussbaum 214.

89 Nussbaum 77.

90 American society is ambivalent about sex and prudery. The latter has a long and unbroken tradition, which surfaces occasionally, especially in times of crisis or when people are provided with an ideological excuse for it. But the sexual revolution has made deep inroads.

91 Martin Buber, *I and Thou*, tr. Walter Kaufmann (New York: Scribner, 1970).

92 Throughout this trilogy, we argue that the end cannot justify the means. (We identify the belief that ends can justify means with ideologies of both the left and the right). And yet we argue here that people may, in some situations, be legitimately "used," "exploited" or "objectified" as the means to other ends. But the inconsistency is more apparent than real. When people say that "ends cannot justify the means," they are using an abbreviation. The whole expression would make it clear that *good* ends cannot justify *evil* means. The question here is whether sexual activity is an evil means. We say no, not necessarily. There are evils *associated* with both porn and prostitution, to be sure, and *those* should be eliminated.

93 Wendy McElroy, *XXX: A Woman's Right to Pornography* (New York: St Martin's Press, 1995).

94 Jacobs and Potter 128. "Passing hate crime laws is now the fallback position for those who wish to denounce prejudiced and bigoted thought and expression via criminal law. By linking hate speech prohibitions to generic criminal law, many well-meaning advocacy groups and politicians seek to shake a fist at the kind of ideas, opinions, and degenerate personalities that 'right-thinking' people abhor. But we must consider whether punishing crimes motivated by politically unpopular beliefs more severely than crimes motivated by other factors itself violates our First Amendment traditions ... In *Wisconsin v. Mitchell*, the Supreme Court drew a sharp line between laws that punish expression per se and those that punish expression that manifests itself in, or is integrally connected to, criminal conduct. Laws that punish expression itself are constitutionally unacceptable, but laws that punish expression linked to

criminal conduct are constitutionally acceptable. Thus, federal and state legislatures have a green light to target politically unpopular prejudices for more severe punishment, whenever these prejudices can be linked to a generic crime" (Jacobs and Potter 128).

95 Jacobs and Potter 121.

96 F.L. Morton and Rainer Knopff, *The Charter Revolution and the Court Party* (Peterborough, ON: Broadview Press, 2000) 66.

97 Alan Borovoy, *The New Anti-Liberals* (Toronto: Canadian Scholars' Press, 1999).

98 Morton and Knopff 15–26.

99 Fisher 110 (her emphasis).

100 Susan G.E. Frayser, *Varieties of Sexual Experience: An Anthropological Perspective on Human Sexuality* (New Haven, CT: HRAS Press, 1985) 9–11.

101 G. Robina Quale, *A History of Marriage Systems* (New York: Greenwood Press, 1988).

102 Nussbaum's position is odd, if you think about it, in view of her belief that female eroticism is a good thing and should never have been repressed in the first place.

103 Inherent in play, therefore, are two seemingly opposed outcomes: unruliness and rebelliousness or even violence on the one hand, imagination and curiosity on the other. The two are only "seemingly" opposed, because the latter would be impossible without some measure of the former.

104 Japan has tried to have it both ways. It could adapt with great speed and relative ease to modernity, an adaptation of colossal proportions, but largely because it carefully maintained traditional social structures at the same time. The corporation and even the state became surrogate families, evoking both loyalty and duty. The system worked very well until quite recently, when corporate efficiency required "downsizing," which has meant abandoning members of what amounts to a national extended family.

105 Communism in China has taken a different route, an innovative one. Although the government still tolerates no political dissent, it tolerates and even encourages economic innovation (at least in some regions). Tacitly, moreover, it tolerates social and cultural change as well. Our point is merely that totalitarian societies must either change in some fundamental way or disappear.

106 The extraordinary popularity of romance novels has been discussed in *Time*: "A few statistics: romance novels are read by 51 million Americans. They account for more than half of all paperback fiction sold in the U.S. If you thought feminist, postmodernism and the Internet had done away with the romance novel, think again. The number of romance-novel readers in the U.S. has risen 18% since 1998" (Lev Grossman, "Rewriting Romance: Bodice Rippers Are More Popular Than Ever, and Julia Quinn Is Taking Them into the Postfeminist Future," *Time*, 3 February 2003: 50). What has

changed is the portrayal of women, not that of men. Women are no longer
fragile and vulnerable.

107 In the SCUM *Manifesto* (London: Olympia Press, 1971), Valerie Solanas
explained her hatred toward men, which resulted in a physical attack on
pop artist Andy Warhol. The title of her tract refers to the Society for Cutting up Men. Solanas was eulogized as insane (and thus not responsible for
her behaviour) but intelligent (and thus of interest to feminists) in a critically
acclaimed movie that was directed by Mary Harron: *I Shot Andy Warhol.*

108 Robin Morgan, *Demon Lover: On the Sexuality of Terrorism* (New York:
Norton, 1989). Morgan is no marginal figure. On the contrary, she has
scaled the heights of mainstream feminism. Once the editor-in-chief of *Ms.*
magazine, she founded the Sisterhood is Global Institute, a feminist think
tank, was named woman of the year in 1990 by the Feminist Majority
Foundation, and has served on the boards of both American and international feminist organizations. In 1990, moreover, she received the National
Endowment for the Arts Prize in poetry.

109 Marilyn French, *Beyond Power: On Women, Men, and Morals.* French is
famous for her feminist fiction, too, notably *The Women's Room* (New
York: Summit, 1977).

110 Marilyn French, *The War against Women* (New York: Summit, 1992).

111 Some religious communities oppose masturbation, at least officially, on
other grounds. Traditional Jews and Christians, for instance, trace the prohibition to Genesis 38:9. Judah has told Onan to have sex with Tamar and
thus continue the lineage of her dead husband Er (Onan's brother). "But
Onan, knowing that the line would not count as his, spilt his seed on the
ground every time he slept with his brother's wife, to avoid providing offspring for his brother" (New Jerusalem Bible). To punish Onan, God kills
him. But punish him for precisely what? For masturbating or for refusing to
do his duty by honouring the custom known as "levirate marriage"? Whatever the original sense of this story, it has been interpreted for many centuries as a prohibition of masturbation – possibly as a way of promoting
marital fidelity. This interpretation has been legitimated, among Catholics,
by the Thomist tradition of natural law. Because the function of semen is
reproduction, masturbation goes against nature. Natural law's rule of "double effect" might have been used by non-Catholics, however, to argue that
masturbation is acceptable. Its main function is to relieve sexual tension, a
useful mechanism that is found not only in all human societies but also in
some primate species; its unintended side effect is to release semen.

112 In the first place, this argument is based on inconsistency. It is one thing for
Christian fundamentalists to take fantasies at face value. They take biblical
passages at face value, after all, and acknowledge literalism as a legitimate
method of interpretation. But ideological feminists are not Christian fundamentalists (although, as ideologues, they are indeed fundamentalists). In

fact, they routinely denounce both the literal *and* the figurative messages of biblical passages. These, they argue, are nothing more, and nothing less, than evil collective fantasies intended to oppress women. For some reason, however, they are willing to accept the most literal approach to *personal* fantasies (at least those of men). Outsiders may be forgiven, then, for suspecting them of intellectual dishonesty and political opportunism.

113 Peter H. Klopfer, and others, "Kids, TV Viewing, and Aggressive Behavior," *Science*, 297.5578 (5 July 2002): 49–50. For a history of studies, see *Children and Television Violence*, [visited] 12 June 2003, <http://www.abelard. org/tv/tv.htm>.

114 Some women, too, like porn. And not only lesbians or those who like the "respectable porn" that we discuss in appendix 5. So do gay men. But when feminists attack porn, those populations are usually ignored. Feminists attack only straight men, because they hold only straight men – that is, supposedly, innate misogynists – responsible for creating and maintaining patriarchy.

115 Frederick Matthews, *The Invisible Boy: Revisioning the Victimization of Male Children and Teens* (Ottawa: Minister of Public Works and Government Services Canada; Health Canada, catalogue no. H72–21/143–1996E, 1996), 16.

116 Lowman 22.

117 Katherine Setzer, "Where the Boys Aren't: The Skinny on Porn for Girls Who Like Girls," *Montreal Hour*, 31 July 1997: 13 (her emphasis).

CHAPTER EIGHT

1 Catharine A. MacKinnon, *Toward a Feminist Theory of the State* (Cambridge: Harvard University Press, 1989) 141.

2 Celia Kitzinger, "Experiential Authority and Heterosexuality," in *Changing Our Lives*, ed. Gabriele Griffin (London: Pluto Press, 1994) 143; cited in Daphne Patai, *Heterophobia: Sexual Harassment and the Future of Feminism* (Lanham, MD: Rowman and Littlefield, 1998) 168.

3 Naomi Wolf, *The Beauty Myth: How Images of Beauty Are Used against Women* (New York: Morrow, 1991).

4 Naomi Wolf, *Fire with Fire: The New Female Power and How It will Change the Twenty-first Century* (New York: Random House, 1993).

5 Naomi Wolf, "The Silent Treatment," *New York Magazine*, 1 March 2004.

6 Naomi Wolf; quoted in Josh Goodman, "Who Else Is Tired of Naomi Wolf?" *Yale Herald*, 27 February 2004.

7 Wolf, "Silent."

8 Anne Applebaum, "Get a Grip, Naomi," *Montreal Gazette*, 29 February 2004: A-11; reprinted from the *Washington Post*.

9 Goodman.

10 Patai xii–xiii.

11 Title IX of the Education Amendments of 1972, 20 U.S.C. §1681 *et seq.*

12 *Williams v. Saxbe*, 413 F. Supp. 654 (D.D.C. 1976).

13 *Alexander v. Yale University*, 631 F. 2d. 178 (2d Cir. 1980).

14 *Moire v. Temple University School of Medicine*, 613 F. Supp. 1360 (E.D. Pa. 1985).

15 *Meritor Savings Bank v. Vinson*, 477 U.S. 57 (1986).

16 In 1992, Congress passed these measures as part of its Higher Education Amendments of 1992. "Victims' Assistance: Campus Sex Assault Victims' Bill of Rights," 2000, *Security on Campus, Inc.*, 3 July 2002, <http://www.campussafety.org/victims/billofrights.html>.

17 "Pamphlet 12 – Sexual Harassment: Part III [Division XV.1] of the *Canada Labour Code* (Labour Standards)," [dated] 21 October 2002, Government of Canada, [visited] 14 February 2004, <http://info.load-otea-hrdc-rhc.gc.ca/publications/labour_standards/harassment.shtml>: 1.

18 "Pamphlet 12" 1.

19 "Harassment and the Canadian Human Rights Act," [undated], *Canadian Human Rights Commission*, [visited] 14 February 2004, <http://www.chrc-ccdp.ca/publications/chra_har-lcdp.asp?l=e>:1.

20 "Pamphlet 12" 1.

21 "Pamphlet 12" 2.

22 Catharine A. MacKinnon, *Sexual Harassment of Working Women: A Case Study of Sexual Discrimination* (New Haven, CT: Yale University Press, 1979).

23 Catharine A. MacKinnon, "Sexual Harassment: Its First Decade in Court," in *Feminism Unmodified: Discourses on Life and Law* (Cambridge: Harvard University Press, 1987) 107; quoted in Patai 47.

24 Patai 28.

25 Patai 28.

26 Patai 41.

27 Patai 170.

28 MacKinnon, *Sexual Harassment* 217–18.

29 Ted Gest and Thom Grier, "Thomas and Hill: Once More with Feeling," *U.S. News and World Report*, 8 June 1992: 10.

30 Barbara Kantrowitz, "Striking a Nerve," *Newsweek*, 21 October 1991: 36 (her emphasis). We looked this up on microfilm, but that particular page had not been photographed!

31 This study is from *Newsweek*. We referred to a similar study, from *Time*, in chapter 3. Both were conducted in 1991. The questions asked were slightly different, but both reveal the same basic pattern: Americans differ widely on how to define sexual harassment.

32 Patai 29.

33 Patai 30.

34 Patai 43.

35 Patai 179.
36 Katie Roiphe, *The Morning After: Sex, Fear, and Feminism* (Boston: Little Brown, 1993) 99–101.
37 Gest and Grier 39.
38 Patai 163–4.
39 *Louis Robinson v. Jacksonville Shipyards Inc.*, 760 F. Supp. 1486 (1991).
40 Gest and Grier 39.
41 Gest and Grier 39.
42 Gest and Grier 39.
43 Patai 26.
44 John Leo, "Harassment's Murky Edges," US *News and World Report*, 21 October 1991: 26.
45 Patai 23.
46 We refer to the Nicene Creed's *filioque* clause. Does the Holy Spirit proceed from the Father alone (as it does according to Eastern Orthodox churches) or from the Father and (*que*) the Son (as it does according to the Roman Catholic Church)?
47 Patai 165.
48 Leo 26.
49 See Paul Nathanson, "I Feel, Therefore I Am: The Princess of Passion and the Implicit Religion of Our Time," *Implicit Religion* 2.2 (1999): 59–87.
50 Kitzinger 143.
51 Kitzinger 143; quoted in Patai 168.
52 Patai 168 (her emphasis).
53 Patai 46.
54 "The Antioch College Sexual Offense Prevention Policy," approved by the Board of Trustees on 8 June 1996, *Antioch College*, 3 July 2002, <http://www.antioch-college.edu/survival/html/sopp.html>.
55 Patai 176.
56 Francine Prose, "Bad Behavior: The Salem Witch Hunts Become a Metaphor for a Trial over a Teacher's Crude Language," *New York Times Magazine*, 26 November 1995: 34–6.
57 Prose 34.
58 Prose 36.
59 Ministry of Education and Training, Ontario, *Framework Regarding Prevention of Harassment and Discrimination in Ontario Universities* (Toronto, 1993).
60 Ministry 2.
61 Paul Benedetti and Andrew Dreschel, "Harassment Policy Stirs Heated Debate in Ontario Universities," *Montreal Gazette*, 20 February 1994: A-5.
62 [William C. Leggett], "Queen's and the 'Zero-Tolerance' Issue: Principal's Statement to the Senate," February 17, 1994.
63 Benedetti and Dreschel A-5.
64 Benedetti and Dreschel A-5.

65 Ministry 4–5.
66 Benedetti and Dreschel A-5. See also Peter Emberley, *Zero Tolerance: Hot Button Politics in Canada's Universities* (Toronto: Penguin, 1996); Graham Good, *Humanism Betrayed: Theory, Ideology, and Culture in the Contemporary University* (Montreal: McGill-Queen's University Press, 2001); Martin Loney, *The Pursuit of Division: Race, Gender, and Preferential Hiring in Canada* (Montreal: McGill-Queen's University Press, 1998); Joan McEwen, *Report in Respect of the Political Science Department of the University of British Columbia* (Vancouver: President's Office, University of British Columbia, 1995).
67 Katie Roiphe, *The Morning After: Sex, Fear, and Feminism* (Boston: Little Brown, 1993) 97.
68 Patai 52.
69 Patai 53.
70 Patai 80.
71 The underlying goal of demonizing men is to separate them from women, says Patai, which "explains why there has never (to my knowledge) been a workshop on, say, how to keep oneself from taking offense at trivial slights or innuendos, or how to respond to an unwanted sexual overture in a spirited way that ends the problem. Instead, the suggested (and, increasingly, mandatory) workshops and training sessions are designed to bring an ever greater range of behavior within the purview of sexual harassment regulations" (Patai 46).
72 Patai 144, referring to Alice Echols, *Daring to Be Bad: Radical Feminism in America, 1967–1975* (Minneapolis, MN: University of Minnesota Press, 1989).
73 Sheila Jeffreys, *Anticlimax: A Feminist Perspective on the Sexual Revolution* (London: Women's Press, 1990).
74 Patai 130.
75 Patai 130–1.
76 Arianne Haley, "Letters," *Ms.*, October 1987: 10.
77 Patai 118.
78 Sue Wilkinson and Celia Kitzinger, eds., *Heterosexuality: A Feminism and Psychology Reader* (London: Sage, 1993).
79 Mary Crawford, "Identity, 'Passing,' and Subversion," in Wilkinson and Kitzinger 44; quoted in Patai 133.
80 Sandra Lee Bartky, "Hypatia Unbound: A Confession," in Wilkinson and Kitzinger 41; quoted in Patai 133.
81 Sandra Lipsitz Bem, "On the Inadequacy of Our Sexual Categories: A Personal Perspective," in Wilkinson and Kitzinger 42; quoted in Patai 133.
82 Patai 133.
83 Patai 139.
84 Patai 140–1.
85 Marilyn Frye, "Willful Virgin, or Do You Have to Be a Lesbian to Be a Femi-

nist?" in *Willful Virgin: Essays in Feminism, 1976–1992* (Freedom, CA: Crossing Press, 1992), 129; quoted in Patai 143. This essay was originally presented as a speech in 1990 at the National Women's Studies Association Conference.

86 Patai 11.

87 Patai 12.

88 Patai 135.

89 Patai 6–7.

90 Patai 160.

91 This book is about men, not women. Nevertheless, it would not do to ignore the effect on women of this preoccupation with sexual harassment. "My own observations of students in women's studies classes," writes Patai, "have led me to believe that years of exposure to feminist-promoted scare statistics have succeeded in imbuing many young women with a foreboding sense of living under constant threat from predatory men. The offer of an escape from this threat is a strong inducement to conformity to feminist blandishments. This, at least, is the more generous interpretation of the vigilante atmosphere promoted in the name of feminism. A less benign explanation is also possible: No social group selflessly refrains from using whatever weapons its historical moment makes available in order to gain money, position, fame (of a sort), and retribution, all in the name of equity and righteousness" (Patai 35).

92 Patai 159.

93 John Stoltenberg, *Refusing to Be a Man: Essays on Sex and Justice* (1989; New York: Meridian, 1990).

94 Patai 150.

95 John Stoltenberg, *End of Manhood: A Book for Men of Conscience* (New York: Dutton, 1993).

96 Today, the Roman Catholic Church focuses heavily on family life. Rejecting the notion of gay marriage to protect the sanctity of marriage is only one example of that. But, as some modern Catholics point out, the tradition has historically ascribed a lower status to family life than to ascetic life.

97 Patai 43.

98 Priscilla Painton, "Woman Power," *Time*, 28 October 1991, 12. And let us not forget the new frontier that could open up for insurance brokers. If employers could be held responsible for misconduct on the part of their employees – even if the former were unaware of it at the time and even if the latter had been correctly indoctrinated – they could hardly afford not to carry insurance against the inevitable plague of law suits. The same goes for individuals. What man could afford to take a job without being insured against charges of sexual harassment? In view of the fact that two female police officers in Long Beach were awarded $3.1 million after three years of sexual taunts from colleagues, it is clear that the financial stakes are truly staggering (Gest and Grier 38). In 1988, a survey of Fortune 500 companies

commissioned by *Working Woman* found that ignoring the problem of sexual harassment can cost up to $6.7 million a year in absenteeism, employee turnover, and lost productivity (Nancy Gibbs, "Office Crimes," *Time*, 21 October 1991, 30). It is hard to see how either the magazine or the companies themselves can possibly know this.

99 "If Your Most Valuable Assets Were at Risk," ad supported by Altria, Kraft Foods, Philip Morris International, and Philip Morris USA, *Harper's Magazine*, March 2004: 1.

100 Training Services by The Edge, [undated], *The Edge*, [visited] 14 February 2004, <http://www3.sympatico.ca/theedgeq/trainserv.html>.

101 Most people but not all. Members of some religious and ethnic communities – the Amish and the Hasidim, say, or some Muslims and Hindus – maintain traditional standards. Because many of them live primarily within their own communities, however, this is not quite the problem that it would be otherwise.

102 Few cultures have admired short hair on women, but they have usually insisted that women either cover their hair or pile it up on their heads. This was certainly true in the West until very recently. No woman with high social status, or the hope of attaining it, would ever "let down her hair" in public; that was reserved for the boudoir. Ancient Egypt was an apparent exception. Egyptian women wore their hair long. In fact, though, women (and men) shaved their heads and wore wigs. This had nothing to do with sex and everything to do with climate and hygiene.

103 Leo 26.

104 Camille Paglia, "A Call for Lustiness," *Time*, 23 March 1998: 54.

CHAPTER NINE

1 Sherene Razack, *Canadian Feminism and the Law: the Women's Legal Education and Action Fund and the Pursuit of Equality* (Toronto: Second Story Press, 1991) 111.

2 Grant A. Brown, "Gender as a Factor in the Response of the Law-enforcement System to Violence against Partners," *Sexuality and Culture* 8:3–4 (summer 2004).

3 Don Macpherson, "Misogynistic Entertainment," *Montreal Gazette*, 6 February 2004: A-15.

4 "[Article 4: Relevancy and Its Limits: Rule] 412: Sex Offense Cases; Relevance of Alleged Victim's Past Sexual Behavior or Alleged Sexual Predisposition," [dated] 1 December 2002, *Federal Rules of Evidence*, [visited] 17 March 2003, <http://www.house.gov/judiciary/Evid202.pdf>: 6–7 [22–3 of 43]. (The first page numbers are those of the document; the second are those of the computer.)

5 Kevin D. Smith, "Navigating the Rape Shield Maze: An Advocate's Guide to MRE 412," [dated] November 2002, [visited] 13 March 2003, <http://www.

jagcnet.army.mil/JAGCNETInternet/Homepages/AC/TJAGSAWeb.nsf/8f7edfd4
48e0ec6c8525694b0064ba51/1cb55669b226e35485256ca3005497a7/$FILE/
Article%201.pdf> : 10. (There is no separate title for the website, although it
seems to be a pamphlet from The Army Lawyer, DA PAM 27-50-357.)

6   "[Article 4: Relevancy and Its Limits: Rule] 413: Evidence of Similar Crimes
    in Sexual Assault Cases," [dated] 1 December 2002, *Federal Rules of Evi-
    dence*, [visited] 14 March 2003, <http://house.gov/judiciary.Evid2002.pdf>: 7
    [23 of 43].

7   "[Article 4: Relevancy and Its Limits: Rule] 414: Evidence of Similar Crimes
    in Child Molestation Cases," [dated] 1 December 2002, *Federal Rules of Evi-
    dence*, [visited] 14 March 2003,
    <http://www.house.gov/judiciary.Evid2002.pdf>: 7–8 [23– 24 of 43]; "[Article
    4: Relevancy and Its Limits: Rule] 415: Evidence of Similar Crimes in Civil
    Cases Concerning Sexual Assault of Child Molestation," [dated] 1 December
    2002, *Federal Rules of Evidence*, [visited] 14 March 2003, <http://www.
    house.gov/judiciary.evid2002.pdf>: 8 [24 of 43].

8   "Section 2246 [of Title 18]," [undated], *U.S. Code*, [visited] 15 March 2003,
    <http://www4.law.cornell.edu/uscode/18/2246.html>: 1; this website is run by
    the Legal Information Institute at Cornell University. Section 2242 of Title 18,
    United States Code, defines a sexual abuser as someone who "knowingly
    causes another person to engage in a sexual act by threatening or placing that
    other person in fear (other than by threatening or placing that other person in
    fear that any person will be subjected to death, serious bodily injury, or kid-
    napping); or engages in a sexual act with another person if that other person
    is – (A) incapable of appraising the nature of the conduct; or (B) physically
    incapable of declining participation in, or communicating unwillingness to
    engage in, that sexual act; or attempts to do so, shall be fined under this title,
    imprisoned not more than 20 years, or both."

9   Charles R. Nesson, Eric D. Green, and Peter L. Murray, "Rule 413: Evidence
    of Similar Crimes in Sexual Assault Cases," [dated] 21 November 1999,
    Problems, Cases and Materials on Evidence, [visited] 19 October 2004,
    <http://www.law.harvard.edu/publications/evidenceiii/main.htm>: 3.

10 Nesson, Green, and Murray 2.

11 "[Article 4: Relevancy and Its Limits: Rule] 403: Exclusion of Relevant Evi-
    dence on Grounds of Prejudice, Confusion, or Waste of Time," [dated] 1
    December 2002, *Federal Rules of Evidence*, [visited] 13 March 2003,
    <http://www.house.gov/judiciary/Evid2002.pdf>: 4 [20 of 43].

12 FRE 404 is on Character Evidence Not Admissible to Prove Conduct; Excep-
    tions; Other Crimes. FRE 405 is on Methods of Proving Character. The former
    states that "Evidence of other crimes, wrongs, or acts is not admissible to
    prove the character of a person in order to show action in conformity there-
    with. It may, however, be admissible for other purposes, such as proof of
    motive, opportunity, intent, preparation, plan, knowledge, identity, or absence

of mistake or accident, provided that upon request by the accused, the prosecution in a criminal case shall provide reasonable notice in advance of trial, or during trial if the court excuses pretrial notice on good cause shown, of the general nature of any evidence it intends to introduce at trial" ([Article 4: Relevancy and Its Limits: Rule] 404: Character Evidence Not Admissible to Prove Conduct; Exceptions; Other Crimes," [dated] 1 December 2002, *Federal Rules of Evidence*, [visited] 13 March 2003, <http://www.house.gov/judiciary/Evid2002.pdf>: 4 [20 of 43]).

13 She was referring to s. 635.

14 Nesson, Green, and Murray 6.

15 Molinari; quoted in Nesson, Green, and Murray 6.

16 Molinari; quoted in Nesson, Green, and Murray 6.

17 "93.671: Family Violence Prevention and Services/Grants for Battered Women's Shelters ..." [undated], *Catalog of Federal Domestic Assistance*, [visited] 18 March 2003, <http://www.cfda.gov/public/viewprog/asp?progid= 1314>: 1. The goal of this act is to "assist States and Indian Tribes in the prevention of family violence and the provision of immediate shelter and related assistance for victims of family violence and their dependents." Here is the history. "The Family Violence Prevention and Services Act (FVPSA) was enacted as Title III of the Child Abuse Amendments of 1984, P.L. 98–457. It was reauthorized and amended for FY 1995 through FY 2000 by P.L. 103–322, the Violent Crime Control and Law Enforcement Act of 1994 (the Crime Bill). The reauthorization of the Child Abuse Prevention and Treatment Act on October 3, 1996 contained a technical amendment affecting funding levels under the FVPSA" ("Legislative authority," [undated], *Family Violence Prevention and Services Programs*, [visited] 20 March 2003, <http://www.acf. dhhs.gov/programs/ocs/01comply/famvio.htm>: 1). ("Legislative authority" is not a separate page of this site, merely a separate section.)

18 James Jacobs and Kimberly Potter, *Hate Crimes: Criminal Law and Identity Politics* (Oxford: Oxford University Press, 1998) 40.

19 Jacobs and Potter 69.

20 Jacobs and Potter 74.

21 Feminists have encouraged women to sue for damages. On 15 May 2000, this new system hit a snag in the United States. Feminists had been agitating for the ability of a victim to sue her rapist in federal court, basing her case on the Constitution's Commerce Clause and its Equal Protection Clause. The test case was *United States v. Morrison*, 529 U.S. 598 (2000). In this case Christy Brzonkala, of Virginia Polytechnic Institute and State University, claimed that she had been raped in September 1994 by Anthony Morrison and James Landale Crawford, two football players who, within an hour of meeting Brzonkala, had allegedly pinned her down on her bed in a dorm and taken turns raping her. The school's disciplinary hearing found only one of them guilty and suspended him for two years. Then, just before the football team's

opening game, the school not only reversed its decision but also gave him a full athletic scholarship. Later, Brzonkala sued both men for violating her civil rights and the school for privately adjudicating a criminal case of rape and for giving preferential treatment to male athletes over female athletes, which was against Title IX of the Civil Rights Act.

The Supreme Court ruled 5 to 4 that "Congress exceeded its authority when it passed the provision of the 1994 Violence Against Women Act that granted victims of rape, stalking and other "gender-motivated" crimes the power to file federal civil lawsuits against their alleged attackers" (Geraldine Sealey, "High Court Nixes Rape Lawsuits: Congress Exceeded Its Authority, Majority Rules," [dated] 15 May 2000, ABC News, [visited] 13 March 2003, <http://abcnews.go.com/sections/us/DailyNews/scotus_raperuling000515. html>: 1). Police power is a local power, according to the majority, not a federal one. And if Congress were to regulate gender-motivated violence, then it would have to regulate all types of violence. According to the minority, on the other hand, Congress had examined a great deal of data to the effect that violence against women affected interstate commerce (Sealey 2). The two female justices took opposing positions. Sandra Day O'Conner voted with the majority, Ruth Bader Ginsburg with the minority. Some observers said that the majority vote might have been intended mainly to support the judicial trend toward protecting states' rights. Other observers said that it usurped the legislative function of Congress.

But the problem for feminists was the government's retreat from its willingness to protect women from violence by men. Patricia Ireland, president of the National Organization of Women (NOW) declared that the "Supreme Court has said not JUST that women's right to be free from violence is not protected by the U.S. Constitution but that the Constitution actually prohibits Congress from providing such protection. I've never seen a more compelling argument for a constitutional amendment guaranteeing women's equality" (Reported in Wendy McElroy, XXX: A Woman's Right to Pornography [New York: St Martin's Press, 1995] 4; no details given).

NOW declared that this case was about limiting the power of women. McElroy declared that it was about limiting the power of Congress, which had been slowly eroding due to expanded interpretations of the Commerce Clause. Had section 13981 of the Violence against Women Act stood, she concludes, it would have been most beneficial to upper-class women fighting divorce cases or educated women with cases against universities. "Unless the application of the VAWA were to be massively expanded to include such issues as child support and alimony – an expansion that may well have been envisioned by its advocates – the VAWA's greatest victory may be as an ideological symbol. It symbolized and institutionalized the political belief that women must receive special protection from men. When confronted with violence and its redress, the VAWA said that women are not to be treated as individuals but to be accorded privileges as the members of a class. Curt Levey, an attorney for the Center for Individual Rights, which provided legal representation for Anthony Morrison, commented that "although today's decision will be viewed as a historic setback for feminist advocacy groups, it is a victory for American women, whose safety is best preserved by strengthening local law enforcement, rather than by relying on federal bureaucrats" (McElroy 5).

22 "Division A – Trafficking Victims Protection Act of 2000," *Violence against Women Office*, 18 June 2002, United States Department of Justice, Office of Justice Programs, 24 June 2002, <http://www.ojp.usdoj.gov/vawo/laws/vawo 2000/stitle_a.htm>.

23 "Division A" 1–2. The Victims of Trafficking and Violence Prevention Act, moreover, held that existing legislation and law enforcement did not acknowledge the gravity of these offenses and were unable either to deter trafficking or to punish traffickers with suitably strong penalties. To improve this situation and to make the reduction of trafficking a priority, it mandated the following: an interagency task force, with members appointed by the president and including the secretary of state, to collect and organize data, consult governmental or nongovernmental agencies, and so forth; a special office within the secretary of state; educational and economic opportunities, including programs to promote women's participation in economic decision making, for victims and potential victims; assistance, including resettlement, through development agencies to victims in foreign countries; assistance to foreign countries, threatening loss of economic aid to those that fail to comply; special benefits or services to victims – even aliens – in the United States, which could be enhanced by special grants from the attorney general; and special "training" for government personnel.

24 "Division B –Violence against Women Act of 2000," 18 June 2002, *Violence against Women Office*, United States Department of Justice, Office of Justice Programs, 24 June 2002 <http://www.ojp.usdoj.gov/vawo/laws/vawo2000/ stitle_b.htm>.

25 "Division B" 20.

26 "Division B" 5.

27 "Division B" 11.

28 "Publications," [undated] *Violence against Women Office*, United States Department of Justice, Office of Justice Programs, [visited] 24 June 2002, <http://www.ojp.usdoj.gov/ vawo/publications.htm>.

29 "Federal Statutes Relating to Crimes against Children," [undated], *Crimes against Children Program*, [visited] 19 November 2001, <http://www.fbi.gov/ hq/cid/cac/federal.htm>. For aggravated sexual abuse, see section 2241(a)(c); for sexual abuse – that is, sexual acts – see section 2243; for prostitution, see section 2421, section 2422, and section 2423(a)(b).

30 National Sex Offender Registry: Crimes against Children, [undated], *Federal Bureau of Investigation*, [visited] 16 June 2005 <http://www.fbi.gov/hq/cid/cac registry.htm>: 1.

31 "Registry" 1.

32 Criminal Code [of Canada], R.S.C. 1985, c. C-46, s. 276.

33 Criminal Code [of Canada], R.S.C. 1985, c. C-46, s. 277.

34 Criminal Code [of Canada], R.S.C. 1985, c. C-46, s. 276.

35 Criminal Code [of Canada], R.S.C. 1985, c. C-46, s. 276.

36 Criminal Code [of Canada], R.S.C. 1985, c. C-46, s. 276.

37 Criminal Code [of Canada], R.S.C. 1985, c. C-46, s. 277.

38 Criminal Code [of Canada], R.S.C. 1985, c. C-46, s. 666. The word "offence" is interesting, because it is broader than the word "assault." *Any* infraction can be cited as evidence of bad character, not only one with some bearing on the case (that is, an assault).

39 *R. v. Seaboyer; R. v. Gayme*, [1991] 2 S.C.R. 577.

40 Razack 112.

41 Christopher P. Manfredi, *The Canadian Feminist Movement, Constitutional Politics, and the Strategic Use of Legal Resources* (Vancouver: Simon Fraser University and University of British Columbia, Centre for the Study of Government and Business, 2000) 35–6.

42 In *Canadian Newspapers Co. v. Canada (A.G.)*, [1988] 2 S.C.R. 122, an Ontario man was tried for committing a sexual assault, contrary to section 246.2(a) of the Criminal Code, R.S.C. 1970, c. C.-34. "At the outset of the trial, the complainant, who was the accused's wife, applied through counsel for an order under s[ection] 442(3) of the Code, directing that the identity of the complainant and any information that could disclose it not be published in any newspaper or broadcast." This presented the problem "of the freedom of the press guaranteed in s[ection] 2(b) of the Canadian Charter of Rights and Freedoms" and whether section 442(3) [was] "justified on the basis of s[ection] 1 of the Canadian Charter of Rights and Freedoms." The Supreme Court found that section 442(3) did infringe the freedom of the press but that section 442(3) did "not infringe or deny the accused's right to a public hearing and that section 442(3) was justified on the basis of s[ection] 1 of the Canadian charter of Rights and Freedoms."

43 "Report by the Government of Canada to the U.N. Commission on Human Rights Special Rapporteur on Violence against Women," [dated] 8 December 1998, *Status of Women Canada*, 2 July 2002 <http;//www.swc-cfc.gc.ca/pubs/ unreport/unreport_e.html>: 3.

44 These cases showed that the legislation could impinge on civil liberties or cause other problems in connection with due process ("The *Victims of Domestic Violence Act* Revisited: A Practitioner's Guide," [dated] December 2001, *The Saskatchewan Advocate*, [visited] 3 March 2004, <http://www.stla. sk.ca/vict1201.shtml>:1). See *Bella v. Bella*, [1995] S.J. No. 253 (Q.B.);

Mosoinier v. Mosoinier, [1997] S.J. No. 732 (Q.B.); *Endicott v. Endicott*, [1995] S.J. No. 317 (Q.B.); *MacDonald v. Kwok*, [1997] S.J. No. 467 (Q.B.); *Dolgopol v. Dolgopol* (1995), 127 Sask. R. 237 Q.B.; and so on.

45 Crimes fall into three categories. Indictable offenses, the most serious, are defined by federal legislation. Summary offenses, less serious, are usually defined by provincial or municipal legislation. Hybrid offenses are those that can be classified as either indictable or summary.

46 "Report" 6.

47 See "Gender-based Analysis [GBA]," 27 December 2001, *Status of Women Canada*, 2 July 2002 <http://www.swc-cfc.gc.ca/gba-acs/english/about/html>.

48 "Report" 10.

49 "Report" 11.

50 "Report" 12.

51 "Women and the Knowledge-based Economy and Society Workshop," 28 October 1998, *Status of Women Canada*, 2 July 2002, <http://www.swc-cfc.gc.ca/publish/kbeswk-e.html> [page 1]; the conference, held on 15 June 1998, was "hosted by Status of Women Canada in partnership with the Policy Research Secretariat."

52 Razack 111. On the fifteenth anniversary of the Montreal Massacre, the same argument was featured. "We know that violence against women persists as a result of women's economic, social and political inequality. This is where violence has its roots. And if we are ever to stop violence against women, we must address the things that contribute to women's inequality such as inadequate wages" (Basil Hargrove, "Inequality at Root of Violence against Women," *National Post*, 6 December 2004: FP-17). The author is president of the Canadian Auto Workers union, so he has an obvious reason for focusing on economics. And his main point is actually about women who lack the financial resources to leave dangerous men. Like many other observers and activists, though, he conflates what causes women not to leave dangerous men with what causes those men to become dangerous in the first place. A few days later and in connection with the same anniversary, something similar was put forward in another newspaper. "Lépine, it was argued, was a madman from whose actions no valid conclusions could be drawn. The other men, the ones responsible for killing 593 women in Quebec since 1989, well, who knows what their problem is? But we do know. It's a refusal to admit women have equal rights, that they have the right to decide what to study, what job to hold, where to live, whether or not to marry or have children" (Janet Bagnall, "Finally, Men Are Catching On," *Montreal Gazette*, 10 December: 2004 A-27). But, feminist orthodoxy notwithstanding, we actually know nothing of the kind. The link between violence and inequality – economic, social, political, or even symbolic – is by no means obvious. A much more obvious link would be between violence and size; bullies (from any group) are usually bigger than their victims (from any group).

53 "Report" 9.

54 One method is to ruin a man's reputation, and often his career, by making false charges of domestic violence (which are hard to recover from even if proven in court to be false). Farrell refers to Thomas Kiernan, who reports (in "Voice of the Bar," letter to the editor, *New Jersey Law Journal* [21 April 1988]: 6) that he attended four seminars for wives seeking divorces and that, in all four cases, a female lawyer advised the women to create records of wife abuse – whether true or false – before filing papers. Doing so makes it far more likely for them to get their husbands kicked out and thus, indirectly, to gain custody of the children (who are already living with their mothers in "stable" environments). Another method is psychological abuse. A great deal has been written over the past thirty years about its use by men. Very little, however, has been written about the other side of that coin (except in connection with these lesbians who abuse their partners). "Now that we know that men are abused at least as much," writes Farrell, "it will be easier to study the entire abuse *system* – male *and* female, psychological *and* physical. What little we do know about heterosexual psychological abuse seems to indicate that the sexes swear and insult each other about equally, and that women threaten men with violence more" (Warren Farrell, *Women Can't Hear What Men Don't Say: Destroying Myths, Creating Love* [New York: Tarcher/Putnam, 1999] 154). Both women and men have distinctive techniques, and these really do conform to stereotypes. "Men are more likely to disappear at work, disappear into a project in the garage, or disappear into a bottle; to withdraw behind a newspaper or in front of the TV; to become addicted to sports or to gambling. Women are more likely to shop and spend, nag and manipulate, or withdraw from sex or into a romance novel. Contrary to popular opinion, both are about equally likely to have affairs. Both sexes employ forms of power intended to compensate for feelings of powerlessness. Both sexes experience Pyrrhic victories" (Farrell 154). Like many other observers, Farrell points out that women usually have an advantage over men in conflicts over relationships: verbal and emotional skills. "In the arena of relationship arguments," he writes, "women are about as much the masters as men are on football fields. But women's misuse of relationship power is legal; men's misuse of physical power is illegal. The illegality of physical abuse makes men more restrained in the use of their physical power than women are in the use of their relationship power. This might be called 'The Great Inequality'" (Farrell 161).

55 Murray A. Straus and Richard J. Gelles, *Physical Violence in American Families: Risk Factors and Adaptations to Violence in 8,145 Families* (New Brunswick, NJ: Transaction Press, 1990); cited in Farrell 139.

56 See, for example, Susan Sorenson and Cynthia A. Telles, "Self-Reports of Spousal Violence in a Mexican-American and Non-Hispanic White Population," *Violence and Victims*, 6.2 (1991): 3–15, or Boyd C. Rollins and Yaw

Oheneba-Sakyi, "Physical Violence in Utah Households," *Journal of Family Violence* 5.4 (1990): 301–9.

57 Coramae Richey Mann, "Getting Even? Women Who Kill in Domestic Encounters," *Justice Quarterly* 5.1 (March 1988): 33–51; cited in Farrell 140.

58 Farrell 129 (his emphasis).

59 Farrell 129.

60 Farrell 131.

61 Farrell 131.

62 U.S. Department of Justice, Federal Bureau of Investigation, Bureau of Justice Statistics, *National Survey of Crime Severity* (Washington, DC: U.S. Government Printing Office, 1985), #NCJ-96017; quoted in Farrell 131, his emphasis). This study was conducted by Marvin E. Wolfgang, Robert M. Figlio, Paul E. Tracy, and Simon I. Singer at the Center for Studies in Criminology and Criminal Law, the Wharton School, University of Pennsylvania.

63 Ileana Arias and Patti Johnson, "Evaluations of Physical Aggression among Intimate Dyads," *Journal of Interpersonal Violence*, 4.3 (September 1989): 303; cited in Farrell 131.

64 Barbara J. Morse, "Beyond the Conflict Tactics Scale: Assessing Gender Differences in Partner Violence," *Violence and Victims*, 10.4 (1995): 251–72; cited in Farrell 128.

65 Farrell 138.

66 Suzanne K. Steinmetz, "Women and Violence," *American Journal of Psychotherapy*, 34.3 (1980): 334–50; cited in Farrell 139.

67 Farrell 130.

68 Suzanne K. Steinmetz, "A Cross-cultural Comparison of Marital Abuse," *Journal of Sociology and Social Welfare*, 8.2 (July 1981): 404–14; cited in Farrell 145. Farrell notes, however, that the samples from some countries – Canada, Puerto Rico, Finland, and the United States – were small.

69 Farrell 145–6.

70 Jerry Adler, "The Numbers Game," *Newsweek*, 25 July 1994: 57–8.

71 Adler 57. In a letter to the editor of *Newsweek*, its director acknowledged this error but without apologizing for it: "Yes, statistics are often misused, confusing and sometimes just plain wrong. Being acutely aware of this fact, we have spent countless hours collecting a broad range of statistical information about domestic violence and its effects. We do not 'assert' that any figure is true. Rather, we give out as much information as possible from a variety of sources so the reader can make an informed decision (Sue Osthoff, "Letters: What's in a Number?" *Newsweek*,29 August 1994: 17).

72 Daniel Maier, of the American Medical Association, had this to say: "In our attempt to add perspective to the number of women killed by husbands and boyfriends, we reported that domestic abuse kills as many women in five years as the total number of Americans who lost their lives in the Vietnam

War. Stated correct, this comparison should read, 'Domestic violence kills *nearly* as many women each *decade* as Americans who lost their lives in the Vietnam War.' The AMA apologizes for the error and any confusion it may have caused" (Daniel J. Maier, "Letters," *Newsweek*, 29 August 1994: 16-17; his emphasis).

73 Adler 57. In another letter to the editor of *Newsweek*, The American Medical Association admitted this error and did apologize. "Stated correctly," noted its director of news and information, "this comparison should read, 'Domestic violence kills *nearly* as many women each *decade* as Americans who lost their lives in the Vietnam War'" (Daniel J. Maier, "Letters: What's in a Number?" *Newsweek*, 29 August 1994, 17; his emphasis).

74 Adler 58.

75 Philip Cook, *Abused Men: The Hidden Side of Domestic Violence* (Westport, CN: Praeger, 1997) 12.

76 Cook 2.

77 Glenda Kaufman Kantor, *1992 National Alcohol and Family Violence Survey*; cited in Farrell 133. This survey was conducted at the University of New Hampshire's Family Research Lab; Farrell's data printout was provided by Jana L. Jasinski. Other studies confirmed fact that women can be violent. According to one on dating couples, women were five times as likely as men to be severely violent (Jan E. Stets and Debra A. Henderson, "Contextual Factors Surrounding a Conflict Resolution While Dating: Results from a National Study," *Family Relations*, 40.1 [January 1991]: 29–36; cited in Farrell 134). According to another, this tendency increased as the emotional stakes got higher for women (Mary Riege Laner and Jeanine Thompson, "Abuse and Aggression in Courting Couples," *Deviant Behavior*, 3.3 (April-June 1982): 229–244; cited in Farrell 134.)

78 Cook, 15–18.

79 Cook 18.

80 Cook 14.

81 "The U.S. Justice Department studied the rates for 1979 through 1988 and found that about 20 percent more females than males were slain by their mates. The figures for 1988 are the most accurate, as the Bureau of Justice Statistics surveyed a larger-than-usual number of homicides, about 8,000 in seventy-five large urban areas. The results of this survey, not released until 1994, show that of all white family murder victims, 62 percent were wives and 38 percent were husbands. For black family spouse murders, wives were just about as likely to kill their husbands as husbands were to kill their wives: 47% of the victims of a spouse were husbands and 53% were wives. For both black and white victims, about 40 percent of the men and 60 percent of the women were killed by their spouses" (Cook 19–20).

82 U.S. Department of Justice, Federal Bureau of Investigation, *Crime in the United States* (Washington, DC: U.S. Government Printing Office, 1990).

The table on page 11, "Victim Offender Relationship by Race and Sex," notes that multiple-offender cases are not broken down by sex; only single-victim-single-offender cases are.

83 Farrell 152.

84 Cited but not named in Patricia Pearson, "Women Behaving Badly," *Saturday Night*, 19 September 1997: 98.

85 Pearson 98.

86 Pearson 100.

87 Farrell 136.

88 Farrell 136.

89 Farrell 127.

90 Farrell 127.

91 Farrell 128.

92 Farrell 128 (our emphasis).

93 Israeli women are indeed conscripted for military service but not for combat.

94 Farrell 149.

95 Farrell 147 (his emphasis).

96 Karl Pillemer and David Finkelhor, "The Prevalence of Elder Abuse: A Random Sample Survey," *Gerontologist*, 28.1 (1988): 51–7; cited in Farrell 147.

97 The National Longitudinal Study of Youth, appendix C, in Murray A. Straus, *Beating the Devil Out of Them: Corporal Punishment in American Families* (New York: Lexington Books, 1994) 25; John Ditson and Sharon Shay, "Use of a Home-based Microcomputer to Analyze Community Data from Reported Cases of Child Abuse and Neglect," *Child Abuse and Neglect*, 8.4 (1984): 503–9; cited in Farrell 147. Mothers are statistically more likely than fathers to abuse their children, it is often said, merely because they spend more time than fathers with their children; fathers might be just as abusive as mothers in different circumstances. But that hardly exonerates abusive mothers. The mere fact that *any* mothers hit their children undermines the angelic stereotype of mothers, one that supports the ideological notion that women in general are innately caring and loving and "nurturing."

98 Farrell 148 (his emphasis).

99 Farrell 148.

100 Lynn Magdol, Terrie E. Moffitt, Avshalom Caspi, and others, "Gender Differences in Partner Violence in a Birth Cohort of 21–year-olds: Bridging the Gap between Clinical and Epidemiological Approaches," *Journal of Consulting and Clinical Psychology*, 65.1 (1997): 68–78; cited in Farrell 148.

101 Farrell 148 (our emphasis).

102 Farrell 134–5.

103 Steinmetz, "Women and Violence"; cited in Farrell 137.

104 Farrell 137.

105 Farrell 124.

106 Alice Myers and Sarah Wright, eds., *No Angels: Women Who Commit Violence* (London: HarperCollins, 1996).

107 Donald G. Dutton, "Patriarchy and Wife Assault: The Ecological Fallacy," *Violence and Victims*, 9.2 (1994): 167–78.

108 Susan C. Turrell, "A Descriptive Analysis of Same-Sex Relationship Violence for a Diverse Sample," *Journal of Family Violence*, 15.3 (2000): 281–93.

109 Farrell 147. Farrell cites one study, according to which 45% of gay women reported physical violence from their latest female partner, versus 32% of straight women who reported physical violence from any of their male partners (Gwat-Yong Lie, Rebecca Schilit, Judy Bush, and others, "Lesbians in Currently Aggressive Relationships: How Frequently Do They Report Aggressive Past Relationships?" *Violence and Victims*, 6.2 (1991): 125–6; cited in Farrell 146). According to another study, 7% of gay women reported that they had been raped by female dates versus 9% of straight women who reported that they had been raped by male dates (Pamela A. Brand and Aline H. Kidd, "Frequency of Physical Aggression in Heterosexual and Female Homosexual Dyads," *Psychological Reports*, 59.3 (1986): 1311; cited in Farrell 146–7).

110 Lenore E.A. Walker, *The Battered Woman Syndrome*, 2d ed. (New York: Springer, 2000).

111 Farrell 140.

112 Brown 65.

113 See U.S. Department of Justice, Bureau of Justice Statistics, *Selected Finding: Violence between Intimates* (Washington, DC: U.S. Department of Justice, Bureau of Justice Statistics, 1994) 6; cited in Farrell 152.

114 Farrell 152.

115 Brown 75–6 (his emphasis).

116 Brown 61.

117 Brown 69.

118 Susan Brownmiller, *Against Our Will: Men, Women, and Rape* (New York: Simon and Schuster, 1975).

119 See Razack.

120 McElroy 2.

121 Intimate-partner violence (current or former spouses, girlfriends, boyfriends) was declining in the United States during the late 1990s; there were fewer murders, too, than in any year since 1976. "Between 1976 and 1998, the number of male victims of intimate partner homicide fell an average 4% per year and the number of female victims fell an average 1%. The number of female victims of intimate violence declined from 1993 to 1998. In 1998 women experienced an estimated 876,340 violent offenses at the hands of an intimate, down from 1.1 million in 1993. In both 1993 and 1998, men were victims of about 160,000 violent crimes by an intimate partner."

("Intimate Partner Violence," [page 1]). This pattern followed other drops in the crime rate; the violent crime rate declined 15% between 1973 and 2000. ("Crime and Victims Statistics," 7 April 2002, *Bureau of Justice Statistics*, United States Department of Justice, Office of Justice Programs, Bureau of Justice Statistics, 21 June 2002, <http://www.ojp.usdoj.gov/bjs/ cvict.htm>).

122 In *United States v. Lanier*, 123 F..3d 945 (1997), MacKinnon wrote the brief for Vivian Archie and the National Coalition against Sexual Assault. She argued that Lanier, a judge, had violated the constitutional equality of five women by raping them. He appealed the case to the Supreme Court, but his appeal was denied. Moreover, MacKinnon has been involved in several Canadian cases of this kind. Her point of view prevailed in *Canadian Newspapers Co. v. Canada (A.G.)*, [1988] 2 S.C.R. 122, which was about preventing anyone from publishing the name of an alleged rape victim. Her position, that names should not be revealed, was partially successful in *Seaboyer 577*. In this case, which involved a challenge to the rape-shield law (see below), she supported the intervention of LEAF with an affidavit and factum. In *M.(K) v. M.(H)*, [1992] 3 S.C.R. 6, MacKinnon successfully supported LEAF in a case before the Supreme Court, arguing that the statute of limitations in proven incest cases violates sexual equality (although the case was decided on another basis: the legal irrelevance of time limitations on discrete torts and breaches of fiduciary responsibilities to children). In *Norberg v. Wynrib* [1992] 2 S.C.R. 226, she successfully supported LEAF once again, this time to argue that equality under the law mandated damages for a woman whose physician had kept her addicted to drugs (in return for sex). MacKinnon has been involved, through LEAF, in other Canadian cases, too. (Kristin Switala, ed., "Catharine MacKinnon," [dated] 1999, *Feminist Theory Website*, [visited] 23 October 2002, <http://www. cddc.vt.edu/feminism/Mackinnon.html>: 6–10). These include: "*Re D.P.* [a reference case about an unnamed minor or other protected person, in which the government has referred a specific question to the court], convicted child molester should not be permitted to be called to the bar in Ontario (won); and *Jane Doe v. Metropolitan Toronto (Municipality) Commissioners of Police* (1990), 74 O.R. (2d) 225, woman raped by serial rapist suing Toronto police for violation of sex equality rights and for negligence in failing to warn (won; going to trial); *A.L.*, battered women's sex equality rights violated by decision not granting her victim compensation (lost, appeal pending)." See also *French Estate v. Ontario (A.G.) [R. v. Bernardo]* (1996), 134 D.L.R. (4th) 587 (Ont. Gen. Div.), affirmed: (1988), 38 O.R. (3d) 347 (C.A.), leave to appeal to S.C.C. refused [1998] S.C.C.A. No. 139.

123 For discussions of *I Shot Andy Warhol* and *Thelma and Louise*, along with many other movies of this type, see Paul Nathanson and Katherine K. Young, *Spreading Misandry: The Teaching of Contempt for Men in Popular Culture* (Albany: State University of New York Press 2001).

124 Catharine MacKinnon, *Only Words* (Cambridge: Harvard University Press, 1994).

125 Carlin Romano, "Between the Motion and the Act," *Nation*, 15 November 1993, 563–70. By that time, many academics agreed with MacKinnon. Some academics at Harvard said so, at any rate; Lindsay Waters and others attacked his "use of rape as a tool for the conduct of criticism" ("Exchange: Words Are All I Have," *The Nation*, 27 December 1993: 786). See also Richard Lacayo, "Assault by Paragraph," *Time*, 17 January 1994: 37.

126 Edward O. Laumann and others, *The Social Organization of Sexuality: Sexual Practices in the United States* (Chicago: University of Chicago Press, 1994).

127 Listen to McElroy: "Ominously, the VAWA does not clearly delineate what constitutes 'gender-motivated violence,' allowing the term to cover conceivably any situation of abuse that involved gender hostility. This is promising for feminists who routinely consider even words and images to be a form of gender violence. Such arguments led Supreme Court Justice Sandra Day O'Connor to state, 'your approach ... would justify a federal remedy for alimony or child support.' Arguably, that is precisely what radical feminists wanted and hoped to achieve through the VAWA. Radical feminists want a war on 'gender violence' similar to the 'War on Drugs' – that is, zero tolerance backed by maximum force. To this end, the VAWA attempted to create a special class of crime defined by ideology. A major tenet of radical feminism is that violence against women is part of a political campaign that men as a class inflict upon women as a class. The fact that real violence against women – e.g., murder, battery, rape – has been steadily and steeply declining since 1990 in no way impacts their passionate cry for harsher enforcement. Facts are often irrelevant to ideology." Jacobs and Potter, too, complain about its loose definition of crime, which "could transform virtually any intergroup crime into a hate crime" (Jacobs and Potter 40). Hate crimes are caused by prejudice, they say, a factor that should increase the punishment. The fact that any woman who has been beaten by a man could already have sued, moreover, made a new law redundant. Its value was purely symbolic. They conclude that its creation was a political response to political demands from a lobby group. It was expedient because it involved no major budgetary consequences, because it provided a way for politicians to appear tough on discrimination and intolerance, and because it was vaguely worded (Jacobs and Potter 78).

128 "Rape," [dated] 2000–2003, *Cool Nurse*, [visited] 10 April 2003, <http://www.coolnurse.com/rape.htm>: 1.

129 Lawrence A. Greenfeld, "Sex Offenses and Offenders: An Analysis of Data on Rape and Sexual Assault," [dated] 7 February 1997, *Violence against Women Online Resources*, [visited] 10 April 2003, <http://www.vaw.umn.edu/documents/sexoff/sexoff.html>: 34, 35.

130 Greenfeld 35.
131 Greenfeld 34.
132 Greenfeld 35.
133 Greenfeld 35.
134 *Criminal Code of Canada*, R.S.C. 1985, C-46, S. 271.
135 "Sexual Harassment: Legal Definitions," [undated], *Memorial University*, [visited] 11 April 2003, <http://www.mun.ca/sexualharassment/Lgality. html>: 3.
136 *Criminal Code of Canada*, R.S.C. 1985, C-46, S. 272.
137 "Sexual Harassment" 3.
138 *Criminal Code of Canada*, R.S.C. 1985, C-46, S. 273.
139 "Sexual Harassment" 3.
140 Maire Gannon, *Feasibility Study on Crime: Comparisons between Canada and the United States*, catalogue number 85F0035XIE (Ottawa: Statistics Canada, Canadian Centre for Justice Statistics, 2001) 11. (The title page indicates that this is an "irregular" periodical.)
141 Gannon 11.
142 Pamela Cross, "The Uniqueness of Sexual Assault Cases, [dated] April 2000, *Ontario Women's Justice Network*, [visited] 13 March 2003, <http://www.owjn.org/issues/assault/unique.htm>: 1.
143 Cross 1.
144 Cross 2.
145 The lower classes worried much less about privacy, mainly because they could not afford it. Until the nineteenth century, for instance, poor people in Europe often lived in one-room dwellings; whole families slept in one bed— if they had beds at all. In the early Middle Ages, even feudal courts often slept together in great halls; whatever privacy they had would have been minimal indeed by Victorian standards. Later kings and queens, moreover, were sometimes observed by courtiers as a matter of policy: to ensure that royal marriages were consummated.
146 Cross 2.
147 Cross 2.
148 Cross 2.
149 Cross 2.
150 Cross 2.
151 Cross 1.
152 Frederick Mathews, *The Invisible Boy: Revisioning the Victimization of Male Children and Teens* (Ottawa: Health Canada, Minister of Public Works and Government Services Canada, 1996) [catalogue no. H72-21/143-1996E] 1996). This noteworthy – indeed almost unprecedented – report is available also at <http://www.hc-sc.gc.ca/hppb/familyviolence/ html/invisible.htm>; from the National Clearinghouse on Family Violence, Health Promotion and Programs Branch, Health Canada Address Locator:

#0201A1, Ottawa, Canada, KIA 1B4; and by calling (613) 957–2938, (613) 941–8930, or 800–267–1291 (fax).

153 In chapter 1, Mathews discusses the sheer prevalence of violence against boys and men (but without ignoring violence against girls and women) in its many forms: sexual abuse; incest involving siblings; physical abuse involving siblings; sexual harassment; prison rape; physical abuse, emotional abuse, and neglect; corporal punishment; communal and institutional violence; suicide; street youth; prostitution; children with disabilities; images of violence against boys and men in the mass media; and professional responses to boys and men as victims as a factor in establishing prevalence. Although Mathews writes primarily about Canada, he does refer to American studies. "In the United States," he writes, "72% of juvenile homicide victims were male" (Mathews 23).

154 Mathews 27, 32.

155 Mathews 28 (our emphasis).

156 Mathews 30; referring to studies by M. Perovich and D. I. Templer in 1984 (59%); A.N. Groth in 1979 (66%); and J. Briere and K. Smiljanich in 1993 (80%).

157 Mathews 30; referring to a study by M.J. O'brien in 1989.

158 Mathews 29.

159 Mathews 29.

160 Mathews 23–4; referring to a American study by the Office of Juvenile Justice and Delinquency Prevention in 1995.

161 Mathews 49 (his emphasis).

162 Molinari; quoted in Nesson, Green, and Murray 7.

163 Canadian feminists recognized this ambivalence, but Pamela Cross argued that "[a]ny ambiguity was to be interpreted as a no, or at least be heard as a demand for further discussion" ("Justice Issues: Defining Consent: What Does R. v. Ewanchuk Mean for Us?" [dated] March 2000, *Ontario Women's Justice Network*, [visited] 20 March 2003, <http://www.owjn.org/issues/assault/consent.htm>: 2.

164 Razack 25.

165 These statements are allowed in every American state. To gauge the importance of this mentality, you have only to examine a website operated by the National Center for Victims of Crime ("Victim Impact Statements," [dated] 2003, *National Center for Victims of Crime*, [visited] 11 April 2003, <http://www.ncvc.org/gethelp/victimimpactstatements/>).

166 Martha C. Nussbaum, *Sex and Social Justice* (Oxford: Oxford University Press, 1999) 180.

167 Nussbaum 180. On its website, the Department of Justice says that "[v]ictims of crime have the right to submit a victim impact statement to the court describing the harm or loss they have suffered from a crime. The victim may choose [to] read their statement aloud at the sentence hearing. The

court must take the victim impact statement into account when sentencing the offender" ("Victims Matter," [dated] 20 December 2002, *Department of Justice*, [visited] 20 March 2003, <http://www.canada.justice.gc.ca/en/dept/pub/voc/victimsmatter.html>: 1).

168 The line separating essentialism from dualism is very thin and probably of more theoretical than practical importance. To believe that all history revolves around your own group, after all, surely implies that it revolves in addition around any opposition to your own group. If history is all about women, then it can also be about an allegedly titanic and historic conspiracy of men to change history in their own favour.

169 Andrea Dworkin, "Suffering and Speech," in *In Harm's Way: The Pornography Civil Rights Hearings*, ed. Catharine A. MacKinnon and Andrea Dworkin (Cambridge: Harvard University Press, 1997) 33–4.

170 Dworkin, "Suffering" 34.

171 Jane Aiken, "Leveling the Playing Field: FRE 412 & 415: Evidence Class as a Platform for Larger (More Important) Lessons," [dated] 28 October 2002, *Washington University in St Louis School of Law, Faculty Working Papers Series, paper no. 02-10-05*, [visited] 13 March 2003, http://law.wustl.edu/Academics/Faculty/Workingpapers/FRE12.pdf: [3]. (There is no home page apart from this one, and since there is no pagination; we counted the pages manually, including the title page.)

172 Aiken [3–4].

173 *Seventy-fifth Annual Academy Awards*, ABC, WVNY, Burlington, VT, 23 March 2003.

174 This might sound like nit-picking, but remember that some legal definitions of rape are very specific indeed. The offense of sexual assault includes any conduct proscribed by Title 18 of the United States Code. Section 2246 of the code defines "sexual act" in a technical way and includes a particular type of contact: "the intentional touching, either directly or through the clothing, of the genitalia, anus, groin, breast, inner thigh, or buttocks of any person with an intent to abuse, humiliate, harass, degrade, or arouse or gratify the sexual desire of any person." ("Section 2246 [of Title 18]," [undated], *U.S. Code*, [visited] 15 March 2003, <http://www4.law.cornell.edu/uscode/18/2246.html>: 1; this website is run by the legal Information Institute at Cornell University.

175 "That was great. I was like, I don't know what the hell is happening here, but I'm gonna go with it!" (Halle Berry; cited by Daniel Fierman, in "The Big Night," *Entertainment Weekly*, 4 April 2003: 28).

176 According to Canada's *Criminal Code*, "No consent is obtained, for the purposes of sections 271, 272 and 273, where (a) the agreement is expressed by the words or conduct of a person other than the complainant; (b) the complainant is incapable of consenting to the activity; (c) the accused induces the complainant to engage in the activity by abusing a position of trust,

power or authority; (d) the complainant expresses, by words or conduct, a lack of agreement to engage in the activity; or (e) the complainant having consented to engage in sexual activity, expresses, by words or conduct, a lack of agreement to continue to engage in the activity" (*Criminal Code of Canada*, R.S.C. 1985, C-46, S.273.

177 Pamela Cross, "Sexual Assault: Introduction to Legal Options, [dated] November 2001, *Ontario Women's Justice Network*, [visited] 13 March 2003, http://www.owjn.org/issues/assault/qa.htm>: 1.

178 *R. v. Ewanchuk*, [1999] 1 S.C.R. 330.

179 "If at any point the complainant has expressed a lack of agreement to engage in sexual activity, then it is incumbent on the accused to point to some evidence from which he could honestly believe consent to have been re-established before he resumed his advances." (Pamela Cross [citing *R. v. Ewanchuk*], "Defining Consent: What Does *R. v. Ewanchuk* Mean for Us?" [dated] March 2000, *Ontario Women's Justice Network*, [visited] 1 April 2003, <http://www.owjn.org/issues/assault/consent.htm>: 8).

180 Mathews 10.

181 Mathews 36; referring to study by J. Brière, D. Evans, M. Runtz, and T. Wall in 1988.

182 Mathews 35; referring to Sepler's "Victim Advocacy and Young Male Victims of Sexual Abuse: An Evolutionary Model," in *The Sexually Abused Male*, ed. Mic Hunter, vol. 1 (Lexington, MA: Lexington Books, 1990), 73–85.

183 Mathews 52–3.

184 Mathews 53.

185 Mathews 12.

186 Mathews 190.

CHAPTER TEN

1 "Women's Studies Program," [undated], *McGill* [*University*], [visited] 11 March 2004, <http://www.mcgill.ca/mcrtw/programs/>: 1.

2 Daphne Patai "Exchange on Heterophobia" [between Daphne Patai and Christine Littleton], [dated] 29 September 2001, *Books on Law, Book Reviews, Jurist: The Law Professors' Network*, [visited] 4 August 2002, <http://jurist.law.pitt.edu/lawbooks/revapr99.htm>: 8–9.

3 Paul R. Gross, Norman Levitt, and Martin W. Lewis, eds., *The Flight from Science and Reason* (New York: New York Academy of Sciences; Baltimore, MD: Johns Hopkins University Press, 1996); Paul R. Gross and Norman Levitt, *Higher Superstition: The Academic Left and Its Quarrels with Science* (Baltimore, MD; Johns Hopkins University Press, 1998).

4 A classic example from the mid-nineteenth century comes from the pen of Charles Dickens. Visited by the ghost of Jacob Marley, in *A Christmas Carol*,

Ebenezer Scrooge refuses to believe his own eyes. "Why do you doubt your senses?" asks the ghost. "Because ... a little thing affects them. A slight disorder of the stomach makes them cheats. You may be an undigested bit of beef, a blot of mustard, a crumb of cheese, a fragment of an underdone potato. There's more of gravy than of grave about you, whatever you are" (Charles Dickens, *A Christmas Carol: A Ghost Story of Christmas* [1843; London: Gollancz, 1983]: 29).

5 In *Higher Superstition*, Gross and Levitt argue that academics in the "hard" sciences have not taken the attack seriously for several reasons. It makes no sense in scientific terms, for instance, and many scientists sympathize with the general goals of ideologies on the political left. In addition, however, they argue that scientists should take it seriously.

6 Gross and Levitt discuss several postmodern variants of the attack on science, including the attacks not only of "radical feminism" but also of radical environmentalism (which includes "ecofeminism" and "Goddess" cults), radical forms of the animal-rights movement, and racism (which includes "Afrocentrism"). Although the authors refer often to ideologies on the political right, including Christian fundamentalism (which sponsors "Creation science"), their book is about ideologies on the political left. Why? Because the latter, unlike the former, are firmly established in universities, including the most prestigious ones, and thus in direct conflict with scientists.

7 Meera Nanda, "The Science Question in Postcolonial Feminism," in Gross, Levitt, and Lewis 420–36. Nanda agrees with other postcolonial (or postmodern) feminists that science has been used by imperialists to exploit and subjugate non-Western societies. She disagrees with their opposition to science, nonetheless, because non-Western societies have used local traditions to exploit and subjugate their own women. The only way to challenge those traditions effectively, she argues, is through science. Following Ernest Gellner, she believes that "while the historic *origin* of reason was culturally bound (à la Durkheim and Weber), scientific rationality, understood as a sensibility, a temperament, a style of thought, can be adopted by diverse cultures situated in different geographical, historical and linguistic spaces. The scientific temper is universally miscible with other cultures – with often unexpected and transformative results – because it is based on one clear and distinct idea that the rational mind cannot ignore, namely, 'that anything which is in conflict with independently, symmetrically established evidence, cannot be true' and must be refused" (Nanda 428; her emphasis). Nanda's opposition to those who attack science is clearly motivated as much by political expediency, though, as any genuine appreciation of science per se. She believes, correctly, that science will make evident – if not immediately, then eventually – all the errors of those who oppress women. But would she accept scientific evidence for things she does not want to believe about women (or men)? Scientific truth is the means to a political end for her, not an end in itself. Many scientists agree

with her, no doubt, but the ultimate primacy of politics over truth is something that should worry them.

8 See Gross and Levitt.

9 For detailed essays defending chaos theory as it is used by scientists from the distortions promoted by postmodernists (and therefore by the ideologues supported by them), see Jean Bricmont, "Science of Chaos or Chaos in Science," in *The Flight from Science and Reason*, ed. Paul R. Gross, Norman Levitt, and Martin W. Lewis (Baltimore: Johns Hopkins University Press for the New York Academy of Sciences, 1996) 131-75. The entire book, however, is useful as a scientific critique of those who have tried to undermine science.

10 Edward de Bono, *Lateral Thinking: A Textbook of Creativity* (London: Ward Lock Educational, 1970).

11 Janet Radcliffe Richards, "Why Feminist Epistemology Isn't," in Gross, Levitt, and Lewis, 385–412; Mary Beth Ruskai, "Are 'Feminist Perspectives' in Mathematics and Science Feminist?" in Gross, Levitt, and Lewis 437–42.

12 Elizabeth Grosz (her emphasis); quoted in Richards 385.

13 Richards 387–8.

14 Richards 389 (her emphasis).

15 Richards 407.

16 Daphne Patai and Noretta Koertge, *Professing Feminism: Cautionary Tales from the Strange World of Women's Studies* (New York: Basic Books, 1994).

17 Noretta Koertge, "Feminist Epistemology: Stalking an Un-dead Horse," in Gross, Levitt, and Lewis, 413–19.

18 Koertge, "Feminist Epistemology" 414.

19 Koertge, "Feminist Epistemology" 414.

20 Koertge, "Feminist Epistemology" 417.

21 Koertge, "Feminist Epistemology" 417.

22 Koertge, "Feminist Epistemology" 418.

23 Research on differences between male and female brains is interpreted by feminists of the ideological – that is, essentialist – school in ways that make men and women fundamentally different (not merely different in some ways or in ways that can be modified by culture).

24 Donna Haraway, "Situated Knowledges," in *Simians, Cyborgs and Women: The Reinvention of Nature*, ed. D. Haraway (New York: Routledge, 1990).

25 Dozens of current books and articles reiterate these fundamental motifs: see L. Nelson, *Who Knows: From Quine to a Feminist Empiricism* (Philadelphia: Temple University Press, 1990); L. Alcoff and E. Otter, eds. *Feminist Epistemologies* (New York: Routledge, 1993); L. Code, *What Can She Know? Feminist Theory and the Construction of Knowledge* (Ithaca, NY: Cornell University Press, 1991); S. Harding, *Whose Science? Whose Knowledge? Thinking from Women's Lives* (Ithaca, NY: Cornell University Press, 1991); H. Longino,

Science as Social Knowledge (Princeton, NJ: Princeton University Press, 1990); K. Lennon and M. Whitford, eds., *Knowing the Difference: Feminist Perspectives in Epistemology* (London: Routledge, 1994).

26 Paul Nathanson, "I Feel, Therefore I Am: The Princess of Passion and the Implicit Religion of Our Time," *Implicit Religion*, 2.2 (1999): 59–87.

27 Patai and Koertge found that many, though not all, female students were hostile toward men. "Some said male students interrupt women, talk too much, question the authority of the female professor, are defensive when the topics of rape or wife battering come up, and in general, 'just don't get it.' Others, however, were appalled at how rudely the more radical women students treated any males who strayed into 'their' classes." In the words of one women's studies professor, "What amazes me is that these students would rather believe men are evil than that they can change"(Patai and Koertge 144).

28 Joy Magezis, *Women's Studies* (Chicago: NTC Publishing Group, 1996).

29 Patai and Koertge 110.

30 Patai and Koertge 8–9.

31 The Canadian link between research on women and feminist activism is evident in the following letter, sent by e-mail, from Monica Hotter, acting director of the McGill Centre for Research and Teaching on Women: "Please circulate to graduate students in your department: Doing research on women? Interested in feminist theory and activism? Didn't know McGill had a Women's Centre?" (7 January 2004).

32 Patai and Koertge 177.

33 Magezis 1.

34 Simon Fraser University, Department of Women's Studies, advertisement, *CAUT Bulletin*, December 2004: B2 (our emphasis).

35 Magezis 13.

36 Patai 8–9.

37 Many of them did so in connection with a controversy over an online colloquy, set up by the *Chronicle of Higher Education*, on Patai's views of women's studies. We will discuss the content of that colloquy later. Here, we refer to the controversy over it: "Daphne Patai, Women's Studies, and the *Chronicle*," WMST-L, [dated] I October 2000, *Chronicle of Higher Education* [visited] 29 September 2002, <http://research.umbc.edu/~korenman/wmst/patai1.html>. Among the very few who actually acknowledged that Patai had a useful point to make was Viki Soady at Valadosta State University: "I do not often agree with Daphne, but if we cannot listen to 'difference' how can we continue to speak to how we must honor it and enjoin others to do so? What I hear coming from Daphne is a legitimate belief that Women's Studies needs to be self-reflexive and to critique its positions and effectiveness" (Soady, "Daphne" 10). But even Soady goes on to say that she knows from personal experience "the transformative effect that feminist theory and ethnic

theory are having way down here in the deep rural South where I have toiled for six years now" (Soady, "Daphne" 10). It is precisely this "transformative effect" that Patai questions in the specific context of education. Soady is surely a model of tolerance, but she still fails to take Patai's critique seriously. Much more representative than Soady, in any case, was Jenea Tallentire, a graduate student at the University of British Columbia: "I guess I should credit people with more ability to think for themselves, but I do believe that those who are predisposed to see the study of women as pointless – or dangerous – can use Patai's voice, supported by such a well-known forum, to damage ws and the study of women in all areas. It is not just the voice, it is the editorial support that is vital here. So what do we do? Solicit editors with our own pieces? Go [to] the newspapers and offer columns?" (Tallentire, "Daphne" 13). Actually, feminists have been doing precisely those things for many years. And for the record, Patai does emphasize the importance of studying women. She just denies the legitimacy of doing so through the exclusive lens of feminist ideology.

38 Daphne Patai, "The State of Women's Studies," [dated] 4 October 2000, *Chronicle of Higher Education: Colloquy Live*, [visited] 4 August 2002, <http://chronicle.com/colloquylive/transcripts/2000/10/20001004patai.htm>: 1.

39 Better still, of course, are testimonials from male academics. "The chair of my department (history)," says Rosa Maria Pegueros at the University of Rhode Island, "stopped by my office yesterday afternoon. He had been on-line and was baffled by Daphne Patai's arguments. He says that he is confused by this controversy because his experience with the feminists on this campus is a very favorable one ... Why is she saying those things? he asked me" (Pegueros, "Daphne" 14).

40 Tallentire, "Daphne," 15.

41 Littleton, "Exchange" 11.

42 Littleton, "Exchange" 15.

43 Beatrice Kachuck, "Rebuttal to Article by Daphne Patai published in *Chronicle of Higher Education*," [dated] 29 September 2001, [visited] 4 August 2002, <http://www.umass.edu/wost/articles/vision2k/kachuck.htm>: 1.

44 Heather S. Kleiner, "State" 7.

45 The same anecdotal evidence is sometimes presented from the perspective of students. Susan Kane, now a librarian at the University of Washington, writes the following: "I was a student in American Studies at the University of Michigan in the early 1990's, where I saw evidence of 'orthodoxies' within Women [*sic*] studies – and in other disciplines. I evaluated each with a critical eye and believed only what made sense to me. Why do you [Patai] assume that undergraduates are stupid?" (Kane, "State" 6).

46 Adrienne McCormick, "State" 13-14.

47 Patai, "State" 14.

48 Diana Blaine, "State" 10.

49 Kristin Rusch, "State" 13.
50 Lisa Jadwin, "State" 8.
51 Patai, "State" 2.
52 Patai, "State" 3.
53 See Katherine K. Young, "Having Your Cake and Eating It Too: Feminism and Religion," in *Journal of the American Academy of Religion*, 67.1 (March 1999): 167–84; Rita M. Gross, "A Rose by Any Other Name ...: A Response to Katherine K. Young," in *Journal of the American Academy of Religion*, 67.1 (March 1999): 185–94; and Katherine K. Young, "Rejoinder to Rita M. Gross," in *Journal of the American Academy of Religion*, 67.1 (March 1999): 195–8.
54 Patai, "State" 4–5.
55 Littleton, "Exchange" 14.
56 Patai, "Exchange" 18.
57 Jane Elza, "State" 9.
58 Patai "State" 9.
59 Except in Britain and Australia, however, the term "women's studies" remains far more common on websites (see appendix 11), than either "gender studies" or "feminist studies" and their variants.
60 *Status of Women Supplement*, in CAUT *Bulletin*, 48:9 (October 2001).
61 Katherine Side, *Status* 3.
62 The academic jargon of feminists (and other postmodernists) clearly spills over into everyday life. Even Gloria Steinem ridicules it deliciously: "[T]hese poor women in academia have to talk this silly language that nobody can understand in order to be accepted, they think. If I read the word 'problematize' one more time, I'm going to vomit. If I hear people talking about 'feminist praxis' – I mean, it's practice, say practice" (Gloria Steinem; interviewed by Cynthia Gorney, "Gloria," [dated] 1995, *Mother Jones* [visited] 23 October 2002, <http://www.motherjones.com/mother_jones/ND95/gorney.html>: 1.)
   Jargon-filled postmodern writing, she says, is "gobbledygook." Our point here, though, is merely to indicate the link between elite feminists and other feminists. Steinem and other celebrated activists can get away with criticism of women's studies. But not academics. Professionally, most find it prudent to toe the line. Those who fail at least to acknowledge and tolerate jargony (or radical) feminist analyses, after all, are accused of not being "inclusive" (referring, of course, only to women).
63 *Routledge Encyclopedia of Philosophy*, ed. Edward Craig, 10 vols. (New York: Routledge, 1998).
64 George Steiner, "Books of Knowledge," review of the *Routledge Encyclopedia of Philosophy*, ed. Edward Craig, *New York Times Book Review*, 5 July 1998: 12.
65 See Joan Korenman, "Internet Resources for Women's Studies," [updated] 29

May 2002, *Monash University*, [visited] 5 August 2002, <http://www.lib.
monash.edu.au/subjecs/WomensStudies/Internet.html>. Listed on the Internet
are no fewer than 1,990 sites, all about resources on women. Korenman is
director of the Center for Women and Information Technology, at the University of Maryland, Baltimore County. Many web pages are produced and
maintained by women's studies departments. See, for example, "Statistical
Sources on Women and Gender," [dated] 22 February 2002, *Women's Studies
Librarian's Office, University of Wisconsin*, [visited 4 August 2002],
<http://www.library.wisc.edu/libraries/WomensStudies/stats.htm>.

66 Gerri Gribi, "Women's Studies Programs Mailing List," [updated] 2 August
2002, *CreativeFolk.com*, [visited] 5 August 2002, <http://creativefolk.com/
ws.html>.

67 Joan Korenman, "E-mail Forums and Women's Studies: The Example of
WMST-L," [undated], *CyberFeminism*, [visited] 5 August 2002, <http://www.
spinifexpress.com.au/cf/cfjoan.htm>): 1; Spinifex Press is an Australian publisher of feminist books.

68 "National Organization for Women Foundation, [undated], *National Organization for Women Foundation*, [visited] 5 August 2002, <http:///www.now-
foundation.org/about.html>: 1.

69 "National Organization for Women Foundation."

70 See, for example, "2002 News Releases," [undated], *National Organization
for Women*, [visited] 5 August 2002], <http://www.now.org/press/00press.
html> 1. One news item, listed for 15 December 2000, was billed "NOW
Activists Vow to Turn Deep Anger into Determined Activism."

71 "Action Center Calendar," [undated], *National Organization for Women*,
[visited] 5 August 2002, <http://www.now.org/calendar.html>.

72 Steinem had an unusual childhood. Even though she did not have much formal education as a child, because her family was constantly on the road, she
eventually went to Smith College. There, she majored in government and
graduated as a Phi Beta Kappa in 1956. After two years in India on a fellow-
ship, she became a freelance columnist and the author of several books,
including *Outrageous Acts and Everyday Rebellions*, 2nd ed. (New York:
Holt, 1995) and *Revolution From Within: A Book of Self-Esteem* (Boston:
Little, Brown, 1993).

73 "About Us," [undated], *Ms Foundation for Women*, [visited] 5 August 2002,
<http://www.ms.foundation.org/about.html>.

74 "About the Feminist Majority Foundation, [undated], *Feminist Majority
Foundation*, [visited] 5 August 2002, <http://www.feminist.org/welcome/
index.html>.

75 "About the Feminist Majority Foundation."

76 "Feminist Bookstores, Publishers, Reviews, Lists and Electronic Versions of
Women's Studies Books," [updated] 22 January 2002, *Women's Studies
Librarian's Office, University of Wisconsin System*, [visited] 5 August 2002,

<http://www.library.wisc.edu/libraries/WomensStudies/books.htm>. One mentions a coalition of thirty "women-centered" presses.

77 The word "elite" refers either to the academic elite or the political elite. Betty Friedan is not an academic, for instance, but she is a member of the upper middle class.

78 Steinem, in fact, argues that feminism is "essentially a populist movement" (Gloria Steinem; interviewed by Cynthia Gorney see note 50.)

79 Untitled, [dated] 31 July 2000, *National Action Committee on the Status of Women*, [visited] 25 October 2002, <http://www2.vpl.vancouver.bc.ca/DBs/cod/orgPgs/4/4870.html>.

80 "Welcome," [updated] 27 May 2002, *Status of Women Canada*, [visited] 23 October 2002, <http://www.swc-cfc.gc.ca/direct.html>.

81 "Women's Program," [updated] 2 February 2000, *Status of Women Canada*, [visited] 5 August 2002, <http://www.swc-cfc.gc.ca/wmnprog/mandate.html>.

82 "National Day of Remembrance and Action on Violence against Women," [updated] 6 December 2001, *Status of Women Canada*, [visited] 5 August 2002, <http://www.swc-cfc.gc.ca/dec6/index.html>.

83 *After the Montreal Massacre* (Gerry Rogers, 1990). This video was produced by the National Film Board of Canada, Studio D (which specialized in feminist productions), and the Canadian Broadcasting Corporation. *Waking Up to Violence* (Sharon Bartlett, 2000). This video features interviews with counselor Dale Trimble.

84 "Promoting Your Research," [updated] 2 February 2002, *Status of Women Canada*, [visited] 5 August 2002, <http://www.swc-cfc.gc.ca/publish/research/020225–promotion-e.html> 6.

85 Pierrette Bouchard, Isabelle Boily and Marie-Claude Proulx, "School Success by Gender: A Catalyst for the Masculinist Discourse, [updated] 15 April 2003, *Status of Women Canada*, [visited] 8 June 2003, <http://www.swc-cfc.gc.ca/pubs/0662882857/200303_0662882857_1_e.html>. This website includes the obligatory disclaimer: "The research and publication of this study were funded by Status of Women Canada's Policy Research Fund of Status of Women Canada. This document expresses the views of the authors and does not necessarily represent the official policy of Status of Women Canada or the Government of Canada" (Bouchard 1). But would Status of Women Canada display this report on its official website if it did not represent the agency's policy?

86 Bouchard, Boily, and Proulx 19–37.

87 Bouchard, Boily, and Proulx 17.

88 Bouchard, Boily, and Proulx 18.

89 On one site mentioned in the report, for instance, someone urges visitors to harass Martin Dufresne (a male feminist): "Call him collect to let him know what you think. Preferably, call him at 3:00 ... in the morning" (Bouchard 71).

90　In our own research, so far, we have focused exclusively on what women are saying about men, but we do at least acknowledge the limitations of this approach. First, it does not represent all women. Second, it does not represent even all feminists but only the feminists we describe as "ideological," and we define that word very carefully indeed. It refers to a mentality that has had a long history, one that originated thousands of years before the advent of feminism and is given expression today by both men and women on both sides of the political spectrum. In fact, we discuss at great length nine specific characteristics of ideology in any form. Feminists who reject those characteristics, or at least most of them, are clearly not ideological feminists (except insofar as they refuse to acknowledge the existence of ideological feminism). We have no problem whatsoever with feminists who believe that sexual equality is something that they must begin to practise now (by treating men with respect as their equals), not some utopian ideal that can be achieved only by practising inequality in the meantime. And it is not a matter only of prudence on the grounds that most people, treated as political pawns, will react negatively in one way or another. It is ultimately a matter of both moral consistency and insight into the human condition. There are, fortunately, many women, including many feminists, who see that both sexes are thoroughly human in a thoroughly ambiguous and complex world. They see that both sexes are morally implicated in existing forms of injustice, though sometimes in different ways, and thus morally obliged to take seriously the needs and problems of those they consider "others," as a way of fostering not merely nominal peace but genuine and enduring reconciliation.

91　Bouchard, Boily, and Proulx 2.

92　"Refused by All-Girl Team, Boys Charge Discrimination," *Montreal Gazette*, 21 December 1994: B1.

93　Bouchard, Boily, and Proulx 132, note 26; the report refers to Martin Dufresne, "Masculinisme et criminalité sexiste," *Recherches féministes*, 11.2 (1998): 125–37; for the sake of variety, possibly, it replaces "masculinist" on several occasions with the less trendy but still common "patriarchal."

94　The report discusses this theory of backlash three times (Bouchard, Boily, and Proulx 46, 49, and 89).

95　The authors have clearly made an effort to avoid words that would be associated immediately with what we call "ideological feminism" (but which others call "gender feminism," "radical feminism," and so on). Although "ideology" itself actually occurs only seven times, possibly because of the dual meaning and consequent ambiguity, it is replaced over and over again with the more fashionable, postmodernist, "discourse." In these cases, both words mean much the same thing.

96　The word "discourse," or "discourses," occurs no fewer than 151 times, often in connection with "masculinism" or "masculinist" (which occurs 105 times).

97 Another postmodernist code word, "deconstruction," is used only once, but in the classic postmodernist sense: "It is important to deconstruct these perceptions and show that girls still have many barriers to overcome in pursuing their chosen educational and professional paths" (Bouchard, Boily, and Proulx 91).

98 Bouchard, Boily, and Proulx 91.

99 Bouchard, Boily, and Proulx 10. The report refers also to "scientific theories developed in the field of women's studies" (Bouchard, Boily, and Proulx 16), even though that field is synonymous with feminism and thus often eschews anything recognizable as a scientific empistemology. Elsewhere, the report "contrasts this [masculinist] discourse with some existing factual data on the same issues" (Bouchard, Boily, and Proulx 4). Whatever the report says is factual or even scientific, in short, but whatever their critics say is "discourse."

100 "Alleged" or "allegedly" occurs 19 times; "apparent," "apparently," or "appears to," 6 times; and "so-called," 4 times.

101 Bouchard, Boily, and Proulx 56–9.

102 Bouchard, Boily, and Proulx 56.

103 Bouchard, Boily, and Proulx 56.

104 In chapter 1, "The Globalization Context," the authors make it clear that when they refer to girls, they refer to both girls and women everywhere. They quote statistics on education, poverty, violence, and so on, from all over the world. When they refer to boys or men, on the other hand, they insist on "contextualization." Here are some examples. All the men's groups in their study, we read, "use the same local, regional or national events as springboards for their claims, always taking care not to mention the benefits and privileges men and boys enjoy around the world. It would certainly be risky for masculinists to acknowledge the low literacy rates and poverty of women in most countries of the world" (Bouchard, Boily, and Proulx 36). But elsewhere we read that the "first aspect of this discourse, beyond its various facets or the arguments it uses, is the fact that it generalizes to an entire gender phenomena that appear in both genders and are present in gender sub-groups" (56). Never mind that this is precisely what they themselves have done on behalf of women. Read this, for instance: "Among these students, researchers have found that school resiliency is essentially a female characteristic" (57). Never mind that the authors condemn essentialism over and over again. For example: "These comments [by men's groups] reflect an essentialist perspective and the concept of [feminist] usurpation [in the lives of boys]" (40). Never mind, in fact, that profoundly essentialist and therefore also dualist forms of feminism have been fashionable and influential for the past thirty years (a major problem that we discussed fully in *Spreading Misandry*). In a note on a survey of violence against women, moreover, Bouchard and her colleagues complain that it "underestimates the real inci-

dence of violence against women because it did not include the Northwest Territories, where violence is especially widespread" (135). In other words, the problem is violence against women as a class; the fact that aboriginal women and other specific groups of women are far more likely to be the victims of violence than other women is considered irrelevant.

105 The report refers to "the political and economic division of power that still subordinates women" (Bouchard, Boily, and Proulx 44). There are other forms of power, but even these are not divided up so neatly. Besides, we keep reading about the need to "contextualize." Consistency alone, therefore, should require these authors to make it clear that not all women have less political or economic power than men.

106 Frederick Mathews, *The Invisible Boy: Revisioning the Victimization of Male Children and Teens* (Ottawa: Health Canada, Minister of Public Works and Government Services Canada, 1996).

107 Mathews, 12.

108 Bouchard, Boily, and Proulx 80.

109 Bouchard, Boily, and Proulx 16, 26–34, 38, 46–9, 54–6.

110 Mathews 9.

111 Mathews 9–10.

112 Mathews 10.

113 F.L. Morton and Rainer Knopff, *The Charter Revolution and the Court Party* (Peterborough, ON: Broadview Press, 2000) 129.

114 Morton and Knopff 129.

115 Morton and Knopff 132.

116 Morton and Knopff 133; referring to Paul Butler, "Racially Based Jury Nullification: Black Power in the Criminal Justice System," *Yale Law Journal* 105.3 (December 1995): 677–725, which was noted in (among many other sources) "When Jurors Ignore the Law," *New York Times*, 27 May 1997: A-24.

117 Morton and Knopff 133; referring to "For Black Scholars Wedded to Prism of Race, New and Separate Goals," *New York Times*, 5 May 1997: A-14.

118 *Women's Law Journal of Legal Theory and Practice*, [visited] 13 June 2003, <http://gort.ucsd.edu/newjour/w/msg02265.html>: 1.

119 Andrea Dworkin, "Against the Male Flood: Censorship, Pornography and Equality," *Harvard Women's Law Journal* 8 (spring 1985): 1–30; Jennifer Gerarda Brown, "'To Give Them Countenance': The Case for a Women's Law School," *Harvard Women's Law Journal* 22 (spring 1999): 1–38; G. Kristian Miccio, "A Reasonable Battered Mother?: Redefining, Reconstructing, and Recreating the Battered Mother in Child Protective Proceedings," *Harvard Women's Law Journal* 22 (spring 1999): 89–122; Margaret A. Baldwin, "Public Women and the Feminist State," *Harvard Women's Law Journal* 20 (spring 1997): 47–162; Emma Coleman Jordan, "Race, Gender, and Social Class in the Thomas Sexual Harassment Hearing: The Hidden

Fault Lines in Political Discourse," *Harvard Women's Law Journal* 15 (spring 1992): 1–24; Jennifer L. Bradfield, "Anti-Stalking Laws: Do They Adequately Protect Stalking Victims?" *Harvard Women's Law Journal* 21 (spring 1998): 229–66; Amy H. Hemko, "Single-Sex Public Education after VMI: The Case for Women's Schools," *Harvard Women's Law Journal* 21 (spring 1998): 19–78; Catharine A. MacKinnon, "Rape, Genocide, and Women's Human Rights," *Harvard Women's Law Journal* 17 (spring 1994): 5–16; Nancy K. Kubasek, Jennifer Johnson, and M. Neil Browne, "Comparable Worth in Ontario: Lessons the United States Can Learn," *Harvard Women's Law Journal* 17 (spring 1994): 103–32; Julie Taylor, "Rape and Women's Credibility: Problems of Recantations and False Accusations Echoed in the Case of Cathleen Crowell Webb and Gary Dotson," *Harvard Women's Law Review* 10 (spring 1987): 59–116; Lenora Ledwon, "Melodrama and Law: Feminizing the Juridical Gaze," *Harvard Women's Law Journal* 21 (spring 1998): 141–78; Rosemary C. Hunter, "Gender in Evidence: Masculine Norms v. Feminist Reforms," *Harvard Women's Law Journal* 19 (spring 1996): 127–68; Elizabeth A. Pendo, "Recognizing Violence against Women: Gender and the Hate Crimes Statistics Act," *Harvard Women's Law Journal* 17 (spring 1994): 157–84; Martha Minow and others, "Perspectives on Our Progress: Twenty Years of Feminist Thought," *Harvard Women's Law Journal* 20 (spring 1997): 1–46; Cynthia Grant Bowman and MaryBeth Lipp, "Legal Limbo of the Student Intern: The Responsibility of Colleges and Universities to Protect Student Interns against Sexual Harassment," *Harvard Women's Law Journal* 23 (spring 2000): 95–132; A.W. Phinney III, "Feminism, Epistemology, and the Rhetoric of Law: Reading *Bowen v. Gilliard*," *Harvard Women's Law Review* 12 (spring 1989): 151–80; Audrey E. Stone and Rebecca J. Fialk, "Criminalizing the Exposure of Children to Domestic Violence: Breaking the Cycle of Abuse," *Harvard Women's Law Journal* 20 (spring 1997): 205–28; Meg Penrose, "I said, 'No,'" *Harvard Women's Law Journal* 23 (spring 2000): 247–8.

120 John Sedgwick, "Beirut on the Charles," *Gentleman's Quarterly*, February 1993, 154–5.

121 Sedgwick 156–7.

122 Sedgwick 201.

123 Morton and Knopff 132.

124 Morton and Knopff 131–3.

125 Morton and Knopff 128.

126 Morton and Knopff 147.

127 "About NWLC," [dated] 2000, *National Women's Law Center*, [visited] 13 June 2005, <http://www.nwlc.org/display.cfm?section=About%20NWLC>:1.

128 *Brentwood Academy v. Tennessee Secondary School Athletic Association*, 531 U.S. 288 (2001).

129 "The Supreme Court and Women's Rights: Fundamental Protections Hang

in the Balance," [dated] June 2001, *National Women's Law Center*, [visited] 5 August 2002, <http://www.nwlc.org/pdf/SupremeCtReport.pdf>. So far, only two women have been appointed to the Supreme Court. Sandra Day O'Connor was appointed in 1981, the first women to hold this position, and Ruth Bader Ginsberg in 1993. As of 1999, 20.6 % of federal court judges were women – up from 9.5 % in 1997." GenderGap in Government," [undated], *GenderGap*, [visited] 25 October 2002, <http:// www.gendergap.com/governme.htm>: 2.

130 Christopher P. Manfredi, *The Canadian Feminist Movement, Constitutional Politics, and the Strategic Use of Legal Resources* (Vancouver: Simon Fraser University and University of British Columbia, Centre for the Study of Government and Business, 2000) 28.

131 "LEAF: Then and Now," [dated] 2000, *Women's Legal Education and Action Fund*, [visited] 3 April 2002, <http://www.leaf.ca/leaf01.html> 1.

132 Manfredi 29.

133 Manfredi 29.

134 Manfredi 29.

135 "About Court Challenges," [undated], *Court Challenges Program of Canada*, [visited] 4 August 2002, <http://www.ccppcj.ca/e/info.html>.

136 "About Court Challenges."

137 Manfredi 30.

138 Manfredi 30.

139 Manfredi 31.

140 The Court Challenges Program's volunteer board of directors has included Shelagh Day (a founder of LEAF and a previous vice-president of the National Action Committee on the Status of Women and a member of the Court Challenges Equality Panel and Chantal Tie (a lawyer with experience in LEAF interventions). The Advisory Committee has included Lynn Smith (a professor of law at the University of British Columbia and a president of LEAF); Juanita Westmoreland (a member of LEAF, a chair of the Ontario Employment Equity Commission, and a Quebec judge); and Sheilah Martin (author, with Kathleen E. Mahoney, of *Equality and Judicial Neutrality* [Toronto: Carswell, 1987]). And the Equality Panel has included Claudyne Bienvenue (who has been on the Quebec Human Rights Tribunal and has been director of the University of Guelph's Human Rights and Equity office); Yvonne Peters (a social worker and lawyer interested in equality and human rights); Leslie MacLeod (who has been on the boards of several Status of Women councils and a consultant on equality and disability); and Martha Jackman (a professor of law at the University of Ottawa and who has been managing editor of the *Canadian Journal of Women and the Law*).

141 Morton and Knopff 128.

142 Morton and Knopff 27.

143 Morton and Knopff 107.

CHAPTER ELEVEN

1   "Gloria Steinem " [undated], *Wisdom Quotes*, [visited] 8 March 2004,
    <http://www.wisdomquotes.com/002551.html>. We are unable to find the
    original source for this quotation.

2   Karen DeCrow, interview by Jack Kammer, in his *Good Will toward Men:
    Women Talk Candidly about the Balance of Power between the Sexes* (New
    York: St Martin's Press, 1994), 58; quoted in Daphne Patai, *Heterophobia:
    Sexual Harassment and the Future of Feminism* (Lanham, MD: Rowman and
    Littlefield, 1998) 129.

3   And just as Jews are not necessarily anti-Christian. We chose the reverse anal-
    ogy, though, because the problem is deeply rooted only in Christianity. Christ-
    ian theology must make sense of the fact that Jews do not believe in Jesus as a
    divine redeemer. As a result, Christians have always been tempted to react
    with hostility toward Jews. But Jewish theology does not refer at all to Chris-
    tianity. If Jews are hostile to Christians – and many are, unfortunately – it is
    due mainly to the history of Christian anti-Judaism (which led to secular anti-
    Semitism).

4   Rabbinic interpreters of scripture have always pointed with pride to the
    ancient Israelites, whose insight into human nature prevented them from try-
    ing to hide the flaws of their heroes. It could be argued less charitably,
    though, that what we see as flaws, the ancients saw as virtues. There is proba-
    bly some truth in both appraisals.

5   Modern Jews explain this away in connection with fear of invasion or disap-
    proval of specific religious practices.

6   Never mind that all of the earliest Christians were themselves Jews. Modern
    Christians, especially academics and theologians who want to dissociate the
    gospel from anti-Semitism, explain this term in the Gospel of John as a result
    of the split between Jews and Christians. At one time, "the Jews" included
    Jewish Christians; now, especially after the influx of gentiles, it no longer did.

7   This should be self-evident to almost everyone, although women have been
    taught by feminists to fear not only men but also life itself. Myrna Blyth,
    retired editor of *Ladies' Home Journal*, has written a scathing attack on
    women's magazines (including her own). These, she says, have supported a
    "culture of fear" and promoted the "victim virus" among women. And pre-
    cisely this mentality, she adds, is what they exploit to sell liberal-to-left-lean-
    ing feminism. See *Spin Sisters: How the Women of the Media Sell Unhappi-
    ness – and Liberalism – to the Women of America* (New York: St Martin's
    Press, 2004).

8   The process had always been politicized to some extent and occasionally –
    think of the Dred Scott case, for instance, which was about slavery to a very
    significant extent.

9   Mircea Eliade would be among the most famous sources for the idea that

there is something quasi-religious about secular political ideologies. He pointed out in *Myths, Dreams and Mysteries: The Encounter between Contemporary Faiths and Archaic Realities* (New York: Harper, 1960) the striking similarities between traditional forms of religion and political ideologies such as communism and fascism. He argued that the only difference, albeit a very important one (because it involves the defining feature of religion), is that traditional religions mediate experiences of the sacred (in some traditions, of God) and purely political ideologies do not. In all other ways – social, economic, political, moral, aesthetic, and so on – political ideologies are the functional equivalents of traditional religions. For Cimini's argument, see Mark Cimini, "Religion versus Religion," [February 1999], DA*DI, [visited] 24 June 2000, <http://www.dadi.org>.

10 Roger Kimball, *Tenured Radicals: How Politics Has Corrupted Our Higher Education* (New York: Harper and Row, 1990). See also Dinesh D'Souza, *Illiberal Education: The Politics of Race and Sex on Campus* (New York: Vintage Books, 1992).

11 It is no accident that Mel Gibson, a very traditional Catholic, produced a movie about Jesus that focuses exclusively and almost sadistically on the latter's suffering: for over two hours, the camera lingers obsessively on the body of a young man being caned, ripped, flayed, crushed, and strangled. In *The Passion of the Christ*, released in 2004, viewers are expected to experience that suffering vicariously and thus feel gratitude for being spared similar suffering – which is to say, gratitude for divine grace. This is consistent with traditional Catholic piety (or at least one form of it). For approximately five hundred years, at least since the fifteenth century, Catholic art has encouraged intense emotional identification with the suffering of Jesus, Mary, and the saints or martyrs. Why, then, has Gibson's movie been so popular among evangelical Protestants? It is true that Protestants rejected the Catholic approach to piety, but some of them gave it new life in a slightly different form. Instead of gruesome suffering, they emphasized sentimental sweetness. Either way, the spotlight is on emotion. Unlike other Protestants, especially the Puritans of early New England, evangelicals have relied heavily on it. To be saved, after all, requires a conversion experience, one that involves a highly emotional passage from the anxiety over sin to joy over conversion; the entire process is accompanied by emotionally charged sermons and ceremonies. This form of Protestantism produced several massively popular "great awakenings" in the nineteenth century. Either directly or indirectly, moreover, it produced anti-intellectual movements such as fundamentalism and pentecostalism in the early twentieth century and the "charismatic movement" in the late twentieth century (often within Anglican, Catholic, and other traditional churches). Evangelical Protestantism now sets the general tone for American religion and also for the secular popular culture that is derived from it. It takes very little imagination to see the continuity between

revival meetings and talk shows – especially that of Oprah Winfrey, who prefers "uplifting" topics and guests to the sleazy ones preferred by other hosts. Both phenomena focus attention on people who testify in public that they were once "in denial" (lost) but are now "in recovery" (saved).

APPENDIX ONE

1 Some people who enjoy popular culture have nothing but scorn for academics who claim to have discovered sinister subtexts almost everywhere in their favourite productions. To some extent, this response reveals anti-intellectualism, but it reveals in addition an understandable rebellion against academic cynicism. At the very least, academics should acknowledge that popular culture has more than one function, that entertainment is one of them, and that not everyone is equally affected by political or ideological subtexts.

2 Warren Farrell, *The Liberated Man: Beyond Masculinity; Freeing Men and Their Relationships with Women* (New York: Random House, 1975); *Why Men Are the Way They Are: The Male-Female Dynamic* (New York: Berkeley, 1986); *The Myth of Male Power: Why Men Are the Disposable Sex* (New York: Simon and Schuster, 1993); and *Women Can't Hear What Men Don't Say: Destroying Myths, Creating Love* (New York: Jeremy Tarcher, 1999).

3 Sacred history is another matter entirely. According to traditional religions, primaeval events – in Western religions, these would include the Creation, the Exodus, the Crucifixion, and so on – are indeed repeatable. In fact, they can be re-experienced by the pious, sacramentally, in connection with rituals and festivals.

4 Protestants rejected Thomist rationalism, based on Aristotelianism, which had long been accepted by Roman Catholicism. They did so as a corollary to their rejection of anything but faith as a way of attaining salvation. The earliest debates were over "good works" as the human contribution to personal salvation, but it soon became clear to Protestants that reason was no more helpful. In fact, they argued, it could be an impediment to salvation. Catholics agreed that reason had its limits; for the specific purpose of salvation, it had to be supplemented by faith. But they were careful not to deny the value of reason for other purposes. This attempt to integrate faith and reason led them to difficulties in the seventeenth century, unfortunately, when reason, in the form of science, actually contradicted some of the doctrines considered necessary for salvation.

APPENDIX TWO

1 Judith Levine: *Harmful to Minors: The Perils of Protecting Children from Sex* (Minneapolis, MN: University of Minnesota Press, 2002) 30.

2 Estelle Freedman, "'Uncontrolled Desires': The Response to the Sexual Psychopath, 1920–1960," *Journal of American History* 71.1 (1987): 83–106; quoted in Levine 31.
3 Levine 32.
4 Levine xxiii–xxiv.
5 Levine 33.
6 Levine 36.
7 Levine 36.
8 Levine 37–8.
9 Levine 26.
10 Levine 27.
11 Levine xxiv.
12 Levine xxviii.
13 Levine xxx.
14 Kee MacFarlane; quoted in Levine 23.
15 Levine 24.
16 Levine 25.
17 Levine 25.
18 Levine xxi.

APPENDIX THREE

1 In avoiding tyrannies of the majority, however, democracies can easily succumb to the opposite problem. When minorities band together, after all, they can become the majority. In one sense, this is an old problem. It has always happened in democracies with multiparty electoral systems, which are based on proportional representation. Because no one party can easily attain a clear majority, coalitions of other parties use their combined power to influence or even dominate the government; it can stay in power only by making deals with them. Even though very few Israelis are religious Jews, for example, Israel's religious parties wield a great deal of power in the country's unstable governments.

In another sense, though, this problem is much more recent and is the result of naive assumptions made in many Western societies about political correctness, on the one hand, and "pluralism," "diversity," or "multiculturalism" on the other. These societies no longer accept the fundamental principle of all democracies: majority rule (albeit with safeguards to prevent tyranny). The whole notion of a majority, in fact, has been "deconstructed" by postmodernists and their ethnic, sexual, or other allies. It is now known pejoratively as "the dominant culture," one that exerts "hegemony" merely by existing. Canada is a good example. Although Canada was founded by Christians and although most Canadians associate themselves at least marginally with Christianity (no matter how secularized), the vaguest reference to Christianity in public life is now considered an affront to Canadian minorities. Even so, not all non-Christians are offended (Josh Freed, "Christmas Part of My Tradition," *Montreal Gazette*, 14 December 2002, A-3; Morton Weinfeld, "Merry ... Oops, Happy Holidays," *Canadian Jewish News*, 9 January 2003: 10).

In 2002, the Royal Canadian Mint referred to the "twelve days of giving," whatever that means (Arthur Kaptainis, "Christmas Trounces Political Correctness," *Montreal Gazette*, 24 December 2002: A-1), and the Gap instructed clerks to say "happy holidays" or "season's greetings" to customers instead of the supposedly offensive "merry Christmas" (Sarah Staples, "Christmas Is In Again at the Gap," *Montreal Gazette*, 14 December 2002: A-15). These examples are trivial. Others are not so trivial. Given their newfound political clout, due to strategic alliances with feminists, gay activists have succeeded in getting elementary schools to use textbooks that promote acceptance of homosexuality (even in places where most parents oppose it on religious grounds) and will almost certainly succeed in the legalization of gay marriage (even though that could, arguably, undermine this institution for the majority) by claiming, apart from anything else, that merely being unmarried is tantamount to lacking human dignity. In other words, the very fact of being a minority is inherently undignified and therefore intolerable, which is a dangerous point of view in any democracy. This particular political strategy, undermining the "dominant" culture, is hardly confined to gay activists. Nor did they invent it. It just so happens that their current demands are among the more dramatic ones.

2 Frans de Waal, *Peacemaking among Primates* (Cambridge: Harvard University Press, 1989) 232–3.

3 Jerry Adler, "The Numbers Game," *Newsweek*, 25 July 1994: 57.

4 One reason for avoiding statistical arguments is simply that statistics go out of date very quickly. Even if nothing changes from one decade to the next, for example, statistics based on the earlier date would normally be considered unacceptable.

5 A social problem is like a disease in one way; it cannot be cured merely by getting rid of symptoms. Even in the most practical sense, therefore, the end cannot be said to justify the means.

6 Adler 56.

7 Philip Sullivan, "Acceptable Scholarship," *University Affairs*, January 1996: 23.

8 Lenore J. Weitzman, *The Divorce Revolution: The Unexpected Social and Economic Consequences for Women and Children in America* (New York: Free Press, 1985).

9 Geoffrey Christopher Rapp, "Lies, Damned Lies, and Lenore J. Weitzman," [undated], [untitled website], [visited] 16 June 2005, <http://www.acbr.com/biglie.htm>: 1–2.

10 Rapp 1. Actually, more than a typo was involved. The carelessness, so to speak, was pervasive. "Once given access to the files," writes Rapp, "Peterson began to recreate Weitzman's study using exactly the same 228-person sample and the methods described in The Divorce Revolution. He found that the information in Weitzman's computer file in many cases did not match up with the paper records of the original respondent interviews. 'The computer file was supposed to be coded from the paper records,' he says, 'but the computer file in fact did not reflect the paper records. For example, suppose the computer file said a person's income was $27,000 last year, but when I looked at the paper records it turned out that it was $37,000'" (Rapp 5).

11 These figures were more in line with those of national studies, writes Rapp, but still misleading. "The problem seems to lie in the 'ratio of income to needs' used by Weitzman, Peterson, and others. Weitzman asked 114 women and 114 men to report pre- and post-divorce income for both themselves and their spouses, adjusting for alimony and child support payments where applicable. Then, she compared these figures to each person's 'economic need,' based on the Bureau of Labor Statistics' Lower Standard Budget for an urban family of four in 1977, to arrive at her ratio. Even as corrected by Peterson, her data was sketchy: income or needs data was missing for 134 of the respondents, and, according to Peterson, the data for family size, age of the household head, oldest child, and other relevant variables was 'problematic' with notable 'inconsistencies.' From this admittedly flawed data set, an income/needs ration was derived, and the results labeled 'standard of living' ...

"In the real world, standard of living is determined not simply by a ratio of income to needs, but also by a lifetime of economic choices, earnings, investments, and purchases. An accurate measure of standard of living would necessarily include property owned, savings, houses, furniture, automobiles, the neighborhood one lives in, clothing, and the like, most of which is typically divided between spouses in a divorce settlement. It seems unlikely that the average man would have a 10 percent higher standard of living after losing half of his marital property, much less a 42 percent increase. Pollock points out that Weitzman's income/needs ratio 'omits completely any prior assets that people have. In divorce settlements, so much of the issue is who gets what, and it's not just alimony or child support but also the division of the others assets. And most of the studies that I've read have omitted that part.'

"Warren Farrell ... agrees with Pollock and adds that Weitzman's and other studies usually omit several expenses which men face. 'There are five expenses that men have after divorce, typically speaking, that Weitzman, just didn't measure,' he says. These include: mortgage payments on a home they no longer live in, rent on a home or apartment they do live in, child support payments, alimony, and higher percentages of dating expenses. Says Farrell, 'No one that I know has controlled for all five of these variables'" (Rapp 5–6).

12 One variable is the different taxation rates of custodial and noncustodial parents (which we discuss in chapter 6). The latter are not allowed to claim child-support payments as tax deductions, but the former are allowed to do that and also to claim children as dependents. Another variable is the money spent by noncustodial parents on visiting children. In other words, custody amounts to a financial prize. Moreover, former wives are often awarded alimony for at least a few years.

13 Atlee Stroup and Gene Pollock, "Economic Consequences of Marital Dissolution," *Journal of Divorce and Remarriage* 22 (1994): 37–54. For additional sources on the economic problems faced by both divorced fathers and divorced mothers, see the Rocky Mountain Family Council's site *Fact Sheet: The Grass Isn't Greener: The Damaging Effects of Divorce*, [visited] 18 December 2002, <http://www.rmfc.org/fs/fs0030.html>. Economic problems are not the only ones faced by divorced or separated men. This site has a very useful bibliography referring to studies showing that they face greater medical and psychiatric risks than married men.

14 Rapp 3.

15 Angela James; quoted in Rapp 3.

16 Rapp 3.

17 Rapp 3–4.

18 Rapp 4.

19 Christina Hoff Sommers; quoted in Rapp 4.

20 F.F. Furstenburg, "Good Dads – Bad Dads: The Two Faces of Fatherhood," in *The Changing American Family and Public Policy*, ed, A.J. Cherlin (Washington, DC: Urban Institute Press, 1988; quoted in Braver 56–7.

21 Cathy Young, "First Wives Club: Some Comments," [undated], *Balance: The Inclusive Vision of Gender Equality*, [visited] 16 December 2002, <http://www.taiga.ca/~balance/index003/wives.html>: 1; also published in the *Philadelphia Inquirer*, 7 October 1996: A-13. According to the criteria that we presented in *Spreading Misandry*, this movie could be classified as misandric. We did not do so in that book, though, because it could also be described as misogynistic. In this case, classification depends heavily on the identity of viewers. For most male (and at least a few female) viewers, the movie is clearly misandric. After all, it ridicules and attacks all three ex-husbands and implies that all husbands are stereotypically worthless louts. And for most female viewers, that presentation is satirical but also justified. But for other female (and at least a few male) viewers, this movie is clearly misogynistic. Why? Because it presents the protagonists – and, by implication, all

wives – as vengeful harpies who should never have been married in the first place. Unfortunately, *First Wives* is not merely misanthropic. It does not attack both men and women, after all, but either men or women. It all depends on who the viewers are and their ability or lack of ability to place the movie in its larger cultural context.

22 Elizabeth Gleick, "Hell Hath No Fury: The First Wives Club Packs Multiplexes with Women Who Recognize the Plot and Want the Message: Get Even, Then Get over It," *Time*, 7 October 1996: 80–5.

23 Maureen Dowd, "Men Behaving Badly," *New York Times*, 29 September 1996: 4, 15.

24 Young 1.

25 Young 2.

26 Erin Pizzey, *Scream Quietly or the Neighbours Will Hear* (Harmondsworth, England: Penguin, 1974).

27 Erin Pizzey, *Prone to Violence* (Feltham, England: Hamlyn, 1982).

28 Suzanne K. Steinmetz, "The Battered Husband Syndrome," *Victimology* 2 (1977–78): 499–500.

29 Murray A. Straus, Richard J. Gelles, and Suzanne K. Steinmetz, *Behind Closed Doors: Violence in the American Family* (New York: Anchor Press/Doubleday, 1980), 40–1; cited in Warren Farrell, *Women Can't Hear What Men Don't Say: Destroying Myths, Creating Love* (New York: Jeremy P. Tarcher/Putnam, 1999) 129.

30 A British survey of the mid-1990s found that more men than women were being assaulted at home. Researchers found that 18% of men and 13% of women claimed to have been the victims of domestic violence. According to Malcolm George in an interview by the British Broadcasting Corporation, "You're confronting here two taboos. One is that women can be violent and the second is that men can be beaten up by their wives. And that is something that nobody wants to take on board" ("Britons Say More Men Assaulted at Home," *Montreal Gazette*, 8 December 1994: A-19).

31 Farrell 142.

32 Farrell 142.

33 Philip W. Cook, *Abused Men: The Hidden Side of Domestic Violence* (Westport, CT: Prasger, 1997), 111 (reporting on the reaction to Suzanne Steinmetz).

34 Cook 112 (reporting on his interview with Steinmetz).

35 Straus; cited in Cook 116.

36 R.L. McNeely; cited in Cook 119.

37 Mark Schulman, "A Survey of Spousal Violence against Women in Kentucky" (Washington, DC: U.S. Government Printing Office, 1979), Study No. 792701. Research was conducted by the Kentucky Commission on Women and sponsored by the Department of Justice, Law Enforcement Assistance Administration; cited in Farrell 143.

38 See Murray A. Straus, "Physical Assaults by Wives: A Major Social Problem," *Current Controversies on Family Violence*, ed. Richard Gelles and Donileen Loseke (Newbury Park, CA: Sage, 1993) 72–3; cited in Farrell 143.

39 Patricia Pearson, "Women Behaving Badly," *Saturday Night*, September 1997: 93.

40 Pearson 94.

41 Leslie W. Kennedy and Donald G. Dutton, "The Incidence of Wife Assault in Alberta," *Canadian Journal of Behavioral Science* 21.1 (1989): 40–54. Research was done at the University of Alberta's Population Research Laboratory.

42 Adler 56.

43 John Fekete, *Moral Panic: Biopolitics Rising* (Montreal: Robert Davies, 1995) 71.

44 See also R. Emerson Dobash, Russell P. Dobash, and others, "The Myth of Sexual Symmetry in Marital Violence," *Social Problems* 39.1 (February 1992): 71– 91. Critiques of what has been dubbed the "Battered Husband Syndrome" (which we discuss in chapter 9) have entered the popular press as well. See Jack C. Straton, "The Myth of the 'Battered Husband Syndrome,'" *Masculinities* 2 (1994): 79–82). The author discusses flaws in Straus' Conflict Tactics Scale studies (CTS). "Perhaps," replied Straus, "the most important conceptual error is the belief that the Conflict Tactics Scale is deficient because it does not measure the consequences of physical assault [such as physical and emotional injury], or the causes [such as a desire to dominate]. This is akin to thinking that a spelling test is inadequate because it does not measure why a child spells badly, or does not measure possible explanations of poor spelling. The concentration ... on acts of physical assault [of specific kinds and degrees of severity] is deliberate and one of its strengths. The attacks ... are examples of blaming the messenger for the bad news. Moreover, no matter what one thinks of the CTS, at least four studies that did not use the CTS also found roughly equal rates of violence by women" (Straus; cited in Cook 116).

45 Fekete 72.

46 Lenore E.A. Walker, *The Battered Woman* (New York: Harper and Row, 1979), xv (our emphasis).

47 Walker 98 (our emphasis).

48 Walker 170.

49 Walker xi.

50 Lenore E.A. Walker, "Psychology and Violence against Women," *American Psychologist* 44.4 (April 1989): 695.

51 Walker, *Battered Woman*, xvii.

52 Walker, *Battered Woman*, 246.

53 Christina Hoff Sommers, "The Spouse Abuse Myth," *USA Today*, 26 October 1994: 13.

54 Christina Hoff Sommers, "The New Mythology," *National Review*, 27 June

1994: 30–4; "More on Superbowl Violence," [undated], *World Wide Web Virtual Library: Men and Domestic Violence Index*, [visited] 18 December 2002, <http://www.vix.com/men/battery/newmyth.html>.

55 Lynda Gorov, "Activists: Abused Women at Risk on Super Sunday," *Boston Globe*, 29 January 1993: 13.

56 Sommers, "Superbowl Violence" 2.

57 Ken Ringle, "Debunking the 'Day of Dread' for Women: Data Lacking for Claim of Domestic Violence Surge after Super Bowl," *Washington Post*, 31 January 1992: A-01; Robert Lipsyte, "Violence Translates at Home," *New York Times*, 31 January 1993: 8.5.

58 Bob Hohler, "Super Bowl Gaffe Groups Back off on Violence Claims," *Boston Globe*, 2 February 1993: 1.

59 Sommers, "Superbowl Violence" 2.

60 Sommers, "The Spouse Abuse Myth" 13.

61 Gloria Steinem, *Revolution from Within: A Book of Self-esteem* (Boston: Little Brown, 1993).

62 "The 'Stolen Feminism' Hoax: Anti-feminist Attack Based on Error-Filled Anecdotes," [dated] September-October 1994, *Extra!* [visited] 19 December 2002, <http://www.fair.org/exra/9409/stolen-feminism-hoax.html>.

63 "Christina Hoff Sommers' Reply to Charges Disseminated by the Left Wing Media Watchdog Group FAIR (Fairness and Accuracy in Reporting, [dated] 15 March 1995, *The Debunker's Domain*, [visited] 19 December 2002, <http://www.debunker.com/texts/fair2.html>: 1.

64 "The Violence against Women Survey," conducted by the Ministry of Industry, Science, and Technology (cat. 11-001E) and reported by Statistics Canada in *The Daily*, 18 November 1993.

65 Fekete 82.

66 Fekete 80–1.

67 Fekete 84–5 (his emphasis).

68 *Changing the Landscape: Ending Violence – Achieving Equality*, Final Report of the Canadian Panel on Violence against Women (Ottawa: Minister of Supply and Services, 1993); cat. no. SW45–1/1993E; quoted in Fekete 99ff.

69 David Thomas, *Not Guilty: The Case in Defense of Men* (New York: Morrow, 1993) 146.

70 Farrell 142–3.

71 Farrell 143.

72 Grant A. Brown, "Gender as a Factor in the Response of the Law-enforcement System to Violence against Partners," forthcoming article.

APPENDIX FOUR

1 William Safire, "Linguistically Correct," *The New York Times Magazine*, 5 May 1991 20.

2 Safire 20.

3 John Sopinka, "Freedom of Speech," *University Affairs*, April 1994, 13.

4 Allan C. Hutchinson, "Like Lunches, Speech is Never Free," *University Affairs*, June–July 1994: 12.

5 Hutchinson 12.

6 Dan Osmond, "Letters," *University Affairs*, April 1996: 28.

7 Sanjay Suri, "Objectionable Toys Withdrawn," *India Abroad*, 12 September 1992: 25.

8 Edward W. Said, *Orientalism* (New York: Vintage Books, 1979) 285–7.

9 The most thorough examination of this problem has been made, ironically (or not), by a German Christian: Katherina von Kellenbach, *Anti-Judaism in Christian-Rooted Feminist Writings: An Analysis of Major American and West German Feminist Theologians* (Ann Arbor, MI: University Microfilms International, 1987). Kellenbach's introduction is intensely moving, and the analysis is brilliant. Even so, she sees no parallel between Jewish-Christian relations and male-female relations. She recognizes "the Fall" as a projection of Original Sin onto Jews, but not onto men. This might be understandable if the context were general. But the context is very specific: feminism. The primary "others" of feminists are men, after all, not Jews. In spite of everything, she fails to make the logical and even obvious connection.

10 Mark Cladis, "Mild-Mannered Pragmatism and Religious Truth," *Journal of the American Academy of Religion* 60.1 (1992): 19–33.

11 James B. Wiggins, "Openings and Closings," *Journal of the American Academy of Religion* 60.1 (1992): 109.

12 George Jonas, "Denying Their Saviour," *Montreal Gazette*, 27 December 1998: A-11.

13 Bob Morris, "A Model Family," *New York Times Magazine*, 12 November 1995: 93 (his emphasis).

14 Jean Bethke Elshtain, "Trial by Fury," review of *The Real Anita Hill: The Untold Story*, by David Brock, *New Republic*, 6 September 1993: 33.

15 Carolyn L. Karcher, *The First Woman in the Republic: A Cultural Biography of Lydia Maria Child* (Durham, NC: Duke University Press, 1994).

16 Drew Gilpin Faust, "Remembering Lydia: The Life of an Abolitionist Who Was Nearly Erased from History," review of *The First Woman in the Republic: A Cultural Biography of Lydia Maria Child*, by Carolyn L. Karcher, *New York Times Book Review*, 8 January 1995: 25.

17 Faust 25.

APPENDIX FIVE

1 In 1985, Juliette Woodruff estimated that 99% of the readers were women ("A Spate of Words, Full of Sound and Fury, Signifying Nothing: Or, How to Read in Harlequin," *Journal of Popular Culture* 19.2 [fall 1985]: 27). There

is no reason to believe that anything has changed in that respect over the past fifteen years.

2 In this respect, though things have changed a lot over the past few decades. By the 1990s, these genres had been successfully integrated – at least in the movies and on television. No one is surprised any more to find female protagonists "kicking butt." We discuss this phenomenon in *Spreading Misandry*.

3 Sarah Bird, "Rules of the Game," *Entertainment Weekly*, 16 August 1991: 32.

4 Angela Miles, "Confessions of a Harlequin Reader: Romance and the Myth of Male Mothers," *Canadian Journal of Political and Social Theory/Revue canadienne de théorie politique et sociale* 12.1–2 (1988): 1–37.

5 Miles 28.

6 Miles 28.

7 Miles 2 (her emphasis).

8 Miles 2.

9 Miles 4.

10 Miles 7–8 (her emphasis).

11 Miles 8.

12 Miles 4.

13 Miles 5 (her emphasis).

14 Miles 16.

15 The filmed version of *Gone with the Wind* (Victor Fleming, 1939) was restored and re-released in 1998.

16 It is the direct ancestor of at least one sitcom, too. Ally, the protagonist of *Ally McBeal*, is not exactly a feminist. She has a high-powered career in law, to be sure, but she spends most of her time whining about her love life, worrying about her biological clock or about her daughter, and indulging in neuroticism. And, as outraged feminists have pointed out, she wears miniskirts in court. (Even worse, Calista Flockhart, who plays Ally, looks emaciated enough to cause rumours that she has anorexia.) Troy Patterson points out that Scarlett and Ally have many characteristics in common. Each belongs to a ruling class (Southern gentry and Northeastern meritocracy); each yearns for an unavailable man (Ashley and Billy); and each "expresses her romantic torment with big eyes that brattishly bug out at a perceived affront and a fat bottom lip alternately trembled in heartbreak, nibbled comically in fluster, and protruded in coquettish pouts. Scarlett and Ally are fairy-tale princesses who bear about as much resemblance to real women as Barbie and Skipper. The fact that there's no longer a place in the fairy tale for Rhett Butler seems one small stop for Girl Power" ("Scarlett Letters," *Entertainment Weekly*, 23 October 1998 82).

17 Helen Taylor, *Scarlett's Women: Gone With the Wind and Its Female Fans* (London: Virago Press, 1989) 139.

18 Taylor 117–18.

19 We have already discussed the contention of Angela Miles that the heroes in

romance novels are really mothers in drag. In one biography (*Margaret Mitchell* [Boston: Twayne, 1991]), Elizabeth Hanson observes that the author of *Gone With the Wind* did indeed apply some of her mother's characteristics to Rhett (and to at least one female character as well). This is hardly surprising for a writer. Like other observers of human nature, she understood that many characteristics – such as strength, courage, endurance, and caring – are commonly found in both men and women. The particular characteristic under discussion here, though, is the potential for violence. Mitchell did not identify this with her mother. Nor is there any evidence to suggest that fans of her book and the movie based on it have ever identified it with either women or mothers. Besides, Rhett is associated specifically with sexual violence, not merely the destructive aspect of nature in general. It is true that motherhood, in both psychoanalytical and mythological terms, has a "dark side." Children do worry about being engulfed or destroyed by their mothers. But for Miles to admit this would defeat her whole argument. She wants to glorify mothers (and, by extension, women), not to demonize them. Her whole article is based on the assumption that mothers (that is, women) are inherently *benevolent*, not that they are both benevolent and malevolent. To say that Rhett Butler is really a "mother," therefore, would mean rejecting the superficial and sentimental notion of motherhood promoted by Miles and seeing him as a Western version of India's Kali, the Great Mother who is associated with cosmic destruction as well as creation.

20 Taylor 115.
21 Tom Kuntz, "Rhett and Scarlett: Rough Sex or Rape? Feminists Give a Damn," *New York Times*, 19 February 1995: iv.7.
22 Friedman; quoted in Kuntz 7.
23 Sommers (her emphasis); quoted in Kuntz 7.
24 When *TV Guide* conducted a survey among celebrities, Tea Leoni observed that in the category of most romantic video rental, "Hands down, it's *Gone with the Wind*. When he grabs her and takes her up the stairs ..." But Julie White disagreed: "That's a rape video! I'm going with *Casablanca* on this one." We wrote to *TV Guide* for this reference but have received no reply.
25 Friedman; quoted in Kuntz 7.
26 Friedman; quoted in Kuntz 7.
27 Margaret Mitchell, *Gone with the Wind* (New York: Pocket Books, 1936) 783. Interviewed about her character in *Mary Reilly*, the servant of Dr Jekyll and Mr Hyde, Julia Roberts said much the same thing: "She gets attracted to someone capable of hurting her. That's the way life is, isn't it?" (quoted in Jeff Gordinier, "Living the Life of Reilly: Clearing Up for Scrutiny of Her Latest Film, Julia Roberts Has Nothing to Hyde," *Entertainment Weekly*, 23 February 1996: 24).
28 Friedman; quoted in Kuntz 7.
29 Sommers; quoted in Kuntz 7.

30 Friedman; quoted in Kuntz 7.
31 Taylor 113.
32 Elaine Gignilliat, "Books of Love," *20/20*, ABC, WVNY-TV, Burlington, VT, 13 August 1981.
33 Juliette Woodruff, "A Spate of Words, Full of Sound and Fury, Signifying Nothing: Or, How to Read in Harlequin," *Journal of Popular Culture* 19.2 (fall 1985): 28.
34 Miles 9.
35 Miles 27.
36 Miles 27.
37 Miles 11.
38 Miles 16.
39 Miles 4.
40 See Nancy Chodorow, *The Reproduction of Mothering: Psychoanalysis and the Sociology of Gender* (Berkeley: University of California Press, 1978). Not all feminists, including ideological feminists, care about psychoanalysis. But many still believe that it can serve their purposes. Chodorow, by no means a marginal figure in feminist circles, is still cited in feminist bibliographies and course reading lists in women's studies. Among her more recent works is *Femininities, Masculinities, Sexualities: Freud and Beyond* (Lexington, KY: University of Kentucky Press, 1994).
41 Miles 21.
42 Miles 25.
43 Miles 2.
44 Ironically, this is linked to the more general dichotomy between mind or spirit (good) and body (evil) that is rejected by most feminists as a characteristically "male" or "patriarchal" way of thinking.
45 See Marilyn French, *Beyond Power: On Women, Men, and Morals* (New York: Ballantyne, 1985). Originally, we intended to discuss French's book, what we call a "Summa feministica," in one volume of this trilogy. Due to lack of space, even with three volumes, we have decided to do so in a separate book on how feminist ideology has been translated into feminist theology. We hope to call this book "Beyond the Fall of Man" (which, confusingly, is what we had originally intended to call this trilogy).
46 Miles 28.
47 Miles 28.
48 Miles 28.
49 Miles 28.
50 See Mary O'Brien, *The Politics of Reproduction* (Boston: Routledge and Kegan Paul, 1981).
51 Miles 23–4.
52 Dorothy Dinnerstein, *The Mermaid and the Minotaur: Sexual Arrangements and Human Malaise* (New York: Harper and Row, 1976); Jane Flax, *Psycho-*

analysis, Feminism, and Postmodernism in the Contemporary West (Berkeley: University of California Press, 1990).

53 Miles 24.

54 Adrienne Rich; quoted in Miles 30.

55 Miles 5.

56 Catherine Keller, *From a Broken Web: Separation, Sexism, and Self* (Boston: Beacon Press, 1966).

57 For a lengthy treatment of this particular argument, see Keller.

58 Miles 7.

59 Kelli Pryor, "Love Takes a Holiday," *Entertainment Weekly*, 16 August 1991: 18.

60 Pryor 18 (our emphasis).

APPENDIX SIX

1 "Fourth World Conference on Women Beijing Declaration," [dated] 18 April 2002, *United Nations, Division for the Advancement of Women*, [visited] 5 August 2002, <http://www.un.org/womenwatch/daw/beijing/platform/ declar.htm>. We will refer to this document as "the Beijing Declaration."

2 "Fourth World Conference on Women Platform for Action," [dated] 18 April 2002, *United Nations, Division for the Advancement of Women*, [visited] 5 August 2002, <http://www.un.org/womenwatch/daw/beijing/platform/ plat1.htm>. We will refer to this document as "the Beijing Platform."

3 General Assembly of the United Nations, "Annex: Further Actions and Initiatives to Implement the Beijing Declaration and Platform for Action," Twenty-third Special Session, Agenda Item 10, A/res/s-23/3, 10 June 2000. We found this document at the following website: <http://www.un.org/womenwatch/ daw/followup/reports.htm>; we will refer to it as "the Annex."

4 *The Optional Protocol, Text and Materials: The Convention on the Elimination of All Forms of Discrimination against Women* (New York: United Nations, Division for the Advancement of Women, Department of Economic and Social Affairs, 2000).

5 *Optional Protocol* 1.

6 United Nations, Universal Declaration of Human Rights; reprinted in *Journal of Religious Pluralism*, 3 (1993): 1–8 (our emphasis).

7 Beijing Platform, section 295.

8 Beijing Platform, section 26.

9 "Fourth World Conference on Women Platform for Action," [dated] 18 April 2002, *United Nations, Division for the Advancement of Women*, [visited] 5 August 2002, <http://www.un.org/womenwatch/daw/beijing/platform/plat2. htm>: 9.

10 Readers are told to see Annex IV to the Beijing Platform, submitted by Canada. See "Amendments to the Initial Position of the Group of 77 (Draft

Platform for Action)" [undated], *Linkages* [visited] 5 August 2002, <http://www.iisd.ca/linkages/4cwc/dpa-012.html>. For some reason, the word "gender" is not defined there, either.

11 Beijing Platform, section 295.

12 Annex 24 (IV.72.e). This is a reference to 24 of the printout, or section iv.72.2 of the document.

13 Annex 2 (I.4).

14 Annex 12 (II.I.27).

15 See, for instance, "Progress has been made to combat negative images of women by establishing professional guidelines and voluntary codes of conduct, encouraging fair gender portrayal and the use of non-sexist language in media programmes" (12; I.J.28) and "Negative, violent and/or degrading images of women, including pornography and stereotyped portrayals, have increased in different forms using new communication technologies in some instances, and bias against women remains in the media" (12; I.J.29).

16 Annex 6 (II.D.13).

17 Annex 31 (IV.B.82.j).

18 Annex 35 (IV.D.93.a).

19 Annex 39 (IV.D.100.c).

20 "NAC Young Womyn," [undated], *National Action Committee on the Status of Women*, [visited] 23 October 2002, <http://www.nac-cca.ca/young/young_e.htm>.

21 Annex 1 (I.1).

22 Annex 8 (II.E.16).

23 Annex 29 (IV.B.79.a).

24 Annex 24.(IV.A.71.a)

25 Annex 38 (IV.98.c).

26 Annex 19 (IV.60).

27 Annex 19 (IV.60).

28 Annex 7 (II.D.14).

29 Annex 23 (IV.A.69.f; IV.A.70.d).

30 Annex 7 (II.D.14).

31 Annex 28 (IV.B.b).

32 Anne Peters, *Women, Quotas and Constitutions: A Comparative Study of Affirmative Action for Women under American, German, European Community and International Law* (The Hague: Kluwer Law International, 2000), 94.

33 Peters 267.

34 Annex 31 (IV.B.82.h).

35 Annex 34 (IV.C.89).

36 Annex 21 (IV.A.66.a).

37 Annex 20 (IV.61).

38 Annex (IV.61).

39 Annex 16 (III.43).
40 Annex 36 (IV.D.95.g).

APPENDIX SEVEN

1 "Our Equality Rights in the Charter," [undated], *Court Challenges Program of Canada*, [visited] 4 August 2002, <http://www.ccppcj.ca/e/info.html>: 2.
2 "Our Equality Rights in the Charter," [undated], *About Court Challenges*, [visited 17 October 2004], <http://www.ccppcj.ca/e/i-charter.html.> *Law v. Canada (Minister of Employment and Immigration)* [1999] 1 S.C.R. 497 requires that claims of discrimination be based on three broad inquiries: whether the law, program, or activity imposes differential treatment between the claimant and others; whether this differential treatment is based on one or more enumerated or analogous grounds, and whether the impugned law, program, or activity has a purpose or effect that is substantially discriminatory.
3 *Eldridge v. British Columbia (A.G.)*, [1997] 3 S.C.R. 624.
4 "Our Equality Rights" 2.
5 Nicholas B. Dirks, *Castes of Mind: Colonialism and the Making of Modern India* (Princeton, N.J.: Princeton University Press, 2001) 15.
6 Dirks 13. Indian society had long been organized into *varnas*, classes or castes, based on occupation: priests (*brahmins*), warriors and rulers (*kshatriyas*), merchants (*vaishyas*), and servants (*shudras*). These groups had gradually been subdivided into thousands of subgroups (*jatis*) based on specific occupations and other criteria. But the vicissitudes of history – invasions, migrations, politics, religious conversions – had allowed some mobility. Not everyone agreed, moreover, on the place of each *jati* or even each *varna* in the hierarchy. The brahmins have articulated one hierarchy, based on ritual purity, but not all Hindus have accepted it. Kshatriyas have sometimes considered political power more important, for instance, than the ritual power of brahmins.
7 This relatively fluid situation changed under the British after 1857. Before that date, the British had felt no need to do much in India except engage in commerce (and take whatever political or military steps were necessary for that purpose, mainly preventing other European powers from capturing their trade routes). British commercial outposts in India, eventually territories, were administered and defended entirely by the British East India Company. After 1857, marked by what the British called the Great Mutiny and what the Indians called the Great Rebellion, British India came under the direct control of Parliament in London. In other words, the British became much more closely involved in the administration of India as a colony. The first step was to create a centralized bureaucracy. The British could not do so very effectively at first, because they knew very little about Indian society and culture. To learn more, they made use of information gathered by missionaries, anthropolo-

gists, soldiers, magistrates, and bureaucrats. Based on this information about caste, they created administrative categories. But because much of their information had come from the brahmins, who were their primary informants, the hierarchy was defined largely by them. And, not surprisingly, they ranked themselves at the top.

8 Dirks 5–6.
9 Dirks 13.
10 The outcastes were so called because they ranked below even the lowest castes. The same thing applied to "tribals."
11 This idea was generally accepted by the time of independence, but some people worried about the possible consequences. They argued that this system would not only perpetuate but also accentuate caste consciousness and even promote "vested interests in backwardness." Others argued that the system should be seen as a temporary measure. Still others argued that neutral factors – illiteracy, lack of land, low income, and so on – should be used instead of caste as the criteria defining eligibility for government help (Dirks 279).
12 Some took drastic action as individuals. "On September 19, 1990, a student from Delhi University poured kerosene over his body and set himself on fire ... in the heat of emotion, in the context of an impassioned protest against a government decision that was seen as taking all future prospects of respectable employment away from young people with upper-caste backgrounds ... Within the next month, more than 159 young people also followed suit, attempting suicide by self-immolation; 63 succeeded. Another 100 people were killed in police firings and clashes that accompanied the widespread protest" (Dirks 275).
13 Dirks 5–6; caste consciousness has been supported not only by Marxists, ironically, but also by postmodernists or postcolonialists.
14 Consider the case of Sri Lanka, which has had a similar history of affirmative action for admission to universities. According to K.M. De Silva, executive director of the International Centre for Ethnic Studies, in Kandy, affirmative action began as a way to bring rural students into the university system but was "transformed in the late 1970s to a regional quota system cutting across ethnic and religious identities. The introduction and implementation of preferential policies in Sri Lanka's university system, and the impassioned resistance to modifying them, much less to reversing them, provide an excellent introduction to the complex nature of Sri Lanka's ethnic conflict and the political ramifications of rivalries between Muslims and Tamils, divisions among Tamils, and, of course, rivalries between Sinhalese and Tamils" (K.M. De Silva, "Affirmative Action Policies: The Sri Lankan Expeience," *Ethnic Studies Report*, 15.2 [July 1997]: 245). "Introduced as a temporary measure, this very limited exercise in affirmative action has survived for over 25 years now, and there is no sign that they [sic] will be abandoned anytime soon ... [T]here have been substantial changes in the system, changes which

unfortunately strengthen the forces opposed to its abandonment or radical reform because with every mutation, one more element is added to a complex system of vested interests that unite to secure its survival ... Here we need to make the point that one result of this system of admissions is that the concept of academic merit has gone by the board. In the hard choice between quality and quantity, quality has been sacrificed to a much greater extent than in most other university systems in the third world" (De Sliva, 282–3).

15 "Our Equality Rights in the Charter" 2.
16 "Our Equality Rights" 4.
17 "Our Equality Rights" 5.
18 "Our Equality Rights" 5.
19 "Our Equality Rights" 4.
20 See, for example, the Employment Equity Act (S.C. 1995, c.44), which regulates employers with 100 or more employees.
21 Grant A. Brown, "The Politics of Preference: A Catalogue of Criticisms of Employment Equity," unpublished manuscript, 16.
22 Following the insight of St Paul, most traditional forms of Christianity insist in one way or another on two fundamental principles. First, that Christ has taken on guilt for the sins of his followers. Second, that he paid the ultimate and complete price for those sins on the cross. That is how Christ liberates Christians from sin. In the secularized version discussed here, however, there is one significant difference. Christ paid the price voluntarily; he sacrificed himself. Men are not sacrificing themselves (even though some convince themselves of that). On the contrary, they are being sacrificed by the state.

APPENDIX EIGHT

1 Grant Brown, "The Politics of Preference: A Catalogue of Criticisms of Employment Equity," unpublished draught paper, 8–9.
2 "Equity," [undated] CAUT/ACPPU, [visited] 25 October 2002, <http://www.caut.ca/english/issues/equity/>: 1.
3 "Equity" 4.
4 "Equity" 1.
5 "Equity" 2.
6 "Equity" 4.
7 In 2004, CAUT called on government officials to amend the Employment Equity Act. Why? In order "to ensure that the Federal Contractors Program is capable of being enforced through the employment equity branch of the Canadian Human Rights Commission" ("Council Adopts Policy Statement on Federal Contractors Program," CAUT Bulletin (January 2004): A-8.
8 "Equity" 4.
9 "Equity" 2.

10 "Equity" 2.
11 *Pay Equity Review*: "Terms of Reference," [dated] 21 January 2002, *Government of Canada*, [visited] 20 October 2002, <http://www.payequityreview.gc.ca/1200–e.html.>: 2.
12 "Introduction," *Pay Equity Review* 2.
13 "Request for Proposals," *Pay Equity Review* 1.

APPENDIX NINE

1 "Lobby Activities: Custody and Access," [dated] 2002, *National Association of Women and the Law*, [visited] 16 December 2002, <http://www.nawl.ca/lob-custody.htm>: 1.
2 American Law Institute, *Principles of the Law of Family Dissolution: Analysis and Recommendations* (Newark, NJ: Matthew Bender, 2002). The Institute outlines several problems confronting anyone seeking to balance the conflicting principles involved in custody disputes.
3 American Law Institute 2.
4 American Law Institute 2.
5 American Law Institute 3.
6 American Law Institute 3.
7 American Law Institute 3.
8 American Law Institute 5.
9 American Law Institute 7.
10 American Law Institute 7–8.
11 American Law Institute 8.
12 American Law Institute 9.
13 American Law Institute 9.
14 American Law Institute 9.
15 American Law Institute 9–10.
16 American Law Institute 10.
17 American Law Institute 13.
18 Gloria Woods, "Father's Rights Groups: Beware Their Real Agenda," [undated], *National NOW Times*, [visited] 1 July 2002 <http://www.now.org/nnt/03–97>: 1.
19 Woods 1.
20 Woods 1.
21 Michael Jackson provoked a journalistic feeding frenzy by dangling his son over the railing of a hotel room in Berlin. The event took less than five seconds, and the boy was in no obvious danger of falling, but Jackson certainly confirmed his widely held reputation for idiosyncratic behaviour. He made things worse several months later in an interview made for the BBC and later shown in the United States on ABC. Jackson referred to his penchant for inviting children to stay with him and his children at Neverland (Jill Lawless,

"Sleepovers in Neverland: Cuddling Kids 'Sweet,' Jackson Says," *Montreal Gazette*, 5 February 2003: D-5). What provoked Gloria Allred to discuss the possibility of launching an investigation or lawsuit to remove any children from Jackson's care, however, was the fact that he encouraged children to sleep with him in his bed. He accused the journalists, in turn, of cynicism. By "sleep," Jackson said, he had meant slumber, not sex. Whatever. Jackson is clearly neurotic. He clearly does things that look shocking to most people now. Children sleeping in the same beds as their parents would not have looked shocking in the nineteenth century or earlier (when most children, except those of the middle and upper classes, routinely did so even if only because they had no beds of their own). Nor would Jackson's childlike sentimentality. Of interest to us here, though, is merely the fact that Jackson reinforced perceptions of fatherhood that are now widespread. No wonder Allred referred over and over again to the inherent danger posed to children by an "adult male" (Gloria Allred, interviewed on *Today*, NBC, WPTZ, Plattsburgh, NY, 7 February 2003).

22 Woods 2.

23 "For the Sake of the Children: Report of the Special Joint Committee on Child Custody and Access [Summary of Recommendations]," [dated] December 1998, *Parliament of Canada*, [visited] 17 July 2002, <http://www.parl.gc.ca?InfoComDoc/36/1/SJCA/Studies/Reports/sjcarp02/10–rec-e.htm>: 3; the committee that prepared this report was jointly chaired by Landon Pearson and Roger Gallaway.

24 "For the Sake" 3.

25 "For the Sake" 3.

26 "For the Sake" 10.

27 "For the Sake" 44.

28 "Violence against Women Survey," [dated] 16 July 2002, *Statistics Canada*, [visited] 17 July 2002 <http://www.statcan.ca/english/sdds/3896.htm>; quoted in "For the Sake" 71.

29 "Genetic Wallets," [dated] 10 April 2002, *Fathers Are Capable Too*, [visited] 3 July 2002, <http://fact.on.ca/news0204/np020410.htm>; also published as an editorial in *National Post*, 10 April 2002: A-17.

30 Bill C-22.

31 Here is section 16(10) of Canada's Divorce Act of 1985: "In making an order under this section, the court shall give effect to the principle that a child of the marriage should have as much contact with each spouse as is consistent with the best interests of the child and, for that purpose, shall take into consideration the willingness of the person for whom custody is sought to facilitate such contact." And here is the proposed revision of 16(10) in Bill C-22: "Without limiting the generality of subsection (7), the court may include in an order under this section a term requiring any person with parental responsi-

bilities who intends to change his or her place of residence or that of the child to notify, at least sixty days before the change or within such other period before the change as the court may specify, any other person with parental responsibilities of the change, the time at which the change will be made and the new place of residence for him or her or the child, as the case may be." The entire section on "maximum contact" was gutted, in short, and replaced with something about notifying either parent about a change of residence.

32 Cristin Schmitz, "'Mother Gets All,' in New Divorce Act," *National Post*, 18 December 2002: A-6.

33 Virginia McRae; quoted in Schmitz A-6.

34 Anne Cools; quoted in Schmitz A-6.

35 Jay Hill; quoted in Schmitz A-6.

36 *Putting Children's Interests First: Custody, Access and Child Support in Canada* (Ottawa: Department of Justice, 2002); see also "Putting Children's Interests First: Custody, Access and Child Support in Canada: Federal, Provincial, Territorial Consultation," [dated] March 2001, *Department of Justice*, [visited] 12 August 2002, <http://www.canada.justice.gc.ca/en/cons/ConsultationDocumetn.pdf>; part of a continuing "consultation process," this document presents the "issues" and is accompanied by a feedback booklet with responses from the public (*Putting Children's Interests First: Custody, Access and Child Support in Canada*, Feedback Booklet [Ottawa: Department of Justice, 2002]).

37 Alar Soever, "The Federal Child Support Guidelines: A Breakdown of Democratic Process and the Canadian Legal System," [dated] 4 April 2002, *Fathers Are Capable Too*, [visited] 17 February 2004, <http://www.fact.on.ca/fathome/header.htm>: 15.

38 *Putting Children's Interests* 43 (the page number is 43 on the printed text; it is 47 on the computer screen); quoted in Soever 21.

39 From a letter of 19 June 2001 by Virginia McRae at the Department of Justice; cited in Soever 22.

40 "Divorce Act, R.S., 1985 c.3 (2nd Suppl.)," *Canada: Department of Justice*, 3 July 2002, <http://laws.justice.gc,ca/en/D-3.4/text.htm/>: section 15.2.6 b.

41 Michael Higgins, "Divorce Laws Violate Charter: Lawsuit," *National Post*, 5 December 2002: A-12.

42 Gerald Chipeur relies on section 15 of the Charter, which is about "equal protection and equal benefit of the law without discrimination and, in particular, without discrimination based on ... sex." (item 42, page 13) and on section 28: "Notwithstanding anything in this Charter, the rights and freedoms referred to in it are guaranteed equally to male and female persons" (43, 14).

According to Chipeur, moreover, "there exists an imbalance in child custody laws and their implementation favouring the mother over the father in the name of the best interests of the child" (6, 3). For evidence, he points to the fact that in Canada "a divorced mother is nearly ten times as likely as is a divorced father to receive sole custody of their children" (26, 8) – the mother 80.4% and father 8.6%. Chipeur uses several other arguments.

Family law proceedings often deny "fathers and men equality and fundamental justice" (27, 8) because of "hearsay and unsworn evidence (collected through child psychologists and others) in custody hearings; a lax approach to due process; and an over-reliance on independent child assessors, who vary widely in their skills, personal preferences, prejudices, and sensitivities" (27, 8). This state of affairs "violates fathers' rights, including equality, liberty and privacy rights, freedom of association and expression, and other common law and statutory rights. Loss of custody stigmatizes fathers as inadequate or unfit (34, 11) and causes them severe distress – loss of custody being analogous to the death of a child or a missing child (41, 13) And this, in turn, constitutes "cruel and unusual punishment" according to section 12 of the Charter.

This bias against fathers not only violates the rights of fathers, says Chipeur, but also interferes with family relationships and improperly deprives children of family relationships (8 and 9, 4).

The test for establishing custody or access "treats parents whose marriage has broken down differently than parents whose marriage is intact by establishing a different test for interference in the relationship between the parents and children" (10, 4).

Section 16(10) of the Divorce Act says that a child "should have as much contact with each spouse as is consistent with the best interests of the child," but subjective interpretations of the "best interests of the child" are given more weight than the idea of contact (28, 9) (although that point might now be irrelevant, given the fact that Bill C-22 no longer refers to the importance of contact).

Family relationships are permanent and independent of marriage or divorce. "Absent a showing of harm or likelihood of harm, the parent-child bond must remain inviolable ... Prima facie, society must trust both parents to look out for the best interests of their child (12, 5).

Because both parents contribute in distinctive ways to parenting, there should be a presumption of joint custody and the state should interfere in the relationship between parent and child only "when the physical or psychological integrity of the child will otherwise be harmed" (23, 7) – and not without hearing from the child.

For good measure, Chipeur cites the Canadian Bill of Rights and several sections of the Divorce Act of 1985, especially 16(10).

43 Higgins; citing the suit.
44 Higgins A-10.
45 Higgins; citing the suit.
46 "Lobby Activities," [dated] 2002, *National Association of Women and the Law*, [visited] 18 January 2004, <http://www.nawl.ca/lob-custody.htm>:1.

47 "Seven out of ten people in Ontario say child-support payments should be withheld from women who deny access to their children to husbands who pay child support, according to a poll for the *Globe and Mail* by the Angus Reid Group. However, Ontario residents are divided over whether women who repeatedly deny access should face jail sentences" ("Poll Addresses Child Access," *Globe and Mail*, 25 May 1998: A-5).

48 Pamela Cross; quoted at "Below[,] Their Propaganda at It's [*sic*] Best," [dated] 30 March 2001, *Fathers Canada*, [visited] 21 December 2002, <http://www.fathers.ca/take_action_2.htm>: 6.

49 "Media Pointers," [dated] October 2002, *Ontario Women's Network on Child Custody and Access (OWNCCA)*, [visited] 19 December 2002, <http://www.owjn.org/custody/media.htm>.

50 This organization has a steering committee that includes representatives from seven other mainstream organizations, including Action Ontarienne contre la violence faite aux femmes, the Disabled Women's Network (DAWN Ontario), Education Wife Assault, the National Association of Women and the Law, the Northwestern Ontario Women's Centre, the Ontario Association of Interval and Transition Houses, and the Ontario Women's Justice Network.

51 "Women's (In)equality, [undated], *Ontario Women's Network on Child Custody and Access (OWNCCA)*, [visited] 12 December 2002, <http://www.owjn.org/custody/inequal.htm>: 4.

52 "The Ontario Women's Network on Child Custody and Access: A Backgrounder," [undated], *Ontario Women's Network on Child Custody and Access (OWNCCA)*, [visited] 19 December 2002, <http://www.owjn.org/custody/.htm>: 1.

53 Cross 8.

54 "Family Law Reform and the Custody of Children: A Backgrounder, [undated], *Ontario Women's Network on Child Custody and Access (OWNCCA)*, [visited] 19 December 2002, <http://www.owjn.org/custody/law.htm>: 3.

55 The Association for Genital Integrity applied to the Court Challenges Program. Their goal was to apply the Canadian ban on female circumcision to include male circumcision as well. Their application was denied. Section 268 of Canada's Criminal Code defines "agggravated assault." One subsection refers specifically to female circumcision. The Court Challenges Program rejected this attempt to create sexual equality, citing the fact that "aggravated assault" could *include* male circumcision. In that case, though, why not either include a subsection for male circumcision or exclude the one on female circumcision? The "program's Equality Rights Panel disagreed with the group's claim of discrimination, said Melina Buckley, acting executive director of the program. 'They are looking at it from a legal perspective in terms of whether or not this is a test case that is going to advance equality for a disadvantaged group and we are not convinced that this was the case,' she said" (Adrian

Humphreys, "Group Denied Public Funding to Fight Circumcision: Charter Equality for Males Sought," *National Post*, 12 February 2001: A-1 and A-2). In other words, female adults should be considered a "disadvantaged group" but not male infants.

56 "Women's (In)equality" 2.

57 Warren Farrell, *Women Can't Hear What Men Don't Say: Destroying Myths, Creating Love* (New York: Tarcher, 1999).

58 "Women's (In)equality" 2.

59 "Media Pointers" 1.

60 Cross 2 (our emphasis).

61 "Lobby Activities" 2.

62 *Willick v. Willick*, [1994] 3 S.C.R. 670.

63 *British Columbia (Public Service Employee Relations Commission) v. British Columbia Government and Service Employees' Union*, (B.C.G.S.E.U.), [1999] 3 S.C.R. 3.

64 "Women's (In)equality" 3.

65 Women's (In)equality 3.

66 "The Best Interests of the Child," [undated], *Ontario Women's Network on Child Custody and Access (OWNCCA)*, [visited] 19 December 2002, <http://www.owjn.org/custody/child.htm>: 1.

67 "Media Pointers" 2.

68 "Best Interests" 2.

69 "Best Interests" 2.

70 "Best Interests" 2.

71 "Best Interests" 3.

72 "Parenting after Separation," [undated], *Ontario Network on Child Custody and Access (OWNCCA)*, [visited] 19 December 2002, <http://www.owjn.org/custody/parent.htm>: 1.

73 "Parenting" 1.

74 In one documentary, viewers watch a male western-lowland gorilla tenderly holds his infant Congo. The mother tries to take it away from him, but he persists (Jean-Yves Collet, *The Strange Adventure of Mabeke the Gorilla* [2001], *Discovery*, 21 January 2003). See also "Headlines and Highlights," [dated] 14 May 2002, *African Wildlife Foundation*, [visited] 22 December 2002, <http://www.awf.org/news/7377>:2; John Allman and others, "Parent That Takes Care of Offspring Tends to Outlive the Other Parent, Study Shows," [dated] 9 June 1998, *Caltech Press Releases*, [visited] 22 December 2002, <http://pr.caltech.edu/media/lead/060898JA.html>: 2; and David Geary and Mark Flinn's study of the evolution of human parenting behaviour: "Evolution of Human Parental Behavior and the Human Family," *Parenting: Science and Practice*, 1.1–2 (2001): 5–61.

In some primate species, females remain with other members of their own birth groups; males do not. Among chimps, bonobos, gorillas, and humans, however, males do; females do not. Geary and Flinn argue, therefore, that we have inherited an inclination toward patrilocality (and patrilineality) from closely related primates. Consider the gorillas. Males have harems and enduring relationships with females. Moreover, they are involved in parenting. Why? Because, say Geary and Flinn, they know their own offspring. This makes them willing to make heavy investments in parenting. Our Australopithecine ancestors, four million years ago, had the same strategy. Gradually, male dominance gave way to pair bonding, though, due to changes – some of which had already occurred in primates – such as the following: the similar size of males and females; the long developmental period necessary for offspring (which made protection and provision more important); concealed ovulation (which reduced mating competition between males); and nonreproductive sexuality (which kept males sexually interested and involved). Females gained from these developments, at least to the extent of recognizing that their offspring needed the involvement of fathers. With females remaining loyal to one male and thus making it clear that their offspring belonged to that one male, the latter no longer needed to supervise his harem so strictly. Geary and Flinn add that primates have found it necessary to prevent, or at least discourage, infanticide. "When infanticide risk is high, females copulate with males who are likely to displace the dominant male and thus confuse paternity. Males generally do not attempt to kill the infants of females with whom they have copulated. Although infanticide might have accompanied hominid evolution, that does not explain concealed ovulation among humans" (Geary and Flinn 23). Why not? Because "an evolved female strategy that confused paternity would be associated with little or no male parenting, which is inconsistent with the finding of male parenting in every human culture that has been studied ... and with the possibility that Australopithecine males parented" (Geary and Flinn 24).

75 "Parenting" 1.
76 "Parenting" 1.
77 "Parenting" 2.
78 "Parenting" 2.
79 "Parenting" 2.
80 "Parenting" 2.
81 "Parenting" 2.
82 "Parenting" 3.
83 "Parenting" 3.
84 "Parenting" 3.
85 "Parenting" 3.
86 "Women's Access to Justice," [undated], *Ontario Women's Network on Child Custody and Access (OWNCCA)*, [visited] 19 December 2002, <http://www. owjn/custody/justice.htm>: 1.
87 "Parenting" 2.

88 "Family Law Reform" 2.
89 "Parenting" 3.
90 "Parenting" 3.
91 "Sample Letter to the Minister of Justice," [dated] 2002, *Ontario Women's Justice Network*, [visited] 19 December 2002, <http://www.owjn.org/custody/lob-let.htm>: 1.
92 "Lobby Activities" 2.
93 "Sample Letter" 1.
94 "Family Law Reform" 2.
95 "Parenting" 3.
96 "Parenting 3.
97 We refer to the media mavens and talk-show gurus for whom self-realization, or "empowerment," long ago replaced self-sacrifice as an ideal worth at least acknowledging. Several factors explain that shift. By the 1980s one result of a lengthy peace and a burgeoning economy, for instance, was rampant hedonism. But another factor was the rise of feminism. Some schools of feminism – the one popularized by Marilyn French in the early 1990s is a good example – have encouraged hedonism as a supposedly female and superior alternative to male asceticism. Underlying that strategy is the belief that women have been taught traditionally to "give" (submit) and men to "take" (dominate). This teaching put women at a severe disadvantage to the extent that this ideal was actualized in everyday life by both women and men – that is, by genuinely submissive wives and genuinely domineering husbands. Feminists are surely correct in arguing against self-sacrifice as an ideal *only* for women. History reveals, however, that self-sacrifice was an ideal for men, too, although it was not supposed to be expressed in the same way. For one thing, men were usually expected to sacrifice their lives for family and society in hunting or in warfare. And this was not merely an abstract ideal. Eventually, it was enforced by the state. Eventually, men were expected to sacrifice much of their time at jobs outside the home that were for most men every bit as boring or degrading as anything women did inside the home. Men neither were, nor are, thrilled at the prospect of spending their lives at jobs that make other people rich; they accept it as a duty they owe to their families – if they can get jobs.

APPENDIX TEN

1 James Gurney, *Dinotopia: A Land Apart from Time* (Atlanta: Turner, 1992).
2 See below. Those topics are almost always closely associated with feminism. All are based on precisely the same assumptions about "engaged scholarship," "hegemonic discourses," "subaltern traditions," "sites of resistance," "trans-

gression," "alterity," "domination," "oppression," and so on. Each differs from the others only in terms of its particular focus. And even the focus is usually understood as one among several closely related ones.

3 *Publications of the Modern Language Association of America* 105.6 (1990): 1353– 1366. The conference took place in Chicago, 27–30 December 1990; 1,892 papers were presented.

4 *Publications of the Modern Language Association of America*, 115.6 (2000): 1413– 1532. The conference took place in Washington, DC, 27–30 December 2000; 2,195 papers were presented.

APPENDIX ELEVEN

1 William Shakespeare, *Romeo and Juliet*, act 2, scene 2, lines 45–6.

2 Paul Nathanson and Katherine K. Young, *Spreading Misandry: The Teaching of Contempt for Men in Popular Culture* (Montreal: McGill-Queen's University Press, 2001) 227.

3 "Mission Statement," [dated] 2002–2003, *University of Chicago, Center for Gender Studies*, [visited] 11 March 2003, <http://humanities.uchicago.edu/org/cgs/mission.html>: 1.

4 "General Course Descriptions," [dated] 26 November 2002, *Gender Studies [at] Indiana University [in] Bloomington*, [visited] 11 March 2003, <http://www.indiana.edu/~gender/textonlyallabout.html>: 1.

5 "Courses," [dated] 2002–2003, *University of Southern California, Gender Studies*, [visited] 11 March 2003, <http://www.usc.edu/dept/LAS/gsp/htm/courses.htm>: 2.

6 "Courses" 2.

7 "Courses" 7–8.

8 "Gender Studies at Northwestern," [dated] 2002–2003, *Northwestern Gender Studies*, [visited] 11 March 2003, <http://www.genderstudies.northwestern.edu/aboutthe program/index.htm>: 1.

9 "Gender Studies at Northwestern" 1.

10 "Gender Studies at Northwestern" 4.

11 "Courses," [dated] 2002–2003, *Northwestern Gender Studies*, [visited] 11 March 2003, <http://www.genderstudies.northwestern.edu/abouttheprogram/index.htm>: 1.

12 "Courses" 2.

13 Edith Zorychta, "The World of Women's Studies," CAUT *Bulletin: Status of Women Supplement*, 48.8 (October 2001): 1.

14 Zorychta 1.

15 Zorychta 1.

16 Laura Mulvey, "Visual Pleasure and Narrative Cinema," in *Feminism and Film Theory*, ed. C. Penley (New York: Routledge, 1988). In this famous

essay, first published in 1975, Mulvey uses psychoanalysis to discuss the "male gaze" of filmmakers.

APPENDIX TWELVE

1 "Funding," [dated] 8 June 2003, *Status of Women Canada*, [visited] 6 January 2004, <http:www.swc-cfc.gc.ca/funding/prfcfp-990902_e.html>.

2 Pierrette Bouchard, Isabelle Boily, and Marie-Claude Proulx, "School Success by Gender: A Catalyst for the Masculinist Discourse," [updated] 15 April 2003, *Status of Women Canada*, [visited] 8 June 2003, <http://www.swc-cfc.gc.ca/pubs/0662882857/200303_0662882857_1_e.html> 17.

3 Institutions – government agencies, universities, and so on – routinely insist on disclaimers. They do so not only to protect themselves but also to assure authors that their academic freedom will be respected, which would be impossible if authors were required to represent any institutional point of view. These institutions routinely commission reports, moreover, and pay for them. In the case of government agencies, they do so in connection with establishing policies, because they can evaluate the potential benefits and risks only on the basis of reliable information and analysis of it. In this case, however, the government agency is not politically neutral – that is, it is not engaged only in gathering and analyzing information on an academic basis. The official mandate of Status of Women Canada is to promote and fund only research that will benefit women. It attracts only those authors, therefore, who are willing – on political grounds – to fulfill that mandate. It is a lamentable but observable fact that authors in this situation tend, whether intentionally or not, to skew either the design of their projects (asking some questions, say, but not others) or their interpretations (or both). This has often been true of some male scholars, as feminists like to point out, and it is just as true of some female scholars – especially those who identify themselves with feminism as a political movement. They justify this as "engaged scholarship," which we discuss in chapter 10. It is for this reason – because the merits of arguments on the other side are not discussed or even acknowledged – that we cast doubt on the academic credibility of the report and draw attention to the outrage of paying for it out of tax dollars – including those of male citizens and female citizens who disagree with doctrines of ideological feminism.

4 Michael Higgins, "Men's Groups Promoting Hatred, Federal Report Says," *National Post*, 30 May 2003: A-6, A-16.

5 See, for example, the following passage: "These [men's] groups are largely composed of white, heterosexual, middle-class men who have not been successful in coping with the challenge to masculinity posed by feminism" (Bouchard, Boily, and Proulx 66; referring to B. Lingard and P. Douglas, *Men Engaging Feminisms: Pro-feminism, Backlashes and Schooling* [Philadelphia: Open Univesity Press, 1999]).

 6 Jon C. Bradley, "Why Boys Drop Out," *Montreal Gazette*, 3 November 2004:
    A-27.
 7 Bouchard, Boily, and Proulx 3.
 8 Bouchard, Boily, and Proulx 3.
 9 Bouchard, Boily, and Proulx 7.
10 Bouchard, Boily, and Proulx 26, 36.
11 Bouchard, Boily, and Proulx 37.
12 Bouchard, Boily, and Proulx 66.
13 Bouchard, Boily, and Proulx 29.
14 We are not referring here to the study of particular goddesses (such as the
    Hindu Kali or Durga and the Buddhist Kuan Yin) in traditional societies. We
    are referring to both academic and public interest in "the Goddess" as a way
    of legitimating ideological feminism in modern Western societies. Much has
    been written about "the Goddess" in the secular fields of history, archaeology,
    and religious studies. Among the most influential books have been Gerda
    Lerner's *The Creation of Patriarchy* (New York: Oxford University Press,
    1986) and Marija Gimbutas's *Civilization of the Goddess* (San Francisco:
    HarperSanFrancisco, 1991). Both authors tried to show that all of history
    since the Neolithic period can be understood as a titanic conspiracy of men
    against women (although neither author claimed that every man consciously
    participates in this conspiracy). Lerner is a historian, her specialty being
    women's history. Gimbutas was an archeologist. Her specific contribution was
    to argue that very ancient Europeans worshipped a "Great Goddess." For
    thousands of years, apparently, they enjoyed equality and peace in what
    amounted to a paradise under the aegis of this female deity; only when men
    rebelled (for some reason that she never explained) under the aegis of a male
    deity did paradise end and the present state of inequality and war – that is,
    patriarchy – begin. Anyone even vaguely familiar with the biblical story of
    Adam and Eve (or, to be more precise, post-biblical interpretations of it) can
    see that this is a feminist revision of what Christians call the "Fall of Man."
    In this version, of course, Original Sin – the ultimate source of evil – is
    blamed on men instead of women.
        This proposition, not exactly easy to prove, has become the historical (and
    ideological) framework that underlies some forms of feminism at both the
    academic and popular levels. In *Changing of the Gods: Feminism and the End
    of Traditional Religions* (Boston: Beacon Press, 1979), for instance, Naomi
    Goldenberg says much the same thing but from the perspective of pop psy-
    chology. So does Mary Daly from that of "thealogy," the feminist version of
    theology. Several "documentaries," moreover, have brought this message to
    the masses. *Beyond the Veil*, for instance, was produced by Canada's National
    Film Board (more specifically by its explicitly feminist Studio D) and thus
    financed by taxpayers. It presents contemporary Irish nuns as latter day
    (albeit subconscious) followers of the "old religion," the good Goddess

religion that was destroyed violently by St Patrick's evil religion and repressed ever since by a sinister church. Goddess revivalism is not a fringe movement either within the university or beyond it. And we do not refer merely to the growing popularity of Wicca, supposedly a survival of (benign) witchcraft. We refer also to the Sophia movement that has taken off (not without resistance) in the Presbyterian and some other mainstream churches, the Holy Spirit being identified with "Sophia" (wisdom) and thus as a female form of God to be recovered after two thousand years of repression.

15 Marija Gimbutas, *The Language of the Goddess* (New York: Harper and Row, 1989); Gerda Lerner, *The Creation of Patriarchy* (New York: Oxford University Press, 1986); *The Goddess Remembered*, directed by Donna Read, script by D.C. Blade, Donna Read, Gloria Demers, 16 mm, 54 min. (Montreal: National Film Board of Canada: Studio D, 1989); *Behind the Veil: Nuns*, directed by Margaret Westcott, script and narration by Gloria Demers, 16 mm., 130 min. (Montreal: National Film Board of Canada, 1984); and *The Burning Times*, directed by Donna Read, script by Erna Buffie, 16 mm., 58 min. (Montreal: National Film Board of Canada, Studio D, 1993).

16 Bouchard, Boily, and Proulx 33.

17 Bouchard, Boily, and Proulx 41.

18 Frederick Mathews, *The Invisible Boy: Revisioning the Victimization of Male Children and Teens* (Ottawa: Minister of Public Works and Government Services Canada; Health Canada [catalogue no. H72–21/143–1996E] 1996), 11.

19 Bouchard, Boily, and Proulx 44.

20 Bouchard, Boily, and Proulx 59.

21 Bouchard, Boily, and Proulx 67.

22 Bouchard, Boily, and Proulx 69, 71.

23 Bouchard, Boily, and Proulx 74, 75.

24 Bouchard, Boily, and Proulx 82, 93.

25 Bouchard, Boily, and Proulx 93.

26 Bouchard, Boily, and Proulx 93.

APPENDIX THIRTEEN

1 Peter Neidig, "Women's Shelters, Men's Collectives, and Other Issues in the Field of Spouse Abuse," *Victimology* 9.3–4 (1984): 464–76.

2 Neidig began his article by pointing out two basic approaches, the ideological and the empirical, in the study of domestic violence. Some feminists, he wrote, presented case studies and analyzed them from an ideological perspective. As examples, he cited Lenore Walker's *The Battered Woman* (New York: Harper and Row, 1979) and Del Martin's *Battered Wives* (New York: Pocket Books, 1976). In addition, Russell Dobash and Rebecca Dobash (*Violence Against Wives* [New York: Free Press, 1979]) represented "a variation of the pure sociological approach in which any pretence of scientific neutrality is aban-

doned for a stance of vigorous advocacy" (Neidig 464). Other researchers, he noted, had emerged from clinically oriented social work. All tended to identify characteristics of the victims, offer descriptions of the victimizers, and recommend new institutional policies or legal reforms. The essays in *Patterns in Family Violence*, edited by Margaret Elbow (New York: Family Service Associates, 1972), exemplified this approach. Still others had written sociological or epidemiological analyses of spousal abuse. This empirical approach had been adopted by Murray Straus, Richard Gelles, and Suzanne Steinmetz (*Behind Closed Doors: Violence in the American Family* [New York: Anchor/Doubleday 1981]). They and their students were using a national survey to identify every conceivable variable that might correlate with domestic violence.

3 Neidig 465.
4 Neidig 465.
5 Neidig 465–6.
6 Neidig 466.
7 Perry London, *The Modes and Morals of Psychotherapy* (New York: Holt, 1964).
8 Neidig 466. It is at least conceivable, however, that this could be a case of "both-and" rather than "either-or." If the recent increase in women's power provokes frustration and even violence on the part of some men, for example, it would hardly be surprising if these men directed their anger and frustration at powerless wives. In short, people generally attack only those who are not in a position to fight back and refrain from attacking those who could retaliate physically or otherwise.
9 Neidig 466.
10 Neidig 466–7.
11 Neidig 467.
12 D. Adams and I. Penn, "Getting Rid of the Excuses Men Use for Abusing Women," *Practice Digest* 4.1 (1981): 5–8.
13 Z. Mettger, "Help for Men Who Batter: Overview of Issues and Programs," *Response* 5 (1982): 1–23. Although Neidig did not comment on this argument, it is worth noting Mettger's assumption that women can understand men better than men can understand themselves. Women have wisely rejected this approach when applied in reverse.
14 E. Hilberman, "Overview: The Wife-Beater's Wife Reconsidered," *American Journal of Psychiatry* 137.11 (1980): 1336–7.
15 Neidig 469, 470.
16 Neidig 469, 470.
17 Neidig 470–1.
18 Andrew McCormack, *Men Helping Men Stop Woman Abuse* (Boston: Emerge, 1979).
19 Neidig 474.

20 Neidig 472.

21 Neidig 472–3.

22 Neidig 467.

23 Neidig 467.

24 Ellen Pence, "Response to Peter Neidig's Article: 'Women's Shelters, Men's Collectives and Other Issues in the Field of Spouse Abuse," *Victimology* 9.3–4 (1984): 479–80.

25 Jeffrey L. Edleson, "Violence is the Issue: A Critique of Neidig's Assumptions," *Victimology* 9.3–4 (1984): 483–9.

26 Edleson 483, 484.

27 Emerge began in 1977 as the first program in the United States devoted specifically to the goal of "challenging men to take responsibility for stopping male violence." Here is the mission statement on its website: "Emerge believes that battering is a learned behavior, not a sickness. Violence against women is a social problem requiring change at the individual, cultural, and institutional levels. Counseling and education for abusive men is one aspect of this change. We support grassroots, institutional, and cultural efforts to stop battery, rape, child abuse, and other degrading treatment of women and children and to build a non-sexist society." See "Emerge: Counseling and Education to Stop Domestic Violence," [dated] 1999, *Emerge*, [visited] 19 September 2002 <http://www.emergedv.com/>.

28 Edleson 486.

29 Neidig 464.

30 Pence 477.

31 Neidig 464.

32 Pence 478.

33 Pence 478.

34 Suzanne K. Steinmetz, "The Battered Husband Syndrome," *Victimology* 2.3–4 (1978): 499–509; Patricia Pearson, "Women Behaving Badly," *Saturday Night*, September 1997: 92–100; Pearson used that article as the basis for *When She Was Bad: Violent Women and the Myth of Innocence* (New York: Viking-Penguin, 1997).

35 Pence 469.

36 Pence 478.

37 Edleson 485.

38 Pence 479.

39 See Neil Boyd, *The Beast Within: Why Men Are Violent* (Vancouver: Greystone Books, 2000). For alcohol: 22, 126, 145, 155–60, 178–9; 180–1; for drugs: 22, 155, 157, 160–1, 179–81.

40 Neidig 472.

41 Edleson 486, 487.

42 Neidig 473.

43 Edleson 486.

44 Edleson 484.

45 This was Lorena Bobbitt's defense, although some feminists disapproved. If she could use it, why not men?

46 "Jean Harris," 20/20, ABC, WVNY-TV, Burlington, VT, 5 March 1993.

47 Barbara Walters, 20/20.

48 Pence 481–2.

49 Pence 481.

50 Neidig 474.

51 Edleson 488.

52 Pearson, "Women Behaving Badly" 96.

Index

Because this book is entirely about the legal regimes that govern men in two countries, the list of entries under the corresponding words – *men*, *law*, *Canada*, and *United States* – would have been extremely long and therefore unhelpful. We have used these words in sub-headings, however, or in parentheses after the names of government agencies, legislation, and so on.

On the other hand, even though this book is also entirely about misandry and ideological feminism – and especially about the close relation between them – the terms denoting these ideas are still unusual enough to merit indexing. Readers should bear in mind, however, that both are often implied even when not actually indexed.

For the sake of brevity, we have used "ideological" instead of the more cumbersome "ideological feminist" (although most of the references would apply to any ideology).

Sometimes this index refers to specific words that appear in the text. At other times, though, it refers instead to general ideas found there. Examples of double standards might appear in the text but not accompanied by the words "double standards," for instance; we have indexed them, nevertheless, under that heading.